AA 1001 GREAT FAMILY DAYS OUT

Cover pictures: Front Cover ltl AA World Travel Library/John Mottershaw; tl AA World Travel Library/Wyn Voysey; tc AA World Travel Library/Eric Meacher; tr AA World Travel Library; rtr AA World Travel Library/Rick Strange; bottom Photodisc; Back Cover ltl AA World Travel Library/Rupert Tennison; tc AA World Travel Library/Tony Souter; tr AA World Travel Library/Andy Midgely; rtr AA World Travel Library/Max Jourdan; lbl AA World Travel Library/Max Jourdan; bl AA World Travel Library/Max Jourdan; cb AA World Travel Library/Max Jourdan; br AA World Travel Library/Wyn Voysey; rbr AA World Travel Library/Derek Forss

The main pictures in this title are from the Automobile Association's own library (AA WORLD TRAVEL LIBRARY) with contributions from the following:
Stuart Abrahams 145; Martyn Adelman 109; Pat Aithie 338; M Alexander 283, 299, 307; Adrian Baker 180; Jeff Beazley 53, 265; M Birkitt 133, 122; Michael Bussele 200; Iim Carnie 294, 316; Derek Croucher 321; Steve Day 270; Derek

Forss 210; Richard Ireland 175; David Jackson 240; Caroline Jones 223; Max Jourdan 1; Paul Kenward 157, 159, 169; Cameron Lees 83; Eric Meacher 261; John Mottershaw 104; Ken Paterson 107, 278, 292; Andrew Perkins 177; Tony Souter 127, Rupert Tenison 226; Richard Turpin 213; Wyn Voysey 46; Tim Woodcock 84, 167

Design by Jamie Wiltshire; Typeset/Repro by Servis Filmsetting Ltd, Manchester
Printed by Everbest, China

The contents of this book are believed correct at the time of printing. Nevertheless, the Publisher cannot be held responsible for any errors or omissions or for changes in the details given in this guide or for the consequence of any reliance on the information provided in the same. This does not affect your statutory rights.

Published by AA Publishing, which is a trading name of Automobile Association Developments Limited, whose registered office is Southwood East, Apollo Rise, Farnborough, Hampshire GU14 0JW Registered number 1878835.

ISBN-10 0749542667   ISBN-13 978-0-7495-4266-5   A02147

Maps prepared by the Cartography Department of The Automobile Association.
Maps © Automobile Association Developments Limited 2005.

Ordnance Survey® This product includes mapping data licensed from Ordnance Survey® with the permission of the Controller of Her Majesty's Stationery Office. © Crown copyright 2005. All rights reserved. Licence number 399221.

Sample entry

❶ ANYVILLE ANYVILLE ZOO

Upton-by-Anyville TV2 1LH
❷ Dir: (2m N of city centre off junct 10 southbound)
❸ Map Ref: *TY99*
❹ ☎ **01234 567890** ▤ **01234 567891**
e-mail: marketing@anyville.co.uk

The largest zoological gardens in the UK, Anyville Zoo has more than 7,000 animals of more than 500 species. Catch feeding time on Penguin Island, visit Desert of Danger with the Giant Sand Lizards, feel the spirit of the Cougar, and visit the awesome Tigers.

❺ Times: Open all year, daily from 10. Last admission varies with season from 5.30pm high summer to 3.30pm winter. (Closed 25
❻ Dec). **Fee:** £12 (£9.50 concessions). Family ticket £39.50
❼ Facilities: ▣ ▙ ✕ licensed ♿ (electric scooters, audio guide, induction loop, Braille) toilets for disabled shop ✖ (ex guide & sensory dogs) ▰

❶ GUIDE ORDER This guide is divided into regions. Within each region counties are listed alphabetically. To find a particular county refer to page opposite. Locations and pub names are listed alphabetically.

❷ DIRECTIONS where shown have been provided by the places of interest themselves. Please telephone for directions where these are not supplied.

❸ MAP REFERENCE is based on the National Grid and can be used with the map at the beginning of each region.

❹ TELEPHONE NUMBERS have the STD code shown before the telephone number. (If dialling Northern Ireland from England, Scotland or Wales, use the STD code, but for the Republic of Ireland you need to prefix the number with 00353, and drop the first zero from the Irish area code).

❺ OPENING TIMES quoted in the guide are inclusive – for instance, where you see Apr-Oct, that place will be open from the beginning of April to the end of October.

❻ FEES for most entries are current. If no price is quoted, please contact the attraction for information.

❼ FACILITIES This section includes information on parking, refreshments, accessibility and whether dogs are allowed admission. Visitors with mobility disabilities should look for the wheelchair symbol showing where all or most of the attraction is accessible to wheelchair users. We strongly recommend that you telephone in advance of your visit to check the exact details, particularly regarding access to toilets and refreshment facilities. Assistance dogs are usually accepted where the attractions show the 'No Dogs' symbol unless otherwise stated.

See below for a key to the Symbols and Abbreviations used in this guide.

PLEASE NOTE Opening times and admission prices are subject to change.

Keys to Symbols and Abbreviations

☎ Telephone number

▤ Fax number

♿ Suitable for visitors in wheelchairs

▣ Parking at Establishments

▣ Parking nearby

▙ Refreshments

✕ Restaurant

✖ No Dogs

▰ No Coaches

✛ Cadw (Welsh Historic Monuments)

♯ English Heritage

♘ National Trust

♚ National Trust for Scotland

▮ Historic Scotland

BH Bank Holidays

PH Public Holidays

Etr Easter

ex except

* indicates that opening dates, times and prices are for 2004. Please telephone to confirm.

Contents

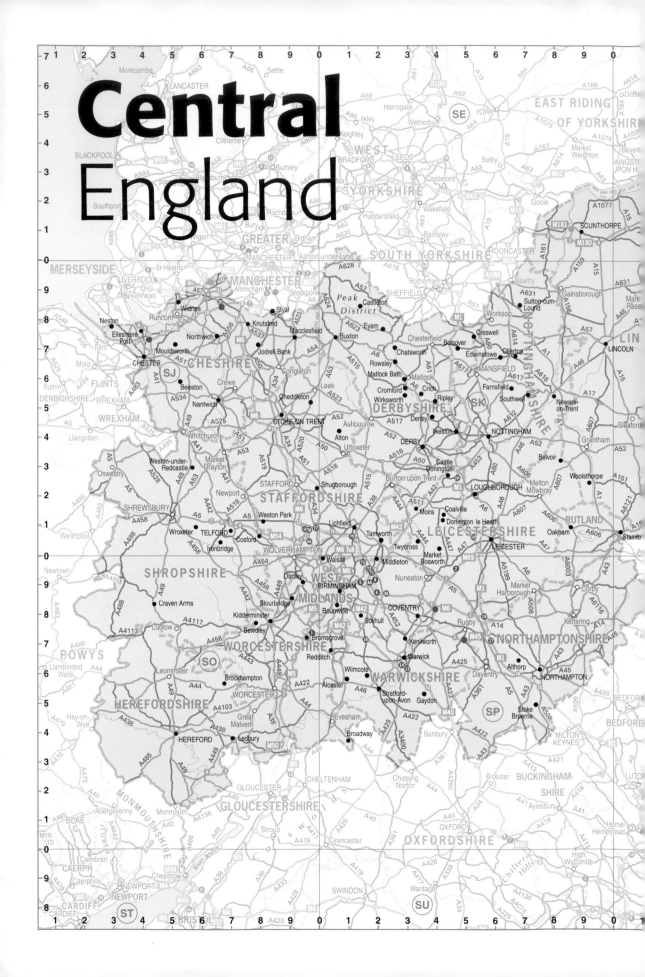

Central
England

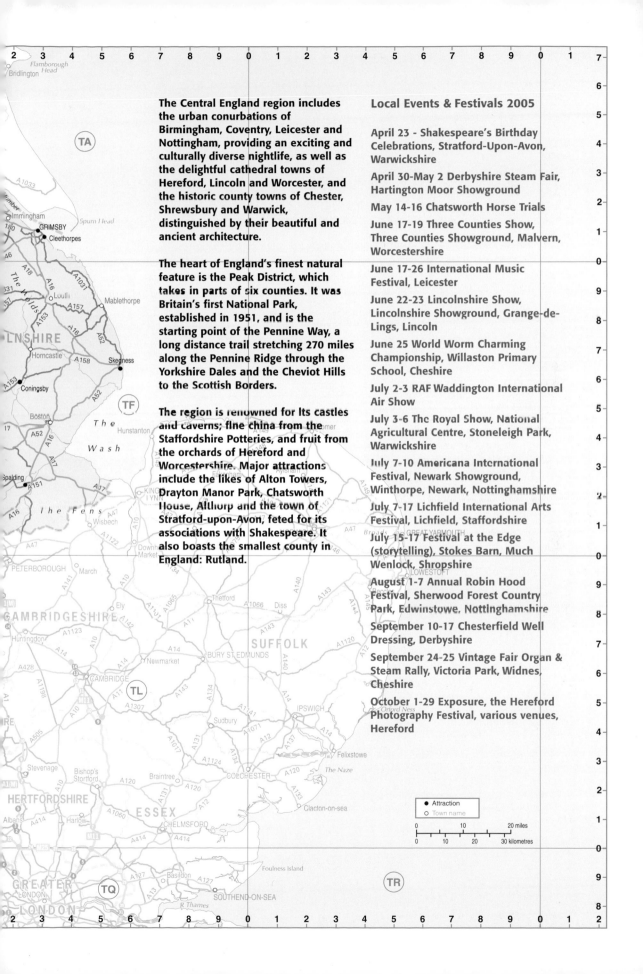

The Central England region includes the urban conurbations of Birmingham, Coventry, Leicester and Nottingham, providing an exciting and culturally diverse nightlife, as well as the delightful cathedral towns of Hereford, Lincoln and Worcester, and the historic county towns of Chester, Shrewsbury and Warwick, distinguished by their beautiful and ancient architecture.

The heart of England's finest natural feature is the Peak District, which takes in parts of six counties. It was Britain's first National Park, established in 1951, and is the starting point of the Pennine Way, a long distance trail stretching 270 miles along the Pennine Ridge through the Yorkshire Dales and the Cheviot Hills to the Scottish Borders.

The region is renowned for its castles and caverns; fine china from the Staffordshire Potteries, and fruit from the orchards of Hereford and Worcestershire. Major attractions include the likes of Alton Towers, Drayton Manor Park, Chatsworth House, Althorp and the town of Stratford-upon-Avon, feted for its associations with Shakespeare. It also boasts the smallest county in England: Rutland.

Local Events & Festivals 2005

April 23 - Shakespeare's Birthday Celebrations, Stratford-Upon-Avon, Warwickshire

April 30-May 2 Derbyshire Steam Fair, Hartington Moor Showground

May 14-16 Chatsworth Horse Trials

June 17-19 Three Counties Show, Three Counties Showground, Malvern, Worcestershire

June 17-26 International Music Festival, Leicester

June 22-23 Lincolnshire Show, Lincolnshire Showground, Grange-de-Lings, Lincoln

June 25 World Worm Charming Championship, Willaston Primary School, Cheshire

July 2-3 RAF Waddington International Air Show

July 3-6 The Royal Show, National Agricultural Centre, Stoneleigh Park, Warwickshire

July 7-10 Americana International Festival, Newark Showground, Winthorpe, Newark, Nottinghamshire

July 7-17 Lichfield International Arts Festival, Lichfield, Staffordshire

July 15-17 Festival at the Edge (storytelling), Stokes Barn, Much Wenlock, Shropshire

August 1-7 Annual Robin Hood Festival, Sherwood Forest Country Park, Edwinstowe, Nottinghamshire

September 10-17 Chesterfield Well Dressing, Derbyshire

September 24-25 Vintage Fair Organ & Steam Rally, Victoria Park, Widnes, Cheshire

October 1-29 Exposure, the Hereford Photography Festival, various venues, Hereford

● Attraction
○ Town name

BEESTON   BEESTON CASTLE

Tarporley CW6 9TX
Dir: (on minor road off A49 or A41) *Map Ref:* *SJ55*
☎ **01829 260464**

Legend tells of a vast treasure hidden here by Richard II, but the real treasure at Beeston lies in its 4,000 years of history waiting to be discovered. The 13th-century castle ruin is set on a rocky summit 500 feet above the Cheshire plain offering breathtaking views from the Pennines to the mountains of Wales.

Times: Open all year, Apr-Sep, daily 10-6; Oct-Mar, daily 10-4. Closed 24-26 Dec & 1 Jan.
Fee: *Prices not confirmed for 2005*
Facilities: 🅿 shop ✖ (in certain areas) ⚓

CHESTER   CHESTER ZOO

Upton-by-Chester CH2 1LH
Dir: (2m N of city centre off A41& M53 junct 10 southbound, junct 12 all other directions) *Map Ref:* *SJ46*
☎ **01244 380280** 📄 **01244 371273**
e-mail: marketing@chesterzoo.co.uk

The largest zoological gardens in the UK, Chester Zoo has more than 7,000 animals of more than 500 species. Catch feeding time on Sealion Beach, visit Islands in Danger with the Komodo Dragons, feel the Spirit of the Jaguar, and the awesome Tsavo - the Black Rhino Experience.

Times: Open all year, daily from 10. Last admission varies with season from 5.30pm high summer to 3.30pm winter. (Closed 25 Dec).
Fee: £12 (£9.50 concessions). Family ticket £39.50 **Facilities:** 🅿 ☕ ✖ licensed ♿ (electric scooters, audio guide, induction loop, Braille) toilets for disabled shop ✖ (ex guide & sensory dogs) 📷

DEVA ROMAN EXPERIENCE

Pierpoint Ln, (off Bridge St) CH1 1NL
Dir: (city centre) *Map Ref:* *SJ46*
☎ **01244 343407** 📄 **01244 347737**

Stroll along reconstructed streets experiencing the sights, sounds and smells of Roman Chester. From the streets of Deva (the Roman name for Chester) you return to the present day on an extensive archaeological 'dig', where you can discover the substantial Roman, Saxon and medieval remains beneath modern Chester.

Times: Open daily Feb-Nov 9-5, Dec-Jan 10-4 . (Closed 25-26 Dec). **Fee:** ✱ £4.25 (ch £2.50, under 5's free, pen & student £3.75). Family ticket £12. Party. **Facilities:** 🅿 (200yds) ♿ shop ✖ (ex guide dogs)

ELLESMERE PORT *BLUE PLANET AQUARIUM*

Cheshire Oaks CH65 9LF
Dir: (off M53 junct 10 at Cheshire Oaks. Follow signs for aquarium) *Map Ref:* SJ47
☎ 0151 357 8804 📠 0151 356 7288
e-mail: info@blueplanetaquarium.co.uk

A voyage of discovery on the longest moving walkway in the world. Beneath the waters of the Caribbean Reef, see giant rays and menacing sharks pass inches from your face and stroke some favourite fish in the special rock pools or pay a visit to the incredible world of poisonous frogs. Divers hand-feed the fish and sharks throughout the day and they can answer questions via state of the art communication systems.

Times: ✱ Open all year, daily from 10. (Closed Xmas). Seasonal variations in closing times, please call to confirm. **Facilities:** 🅿 ✖ licensed ♿ (wheelchair hire, lifts) toilets for disabled shop 🐾 (ex guide dogs) 📱

BOAT MUSEUM

South Pier Rd CH65 4FW
Dir: (M53 junct 9) *Map Ref:* SJ47
☎ 0151 355 5017 📠 0151 355 4079
e-mail: bookings@thewaterwaystrust.org

Occupying a historic dock complex at the junction of the Shropshire Union and Manchester Ship Canals, this museum has the world's largest collection of floating canal craft, from a small weedcutter to a 300-ton coaster. Boat trips are also available. There are indoor exhibitions on canal life and local history, together with period workers' cottages, a blacksmith's forge and working engines.

Times: Open Summer daily 10-5. Winter daily (ex Thu & Fri) 11-4. (Closed 25 & 26 Dec). **Fee:** ✱ £5.50 (ch £3.70, pen & student £4.30). Family ticket £16.50, pen family ticket £14.50. **Facilities:** 🅿 🍴 ♿ (tactile map for blind, wheelchairs) toilets for disabled shop 🐾 ex guide dogs 📱

JODRELL BANK *JODRELL BANK VISITOR CENTRE & ARBORETUM*

SK11 9DL
Dir: (M6 junct 18, A535 Holmes Chapel to Chelford road) *Map Ref:* SJ77
☎ 01477 571339 📠 01477 571695
e-mail: visitorcentre@jb.man.ac.uk

At Jodrell Bank, a scientific and engineering wonder awaits you - the magnificent Lovell telescope, one of the largest radio telescopes in the world. A pathway leads you 180 degrees around the telescope as it towers above you surveying and exploring the universe. Then, you can wander along pathways amongst the trees of the extensive arboretum. The Centre is currently under a redevelopment, which will take two to three years to complete.

Times: Open daily Nov-mid Mar 10.30-3, wknds 11-4; mid Mar-end Oct 10.30-5.30 **Fee:** £3 per car, £1 for 3D Show. **Facilities:** 🅿 (charged) 🍴 ♿ (wheelchair loan) toilets for disabled shop 🐾 (ex guide dogs) 📱

KNUTSFORD TATTON PARK

WA16 6QN
Dir: (5m from M6 junct 19, or M56 junct 7. Signed on A556, 4m S
of Altrincham. Entrance to Tatton Park on Ashley Rd, 1.5m NE of
junct A5034 with A50) *Map Ref:* SJ77
☎ **01625 534400** 📠 **01625 534403**
e-mail: tatton@cheshire.gov.uk

Tatton is one of England's most complete historic estates with
gardens and a 1,000-acre country park. The centrepiece is the
Georgian mansion, with gardens by Humphry Repton and Sir Joseph
Paxton. More recently, a Japanese garden with a Shinto temple was
created. The Tudor Old Hall is the original manor house.

Times: Open mid Mar-early Oct, Tue-Sun & BH 1-5; Gardens &
parkland all year Tue-Sun & BH. **Fee:** ✱ Mansion, £3 (ch £2), family
£8, groups 12+ £2.40 (ch £1.60) Saver tickets available
Facilities: 🅿 (charged) 🍽 ✗ licensed ♿ (old hall & areas of farm
not accessible, Braille guides) toilets for disabled shop garden centre
✖ (ex in parkland) 🐾 📷

MACCLESFIELD MACCLESFIELD SILK MUSEUM

Heritage Centre, Roe St SK11 6UT
Dir: (Turn off A523 & follow brown signs. Museum in town
centre) *Map Ref:* SJ97
☎ **01625 613210** 📠 **01625 617880**
e-mail: silkmuseum@tiscali.co.uk

The story of silk, from its origins in China to its establishment in
Macclesfield is told through a colourful audio-visual programme,
exhibitions, textiles, garments, models and room settings. The Silk
Museum is part of the Heritage Centre, a restored Georgian
Sunday School, which runs a full programme of musical and
artistic events throughout the year.

Times: Open all year, Mon-Sat 11-5, Sun & BH
Mon 12-5. Closed 25-26 Dec, 1 Jan & Good Fri.
Please ring for winter opening times.
Fee: ✱ £3.20 (concessions £2.20). Family ticket
£9 Joint ticket with Paradise Mill £3.75
(concessions £2.75). Family ticket £10.80.
Facilities: 🅿 (50mtrs) 🍽 ✗ licensed ♿ (ramps,
chairlift, audio guides, induction loop) toilets for
disabled shop ✖ (ex guide dogs) 📷

PARADISE MILL & SILK INDUSTRY MUSEUM

Park Ln SK11 6TJ
Dir: (turn off A523 'The Silk Rd' & follow brown signs)
Map Ref: SJ97
☎ **01625 612045** 📠 **01625 612048**
e-mail: silkmuseum@tiscali.co.uk

This was a working silk mill until 1981, and has restored jacquard
hand looms in their original location. Knowledgeable guides,
many of them former silk mill workers, illustrate the silk
production process with the help of demonstrations from
weavers. Exhibitions and room settings give an impression of
working conditions at the mill during the 1930s.

Times: Open all year, BH Mon & Mon-Sat from
11-5 (Closed Sundays, 25-26 Dec & 1 Jan, Good
Fri). Ring for winter opening **Fee:** ✱ £3.75
(ch £2.75), family £10.80
Facilities: 🅿 (100yds) ♿ (care needed on
uneven floors) ✖ (ex guide dogs) 📷

MOULDSWORTH MOULDSWORTH MOTOR MUSEUM

Smithy Ln CH3 8AR
Dir: (6m E of Chester, off B5393, close to Delamere Forest & Oulton Park Racing Circuit, signposted. Or M56 junct 12 into Frodsham then B5393 into Mouldsworth, follow brown heritage signs in village) *Map Ref:* SJ57
☎ 01928 731781

Housed in a 1937 large Art Deco building close to Delamere Forest, this is a superb collection of over 60 motor cars, motorcycles and bicycles. There is also a massive collection of automobilia - old signs, pumps, tools, mascots and badges, as well as old motoring toys, Dinky cars and pedal cars. These are complemented by a motoring art gallery, with posters and advertising material. School parties are encouraged to take a guided tour and structured talk. Motoring clubs visit on Sundays. There is also a Harry Potter car for children to sit in.

Times: Open Feb-Nov (Sun only), Etr wknd, early May BH Mon, Spring BH Sun-Mon & Aug BH wknd; Sun, Feb-Nov; also Wed, Jul-Aug, noon-5. **Fee:** ✱ £3 (ch £1.50) **Facilities:** 🅿 ♿ (hands on items) shop

NANTWICH STAPELEY WATER GARDENS

London Rd, Stapeley CW5 7LH
Dir: (off M6 junct 16, 1m S of Nantwich on A51) *Map Ref:* SJ65
☎ 01270 623868 & 628628 🖷 01270 624919
e-mail: info@stapeleywg.com

Stapeley Water Gardens consists of three main areas. The Palms Tropical Oasis is a glass pavilion which is home to Koi carp, Giant Amazon water-lilies, sharks, piranhas, parrots and exotic flowers. The two-acre Water Garden Centre houses the national collection of water-lilies, and there is also a garden centre with a children's play area.

Times: Open Summer: Mon-Sat 9-6, BHs 10-6, Sun 10-4, Wed 9-8; Winter: Mon-Sat 9-5, BHs 10-5, Sun 10-4, (Wed 9-8 Angling dept only). The Palms Tropical Oasis open from 10am. **Fee:** The Palms Tropical Oasis £4.45 (ch £2.60, pen £3.95). Family ticket (2 ad & 2 ch) £12.10 (2 ad & 3 ch) £14.30. **Facilities:** 🅿 🍽 ✗ licensed ♿ (free wheelchair loan service) toilets for disabled shop garden centre ✖ (ex guide dogs) 🛍

NESTON LIVERPOOL UNIVERSITY BOTANIC GARDENS (NESS GARDENS)

Ness Gardens CH64 4AY
Dir: (off A540 near Ness-on-Wirral, follow signs) *Map Ref:* SJ27
☎ 0151 353 0123 🖷 0151 353 1004
e-mail: nessgdns@liv.ac.uk

A long association with plant collectors ensures a wide range of plants, providing interest for academics, horticulturists and amateurs alike. There are tree and shrub collections, water and rock gardens, herbaceous borders and glasshouses. A regular programme of lectures, courses and special events takes place throughout the year for which tickets must be obtained in advance.

Times: Open all year, Nov-Feb, daily 9.30-4; Mar-Oct, daily 9.30-5. (Closed 25 Dec). **Fee:** ✱ £4.70 (ch free admission when accompanied with an adult, concessions £4.30) **Facilities:** 🅿 🍽 ♿ (wheelchair route, induction loop in lecture theatre) toilets for disabled shop garden centre ✖ (ex guide dogs) 🛍

NORTHWICH SALT MUSEUM

162 London Rd CW9 8AB
Dir: (on A533 0.5m S of town centre and 0.5m N of A556. Well signposted from A556) *Map Ref:* SJ67
☎ **01606 41331** 📠 **01606 350420**
e-mail: cheshiremuseums@cheshire.gov.uk

Britain's only salt museum tells the fascinating story of Cheshire's oldest industry. Salt has been produced in Northwich for 2,000 years and is still produced on a large scale in the town today. Models, reconstructions, original artefacts and audio-visual programmes throw new light on a commodity that we all tend to take for granted.

Times: Open Tue-Fri 10-5, wknds 2-5 (Sun 12-5 in Aug). Open BH & Mons in Aug 10-5.
Fee: £2.40 (ch £1.20, concessions £2) Family ticket (2 adults + 2 ch) £6 **Facilities:** 🅿 ☕ ♿ (inductory video with induction loop facilities) toilets for disabled shop garden centre ✖ (ex guide dogs) 🍴

STYAL QUARRY BANK MILL & STYAL ESTATE

SK9 4LA
Dir: (1.5m N of Wilmslow off B5166, 2.5m from M56 junct 5, 10m S of Manchester. Heritage signs from A34 and M56)
Map Ref: SJ88
☎ **01625 527468** 📠 **01625 539267**
e-mail: quarrybankmill@nationaltrust.org.uk

Quarry Bank Mill is a working water and steam powered cotton mill. Spinning and weaving techniques from throughout the industrial revolution are demonstrated every day and items made from the cloth are sold in the shop. The mill and its colony village are set in the beautiful Styal Estate beside the River Bollin. There are lots of practical 'hands-on' activities plus a children's playground and railway. The Apprentice House and its Victorian vegetable garden show how life was for the mill apprentices.

Times: Mill open all year, Apr-Sep daily 10.30-5.30 (last admission 4); Oct-19 Mar, daily 10.30-5 (closed Mon in term time). Last admission 3.30. Apprentice House & Garden, Tue-Fri from 11 (2-3.30 term time), Sat-Sun & Aug from 11. Closed Mon (ex school hols).
Fee: ✱ Mill & Apprentice House £7.30 (ch £4.50). Family ticket £18. Mill only £5.20 (ch £3.50). Family ticket £15. Estate fee £2.50.
Facilities: 🅿 (charged) ☕ ✖ licensed ♿ (wheelchairs, chairlift, ramps, Braille & large print guide) toilets for disabled shop ✖ (ex in park) 🌿 🍴

WIDNES *CATALYST SCIENCE DISCOVERY CENTRE*

Mersey Rd WA8 0DF
Dir: (signed from M62 junct 7 and M56 junct 12) *Map Ref:* SJ58
☎ **0151 420 1121** 📠 **0151 495 2030**
e-mail: info@catalyst.org.uk

Discover a world where science and technology come alive, with over 100 interactive exhibits and hands-on displays which guarantee a fun-filled day out for all the family. Take a trip in an all-glass lift to the Observatory, 100 feet above the River Mersey. A range of special events is planned throughout the year. Please ring for details.

Times: ✱ Open all year, Tue-Fri daily & BH Mon 10-5, wknds 11-5. (Closed Mon ex BH's, 24-26 Dec & 1 Jan). **Facilities:** 🅿 ☕ ♿ toilets for disabled shop ✖ (ex guide dogs) 🍴

BOLSOVER BOLSOVER CASTLE

Castle St S44 6PR
Dir: (on A632) **Map Ref:** *SJ47*
☎ **01246 822844** 🖷 **01246 241569**

This award-winning property has the air of a romantic storybook castle, with its turrets and battlements rising from a wooded hilltop. It was built on the site of a medieval castle, beginning in 1612. See the stunning Venus Garden, beautifully restored with its 23 new statues and fountain. The stables have been converted into a Discovery Centre, and state-of-the-art audio tours of the castle are available.

Times: Open all year, Apr & Sep-Oct, Thu-Mon 10-5; May-Jul, daily 10-6; Aug, daily 10-7; Nov-Mar, Thu-Mon 10-4. (Closed 24-26 Dec & 1 Jan). **Fee:** ✱ £6.50 (ch £3.30, concessions £4.90). Family £16.30. Prices & opening times relate to 2004, for further details phone or log onto www.english-heritage.org.uk/visits
Facilities: 🅿 🍽 ♿ (keep not accessible) shop ✖ ⚏

BUXTON POOLE'S CAVERN (BUXTON COUNTRY PARK)

Green Ln SK17 9DH
Dir: (1m from Buxton town centre, off A6 and A515)
Map Ref: *SK07*
☎ **01298 26978** 🖷 **01298 73563**
e-mail: info@poolescavern.co.uk

Limestone rock, water and millions of years created this natural cavern containing thousands of crystal formations. A 45-minute guided tour leads the visitor through chambers used as a shelter by Bronze-Age cave dwellers, Roman metal workers and as a hideout by the infamous robber Poole. Attractions include the underground source of the River Wye, the 'Poached Egg Chamber', Mary, Queen of Scots' Pillar, the Grand Cascade and underground sculpture formations.

Times: ✱ Open Mar-Oct, daily 10-5. (Open in winter for groups only).
Facilities: 🅿 ♿ toilets for disabled shop ✖ (ex guide dogs or in park) 🍴

CASTLETON BLUE-JOHN CAVERN & MINE

Buxton Rd S33 8WP
Dir: (follow brown "Blue-John Cavern" signs from Castleton)
Map Ref: *SK18*
☎ **01433 620638 & 620642** 🖷 **01433 621586**
e-mail: lesley@bluejohn.gemsoft.co.uk

The Blue John Cavern is a remarkable example of a water-worn cave, over a third of a mile long, with chambers 200 feet high. It contains eight of the 14 veins of Blue John stone, and has been the major source of this unique form of fluorspar for nearly 300 years - the cavern is still mined during the winter months. Guided tours take 45 minutes to an hour, and visitors can see stalactites, stalagmites and magnificent caverns as well as Blue John veins in the limestone.

Times: ✱ Open all year, daily, 9.30-5 (or dusk). Guided tours of approx 1hr every 10 mins tour.
Facilities: 🅿 🍽 (not suitable for disabled visitors) shop 🍴

PEAK CAVERN

S33 8WS
Dir: (on A6187, in centre of Castleton) **Map Ref:** SK18
☎ **01433 620285**
e-mail: info@peakcavern.co.uk

One of the most spectacular natural limestone caves in the Peak District, with an electrically-lit underground walk of about half a mile. Ropes have been made for over 500 years in the 'Grand Entrance Hall', and traces of a row of cottages can be seen. Rope-making demonstrations are included on every tour.

Times: Open Etr-Oct, daily 10-5. Nov-Etr, wknds only 10-5
Facilities: 🅿 (charged) shop 🔳

SPEEDWELL CAVERN

Winnats Pass S33 8WA
Dir: (A625 becomes A6187 at Hathersage. 0.5m W of Castleton)
Map Ref: SK18
☎ **01433 620512** 📄 **01433 621888**
e-mail: info@speedwellcavern.co.uk

Speedwell Cavern is located at the foot of Winnats Pass, just west of Castleton in a former lead mine. A staircase of 105 steps leads down to an artificial tunnel, now filled with water and a boat takes you on a one-mile underground exploration of the floodlit chamber called the Bottomless Pit, which is about 100 metres high and features a 20-metre-high waterfall.

Times: Open all year, Etr-Oct daily 9.30-5.30, Nov-Etr 10-5. (Closed 25 Dec). Phone to check Winter opening times due to weather.
Fee: ✱ £6 (ch £4). **Facilities:** 🅿 (charged) shop 🔳

TREAK CLIFF CAVERN

S33 8WP
Dir: (0.75m W of Castleton on A6187) **Map Ref:** SK18
☎ **01433 620571** 📄 **01433 620519**
e-mail: treakcliff@bluejohnstone.com

An underground world of stalactites, stalagmites, flowstone, rock and cave formations, minerals and fossils is to be discovered at Treak Cliff Cavern. There are rich deposits of the rare and beautiful Blue John Stone, and the show caves include the Witch's Cave, Aladdin's Cave and Fairyland Grotto and some of the finest stalactites in the Peak District.

Times: Open all year, Mar-Oct, daily 10-last tour 4.20, Aug only, last tour 4.45; Nov-Feb daily 10-last tour at 3.20. All tours are guided & last about 40 mins. Enquire for last tour of day & possible closures.
Fee: ✱ £5.80 (ch 5-15 £3.20). Family ticket (2 ad & 2 ch) £16.
Facilities: 🅿 ☕ (establishment can only cater for walking disabled) shop 🔳

CHATSWORTH CHATSWORTH

DE45 1PP
Dir: (8m N of Matlock off B6012. 16m from M1 junct 29,
signposted via Chesterfield, follow brown signs) **Map Ref:** SK27
☎ 01246 582204 ▤ 01246 583536
e-mail: visit@chatsworth.org

The magnificent stately home of the Duke and Duchess of
Devonshire, Chatsworth contains a massive private collection of
fine and decorative arts. There is a splendid painted hall, and a
great staircase leads to the chapel, decorated with statues and
paintings. There are pictures, furniture and porcelain, and a
trompe l'oeil painting of a violin on the music room door. The
park was laid out by 'Capability' Brown, but is most famous as the
work of Joseph Paxton, head gardener in the 19th century.

Times: Open 17 Mar-19 Dec, House & Garden
11-5.30, Farmyard 10.30-5.30. **Fee:** ✱ House &
Garden: £9 (ch £3.50, students & pen £7). Family
ticket £21.50. Pre-booked group discounts
available. Garden only: £5.50 (ch £2.50, students
& pen £4). Family ticket £13.50. Farmyard &
Adventure Playground: £4 (ch under 3 free, pen
£3). Groups 5+ £3.50. Family pass to all
attractions £35. **Facilities:** 🅿 (charged) ☕
✕ licensed ♿ (3 electric wheelchairs available for
garden) toilets for disabled shop garden centre
🐕 (ex park & gardens on lead) ◀

CRESWELL CRESWELL CRAGS MUSEUM AND EDUCATION CENTRE

Crags Rd, Welbeck S80 3LH
Dir: (on the B6042, Crags Road, between A616 and A60, 1m E of
Creswell village) **Map Ref:** SK57
☎ 01909 720378 ▤ 01909 724726
e-mail: info@creswell-crags.org.uk

Creswell Crags, a picturesque limestone gorge with lakes and
caves, is one of Britain's most important archaeological sites. The
many caves on the site have yielded Ice Age remains, including
bones of woolly mammoth, reindeer, hyena and bison, and the
stone tools of Ice Age hunters from over 10,000 years ago. Visit
the museum and education centre to learn more about your Ice
Age ancestors through an exhibition, touch screen computers and
video. Join a 'Virtually the Ice Age' cave tour, picnic in Crags
Meadow, or try the new activity trail.

Times: Open all year, Feb-Oct, daily, 10.30-4.30;
Nov-Jan, Sun only 10.30-4.30. **Fee:** ✱ Free. Cave
& site tour £2.75 (ch £2, no under 5's). £1
parking donation requested.
Facilities: 🅿 ♿ (mobility scooter, tour may be
unsuitable due to steps) toilets for disabled
shop ◀

CRICH CRICH TRAMWAY VILLAGE

DE4 5DP
Dir: (off B5035, 8m from M1 junct 28) **Map Ref:** SK35
☎ 0870 758 7267 ▤ 01773 852326
e-mail: enquiry@tramway.co.uk

Visitors can enjoy unlimited vintage tram rides at Crich Tramway
Village, which provides a mile-long scenic journey through a
period street to open countryside with panoramic views. The
exhibition hall houses the largest collection of vintage electric
trams in Britain and from the viewing gallery you can see
restoration work underway. Children will enjoy the indoor
Discovery Depot or outdoor adventure playground. Refreshments
are available within the village at the Red Lion pub or the Village
Tea Room. Ring for details of special events.

Times: Open Apr-Oct, daily 10-5.30 (6.30 wknds Jun-Aug & BH
wknds). Nov-Dec wknds 10.30-4 **Fee:** ✱ £8 (ch 3-15 £4, pen £7).
Family ticket (2ad+3ch) £21 **Facilities:** 🅿 ☕ ✕ licensed ♿ (Braille
guidebooks, converted tram, talktype facility) toilets for disabled
shop ◀

CROMFORD ARKWRIGHT'S CROMFORD MILL

Mill Ln DE4 3RQ
Dir: (off A6, 3m S of Matlock) *Map Ref:* SK25
☎ 01629 824297 📄 01629 823256
e-mail: info@cromfordmill.co.uk

Sir Richard Arkwright established the world's first successful water-powered cotton spinning mill at Cromford in 1771, and the Arkwright Society is involved in a major restoration to create a lasting monument to an extraordinary genius. Guided tours are available, and there is a programme of lectures and visits - ring for details. The mill is part of the Derwent Valley Mill World Heritage site.

Times: Open all year, daily 9-5 (Closed 25 Dec). **Fee:** Guided tour & exhibitions £2 (ch & pen £1.50). Mill site Free. **Facilities:** 🅿 ✗ ♿ ramps toilets for disabled shop 🛍

DENBY DENBY POTTERY VISITOR CENTRE

Derby Rd DE5 8NX
Dir: (8m N of Derby off A38, on B6179) *Map Ref:* SK34
☎ 01773 740799 📄 01773 740749
e-mail: visitor.centre@denby.co.uk

The visitor centre is situated around a cobbled courtyard including shops and a restaurant. Pottery tours are available daily and offer hands-on activities such as painting a plate and making a clay souvenir. The extensive cookshop runs free half-hour demonstrations daily. There is a factory shop selling Denby seconds, hand-made blown glass from the Glass Studio, a Dartington Crystal Shop, and local artists' gallery.

Times: Open all year. Factory tours, Mon-Thu 10.30 & 1. Craftroom tour, daily 11-3. Visitor Centre Mon-Sat 9.30-5, Sun 10-5. Closed 25-26 Dec. **Fee:** Free. Factory tour £4.95 (ch £3.95). Craftroom tour £3.50 (ch £2.50) **Facilities:** 🅿 ☕ ✗ licensed ♿ (lift) toilets for disabled shop garden centre (outside only, ex guide dogs) 🛍

DERBY DERBY MUSEUM & ART GALLERY

The Strand DE1 1BS
Dir: (follow directions to city centre) *Map Ref:* SK33
☎ 01332 716659 📄 01332 716670
e-mail: david.fraser@derby.gov.uk

FREE

The museum has a wide range of displays, most notably the collection of Derby porcelain, made in the city since 1750, and the largest collection in the world of paintings by local artist Joseph Wright (1734-97). There are also archaeology and militaria galleries, a Bonnie Prince Charlie Room commemorating Derby's role in the Jacobite uprising, and a Derbyshire geology and wildlife feature. The museum also has a temporary exhibition programme and school holiday activities.

Times: Open all year, Mon 11-5, Tue-Sat 10-5, Sun & BHs 2-5. Closed Xmas & New Year, telephone for details. **Facilities:** 🅿 (50yds) ♿ (lift to all floors, portable mini-loop, large print labels) toilets for disabled shop ✈ (ex guide dogs)

EYAM   EYAM HALL

S32 5QW
Dir: (Turn off A623 just after Calver Crossroads & village of Stoney Middleton. Turn left at the top of the hill. Eyam Hall in centre of village opposite the stocks) **Map Ref:** *SK27*
☎ **01433 631976** 📠 **01433 631603**
e-mail: nicola@eyamhall.com

An intimate 17th-century manor house in the heart of the famous 'plague village'. Home to the Wright family since 1671, the Hall offers a glimpse of domestic history through the eyes of one family, in portraits, furniture, tapestries, costumes and memorabilia. Converted farm buildings house the Eyam Hall Craft Centre. Please telephone for details of musical and theatrical events throughout the season.

Times: Open House: Jun-Aug, Wed-Thu, Sun & BH Mon 11-4. Craft Centre open all year Tue-Sun 11-5. **Fee:** House £4.75 (ch £3.50, pen £4.25). Family ticket £14.50. Craft centre free admission. **Facilities:** 🅿 💷 ✕ licensed ♿ (disabled entrance via special gate, ramps) toilets for disabled shop ✈ (ex guide & dogs in grounds) ◀

ILKESTON   *AMERICAN ADVENTURE THEME PARK*

DE7 5SX
Dir: (off M1 junct 26, signed, take A610 to A608 then A6007)
Map Ref: *SK44*
☎ **0845 330 2929** 📠 **01773 716140**
e-mail: sales@americanadventure.co.uk

This is one of Britain's few fully themed parks, based on the legend of a whole continent. The experiences here are widely varied, from the Missile Rollercoaster in Spaceport USA, to the wet and wild excitement of the Rocky Mountain Rapids ride and the Nightmare Niagara log flume. There's also a Mississippi paddle steamer, a horse-show in Silver City, glamorous Lazy Lil's Saloon Show, and Skycoaster, a 200-foot free fall.

Times: ✳ Open 23 Mar-3 Nov, daily from 10. **Facilities:** 🅿 💷 ✕ licensed ♿ (free wheelchair hire, must pre book, call 0845 330 2929) toilets for disabled shop ✈ (ex guide dogs) ◀

MATLOCK BATH   HEIGHTS OF ABRAHAM CABLE CARS, CAVERNS, HILLTOP PARK

DE4 3PD
Dir: (on A6, signed from M1 junct 28. Base station by rail station)
Map Ref: *SK25*
☎ **01629 582365** 📠 **01629 581128**
e-mail: enquiries@h-of-a.co.uk

The visit begins with a spectacular cable car journey to the summit of the hill-top country park. The two spectacular show caverns provide exciting tours to an underground world. There's the 'miners tale', in the Great Rutland Cavern and the 'story of the rock' at the Masson Cavern Pavilion.

Times: Open daily 14-22 Feb & Etr-Oct 10-5 (later in high season), 28 Feb-26 Mar wknds only, for Autumn & Winter opening telephone for details. **Fee:** ✳ £8.50 (ch £5.50, pen £6.50) **Facilities:** 🅿 (300mtrs) 💷 ✕ licensed ♿ (please ring for details) toilets for disabled shop ✈ (ex in grounds & cable car) ◀

PEAK DISTRICT MINING MUSEUM

The Pavilion DE4 3NR
Dir: (On A6 alongside River Derwent) *Map Ref:* SK25
☎ 01629 583834
e-mail: mail@peakmines.co.uk

A large display explains the history of the Derbyshire lead industry from Roman times to the present day. The geology of the area, mining and smelting processes, the quarrying and the people who worked in the industry, are illustrated by a series of static and moving exhibits. The museum also features an early 19th-century water pressure pumping engine. There is a new recycling display in the Pump Room.

Times: ✱ Open all year, daily 11-4 (later in summer season). Closed 25 Dec.
Facilities: ℙ (charged) ☕ & (chair lift to mezzanine) shop ✖ (ex guide dogs)

TEMPLE MINE

Temple Rd DE4 3NR
Dir: (off A6) *Map Ref:* SK25
☎ 01629 583834
e-mail: mail@peakmines.co.uk

Temple Mine is a typical Derbyshire mine, which was worked from the early 1920s until the mid 1950s for fluorspar and associated minerals. A visit to the mine brings to life the processes explained in the nearby Peak District Mining Museum, showing examples of mining methods and providing insight into working conditions underground.

Times: ✱ Open all year, Summer 10-5, Winter timed visits during afternoon.
Facilities: ℙ (100mtrs) ✖ (ex guide dogs)

RIPLEY MIDLAND RAILWAY BUTTERLEY

Butterley Station DE5 3QZ
Dir: (1m N of Ripley on B6179, signposted from A38)
Map Ref: SK35
☎ 01773 747674 & 749788 📄 01773 570721
e-mail: mrc@rapidial.co.uk

A regular steam-train passenger service runs here, to the Midland Railway Centre, where the aim is to depict every aspect of the golden days of the Midland Railway and its successors. Exhibits range from the steam locomotives of 1866 to an electric locomotive. There is also a large section of rolling stock spanning the last 100 years. Special events are held throughout the year, please phone for details.

Times: Open all year, wknds. May-Oct and most school hols. **Fee:** ✱ £8.95 (ch 5-16 £4.50, pen £7.95) children under 5 free. Party 15+.
Facilities: ℙ ☕ & (special accommodation on trains) toilets for disabled shop ◀

ROWSLEY *THE WIND IN THE WILLOWS*

Peak Village DE4 2NP
Dir: (at junct of A6 & B6012) *Map Ref:* SK26
☎ **01629 733433** 📄 **01629 734850**
e-mail: enquiries@windinthewillows.info

Based on the charming book written by Kenneth Grahame and illustrated by E H Shepard, this attraction brings to life the characters of Mole, Ratty, Toad and Badger in an indoor recreation of the English countryside. The Wind in the Willows attraction was designed by the same team that created The World of Beatrix Potter in Cumbria.

Times: Open Apr-Sep, daily 10-5.30; Oct-Mar, daily 10-4.30. (Closed 25 Dec & 28-30 Jan).
Facilities: 🅿 🍽 ♿ toilets for disabled shop ✖ (ex guide dogs) ▰

WIRKSWORTH WIRKSWORTH HERITAGE CENTRE

Crown Yard DE4 4ET
Dir: (on B5023 off A6 in centre of Wirksworth) *Map Ref:* SK25
☎ **01629 825225**
e-mail: heritage@crownyard.fsnet.co.uk

The centre has been created in an old silk and velvet mill, with three floors of interpretative displays on the town's history as a prosperous lead-mining centre. These include a computer game called 'Rescue the injured lead-miner', a mock-up of a natural cavern, and a Quarryman's House. During the Spring Bank Holiday you can also see the famous well dressings. A new exhibition honours the achievements of local girl Ellen MacArthur and there is a gallery selling the work of local artists.

Times: Open Mar-Etr & Nov, Wed-Sat, 11-4, Sun 1.30-4; Etr-Jun & Oct, Tue-Sat, 11-4, Sun 1.30-4; Jul-Sep, Tue-Sat 10-5, Sun 1.30-5. Also open BH Mon 10-5. Last admission 40 mins before closing.
Fee: £3 (ch £1, pen £2). Party 20+ 10% discount **Facilities:** 🅿 (80yds) (pay & display) 🍽 ✖ licensed shop ✖ (ex guide dogs)

BROCKHAMPTON BROCKHAMPTON ESTATE

WR6 5TB
Dir: (2m E of Bromyard on A44) *Map Ref:* SO65
☎ **01885 482077 & 488099** 📄 **01885 482151**
e-mail: brockhampton@nationaltrust.org.uk

Lower Brockhampton on the Brockhampton Estate near Bromyard is a late 14th-century moated manor house, with an attractive half-timbered, 15th-century gatehouse, a rare example of this type of structure, and the ruins of a 12th-century chapel. It is part of a larger National Trust property covering over 1,700 acres of Herefordshire/Worcestershire countryside, with various walks including a sculpture trail.

Times: Open Mar-Oct daily (ex Mon & Tue) but open BH Mons Apr-Oct 12-5 (12-4 in Oct). Woodland walks open to dusk throughout the year. **Fee:** ✱ Lower Brockhampton £3.50 (ch £1.75) Family £8.50 **Facilities:** 🅿 🍽 ♿ (special parking, ramps, Braille guide) toilets for disabled shop ✿ ▰

HEREFORD   *HEREFORD CATHEDRAL*

HR1 2NG
Dir: (A49 signed from city inner ring roads) *Map Ref:* SO53
☎ 01432 374200   📄 01432 374220
e-mail: office@herefordcathedral.co.uk

The first bishop was appointed to the See of Hereford in AD 676. The cathedral is mainly Norman with a 13th-century Lady Chapel. Hereford's two outstanding treasures are exhibited together in the museum building at the west front: the Mappa Mundi, drawn in 1289, and the famous chained library, containing over 1,400 chained books and 227 manuscripts dating from the 8th century.

Times: ✻ Cathedral open daily for visitors 9.30-5; Mappa Mundi & Chained Library Exhibition Summer: Mon-Sat 10-4.15, Sun 11-3.15. Winter: Mon-Sat 11-3.15 (closed Sun).
Facilities: P (0.25m) 🍵 ⴺ (touch facility for blind, braille & large print info) toilets for disabled shop ✕ (ex guide dogs) ◼

OLD HOUSE

High Town HR1 2AA
Dir: (located in the centre of the High Town) *Map Ref:* SO53
☎ 01432 260694

The Old House is a fine half-timbered Jacobean building dating from around 1621, and was once part of a row of similar houses. It became a museum in 1929, and its rooms are furnished in 17th-century style giving visitors the chance to learn what life was like in Cromwell's time. A virtual tour is offered on the ground floor for those unable to access the upper floors.

Times: ✻ Open all year, 10-5. Apr-Sep, Tue-Sat 10-5, Sun & BH Mon 10-4. **Facilities:** P ⴺ shop (very small) ✕ (ex guide dogs)

LEDBURY   *EASTNOR CASTLE*

Eastnor HR8 1RL
Dir: (2.5m E of Ledbury on A438 Tewkesbury road)
Map Ref: SO73
☎ 01531 633160   📄 01531 631776
e-mail: eastnorcastle@eastnorcastle.com

A magnificent Georgian castle in a lovely setting, complete with a deer park, arboretum and lake. Inside, the Italianate and Gothic interiors have been beautifully restored and there are tapestries, fine art and armour on display. An adventure playground, nature trails and lakeside walks all add to the enjoyment of your visit.

Times: Open 27 Mar-2 Oct, Sun & BH Mon; Jul & Aug, Sun-Fri 11-5.
Fee: Castle & grounds £7 (ch £4, pen £6) Family £18. Grounds only £5 (ch £3, pen £4). **Facilities:** P 🍵 ⴺ (please telephone for access & facilities details) shop ◼

BELVOIR BELVOIR CASTLE

NG32 1PD
Dir: (between A52 & A607, follow the brown heritage signs from A1, A52, A607 & A46) *Map Ref:* SK83
☎ **01476 871002** ▤ **01476 871018**
e-mail: info@belvoircastle.com

Although Belvoir Castle has been the home of the Dukes of Rutland for many centuries, the turrets, battlements, towers and pinnacles of the house are a 19th-century fantasy. Amongst the many treasures to be seen inside are paintings by Murillo, Holbein and other famous artists. The castle also houses the museum of the Queens Royal Lancers. The lovingly restored gardens are also open to visitors. Special events are planned every weekend throughout the season, please phone for details.

Times: Open 16-20 Feb; Apr-Sep, daily (closed Mon & Thu); Mar & Oct Sun only. **Fee:** ✳ £9 (ch £7 pen £8). **Facilities:** ▣ ▃ ✕ licensed ⑤ (permitted to be driven/drive right up to castle entrance) toilets for disabled shop ✖ (ex guide dogs) ◀

CASTLE DONINGTON DONINGTON GRAND PRIX COLLECTION

Donington Park DE74 2RP
Dir: (2m from M1 junct 23a/24 and M42/A42 close to Nottingham, Derby and Leicester) *Map Ref:* SK42
☎ **01332 811027** ▤ **01332 812829**
e-mail: enquiries@doningtoncollection.co.uk

Donington has the largest collection of McLaren racing cars on public display; the world's only complete collection of Racing Green Vanwalls, every William F1 car from 1983 to 1999, a superb BRM display, more rare four-wheel drive racing cars than you'll see anywhere else, Ferraris driven by Asvar, and Ickx, Senna's winning McLaren from the 1993 European Grand Prix at Donington, Stirling Moss's Lotus which defeated the Ferraris at Monaco in 1961, Jim Clark's beautiful Lotus 25, and Ronnie Peterson's unique six-wheel Tyrell.

Times: ✳ Open daily 10-5 (last admission 4). Open later on race days. Closed over Xmas period - telephone to confirm opening times.
Facilities: ▣ ▃ ✕ licensed ⑤ shop ✖ (ex guide dogs) ◀

COALVILLE SNIBSTON DISCOVERY PARK

Ashby Rd LE67 3LN
Dir: (4.5m from M1 junct 22/2m or from A42/M42 junct 13 on A511 on W side of Coalville) *Map Ref:* SK41
☎ **01530 278444** ▤ **01530 813301**
e-mail: snibston@leics.gov.uk

At Leicestershire's all-weather science and industry museum, visitors can try their hands at over 50 hands-on experiments, or explore our rich heritage in the Transport, Extractive, Engineering and Textile and Fashion Galleries. Ex-miners give tours of Snibston's colliery buildings, and kids can let off steam in the outdoor science and water playgrounds.

Times: Open daily, 10-5. Closed 1 week in Jan & Christmas period. **Fee:** ✳ £5.70 (ch £3.60, concessions £3.90). Family ticket £17.50. Party. **Facilities:** ▣ ▃ ⑤ (Braille labels, touch tables, parking available) toilets for disabled shop ✖ (ex guide dogs) ◀

DONINGTON-LE-HEATH DONINGTON-LE-HEATH MANOR HOUSE

Manor Rd LE67 2FW
Dir: (S of Coalville) **Map Ref:** *SK41*
☎ **01530 831259** 📄 **01530 831259**
e-mail: museum@leics.gov.uk

FREE

This is a rare example of a medieval manor house, tracing its history back to about 1280. It has now been restored as a period house, with fine oak furnishings. The surrounding grounds include period gardens, and the adjoining stone barn houses a restaurant. A monthly programme of events includes crafts, demonstrations, re-enactments and hands-on activities.

Times: Open Apr-Sep, 11-5; Oct, Nov & Mar 11-3. Dec-Feb wknds only **Facilities:** 🅿 💺 ✗ ♿ toilets for disabled shop ✈ (ex guide dogs)

LEICESTER ABBEY PUMPING STATION

Corporation Rd, Abbey Ln LE4 5PX
Dir: (off A6, 1m N from city centre) **Map Ref:** *SK50*
☎ **0116 299 5111** 📄 **0116 299 5125**

Built as a sewage pumping station in 1891, this fascinating museum features some of the largest steam beam engines in the country, and an exhibition on the history and technology of toilets, water and hygiene. The famous interactive loo is quite a talking point, and there is a steam shovel and a passenger carrying narrow gauge railway. The historic vehicle collection also on site stars a coal-fired fish and chip van.

Times: Open Apr-Sep, Mon-Sat 10-5, Sun 1-5; Oct-Mar, Mon-Sat 10-4, Sun 1-4. Closed 24-26 & 31 Dec-1 Jan. **Facilities:** 🅿 ♿ (loan of wheelchairs, wheelchair lift) toilets for disabled shop ✈ (ex guide dogs) 🍴

JEWRY WALL MUSEUM & SITE

St Nicholas Circle LE1 4LB
Dir: (opposite The Holiday Inn) **Map Ref:** *SK50*
☎ **0116 225 4971** 📄 **0116 225 4966**

The museum is set behind the massive fragment of the Roman Jewry Wall, one of Leicester's best known landmarks, and a Roman Baths site of the 2nd century AD. It is a museum of Leicestershire archaeology, which covers finds from the earliest times to the Middle Ages. A multi-media exhibition, 'The Making of Leicester' focuses on the people behind the city's history, demonstrating how archaeology reveals their secrets. Children have the opportunity to dress up in historical costumes and to become 'archaeological detectives'.Portraits of Leicester through the ages are another feature.

Times: Open Apr-Sep, Mon-Sat 10-5, Sun 1-5; Oct-Mar, Mon-Sat 10-4, Sun 1-4. Closed 24-26 & 31 Dec & 1 Jan. **Facilities:** 🅿 (300yds) (limited on-street parking) ♿ toilets for disabled shop ✈ (ex guide dogs)

LEICESTERSHIRE MUSEUM & ART GALLERY

53 New Walk LE1 7EA
Dir: (situated on New Walk. Access by car from A6 onto Waterloo
Way at Railway Stn. Right into Regent Rd, right onto West St, right
onto Princess Rd which leads to car park) ***Map Ref:*** *SK50*
☎ 0116 225 4900 ▤ 0116 225 4927

Leicester's oldest museum is a major regional venue housing
local and national collections. Major exhibits include 'Wild Space'
a hands-on exhibition interpreting biodiversity and the widely
varying habitats of the world, along with the self-explanatory
'Mighty Dinosaurs', 'Leicestershire's Rocks' and 'Ancient Egyptians'.
Newly refurbished first floor art galleries include a new 'World
Arts' gallery, while 'Gallery Nine' reflects the city's diversity,
providing space for communities to show their own exhibitions.
Specifically for children is 'Discover', a gallery where two to eight-
year-olds are encouraged to play and interact with objects. There
is also a programme of special exhibitions.

Times: Open all year, Apr-Sep, Mon-Sat 10-5, Sun
1-5. Oct-Mar, Mon-Sat 10-4, Sun 1-4. Closed
24-26 & 31 Dec & 1 Jan) **Facilities:** P 🅿
♿ (wheelchairs for loan, minicom, induction loop)
toilets for disabled shop ✖ (ex guide dogs) ◀

NATIONAL SPACE CENTRE

Exploration Dr LE4 5NS
Dir: (off A6, 2m N of Leicester city centre midway between
Leicester's central & outer ring roads. Follow brown signs from M1
junct 21, 21a or 22) and all arterial routes around Leicester)
Map Ref: *SK50*
☎ 0116 261 0261 ▤ 0116 258 2100
e-mail: info@spacecentre.co.uk

Offering five themed galleries, cutting-edge audio-visual
technology and glimpses into genuine space research, the
National Space Centre is a unique experience. Learn about the
planets, the life of an astronaut, weather forecasting, space-
stations and satellites. Visit the Space Theatre and the Newsdesk,
and take a look at the scientists and astronomers doing genuine
research in the Space Science Research Unit.

Times: During school term: Tue-Fri, 10-5 (last
entry 3.30) Sat & Sun 10-6 (last entry 4.30).
Closed Mon. During school holidays: Mon 12-6
(last entry 4.30) Tue-Sun 10-6 (last entry 4.30).
Open all Bank Hols 10-6 (last entry 6.30)
Fee: £8.95 (ch 4-16yrs, concessions & students
£6.95). Family of 4 £28, family of 5 £34
Facilities: P 🅿 ✖ licensed ♿ toilets for disabled
shop ✖ (ex guide dogs) ◀

NEWARKE HOUSES

The Newarke LE2 7BY
Dir: (opposite De Montfort University) ***Map Ref:*** *SK50*
☎ 0116 225 4980 ▤ 0116 225 4982

Newarke Houses Museum comprises two houses, Wygston's
Chantry House dating from around 1511, and Skeffington House
built by Sir Thomas Skeffington between 1560 and 1583, both set
in lovely gardens. William Wygston built the Chantry House to
accommodate two chantry priests to sing masses for his soul in a
nearby church, long since demolished. Reopening in Autumn
2005 after a period of refurbishment, the new emphasis of the
museum will be on the daily life of the 'everyman' in Leicester in
the 20th century, with exhibits on immigration, leisure and
shopping.

Times: Open Apr-Sep, Mon-Sat 10-5, Sun 1-5;
Oct-Mar, Mon-Sat 10-4, Sun 1-4. Closed 24-26 &
31 Dec & 1 Jan. **Facilities:** P (200yds) ♿ (car
parking can be arranged) shop ✖ (ex guide dogs)

UNIVERSITY OF LEICESTER HAROLD MARTIN BOTANIC GARDEN

Beaumont Hall, Stoughton Dr South, Oadby LE2 2NA
Dir: (3m SE A6, entrance at 'The Knoll', Glebe Rd, Oadby)
Map Ref: SK50
☎ 0116 271 7725   FREE

The grounds of four houses, now used as student residences, which are not open to the public, make up this 16-acre garden. Here you can see a great variety of plants in different settings, in what is a delightful place to walk. There are rock, water and sunken gardens, trees, borders, heathers and glasshouses.

Times: Open Mon-Fri 10-4, Sat & Sun 10-4 (from 3rd wknd in Mar to 2nd wknd in Nov inclusive). Closed 25-26 Dec & 1 Jan.
Facilities: P (adjacent) ♿ toilets for disabled ✗ (ex guide dogs)

LOUGHBOROUGH   GREAT CENTRAL RAILWAY

Great Central Rd LE11 1RW
Dir: (signed from A6) *Map Ref:* SK51
☎ 01509 230726   📄 01509 239791
e-mail: booking_office@gcrailway.co.uk

The Great Central is Britain's only main line railway, with full-sized steam engines running on a double track, with freight and passenger trains. The lines run over eight miles from Loughborough Central to Leicester North, with all trains calling at Quorn & Woodhouse and Rothley. The locomotive depot and museum are at Loughborough Central. A buffet car runs on most trains, and the classic corridor trains are steam heated in winter.

Times: Open all year daily, Jun-Aug & school hols; Sep-May, Sat, Sun & BH Mon **Fee:** ✱ Runabout (all day unlimited travel) £11 (ch & pen £7.50). Family ticket £27.50 **Facilities:** P ☕ ✗ licensed ♿ (disabled coach available on most trains, check beforehand) toilets for disabled shop 🛍

MARKET BOSWORTH   *THE BATTLEFIELD LINE*

Shackerstone Station, Shackerstone, Nuneaton CV13 6NW
Dir: (from A444/A447 take B585 to Market Bosworth and follow signs for Congerstone/Shackerstone) *Map Ref:* SK40
☎ 01827 880754   📄 01827 881050

The Battlefield Line runs a regular railway service (mainly steam) from Shackerstone to Shenton. It is a voluntary organisation, now employing paid staff, which has been going since the late 1960s. The railway's base at Shackerstone Station has been fully restored and accommodates an extensive railway museum with a collection of rolling stock and many other relics from the age of steam, plus a shop selling souvenirs.

Times: ✱ Open all year, Passenger steam train service operates Apr-Oct, Sat, Sun & BH Mon. Heritage Railcar Wed Jul-Aug **Facilities:** P ☕ ✗ ♿ toilets for disabled shop 🛍

BOSWORTH BATTLEFIELD VISITOR CENTRE & COUNTRY PARK

Ambion Hill, Sutton Cheney CV13 0AD
Dir: (follow brown tourist signs from A447, A444 & A5)
Map Ref: SK40
☎ **01455 290429** 🗎 **01455 292841**
e-mail: bosworth@leics.gov.uk

The Battle of Bosworth Field was fought in 1485 between the armies of Richard III and the future Henry VII, the latter emerging the victor. The visitor centre offers a comprehensive interpretation of the battle, with exhibitions, models and a film theatre, plus a great insight into medieval life. Special medieval attractions are held in the summer months.

Times: Open Country Park and Battle Trails all year. Visitor Centre open Apr-Oct, daily, 11-5; Nov-Dec, Sun 11-4; Mar, wknds 11-5. Parties all year by arrangement. **Facilities:** 🅿 (charged) ☕ 🚻 (wheelchair & electric scooter hire, tactile exhibits) toilets for disabled shop 🛍

MOIRA CONKERS

Millennium Av, Rawdon Rd DE12 6GA
Dir: (on B5003 in Moira, signed from A444 and M42)
Map Ref: SK31
☎ **01283 216633** 🗎 **01283 210321**
e-mail: info@visitconkers.com

Conkers, located at the heart of the National Forest, is a unique mix of indoor and outdoor hands on experiences. Indoors there are four discovery zones, where children and adults of all ages can get really close to the forest and experience its life and energy. Newer additions are Waterside, an indoor play centre for children, and the Gallery Restaurant. Visitors can travel between the centres on a miniature railway. Outdoors there are 23 different activities including nature trails, an assault course, playgrounds, mazes, Tree Top Tremor and a feature Timber Ramp.

Times: Open daily, summer 10-6, winter 10-5. Closed 25 Dec. **Fee:** £5.95 (ch 3-15yrs £3.95, concessions £4.95). Family ticket (2ad+2ch) £17.50 **Facilities:** 🅿 ☕ ✗ licensed 🚻 (multi access walks & trails accessible to wheelchairs) toilets for disabled shop garden centre 🐕 (ex guide dogs) 🛍

TWYCROSS TWYCROSS ZOO PARK

CV9 3PX
Dir: (on A444 Burton to Nuneaton road, off M42 junct 11)
Map Ref: SK30
☎ **01827 880250** 🗎 **01827 880700**

Set in 50 acres of parkland, the zoo is home to around 1,000 animals, most of which are endangered species. Twycross is the only zoo in Britain to house Bonobos - humans' closest living relative. There are also various other animals such as lions, elephants and giraffes, and a pets' corner for younger children. Other attractions include a penguin pool with underwater viewing and a children's adventure playground.

Times: Open all year, daily 10-6 (4 in winter). Closed 25 Dec. **Fee:** ✱ Please telephone for prices. **Facilities:** 🅿 (charged) ☕ 🚻 toilets for disabled shop 🐕 (ex guide dogs) 🛍

CLEETHORPES *PLEASURE ISLAND FAMILY THEME PARK*

Kings Rd DN35 0PL
Dir: (Follow signs to Pleasure Island from A180) **Map Ref:** *TA30*
☎ **01472 211511** 🖹 **01472 211087**
e-mail: pleasureisland@btinternet.com

Pleasure Island is packed with over 70 rides and attractions. Hold on tight as the colossal wheel of steel rockets you into the sky at a G-force of 2.5, then hurtles you around 360 degrees, sending riders into orbit and giving the sensation of complete weightlessness. It's not just grown ups and thrill seekers who are catered for at Pleasure Island. For youngsters there's hours of fun in Tinkaboo Town, an indoor themed area full of rides and attractions.

Times: ✱ Open 6 Apr-7 Sep, daily from 10. Plus wknds during Sep-Oct & daily during half term (25 Oct-2 Nov). **Facilities:** 🅿 ☕ ✗ licensed ♿ toilets for disabled shop 🖼

CONINGSBY *BATTLE OF BRITAIN MEMORIAL FLIGHT VISITOR CENTRE*

LN4 4SY
Dir: (on A153) **Map Ref:** *TF25*
☎ **01526 344041** 🖹 **01526 342330**
e-mail: bbmf@lincolnshire.gov.uk

View the aircraft of the Battle of Britain Memorial Flight at this visitor centre based at RAF Coningsby. It comprises the only flying Lancaster in Europe, five Spitfires, two Hurricanes, a Dakota and two Chipmunks. There is a permanent gallery and a temporary exhibition space. Guided tours of the hangar, which take about an hour, can also be booked. Because of operational commitments, specific aircraft may not be available. Please ring for information before planning a visit.

Times: Open all year, Mon-Fri, conducted tours 10-3.30. (Closed 2 wks Xmas). (Phone prior to visiting to check security situation) **Fee:** £3.70 (concessions £2.20) Family £9.60 **Facilities:** 🅿 ☕ ♿ (electric wheelchairs not allowed in hangar) toilets for disabled shop 🐕 (ex guide dogs) 🖼

GRIMSBY *NATIONAL FISHING HERITAGE CENTRE*

Alexandra Dock DN31 1UZ
Dir: (follow signs off M180) **Map Ref:** *TA20*
☎ **01472 323345** 🖹 **01472 323555**

The National Fishing Heritage Centre recreates the life of a fisherman as it was in the port of Grimsby's heyday in the 1950s. Here you can sign on as a crew member for a journey of discovery, and experience the harsh reality of life on board a deep sea trawler - without leaving the building. Through interactive games and displays, your challenge is to navigate the icy waters of the Arctic in search of the catch. You can also explore the backstreets of Grimsby, where the fishermen's families lived, shopped and drank.

Times: ✱ Open Apr-Sep, Mon-Thu 10-4, Sat-Sun 11-5 (10.30-5.30 Jul-Sep). **Facilities:** 🅿 ☕ ♿ (easy access route) toilets for disabled shop 🐕 (ex guide dogs) 🖼

LINCOLN MUSEUM OF LINCOLNSHIRE LIFE

Burton Rd LN1 3LY
Dir: (100mtr walk from Lincoln Castle) *Map Ref:* SK97
☎ 01522 528448 ▤ 01522 521264
e-mail: lincolnshirelife.museum@lincolnshire.gov.uk

The museum is located in the former Loyal North Lincoln Militia barracks, dating from 1857. It is a large and varied social history museum, where two centuries of Lincolnshire life are illustrated by displays of domestic implements, industrial machinery, agricultural tools and a collection of horse-drawn vehicles. There is also a collection belonging to the Royal Lincolnshire Regiment. Temporary exhibitions, events and activities are held on a regular basis.

Times: Open all year, May-Sep, daily 10-5.30; Oct-Apr, Mon-Sat 10-5.30, Sun 2-5.30. Closed Sun Oct-Apr **Fee:** ✱ £2.05 (concessions £1.25). Family (2ad 1 3ch) £5.35. **Facilities:** ▣ ▧ ⌖ (wheelchair available, parking space) toilets for disabled shop ✖

USHER GALLERY

Lindum Rd LN2 1NN
Dir: (in city centre, signed) *Map Ref:* SK97
☎ 01522 527980 ▤ 01522 560165
e-mail: usher.gallery@lincolnshire.gov.uk

FREE

Built as the result of a bequest by Lincoln jeweller James Ward Usher, the gallery houses his magnificent collection of watches, porcelain and miniatures, as well as topographical works, watercolours by Peter de Wint, Tennyson memorabilia and coins. The gallery has a popular and changing display of contemporary visual arts and crafts. There is a lively lecture programme and children's activity diary.

Times: Open all year, Tue-Sat 10-5 (last entry 4.30), Sun 1-5 (last entry 4.30), from 1 Jun daily 10-5. Open BHs. Closed 24-26 Dec & 1 Jan. **Facilities:** ▣ ▧ ⌖ (large print guides, induction loop, parking) toilets for disabled shop ✖ (ex guide dogs) ▰

SCUNTHORPE NORMANBY HALL COUNTRY PARK

Normanby DN15 9HU
Dir: (4m N of Scunthorpe off B1430) *Map Ref:* SE81
☎ 01724 720588 ▤ 01724 721248
e-mail: normanbyhall@northlincs.gov.uk

A whole host of activities and attractions is offered in the 300 acres of grounds that surround Normanby Hall, including riding, nature trails and a farming museum. Inside the Regency mansion the fine rooms are decorated and furnished in period style. Outside there is a fully restored and working Victorian kitchen garden and a Victorian walled garden with a nursery selling a wide range of Victorian specialities and other unusual plants.

Times: Open, Park all year, daily, 9-dusk. Walled garden: daily 10.30-5 (4 in winter). Hall & Farming Museum: Apr-Sep daily 1-5. **Fee:** ✱ Apr-Sep £4 (ch £2, concessions £3.60). Family ticket £12. Season ticket (resident) £12 (non resident) £16, Oct-Mar £2.20 per car. **Facilities:** ▣ (charged) ▧ ✖ licensed ⌖ (audio tour, sensory bed in garden, wheelchair/scooter) toilets for disabled shop garden centre ✖ (ex guide dogs & park on lead) ▰

SKEGNESS CHURCH FARM MUSEUM

Church Rd South PE25 2HF
Dir: (follow brown museum signs on entering Skegness)
Map Ref: *TF56*
☎ **01754 766658** 🖹 **01754 898243**
e-mail: churchfarmmuseum@lincolnshire.gov.uk

Church Farm Museum comprises a farmhouse and outbuildings
restored to show the way of life on a Lincolnshire farm at the end
of the 19th century. Items on display include farm implements
and machinery plus household equipment. Temporary exhibitions
are held in the barn with special events throughout the season. A
timber framed mud and stud cottage has been restored on site.

Times: Open Apr-Oct, daily 10-5
Facilities: 🅿 ☕ ♿ (wheelchair available,
grounds accessible with care) toilets for disabled
shop ✖ (ex guide dogs)

SKEGNESS NATURELAND SEAL SANCTUARY

North Pde PE25 1DB
Dir: (N end of seafront) ***Map Ref:*** *TF56*
☎ **01754 764345** 🖹 **01754 764345**
e-mail: natureland@fsbdial.co.uk

Natureland houses seals, penguins, tropical birds, an aquarium,
reptiles and a pets' corner. You can also see tropical butterflies
flying free from May to October. The sanctuary is well known for
its rescue of abandoned seal pups, and has successfully reared
and returned to the wild a large number of them. The hospital
unit incorporates a public viewing area, and a large seascape seal
pool with underwater viewing.

Times: Open all year, daily at 10. Closing times vary according to
season. Closed 25-26 Dec & 1 Jan. **Fee:** ✳ £4.95 (ch under 3 free,
ch £3.25, pen £3.95). Family ticket £14.70. **Facilities:** 🅿 (100yds)
☕ ♿ (low windows on seal pools) toilets for disabled shop ◀

SPALDING BUTTERFLY & WILDLIFE PARK

Long Sutton PE12 9LE
Dir: (off A17 at Long Sutton) ***Map Ref:*** *TF22*
☎ **01406 363833 & 363209** 🖹 **01406 363182**
e-mail: butterflypark@hotmail.com

The park has one of Britain's largest walk-through tropical houses,
in which hundreds of butterflies and birds from all over the world
fly freely. See the ant room where you can observe leaf-cutting
ants in their natural working habitat, and Reptile Land, home to
crocodiles and snakes. Outside are 15 acres of butterfly and bee
gardens, wildflower meadows, a nature trail, farm animals, a pets'
corner and a large adventure playground. At the Lincolnshire Birds
of Prey Centre, also on site, there are daily flying displays.

Times: Open 20 Mar-end Oct, daily 10-5. (Sep &
Oct 10-4). **Fee:** ✳ £5.50 (ch 3-16 £3.80, pen
£4.80). Family ticket £17-£20. Party rates on
application. **Facilities:** 🅿 ✖ licensed
♿ (wheelchairs available) toilets for disabled shop
✖ (ex guide dogs) ◀

STAMFORD BURGHLEY HOUSE

PE9 3JY
Dir: (1.5m off A1 at Stamford) **Map Ref:** *TF00*
☎ **01780 752451** 📄 **01780 480125**
e-mail: burghley@burghley.co.uk

This great Elizabethan palace, built by William Cecil, has all the hallmarks of that ostentatious period. The vast house is three storeys high and the roof is a riot of pinnacles, cupolas and paired chimneys in classic Tudor style. However, the interior was restyled in the 17th century, and the state rooms are now Baroque, with silver fireplaces, elaborate plasterwork and painted ceilings. These were painted by Antonio Verrio, whose Heaven Room is quite awe-inspiring.

Times: Open end Mar-Oct, daily. Please telephone for details. **Fee:** ✱ £7.80 (ch 5-11 £3.50, pen £6.90) Family £19.50
Facilities: 🅿 🍴 ✗ licensed ♿ (chairlift access, some mobility required) toilets for disabled shop ✗ (ex guide dogs) ▬

STAMFORD MUSEUM

Broad St PE9 1PJ
Dir: (from A1 follow town centre signs from any Stamford exit)
Map Ref: *TF00*
☎ **01780 766317** 📄 **01780 480363**   **FREE**
e-mail: stamford_museum@lincolnshire.gov.uk

Displays illustrate the history of this fine stone town and include Stamford Ware pottery, the visit of Daniel Lambert and the town's more recent industrial past. The new Stamford Tapestry depicts the history of the town in wool. Holiday activities are provided for children, and there are information sheets on Daniel Lambert, the Stamford Spitfire, Sir Malcolm Sargent, and the filming of 'Middlemarch'.

Times: Open all year, Apr-Sep, Mon-Sat 10-5, Sun 1-4; Oct-Mar Mon-Sat 10-5. Closed 24-26 & 31 Dec & 1 Jan. **Facilities:** 🅿 (200yds) (on street parking is limited waiting) ♿ (audio loop at reception, Braille leaflets) shop ✗ (ex guide dogs)

WOOLSTHORPE WOOLSTHORPE MANOR

23 Newton Way NG33 5NR
Dir: (7m S of Grantham, 1m W of A1) **Map Ref:** *SK92*
☎ **01476 860338** 📄 **01476 860338**
e-mail: woolsthorpemanor@nationaltrust.org.uk

A fine stone-built, 17th-century farmhouse, Woolsthorpe Manor was the birthplace of the scientist and philosopher Sir Isaac Newton. He also lived at the house from 1665-67 during the Plague, and an early edition of his book '*Principia Mathematica*' (1687) is on display. There is a 'Young Newton' exhibition in the house and a Science Discovery Centre in the barn. In the orchard is a descendant of the famous apple tree.

Times: Open Apr-Sep, Wed-Sun 1-5; Oct, Sat & Sun 1-5, BH Mon **Fee:** £4.20 (ch £2.10). Family ticket £10.50 **Facilities:** 🅿 ♿ (Braille & large print guide, wheelchair available) toilets for disabled ✗ (ex guide dogs) ▬

ALTHORP ALTHORP

NN7 4HQ
Dir: (from S, exit M1 junct 16, & N junct 18, follow signs towards Northampton until directed by brown signs) **Map Ref:** *SP66*
☎ **01604 770107 & 0870 167 9000** 🖷 **01604 770042**
e-mail: mail@althorp.com

Althorp House has been the home of the Spencer family since 1508. The house was built in the 16th century, but has been changed since, most notably by Henry Holland in the 18th century. Now restored by the present Earl, the house is carefully maintained and in immaculate condition. The award-winning exhibition 'Diana, A Celebration' is located in six rooms and depicts the life and work of Diana, Princess of Wales. There is in addition, a room which depicts the work of the Diana, Princess of Wales Memorial Fund.

Times: Open Jul-Sep, daily 11-5. Closed 31 Aug. **Fee:** £11.50 (ch £5.50 & pen £9.50). Family ticket £28.50. Tickets discounted if pre-booked (not confirmed) **Facilities:** 🅿 ⬛ & (disabled parking, wheelchairs, audio tour, shuttle) toilets for disabled shop ✖ (ex guide dogs) ◀

STOKE BRUERNE CANAL MUSEUM

NN12 7SE
Dir: (A508, 4m S of M1 junct 15. 5m from Towcester A43/A5 junct) **Map Ref:** *SP74*
☎ **01604 862229** 🖷 **01604 864199**
e-mail: canal.museum@thewaterwaystrust.co.uk

Housed on three floors of an old corn mill, the colourful collection at the Canal Museum vividly portrays the many aspects of inland waterways from their origins to the present day. It is located beside the flight of locks and long Blisworth Tunnel on the Grand Union Canal in the picturesque village of Stoke Bruerne.

Times: Open Etr-Oct daily, 10-5; Nov-Etr Tue-Sun, 10-4. Closed 25-26 Dec. (Last admission 30 mins before closing time). **Facilities:** 🅿 (charged) & toilets for disabled shop ✖ (ex guide dogs) ◀

EDWINSTOWE SHERWOOD FOREST COUNTRY PARK & VISITOR CENTRE

NG21 9HN
Dir: (on B6034 N of Edwinstowe between A6075 and A616)
Map Ref: *SK66*
☎ **01623 823202 & 824490** 🖷 **01623 823202**   `FREE`
e-mail: sherwood.forest@nottscc.gov.uk

At the heart of the Robin Hood legend is Sherwood Forest. Today it offers a country park and visitor centre with 450 acres of ancient oaks and shimmering silver birches. Waymarked pathways are provided to help guide walkers through the forest. A year round programme of events includes the spectacular Robin Hood Festival held annually in late July-early August.

Times: Country Park: open daily dawn to dusk. Visitor Centre: open daily 10-5 (4.30 Nov-Mar) **Facilities:** 🅿 (charged) ✖ & (wheelchair loan) toilets for disabled shop ◀

FARNSFIELD   WHITE POST FARM CENTRE

NG22 8HL
Dir: (12m N of Nottingham on A614) *Map Ref:* SK65
☎ 01623 882977 & 882026   ▤ 01623 883499
e-mail: tim@whitepostfarmcentre.co.uk

This award-winning working farm gives an introduction to a variety of modern farming methods. It explains how farms work, with exhibits such as llamas, deer, pigs, cows, snails, quails, snakes and fish. Indoors you can see the incubator room, mousetown and a reptile house. There is also a large indoor play area including a sledge run, trampoline and a large bouncy slide.

Times: Open daily from 10 **Fee:** ✱ £6.75 (ch 3-16 £6, under 3's free) **Facilities:** 🅿 💺 ♿ (free hire wheelchairs, book if more than 6) toilets for disabled shop ✖ (ex guide dogs) ◄

NEWARK-ON-TRENT   MILLGATE MUSEUM

48 Millgate NG24 4TS
Dir: (easy access from A1 & A46) *Map Ref:* SK75
☎ 01636 655730   ▤ 01636 655735   FREE
e-mail: museums@nsdc.info

The Millgate Museum shows some fascinating exhibitions such as recreated streets, shops and houses in period settings. These displays illustrate the working and domestic life of local people from Victorian times to 1950. The mezzanine gallery is used as a temporary exhibition space showcasing the work of local artists, designers and photographers.

Times: Open all year, Mon-Fri 10-5, Sat & Sun & BH 1-5. (Last admission 4.30).
Facilities: 🅿 (250yds) 💺 ♿ toilets for disabled shop ✖ (ex assistance dogs)

NEWARK AIR MUSEUM

The Airfield, Winthorpe NG24 2NY
Dir: (easy access from A1, A46, A17 & Newark relief road, follow tourist signs) *Map Ref:* SK75
☎ 01636 707170   ▤ 01636 707170
e-mail: newarkair@onetel.com

Newark Air Museum, the largest volunteer-managed aviation museum in the country, houses a diverse collection of more than 60 items. These include transport, training and reconnaissance aircraft, jet fighters, bombers and helicopters. An undercover aircraft display hall and an engine hall make the museum an all-weather attraction, with everything set around a World War II airfield.

Times: Open all year, Mar-Sep daily 10-5; Oct-Feb, daily 10-4. Closed 24-26 Dec & 1 Jan. Other times by appointment. **Fee:** £4.75 (ch £3, pen £4). Family ticket £13.50. Party 10+.
Facilities: 🅿 💺 ♿ toilets for disabled shop ◄

VINA COOKE MUSEUM OF DOLLS & BYGONE CHILDHOOD

The Old Rectory, Cromwell NG23 6JE
Dir: (5m N of Newark off A1) **Map Ref:** *SK75*
☎ **01636 821364**

All kinds of childhood memorabilia are displayed in this 17th-century dower house: prams, toys, dolls' houses, costumes and a large collection of Victorian and Edwardian dolls. Vina Cooke hand-made character dolls, crafts and other items are available for sale, and there is also a dolls' hospital. There is a tearoom and picnic area in the delightful garden, and a special event on Easter Monday with crafts, morris and clog dancing.

Times: ✱ Open Apr-Sep, Sat-Thu 10.30-12 & 2-5. Oct-Mar, opening times vary.
Facilities: 🅿 & shop

NOTTINGHAM   THE CAVES OF NOTTINGHAM

Upper Level, Broadmarsh Shopping Centre NG1 7LS
Dir: (within Broadmarsh Shopping Centre, on first floor)
Map Ref: *SK53*
☎ **0115 924 1424** 🖹 **0115 924 1430**
e-mail: info@cavesofnottingham.co.uk

The Caves of Nottingham is a unique 750-year-old cave system situated beneath a modern day shopping centre. A digital audio tour guides you through the only remaining underground medieval tannery in England, beer cellars, an air raid shelter and the remains of Drury Hill, one of the oldest streets in Nottingham.

Times: ✱ Open daily 10-5, Sun 11-5 (last admission 4.15, Sun 4). Closed 24-26 Dec, 1 Jan & Etr Sun. **Facilities:** 🅿 (charged) & (non-accessible to w/chairs, induction loop, textual guide) shop ✖ (ex guide dogs) 🍴

GALLERIES OF JUSTICE

The Shire Hall, High Pavement, Lace Market NG1 1HN
Dir: (follow signs to city centre, brown heritage signs to Lace Market & Galleries of Justice) **Map Ref:** *SK53*
☎ **0115 952 0555** 🖹 **0115 993 9828**
e-mail: info@galleriesofjustice.org.uk

The Galleries of Justice are located on the site of an original court and county gaol. Visitors can take a tour through three centuries of crime and punishment, witnessing a trial re-created in the authentic Victorian courtroom before being 'sent down' to the original cells and medieval caves. In the Edwardian police station, an interactive forensic science display allows visitors to 'crack the case'. A series of innovative and stimulating temporary exhibitions runs throughout the year, with special activities for all the family run in school holidays.

Times: ✱ Open all year, Tue-Sun & BH Mon 10-5 (also open Mon in school hols). (Last admission one hour before closing). Contact for Xmas opening times. **Facilities:** 🅿 (5 mins walk) 💷 & (Braille control lifts, induction loop, large print lables) toilets for disabled shop ✖ (ex guide dogs) 🍴

THE MUSEUM OF NOTTINGHAM LIFE

Brewhouse Yard, Castle Boulevard NG7 1FB
Dir: (follow signs to city centre) *Map Ref:* *SK53*
☎ **0115 915 3600 & 0115 915 3640** 🖹 **0115 915 3601**

Nestled in the rock below Nottingham Castle and housed in a row of 17th-century cottages, the museum presents a realistic glimpse of life in Nottingham over the last 300 years. Discover the caves behind the museum and peer through 1920's shop windows. You can also visit a World War II bomb shelter and a Victorian home.

Times: Open daily, 10-4.30. Last admission 4. **Fee:** ✱ Free Mon-Fri but donations appreciated. Wknds & BHs £1.50 (concessions 80p). Family ticket £3.80. **Facilities:** P (100yds) ♿ (call 0115 915 3700 for info on access) toilets for disabled shop ✖ (ex guide dogs)

NOTTINGHAM CASTLE

NG1 6EL
Map Ref: *SK53*
☎ **0115 915 3700** 🖹 **0115 915 3653**

This 17th-century building is both a museum and art gallery, with major temporary exhibitions by historical and contemporary artists, as well as the permanent collections. There is a 'Story of Nottingham' exhibition and a gallery designed especially to entertain young children. Guided tours of the underground passages take place on most days.

Times: ✱ Open all year, daily 10-5. Grounds 8-dusk. Closed 25-26 Dec. **Facilities:** P (400yds) ☕ ♿ (parking at castle, for more info call 0115 915 3700) toilets for disabled shop ✖ (ex guide dogs)

TALES OF ROBIN HOOD

30-38 Maid Marian Way NG1 6GF
Dir: (in city centre, follow brown & white signs) *Map Ref:* *SK53*
☎ **0115 948 3284** 🖹 **0115 950 1536**
e-mail: robinhoodcentre@mail.com

Using a combination of adventure cars and special effects, visitors to the Tales of Robin Hood are transported back to medieval Nottingham and Sherwood Forest, legendary home of Robin Hood. Portable CD players provide a commentary in seven languages. Other attractions include the Silver Arrow Trail detective game, Shoot the Sheriff archery practice and storytelling workshops. By night the centre becomes the setting for medieval banquets. Special events take place throughout the year.

Times: Open all year, daily 10-5.30. Last admission 4. Closed 25-26 Dec. **Fee:** £6.95 (ch £4.95, pen & students £5.95) Family ticket from £21.50. **Facilities:** P (NCP 200 yds) ☕ ♿ (specially adapted 'car', lift) toilets for disabled shop ✖ (ex guide dogs) ◀

WOLLATON HALL & PARK

Wollaton NG8 2AE
Dir: (M1 junct 25 signed from A52, A609, A6154, A60 and city centre) *Map Ref:* SK53
☎ 0115 915 3900 🖹 0115 915 3932
e-mail: info@wollatonhall.org.uk

Built in the late 16th century, and extended in the 19th, Wollaton Hall and Park holds Nottingham's Natural History Museum, Nottingham's Industrial Museum, the Wollaton Park Visitor Centre, and the Yard Gallery, which has changing exhibitions exploring art and the environment. The hall itself is set in 500 acres of deer park, with herds of red and fallow deer roaming wild. There are also formal gardens, a lake, nature trails, adventure playgrounds, a sensory garden and a water garden. The many events throughout the year include pop concerts, opera, and twilight bat walks.

Times: Open Hall, visitor centre, shop, yard gallery daily, Oct-Mar 11-4, Apr-Sep 11-5. Industrial Museum open Apr-Sept, daily 11-5. Park & grounds wkdays 8-dusk, wknds 9-dusk.
Fee: ✱ Free wkdays. Ticket for either Hall or Museum £1.50 (ch & concessions 80p), family ticket £3.80. Ticket for Hall & Museum £2 (concessions £1) family ticket £5. Charge made at wknds & BHs only. **Facilities:** 🅿 (charged) ☕ ♿ (call 0115 915 3700 for info on access) toilets for disabled shop ✖ (ex guide dogs) ◀

OLLERTON   RUFFORD ABBEY AND COUNTRY PARK

NG22 9DF
Dir: (2m S of Ollerton, adjacent to A614) *Map Ref:* SK66
☎ 01623 822944 🖹 01623 824840   FREE
e-mail: marilyn.louden@nottscc.gov.uk

At the heart of the wooded country park stand the remains of a 12th-century Cistercian Abbey, housing an exhibition on the life of Cistercian Monks at Rufford. Many species of wildlife can be seen on the lake, and there are lovely formal gardens, with sculptures and Britain's first centre for studio ceramics.

Times: Open all year 10.30-5.30 (craft centre closes 4pm Jan & Feb). For further details of opening times telephone establishment.
Facilities: 🅿 (charged) ☕ ✖ licensed ♿ (lift to craft centre gallery, free parking,wheelchair loan) toilets for disabled shop garden centre ✖ (ex guide dogs) ◀

SOUTHWELL   THE WORKHOUSE

Upton Rd NG25 0PT
Map Ref: SK65
☎ 01636 817250 🖹 01636 817251
e-mail: theworkhouse@nationaltrust.org.uk

Enter this 19th-century brick-built institution and discover the thought-provoking story of the 'welfare' system of the New Poor Law. The least altered workhouse in existence today, it survives from hundreds that once covered the country. Explore the segregated stairs and rooms, use the audio guide, based on archive records, to bring the 19th-century inhabitants to life in the empty rooms, then try the interactive displays exploring poverty through the years and across the country.

Times: Open 28 Mar-Oct, Thu-Mon noon-5 (Aug 11-5). (Last admission 1hr before closing).
Fee: £4.60 (ch £2.30). Family ticket £11.50
Facilities: 🅿 ♿ (virtual tour, photo album, wheelchairs available) toilets for disabled ✖ (ex guide dogs) ✤

SUTTON-CUM-LOUND *WETLANDS WATERFOWL RESERVE & EXOTIC BIRD PARK*

Off Loundlow Rd DN22 8SB
Dir: (signed on A638) ***Map Ref:*** *SK68*
☎ **01777 818099**

The reserve is a 32-acre site for both wild and exotic waterfowl. Visitors can see a collection of birds of prey, parrots, geese, ducks, and wigeon among others. There are also many small mammals and farm and wild animals to see, including llamas, wallabies, emus, monkeys, red squirrels, deer and goats.

Times: ✱ Open all year, daily 10-5.30 (or dusk - whichever is earlier). Closed 25 Dec.
Facilities: 🅿 🍽 ♿ (wheelchair available) shop ✘ (ex guide dogs)

OAKHAM *RUTLAND COUNTY MUSEUM*

Catmos St LE15 6HW
Dir: (on A6003, S of town centre) ***Map Ref:*** *SK80*
☎ **01572 758440** 📄 **01572 758445**   FREE
e-mail: museum@rutland.gov.uk

Rutland County Museum displays collections of farming equipment, machinery and wagons, rural tradesmen's tools, domestic artefacts and local archaeology, all housed in a splendid late 18th-century cavalry riding school. The new 'Welcome to Rutland' gallery provides a guide to the history of Rutland and includes a shop and study area.

Times: Open all year, Mon-Sat 10.30-5, Sun 2-4. Closed Good Fri & Xmas. **Facilities:** 🅿 (adjacent) (pay & display, free on Sun) ♿ (induction loop in meeting room) toilets for disabled shop ✘ (ex guide dogs)

COSFORD *ROYAL AIR FORCE MUSEUM*

TF11 8UP
Dir: (on A41, 1m S of M54 junct 3) ***Map Ref:*** *SJ70*
☎ **01902 376200** 📄 **01902 376211**
e-mail: cosford@rafmuseum.org

The Royal Airforce Museum at the Shropshire RAF base has one of the largest aviation collections in the UK. Exhibits include the Victor and Vulcan bombers, the Hastings, York and British Airways airliners, the Belfast freighter and the last airworthy Britannia. The research and development collection includes the notable TSR2, Fairey Delta, Bristol 188 and many more important aircraft.

Times: Open all year daily, 10-6 (last admission 4). Closed 24-26 Dec & 1 Jan
Facilities: 🅿 ✘ licensed ♿ (free loan of 3 manual wheelchairs) toilets for disabled shop ✘ (ex guide dogs)

CRAVEN ARMS SECRET HILLS, THE SHROPSHIRE HILLS DISCOVERY CENTRE

School Rd SY7 9RS
Dir: (on A49, on S edge of Craven Arms) **Map Ref:** SO48
☎ **01588 676000** 📄 **01588 676030**
e-mail: jill.jarrett@shropshire-cc.gov.uk

This attraction explores the history, nature and geography of the Shropshire Hills through a series of interactive displays and simulations, including a simulated balloon flight. The centre has 23 acres of meadowlands, with a network of cycle routes and walks. On summer weekends, a shuttle bus operates which allows visitors to explore the local landscape, and market towns.

Times: Open all year, daily from 10. (Last admission 3.30 Nov-Mar, 4.30 Apr-Oct). **Fee:** ✱ £4.25 (ch £2.75 & pen £3.75, ch under 5 free). Family ticket £12.20. Groups 20+ £3.75 each, ch £2.50 each. **Facilities:** 🅿 ☕ ✕ licensed ♿ (wheelchair available) toilets for disabled shop ✖ (ex guide dogs) ◼

IRONBRIDGE *IRONBRIDGE GORGE MUSEUMS*

Coach Rd TF8 7DQ
Dir: (M54 junct 4, signed) **Map Ref:** SJ60
☎ **01952 433522 & 0800 590258** 📄 **01952 432204**
e-mail: info@ironbridge.org.uk

Ironbridge is the site of the world's first iron bridge, cast and built here in 1779 to span a narrow gorge over the River Severn. Now Ironbridge is the site of a remarkable series of museums relating the story of the bridge, recreating life in Victorian times and featuring ceramics and social history displays. These are the Coalbrookdale Museum of Iron and Darby Houses, Blists Hill Victorian Town, the Coalport China Museum and Tar Tunnel, the Museum of the Gorge, the Iron Bridge and Tollhouse, the Jackfield Tile Museum, Broseley Pipeworks, and Enginuity, an interactive design and technology centre.

Times: ✱ Open all year, 10-5. Some small sites closed Nov-Mar. Telephone or write for exact winter details. **Facilities:** 🅿 ☕ ✕ licensed ♿ (wheelchairs, potters wheel, Braille guide, hearing loop) toilets for disabled shop ✖ (ex Blists Hill & guide dogs) ◼

TELFORD *HOO FARM ANIMAL KINGDOM*

Preston-on-the-Weald Moors TF6 6DJ
Dir: (M54 junct 6, follow brown tourist signs) **Map Ref:** SJ60
☎ **01952 677917** 📄 **01952 677944**
e-mail: info@hoofarm.com

Hoo Farm is clean, friendly farm that offers close contact with animals from fluffy yellow chicks and baby lambs to foxes, llamas, deer and ostriches. A daily programme of events encourages audience participation in bottle feeding lambs, pig feeding and collecting freshly laid eggs. They even have ferret racing! The craft area offers candle dipping, glass or pottery painting or throwing a pot on the potter's wheel. There are junior quad bikes, a rifle range, pony rides and powered mini tractors as well as indoor and outdoor play areas and a games room.

Times: ✱ Open 23 Mar-8 Sep, daily 10-6 (last admission 5). 10 Sep-22 Nov, Tue-Sun 10-5 (last admission 4. Closed Mon ex Halloween). 23 Nov-24 Dec daily 10-5 (closes at 1pm 24 Dec). Closed 25 Dec-mid Mar. **Facilities:** 🅿 ☕ ♿ toilets for disabled shop ✖ (ex guide dogs) ◼

WESTON-UNDER-REDCASTLE HAWKSTONE HISTORIC PARK & FOLLIES

SY4 5UY
Dir: (3m from Hodnet off A53, follow brown heritage signs)
Map Ref: SJ52
☎ **01939 200611** 📄 **01939 200311**
e-mail: info@hawkstone.co.uk

After a century of neglect, this 100-acre 18th-century park has been restored and given a Grade I listing. Visitors can once again experience the magical world of intricate pathways, arches, bridges, towering cliffs and follies, and an awesome grotto. There are centuries-old oaks, wild rhododendrons and lofty monkey puzzles. Visitors should allow three to four hours for the tour (map provided). Wear sensible footwear and bring a torch.

Times: ✱ Open from 10, Jan-Mar, Sat & Sun; Apr-May, & Sep-Oct, Wed-Sun; Jun-Aug, daily. Closed Nov & Dec. **Fee:** *Prices not confirmed for 2005* **Facilities:** 🅿 ☕ ✗ licensed ♿ (no access to follies due to terrain access Valley only) toilets for disabled shop 🛍

WROXETER WROXETER ROMAN CITY

SY5 6PH
Dir: (5m E of Shrewsbury, 1m S of A5) *Map Ref:* SJ50
☎ **01743 761330**

Discover what urban life was like 2,000 years ago in Wroxeter (Viroconium), the fourth largest city in Roman Britain and a fine example of Roman civic planning. It began as a legionary fortress and developed into a flourishing city covering 200 acres with two miles of walls. See the remains of the impressive 2nd-century municipal baths and view the excavated treasures in the museum.

Times: Open all year, Mar-May, daily, 10-5; Jun-Aug, daily, 10-6; Sep-Oct, daily, 10-5; Nov-Feb, daily, 10-4. Closed 24-26 Dec & 1 Jan
Fee: ✱ £4 (ch £2, concessions £3, family £10). Prices & opening times relate to 2004, for further details phone or log onto www.english-heritage.org.uk/visits
Facilities: 🅿 ♿ shop ⌗

ALTON ALTON TOWERS

ST10 4DB
Dir: (from S - M1 junct 23a or M6 junct 15 from N - M1 junct 28 or M6 junct 16) *Map Ref:* SK04
☎ **08705 204060** 📄 **01538 704097**
e-mail: info@alton-towers.com

Alton Towers is a fantastic day out for all the family. With some of the country's favourite rides and attractions as well as some beautiful gardens. The park is divided into ten areas or 'lands', with thrill-seekers generally heading for Forbidden Kingdom. There is fun for everyone at HEX, set in the Towers' ruins, the runaway train ride and the stone-age land of UG. Younger children will be delighted by Storybook Land, Cred Street and Old MacDonald's Farm. A new addition is the Spinball Whizzer, a fabulous spinner coaster.

Times: Open daily 12 Mar-30 Oct **Fee:** ✱ From £20 (ch from £17) **Facilities:** 🅿 (charged) ☕ ✗ licensed ♿ (disabled guest guide books) toilets for disabled shop 🐕 (ex guide dogs) 🛍

CHEDDLETON CHEDDLETON FLINT MILL

Beside Caldon Canal, Leek Rd ST13 7HL
Dir: (3m S of Leek on A520) *Map Ref:* SJ95
☎ 01782 502907

FREE

Twin water-wheels on the River Churnet drive flint-grinding pans in the two mills. The mill museum shows a collection of machinery used in the preparation of materials for the ceramic industry. This includes a 100 HP Robey horizontal steam engine, a model Newcomen beam engine, an edge-runner mill, and the narrow boat 'Vienna', moored on the Caldon Canal. Display panels explain the processes of winning and treating clays, stone and flint for the pottery industry.

Times: Open all year, Sat & Sun 2-5, Mon-Fri 10-5 (by arrangement). Phone to check **Facilities:** P & toilets for disabled

CHURNET VALLEY RAILWAY

The Station ST13 7EE
Dir: (3m S from Leek, 3m N from Cellarhead along A520)
Map Ref: SJ95
☎ 01538 360522 📄 01538 361848
e-mail: mgt@cheddcvr.freeserve.co.uk

The Churnet Valley Railway runs through the hidden countryside between Cheddleton, with its Grade II Victorian station, and Froghall, with the newly built station and Canal Wharf. The journey incorporates Consall, which has a sleepy rural station and nature reserve, and Leekbrook with one of the longest tunnels on a preserved railway. Special event days are a feature.

Times: Open every Sun, Mar-mid Oct; Wed & Sat, Jun-Aug; Diesel trains every Tue & Thu in Aug & all BHs. **Fee:** ✱ Return ticket £7 (ch £4, pen £6). **Facilities:** P 💻 & (ramps) toilets for disabled shop ◀

LICHFIELD LICHFIELD HERITAGE CENTRE

Market Square WS13 6LG
Dir: (in city centre) *Map Ref:* SK10
☎ 01543 256611 📄 01543 414749
e-mail: info@lichfieldheritage.org.uk

At the heritage centre a colourful exhibition called 'The Lichfield Story' gives a vivid account of Lichfield's rich and varied history over 2,000 years. It is also home to the Staffordshire Millennium Embroideries, which are displayed within their own gallery. There are fine examples of city, diocesan and regimental silver, ancient charters and archives. Two audio visual presentations, a family trail and a mouse hole trail for younger children provide interest and fun for all the family.

Times: ✱ Open all year, daily 10-5, Sun 10.30-5. (Last admission 4). Closed Xmas & New Year. **Facilities:** P (200yds) 💻 & (lift to first floor) toilets for disabled shop ✖ (ex guide dogs) ◀

SHUGBOROUGH *SHUGBOROUGH ESTATE*

ST17 0XB
Dir: (6m E of Stafford off A513, signposted from M6 junct 13)
Map Ref: SJ92
☎ 01889 881388 📄 01889 881323
e-mail: shugborough.promotions@staffordshire.gov.uk

Shugborough is the magnificent 900-acre seat of the Earls of
Lichfield on the edge of Cannock Chase, an 18th-century mansion
house with fine ceramics, silver, paintings and French furniture.
Visitors can enjoy the Grade I listed historic garden and unique
neo-classical monuments. Other attractions include the museum,
the servants' quarters, laundry, kitchens, brewhouse and
coachhouses, all restored and fully operational. Shugborough Park
Farm is a Georgian farmstead with an agricultural museum,
working corn mill and rare breeds centre.

Times: Open 27 Mar-26 Sep, daily (ex Mon, but
open BH Mon) 11-5. Sun only during Oct. Site
open all year to pre-booked parties.
Facilities: 🅿 (charged) 🍴 ✗ licensed ♿ (step
climber for wheelchairs, 2 Batricars) toilets for
disabled shop ✗ (ex guide dogs & in parkland)

STOKE-ON-TRENT *CERAMICA*

Market Place, Burslem ST6 3DS
Dir: (exit M6 junct 15/16 take A500 leave at A4527 (signposted
Tunstall). After 0.5m right onto B5051 for Burslem. Ceramica is in
Old Town Hall in centre of town) *Map Ref:* SJ84
☎ 01782 832001 📄 01782 823300
e-mail: info@ceramicauk.com

A unique experience for all the family, Ceramica is housed in the
Old Town Hall in the centre of Burslem, Mother Town of the
Potteries. Explore the hands-on activities in Bizarreland, and learn
how clay is transformed into china. Dig into history with the time
team and take a magic carpet ride over the town. Discover the
past, present and future of ceramics with the interactive displays
in the Pavillions. Explore the Memory Bank and read the local
news on Ceramica TV.

Times: Open Mon-Sat 9.30-5, Sun 10.30-4.30.
For Xmas opening please telephone.
Fee: ✱ £3.75, (concessions £2.50, under 4's
free). Family ticket (2ad+2ch) £10. Group of 12
£2.50 per person. **Facilities:** 🅿 (charged)
♿ (ramps, lift to all floors, tactile displays) toilets
for disabled shop ✗ (ex guide dogs) 🔊

GLADSTONE WORKING POTTERY MUSEUM

Uttoxeter Rd, Longton ST3 1PQ
Dir: (M6 junct 15, follow A500 to A50 then follow brown heritage
signs. From M1 follow A50 westbound then follow brown signs)
Map Ref: SJ84
☎ 01782 319232 📄 01782 598640
e-mail: gladstone@stoke.gov.uk

At the last remaining Victorian Pottery in the heart of the Potteries
you can see what it was like for the men, women and children
who lived and worked in a potbank during the era of the coal
firing bottle ovens. Working potters can be found demonstrating
traditional pottery skills in original workshops, and you can also
throw your own pot, make china flowers and decorate pottery
items to take home. Explore 'Flushed With Pride', dedicated to
development of the toilet, and the Tile Gallery, tracing the
development of decorative tiles.

Times: Open all year, daily 10-5 (last admission
4). Limited opening Xmas & New Year.
Fee: £4.95 (ch £3.50, students & pen £3.95).
Family ticket £14 (2ad+3ch 4-16yrs). Passport
ticket available annual admission to Gladstone
Pottery Museum £7.50 (concessions £6.50),
Family £16. **Facilities:** 🅿 🍴 ✗ licensed
♿ (electric buggy available to loan) toilets for
disabled shop ✗ (ex guide dogs) 🔊

TAMWORTH DRAYTON MANOR THEME PARK & ZOO

B78 3TW
Dir: (M42 junct 9, follow brown tourist signs on A409. Exit at T2 on M6 toll) *Map Ref:* SK20
☎ **01827 287979** 📄 **01827 288916**
e-mail: info@draytonmanor.co.uk

A popular family theme park with over 100 brilliant rides and attractions set in 280 acres of parkland and lakes. Drayton Manor features world-class rides like 'Apocalypse', the world's first stand-up tower drop; 'Stormforce 10', the best water ride in the country and 'Shockwave', Europe's only stand-up rollercoaster. There are fantastic family thrills in 'Excalibur - a Dragon's Tale' and 'Private Adventure', plus a host of children's rides, zoo, museum, shops and attractions.

Times: Park open end Mar-Oct. Rides from 10.30-5 or 6. Zoo open all year. **Fee:** ✱ Please telephone for details. **Facilities:** 🅿 💺 ✗ licensed ♿ (ramps or lifts to most rides, some rides limited access) toilets for disabled shop garden centre 🐾 (ex in park) ◀

TAMWORTH CASTLE

The Holloway, Ladybank B79 7NA
Dir: (M42 junct 10 & M6 junct 12, access via A5) *Map Ref:* SK20
☎ **01827 709629 & 709626** 📄 **01827 709630**
e-mail: heritage@tamworth.gov.uk

Tamworth Castle, with its dramatic Norman motte and bailey, was once the home of England's Royal Champions and today is reputed to be haunted by two lady ghosts. It is located in the centre of town, overlooking the Castle Pleasure Gardens, with its play areas, band stand, river walks, crazy golf, tennis and pavilion café. Quizzes, dressing-up, brass rubbing and a 'feelie' box make it a great family destination.

Times: Open mid Feb-Oct: Tue-Sun noon- 5.15, (last admission 4.30). Nov-mid Feb: Thu-Sun 12-5.15, (last admission 4.30). **Fee:** £4.75 (ch £2.75 & pen £3.75). Family £13. Prices subject to change. **Facilities:** 🅿 (100yds & 400yds) 💺 ♿ (one wheelchair for use inside the castle) shop 🐾 (ex guide dogs & hearing dogs) ◀

WESTON PARK *WESTON PARK*

TF11 8LE
Dir: (on A5 at Weston-under-Lizard, 30min from central Birmingham. 3m off M54 junct 3 and 8m off M6 junct 12)
Map Ref: SJ81
☎ **01952 852100** 📄 **01952 850430**
e-mail: enquiries@weston-park.com

Built in 1671, this fine mansion stands in elegant gardens and a vast park designed by 'Capability' Brown. Three lakes, a miniature railway, and a woodland adventure playground are to be found in the grounds, and in the house itself there is a magnificent collection of pictures, furniture and tapestries. Also on site are an animal centre and deer park.

Times: Open wknds from 19 Apr-Jul, then daily until 7 Sep. **Facilities:** 🅿 💺 ✗ licensed ♿ (disabled route, access to restaurant & shop) toilets for disabled shop ◀

ALCESTER *RAGLEY HALL*

B49 5NJ
Dir: (8m SW of Stratford-upon-Avon, off A46/A435, follow brown tourist signs) *Map Ref:* SP05
☎ 01789 762090 📄 01789 764791
e-mail: info@ragleyhall.com

Built in 1680, Ragley is the family home of the Marquess and Marchioness of Hertford and houses a superb collection of 18th-century paintings, porcelain and furniture. The house is set in 27 acres of gardens and 400 acres of parkland, and has a stunning mural by Graham Rust, 'The Temptation', and England's finest Baroque plasterwork dated 1750. Admission includes the house, the terrace tea rooms overlooking the rose garden, a gift shop, adventure playground, unique 3D maze, lakeside picnic area, woodland walk and stables filled with equestrian memorabilia.

Times: ✱ Open mid Apr-end Sep, Thu-Sun & BH Mon. Park & Garden open daily, mid Jul-end Aug.
Facilities: 🅿 ☕ ♿ (lift to first floor) toilets for disabled shop

GAYDON HERITAGE MOTOR CENTRE

Banbury Rd CV35 0BJ
Dir: (M40 junct 12, B4100. Centre signed) *Map Ref:* SP35
☎ 01926 641188 📄 01926 641555
e-mail: enquiries@heritage-motor-centre.co.uk

Home to the largest collection of historic British cars anywhere in the world, the Heritage Motor Centre is set in 65 acres of grounds. Attractions at the centre include the Time Road, a fascinating journey through Britain's motoring and social history, the motoring cinema, and the 'Get Behind the Wheel' zone. Outside, there are go-kart tracks and a children's electric roadway.

Times: Open daily 10-5. (Closed 24-26 Dec). **Fee:** ✱ £8 (ch 5-16 £6, under 5 free, & pen £7). Family ticket £25. Additional charges apply to outdoor activities **Facilities:** 🅿 ☕ ♿ (lift to all floors, limited number of manual wheelchairs) toilets for disabled shop 🐕 (ex guide/hearing dogs) ◀

KENILWORTH KENILWORTH CASTLE

CV8 1NE
Map Ref: SP27
☎ 01926 852078 📄 01926 851514

Explore the largest and most extensive castle ruin in England, with a past rich in famous names and events in history. Its massive red sandstone towers, keep and wall glow brightly in the sunlight. The Norman keep is one of the oldest parts of the castle, designed to be impregnable with walls 20 feet thick. Visitors can discover the history of Kenilworth through the interactive model in Leicester's Barn.

Times: Open all year, Mar, daily, 10-5; Apr-May, daily, 10-5; Jun-Aug, daily, 10-6; Sep-Oct, daily, 10-5; Nov-Feb, daily, 10-4. Closed 24-26 Dec & 1 Jan **Fee:** ✱ £4.80 (ch £2.40, concessions £3.60, family £12). Prices & opening times relate to 2004, for further details phone or log onto www.english-heritage.org.uk/visits
Facilities: 🅿 ☕ ♿ shop ♯

MIDDLETON ASH END HOUSE CHILDREN'S FARM

Middleton Ln B78 2BL
Dir: (signed from A4091) *Map Ref:* SP19
☎ **0121 329 3240** ▤ **0121 329 3240**
e-mail: contact@thechildrensfarm.co.uk

Ideal for young children, this is a small family-owned farm with many friendly animals to feed and stroke, including some rare breeds. There are play areas on site and lots of under cover activities, plus a café, picnic barns, theatre barn and gift shop. Pony rides are available and bottle feeding of lambs in the spring.

Times: Open daily 10-5 or dusk in winter. Closed 25 Dec-1 Jan and wkdays in Jan. **Fee:** £3.90 (ch £4.90 includes animal feed, pony ride, farm badge & all activities). **Facilities:** P ☕ ♿ toilets for disabled shop ✖ (ex guide dogs) 🎥

STRATFORD-UPON-AVON ROYAL SHAKESPEARE COMPANY COLLECTION

Royal Shakespeare Theatre, Waterside CV37 6BB
Dir: (M40 junct 14 take A46 S. At 1st rdbt take 1st exit (A439). Park in town centre, follow RSC signs) *Map Ref:* SP25
☎ **01789 262870** ▤ **01789 262870**
e-mail: info@rsc.org.uk

The RSC gallery opened in 1881, and was part of the first Shakespeare Memorial Theatre. In 1926 fire destroyed the theatre leaving only a semi circular wall and the gallery. The exhibition space now displays costumes from past RSC productions, paintings and other theatre memorabilia. The gallery shares its entrance with the Swan Theatre.

Times: ✱ Open all year, Mon-Fri 1.30-6.30, Sat 10.30-6.30 & Sun 11.30-4.30. Closed 24-25 Dec. Theatre tours usually Mon-Fri (ex matinee days), 1.30 & 5.30, Sun 12, 1, 2 & 3. **Facilities:** P (charged) ☕ ✖ ♿ (services for hearing impaired, Braille books/reading room) toilets for disabled shop ✖ (ex guide dogs)

SHAKESPEARE'S BIRTHPLACE

Henley St CV37 6QW
Dir: (in town centre) *Map Ref:* SP25
☎ **01789 204016** ▤ **01789 292083**
e-mail: info@shakespeare.org.uk

Shakespeare was born in this half-timbered house in 1564. It has been beautifully restored and has been presented in period style as it might have been when Shakespeare was a boy. The ticket price includes entrance to an exhibition of the author's life.

Times: Open Nov-Mar, Mon-Sat 10-4, Sun 10.30-4; Apr-May & Sep-Oct, Mon-Sat 10-5, Sun 10.30-5; Jun-Aug, Mon-Sat 9-5, Sun 9.30-5. **Fee:** ✱ £6.70 (ch £2.60, concessions £5.50) Family ticket £15. All five Shakespeare Houses £13 (ch £6.50, concessions £12) Family ticket £29. All three Town Shakespeare Houses £10 (ch £5, concessions £8) Family ticket £20. **Facilities:** P ♿ (computer based virtual reality tour of upper floor) toilets for disabled shop ✖ (ex assist dogs) 🎥

STRATFORD BUTTERFLY FARM

Tramway Walk, Swan's Nest Ln CV37 7LS
Dir: (south bank of River Avon opposite RSC) **Map Ref:** *SP25*
☎ **01789 299288** 🖹 **01789 415878**
e-mail: sales@butterflyfarm.co.uk

Europe's largest live butterfly and insect exhibit. Hundreds of the world's most spectacular and colourful butterflies live in the unique setting of a lush tropical landscape, with splashing waterfalls and fish-filled pools. See also the strange and fascinating Insect City, a bustling metropolis of ants, bees, stick insects, beetles and other remarkable insects. And don't miss the dangerous and deadly residents of Arachnoland!

Times: Open daily 10-6 (winter 10-dusk). Closed 25 Dec. **Fee:** ✱ £4.45 (ch £3.45, pen & students £3.95). Family £12.95 **Facilities:** P (opposite entrance) (site parking orange badge holders only) ♿ toilets for disabled shop ✕ ◀

THE TEDDY BEAR MUSEUM

19 Greenhill St CV37 6LF
Dir: (M40 junct 15, follow signs to town centre) **Map Ref:** *SP25*
☎ **01789 293160**
e-mail: info@theteddybearmuseum.com

The museum has a collection of some of the oldest and rarest teddy bears in the world, displayed in a house once owned by Henry VIII. There are lots of modern teddy bear stars too, including the original Fozzie Bear, Paddington Bear from the earliest television series, Mr Bean's bear, and many more.

Times: Open all year, daily 9.30-5.30 (ex Jan & Feb 10-4.30). Closed 25-26 Dec. **Fee:** £2.95 (ch £1.95, concessions £2.45). Family ticket £9.50 (2ad+3ch or 1ad+4ch) **Facilities:** P (30yds & 200yds) (access to ground floor shop only) shop ✕ (ex guide dogs) ◀

WARWICK WARWICK CASTLE

CV34 4QU
Dir: (2m from M40 junct 15) **Map Ref:** *SP26*
☎ **0870 442 2000** 🖹 **0870 442 2394**
e-mail: customer.information@warwick-castle.com

From the days of William the Conqueror to the reign of Queen Victoria, Warwick Castle has provided a backdrop for many turbulent times. Attractions include the gloomy dungeon and torture chamber, the grand state rooms, the great hall, and a reconstruction of the royal weekend party of 1898, where 'Daisy', Countess of Warwick held sway.

Times: Open all year, daily 10-6 (5pm Nov-Mar, 7pm Aug wknds). Closed 25 Dec.
Fee: ✱ £11.50-£14.50 (ch 4-16 £7.25-£8.75, pen £8.20-£10.50, students £8.75-£10.75). Family ticket (2ad+2ch) £33-£39. Wheelchair bound visitors free. Group discounts are available.
Facilities: P (charged) ◘ ✕ licensed ♿ (free parking, wheelchair hire, advance notice needed) toilets for disabled shop ✕ (ex assistance dogs) ◀

Warwickshire continued

WILMCOTE MARY ARDEN'S HOUSE AND THE SHAKESPEARE COUNTRYSIDE MUSEUM

Station Rd CV37 9UN
Dir: (3m NW of Stratford-upon-Avon off A3400) **Map Ref:** SP15
☎ **01789 293455** 📠 **01789 292083**
e-mail: info@shakespeare.org.uk

This picturesque, half-timbered Tudor house was the childhood home of Shakespeare's mother, Mary Arden. The site also includes Palmers Farm - a working farm with rare breed farm animals, including Gloucester Old Spot pigs, Cotswold sheep and Longhorn cattle. Falconry displays take place regularly and there is a children's adventure playground.

Times: Open Nov-Mar, Mon-Sat 10-4, Sun 10.30-4; Apr-May & Sep-Oct, Mon-Sat 10-5, Sun 10.30-5; Jun-Aug, Mon-Sat 9.30-5, Sun 10-5.
Fee: ✱ £5.70 (ch £2.50, concessions £5) Family ticket £13.50. All five Shakespeare Houses £13 (ch £6.50, concessions £12) Family ticket £29.
Facilities: 🅿 💺 & toilets for disabled shop ✖ (ex assist dogs) 🎦

BIRMINGHAM BIRMINGHAM BOTANICAL GARDENS & GLASSHOUSES

Westbourne Rd, Edgbaston B15 3TR
Dir: (2m W of city centre, follow Edgbaston and brown signs)
Map Ref: SP08
☎ **0121 454 1860** 📠 **0121 454 7835**
e-mail: admin@birminghambotanicalgardens.org.uk

The Birmingham Botanical Gardens feature the Tropical House, which has 24 foot-wide lily pool; the Mediterranean House, with a wide variety of citrus fruits, and the Arid House with its desert scene. Outside you will find a collection of over 200 trees and a young children's discovery garden.

Times: Open daily all year, wkdays 9-7 or dusk, Sun 10-7 or dusk whichever is earlier. Closed 25 Dec. **Fee:** ✱ £5.70 (concessions £3.30); £6 summer Sun & BHs. Family £16 (£17 summer & BHs) Groups 10+ £4.70 (concessions £3) **Facilities:** 🅿 💺 ✖ licensed & (3 wheelchairs, 2 electric scooters & Braille guides) toilets for disabled shop garden centre ✖ (ex guide dogs) 🎦

MUSEUM OF THE JEWELLERY QUARTER

75-79 Vyse St, Hockley B18 6HA
Dir: (off A41 into Vyse St, museum on left after 1st side street)
Map Ref: SP08
☎ **0121 554 3598** 📠 **0121 554 9700**   〔FREE〕
e-mail: bmag-enquiries@birmingham.gov.uk

The museum tells the story of jewellery-making in Birmingham from its origins in the Middle Ages right through to the present day. Discover the skill of the craft and enjoy a unique tour of an original jewellery factory frozen in time. The Jewellery Quarter is still very much at the forefront of its manufacture in Britain and the museum showcases the work of the city's most exciting new designers.

Times: Open Etr-Oct, Tue-Sun 11.30-4. (Closed Mon ex BH Mon) **Facilities:** 🅿 (limited 2hr stay/pay & display) 💺 & (tours for hearing/visually impaired booked in advance) toilets for disabled shop ✖ (ex guide dogs) 🎦

RSPB SANDWELL VALLEY NATURE RESERVE

20 Tanhouse Av, Great Barr B43 5AG
Dir: (off B4167 Hamstead Rd into Tanhouse Ave) **Map Ref:** SP08
☎ **0121 357 7395** ▤ **0121 358 3013**

Opened in 1983 on the site of an old colliery, Sandwell Valley is home to hundreds of bird, animal and insect species in five different habitats. Summer is the best time to see the yellow wagtail or reed warblers, while wintertime attracts goosanders, snipe, and redshanks. There are guided walks and bug hunts for the kids in summer, and a shop and visitor centre all year round.

Times: Open Tue-Fri 9-5, Sat & Sun 10-5 (closes at dusk in winter). Closed Mon, 24 Dec-2 Jan
Facilities: ▣ & toilets for disabled shop

SAREHOLE MILL

Cole Bank Rd, Hall Green B13 0BD
Dir: (M42 junct 4. Take A34 towards Birmingham. After 5m turn left on B4146, Mill on left) **Map Ref:** SP08
☎ **0121 777 6612** ▤ **0121 303 2891**   **FREE**

Birmingham's only working watermill was built in the 1760s. Used for both flour production and metal rolling up to the last century, the mill can still be seen in action during the summer months. It was restored with financial backing from J R R Tolkien, who grew up in the area and cites Sarehole as an influence for writing 'The Hobbit' and 'Lord of the Rings'.

Times: Open Etr-Oct, Tue-Sun 11.30-4. (Closed Mon, ex BH Mon) **Facilities:** ▣ ✖ (ex guide dogs)

THINKTANK AT MILLENNIUM POINT

Millennium Point, Curzon St B4 7XG
Map Ref: SP08
☎ **0121 202 2222** ▤ **0121 202 2280**
e-mail: findout@thinktank.ac

Thinktank is the Birmingham Museum of Science and Discovery. It has four floors with ten themed galleries packed with interactive exhibits that explore everything from locomotives and aircraft to intestines and spit glands! The special LEGO lab offers kids the chance to programme their own LEGO robots and find out how LEGO itself evolved.

Times: ✱ Open daily 10-5 (last entry 4). Closed 24-26 Dec **Facilities:** ▣ (charged) � & toilets for disabled shop ✖ (ex guide dogs) ◼

BOURNVILLE *CADBURY WORLD*

Linden Rd B30 2LD
Dir: (1m S of A38 Bristol Rd, on A4040 Ring Rd) *Map Ref:* SP08
☎ **0121 451 4159** 📄 **0121 451 1366**
e-mail: cadbury.world@csplc.com

Recent changes have meant that Cadbury World now has much more to see, do and taste. There is the chance to get involved in the chocolate making process, and to find out how the chocolate is used to make famous confectionery. Visitors can learn about the early struggles and triumphs of the Cadbury business, and follow the history of their television advertising. Besides all this, visitors can relax on the gentle Cadabra ride, and be a big kid in CadburyLand, the Fantasy Factory, and on the Cocoa Road.

Times: ✱ Contact information line 0121 451 4180 for opening times. **Facilities:** P 🍴 ✕ ♿ (adapted ride & lift to 2nd floor, subtitles) toilets for disabled shop ✖ (ex guide dogs) ◀

COVENTRY *COVENTRY CATHEDRAL & VISITOR CENTRE*

7 Priory Row CV1 5ES
Dir: (signposted on all approaches to the city) *Map Ref:* SP37
☎ **024 7622 7597** 📄 **024 7663 1448**
e-mail: information@coventrycathedral.org

Coventry's old cathedral was bombed during an air raid on November 1940, which devastated the city, and the remains have been carefully preserved. The new cathedral was designed by Sir Basil Spence and consecrated in May 1962. It contains outstanding modern works of art, including a huge tapestry designed by Graham Sutherland, the west screen (a wall of glass engraved by John Hutton with saints and angels), bronzes by Epstein, and the great baptistry window by John Piper.

Times: Open all year, daily, Etr-Oct 8.30-6, Oct-Etr 8.30-5.30. **Facilities:** P (250yds) 🍴 ♿ (lift, touch and hearing centre, paved wheelchair access) toilets for disabled shop ✖ (ex guide dogs)

COVENTRY TRANSPORT MUSEUM

Hales St CV1 1PN
Dir: (just off junct 1, Coventry ring road, Tower St in city centre)
Map Ref: SP37
☎ **024 7683 2425** 📄 **024 7683 2465**
e-mail: museum@mbrt.co.uk

Coventry is the traditional home of the motor industry, and the Coventry Transport Museum displays the largest collection of British cars, buses, cycles and motorcycles in the world. Visitors can learn about motoring's early days in 'Landmarques', how royalty travelled, and see Thrust 2 and Thrust SSC, the world land speed record cars.

Times: Open all year, daily 10-5. Closed 24-26 Dec. **Facilities:** P (adjacent) (pay & display) 🍴 ♿ (audio tour, tactile floor & models, wheelchairs for hire) toilets for disabled shop ✖ (ex guide dogs) ◀

HERBERT ART GALLERY & MUSEUM

Jordan Well CV1 5QP
Dir: (in city centre near Cathedral) **Map Ref:** SP37
☎ **024 7683 2381 & 7683 2565** 📄 **024 7683 2410**
e-mail: artsandheritage@coventry.gov.uk

As Coventry's premier museum hosting a range of exhibitions and events, the Herbert provides a focus for the city's cultural heritage. 'Godiva City' tells Coventry's story over 1,000 years, through interactive exhibits, objects, pictures and words. 'My World' is a fun exhibition for three to five-year-olds. There are also changing displays of art, craft, social and industrial history. The museum is in the midst of a four-year programme of re-development which will bring many new facilities.

Times: Open all year, Mon-Sat 10-5.30, Sun 12-5. Closed 24-26, 31 Dec & 1 Jan
Facilities: 🅿 (500yds) 🍵 ♿ (disabled parking, automatic doors, tactile/audio displays) toilets for disabled shop 🐕 (ex guide/assistance dogs)

LUNT ROMAN FORT

Coventry Rd, Baginton CV8 3AJ
Dir: (S side of city, off Stonebridge highway, A45) **Map Ref:** SP37
☎ **024 7683 2381 & 7683 2565** 📄 **024 7683 2410**
e-mail: artsandheritage@coventry.co.uk

Lunt Roman Fort is a turf and timber construction which was occupied by the Romans for around 20 years between AD 60 and 80, after the Boudiccan rebellion. There were extensive excavations of the site between 1965 and 1973, and what you see today is a partial reconstruction. The fort was repaired in 2004 and the facilities upgraded. An interpretation centre and museum of the Roman army is housed in the granary.

Times: Open 27 Mar-Oct, Sat-Sun & BH Mon 10-5; mid Jul-end Aug, Thu-Tue 10-5; Spring BH wk, Thu-Tue 10-5. **Facilities:** 🅿 ♿ (ramp to Granary Interpretation Centre) toilets for disabled shop 🐕 (ex guide/assistance dogs)

DUDLEY BLACK COUNTRY LIVING MUSEUM

Tipton Rd DY1 4SQ
Dir: (on A4037, nr Showcase Cinema) **Map Ref:** SO99
☎ **0121 557 9643 & 0121 520 8054** 📄 **0121 557 4242**
e-mail: info@bclm.co.uk

On the 26-acre site is a recreated canal-side village, with shops, houses and work places. Meet the costumed guides and find out what life was like around 1900. Ride on a tramcar, take a trip down the underground mine, venture into the limestone caverns or visit the olde tyme fairground (additional charge). There are also demonstrations of chainmaking, glass engraving and sweet-making. Watch a silent movie in the Limelight cinema, taste fish and chips cooked on a 1930's range, and finish your visit with a glass of real ale in the Bottle and Glass Inn.

Times: Open all year, Mar-Oct daily 10-5; Nov-Feb, Wed-Sun 10-4. (Telephone for Xmas closing) **Fee:** ✱ £9.95 (ch 5-18 £5.75, pen £8.75). Family ticket (2ad+3ch) £28.
Facilities: 🅿 (charged) 🍵 ✕ licensed ♿ (ramps available) toilets for disabled shop 🐕 (ex guide dogs) 🛶

DUDLEY ZOOLOGICAL GARDENS

2 The Broadway DY1 4QB
Dir: (M5 junct 2 towards Wolverhampton/Dudley, signed)
Map Ref: SO99
☎ **01384 215313** 🖷 **01384 456048**
e-mail: marketing@dudleyzoo.org.uk

From lions and tigers to snakes and spiders, enjoy animal encounters and feeding times at Dudley Zoological Gardens. Get closer to some furry, and some not so furry creatures, and have fun on the fair rides, land train, and the adventure playground. Step back in time and see history come to life in the castle.

Times: Open all year, Etr-mid Sep, daily 10-4; mid Sep-Etr, daily 10-3. Closed 25 Dec. **Fee:** ✱ £8.50 (ch 4-15 £5.25, concessions £5.75). Family ticket £28.50 (2ad+3ch) **Facilities:** 🅿 (charged) ☕ ✗ licensed & (land train from gates-castle, wheelchair hire) toilets for disabled shop ✶ (ex guide dogs) ◀

SOLIHULL NATIONAL MOTORCYCLE MUSEUM

Coventry Rd, Bickenhill B92 0EJ
Dir: (M42 junct 6, off A45 near NEC) *Map Ref:* SP17
☎ **01675 443311** 🖷 **0121 711 3153**

Five exhibition halls show British motorcycles built during the golden age of motorcycling at this national museum. Spanning 90 years, the immaculately restored machines are the products of around 150 different factories. Over 700 machines are on show, most owned by the museum, others from collections or private owners. Restoration work is carried out by enthusiasts, and new motorcycles are acquired from all over the world.

Times: Open all year, daily 10-6. Closed 24-26 Dec. **Fee:** ✱ £5.95 (ch 12 & pen £4.75). Party 20+ £4.95 **Facilities:** 🅿 ✗ licensed & toilets for disabled shop ✶ (ex guide dogs) ◀

STOURBRIDGE *THE FALCONRY CENTRE*

Hurrans Garden Centre, Kidderminster Rd South, Hagley DY9 0JB
Dir: (off A456) *Map Ref:* SO88
☎ **01562 700014** 🖷 **01562 700014**

The centre houses some 70 birds of prey including owls and hawks as well as falcons, and it is also a rehabilitation centre for sick and injured birds of prey. Spectacular flying displays are put on daily from midday. Picnic areas are provided and special fun days and training courses are arranged.

Times: Open all year, daily 10-5 & Sun 11-5. Closed 25, 26 Dec & Etr Sun. **Facilities:** 🅿 ☕ & toilets for disabled shop garden centre ✶ (ex guide dogs) ◀

WALSALL   NEW ART GALLERY WALSALL

Gallery Square WS2 8LG
Dir: (signed from all major routes into town centre)
Map Ref: SP09
☎ 01922 654400 📠 01922 654401   FREE
e-mail: info@artatwalsall.org.uk

This exciting art gallery has at its core the Garman Ryan
Collection, donated to the borough by Lady Kathleen Epstein, and
a permanent collection of works acquired by the Walsall Museum
and Art Gallery since 1892. Admission to the gallery is free and
children are very welcome. An innovative approach is taken in the
Children's Discovery Gallery, which offers access to the very best
in contemporary art in the only interactive art gallery designed
especially for young people. The gallery also has an vibrant
programme of temporary exhibitions.

Times: Open all year Tue-Sat 10-5, Sun noon-5.
Closed Mon ex BH Mon. **Facilities:** 🅿 🍴 ✗
♿ (lift access to facilties, induction loop, large
print) toilets for disabled shop ✗ (ex guide dogs)

BEWDLEY   WEST MIDLAND SAFARI & LEISURE PARK

Spring Grove DY12 1LF
Dir: (on A456 between Kidderminster & Bewdley)
Map Ref: SO77
☎ 01299 402114 📠 01299 404519
e-mail: info@wmsp.co.uk

Located in the heart of rural Worcestershire, this 200-acre site is
the home to a drive-through safari and the Kingdom of the White
Lions. There is a variety of rides, amusements and live shows
suitable for all members of the family. Other features include the
Discovery Trail, Hippo Lakes, Goat Walk, Seal Aquarium, a Creepy
Crawlies exhibit, animal and reptile encounters and Sealion
Theatre.

Times: Open Apr-Oct, daily from 10 including
BHs. **Fee:** ✱ £7.25 (ch 4 free). Multi ride
wristband £8.50. Junior restricted £7 (restricted
rides only). Ride tickets £3 for two tickets from
machines (various no of tickets per ride).
Facilities: 🅿 🍴 ✗ licensed ♿ (most area
accessible slopes/tarmac paths) shop ✗ (ex guide
dogs) 🍴

BROADWAY   BROADWAY TOWER & ANIMAL PARK

WR12 7LB
Dir: (off A44, 1m SE of village) *Map Ref:* SP03
☎ 01386 852390 📠 01386 858038
e-mail: info@broadwaytower.co.uk

The 65-foot Broadway Tower was designed by James Wyatt for
the 6th Earl of Coventry, and built in 1799. The unique building
now houses exhibitions depicting its colourful past and various
uses such as a holiday retreat for artist and designer William
Morris. The viewing platform is equipped with a telescope, giving
wonderful views over 13 counties.

Times: Open Apr-Oct, daily 10.30-5. Nov-Mar
(tower only) wknds weather permitting 11-3 or by
prior booking. **Fee:** Tower, £3.50 (ch 4-4 £2,
concessions £3) Family £10 (2ad+3ch)
Facilities: 🅿 🍴 ✗ licensed shop 🍴

BROMSGROVE *AVONCROFT MUSEUM OF HISTORIC BUILDINGS*

Stoke Heath B60 4JR
Dir: (2m S, off A38) *Map Ref:* SO97
☎ **01527 831886** 📄 **01527 876934**
e-mail: avoncroft1@compuserve.com

A visit to Avoncroft takes you through nearly 700 years of history. Here you can see 25 buildings rescued from destruction and authentically restored on a 15-acre rural site. There are 15th and 16th-century timber framed buildings, 18th-century agricultural buildings and a cockpit. There are industrial buildings and a working windmill from the 19th century; and from the 20th century a fully furnished pre-fab.

Times: ✱ Open Jul-Aug daily 10.30-5; Apr-Jun & Sep-Oct 10.30-4.30 (wknds 5.30), (Closed Mon); Mar & Nov 10.30-4, (Closed Mon & Fri). Open BHs. **Facilities:** 🅿 ☕ ♿ (ramps, wheelchair available) toilets for disabled shop 🍴

KIDDERMINSTER *SEVERN VALLEY RAILWAY*

Comberton Hill DY10 1QN
Dir: (on A448, clearly signed) *Map Ref:* SO87
☎ **01299 403816** 📄 **01299 400839**

The Severn Valley is the leading standard gauge steam railway, with one of the largest collections of locomotives and rolling stock in the country. Services operate from Kidderminster and Bewdley to Bridgnorth through 16 miles of picturesque scenery along the River Severn. Special steam galas and 'Day out with Thomas' weekends take place during the year along with Santa Specials.

Times: Trains operate wknds throughout year, daily, early May to late Sep, school hols & half terms, Santa Specials, phone for details.
Fee: ✱ Subject to Review. (Train fares vary according to journey. Main through ticket £10.80 return, Family ticket £29)
Facilities: 🅿 (charged) ☕ ♿ (some specially adapted trains, call for details) toilets for disabled shop (at Kidderminster/Bridgnorth) 🍴

WORCESTERSHIRE COUNTY MUSEUM

Hartlebury Castle, Hartlebury DY11 7XZ
Dir: (4m S of Kidderminster clearly signed from A449)
Map Ref: SO87
☎ **01299 250416** 📄 **01299 251890**
e-mail: museum@worcestershire.gov.uk

Housed in the north wing of Hartlebury Castle, the County Museum contains a delightful display of crafts and industries. There are unique collections of toys and costume, displays on domestic life, period room settings and horse-drawn vehicles. Visitors can also see a reconstructed forge, a schoolroom, a wheelwright's and tailor's shop.

Times: Open Feb-Nov, Mon-Thu 10-5, BHs 11-5, Fri & Sun 2-5. (Closed Sat & Good Fri).
Facilities: 🅿 ☕ ♿ (car parking spaces, close to main building) toilets for disabled shop
✖ (ex guide dogs & in grounds) 🍴

REDDITCH *FORGE MILL NEEDLE MUSEUM & BORDESLEY ABBEY VISITOR CENTRE*

Forge Mill, Needle Mill Ln, Riverside B98 8HY
Dir: (N side of Redditch, off A441. M42 junct 2) *Map Ref:* SP06
☎ **01527 62509**
e-mail: museum@redditchbc.gov.uk

The Needle Museum tells the fascinating and sometimes gruesome story of how needles are made. Working, water-powered machinery can be seen in an original needle-scouring mill - the only one left in the world, which is located in the grounds of a 12th-century Cistercian Abbey. The visitor centre accommodates an archaeological museum showing finds from excavations at Bordesley Abbey.

Times: ✱ Open Etr-Sep, Mon-Fri 11-4.30, Sat-Sun 2-5; Feb-Etr & Oct-Nov, Mon-Thu 11-4 & Sun 2-5. Parties by arrangement.
Facilities: 🅿 ᴕ (wheelchair available, audio tour of museum) toilets for disabled shop ✖ (ex guide dogs) ◀

WORCESTER *ELGAR'S BIRTHPLACE MUSEUM*

Crown East Ln, Lower Broadheath WR2 6RH
Dir: (3m W of Worcester, signed off A44 to Leominster)
Map Ref: SO85
☎ **01905 333224** 🖹 **01905 333426**
e-mail: birthplace@elgarmuseum.org

The Elgar Centre was opened to complement the historic Birthplace Cottage and to provide additional exhibition space for more treasures from this unique collection, telling the story of Elgar's musical development and inspirations. Listen to his music as the audio tour guides you round the easily accessible displays.

Times: Open daily 11-5, last admission 4.15. (Closed 23 Dec-end Jan). **Fee:** ✱ £4.50 (ch £2 & pen £4) Family ticket £11. Party rates available.
Facilities: 🅿 ᴕ (large print guides, audio facilities, wheelchair) toilets for disabled shop ✖ (ex guide dogs) ◀

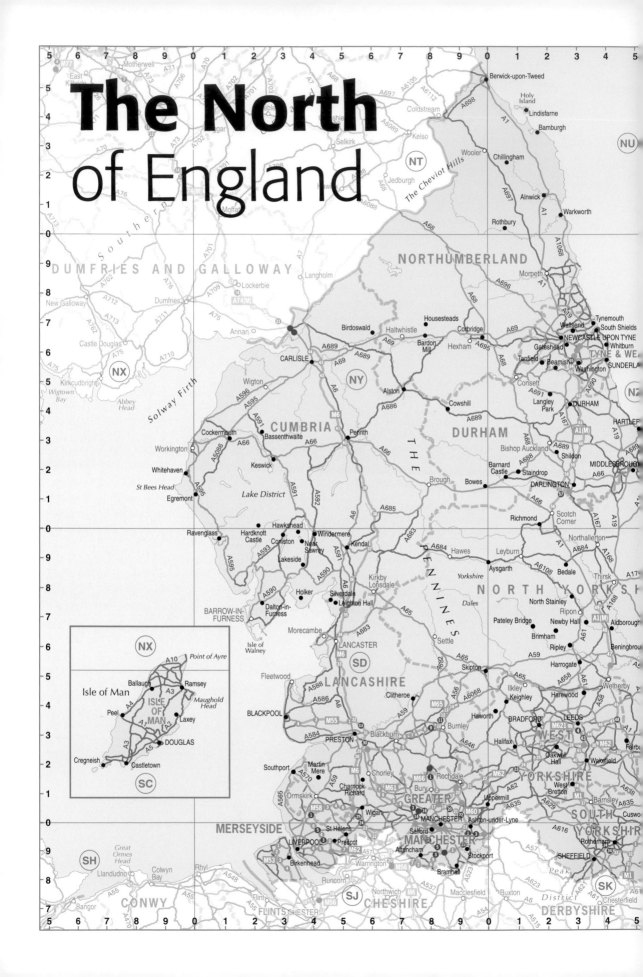

The North
of England

The big industrial cities of the north – Liverpool, Manchester, Leeds, Sheffield, Bradford and Newcastle – have shaken off much of their dour image in recent decades and in parts have enough cultural cachet to challenge the capital. Blackpool is Europe's top seaside resort attracting six million plus visitors annually; York and Durham are two of England's finest cathedral cities, and genteel towns like Harrogate, Windermere and Haworth offer all that's best in tea shops and literary associations. Fabulous natural landscapes take in the Lake District, the Yorkshire Dales, and the North York Moors National Park. The North Pennines, spanning Northumberland, Durham and Cumbria, is the country's most recently declared 'Area of Outstanding National Beauty'.

Favourite tourist attractions in the region are Flamingo Land Theme Park; Pleasureland in Southport; Beamish, the North of England Open Air Museum; Merseyside Maritime Museum, The National Museum of Photography, Film & Television; The National Railway Museum; Castle Howard, and Windermere Lake Cruises.

Events & Festivals

March 28 World Coal Carrying Championship, Royal Oak pub, Owl Lane, Ossett, West Yorkshire

April 29-May 1 Moor & Coast Festival, Whitby, North Yorkshire

June 2-8 Appleby Horse Fair, Roman Road, Appleby-in-Westmorland, Cumbria

June (tbc) Sheffield Children's Festival

June 11-12 Greater Manchester Youth Games, Robin Park Stadium, Wigan

June 26-July 3 Alnwick Medieval Fair, Alnwick, Northumberland

July 9 Durham Miners Gala, colourful miners' banners paraded through the streets of Durham

July 12-14 Great Yorkshire Show, Great Yorkshire Showground, Harrogate, North Yorkshire

July (tbc) Manchester Mega Mela, Platt Fields Park, Rusholme

July 30-31 Sunderland International Air Show, Promenade, Seaburn, Sunderland

August 6 Powburn Show & Sheepdog Trials, Northumberland

August 27-29 International Beatles Week & Convention, Liverpool

August 28-29 Durham Light Infantry Vehicle Rally, DLI Museum & Durham Art Gallery, Co Durham

August 29 Lancaster Georgian Festival & National Sedan Chair Carrying Championships

September 2-3 Sea Fever 2005, International Sea Shanty Festival, Hull

September 16-18 Harrogate Autumn Flower Show, Harrogate, North Yorkshire

September 17 Egremont Crab Fair (including gurning contest), Cumbria

NORTH

SEA

Redcar
Saltburn-by-the-Sea
Skinningrove
isborough A174
A171 Whitby

Danby

rth York
Moors A169 A171

lmsley
Pickering A170
Kirby Misperton

Bempton Flamborough
A64 Head
Malton A165
Sewerby
SE Bridlington

A166 A614
Driffield TA

RK
EAST RIDING A164
Elvington A1079 OF YORKSHIRE A165
A163 Market A1079 Beverley
by. A614 Weighton
A63 A19 A164
KINGSTON UPON HULL
M62 A63 A1033
R.Humber
Goole

M18
A15 A160 Immingham Spurn Head
M180 A180
SCUNTHORPE A18 GRIMSBY Cleethorpes
ONCASTER A161 A46

(M) Bawtry A159 A15 Market A16 A1031
A631 Gainsborough Rasen Louth TF
rksop A620 A631 A46 A157
A1 A156 A158 A153 A16
A57 A158 A46 A62
LINCOLN LINCOLNSHIRE
16 A614
TINGHAMSHIRE Horncastle

| ● Attraction |
| ○ Town name |

0   10   20 miles
0   10   20   30 kilometres

ALSTON NENT VALLEY

Nenthead Mines Heritage Centre, Nenthead CA9 3PD
Dir: *(5m E of Alston, on A689)* **Map Ref:** *NY74*
☎ **01434 382726** 📄 **01434 382294**
e-mail: administration.office@virgin.net

Set in 200 acres in the North Pennines, this hands-on heritage centre contains exhibitions and displays on geology, local wildlife and social history. Visitors can operate three enormous water wheels, gaze down a 328-foot deep brewery shaft, and take an underground trip through the Nenthead Mines, which were last worked for lead in 1915.

Times: Open Etr-Oct, daily 10.30-5. Mine tours at 12, 1.30 & 3 daily **Fee:** ✱ £4-£6.50 (pen £3.25-5.50, ch site free, mine £2). Family ticket £15.30 **Facilities:** 🅿 ☕ ♿ (ramps & motorised scooter) toilets for disabled shop 🛍

SOUTH TYNEDALE RAILWAY

The Railway Station, Hexham Rd CA9 3JB
Dir: *(0.25m N, on A686)* **Map Ref:** *NY74*
☎ **01434 381696 & 382828**

Running along the beautiful South Tyne Valley, this narrow-gauge railway follows the route of the former Alston to Haltwhistle branch. At present the line runs between Alston in Cumbria and Kirkhaugh in Northumberland, a scenic route some two and a quarter miles' long. Money is being raised to extend the line by the same length again to Slaggyford.

Times: Open Apr-Oct & Dec, wknds and BHs; 20 Jul-Aug, daily. Also open school hols & some wknds in Dec. Please enquire for times of trains. **Fee:** ✱ Return £5 (ch 3-15 £2). Single £3 (ch 3-15 £1.50). All day £12.50 (ch 3-15 £5). **Facilities:** 🅿 ☕ ♿ (railway carriage for wheelchairs, pre-booking required) toilets for disabled shop

BASSENTHWAITE TROTTERS WORLD OF ANIMALS

Coalbeck Farm CA12 4RD
Map Ref: *NY23*
☎ **017687 76239** 📄 **017687 76598**
e-mail: info@trottersworld.com

Trotters is home to hundreds of friendly animals including lemurs, wallabies and other exotic ceatures along with reptiles and birds of prey and a family of gibbons, which will keep families amused for hours. Informative and amusing demonstrations held on a daily basis bring visitors closer to the animals. 'Clown About' is an indoor play centre with a soft play area and ballpools for toddlers upwards.

Times: Open all year, except 25 Dec & 1 Jan. Summer 10-5.30, Winter 11-4.30 **Fee:** £5.50 (ch £4.25, under 3yrs free) **Facilities:** 🅿 ☕ ♿ toilets for disabled shop ✖ (ex guide dogs) 🛍

BIRDOSWALD BIRDOSWALD ROMAN FORT

CA8 7DD
Dir: (signposted off A69 between Brampton & Hexham)
Map Ref: NY66
☎ **016977 47602** 📄 **016977 47605**
e-mail: birdoswald@dial.pipex.com

A visitor centre introduces you to Hadrian's Wall and the Roman Fort. This unique section of Hadrian's Wall overlooks the Irthing Gorge, and is the only point along the Wall where all the components of the Roman frontier system can be found together. Birdoswald isn't just about the Romans, though, it's also about border raids in the Middle Ages, and recent archaeological discoveries.

Times: Open Mar-Oct, 10-5.30. Winter season exterior only
Fee: ✱ English Heritage members half price. Prices & opening times relate to 2004, for further details phone or log onto www.english-heritage.org.uk/visits **Facilities:** 🅿 ☕ ♿ (ramp outside, disabled parking, lift) toilets for disabled shop 🛍

CARLISLE CARLISLE CASTLE

CA3 8UR
Dir: (north side of city centre, close to station) *Map Ref:* NY35
☎ **01228 591992** 📄 **01228 514880**

At this medieval fortress you can discover a thrilling and bloody past and enjoy panoramic views over the city and on to the hills of the Lake District and southern Scotland. Explore ancient chambers, staircases and dungeons and uncover an exciting history through lively exhibitions, which tell of William Rufus, Mary, Queen of Scots and Bonnie Prince Charlie.

Times: Open all year, Apr-Sep, daily 9.30-6; Oct-Mar, daily 10-4. (Closed 24-26 Dec & 1 Jan).
Fee: ✱ £3.80 (ch £1.90, concessions £2.90) Prices & opening times relate to 2004, for further details phone or log onto www.english-heritage.org.uk/visits
Facilities: 🅿 (400yds) ♿ (parking for disabled at Castle) shop 🐕 (ex on lead in certain areas) ⊞

TULLIE HOUSE MUSEUM & ART GALLERY

Castle St CA3 8TP
Dir: (M6 junct 42, 43 or 44 follow signs to city centre. Car park located in Devonshire Walk) *Map Ref:* NY35
☎ **01228 534781** 📄 **01228 810249**
e-mail: barbaral@carlisle.gov.uk

Dramatic audio-visual displays, striking recreations of long vanished scenes and imaginative hands-on displays - there is something for everyone at Tullie House. This unique project combines the museum's own collections with cutting edge contemporary art. The new multi-media room features touch sensitive computer screens and a short film. Don't miss the stunning underground Millennium Gallery or the Border River pathway linking to Carlisle Castle.

Times: Open: Nov-Mar, Mon-Sat 10-4, Sun 12-4; Apr-Jun & Sep-Oct, Mon-Sat 10-5, Sun 12-5; Jul-Aug, Mon-Sat 10-5, Sun 11-5. Closed 25-26 Dec & 1 Jan. **Fee:** ✱ Ground floor (including Art Gallery & Old Tullie House) - Free. Upper floors & New Millenium Gallery - £5.20 (ch £2.60 concessions £3.60) Family ticket (2ad+3ch) £14.50 **Facilities:** 🅿 (5mins walk) (disabled parking on site by request) ☕ ✗ licensed ♿ (chair lift) toilets for disabled shop 🐕 (ex guide dogs) 🛍

COCKERMOUTH LAKELAND SHEEP & WOOL CENTRE

Egremont Rd CA13 0QX
Dir: (M6 junct 40, W on A66 to rdbt at Cockermouth on
A66/A586 junct) *Map Ref: NY13*
☎ **01900 822673** 📄 **01900 822673**
e-mail: reception@sheep-woolcentre.co.uk

Come face to face with 19 different breeds of live sheep at the
Lakeland Sheep & Wool Centre. A stage show with 'One Man and
his Dog' demonstrations and a resident Jersey cow are a feature.
These are held four times daily from March till the end of October,
and are all indoors.

Times: Open all year, daily 9.30-5.30 (Closed 25
Dec & 4-18 Jan). **Fee:** £4 (ch £3) for sheep
shows **Facilities:** 🅿 💻 ✗ licensed ♿ (hearing
loop system) toilets for disabled shop
✈ (ex guide/hearing dogs) ◀

CONISTON STEAM YACHT GONDOLA

Coniston Pier LA22 8AN
Dir: (A593 to Coniston, follow signs near garage 'to boats' & S Y
Gondola. Coniston Pier is at end of Lake Road) *Map Ref: SD39*
☎ **015394 41288** 📄 **015394 41288**
e-mail: gondola@nationaltrust.org.uk

Originally launched in 1859, the graceful 'Gondola' is a coal-fired
steam yacht that worked on Coniston Water until 1936.
Beautifully rebuilt, she came back into service in 1980, and
visitors can once again enjoy her silent progress and old-
fashioned comfort in daily trips from Coniston Pier to Brantwood
Jetty between April and October.

Times: Open Apr-Oct to scheduled daily
timetable. Trips commence from 11 at Coniston
Pier. Piers at Coniston & Brantwood.
Fee: ✱ Ticket prices on application.
Facilities: 🅿 shop 🌿 ◀

DALTON-IN-FURNESS SOUTH LAKES WILD ANIMAL PARK

Crossgates LA15 8JR
Dir: (M6 junct 36, A590 to Dalton-in-Furness, follow tourist signs)
Map Ref: SD27
☎ **01229 466086** 📄 **01229 461310**
e-mail: office@wildanimalpark.co.uk

Here visitors can walk with kangaroos and emus in the bush,
watch parrots fly free in the trees and hand-feed families of nine
different species of lemur. In an approximation of an African plain
four rhino, six giraffes and a family of baboons are kept in the
same field. You can also see lions, tigers, spectacled bears,
cheetah, red pandas, gibbons, macaques and spider monkeys,
among over 100 species. This is an active conservation park with
partnerships all over the world to save animals and their habitats.

Times: Open all year, daily 10-5 (last admission
4.15); Nov-Feb 10-4.30 (last admission 3.45).
(Closed 25 Dec). **Fee:** ✱ £9.50 (ch, pen,
wheelchair users & registered blind £6). Reduced
prices Nov-Mar. **Facilities:** 🅿 💻 ♿ (wheelchair
users may need help) toilets for disabled shop
✈ ◀

EGREMONT   FLORENCE MINE HERITAGE CENTRE

Florence Mine CA22 2NR
Dir: (on A595 Egremont by-pass. Exit at Wilton/Haile, follow
signs) *Map Ref:* NY01
☎ 01946 825830 📠 01946 825830
e-mail: info@florencemine.co.uk

Based in the last deep working, iron ore mine in Western Europe,
the centre offers a mining museum, geology and mineral room, a
reconstructed drift (or tunnel) and a research facility.
Underground tours are also available all year, including weekdays,
by prior arrangement. Please phone the mine for details. Suitable
footwear and old clothes are advised for underground tours.

Times: Open Apr-Oct, daily, 10-4. Nov-Mar,
wkdays only **Fee:** ✱ Centre: £2 (ch £1); Mine
Tour: £6.50 (ch £4.50) **Facilities:** 🅿 ☕
♿ (hands-on display) toilets for disabled shop
✖ (ex guide dogs)

HARDKNOTT CASTLE ROMAN FORT   HARDKNOTT CASTLE ROMAN FORT

Dir: (9m NE of Ravenglass, at W end of Hardknott Pass)
Map Ref: NY20   FREE

Hardknott Roman Fort, called Mediobogdum by the Romans, is
one of the most dramatic Roman sites in Britain, with stunning
views over the Lakeland fells. Built between AD 120 and AD 138,
the fort controlled the road from Ravenglass to Ambleside and
500 infantrymen were stationed here. The remains include the
headquarters building, commandant's house and granaries, with a
bath house and parade ground outside the walls.

Times: Open any reasonable time. Access may
be hazardous in winter. **Facilities:** ✖ (ex dogs
on leads) 🚐 ♿

HAWKSHEAD   BEATRIX POTTER GALLERY

Main St LA22 0NS
Dir: (in village centre) *Map Ref:* SD39
☎ 015394 36355 📠 015394 36187
e-mail: beatrixpottergallery@nationaltrust.org.uk

The Beatrix Potter Gallery shows an annually changing exhibition
of Beatrix Potter's original sketches and watercolors, with which
she illustrated her children's stories. The exhibition is housed in a
17th-century building, the former office of her husband, solicitor
William Heelis, and retains the authentic look of an Edwardian
law firm. The building was also the model for Tabitha Twitchit's
shop in 'The Tale of Ginger & Pickles'.

Times: Open 3 Apr-Oct & Good Fri, Sat-Wed
10.30-4.30 (last admission 4). Admission is by
timed ticket including NT members. **Fee:** ✱ £3
(ch £1.50) Family ticket £7.50 (2ad+3ch)
Facilities: 🅿 (300mtrs) No parking in village
centre (Braille guide) shop ✖ 🚐 ♿

55

HOLKER   HOLKER HALL & GARDENS

Cark in Cartmel, Grange over Sands LA11 7PL
Dir: (from M6 junct 36, follow A590, signposted)   **Map Ref:** *SD37*
☎ 015395 58328   015395 58378
e-mail: **publicopening@holker.co.uk**

The Hall dates from the 16th century, though one wing was rebuilt in 1871 after a fire. Inside there is a notable woodcarving and many fine pieces of furniture, which mix happily with family photographs from the present day. Outside are the magnificent gardens, with both formal and woodland areas. Additional attractions include the Lakeland Motor Museum, exhibitions, the deer park and adventure playground.

Times: Open 28 Mar-29 Oct, Sun-Fri 10-6. Hall open 10.30-4.45. (Closed Sat). **Fee:** ✱ Gardens & Grounds £4.50 (ch 6-15 £2.75) Family ticket £13.75. All 3 attractions £9.25 (ch £4.65) Family ticket £27.75. **Facilities:** 🅿 💻 ✗ licensed ♿ (ramps, wheelchairs & scooters available for hire) toilets for disabled shop on lead, not in garden ▰

KENDAL   MUSEUM OF LAKELAND LIFE

Abbot Hall LA9 5AL
Dir: (M6 junct 36, follow signs to Kendal. Located at south end of Kendal beside Abbot Hall Art Gallery)   **Map Ref:** *SD59*
☎ 01539 722464   01539 722494
e-mail: **info@lakelandmuseum.org.uk**

The life and history of the Lake District is captured by the displays in this museum, housed in Abbot Hall's stable block. The working and social life of the area are well illustrated by a variety of exhibits including period rooms, a Victorian Cumbrian street scene and a farming display. Two of the rooms are devoted to the memory of the writer Arthur Ransome, best known for his '*Swallows and Amazons*' series of children's books.

Times: Open 20 Jan-23 Dec, Mon-Sat 10.30-5. (Closing at 4pm Jan, Feb, Mar, Nov, Dec) **Fee:** ✱ £3.50 (ch & students £2). Family ticket £9.50. Combined ticket with Abbot Hall & Lakeland Life (same day), £6.50. **Facilities:** 🅿 💻 ♿ (listening posts, large print labels) toilets for disabled shop ✗ (ex guide dogs) ▰

KESWICK   CUMBERLAND PENCIL MUSEUM

Southey Works, Greta Bridge CA12 5NG
Dir: (M6 N onto A66 at Penrith. Left at 2nd Keswick exit, left at T-junct, left over Greta Bridge)   **Map Ref:** *NY22*
☎ 017687 73626   017687 74679
e-mail: **museum@acco-uk.co.uk**

The Cumberland Pencil Museum investigates the history and technology of an object most of us take utterly for granted. Its interesting exhibits include a replica of the Borrowdale mine where graphite was first discovered, the world's largest pencil, and displays on brass-rubbing and various artistic techniques that are based on the humble pencil.

Times: ✱ Open daily 9.30-4 (hours may be extended during peak season). (Closed 25-26 Dec & 1 Jan) **Facilities:** 🅿 ♿ toilets for disabled shop ▰

MIREHOUSE

CA12 4QE
Dir: (3m N of Keswick on A591) **Map Ref:** *NY22*
☎ **017687 72287** 📄 **017687 72287**
e-mail: info@mirehouse.com

Visitors return to Mirehouse for many reasons, but chief among them are its close links to both Tennyson and Wordsworth, the spectacular setting of mountain and lake, the varied gardens, the changing displays on the Poetry Walk, the free children's nature notes, four woodland playgrounds, live classical piano music in the house, generous Cumbrian cooking in the tearoom, and a relaxed, friendly welcome.

Times: Open Apr-Oct. Grounds: daily 10.30 5.30 House: Wed, Sun, (also Fri in Aug) 2-last entry 4.30. Parties by arrangement.
Fee: ✱ House & grounds £4.60 (ch £2.30). Grounds only £2.20 (ch £1.10). Family ticket £13.80 (2 ad & 4 ch)
Facilities: 🅿 (charged) ☕ ♿ toilets for disabled ✖ (ex on leads & guide dogs)

Alfred Lord Tennyson

LAKESIDE AQUARIUM OF THE LAKES

LA12 8AS
Dir: (M6 junct 36, take A590 to Newby Bridge. Turn right over bridge, follow Hawkshead rd to Lakeside. Well signed)
Map Ref: *SD38*
☎ **015395 30153** 📄 **015395 30152**
e-mail: aquariumofthelakes@reallive.co.uk

Set on the southern shore of Lake Windermere at Lakeside, the award-winning Aquarium of the Lakes is the UK's largest collection of freshwater fish. Over 30 displays recreate the journey of a Lakeland river from mountain top to the open sea. Naturally themed habitats are home to everything from diving ducks and mischievous otters to sharks and rays. An all-weather experience for all ages.

Times: Open all year, daily from 9. Closed 25 Dec. **Fee:** ✱ £5.95 (ch £3.75, pen £4.95). Family ticket (2ad+2ch £16.95, 2ad+3ch £19.95, 2ad+4ch £22.95). **Facilities:** 🅿 (charged) ☕ ♿ (lift to first floor, wheelchairs) toilets for disabled shop ✖ (ex guide dogs) ▰

NEAR SAWREY HILL TOP

LA22 0LF
Dir: (2m S of Hawkshead. Behind The Tower Bank Arms)
Map Ref: *SD39*
☎ **015394 36269** 📄 **015394 36811**
e-mail: hilltop@nationaltrust.org.uk

This small 17th-century house is where Beatrix Potter wrote many of her famous children's stories. It remains just as she left it, and in each room you can spot something that has appeared in one of her books. It is a small property, so a timed entry system is operated to avoid overcrowding. Outside, there is a pretty cottage garden where vegetables, fruit, herbs and flowers are grown, just as they were in Beatrix Potter's time.

Times: Open 3 Apr-Oct, Sat-Wed 10.30-4.30, last admission 4. Garden only: 8 Apr-29 Oct, Thu-Fri 11-4. Shop 3 Apr-Oct, Sat-Wed 10.30-5; 8 Apr-29 Oct, Thu-Fri 11-4. **Fee:** ✱ £4.50 (ch £2) Family ticket £11(2ad+3ch) **Facilities:** 🅿 (200 mtrs) (no parking for coaches) (Braille guide,handling items,accessibility by arrangement) shop ✖ (ex guide dogs) ♨ ▰

PENRITH RHEGED - THE VILLAGE IN THE HILL

Redhills CA11 0DQ
Dir: (M6 junct 40, on A66 towards Keswick) *Map Ref:* NY53
☎ **01768 868000** 🖹 **01768 868002**
e-mail: enquiries@rheged.com

Named after Cumbria's Celtic kingdom, this incredible attraction is the largest grass-covered building in Europe, and is designed to look like a Lakeland hill. Inside is a state-of-the-art Mega Systems cinema with a screen that measures 60-feet wide and 48-feet high. Among the films shown on this massive screen are *'Rheged - The Movie'*, a journey through the myths, legends and scenery of Cumbria; and *'Everest - The Movie'*, a breathtaking trip to the top of the world. Rheged also contains the permanent Helly Hansen National Mountaineering Exhibition.

Times: Open daily 10-5.30. (Closed 25 Dec) **Fee:** ✱ Each attraction £5.50 (ch £3.90 & pen £4.70). Family ticket £16 **Facilities:** 🅿 ☕ ✕ licensed ♿ toilets for disabled shop ✈ (ex guide dogs) 🍴

WETHERIGGS COUNTRY POTTERY

Clifton Dykes CA10 2DH
Dir: (approx 2m off A6, S from Penrith, signed) *Map Ref:* NY53
☎ **01768 892733** 🖹 **01768 892733 ext 231**   **FREE**
e-mail: info@wetheriggs-pottery.co.uk

The only steam-powered pottery in Britain, Wetheriggs is a 19th-century industrial monument. The pottery was founded in the 1860s by John Schofield and Margaret Thorburn and restored in the mid 1990s. Guided tours are available all through the year and you can see designer-makers at work. There are 7.5 acres of things to do, including the Pots of Fun Studio, where you can throw or paint a pot, the pottery museum, play areas, newt pond, café, bistro and shops.

Times: Open daily, Winter 10-5, Summer 10-5.30
Facilities: 🅿 ☕ ✕ licensed ♿ toilets for disabled shop (ex guide dogs) 🍴

RAVENGLASS RAVENGLASS & ESKDALE RAILWAY

CA18 1SW
Dir: (close to A595, Barrow to Carlisle road) *Map Ref:* SD09
☎ **01229 717171** 🖹 **01229 717011**
e-mail: steam@ravenglass-railway.co.uk

From the Lake Disrict National Park's only coastal village of Ravenglass, small steam engines haul trains through seven miles of outstanding, unspoilt beauty to the foot of England's highest mountains in Eskdale. Ravenglass & Eskdale Railway offers both open topped or cosy covered carriages, and children learn about steam with 'La'al Ratty', the water-vole stationmaster.

Times: Open: trains operate daily mid Mar-early Nov. Most winter wknds, plus daily in Feb Half term. **Fee:** ✱ Return fare £8.20 (ch 5-15 £4.10). 1 adult half price with 2+ fare paying children. **Facilities:** 🅿 (charged) ☕ ✕ ♿ (special coaches - prior notice advisable) toilets for disabled shop 🍴

WHITEHAVEN THE BEACON

West Strand CA28 7LY
Dir: (A595, after Porton right onto New Rd. Follow one-way
system & tourist signs to The Beacon) **Map Ref:** NX91
☎ **0845 095 2131** 🖷 **01946 598150**
e-mail: thebeacon@copelandbc.gov.uk

Home to the town's museum collection, The Beacon traces the
social, industrial and maritime heritage of the area using local
characters, audio-visual displays and museum pieces. Through
these, you can explore Whitehaven's connections with rum, sugar,
the slave trade and smuggling, and local industries, including coal
mining, iron mining, pottery and ship building. Visitors can enjoy
panoramic views of the town and coast from the Met Office
Weather Gallery.

Times: Open Tue-Sun, Etr-Oct 10-5.30, Nov-Mar
10-4.30. Open school & BHs. Closed 25 Dec.
Fee: ✱ £4.40 (ch £2.90, pen £3.60) Family
£13.25. Art gallery free. **Facilities:** 🅿 (charged)
🍽 & (chair/stair lift, Braille signs) toilets for
disabled shop ✈ 🎞

THE RUM STORY

27 Lowther St CA28 7DN
Dir: (A595, follow town centre signs) **Map Ref:** NX91
☎ **01946 592933** 🖷 **01946 590595**
e-mail: dutymanagers@rumstory.co.uk

Set in the original shop, courtyards, cellars and bonded
warehouses of the Jefferson family - the oldest rum trading family
in the UK - this fascinating story takes the visitor back in time to
the days of the rum trade, its links with the slave trade, sugar
plantations, the Royal Navy, barrel-making and more.

Times: Open daily, Apr-Sep 10-5, Oct-Mar 10-4
Closed 25 Dec & 1 Jan. **Fee:** ✱ £4.95 (ch £2.95,
concessions £3.50) Family £13.60. Groups 15+
£3 **Facilities:** 🅿 (various in area) (disc zones up
to 1hr) 🍽 ✗ licensed & (wheelchairs, wide
doors, lifts) toilets for disabled 🎞

WINDERMERE *LAKE DISTRICT VISITOR CENTRE AT BROCKHOLE*

LA23 1LJ
Dir: (on A591, between Windermere and Ambleside, follow
brown tourist signs) **Map Ref:** SD49
☎ **015394 46601** 🖷 **015394 45555**
e-mail: infodesk@lake-district.gov.uk

Set in 32 acres of landscaped gardens and grounds, on the shore
of Lake Windermere, this house became England's first National
Park Visitor Centre in 1969. It offers exhibitions, audio-visual
programmes, an adventure playground and an extensive events
programme. Cruises on Lake Windermere are available from the
centre's jetty in high season.

Times: Open Etr-Oct, daily, 10-5. Grounds &
gardens open all year. **Facilities:** 🅿 (charged)
🍽 ✗ licensed & (manual & electric wheelchairs,
lifts, induction loops) toilets for disabled shop 🎞

Cumbria continued

WINDERMERE STEAMBOAT CENTRE

Rayrigg Rd LA23 1BN
Dir: (0.5m N of Bowness-on-Windermere on A592)
Map Ref: SD49
☎ 015394 45565 📄 015394 48769
e-mail: steamboat@ecosse.net

The Windermere Steamboat Centre has a unique collection of Victorian and Edwardian steamboats and vintage motorboats, including the oldest steamboat in the world, the 'S L Dolly', which dates from 1850. Museum displays tell the social and commercial history of England's largest lake, and there are steamboat trips daily, weather permitting.

Times: Open 17 Mar-7 Nov daily, 10-5. Steamboat trips subject to availability & weather. **Fee:** £4.25 (ch £2.25). Family ticket £8.50, season ticket £15. **Facilities:** 🅿 ☕ & toilets for disabled shop 🖬

BARNARD CASTLE   BARNARD CASTLE

DL12 9AT
Map Ref: NZ01
☎ 01833 638212

The imposing remains of one of England's largest medieval castles are perched high on a rugged escarpment above the banks of the River Tees. The castle was built by Bernard Balliol in 1125, and the market town of Barnard Castle has developed over the centuries in its protective shadow.

Times: Open all year, Apr-Sep, daily 10-6; Oct, daily 10-4; Nov-Mar, Thur-Mon 10-4. Closed 24-26 Dec & 1 Jan. **Fee:** ✱ £3 (ch £1.50, concessions £2.30). Prices & opening times relate to 2004, for further details phone or log onto www.english-heritage.org.uk/visits
Facilities: & shop ⌗

THE BOWES MUSEUM

DL12 8NP
Dir: (located in Barnard Castle, just off A66) **Map Ref:** NZ01
☎ 01833 690606 📄 01833 637163
e-mail: info@bowesmuseum.org.uk

Enjoy a great family day out at the Bowes Museum, as you immerse yourself in the atmosphere of this magnificent French-style château, and explore the extravagant life stories of founders John and Joséphine Bowes. The museum contains an outstanding collection of fine and decorative art, including the world-famous Silver Swan. There is something for all the family, including dining, shopping and beautiful parkland.

Times: Open daily 11-5. Closed 25-26 Dec & 1 Jan. **Fee:** £6 (concessions £5, ch under 16 free) **Facilities:** 🅿 ☕ & (lift, ramped entrance, reserved parking) toilets for disabled shop (grounds only, ex guide dogs) 🖬

BEAMISH BEAMISH, THE NORTH OF ENGLAND OPEN-AIR MUSEUM

DH9 0RG
Dir: (off A693 & A6076) *Map Ref:* NZ25
☎ **0191 370 4000** 📄 **0191 370 4001**
e-mail: museum@beamish.org.uk

Set in 200 acres of countryside, the award-winning museum at Beamish recreates life in the early 1800s and 1900s. Costumed staff welcome visitors to a 1913 town street, a colliery village, farm and railway station, and there is a display of how people lived and worked. You can ride on early electric tramcars, or a replica of an 1825 steam railway, and visit Pockerley Manor where a yeoman farmer and his family would have lived.

Times: Open 3 Apr-Oct, daily 10-5; Nov-18 Mar, 10-4 (ex Mon & Fri). Closed 13 Dec-3 Jan (last admission 3). **Fee:** ✱ Summer £14 (ch £7, pen £11). Group 20+ £9, £5 & £8. Winter £5 (ch & pen £5). Winter visit is centered on town & tramway only, other areas are closed. **Facilities:** 🅿 🍽 ♿ (not ideal for wheelchairs, free entry, helpers essential) toilets for disabled shop 🛍

BOWES THE OTTER TRUST'S NORTH PENNINES RESERVE

Vale House Farm DL12 9RH
Dir: (S side of A66 Scotch Corner to Penrith Rd, 2m W of Bowes)
Map Ref: NY91
☎ **01833 628339** 📄 **01986 892461**

Set in 230 acres of upland farmland, the Otter Trust reserve isn't just about otters, although there is an ongoing release programme that aims to protect the otter from extinction. Visitors can also see red and fallow deer, mouflon sheep, and a wide range of birds including curlew, oystercatchers, snipe, and black grouse. The visitor centre contains exhibits on some of the animals as well as local history, and overlooks the River Greta.

Times: Open Apr-Oct, daily 10.30-6 **Fee:** ✱ £5 (ch £3) **Facilities:** 🅿 🍽 ♿ toilets for disabled shop 🐕 (ex guide dogs)

COWSHILL KILLHOPE THE NORTH OF ENGLAND LEAD MINING MUSEUM

DL13 1AR
Dir: (beside A689 midway between Stanhope & Alston)
Map Ref: NY84
☎ **01388 537505** 📄 **01388 537617**
e-mail: killhope@durham.gov.uk

Equipped with hard hats and lamps, you can explore the working conditions of lead miners at Kilhope. The lead mine and 19th-century crushing mill have been recreated to look as they would have done in the 1870s, and the 34-foot water wheel has been restored to working order. There is also a visitor centre and mineral exhibition, a woodland walk, children's play area and a red squirrel and bird hide.

Times: Open 19-20 & 25 Mar-Oct, daily 10.30-5 (BHs & summer school hols open until 5.30); Open Dec 3-4 & 10-11 **Fee:** Mine & Site: £6 (ch £3, concessions £5.50). Family £17. Site: £4.50 (ch £1.70, concessions £4). Family £11 **Facilities:** 🅿 🍽 ♿ (electric scooter, sympathetic hearing scheme) toilets for disabled shop 🛍

DARLINGTON   DARLINGTON RAILWAY CENTRE & MUSEUM

North Rd Station DL3 6ST
Dir: (0.75m N, off A167) *Map Ref: NZ21*
☎ 01325 460532 ▤ 01325 287746
e-mail: museum@darlington.gov.uk

Housed in the carefully restored North Road Station, this museum's prize exhibit is 'Locomotion', which pulled the first passenger train on the Stockton to Darlington railway and was built by Robert Stephenson & Co in 1825. Several other steam locomotives are also shown, together with models and other exhibits relating to the Stockton and Darlington and the North Eastern Railway companies. Recently arrived at the museum for a two year period is an A2 Pacific No 60532 'Blue Peter'. Refreshments are available.

Times: Open daily 10-5. Closed 25-26 Dec & 1 Jan. **Fee:** ✱ £2.50 (ch £1.50, pen £1.50). **Facilities:** ▣ ও toilets for disabled shop ✖ (ex guide dogs) ◾

DURHAM   DURHAM CATHEDRAL

DH1 3EH
Dir: (A690 into city, follow signs to car parks) *Map Ref: NZ24*
☎ 0191 386 4266 ▤ 0191 386 4267
e-mail: enquiries@durhamcathedral.co.uk

Founded in 1093 as a shrine to St Cuthbert, the 7th-century Bishop of Lindisfarne, the cathedral is one of the country's finest. It is a remarkable example of Norman architecture, set in an impressive position high above the River Wear, and is part of a designated World Heritage Site. The cathedral also houses the tomb of St Bede, England's first historian, who chronicled the life of St Cuthbert. A full programme of concerts is run throughout the year.

Times: ✱ Open all year, daily 9.30-6.15; 21 Jun-8 Sep 9.30-8. (Sun 12.30-5). Cathedral is closed to visitors during evening recitals & concerts. **Facilities:** ▣ (in city centre) ✖ licensed ও (Braille guide, touch/hearing centre, stairclimber) toilets for disabled shop ✖ (ex guide dogs)

ORIENTAL MUSEUM

University of Durham, Elvet Hill DH1 3TH
Dir: (signed from A167 & A177) *Map Ref: NZ24*
☎ 0191 334 5694 ▤ 0191 334 5694
e-mail: oriental.museum@durham.ac.uk

The Oriental Museum is part of the University of Durham, and 'Oriental' is used in the 19th-century sense, relating to the cultures of Asia, the Near East and Islamic Africa. The Marvels of China gallery introduces the visitor to contemporary China, its history and decorative arts. Other displays cover the Islamic world, Buddhism, Chinese archaeology, the story of writing, a Javanese gamelan orchestra and an Egyptian gallery containing everything from mummies to magic amulets.

Times: Open Mon-Fri 10-5, wknds 12-5. Closed Xmas-New Year. **Fee:** £1.50 (concessions 75p). Family ticket £3.50. **Facilities:** ▣ ▣ ও (lifts to all floors) toilets for disabled shop ✖ ◾

HARTLEPOOL HMS TRINCOMALEE

Jackson Dock TS24 0SQ
Dir: (From A19 take A689 or A179, follow signs for Hartlepool Historic Quay) **Map Ref:** NZ53
☎ **01429 223193** 🖹 **01429 864385**
e-mail: office@hms-trincomalee.co.uk

'HMS Trincomalee' is the oldest ship afloat in the UK and the last of Nelson's frigates, built in 1817. It has been fully restored in an award-winning project and is berthed at the Hartlepool's historic quay. Visitors can come aboard for a unique experience of navy life two centuries ago. The 'Trincomalee' can also be chartered for events, tours and weddings.

Times: Open all year, Summer: 10-5, Winter: 10.30-4. Closed Xmas & New Year. **Fee:** ✱ £4.25 (ch, students, disabled, pen & unemployed £3.25. Family ticket (2ad+3ch) £11.75. Group tickets available. **Facilities:** 🅿 ♿ (3 out of the 4 decks are accessible by lift) shop ✖ (ex guide dogs) ◀

MUSEUM OF HARTLEPOOL

Jackson Dock, Maritime Av TS24 0XZ
Dir: (Historic Quay & Museum towards Marina) **Map Ref:** NZ53
☎ **01429 860077** 🖹 **01429 523477**

This museum tells the story of Hartlepool from prehistory to the present day and includes many original artefacts, models, computer interactives and hands-on exhibits. See how iron and steel ships were built in the town and climb aboard the Humber ferry 'Wingfield Castle', a paddle steamer built in Hartlepool in 1934.

Times: ✱ Open all year, daily. Closed 25-26 Dec & 1 Jan. **Facilities:** 🅿 🅿 ♿ toilets for disabled shop ✖ (ex guide dogs)

LANGLEY PARK DIGGERLAND

DH7 9TT
Dir: (A1(M) junct 62. A690 W (then A691) follow signs to Consett. After 6m left at rdbt, signed Langley Park, then right into Riverside Ind Est) **Map Ref:** NZ24
☎ **08700 344437** 🖹 **09012 010300**
e-mail: mail@diggerland.com

An adventure park with a difference, where kids of all ages can experience the thrills of driving real earth moving equipment. Choose from various types of diggers and dumpers ranging from a ton to 8.5 tons. Supervised by an instructor, you can complete the Dumper Truck Challenge or dig for buried treasure. New rides include JCB Robots, the Supertrack, Landrover Safari and Spin Dizzy. Even under fives can join in, with mum or dad's help.

Times: Open 12 Feb-27 Nov, 10-5 wknds BHs & school hols **Fee:** £2.50 (pen £1.25, under 2's free). Additional charge to drive/ride machinery. **Facilities:** 🅿 🅿 ♿ toilets for disabled shop ✖ (ex guide dogs) ◀

SHILDON LOCOMOTION: THE NATIONAL RAILWAY MUSEUM AT SHILDON

DL4 1PQ
Dir: (A1(M) junct 68, take A68 & A6072 to Shildon, museum is 0.25m SE of town centre) **Map Ref:** NZ22
☎ **01388 777999** 📠 **01388 777999**   FREE
e-mail: gill@hamer-loco.fsnet.co.uk

Timothy Hackwood (1786-1850) was an important figure in the development of steam travel. He constructed 'Puffing Bill' for William Hedley, ran Stephenson's Newcastle Works, and also became the first superintendent of the Stockton & Darlington Railway. The museum and house detail Hackwood's life and the steam transport revolution, as well as displaying working models and locomotives from various periods. Steam train rides are available throughout the year.

Times: Open 3 Nov-18 Mar, Wed-Sun 10-4. Closed 13 Dec-5 Jan. 19 Mar-30 Oct daily 10-5
Facilities: 🅿 🍽 ♿ (bus available to transport guests, please contact) toilets for disabled shop 🐕 (ex guide dogs)

STAINDROP RABY CASTLE

DL2 3AH
Dir: (on A688, Barnard Castle to Bishop Auckland road, 1m N of Staindrop) **Map Ref:** NZ12
☎ **01833 660202** 📠 **01833 660169**
e-mail: admin@rabycastle.com

This dramatic 14th-century castle, built by the Nevills, has been home to Lord Barnard's family since 1626. It has an impressive gateway, nine towers, a vast hall and an octagonal Victorian drawing room that has re-emerged as one of the most striking interiors from the 19th century. Rooms contain fine furniture, impressive artworks and elaborate architecture. In the grounds are a deer park, large walled gardens, coach and carriage collections, a woodland adventure playground, a picnic area and gift shop.

Times: Open May & Sep, Wed & Sun only. Jun-Aug, Sun-Fri. Castle open 1-5. Park & gardens 11-5.30, (last admission 4.30). Open BH wknds.
Fee: Castle, Park & Gardens £9 (ch £4 & pen £8). Family ticket £25 (2ad+3ch). Park & Gardens £4 (ch £2.50 & pen £3.50). Group rates available.
Facilities: 🅿 🍽 ♿ (most of ground floor accessible) toilets for disabled shop 🐕 (ex guide dogs & on lead) 🍴

TANFIELD TANFIELD RAILWAY

Old Marley Hill NE16 5ET
Dir: (on A6076 1m S of Sunniside) **Map Ref:** NZ15
☎ **0191 388 7545** 📠 **0191 387 4784**
e-mail: tanfield@ingsoc.demon.co.uk

Tanfield is a three-mile working steam railway and the oldest existing railway in the world. The Causey Arch, the first large railway bridge of its era, is the centrepiece of a deep wooded valley with picturesque walks. You can ride in carriages that first saw use in Victorian times, and visit Marley Hill shed, the home of 35 engines. Here you can see the stationary steam engine at work driving some of the vintage machine tools. Special events are held throughout the year.

Times: ✱ Open all year, Summer daily 10-5; Winter daily 10-4. Trains: Sun & Summer BHs wknds; also Thu & Sat mid Jul-Aug. Santa's Specials Sat & Sun in Dec (booking essential). Mince pie specials Boxing Day. **Facilities:** 🅿 🍽 ♿ (all trains carry ramps for wheelchair access) toilets for disabled shop

ALTRINCHAM DUNHAM MASSEY

WA14 4SJ
Dir: (3m SW of Altrincham (off A56), off M6 junct 19 or off M56 junct 7, then follow brown signs) *Map Ref:* SJ78
☎ 0161 941 1025 📠 0161 929 7508
e-mail: dunhammassey@nationaltrust.org.uk

This fine 18th-century house, garden and park, was home to the Earls of Stamford until 1976. Its 30 rooms include the library, billiard room, fully-equipped kitchen, butler's pantry and laundry. The garden is on an ancient site with waterside plantings, mixed borders and lawns. There is also 300-acre deer park. Please telephone for details of special events.

Times: Open: Park, restaurant & shop open all year. House open 27 Mar-3 Nov, 12-5 (11 Sun & BH Mon, closes at 4 during late Oct). Garden, 11-5.30 (closes 4.30 in late Oct). Last entry to house 30mins before closing time. **Fee:** ✱ House & Garden £6 (ch £3). House only £4 (ch £2). Garden only £4 (ch £2). Family ticket £15. Park only, £3.50 per car. £1 per motorbike
Facilities: 🅿 (charged) ✗ licensed ♿ (loan of batricar/wheelchairs, lift, braille guide, parking) toilets for disabled shop ✖ (ex on lead in Park) ✿ ▰

ASHTON-UNDER-LYNE PORTLAND BASIN MUSEUM

Portland Place OL7 0QA
Dir: (M60 junct 23 into Ashton town centre. Museum is near Cross Hill Street & car park) *Map Ref:* SJ99
☎ 0161 343 2878 📠 0161 343 2869   **FREE**
e-mail: portland.basin@tameside.gov.uk

Exploring the social and Industrial history of Tameside, this museum is part of the rebuilt Ashton Canal Warehouse, dating from 1834. Visitors can walk around a 1920's street, dress up in old hats and gloves, steer a virtual canal boat, and see the original canal powered waterwheel that once drove the warehouse machinery. Portland Basin Museum also features changing exhibitions and event programme - so there's always something new to see!

Times: Open all year, Tue-Sun 10-5. (Closed Mon, ex BHs) **Facilities:** 🅿 ▰ ♿ (wheelchair, lift, loop system) toilets for disabled shop ✖ (ex guide dogs) ▰

BRAMHALL BRAMALL HALL & PARK

SK7 3NX
Dir: (from A6 right at Blossoms public house through Davenport village then right - signed) *Map Ref:* SJ88
☎ 0161 485 3708 📠 0161 486 6959
e-mail: bramall.hall@stockport.gov.uk

This large timber-framed hall dates from the 14th century, and is one of the finest black-and-white houses in the northwest. It has rare 16th-century wall paintings and period furniture, and was the home of the Davenport family for 500 years. Much of the house is open to the public and available for hire. Open air concerts and plays are a feature in summer.

Times: Open all year, Good Fri-Sep, Mon-Sat 1-5, Sun & BHs 11-5; Oct-New Year's Day Tue-Sat 1-4, Sun & BHs 11-4; 2 Jan-Good Fri Sat & Sun 12-4. Closed 25-26 Dec. **Facilities:** 🅿 (charged) ▰ ♿ (access for wheelchair users) toilets for disabled shop ✖ (ex guide dogs) ▰

MANCHESTER GALLERY OF COSTUME

Platt Hall, Rusholme M14 5LL
Dir: (situated in Platt Fields Park, Rusholme, access from Wilmslow Rd. 2m S of city centre) **Map Ref:** *SJ89*
☎ **0161 224 5217** 📄 **0161 256 3278**
e-mail: a.jarvis@notes.manchester.gov.uk

With one of the most comprehensive costume collections in Great Britain, this gallery makes captivating viewing. Housed in a fine Georgian mansion, the displays focus on the changing styles of everyday fashion and accessories over the last 400 years. Contemporary fashion is also illustrated. Because of the vast amount of material in the collection, no one period is permanently illustrated.

Times: Open to public on last Sat of month. Mon-Fri by appointment, please ring; 0161 224 5217 **Facilities:** 🅿 & shop ✖ (ex guide dogs)

IMPERIAL WAR MUSEUM NORTH

The Quays, Trafford Wharf Rd, Trafford Park M17 1TZ
Dir: (M60 junct 9, A5081 towards Trafford Park. At 1st island 3rd exit onto Village Way. At next island 2nd exit onto Warren Bruce Rd. Right at T-junct onto Trafford Wharf Rd. Or M602 junct 2, follow signs) **Map Ref:** *SJ89*
☎ **0161 836 4000** 📄 **0161 836 4012**
e-mail: info@iwmnorth.org.uk

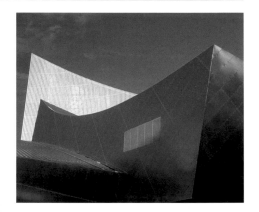

This new war museum is built to resemble three shards of a shattered globe, representing conflict on land, sea, and in the air and was designed by Daniel Libeskind. Inside are thousands of exhibits, interactive sessions, performances and recreations that explore the way that 20th-century conflict has shaped our lives.

Times: Open daily Mar-Oct 10-6, Nov-Feb 10-5. Closed 24-26 Dec. **Facilities:** 🅿 (charged) ✖ licensed & (lifts, parking, manual wheelchairs) toilets for disabled shop ✖ (ex guide dogs)

MANCHESTER ART GALLERY

Mosley St/Princess St M2 3JL
Dir: (from M60 follow signs to city centre) **Map Ref:** *SJ89*
☎ **0161 235 8888** 📄 **0161 235 8899**

The Mosley Street Galleries in Manchester have permanent displays of European art, ceramics and silver, displayed along with furniture in an elaborate decorative scheme. There is a superb collection of Victorian art, including some major Pre-Raphaelite paintings. Decorative and applied arts, including porcelain, furniture and sculpture, can also be seen.

Times: Open Tue-Sun, 10-5 (closed Mon except BH). Closed Good Fri, 24-26 & 31 Dec & 1 Jan. **Facilities:** 🅿 (NCP-5 mins walk) 🍴 ✖ & toilets for disabled shop ✖ (ex guide dogs)

MANCHESTER MUSEUM

The University, Oxford Rd M13 9PL
Dir: (S of city centre on B5117) *Map Ref:* *SJ89*
☎ **0161 275 2634 0161 275 2643** 📄 **0161 275 2676**
e-mail: anna.j.davey@man.ac.uk   FREE

The Manchester Museum has undergone major refurbishment
and rebuilding. It has leading research facilities and collections in
archaeology, botany, Egyptology, ethnology, mineralogy,
numismatics and zoology, among others, including some six
million items from all over the world. There are large galleries
devoted to most of these departments, but the Egyptology
collection is particularly impressive, featuring mummies excavated
by Sir William Flinders Petrie.

Times: Open all year, Mon-Sat 10-5, Sun & BHs
11-4. **Facilities:** 🅿 (charged) 🍴 ♿ (lift access,
hearing loop, accessible parking) toilets for
disabled shop ✖ (ex guide dogs) 🔊

MANCHESTER UNITED MUSEUM & TOUR CENTRE

Sir Matt Busby Way, Old Trafford M16 0RA
Dir: (2m from city centre, off A56) *Map Ref:* *SJ89*
☎ **0870 442 1994** 📄 **0161 868 8861**
e-mail: tours@manutd.co.uk

This museum was opened in 1986 and is the first purpose built
British football museum. It covers the history of Manchester United
in words, pictures, sound and vision, from its inception in 1878 to
the present day. Stadium tours can also be booked, for a birds' eye
view of the pitch, a visit to the home changing rooms and the
chance to emerge from the players tunnel to the roar of the crowd.

Times: Open daily 9.30-5 (open until 30mins before kick off on
match days). Closed some days over Xmas & New Year.
Fee: ✱ Stadium tour & Museum: £9 (ch & pen £6) Family ticket £25.
Museum only: £5.50 (ch & pen £3.75) Family ticket £15.50.
Facilities: 🅿 🍴 ✖ licensed ♿ (w/chair, audio visual scripts, part of
tour not accessible) toilets for disabled shop ✖ (ex guide dogs) 🔊

THE MUSEUM OF SCIENCE AND INDUSTRY IN MANCHESTER

Liverpool Rd, Castlefield M3 4FP
Dir: (follow brown tourist signs from city centre) *Map Ref:* *SJ89*
☎ **0161 832 2244 & 0161 832 1830** 📄 **0161 833 1471**
e-mail: marketing@msim.org.uk

This museum is housed in the buildings of the world's oldest
passenger railway station. Colourful galleries packed full of
fascinating facts and amazing artefacts bring the past to life. Walk
away from your own shadow in Xperiment! - the mind bending
science centre. See wheels of industry turning in the Power Hall,
and the planes that made flying history in the Air and Space Hall.
There is also a programme of changing exhibitions.

Times: Open all year, daily 10-5. Last admission
4.30. Closed 24-26 Dec. **Facilities:** 🅿 (charged)
🍴 ✖ licensed ♿ (lifts, wheelchair loan service)
toilets for disabled shop ✖ (ex guide dogs) 🔊

MUSEUM OF TRANSPORT

Boyle St, Cheetham M8 8UW
Dir: (museum adjacent to Queens Rd bus depot, 1.25m N of city centre) *Map Ref:* SJ89
☎ **0161 205 2122** 📄 **0161 205 2122**
e-mail: Gmts.enquire@btinternet.com

This museum is a must-see for fans of public transport! Among the many interesting exhibits are more than 80 beautifully restored buses and coaches from the region - the biggest collection in the UK. Displays of old photographs, tickets and other memorabilia complement the vehicles, some of which date back to 1890. Please telephone for details of special events.

Times: ✱ Open all year, Wed, Sat, Sun & BH 10-5 ex Xmas.
Facilities: 🅿 💺 ♿ toilets for disabled shop 📼

URBIS

Cathedral Gardens M4 3BG
Dir: (next to Victoria Railway Station) *Map Ref:* SJ89
☎ **0161 907 9099** 📄 **0161 605 8201** **FREE**
e-mail: info@urbis.org.uk

Urbis is a unique institution dedicated to the exploration of contemporary urban culture. The Level One Gallery offers a programme of large-scale international exhibitions, while Project Space on the ground floor shows the best of Manchester's creativity. Levels two, three and four feature interactive exhibits exploring cities around the world from Tokyo to Paris, revealing how different cities work, how they change and how they affect others.

Times: Open all year daily 10-6
Facilities: 🅿 (200yds) 💺 ✕ licensed ♿ toilets for disabled shop ✖ (ex guide dogs) 📼

THE WHITWORTH ART GALLERY

The University of Manchester, Oxford Rd M15 6ER
Dir: (follow brown tourist signs, on Oxford Rd on B5117 to S of city centre. Gallery in Whitworth Park, opp Manchester Royal Infirmary) *Map Ref:* SJ89
☎ **0161 275 7450** 📄 **0161 275 7451** **FREE**
e-mail: whitworth@man.ac.uk

The Whitworth Art Gallery houses an impressive range of modern and historic drawings, prints, paintings and sculpture. It has the largest collection of textiles and wallpapers outside London, and an internationally famous collection of British watercolours. The gallery hosts an innovative programme of touring exhibitions. A selection of tour lectures, workshops and concerts complement the exhibition programme.

Times: Open Mon-Sat 10-5, Sun 2-5. Closed Good Fri & Xmas-New Year. **Facilities:** 🅿 💺 ♿ (wheelchair available, induction loop, Braille lift buttons) toilets for disabled shop ✖ (ex guide dogs)

SALFORD THE LOWRY

Pier Eight, Salford Quays M50 3AZ
Dir: (M60 junct 12 for M602. Salford Quays is 0.25m from junct 3 of M602, follow brown Lowry signs) ***Map Ref:*** *SJ89*
☎ 0870 787 5774 📠 0161 876 2001 FREE
e-mail: info@thelowry.com

The Lowry is a stunning waterside complex at Salford Quays, taking in galleries, shops, cafés and a restaurant, plus two theatres showing everything from West End plays and musicals to comedians, ballet and live bands. In addition to the L S Lowry gallery, a tribute to the celebrated local artist, contemporary art exhibitions are also a feature. With regular family activities, too, you can make a whole day of your visit.

Times: Open daily from 10. Galleries, Sun-Fri from 11, Sat from 10. Closed 25 Dec. **Facilities:** P (charged) licensed (Sennheiser System) toilets for disabled shop (ex guide dogs)

SALFORD MUSEUM & ART GALLERY

Peel Park, Crescent M5 4WU
Dir: (from N leave M60 junct 13, A666. From S follow signs from end of M602. Museum on A6) ***Map Ref:*** *SJ89*
☎ 0161 736 2649 📠 0161 745 9490 FREE
e-mail: salford.museum@salford.gov.uk

The museum features a reconstruction of a 19th-20th century northern street with original shop fronts. Upstairs in the galleries there are temporary exhibitions and a gallery displaying paintings, sculptures and ceramics. Recent additions include the lifetimes gallery, featuring audio presentations, IT zones, temporary exhibitions, a spectacular Pilkington's display and lots of hands-on activities and dressing-up areas.

Times: Open all year Mon-Fri 10-4.45, Sat & Sun 1-5. Closed Good Fri, Etr Sat, 25 & 26 Dec, 1 Jan. **Facilities:** P (Braille & large print labels & visitor packs, hearing loop) toilets for disabled shop (ex guide dogs)

STOCKPORT HAT WORKS MUSEUM

Wellington Mill, Wellington Rd South SK3 0EU
Dir: (M60 junct 1, follow signs for town centre. Museum opposite bus station) ***Map Ref:*** *SJ89*
☎ 0161 355 7770/6 📠 0161 480 8735
e-mail: hatworks@stockport.gov.uk

Hat Works is the UK's only museum of the hatting industry, hats and headwear, offering an insight into a once flourishing industry. See how hats are made with a unique working collection of Victorian millinery machinery and take a tour with expert guides who will give visitors an insight into the hatter's world. Browse an extensive collection of hats before relaxing in the Level 2 café.

Times: Open daily Mon-Fri 10-5, Sat & Sun 1-5. Closed 25-26 Dec & 1 Jan. **Fee:** £3.95 (ch £2.50 & concessions £2.50, under 5's free). Family ticket £11 **Facilities:** P (limited pay & display parking) toilets for disabled shop (ex guide dogs)

Greater Manchester continued

UPPERMILL *SADDLEWORTH MUSEUM & ART GALLERY*

High St OL3 6HS
Dir: (M62 E junct 22 or M62 W junct 21. On A670)
Map Ref: SD90
☎ **01457 874093** 📄 **01457 870336**
e-mail: museum-curator@saddleworth.net

Based in an old mill building next to the Huddersfield Canal, the museum explores the history of the Saddleworth area. Wool weaving is the traditional industry, displayed in the 18th-century Weaver's Cottage and Victoria Mill Gallery. The textile machinery is run regularly by arrangement. The art gallery has regular exhibitions.

Times: Open all year, Nov-late Mar, daily 1-4; late Mar-Oct, Mon-Sat 10-5, Sun 12-5. Closed 24-25 Dec & 31 Dec-1 Jan. **Facilities:** 🅿 ♿ (stairlift, ramps, Braille & large print guides, wheelchair) toilets for disabled shop ✖ (ex guide dogs)

WIGAN *WIGAN PIER*

Trencherfield Mill WN3 4EF
Dir: (follow brown tourist signs from M6 junct 25-27/M61 junct 6-8) *Map Ref:* SD50
☎ **01942 323666** 📄 **01942 701927**
e-mail: wiganpier@wlct.org

Wigan Pier is a journey never to be forgotten. Part museum, part theatre, it is a mixture of entertainment and education. Step back in time at 'The Way We Were' heritage centre and visit the world's largest original mill steam engine. You can also enjoy trips along the Leeds-Liverpool canal or walks in the grounds. There is also a regular programme of events.

Times: Open all year, Mon-Thu 10-5; Sat & Sun 11-5. Closed every Fri ex Good Fri, 25-26 Dec, 1 Jan. **Fee:** ✱ £8.50 (concessions £6.25). Site ticket £23.50 (2 ad & 2 concessions). **Facilities:** 🅿 ☕ ✖ licensed ♿ (Braille guide, audio tape, large text leaflet, minicom) toilets for disabled shop ✖ (ex guide dogs) ◀

BALLAUGH *CURRAGHS WILD LIFE PARK*

IM7 5EA
Dir: (on main road halfway between Kirk Michael & Ramsey)
Map Ref: SC27
☎ **01624 897323** 📄 **01624 897327**
e-mail: curraghswlp@gov.im

This park has been developed adjacent to the reserve area of the Ballaugh Curraghs, and a large variety of animals and birds can be seen. A walk through enclosure lets visitors explore the world of wildlife, including local habitats along the Curraghs nature trail. On Sundays you can also take a ride on the miniature railway.

Times: Open all year Etr-Oct, daily 10-6. (Last admission 5). Oct-Etr, Sat & Sun 10-4. **Fee:** ✱ £4.50 (ch £2.50, under 5's free, pen £3). Party. **Facilities:** 🅿 ☕ ♿ (loan of wheelchair & electric wheelchair) toilets for disabled shop ✖ (ex guide dogs by arrangement)

CASTLETOWN *CASTLE RUSHEN*

The Quay IM9 1LD
Dir: (centre of Castletown) *Map Ref:* SC26
☎ **01624 648000** ▤ **01624 648001**
e-mail: enquiries@mnh.gov.im

One of Britain's most complete medieval castles, Castle Rushen is a limestone fortress rising out of the heart of the old capital of the island, Castletown. Once the fortress of the Kings and Lords of Mann, Castle Rushen is bought alive with rich decorations, and the sounds and smells of a bygone era. In summer battles are re-enacted and the lifestyle of the period recreated by enthusiasts.

Times: ✱ Open daily, 10-5, Apr-late Oct.
Facilities: ℗ (100 yds) (disc zone parking) ♿ shop ✖ (ex guide dogs) ▬

NAUTICAL MUSEUM

Dir: (From Castletown centre, cross the footbridge over the harbour. Museum is on the right) *Map Ref:* SC26
☎ **01624 648000** ▤ **01624 648001**
e-mail: enquiries@mnh.gov.im

Set at the mouth of Castletown Harbour, this museum is home to an 18th-century armed yacht, 'The Peggy', built by a Manxman in 1791. A replica sailmaker's loft, ship model and a collection of photographs brings the story of maritime Manx and trade in the days of sail to life.

Times: ✱ Open daily 10-5, Apr-late Oct.
Facilities: ℗ ♿ shop ✖ (ex guide dogs) ▬

OLD GRAMMAR SCHOOL

IM9 1LE
Dir: (centre of Castletown, opposite the castle) *Map Ref:* SC26
☎ **01624 648000** ▤ **01624 648001**
e-mail: enquiries@mnh.gov.im

This small whitewashed building, built around AD 1200, was originally the church in the former capital, Castletown. Its main wing is the oldest roofed building on the island. St Mary's has played a significant role in Manx education. It was used as a school from at least 1570, and exclusively so from 1702 until 1930, and these days recalls the experience of Victorian school life.

Times: ✱ Open daily 10-5, Apr-late Oct.
Facilities: ℗ shop ✖ (ex guide dogs)

CREGNEISH *CREGNEASH VILLAGE FOLK MUSEUM*

Dir: (2m from Port Erin/Port St Mary, signed) *Map Ref:* SC16
☎ 01624 648000 📄 01624 648001
e-mail: enquiries@mnh.gov.im

The Cregneash story begins in Cummal Beg - the village
information centre - where you can experience what life was
really like in a Manx crofting village during the early 19th century.
As you stroll around this attractive village, set in beautiful
countryside, call into Harry Kelly's cottage, a turner's shed, a
weaver's house, and the smithy. The Manx four-horned Loghtan
sheep can be seen grazing along with other animals from the
village farm.

Times: * Open Apr-late Oct, daily 10-5.
Facilities: 🅿 💷 shop ✖ (ex guide dogs) ◀

DOUGLAS *MANX MUSEUM*

IM1 3LY
Dir: (signed in Douglas) *Map Ref:* SC37
☎ 01624 648000 📄 01624 648001
e-mail: enquiries@mnh.gov.im

The island's treasure house provides an exciting introduction to
the 'Story of Mann' where a specially produced film portrayal of
Manx history complements the award-winning displays. Galleries
depict natural history, archaeology and the social development of
the Island. There are also examples of famous Manx artists in the
National Art Gallery together with the island's national archive and
reference library.

Times: * Open daily all year, Mon-Sat 10-5.
Closed 25-26 Dec & 1 Jan.
Facilities: 🅿 ✖ licensed ♿ (lift) toilets for
disabled shop ✖ (ex guide dogs) ◀

SNAEFELL MOUNTAIN RAILWAY

Banks Circus IM1 5PT
Dir: (Manx Electric Railway from Douglas and change at Laxey)
Map Ref: SC37
☎ 01624 663366 📄 01624 663637
e-mail: info@busandrail.dtl.gov.im

Snaefell is the Isle of Man's highest mountain at 2,036 feet.
Running up it is Britain's oldest working mountain railway, which
was laid in 1895. It is a total of four miles from the village of
Laxey to the summit, where there is a café, pub and small
museum. From the top of Snaefell, on a clear day, England,
Ireland, Scotland and Wales are all visible.

Times: Open 25 Apr-25 Sep **Fee:** Various fares
charged. **Facilities:** 🅿 💷 shop ◀

LAXEY *GREAT LAXEY WHEEL & MINES TRAIL*

Dir: (signed in Laxey village) ***Map Ref:*** *SC48*
☎ **01624 648000** ▤ **01624 648001**
e-mail: enquiries@mnh.gov.im

Built in 1854, the Great Laxey Wheel, 22 metres in diameter, is
the largest working water wheel in the world. It was designed to
pump water from the lead and zinc mines and is an
acknowledged masterpiece of Victorian engineering. The wheel
was christened by Lady Isabella, the wife of the Lieutenant
Governor of the Isle of Man.

Times: ✱ Open Apr-late Oct, daily 10-5. **Facilities:** 🅿 ♿ shop
🐕 (ex guide dogs) ▤

PEEL *HOUSE OF MANANNAN*

Mill Rd IM5 1TA
Dir: (signed in Peel) ***Map Ref:*** *SC28*
☎ **01624 648000** ▤ **01624 648001**
e-mail: enquiries@mnh.gov.im

This £6 million centre is an unforgettable experience. Here, the
mythical god of the sea, Manannan, guides you through the
Celtic, Viking and maritime traditions of the Isle of Man.
Reconstructions, interactive displays, audio visual presentations
and original material help you to explore these themes. A visit will
leave you in awe of the diversity of Manx heritage and eager to
learn more.

Times: ✱ Open daily, 10-5. Closed 25-26 Dec &
1 Jan. **Facilities:** 🅿 ♿ toilets for disabled shop
🐕 (ex guide dogs) ▤

PEEL CASTLE

IM5 1TB
Dir: (on St Patrick's Isle, facing Peel Bay, signed) ***Map Ref:*** *SC28*
☎ **01624 648000** ▤ **01624 648001**
e-mail: enquiries@mnh.gov.im

Peel Castle is one of the island's principle historic centres. The
great natural fortress, with an imposing curtain wall, is set
majestically at the mouth of Peel Harbour and is steeped in Viking
heritage. The sandstone walls of the castle enclose an 11th-
century church and round tower, the 13th-century St German's
Cathedral and the later apartments of the Lords of Mann.

Times: ✱ Open Apr-late Oct, daily 10-5.
Facilities: 🅿 shop 🐕 (ex guide dogs)

Isle of Man continued

RAMSEY 'THE GROVE' RURAL LIFE MUSEUM

IM8 3UA
Dir: (on W side of Andreas Rd. Signed in Ramsey)
Map Ref: *SC49*
☎ **01624 648000** 🖶 **01624 648001**
e-mail: enquiries@mnh.gov.im

This Victorian time capsule was a country house built as a
summer retreat for a Liverpool shipping merchant. Rooms are
filled with period furnishings together with a costume exhibition.
In the adjacent farmyard are buildings with displays on farming
and 19th-century vehicles. Around the grounds you may see
Loghtan sheep, ducks and perhaps a Manx cat.

Times: ✻ Open Apr-late Oct, daily 10-5.
Facilities: 🅿 🍽 🚻 shop ✖ (ex guide dogs) 🛍

BLACKPOOL BLACKPOOL ZOO PARK

East Park Dr FY3 8PP
Dir: (M55 junct 4, follow brown tourist signs) **Map Ref:** *SD33*
☎ **01253 830830** 🖶 **01253 830800**
e-mail: info@blackpoolzoo.freeserve.co.uk

This modern zoo, built in 1972, houses over 1,500 animals within
its 32 acres of landscaped gardens. There are plenty of
opportunities for close encounters with animals, and to see
animals in action, including highlights such as animal feeding
times and keeper talks throughout the day. Other attractions are
the miniature railway and a children's play area.

Times: Open all year daily, summer 10-6; winter
10-5 or dusk. Closed 25 Dec. **Fee:** ✻ £8.50
(ch £6.50). Family (2ad+2ch) £26, (2ad+3 ch)
£31. Concessions for seniors, disabled, carers and
groups. **Facilities:** 🅿 🍽 ✖ licensed
🚻 (wheelchair loan, Braille factsheets, sensory
experiences) toilets for disabled shop ✖ 🛍

CHARNOCK RICHARD CAMELOT THEME PARK

PR7 5LP
Dir: (from M6 junct 27/28, or M61 junct 8 follow brown tourist
signs) **Map Ref:** *SD51*
☎ **01257 453044** 🖶 **01257 452320**
e-mail: kingarthur@camelotthemepark.co.uk

Join Merlin, King Arthur and the Knights of the Round Table at the
magical kingdom of Camelot. Explore five magic lands filled with
thrilling rides, spectacular shows, and many more attractions. From
white-knuckle thrills on spinning rollercoaster to wet-knuckle thrills
on Pendragon's Plunge there's something for everyone.

Times: Open Etr-Oct. Telephone for further details. **Fee:** ✻ £15
(ch over 1mtr £12, under 1mtr free, pen & disabled £11)
Facilities: 🅿 🍽 🚻 (disabled car parking) toilets for disabled shop
✖ (ex guide dogs) 🛍

CLITHEROE CLITHEROE CASTLE MUSEUM

Castle Gate, Castle St BB7 1BA
Dir: (follow Clitheroe signs from A59 Preston-Skipton by-pass. Museum located in castle grounds near town centre)
Map Ref: *SD74*
☎ **01200 424635**
e-mail: museum@ribblevalley.gov.uk

The museum has a good collection of carboniferous fossils, and items of local interest. Displays include local history and the industrial archaeology of the Ribble Valley, while special features include the restored Hacking ferry boat believed to be the inspiration for Buckleberry Ferry featured in JRR Tolkien's *'Fellowship of the Ring'.*

Times: Open late Feb-Etr, Sat-Wed, 11-4.30; Etr-Oct, daily inc BH; Nov, Dec & Feb, wknds & school half terms. Closed Jan **Fee:** ✱ £1.70 (ch 25p, pen 85p). Family ticket £3.65 **Facilities:** P (500yds) (disabled only parking at establishment) 🍴 ♿ shop ✖ (ex guide dogs)

LEIGHTON HALL LEIGHTON HALL

LA5 9ST
Dir: (M6 junct 35 onto A6 & follow signs) **Map Ref:** *SD47*
☎ **01524 734474** 📠 **01524 720357**
e-mail: info@leightonhall.co.uk

This is the historic family home of the Gillow furniture makers, and early Gillow furniture is displayed among other treasures in the fine interior of the neo-Gothic mansion. Outside a large collection of birds of prey can be seen, and flying displays are held each afternoon. There are also lovely gardens, a maze and a woodland walk to enjoy. The hall is a romantic venue for civil weddings and is popular too for other events.

Times: Open May-Sep, Sun, Tue-Fri & BH Mon from 2. For Aug only 12.30. (Last admission 4.30). **Fee:** ✱ £5 (ch 5-16 £3.50, pen & student £4.50). Family ticket £15. **Facilities:** P 🍴 ♿ toilets for disabled shop garden centre ✖ (ex guide dogs & in park)

MARTIN MERE WWT MARTIN MERE

L40 0TA
Dir: (signed from M61, M58 & M6. 6m from Ormskirk, off A59)
Map Ref: *SD41*
☎ **01704 895181** 📠 **01704 892343**
e-mail: info@martinmere.co.uk

One of Britain's most important wetland sites, where you can get really close to a variety of ducks, geese and swans from all over the world as well as two flocks of flamingos. Thousands of wildfowl, including pink-footed geese, Bewick's and Whooper swans, winter here. Other features include a children's adventure playground, exhibition gallery, craft area and an educational centre. The Annual North West Bird Fair takes place during November and wild swans by floodlight from 1st November to 31st January.

Times: Open all year, daily 9.30-5.30 (5 in winter). Closed 25 Dec. **Fee:** £5.75 (ch £3.75, concessions £4.75). Family ticket £15. £1 off each for group members **Facilities:** P 🍴 ♿ (wheelchair loan, Braille trail, heated hide, audio tours) toilets for disabled shop ✖ (ex guide dogs) 🍴

PRESTON HARRIS MUSEUM & ART GALLERY

Market Square PR1 2PP
Dir: (M6 junct 31, follow signs for city centre, park at bus station car park) *Map Ref:* SD52
☎ **01772 258248** 🖹 **01772 886764** FREE
e-mail: harris.museum@preston.gov.uk

This museum and art gallery is located in an impressive Grade I listed Greek Revival building and shows extensive collections of fine and decorative art, including a gallery of clothes and fashion. The Story of Preston covers the city's history and the lively exhibition programmes of contemporary art and social history are accompanied by events and activities throughout the year.

Times: Open all year, Mon-Sat 10-5, Sun 11-4. Closed BHs. **Facilities:** P (5 mins walk) (blue badge disabled parking only) 🛗 ♿ (wheelchair available, chair lift to mezzanine galleries) toilets for disabled shop ✖ (ex guide & assistance dogs) 🍴

THE NATIONAL FOOTBALL MUSEUM

Sir Tom Finney Way, Deepdale PR1 6RY
Dir: (2m from M6 junct 31, 31A or 32. Follow brown tourist signs) *Map Ref:* SD52
☎ **01772 908442** 🖹 **01772 908433** FREE
e-mail: enquiries@nationalfootballmuseum.com

What location could be more fitting for a National Football Museum than Deepdale Stadium, the home of Preston North End, first winners of the professional football league in 1888-9? This fascinating trip through football past and present includes the FIFA Museum Collection, a fine display of memorabilia and artefacts; interactive displays that allow visitors to commentate on matches, and take virtual trips to every league ground in the country; and an art gallery dedicated to the Beautiful Game.

Times: Open Tue-Sat 10-5, Sun 11-5. Closed Mon ex BHs. Contact for opening times on match days. **Facilities:** P 🛗 ♿ (lifts, multi-sensory exhibitions) toilets for disabled shop ✖ (ex guide dogs) 🍴

SILVERDALE RSPB NATURE RESERVE

Myers Farm LA5 0SW
Dir: (M6 junct 35, west on A501(M) for 0.5m. Turn right and N on A6. Follow brown tourist signs) *Map Ref:* SD47
☎ **01524 701601** 🖹 **01524 701601**
e-mail: leighton.moss@rspb.org.uk

The reserve covers 321 acres comprising a large reed swamp with meres; willow and alder scrub in the valley, and woodland on the limestone slopes. It is home to the North West's largest concentration of bitterns, together with reed, sedge and grasshopper warblers; bearded tits, pochards, tufted ducks and marsh harriers. Black terns and ospreys regularly pass through in spring and greenshanks and various sandpipers in the autumn. Wintering wildfowl include large flocks of mallards, teals, wigeons, and shovelers.

Times: Reserve: open daily 9-dusk (or sunset if earlier). Visitor Centre daily 9.30-5. Feb-Oct 9.30-4.30 Nov-Jan. Closed 25 Dec. **Fee:** ✱ £4.50 (ch £1, concessions £3) Family £9. RSPB members Free **Facilities:** P 🛗 ✖ ♿ (stairlift available to tea room) toilets for disabled shop ✖ (ex guide dogs) 🍴

BIRKENHEAD *HISTORIC WARSHIPS*

East Float, Dock Rd CH41 1DJ
Dir: (end of M53 all docks turn off follow tourist signs. From Liverpool Wallasey tunnel 1st exit after toll & follow brown heritage signs) *Map Ref:* *SJ38*
☎ 0151 650 1573 📄 0151 650 1473
e-mail: manager@warships.freeserve.co.uk

The Warship Preservation Trust has the largest collection of preserved 20th-century warships in Europe, and displays them at Birkenhead. The collection includes 'HMS Onyx', which served in the Falklands and is the only submarine afloat in the UK that visitors can explore; 'HMS' Plymouth', an anti-submarine frigate, which also served in the Falklands; and the U534, the only World War II German U-Boat to be raised from the sea bed. Pre-booking is required for guided tours; only adults and accompanied children over 12 are admitted to the U-Boat tour.

Times: ✱ Open all year, Sep-Mar daily 10-4, Apr-Aug daily 10-5. Closed 24-26 Dec, only open wknds for first 6 wks of year. **Facilities:** 🅿 ☕ ♿ (museum only, access to HMS Plymouth, multimedia tour of U534) shop ✖ (ex guide dogs) ◀

LIVERPOOL THE BEATLES STORY

Britannia Pavilion, Albert Dock L3 4AD
Dir: (follow signs to Albert Dock. Located outside Britannia Pavilion, next to Premier Lodge Hotel) *Map Ref:* *SJ39*
☎ 0151 709 1963 📄 0151 708 0039
e-mail: info@beatlesstory.com

At this award-winning attraction you can relive the story of the four lads from Liverpool who took the world by storm and changed the face of popular music for ever. It is a walk through experience located in the vaults of the Britannia Pavilion in the Albert Docks. The tour takes you through the cobbled streets of Hamburg, the Cavern Club in 1962, masses of screaming fans, Beatlemania, flower power, and the White Room dedicated to the memory of John Lennon.

Times: Open all year 10-6 (last admission 5). Closed 25-26 Dec. **Fee:** £8.45 (ch 5-16yrs £4.95 & concessions £5.75). Family ticket (2ad+3ch) £23 **Facilities:** 🅿 ♿ shop ✖ (ex guide dogs) ◀

THE GRAND NATIONAL EXPERIENCE

Aintree Racecourse, Ormskirk Rd L9 5AS
Dir: (Aintree Racecourse on A59 (Liverpool to Preston road), clearly signed) *Map Ref:* *SJ39*
☎ 0151 522 2921 📄 0151 522 2920
e-mail: aintree@rht.net

The visitor centre at Aintree Racecourse offers a fascinating look at Britain's most famous horserace, The Grand National. Visitors can sit in the jockeys' weighing-in chair, walk around the dressing rooms, and take part in The Grand Finale, a virtual Grand National ride. There is also the opportunity to watch video presentations and view a gallery of paintings and photography depicting the race.

Times: Open 23 May-14 Oct **Fee:** ✱ £7 (concessions £4) **Facilities:** 🅿 ✖ licensed ♿ toilets for disabled shop ✖ (ex guide dogs) ◀

HM Customs & Excise National Museum

Merseyside Maritime Museum, Albert Dock L3 4AQ
Dir: (in Albert Dock - follow brown signs) **Map Ref:** SJ39
☎ 0151 478 4499 📄 0151 478 4590   FREE

Enter the exciting world of smuggle busting where everyday items reveal their hidden secrets. Find a fake, rummage for hidden goods and spot a suspect traveller. Look into the illustrious history of HM Customs & Excise, it's the longest battle in history and it's still going on today! Exhibits include the tools of the trade, prints, paintings and photographs, plus some fascinating confiscated goods.

Times: Open daily 10-5. Closed 23-26 Dec & 1 Jan. **Facilities:** 🅿 ☕ ✗ licensed ♿ (restricted wheelchair access, no access to basement) toilets for disabled shop ✗ (ex guide dogs) ◼

Liverpool Football Club Visitors Centre Tour

Anfield Rd L4 0TH **Map Ref:** SJ39
☎ 0151 260 6677 📄 0151 264 0149
e-mail: Museum1@liverpoolfc.tv

Touch the famous 'This is Anfield' sign as you walk down the tunnel to the sound of the crowd at the LFC museum and tour centre. Celebrate all things Liverpool, past and present. Bright displays and videos chart the history of England's most successful football club and more recent glories are recalled.

Times: Open all year: Museum daily 10-5 last admission 4. Closed 25-26 Dec. Match days 9 until last admission - 1hr before kick off. Museum & Tour - tours are run subject to daily demand. Advance booking is essential to avoid disappointment. **Fee:** Museum only, £5 (ch under 6 & pen £3) Family £13. Museum & Tour £9.00 (ch under 16 & pen £5.50) Family £23. Special deals for schools & groups. **Facilities:** 🅿 ☕ ✗ licensed ♿ (lifts, ramps to all areas for wheelchairs) toilets for disabled shop ✗ (ex guide dogs) ◼

World Museum Liverpool (formerly Liverpool Museum)

William Brown St L3 8EN
Dir: (in city centre next to St George's Hall and Lime St, follow brown signs) **Map Ref:** SJ39
☎ 0151 478 4393   FREE
e-mail: themuseum@liverpoolmuseums.org.uk

One of Britain's most interesting museums, the Liverpool Museum has diverse collections ranging from the Amazonian rain forests to the mysteries of outer space. Special attractions include the award-winning hands-on Natural History Centre and the Planetarium. The museum is undergoing extensive building improvements and refurbishment for its 'Into the Future' project which will lead it to double in size.

Times: Open Mon-Sat 10-5, Sun noon-5. Closed 23-26 Dec & 1 Jan. **Facilities:** 🅿 ☕ ♿ toilets for disabled shop ✗ (ex guide dogs)

MERSEYSIDE MARITIME MUSEUM

Albert Dock L3 4AQ
Dir: (Entry into Dock is from The Strand) *Map Ref:* SJ39
☎ **0151 478 4499** 📄 **0151 478 4590**

Set in the heart of Liverpool's magnificent waterfront, the Merseyside Maritime Museum is located in a former bonded warehouse on Albert Dock. The museum offers a unique insight into the history of the great port of Liverpool, its ships and its people, and the archive has one of the finest collections of merchant shipping records in the UK. There are exhibits on transatlantic slavery, the mass emigration from Liverpool to the New World between 1830 and 1930, and the opulent liners 'Titanic' and 'Lusitania'.

Times: Open daily 10-5. Closed 23-26 Dec & 1 Jan. **Facilities:** 🅿 ✗ licensed ♿ (lifts, wheelchairs, ramps, ex pilot boat & basement) toilets for disabled shop ✗ (ex guide dogs) ◼

MUSEUM OF LIVERPOOL LIFE

Pier Head L3 4AA
Dir: (follow signs for Albert Dock, museum is on Pier Head side)
Map Ref: SJ39
☎ **0151 478 4080** 📄 **0151 478 4090**
e-mail: liverpoollife@liverpoolmuseums.org.uk

The Museum of Liverpool Life celebrates the contribution of the people of Liverpool to national life. It has now expanded to include three new galleries: 'City Lives' exploring the richness of Liverpool's cultural diversity, 'The River Room' featuring life around the River Mersey and 'City Soldiers' about the King's Regiment. Other galleries include 'Mersey Culture' from Brookside to the Grand National, 'Making a Living' and 'Demanding a Voice'.

Times: Open daily 10-5. Closed from 2 on 24 Dec and all day 25-26 Dec & 1 Jan) **Facilities:** 🅿 (charged) ♿ (wheelchairs, audio handsets, subtitles on video terminals) toilets for disabled shop ✗ (ex guide/hearing dogs) ◼

TATE LIVERPOOL

Albert Dock L3 4BB
Dir: (within walking distance of Liverpool Lime Street train station) *Map Ref:* SJ39
☎ **0151 702 7400 & 0151 702 7402** 📄 **0151 702 7401**
e-mail: liverpoolinfo@tate.org.uk

A converted Victorian warehouse with stunning views across the River Mersey, Tate Liverpool displays the best of the National Collection of 20th-Century Art. A changing programme of exhibitions draws on works from public and private collections from across the world. Although admission to the Tate and the permanent collection is free, there are sometimes charges for specific temporary exhibitions.

Times: ✳ Open Tue-Sun, 10-5.30. Closed Mon ex BH Mon, 25-26 Dec, 1 Jan & Good Fri. **Facilities:** 🅿 🅿 ♿ (wheelchairs available, leaflets in Braille, hearing loop) toilets for disabled shop ✗ ◼

PRESCOT KNOWSLEY SAFARI PARK

L34 4AN
Dir: (M62 junct 6 onto M57 junct 2. Follow 'safari park' signs)
Map Ref: SJ49
☎ 0151 430 9009 📄 0151 426 3677
e-mail: safari.park@knowsley.com

A five-mile drive through the reserves at Knowsley Safari Park enables visitors to see lions, tigers, elephants, rhinos, monkeys and many other animals in spacious, natural surroundings. You can also visit the reptile house and pets' corner, and take in a sea lion show. Other attractions include a children's amusement park and a miniature railway.

Times: Open all year, Mar-Oct, daily 10-4. Winter Nov-Feb, 11-3. **Fee:** £9 (ch & pen £6).
Facilities: 🅿 💺 ♿ toilets for disabled shop ✈ (kennels provided) 🍴

ST HELENS WORLD OF GLASS

Chalon Way East WA10 1BT
Dir: (5mins from M62 junct 7) *Map Ref:* SJ59
☎ 08700 114466 📄 01744 616966
e-mail: info@worldofglass.com

Ideal for all the family, this fascinating attraction is in the heart of St Helens, a town shaped by glass-making. Features include the world's first continuous glass-making furnace, and two museum galleries that show glass in the ancient world and Victorian life in St Helens. There is also a mirror maze where Wizard Filligrano works, a newly refurbished café and a gift shop.

Times: Open Tue-Sun & BH, 10-5. Closed 25-26 Dec & 1 Jan.
Fee: £5.30 (ch £3.80, pen £3.80) Family & group discounts.
Facilities: 🅿 💺 ♿ toilets for disabled shop ✈ (ex guide dogs) 🍴

SOUTHPORT PLEASURELAND

Marine Dr PR8 1RX
Dir: (signed from Southport Town Centre) *Map Ref:* SD31
☎ 0870 220 0204 📄 01704 537936
e-mail: mail@pleasurelandltd.freeserve.co.uk

Pleasureland is home to over 100 rides and attractions, including the awesome TRAUMAtizer suspended rollercoaster. You can also go all Jurassic on the new Lost Dinosaurs of the Sahara - a mysterious boat ride to prehistoric times. A diverse programme of special events includes an annual 'Fame' talent show, the Nairobi International Circus and a Halloween Festival.

Times: Open Mar-Nov opening times vary please call for information. **Fee:** ✶ £17 all day (juniors £12). Entry for 4 (adults and/or children) £60.
Facilities: 🅿 (charged) 💺 ✗ licensed ♿ (access on some rides) toilets for disabled shop ✈ (ex guide dogs) 🍴

ALNWICK *ALNWICK CASTLE*

NE66 1NQ
Dir: (off A1 on outskirts of town, follow signs for The Alnwick
Garden & Castle) *Map Ref:* NU11
☎ 01665 510777 📠 01665 510876
e-mail: enquiries@alnwickcastle.com

Alnwick Castle is the main seat of the Duke of Northumberland
whose family have lived here since 1309. The stern, medieval
exterior belies the treasure house within, furnished in
Renaissance style, with paintings by Titian, Van Dyck and
Canaletto, and an exquisite collection of Meissen china. The
Regiment Museum of the Royal Northumberland Fusiliers is
housed in the Abbot's Tower of the castle. The refurbished towers
accommodate museums of local archaeology and the Percy
Tenantry volunteers.

Times: ✳ Open 28 Mar-25 Oct, daily 11-5 (last
admission 4.15). **Facilities:** 🅿 🍽 & (Castle lift
for those able to walk a little) toilets for disabled
shop ✘ (ex guide dogs) ◀

BAMBURGH *BAMBURGH CASTLE*

NE69 7DF
Dir: (A1 Belford by-pass, E on B1342 to Bamburgh)
Map Ref: NU13
☎ 01668 214515 & 214208 📠 01668 214060
e-mail: bamburghcastle@aol.com

Rising dramatically from a rocky outcrop, Bamburgh Castle is a
huge, square Norman castle looking out to sea towards Holy
Island and the Farne Islands and inland to the Cheviot Hills. Two
museums are accommodated in the castle, one dedicated to the
life of the first Baron Armstrong and his engineering prowess, and
the other a museum of aviation artefacts. Guide services are
available.

Times: ✳ Open 15 Mar-Oct, daily 11-5 (last
admission 4.30). Other times by prior
arrangement. **Facilities:** 🅿 (charged) 🍽 & shop
✘ (ex guide dogs)

BARDON MILL *VINDOLANDA (CHESTERHOLM)*

Vindolanda Trust NE47 7JN
Dir: (signed from A69 or B6318) *Map Ref:* NY76
☎ 01434 344277 📠 01434 344060
e-mail: info@vindolanda.com

Vindolanda was a Roman fort and frontier town. It was started
well before Hadrian's Wall, and became a base for 500 soldiers.
The civilian settlement lay just west of the fort and has been
excavated. The excellent museum in the country house of
Chesterholm nearby has displays and reconstructions. There are
also formal gardens and an open-air museum with a Roman
temple, shop, house and Northumbrian croft.

Times: Open Feb-Mar, daily 10-5. Apr-Sep 10-6,
Oct & Nov 10-5. **Fee:** ✳ £4.50 (ch £2.90,
student & pen £3.80, free admission for disabled).
Saver ticket for joint admission to sister site - The
Roman Army Museum £6.50 (ch £4.30, pen
£5.50) Party. **Facilities:** 🅿 🍽 & (please contact
for further info) toilets for disabled shop
✘ (ex guide dogs) ◀

BERWICK-UPON-TWEED *PAXTON HOUSE*

TD15 1SZ
Dir: (3m from A1 Berwick-upon-Tweed bypass on B6461 Kelso
road) *Map Ref:* NT95
☎ 01289 386291 📠 01289 386660
e-mail: info@paxtonhouse.com

Built in 1758 by the Adam brothers for the Laird of Wedderburn,
the house is a fine example of neo-Palladian architecture. Much
of the house is furnished by Chippendale and there is a picture
gallery showing a large collection of publicly owned art. The
house is set in 80 acres beside the River Tweed, and the grounds
include an adventure playground. An extensive programme of
events and exhibitions is run throughout the season.

Times: ✱ Open daily from Apr-Oct, House &
gallery 11-5 (last tour of house 4.15). Grounds
10-sunset. **Facilities:** 🅿 ☕ ✗ licensed ♿ (lifts
to main areas of house, parking close to
reception) toilets for disabled shop 🛍

CHILLINGHAM CHILLINGHAM WILD CATTLE PARK

NE66 5NP
Dir: (off B6348, follow brown tourist signs off A1 and A697)
Map Ref: NU02
☎ 01668 215250 📠 01668 215250

The park, a registered charity at Chillingham, boasts an
extraordinary survival: a herd of wild white cattle descended from
animals trapped in the park when the wall was built in the 13th
century; they are the sole surviving pure-bred examples of their
breed in the world. Binoculars are recommended for a close view.
Visitors are accompanied into the park by the warden.

Times: Open Apr-Oct, daily 10-12 & 2-5, Sun 2-5.
(Closed Tue). **Fee:** £4 (ch £1.50 & pen £3).
Facilities: 🅿 ✗

CORBRIDGE CORBRIDGE ROMAN SITE AND MUSEUM

NE45 5NT
Dir: (0.5m NW of Corbridge on minor road - signed)
Map Ref: NY96
☎ 01434 632349

Originally a fort, which evolved into a prosperous town during the
Roman era, the Corbridge Roman Site and Museum is an
excellent starting point for exploring Hadrian's Wall. The museum,
built in the Roman style, houses a fascinating collection of finds,
including the famous stone fountainhead - the Lion of Corbridge.

Times: Open all year, Apr-Sep, daily 10-6; Oct,
daily 10-4; Nov-Mar, Sat-Sun 10-4. Closed 24-26
Dec & 1 Jan. **Fee:** ✱ £3.50 (ch £1.80,
concessions £2.60). Prices & opening times relate
to 2004, for further details phone or log onto
www.english-heritage.org.uk/visits
Facilities: 🅿 ♿ toilets for disabled ⌗

HOLY ISLAND (LINDISFARNE) LINDISFARNE PRIORY

TD15 2RX
Dir: (can only be reached at low tide across a causeway. Tide tables posted at each end of the causeway) *Map Ref:* NU14
☎ **01289 389200**

One of the holiest Anglo-Saxon sites in England, Lindisfarne Priory is renowned as the original burial place of St Cuthbert whose corpse was discovered 11 years after his burial and found to be mysteriously undecayed. The remains of the priory can be visited, and the visitor centre tells the story of the monks' lives on the island. Please note that the causeway to the island can only be crossed at low tide.

Times: Open all year, Apr-Sep, daily 10-6; Oct, daily 10-4; Nov-Jan, Sat & Sun 10-4; Feb-Mar, daily, 10-4. Closed 24-26 Dec & 1 Jan.
Fee: ✱ £3.50 (ch £1.80, concessions £2.60). Prices & opening times relate to 2004, for further details phone or log onto www.english-heritage.org.uk/visits **Facilities:** shop ♿

HOUSESTEADS HOUSESTEADS ROMAN FORT

Haydon Bridge NE47 6NN
Dir: (2.5m NE of Bardon Mill on B6318) *Map Ref:* NY76
☎ **01434 344363**

Housesteads Roman Fort is the jewel in the crown of Hadrian's Wall and the most complete Roman fort in Britain. The wall was built in about AD 122 and Housesteads is one of 16 permanent bases built along its length. The superb remains offer a fascinating glimpse into the past glories of one of the world's greatest empires.

Times: Open all year, Apr-Sep, daily 10-6; Oct-Mar, daily 10-4. Closed 24-26 Dec & 1 Jan.
Fee: ✱ £3.50 (ch £1.80, concessions £2.60, family £8.80). Prices & opening times relate to 2004, for further details phone or log onto www.english-heritage.org.uk/visits
Facilities: P (0.25m from fort) (charge payable) (disabled parking) shop ♿

ROTHBURY *CRAGSIDE*

NE65 7PX
Dir: (1m NW of Morpeth on A697, left onto B6341, entrance 1m N of Rothbury) *Map Ref:* NU00
☎ **01669 620333 & 620150** 📠 **01669 620066**
e-mail: ncrvmx@smtp.ntrust.org.uk

Cragside, a Victorian mansion, was the first building in the world to be lit by hydro-electricity. In the 1880s the house had hot and cold running water, central heating, telephones and a passenger lift. There is a vast forest garden to explore containing one of Europe's largest rock gardens, formal gardens, lakes and an adventure play area.

Times: ✱ Open, Estate & Gardens: 23 Mar-4 Nov, Tue-Sun & BH Mons 10.30-7 (last admission 5); House: 23 Mar-Sep 1-5.30. Oct-3 Nov 1-4 (last admission 1hr before closing).
Facilities: P ✗ licensed ♿ (ltd access, Braille guide, wheelchair path, lift) toilets for disabled shop ♿

Northumberland continued

WARKWORTH WARKWORTH CASTLE & HERMITAGE

NE66 0UJ
Map Ref: NU20
☎ 01665 711423

The magnificent eight-towered keep of Warkworth Castle stands
on a hill high above the River Coquet, dominating all around it. A
complex stronghold, it was home to the Percy family, which at
times wielded more power in the North than the king himself.
The most famous member of the family was Harry Hotspur
(Sir Henry Percy), immortalised in Shakespeare's *Henry IV*.

Times: Open all year. Castle; Apr-Sep, daily 10-6; Oct, daily 10-4;
Nov-Mar, Sat-Mon 10-4. Hermitage; Apr-Sep, Wed, Sun & Bank Hols
(Closed 24-26 Dec & 1 Jan). **Fee:** ✱ Castle; £3 (ch £1.50,
concessions £2.30). Hermitage; £2 (ch £1, concessions £1.50). Prices
& opening times relate to 2004, for further details phone or log onto
www.english-heritage.org.uk/visits **Facilities:** 🅿 ♿ (limited access)
shop ⌗

GATESHEAD BALTIC CENTRE FOR CONTEMPORARY ART

South Shore Rd NE8 3BA
Dir: (follow signs for Quayside, Millennium Bridge. 15 mins' walk
from Gateshead Metro & Newcastle Central Station)
Map Ref: NZ26
☎ 0191 478 1810 0191 440 4944 📄 0191 478 1922
e-mail: info@balticmill.com

FREE

Once a 1950's grain warehouse, part of the old Baltic Flour Mills,
the Baltic Centre for Contemporary Art is an international centre
presenting a dynamic and ambitious programme of
complementary exhibitions and events. It comprises five art
spaces, cinema, auditorium, library and archive, eating and
drinking areas and a shop. Check the website for current events
information.

Times: Please see website for details
(www.balticmill.com) **Facilities:** 🅿 (charged) 🖥
✖ licensed ♿ (wheelchairs/scooters,
Braille/large-print guides toilets for disabled shop
✖ (ex guide dogs & hearing dogs)

NEWCASTLE UPON TYNE HANCOCK MUSEUM

Barras Bridge NE2 4PT
Dir: (follow exit signs for city centre A167 off the A1)
Map Ref: NZ26
☎ 0191 222 7418 📄 0191 261 7537
e-mail: hancock@twmuseums.org.uk

Newcastle's premier natural history museum unravels the natural
world through sensational galleries and close encounters with
resident reptiles and insects. For more than 100 years the
Hancock Museum has provided visitors with a glimpse of the
animal kingdom and the powerful and often destructive forces of
nature. From the dinosaurs to live animals it is home to creatures
past and present and the odd Egyptian mummy or two.

Times: Open all year, Mon-Sat, 10-5, Sun 2-5.
Closed 25-26 Dec & 1 Jan. **Fee:** Prices vary with
special exhibitions. Phone for details
Facilities: 🅿 🖥 ♿ (stair lift, audio & Braille
guide, sign language) toilets for disabled shop
✖ (ex guide dogs) 📷

LIFE SCIENCE CENTRE

Times Square NE1 4EP
Dir: (A1M, A69, A184, A1058 & A167, follow signs to Life Science Centre or Central Station) **Map Ref:** NZ26
☎ **0191 243 8223 & 0191 243 8210** 📠 **0191 243 8201**
e-mail: bookings@lifesciencecentre.co.uk

The Life Science Centre is an interactive, action-packed day out that takes the visitor to the beginning of life and back again. From single-celled organisms to dinosaurs, from four billion years ago to today, this is a fascinating attraction that deals with perhaps the most fundamental subject of all: life itself. Temporary exhibitions are also a feature.

Times: ✳ Open Mon-Sat 10-6, Sun 11-6 . Closed 25 Dec & 1 Jan. (Last entry subject to seasonal demand). **Facilities:** 🅿 (charged) 🍴 ✗ licensed ♿ (ramps, wheelchairs, induction loops) toilets for disabled shop ✗ (ex guide dogs) 🎞

MUSEUM OF ANTIQUITIES

The University NE1 7RU
Dir: (Situated on main campus of Newcastle University between The Haymarket and Queen Victoria Rd) **Map Ref:** NZ26
☎ **0191 222 7849** 📠 **0191 222 8561**   FREE
e-mail: m.o.antiquities@ncl.ac.uk

Artefacts from the north-east of England dating from prehistoric times to AD 1600 are on display at Newcastle's Museum of Antiquities, which belongs jointly to the Society of Antiquaries and the University of Newcastle upon Tyne. The principal museum for Hadrian's Wall, this collection includes models of the wall, life-size Roman soldiers and a newly refurbished reconstruction of the Temple of Mithras.

Times: Open all year, daily (ex Sun), 10-5. Closed Good Fri, 24-26 Dec & 1 Jan.
Facilities: 🅿 (400yds) ♿ (large print guide) shop ✗ (ex guide dogs) 🎞

SOUTH SHIELDS ARBEIA ROMAN FORT & MUSEUM

Baring St NE33 2BB
Dir: (5 mins' walk from town centre) **Map Ref:** NZ36
☎ **0191 456 1369 & 454 4093** 📠 **0191 427 6862**

In South Shields town are the extensive remains of Arbeia, a Roman fort in use from the 2nd to the 4th century. It was the supply base for the Roman army's campaign against Scotland. On site there are full size reconstructions of a fort gateway, a barrack block and part of the commanding officer's house. Archaeological evacuations are in progress throughout the summer.

Times: ✳ Open all year, Etr-Sep, Mon-Sat 10.30-5.30, Sun 1-5; Oct-Etr, Mon-Sat 10-4. Closed 25-26 Dec, 1 Jan & Good Fri.
Facilities: 🅿 ♿ (Minicom system) toilets for disabled shop 🎞

SUNDERLAND *MUSEUM & WINTER GARDENS*

Burdon Rd SR1 1PP
Dir: (in city centre) **Map Ref:** NZ35
☎ 0191 553 2323 📄 0191 553 7828
e-mail: sunderland.museum@tyne-wear-museums.org.uk

An award-winning attraction with wide-ranging displays, that many hands-on exhibits that cover the archaeology and geology of Sunderland, the coal mines and shipyards of the area and the spectacular glass and pottery made on Wearside. Other galleries show the changes in the lifestyles of Sunderland women over the past century, works by LS Lowry and wildlife from all corners of the globe. The Winter Gardens is a horticultural wonderland where the exotic plants from around the world can be seen growing to their full natural height in a spectacular glass and steel rotunda.

Times: * Open all year, Mon 10-4, Tue-Sat 10-5, Sun 2-5. **Facilities:** P (150 yds) ✗ licensed ♿ (lifts to all floors, induction loops) toilets for disabled shop ✗ (ex guide dogs) ◼

NATIONAL GLASS CENTRE

Liberty Way SR6 0GL
Dir: (A19 onto A1231, signposted from all major roads)
Map Ref: NZ35
☎ 0191 515 5555 📄 0191 515 5556
e-mail: info@nationalglasscentre.com

Housed in a striking modern building, the National Glass Centre celebrates the unique material and explains its history. Visitors can see the changing exhibitions of glass art, featuring pieces by leading artists. There is also the opportunity to witness the glass-making process and learn more about the substance and how it impacts on our lives. The brave can even walk on the glass roof 30 feet above the riverside.

Times: Open daily 10-5 (last admission to glass tour 4). Closed 25 Dec & 1 Jan. **Fee:** £5 (concessions £3). Family ticket £12. **Facilities:** P ✗ licensed ♿ (lifts, ramps, parking facilites) toilets for disabled shop ✗ (ex guide dogs) ◼

TYNEMOUTH BLUE REEF AQUARIUM

Grand Pde NE30 4JF
Dir: (follow A19, taking A1058 (coast road), signed Tynemouth. Situated on seafront) **Map Ref:** NZ36
☎ 0191 258 1031 📄 0191 257 2116
e-mail: tynemouth@bluereefaquarium.co.uk

From its position overlooking one of the north-east's prettiest beaches, Blue Reef is home to a dazzling variety of creatures including seahorses, puffer fish, octopi, and even the deadly piranha. Visitors can walk through an underwater tunnel in a 250,000 litre tropical ocean tank. This offers close encounters with all manner of undersea wonders such as sharks and stingrays.

Times: Open daily from 10. Closed 25 Dec **Fee:** * £4.95 (ch £3.25, pen & students £4.25). Family ticket (2ad+3ch) £14.95 **Facilities:** P (charged) 🖪 ♿ toilets for disabled shop ✗ (ex guide dogs) ◼

WALLSEND SEGEDUNUM ROMAN FORT, BATHS & MUSEUM

Buddle St NE28 6HR
Dir: (A187 from Tyne Tunnel, signposted) *Map Ref:* NZ26
☎ 0191 236 9347 ▤ 0191 295 5858
e-mail: segedunum@twmuseums.org.uk

Hadrian's Wall was built by the Roman Emperor, Hadrian in AD 122, Segedunum was built as part of the Wall, serving as a garrison for 600 soldiers until the collapse of Roman rule around AD 410. This major historical venture shows what life would have been like then, using artefacts, audio-visuals, reconstructed buildings and a 34-metre high viewing tower.

Times: Open all year, 9 Apr-Aug 9.30-5.30, Sep-Oct 10-5, Nov-Apr 10-3.30 **Fee:** ✱ £3.50 (ch, pen & concessions £1.95). Family ticket £9 **Facilities:** 🅿 ▭ ♿ (lifts) toilets for disabled shop ✖ (ex guide dogs) ▰

WASHINGTON WWT WASHINGTON

District 15 NE38 8LE
Dir: (signposted off A195, A1231 & A182) *Map Ref:* NZ35
☎ 0191 416 5454 ▤ 0191 416 5801
e-mail: washington@wwt.org.uk

In a parkland setting, on the north bank of the River Wear, WWT Washington is the home of a wonderful collection of exotic wildfowl from all over the world. There is also a heronry where visitors can watch a colony of wild grey herons on CCTV. The 100-acre site includes an area for wintering wildfowl which can be observed from hides, and a flock of Chilean flamingos. Other features include a discovery centre, waterfowl nursery, picture windows and a viewing gallery from which to observe the birds.

Times: Open all year, daily 9.30-5 (summer) or 9.30-4 (winter). Closed 25 Dec. **Fee:** ✱ £5.75 (ch £3.75, concessions £4.75). Family £15. **Facilities:** 🅿 ▭ ✖ licensed ♿ (lowered windows in certain hides, wheelchairs to hire free) toilets for disabled shop ✖ (ex guide/hearing dogs) ▰

WHITBURN SOUTER LIGHTHOUSE

Coast Rd SR6 7NH
Dir: (on A183 coast road, 2m S of South Shields, 3m N of Sunderland) *Map Ref:* NZ46
☎ 0191 529 3161 & 01670 773966 ▤ 0191 529 0902
e-mail: nslhse@smtp.ntrust.org.uk

When it opened in 1871, Souter was the most advanced lighthouse in the world. Painted red and white and standing 150 feet high, it is a dramatic building and hands-on displays and volunteers help bring it to life. The engine and battery rooms are all in working order and are included in the guided tour, along with the light tower and museum cottage.

Times: ✱ Open Apr-Oct daily (ex Fri but open Good Fri), 11-5. (Last admission 4.30). Please contact for opening at other times. **Facilities:** 🅿 ✖ ♿ (Braille guide, induction loops, tactile exhibits) toilets for disabled shop ✖ (ex guide dogs) ⚘ ▰

BEMPTON RSPB NATURE RESERVE

YO15 1JD
Dir: (take cliff road from B1229, Bempton village and follow
brown tourist signs) *Map Ref: TA17*
☎ 01262 851179 📄 01262 851533

Part of the spectacular chalk cliffs that stretch from Flamborough
Head to Speeton, rising to 400 feet, this is one of the best sites in
England to see thousands of nesting seabirds at close quarters.
Viewpoints overlook the cliffs, which are best visited from April to
July. Gannets, puffins guillemots, razorbills, kittiwakes, fulmars,
herring gulls and several pairs of shag nest here, and many
migrants pass off-shore including terns, skuas and shearwaters.
Wheatears, ring ouzels and merlins frequent the clifftop on
migration. Grey seal and porpoise are sometimes seen offshore.

Times: Visitor centre open daily, Mar-Nov 10-5.
Dec-Feb 9.30-4. **Fee:** £3.50 per car, £6 per
minibus, £10 per coach. **Facilities:** 🅿 (charged)
🍵 ♿ toilets for disabled shop ◀

GOOLE THE WATERWAYS MUSEUM

Dutch River Side DN14 5TB
Dir: (M62 junct 36, enter Goole & turn right at next 3 sets of
traffic lights onto Dutch River Side. 0.75m, follow brown signs)
Map Ref: SE72
☎ 01405 768730 📄 01405 769868
e-mail: waterwaysmuseum@btinternet.com

The waterways referred to in the museum and activity centre's
title are the Aire and Calder Navigation and the Port of Goole. The
story of their origins and development are told in a variety of
media, including over 5,000 photographs, model boats and
interactive exhibits. There is a changing programme of exhibitions
in the new foyer, and events such as family fun days, pirate days,
pumpkin festivals, children's art and talks on shipping. Courses
are also run, in arts, crafts, practical conservation and waterways
work.

Times: Open: Mon-Fri 9-4 (Apr-Sep, Sun 12-5)
Fee: ✱ £2.50 (concessions £1.50) Boat Trip £3.
Facilities: 🅿 🍵 ♿ (disabled access on boats,
nature trail) toilets for disabled shop ✖ (ex guide
dogs)

KINGSTON UPON HULL MARITIME MUSEUM

Queen Victoria Square HU1 3DX
Dir: (from M62 follow A63 to town centre, museum is within
pedestrian area of town centre) *Map Ref: TA02*
☎ 01482 613902 📄 01482 613710
e-mail: museums@hullcc.gov.uk

Hull's maritime history is illustrated here, in the former town
docks' office, with displays on whales and whaling, ships and
shipping, and other aspects of this Humber port. There is also a
Victorian court room which is used for temporary exhibitions. The
restored dock area, with its fine Victorian and Georgian buildings,
is well worth exploring too.

Times: ✱ Open all year, Mon-Sat 10-5 & Sun
1.30-4.30. Closed 25 Dec-2 Jan & Good Fri)
Facilities: 🅿 (100yds) ♿ shop ✖ (ex guide
dogs)

'STREETLIFE' - HULL MUSEUM OF TRANSPORT

High St HU1 1PS
Dir: (A63 from M62, follow signs for Old Town) **Map Ref:** TA02
☎ **01482 613902** 🖹 **01482 613710**
e-mail: museums@hullcc.gov.uk

This purpose built museum uses a 'hands-on' approach to trace 200 years of transport history. With a vehicle collection of national importance, state-of-the-art animatronic displays and authentic scenarios, you can see Hull's Old Town brought vividly to life. The mail coach ride uses the very latest in computer technology to recreate a Victorian journey by four-in-hand.

Times: ✱ Open all year, Mon-Sat 10-5, Sun 1.30-4.30. Closed 24-25 Dec & Good Fri
Facilities: Ⓟ (500mtrs) ♿ toilets for disabled shop ✖ (ex guide dogs)

THE DEEP

HU1 4DP
Dir: (follow signs from city centre) **Map Ref:** TA02
☎ **01482 381000** 🖹 **01482 381010**
e-mail: info@thedeep.co.uk

The World's Only Submarium tells the story of the oceans, from the Big Bang to the present day and into the future using stunning aquaria and the latest hands-on interactives. Highlights of Europe's deepest aquarium centre include a massive fossil wall, Europe's first pair of green sawfish and a lift ride through the waters of the tanks, bringing you face to face with sharks, eels and hundreds of other marine creatures.

Times: Open daily 10-6. Closed 24-25 Dec **Fee:** £6.75 (ch under 16 £4.75, pen £5.25). Family ticket (2ad+2ch) £21, (2ad+3ch) £24
Facilities: Ⓟ (charged) 🍽 ♿ (signing for the deaf if booked in advance, Braille) toilets for disabled shop ✖ (ex guide dogs) 🍴

SEWERBY   SEWERBY HALL & GARDENS

YO15 1EA
Dir: (2m NE of Bridlington on B1255 towards Flamborough)
Map Ref: TA16
☎ **01262 673769** 🖹 **01262 673090**
e-mail: sewerby.hall@eastring.gov.uk

Sewerby Hall and Gardens, set in 50 acres of parkland overlooking Bridlington Bay, dates back to 1715. The Georgian House, with its 19th-century Orangery, contains art galleries, archaeological displays and an Amy Johnson room with a collection of her trophies and mementoes. The grounds include magnificent walled Old English and Rose gardens and host many events throughout the year. Activities for all the family include a children's zoo and play areas, golf, putting, bowls, plus woodland and cliff top walks. Phone for details of special events.

Times: Estate open all year, dawn-dusk. Hall open Etr-end Oct. Please contact for further details.
Fee: ✱ £3.10 (ch 5-15 £1.20, pen £2.30). Family ticket £7.50. Group 10+ **Facilities:** Ⓟ 🍽 ♿ toilets for disabled shop 🍴

ALDBOROUGH ALDBOROUGH ROMAN SITE

YO5 9ES
Dir: (0.75m SE of Boroughbridge, on minor road off B6265 within
1m of junct of A1 & A6055) *Map Ref:* SE46
☎ **01423 322768**

At the Aldborough Roman Site you can view two spectacular
mosaic pavements and parts of the town walls, which are all that
is left of the once principal Roman town of Isurium Brigantum,
the administrative centre of the Brigantes, the largest tribe in
Roman Britain. A museum at the site exhibits archaeological finds.

Times: Open Apr-Jun, Thu-Mon, 10-5; Aug, daily,
10-6; Sep, Thu-Mon, 10-5. **Fee:** ✻ £2 (ch £1,
concessions £1.50). Prices & opening times relate
to 2004, for further details phone or log onto
www.english-heritage.org.uk/visits
Facilities: shop ⌗

AYSGARTH NATIONAL PARK CENTRE

DL8 3TH
Dir: (off A684, Leyburn to Hawes road at Falls junct, Palmer Flatt
Hotel & continue down hill over river, centre 500yds on left)
Map Ref: SE08
☎ **01969 663424** 🖹 **01969 663105**   **FREE**
e-mail: aysgarth@ytbtic.co.uk

This is a visitor centre for the Yorkshire Dales National Park, with
maps, guides, walks and local information. Interactive displays
explain the history and natural history of the area. Plan the day
ahead with a light lunch in the coffee shop. Various guided walks
set off from here throughout the year.

Times: Open Apr-Oct, daily 10-5; Winter open
Fri-Sun, 10-4. **Facilities:** 🅿 (charged) ☕
& (viewing platform at Falls) toilets for disabled
shop ✈ (ex guide dogs) ◣

BEDALE *BEDALE MUSEUM*

DL8 1AA
Dir: (on A684, 1.5m W of A1 at Leeming Bar. Opposite church, at
N end of town) *Map Ref:* SE28
☎ **01677 423797** 🖹 **01677 425393**

Situated in a building dating back to the 17th century, the Bedale
is a fascinating museum. The central attraction is the Bedale fire
engine, which dates back to 1742. Other artefacts include
documents, toys, craft tools and household utensils, which all
help to give an authentic picture of the lifestyle of the times.

Times: Open Tue & Fri 10-12.30 & 2-4, Wed 2-4,
Thu-Sat 10-12 **Facilities:** 🅿 & ✈ (ex guide
dogs)

BENINGBROUGH *BENINGBROUGH HALL*

YO6 1DD
Dir: (off A19, 8m NW of York. Entrance at Newton Lodge)
Map Ref: SE55
☎ 01904 470666 ▤ 01904 470002
e-mail: ybbrgb@smtp.ntrust.org.uk

Beningbrough Hall was built around 1716 and has an impressive baroque interior, with ornately carved wooden panelling as a feature in several of the rooms. A central corridor runs the full length of the house, and 100 pictures from the National Portrait Gallery in London are exhibited. The other side of country house life can be seen in the restored Victorian laundry, while outside there is a walled garden and sculptures in the wood.

Times: ✱ Open 23 Mar-3 Nov daily (ex Thu & Fri) open Good Fri, Jul-Aug daily (ex Thu) 12-5. Grounds 11-5.30. **Facilities:** ⓟ ✗ licensed 🚻 (access to Victorian laundry, shop & restaurant) toilets for disabled shop ✖ ♨

BRIMHAM *BRIMHAM ROCKS*

Summerbridge HG3 4DW
Dir: (10m NW of Harrogate, off B6265) *Map Ref:* SE26
☎ 01423 780688 ▤ 01423 781020
e-mail: brimhamrocks@nationaltrust.org.uk

Brimham Rocks stand on open National Trust moorland at a height of 950 feet, affording spectacular views over the surrounding countryside. The area is filled with strange and fascinating rock formations and is rich in wildlife. An old shooting lodge in the area has been converted to provide an information point and shop.

Times: Open 8-dusk, (facilities may close in bad weather): shop with exhibition room, kiosk 20 Mar-23 May & Oct, Sat & Sun 11-5, 29 May-Sep daily 11-5, 7 Nov-19 Dec, Sun 11-5. Also open daily; local school hols, BHs, 26 Dec & 1 Jan (weather permitting). **Fee:** Cars (up to 4hrs £3, over 4hrs £4). Minibuses £7. Coaches £12. Motorcycles free. **Facilities:** ⓟ (charged) ☕ ✗ 🚻 (specially adapted path steep in places, Braille guide) toilets for disabled shop ♨ ▤

DANBY *MOORS CENTRE*

Lodge Ln YO21 2NB
Dir: (turn S off A171 signed Moors Centre Danby. Turn left at crossroads in Danby, follow road for 2m, The Moors Centre is at a bend on the right) *Map Ref:* NZ70
☎ 01287 660654 ▤ 01287 660308   FREE
e-mail: moorscentre@ytbtic.co.uk

The Moors Centre, located in the Esk Valley, is the ideal starting place for exploring the North York Moors National Park. There is an exhibition about the area and a National Park video, as well as a wild flower garden, walks, trails and quizzes. Facilities include a shop, tearooms, wheelchair loan, and an accommodation booking service. Moorsbus Park-and-Ride operates from this site, please phone for details.

Times: Open all year, Apr-Oct, daily 10-5. Nov, Dec & Mar daily 11-4. Jan & Feb wknds only 11-4. **Facilities:** ⓟ (charged) ☕ 🚻 (woodland & garden trails, motorised & manual wheelchairs) toilets for disabled shop ✖ (ex guide dogs & in grounds) ▤

ELVINGTON YORKSHIRE AIR MUSEUM & ALLIED AIR FORCES MEMORIAL

Halifax Way YO41 4AU
Dir: (from York take A1079 then immediate right onto B1228, museum is signposted on right) *Map Ref:* SE74
☎ 01904 608595 📠 01904 608246
e-mail: museum@yorkshireairmuseum.co.uk

This award-winning museum and memorial is based around the largest authentic former World War II bomber command station open to the public. There is a restored tower, an air gunners' museum, archives, an airborne forces display, squadron memorial rooms, and much more. Among the exhibits are replicas of the pioneering Cayley Glider and Wright Flyer, along with the Halifax Bomber and modern jets like the Harrier GR3.

Times: Open daily, 10-5 (summer), 10-3.30 (winter). Closed 25 & 26 Dec. **Fee:** £5 (ch £3 & pen £4). **Facilities:** 🅿 ☕ ✕ licensed ♿ toilets for disabled shop 🛍

FAIRBURN RSPB NATURE RESERVE

Fairburn Ings, The Visitor Centre, Newton Ln WF10 2BH
Dir: (W of A1, N of Ferrybridge. Signed from Allerton Bywater off A656. Signed Fairburn Village off A1) *Map Ref:* SE24
☎ 01977 603796
e-mail: chris.drake@rspb.org.uk

One-third of this 700-acre RSPB Nature Reserve is open water. Over 270 species of birds have been recorded here and it is a great place for seeing wetland birds close up. There are thousands of ducks and geese in winter, and in summer look out for terns, swallows, snipe and lapwings. A visitor centre provides information, and there is an elevated boardwalk, which is suitable for disabled visitors.

Times: ✱ Access to the reserve via car park, open 9-dusk. Centre open 10-5 wknds and 11-4 wkdays. Closed 25-26 Dec.
Facilities: 🅿 ♿ (raised boardwalk for wheelchair) toilets for disabled shop ✈ (ex guide dogs)

HARROGATE THE ROYAL PUMP ROOM MUSEUM

Crown Place HG1 2RY
Dir: (A61 into town centre and follow brown heritage signs)
Map Ref: SE35
☎ 01423 556188 📠 01423 556130
e-mail: lg23@harrogate.gov.uk

Housed in a delightful early Victorian pump room over the town's sulphur wells, the museum tells the story of Harrogate's heyday as England's European spa. Visitors discover some of the amazing spa treatments, taste the sulphur water, and explore stories of Russian royalty, communal ox-roasts and early bicycles. A programme of changing exhibitions complements the permanent displays.

Times: Open all year, Apr-Oct, Mon-Sat 10-5, Sun 2-5, (Nov-Mar close at 4). Closed 24-26 Dec & 1 Jan. **Fee:** ✱ £2.50 (ch £1.25, concessions £1.50). Family rate £6.50 (2ad+2ch). Party. Combined seasonal tickets available for The Royal Pump Room Museum & Knaresborough Castle & Museum. **Facilities:** 🅿 (100yds) (restricted to 3hrs, need parking disc) ♿ toilets for disabled shop ✈ (ex guide dogs) 🛍

HELMSLEY DUNCOMBE PARK

YO62 5EB
Dir: (located within North York Moors National Park, off A170
Thirsk-Scarborough road, 1m from Helmsley market place)
Map Ref: SE68
☎ **01439 770213** 📄 **01439 771114**
e-mail: liz@duncombepark.com

Duncombe Park is set in a 30-acre early 18th-century landscaped
garden, amid 300 acres of parkland on the River Rye. Built in
1713, the house was gutted by fire in 1879 and rebuilt in grand
style in 1895. It was the home of the Duncombes for 300 years,
and then a girls' school for some time. In 1985 the present Lord
and Lady Feversham made it a family home again and after major
restoration, opened the house to the public in 1990. Part of the
garden and parkland were designated a 250-acre National Nature
Reserve in 1994. Special events are held throughout the year.

Times: Open: 13 Apr-24 Oct, Sun-Thu; Gardens,
Parkland Centre tea room & shop & Parkland
walks 11-5.30. House by guided tour only every
hour from 12.30-3.30. **Fee:** ✱ House & Gardens
£6.50 (ch 10-16, £3, concessions £5) Gardens &
Parkland £3.50 (ch £1.50, concessions £3)
Parkland only £2 (ch £1).
Facilities: 🅿 ✕ licensed ♿ (portable ramp, lift,
wheelchair for loan) toilets for disabled shop
✈ (ex park & guide dogs) ◀

KIRBY MISPERTON *FLAMINGO LAND THEME PARK & ZOO*

The Rectory YO17 6UX
Dir: (turn off A64 onto A169, Pickering to Whitley road)
Map Ref: SE77
☎ **01653 668287** 📄 **01653 668280**
e-mail: info@flamingoland.co.uk

Set in 375 acres of North Yorkshire countryside, Flamingo Land
comprises a zoo, a dozen white knuckle rides, Kiddie's Kingdom,
and no less than five daily family shows. There are over 100 rides
and attractions, to suit all ages, and the largest flock of pink
flamingos in the country, which gave the park its name. New
additions are Little Monster's Wacky Races, and the Lost River
Ride in the Lost Kingdom. Take a stroll through the extensive zoo,
where there are over 1,000 animals including tigers, giraffes,
hippos, rhinos, monkeys, penguins, sea lions and meerkats.

Times: ✱ Open end Mar-2 Nov from 10. Closing
times vary depending upon season.
Facilities: 🅿 🍽 ✕ licensed ♿ (parking,
wheelchair hire) toilets for disabled shop ◀

MALTON CASTLE HOWARD

YO60 7DA
Dir: (15m NE of York, off A64, follow brown signs) **Map Ref:** SE77
☎ **01653 648333** 📄 **01653 648529**
e-mail: house@castlehoward.co.uk

Castle Howard is one of Britain's finest historic houses, with
magnificent 18th-century architecture set in a dramatic landscape
featuring temples, lakes, statues and fountains. Guides in the
guise of historical character are available inside the house, and
visitors can join outdoor tours. Additional attractions include a
children's adventure playground and boat trips.

Times: Open March-Oct. Grounds open 11-6.30/dusk, (last admission
4). Stable courtyard open 10-5 all yr **Fee:** ✱ £10 (ch £7, pen £9).
Grounds only £7 (ch £5, pen £6.50). **Facilities:** 🅿 🍽 ✕ licensed
♿ (wheelchair lift, free adapted transport to house) toilets for disabled
shop garden centre ✈ (ex guide dogs) ◀

EDEN CAMP MODERN HISTORY THEME MUSEUM

Eden Camp YO17 6RT
Dir: (junct of A64 & A169, between York & Scarborough)
Map Ref: SE77
☎ **01653 697777** 📄 **01653 698243**
e-mail: admin@edencamp.co.uk

The story of the people's war unfolds in this museum, which is devoted to civilian life in World War II. The displays, covering the blackout, rationing, the Blitz and the Home Guard, are housed in a former prisoner-of-war camp built in 1942 for German and Italian soldiers. Hut 13, part of a Millennium project, looks at the conflicts that Britain has been involved with from 1945 to the present day. Huts 24-29 cover the military and political events of the war, while Hut 11 tells the story of World War I.

Times: Open 2nd Mon in Jan-23 Dec, daily 10-5. (Last admission 4) **Fee:** £4.50 (ch & pen £3.50) Party 10+.£3.50 (ch & pen £2.50) **Facilities:** 🅿 ☕ & (taped tours, Braille guides) toilets for disabled shop

MIDDLESBROUGH CAPTAIN COOK BIRTHPLACE MUSEUM

Stewart Park, Marton TS7 8AT
Dir: (3m S on A172) **Map Ref:** NZ42
☎ **01642 311211** 📄 **01642 515659**
e-mail: captcookmuseum@middlesbrough.gov.uk

Opened to mark the 250th anniversary of the birth of the voyager in 1728, this museum illustrates the early life of James Cook and his discoveries with permanent and temporary exhibitions. Located in spacious and rolling parkland, the site also offers outside attractions for the visitor. Now refurbished, the museum has a special resource centre which has fresh approaches to presentation with computers, films, special effects, interactives and educational aids.

Times: Open all year: Mar-Oct, Tue-Sun, 10-5.30. Nov-Feb 9-3.30. (Last entry 45 mins before closure). Closed Mon except BH, 24-28 Dec & 31 Dec-7 Jan. **Fee:** £2.40 (pen £1.20). Family ticket £6. **Facilities:** 🅿 ☕ ✕ & (lift to all floors, car parking) toilets for disabled shop ✖ (ex guide dogs) ◀

NEWBY HALL & GARDENS NEWBY HALL & GARDENS

HG4 5AE
Dir: (4m SE of Ripon & 2m W of A1M, off B6265) **Map Ref:** SE36
☎ **01423 322583** 📄 **01423 324452**
e-mail: info@newbyhall.com

Newby Hall is a late 17th-century house with beautifully restored Robert Adam interiors and an important collection of classical sculpture, Chippendale furniture and Gobelin tapestries. The award-winning gardens include a miniature railway, a woodland discovery walk with a sculpture park, and an adventure garden for children.

Times: Open Apr-Sep, Tue-Sun & BHs, also Mon in school hols; Gardens 11-5.30; House 12-5. (Last admission 5 Gardens, 4.30 House) **Fee:** ✱ House & Garden £7.20, (ch £4.70, pen £6.20). Gardens only £5.70 (ch £4.20, pen £4.70). Party rates and family tickets on application. **Facilities:** 🅿 ☕ ✕ licensed & (wheelchairs available, maps of wheelchair routes) toilets for disabled shop garden centre ✖ (ex guide dogs) ◀

NORTH STAINLEY   *LIGHTWATER VALLEY THEME PARK*

HG4 3HT
Dir: (3m N of Ripon on the A6108) *Map Ref:* *SE27*
☎ 0870 458 0060 & 458 0040 📄 01765 635359
e-mail: leisure@lightwatervalley.co.uk

The family sized theme park with thrills of all sizes, from Europe's longest rollercoaster; 'The Ultimate' and 'The Grizzly Bear' log flume to family favourites such as the 'ladybird' rollercoaster and Grand Prix Go Karting along with spinning teacups, vintage cars and much more for younger children. You just pay once and enjoy the fun all day long! Other attractions include the Lightwater Country Shopping Village and special seasonal events.

Times: ✱ Open 23 Mar-7 Apr, wknds only; 13 Apr-26 May inc BH Mon; daily from Jun-2 Sep, wknds only, 7 Sep-13 Oct, daily 19 Oct-27 Oct. **Facilities:** 🅿 🍽 ✗ licensed ♿ (even pathways) toilets for disabled shop ✈ (ex guide dogs) ◀

PATELEY BRIDGE   *STUMP CROSS CAVERNS*

Greenhow HG3 5JL
Dir: (situated on B6265 between Pateley Bridge and Grassington) *Map Ref:* *SE16*
☎ 01756 752780 📄 01756 752780

Discovered by the brothers Mark and William Newbould in 1860, Stump Cross Caverns have been an attraction for visitors since 1863 when one shilling was charged for entrance. Among the few limestone show caves in Britain, these require no special clothing, experience or equipment, as walkways are gravel and concrete and floodlighting is provided. Stalagmites, stalagtites and calcite precipitation make this an eerie day out.

Times: ✱ Open daily, mid Mar-2 Nov, then wknds (winter) 10-5. **Facilities:** 🅿 🍽 shop ✈ (ex guide dogs) ◀

PICKERING   NORTH YORKSHIRE MOORS RAILWAY

Pickering Station YO18 7AJ
Dir: (from A169 take road towards Kirkbymoorside, right at traffic lights, Station 400yds on left) *Map Ref:* *SE78*
☎ 01751 472508 📄 01751 476970
e-mail: admin@nymr.pickering.fsnet.co.uk

Running from Pickering to Grosmont, through the heart of the North York Moors National Park and some magnificent scenery, this preserved steam railway covers a distance of 18 miles. The locomotive sheds at Grosmont are open to the public, and there is a shop there selling souvenirs. Events throughout the year include Day Out with Thomas events, Steam Galas and Santa Specials.

Times: Open 29 Mar-Oct, daily; Dec, Santa specials and Christmas to New Year running. Further information available from Pickering Station. **Fee:** Return: £12 (ch £6, pen £10.50). Family ticket £27 (2ad+3ch), others on request. Party 20+. **Facilities:** 🅿 (charged) 🍽 ✗ licensed ♿ (ramp for trains) toilets for disabled shop (at Pickering, Goathland & Grosmont) ◀

RICHMOND RICHMOND CASTLE

DL10 4QW
Map Ref: NZ10
☎ **01748 822493**

The views from the Richmond Castle are stunning, overlooking the River Swale and the market town of Richmond, which has grown up around it. The castle was built by Alan the Red of Brittany in 1071, on land given to him by William the Conqueror. The keep, a 12th-century addition to the building, is the best preserved part, standing 100 feet above the town. The castle now houses an exciting interactive exhibition and a display of artefacts excavated from the site.

Times: Open all year, Apr-Sep, daily, 10-6; Oct-Mar, Thu-Mon, 10-4. Closed 24-26 Dec & 1 Jan. **Fee:** ✱ £3.50 (ch £1.80, concessions £2.60, family £8.80). Prices & opening times relate to 2004, for further details phone or log onto www.english-heritage.org.uk/visits
Facilities: P (800 yds) & toilets for disabled shop ✿

RIPLEY RIPLEY CASTLE

HG3 3AY
Dir: (off A61, Harrogate to Ripon road) *Map Ref:* SE26
☎ **01423 770152** 📄 **01423 771745**
e-mail: enquiries@ripleycastle.co.uk

Ripley Castle has been home to the Ingilby family since 1320, and stands at the heart of an estate with a deer park, lake and gardens. The castle has a rich history and a fine collection of Royalist armour housed in the 1555 tower. There are also walled gardens, tropical hot houses, woodland walks, pleasure grounds and the National Hyacinth Collection in spring.

Times: Open Sep-Jun, Tue, Thu, Sat & Sun 10.30-3, Jul-Aug daily 10.30-3, also BH and school holidays. Groups all year by prior arrangement. Gardens open daily 9-5.30. **Fee:** Castle & Gardens £6 (ch £3.50, pen £5). Gardens only £3.50 (ch £2, pen £3). Party £3.
Facilities: P ▣ ✗ licensed & (mobility buggy for hire, audio loop) toilets for disabled shop garden centre ✖ (ex guide dogs) ◄

SALTBURN-BY-THE-SEA SALTBURN SMUGGLERS HERITAGE CENTRE

Old Saltburn TS12 1HF
Dir: (adjoining Ship Inn, on A174) *Map Ref:* NZ62
☎ **01287 625252** 📄 **01287 625252**

The Saltburn Smugglers Heritage Centre is housed in old fisherman's cottages and skilfully blends costumed characters with authentic sounds and smells. Here you can follow the story of John Andrew 'King of Smugglers', who was at the heart of illicit local trade 200 years ago. You may also catch a glimpse of where the contraband is hidden.

Times: Open Apr-Sep, daily 10-6: Winter open by arrangement only telephone 01642 470836.
Fee: ✱ £1.95 (ch £1.45). Family ticket £5.80. Party. **Facilities:** P (200 mtrs) (charged) shop ✖

SCARBOROUGH SCARBOROUGH CASTLE

Castle Rd YO11 1HY
Dir: (E of town centre) **Map Ref:** *TA08*
☎ **01723 372451**

A 12th-century fortress in a naturally well defended spot looking out to sea, Scarborough Castle has housed many important figures in history. The remains of the great keep still stand over three storeys high affording spectacular coastal views from 300 feet above the town and harbour. Visitors can hear about the castle's exciting history through the free audio tour.

Times: Open all year, Apr-Sep, daily 10-6; Oct-Mar, Thu-Mon, 10-4. Closed 24-26 Dec & 1 Jan. **Fee:** ✱ £3.20 (ch £1.60, concessions £2.40, family £8). Prices & opening times relate to 2004, for further details phone or log onto www.english-heritage.org.uk/visits
Facilities: P (100yds) & (ex in keep) ⌗

SEA LIFE & MARINE SANCTUARY

Scalby Mills Rd, North Bay YO12 6RP
Dir: (follow brown tourist signs after entering Scarborough. Centre in 'North Bay Leisure Parks' area of town) **Map Ref:** *TA08*
☎ **01723 376125** ▤ **01723 376285**

With a striking design comprising three large white pyramids, this impressive marine sanctuary overlooks the white sandy beaches of the North Bay, Scarborough's Castle and Peasholm Park. The centre provides a home for thousands of sea creatures including jellyfish, otters, penguins and sea turtles, and a sanctuary for orphaned or poorly seal pups. A new addition is the Lair of the Octopus exhibition.

Times: Open daily. Closed 25 Dec. **Fee:** ✱ Prices to be confirmed. **Facilities:** P (charged) ☕ & (lift to cafe) toilets for disabled shop ✖ (except guide dogs) ◀

SKINNINGROVE CLEVELAND IRONSTONE MINING MUSEUM

Deepdale TS13 4AP
Dir: (in Skinningrove Valley, just off A174 near coast between Middlesbrough and Whitby) **Map Ref:** *NZ71*
☎ **01287 642877** ▤ **01287 642970**
e-mail: visits@ironstonemuseum.co.uk

On the site of the old Loftus Mine, this museum offers visitors a glimpse into the underground world of Cleveland's ironstone mining past. Here you can discover the special skills and customs of the miners who helped make Cleveland the most important ironstone mining district in Victorian and Edwardian England. Hear about a 'trappy lad' on his first day underground and visit the museum gallery with its collection of mining photographs.

Times: Open Apr-Oct, daily from 1 (last admission 4). Nov-Mar, pre-booked parties can be arranged at any time **Fee:** ✱ £4 (ch £2). Family ticket (2ad+2ch) £10. **Facilities:** P & (Please telephone to discuss) toilets for disabled shop ✖ (ex guide dogs)

SKIPTON SKIPTON CASTLE

BD23 1AQ
Dir: (in town centre at head of High Street) **Map Ref:** *SD95*
☎ **01756 792442** 📄 **01756 796100**
e-mail: info@skiptoncastle.co.uk

Skipton is one of the most complete and well-preserved medieval castles in England. Some of the castle dates from the 1650s when it was rebuilt after being partially damaged following the Civil War. However, the original castle was erected in Norman times and became the home of the Clifford family in 1310 and remained so until 1676. Illustrated tour sheets are available in a number of languages.

Times: Open daily from 10, Sun noon. (Last admission 6, 4pm Oct-Feb). Closed 25 Dec. **Fee:** ✱ £5 (inc illustrated tour sheet) (ch under 18 £2.50, under 5 free, concessions £4.40). Family ticket £13.90. Party 15+. **Facilities:** P (200m) ☕ shop garden centre 🍴

YORK THE ARC

St Saviourgate YO1 8NN
Dir: (follow A19 or A64 to York city centre then pedestrian signs for the attraction) **Map Ref:** *SE65*
☎ **01904 543403** 📄 **01904 627097**
e-mail: enquiries@vikingjorvik.com

The ARC offers a unique opportunity to experience York's Viking history in the most unusual way. Visitors can take on the role of the archaeologist and handle genuine 1,000-year-old objects that once belonged to the Vikings themselves. With the help of a special detective guidebook, it is possible to deduce what life was really like at that time.

Times: Open: School term time Mon-Fri 10-3.30. School hols Mon-Sat 11-3 **Fee:** ✱ £4.50. (ch, students & pen £4) Family £15. Group rates available on request. **Facilities:** P (50yds) ♿ (induction loop, sensory garden, hearing posts) toilets for disabled shop 🐕 (ex guide dogs) 🍴

JORVIK

Coppergate YO1 9WT
Dir: (City centre, attraction signed) **Map Ref:** *SE65*
☎ **01904 543403** 📄 **01904 627097**
e-mail: enquiries@vikingjorvik.com

Explore York's Viking history on the very site where archaeologists discovered remains of the city of Jorvik. Encounter Viking residents, learn what life was like here 1,000 years ago, and journey through a reconstruction of actual Viking streets.

Times: Open all year, Apr-Oct daily 10-5; and Viking festival Nov-Mar daily 10-4. Closed 25 Dec. Opening times subject to change, please telephone for up to date details. **Fee:** ✱ £7.20 (ch 5-15 £5.10, under 5 free, student & pen £6.10) Family of 4 £21.95 & family of 5 £26.50. Telephone bookings on 01904 543403 (£1 booking fee per person at peak times). **Facilities:** P (400 yds) (limited to 3 hours) ☕ ♿ (lift & time car designed to take wheelchair, hearing loop) toilets for disabled shop 🐕 (ex guide dogs) 🍴

NATIONAL RAILWAY MUSEUM

Leeman Rd YO26 4XJ
Dir: (situated behind railway station. Signed from all major
approach roads) *Map Ref:* SE65
☎ **01904 621261** 🖷 **01904 611112**
e-mail: nrm@nmsi.ac.uk

York boasts the world's largest railway museum, and families can
spend all day exploring the three giant halls that house this
impressive collection. Among the exhibits are the huge Chinese
Locomotive, built in 1935 and weighing in at 193 tons with
tender; the Mallard, which still holds the world speed record for
steam traction on rail (126mph in 1938); the legendary
Stephenson's Rocket; and various rail-related items like winding
engines, bridges and a horse-drawn ambulance for injured horses.

Times: Open all year, Mon-Sun 10-6. Closed
24-26 Dec. **Fee:** Admission may be charged for
special events **Facilities:** 🅿 (charged) 🍵
✕ licensed & ("Please Touch" evenings usually in
June) toilets for disabled shop
✈ (ex guide/hearing dogs) ■

TREASURER'S HOUSE

Chapter House St YO1 7JL
Dir: (in Minster Yard, on N side of Minster *Map Ref:* SE65
☎ **01904 624247** 🖷 **01904 647372**
e-mail: yorkth@smtp.ntrust.org.uk

Named after the Treasurer of York Minster and built over a Roman
Road, this house is not all it seems. Come and discover why!
Nestled behind the Minster, the size, splendour and contents of
the house are a constant surprise to visitors - as are the famous
ghost stories. Children's trails and access to the tea room is free.

Times: ✱ Open Apr-Oct, daily except Fri, 11-5.
Facilities: 🅿 (800 mtrs) 🍵 ✕ & (Braille
guide/tactile pictures/induction loop/scented
path) ✈ (ex guide dogs) ♨

YORK CASTLE MUSEUM

The Eye of York YO1 IRY
Dir: (city centre, next to Clifford's Tower) *Map Ref:* SE65
☎ **01904 653611** 🖷 **01904 671078**

Fascinating exhibits at York Castle Museum are imaginatively
displayed through reconstructions of period rooms and two
indoor streets, complete with shops, cobbles, a Hansom cab and
a park. It is housed in the city's former prison - featuring the cell
where highwayman Dick Turpin was held - and is based on an
extensive collection of bygones acquired at the beginning of the
20th century. A fine collection of Militaria includes an Anglo-Saxon
helmet - one of only three known. Please contact the museum for
details of exhibition and events.

Times: ✱ Open all year, Apr-Oct Mon-Sat
9.30-5.30, Sun 10-5.30; Nov-Mar, Mon-Sat 9.30-4,
Sun 10-4. Closed 25-26 Dec & 1 Jan.
Facilities: 🍵 & toilets for disabled shop ✈ ■

Yorkshire, North continued

THE YORK DUNGEON

12 Clifford St YO1 9RD
Dir: (A64/A19/A59 to city centre) *Map Ref:* SE65
☎ 01904 632599 📄 01904 612602
e-mail: yorkdungeons@merlinentertainments.biz

Deep in the heart of historic York, buried beneath the paving stones, lies the York Dungeon, bringing more than 2,000 years of gruesomely authentic history vividly to life. The darkest chapters of our grim and bloody past are recreated in all their dreadful detail. In the dungeon's dark catacombs it pays to keep your wits about you - the 'exhibits' have an unnerving habit of coming back to life! The journey features Dick Turpin, Guy Fawkes, Witch Trails, Clifford's Tower, Pit of Despair and Gorvik - the real Viking experience.

Times: ✻ Open all year, daily 10.30-5 (closes 4.30 Oct-Mar). Closed 25 Dec.
Facilities: P (500yds) ♿ (wheelchair ramps, stairlifts, award winning access) toilets for disabled shop 🛍

YORK MINSTER

Deangate YO1 7EW
Dir: (easy access via A19, A1 or A64) *Map Ref:* SE65
☎ 01904 557216 📄 01904 557218
e-mail: visitors@yorkminster.org

Enjoy the peaceful atmosphere of the largest Gothic cathedral in Northern Europe, a place of worship for over 1,000 years, and a treasure house of stained glass. Take an audio tour of the undercroft to find out more about the Minster's fascinating history and climb the tower for an amazing view over the city. A comprehensive programme of events is held at the Minster throughout the year.

Times: Open from 7 for services. Visitors Mon-Sat 9-4.45 (9.30 in winter), Sun noon-3.45. Phone for 2005 details. **Fee:** ✻ £4.50 (ch16 free, concessions £3). Small charge also for the Undercroft and Tower). **Facilities:** P (440yds) ♿ (tactile model, Braille & large print guide) toilets for disabled shop 🐕 (ex guide dogs) 🛍

CUSWORTH THE MUSEUM OF SOUTH YORKSHIRE LIFE CUSWORTH HALL

Cusworth Ln DN5 7TU
Dir: (3m NW of Doncaster) *Map Ref:* SE50
☎ 01302 782342 📄 01302 782342
e-mail: museum@doncaster.gov.uk

The Museum of South Yorkshire is located in Cusworth Hall, an 18th-century country house set in a landscaped park. The displays illustrate the way local people lived, worked and entertained themselves over the last 200 years, with a particular focus on the Victorian era. Local industries represented include farming, mining and the railway. Following a grant from the Heritage Lottery Fund, substantial refurbishment of the museum is ongoing.

Times: ✻ Open Mon-Fri 10-5, Sat 11-5 & Sun 1-5. (4 Dec & Jan). Closed Good Fri, Xmas & 1 Jan. Hall & Park undergoing restoration and at times some areas may not be open to the public. Telephone for details. **Facilities:** P 🍴 ♿ (wheelchair available) toilets for disabled shop 🐕 (ex guide dogs)

DONCASTER *EARTH CENTRE*

Denaby Main DN12 4EA
Dir: (A1(M) junct 36, follow brown Earth Centre signs along A630, then A6023 towards Mexborough. Earth Centre next right after Coniston Train Stn) *Map Ref:* SE50
☎ **01709 513933** 📄 **01709 512010**
e-mail: info@earthcentre.org.uk

This is a centre dedicated to the understanding and application of sustainable development. It offers indoor and outdoor exhibitions, unique buildings, gardens, wetlands, a country park and safe play areas. There are animals to visit, dinosaurs to dig for and a sensory walk that you do bare foot. Visitors can also enjoy a guided tour on Hope's Express, the bright red road train. Special events are a regular feature.

Times: Open all year, daily 10-5 summer, 10-4 winter, 10-7 school hols. Closed 25 Dec
Facilities: 🅿 (charged) 🍴 ✕ licensed ♿ (prebooked wheelchairs/electric cars for hire) toilets for disabled shop ✖ (ex guide dogs) ■

ROTHERHAM *MAGNA SCIENCE ADVENTURE CENTRE*

Sheffield Rd, Templeborough S60 1DX
Dir: (M1 junct 34, follow Templeborough sign off rdbt, then brown heritage signs) *Map Ref:* SK49
☎ **01709 720002** 📄 **01709 820092**
e-mail: jeyre@magnatrust.co.uk

Magna is the UK's first Science Adventure Centre, an exciting exploration of Earth, Air, Fire, Water and Power. A chance for visitors to create their own adventure through hands-on interactive challenges. Visit the five adventure pavilions, two shows and the outdoor adventure park and have fun unearthing the mysteries of our world.

Times: Please phone for 2005 details
Facilities: 🅿 🍴 ✕ licensed ♿ (lifts, portable seating, wheelchair hire) toilets for disabled shop ✖ (ex guide dogs) ■

SHEFFIELD *KELHAM ISLAND MUSEUM*

Alma St S3 8RY
Dir: (0.5m NW of city centre, A61 N to West Bar, follow signs)
Map Ref: SK38
☎ **0114 272 2106** 📄 **0114 275 7847**
e-mail: postmaster@simt.co.uk

The story of Sheffield, its industry and life, is told at Kelham Island Museum. It has the most powerful working steam engine in Europe, reconstructed workshops, and craftspeople demonstrating traditional 'made in Sheffield' skills - this is a 'living' museum. During the year Kelham Island stages events, displays and temporary exhibitions culminating in the annual Christmas Victorian Market.

Times: ✱ Open Mon-Thu 10-4, Sun 11-4.45. Closed Fri and Sat. Check opening days/times at Xmas & New Year before travelling.
Facilities: 🅿 🍴 ♿ (wheelchair on request) toilets for disabled shop ✖

MILLENNIUM GALLERIES

Arundel Gate S1 2PP
Map Ref: *SK38*
☎ **0114 278 2600** 🖹 **0114 278 2604**
e-mail: info@sheffieldgalleries.org.uk

With four different galleries under one roof, the Millennium Galleries have something for everyone. Enjoy new blockbuster exhibitions drawn from the collections of Britain's national galleries and museums, including the Victoria & Albert Museum and Tate Gallery. See the best of contemporary craft and design in a range of exhibitions by established and up-and-coming makers. Be dazzled by Sheffield's magnificent and internationally important collection of decorative and domestic metalwork and silverware. Discover the Ruskin Gallery with its wonderful array of treasures by Victorian artist and writer John Ruskin.

Times: ✱ Open daily Mon-Sat 10-5, Sun 11-5.
Facilities: P 💺 ✗ licensed ♿ (hearing loop) toilets for disabled shop ✖ (ex guide dogs) ◀

BRADFORD BRADFORD INDUSTRIAL MUSEUM AND HORSES AT WORK

Moorside Mills, Moorside Rd, Eccleshill BD2 3HP
Dir: (off A658) **Map Ref:** *SE13*
☎ **01274 435900** 🖹 **01274 636362**   FREE

Moorside Mills is an original spinning mill, now part of a museum that brings vividly to life the story of Bradford's woollen industry, with the machinery that once converted raw wool into cloth. The mill yard rings with the sound of iron on stone as shire horses pull trams, haul buses and give rides. There are daily demonstrations and a programme of changing exhibitions.

Times: Open all year, Tue-Sat 10-5, Sun 12-5. Closed Mon ex BH, Good Fri, 25-26 Dec
Facilities: P 💺 ♿ (induction loop in lecture theatre, lift) toilets for disabled shop ✖ (ex guide dogs)

COLOUR MUSEUM

Perkin House, 1 Providence St BD1 2PW
Dir: (from city centre follow signs B6144 (Haworth), then brown heritage signs) **Map Ref:** *SE13*
☎ **01274 390955** 🖹 **01274 392888**
e-mail: museum@sdc.org.uk

Europe's only museum of colour is run by the Society of Dyers and Colourists. It comprises two galleries packed with visitor-operated exhibits demonstrating the effects of light and colour, including optical illusions, and the story of dyeing and textile printing. There is a programme of special exhibitions and events. Please telephone for details.

Times: Open 2 Jan-18 Dec, Tue-Sat, 10-4.
Fee: ✱ £2 (concessions £1.50). Family ticket £4
Facilities: P (300 yds) ♿ (lifts, ramps at door) toilets for disabled shop ✖ (ex guide dogs) ◀

NATIONAL MUSEUM OF PHOTOGRAPHY, FILM & TELEVISION

BD1 1NQ
Dir: (2m from end of M606, follow signs for city centre)
Map Ref: SE13
☎ 0870 7010200   📠 01274 394540
e-mail: talk.nmpft@nmsi.ac.uk

This newly refurbished museum is one of the North of England's most popular attractions. Here you can experience the past, present and future of photography, film and television. Expect amazing interactive displays and a spectacular 3D IMAX cinema. A full programme of events, talks and exhibitions is also offered.

Times: Open all year, Tue-Sun, BHs & main school hols 10-6. Closed Mon. **Fee:** ✱ Admission to permanent galleries free, IMAX Cinema £5.95 (concessions £4.20). Groups 20% discount.
Facilities: 🅿 (adjacent) 💻 ✗ licensed ♿ (tailored tours, Braille signs, induction loop, cinema seating) toilets for disabled shop ✖ (ex guide dogs) 🎞

HALIFAX   *BANKFIELD MUSEUM*

Boothtown Rd, Akroyd Park HX3 6HG
Dir: (on A647 Bradford via Queensbury road, 0.5m from Halifax town centre) *Map Ref:* SE02
☎ 01422 354823 & 352334   📠 01422 349020
e-mail: bankfield-museum@calderdale.gov.uk

Built by Edward Akroyd in the 1860s, this Renaissance-style building is set in parkland on a hill overlooking the town. It has an outstanding collection of costumes and textiles from many periods and parts of the world, including a new gallery featuring East European textiles. There is also a section on toys, and the museum of the Duke of Wellington's Regiment is housed here. Temporary exhibitions are held and there is a lively programme of events, workshops and activities. Please ring for details.

Times: ✱ Open all year, Tue-Sat 10-5, Sun 2-5, BH Mon 10-5. (Extended closing times at Xmas and New Year, phone for details)
Facilities: 🅿 ♿ (audio guide & tactile objects) toilets for disabled shop ✖ (ex guide dogs) 🎞

EUREKA! THE MUSEUM FOR CHILDREN

Discovery Rd HX1 2NE
Dir: (M62 junct 24 follow brown heritage signs to Halifax centre - A629) *Map Ref:* SE02
☎ 01422 330069   📠 01422 330275
e-mail: info@eureka.org.uk

With over 400 'must touch' exhibits, interactive activities and challenges, visitors are invited to embark upon a journey of discovery through four main gallery spaces: Me and My Body, Living and Working Together, Our Global Garden and Sound Space, an amazing new music gallery inviting children to explore the science behind sound, rhythm and technology. They can find out how their bodies and senses work, discover the realities of daily life, travel from the familiar 'backyard' to amazing and faraway places and explore the world of communications.

Times: Open all year, daily 10-5. Closed 24-26 Dec **Fee:** ✱ £5.95 (ch under 3 free) Family Saver ticket £27.50 **Facilities:** 🅿 (charged) 💻 ♿ (lift, staff trained in basic sign language, large print) toilets for disabled shop ✖ (ex guide dogs) 🎞

PIECE HALL

HX1 1RE
Dir: (follow brown tourist signs, close to railway station)
Map Ref: SE02
☎ **01422 358087** 🖹 **01422 349310**
e-mail: karen.belshaw@calderdale.gov.uk

The merchants of Halifax built this elegant and unique hall in 1779, and it has over 300 merchant's rooms around a courtyard, now housing an industrial museum, art galleries and shops selling antiques, books and so on. Open markets are held on Friday and Saturday and a flea market on Thursday. There is a lively programme of exhibitions, workshops, activities and events throughout the year, and a festival in the summer. Please ring for details.

Times: ✱ Open all year daily. Closed 25-26 Dec. Art Gallery, Tue-Sun & BH Mon 10-5.
Facilities: 🅿 (50 yds) ☕ 👩‍🦽 (lifts, shopmobility on site & audio guide available) toilets for disabled shop 🛍

HAREWOOD HAREWOOD HOUSE & BIRD GARDEN

LS17 9LQ
Dir: (junct A61/A659 Leeds to Harrogate road) *Map Ref:* SE34
☎ **0113 218 1010** 🖹 **0113 218 1002**
e-mail: business@harewood.org

Designed in 1759 by John Carr, Harewood House is the home of the Queen's cousin, the Earl of Harewood. The House, renowned for its stunning architecture and exquisite Adam interiors, contains a rich collection of Chippendale furniture, fine porcelain and outstanding art collections from Italian Renaissance masterpieces and Turner watercolours to contemporary works. The old kitchen has the best collection of noble household copperware in the country. The grounds include a restored parterre terrace, oriental rock garden, walled garden, lakeside and woodland walks, a bird garden and, for youngsters, an adventure playground.

Times: Open 4 Feb-mid Nov, (grounds until mid Dec), Grounds (inc Bird Gardens) daily from 10, House from 11. **Fee:** ✱ 'Freedom ticket' (house, grounds, bird garden, terrace gallery) Mon-Sat £10 (ch £5.50, pen £8.25) Family £30.50. Sun & BH £11 (ch £6, pen £9.25) Family £33.50. Bird Garden & Grounds: £7.25 (ch £4.25 pen £6.25) Family £23. Sun & BH £8.25 (ch £5, pen £7.25) Family £26. **Facilities:** 🅿 ☕ ✕ licensed 👩‍🦽 (electric ramp, lift, free audio tour) toilets for disabled shop ✈ (ex guide dogs or in gardens) 🛍

HAWORTH KEIGHLEY & WORTH VALLEY RAILWAY & MUSEUM

Keighley BD22 8NJ
Dir: (1m from Keighley on A629 Halifax road, follow brown signs)
Map Ref: SE03
☎ **01535 645214 & 677777** 🖹 **01535 647317**

The line was built mainly to serve the valley's mills, and goes right through the heart of Brontë country. Beginning at Keighley (shared with Railtrack), it climbs up to Haworth, and terminates at Oxenhope, which has a storage and restoration building. At Haworth there are locomotive workshops and at Ingrow West an award-winning museum.

Times: ✱ All year wknd service, but daily all BH wks & 19 Jun-1 Sep
Facilities: 🅿 (charged) ☕ 👩‍🦽 (wheelchairs can be accommodated in brake car) toilets for disabled shop 🛍

KEIGHLEY CLIFFE CASTLE MUSEUM & GALLERY

Spring Gardens Ln BD20 6LH
Dir: (NW of town off A629) *Map Ref:* SE04
☎ **01535 618231** 📄 **01535 610536**

FREE

French furniture from the Victoria & Albert Museum is displayed at Cliffe Castle, together with collections of local and natural history, ceramics, dolls, geological items and minerals. The grounds of the 19th-century mansion include a play area and an aviary.

Times: Open all year, Tue-Sat 10-5, Sun 12-5. Open BH Mon. Closed Good Fri & 25-28 Dec.
Facilities: 🅿 ♿ toilets for disabled shop garden centre ✖ (ex guide dogs)

LEEDS ABBEY HOUSE MUSEUM

Abbey Walk, Abbey Rd, Kirkstall LS5 3EH
Dir: (3m W of city centre on A65) *Map Ref:* SE33
☎ **0113 230 5492** 📄 **0113 230 5499**
e-mail: abbeyhouse.museum@virgin.net

Displays at this museum include an interactive childhood gallery, a look at Kirkstall Abbey, and an exploration of life in Victorian Leeds. Three reconstructed streets allow the visitor to immerse themselves in the sights and sounds of the late 19th century, from the glamorous art furnisher's shop to the impoverished widow washerwoman.

Times: ✱ Open all year Tue-Fri 10-5, Sat noon-5, Sun 10-5. Closed Mon ex BH Mon (open 10-5)
Facilities: 🅿 ✖ licensed ♿ (Braille plaques on wall, tactile tours by request) toilets for disabled shop ✖ (ex guide dogs) ◼

LEEDS INDUSTRIAL MUSEUM AT ARMLEY MILLS

Canal Rd, Armley LS12 2QF
Dir: (2m W of city centre, off A65) *Map Ref:* SE33
☎ **0113 263 7861**

Once the world's largest woollen mill, Armley Mills evokes memories of the 18th-century woollen industry, showing the progress of wool from the sheep to knitted clothing. The museum has its own 1930's cinema illustrating the history of cinema projection, including the first moving pictures taken in Leeds. There are demonstrations of static engines and steam locomotives, a printing gallery and a journey through the working world of textiles and fashion.

Times: Open all year, Tue-Sat 10-5, Sun 1-5. (Last entry 1 hr before closing). Closed Mon ex BHs.
Fee: ✱ £2 (ch 50p, pen, students & UB40's £1) Friends & Family ticket £5 (2ad+3ch)
Facilities: 🅿 ♿ (chair-lifts between floors) toilets for disabled shop ✖ ◼

ROYAL ARMOURIES MUSEUM

Armouries Dr LS10 1LT
Dir: (off A61 close to Leeds centre, follow brown heritage signs)
Map Ref: SE33
☎ **0113 220 1999 & 0990 106 666** 📠 **0113 220 1934**
e-mail: enquiries@armouries.org.uk

The museum is an impressive contemporary home for the renowned national collection of arms and armour. The collection is divided between five galleries: War, Tournament, Self-Defence, Hunting and Oriental. The Hall of Steel features a 100 foot-high mass of 3,000 pieces of arms and armour. Extensive interactive displays, dramatisations of jousting tournaments, and the chance to see leather workers and armourers at work all make for an exciting day out.

Times: ✱ Open daily, from 10-5. Closed 24-25 Dec **Facilities:** 🅿 (charged) 🍽 ✗ licensed ♿ (induction loops, wheelchairs, signers, low level counter) toilets for disabled shop 🐕 (ex guide & hearing dogs) 🍴

TEMPLE NEWSAM HOUSE & PARK

LS15 0AE
Dir: (off A63) *Map Ref:* SE33
☎ **0113 264 7321 (House) & 264 5535 (Park)**
📠 **0113 260 2285**

This Tudor and Jacobean mansion boasts extensive collections of decorative arts in their original room settings, including an incomparable Chippendale collection. The house is set in 1,500 acres of parkland landscaped by 'Capability' Brown, where you will find a rare breeds centre and gardens with a magnificent display of rhododendrons in season. Free audio guides talk you around the house and tell you more about the people who lived there. On special days, visitors can join in with the laundry maids washing at the dolly tub, watch the blacksmith hammer out shoes and see logs cut at the saw-mill.

Times: Open all year. House: Tue-Sat 10-5, Sun 1-5; Nov-28 Dec & Mar, Tue-Sat 10-4, Sun 12-5. Open Bank Hols. Home Farm: Tue-Sun, 10-4 (3 in winter); Gardens: 10-dusk. Estate: daily, dawn-dusk. Closed Jan-Feb re-opens 28 Feb. **Fee:** ✱ Joint ticket £5 (ch £3). Family tickets £13 (2ad+2ch) **Facilities:** 🅿 (charged) 🍽 ♿ (ramps for full access to parkland, electric wheelchairs) toilets for disabled shop 🐕 (ex guide dogs) 🍴

THACKRAY MUSEUM

Beckett St LS9 7LN
Dir: (M1 junct 43, onto M621 junct 4. Follow signs for Harrogate & St James Hospital, then brown tourist signs) *Map Ref:* SE33
☎ **0113 244 4343** 📠 **0113 247 0219**
e-mail: info@thackraymuseum.org

Housed in a large Victorian building, next to the famous St James's Hospital, the Thackray Museum offers a unique hands-on experience. A cow from Gloucester, green mould and smelly toilets - all these things have helped transform our lives. Find out how by walking back in time and exploring the sights, sounds and smells of Victorian slum life.

Times: Open all year, daily 10-5. Closed 24-26 & 31 Dec & 1 Jan **Fee:** ✱ £4.90 (ch 4-16 £3.50, pen, students & unemployed £3.90). Family ticket (2ad+3ch) £16. Group rates available. **Facilities:** 🅿 (charged) 🍽 ♿ (wheelchairs, induction loop, texts) toilets for disabled shop 🐕 (ex guide dogs) 🍴

TROPICAL WORLD

Canal Gardens, Roundhay Park LS8 2ER
Dir: (3m N of city centre off A58 at Oakwood) *Map Ref: SE33*
☎ 0113 266 1850 📄 0113 237 0077

The atmosphere of the tropics is recreated here as visitors walk on the beach among exotic trees. A waterfall cascades into a rock-pool and other pools contain terrapins and carp. There are reptiles, insects and more than 30 species of butterfly. Feel the dry heat of the desert and the darkness of the nocturnal zone, and watch out for the piranhas and other exotic fish in the depths of the aquarium.

Times: Open Winter (GMT), daily 10-4 (last admission 3.30); Summer (BST), 10-6 (last admission 5.30) **Fee:** ✱ f3 (ch 8-15 £2, under 8's & Leeds card holders free) **Facilities:** 🅿 💷 ♿ toilets for disabled shop ✖ (ex guide dogs) 🖃

MIDDLESTOWN   NATIONAL COAL MINING MUSEUM FOR ENGLAND

Caphouse Colliery, New Rd WF4 4RH
Dir: (on A642 between Wakefield & Huddersfield)
Map Ref: SE21
☎ 01924 848806 📄 01924 844567   FREE
e-mail: info@ncm.org.uk

A unique opportunity to go 140 metres underground down one of Britain's oldest working mines. Take a step back in time with one of the museum's experienced local miners who will guide parties around the underground workings, where models and machinery depict methods and conditions of mining from the early 1800s to the present day. Other attractions include the pithead baths, Victorian steam winder, nature trail and adventure playground and meet the last ever working pit ponies. You are strongly advised to wear sensible footwear and warm clothing.

Times: Open all year, daily 10-5. Closed 24-26 Dec & 1 Jan. **Facilities:** 🅿 💷 ✖ licensed ♿ (nature trail not accessible) toilets for disabled shop ✖ (ex guide dogs) 🖃

OAKWELL HALL   OAKWELL HALL

Nutter Ln, Birstall WF17 9LG
Dir: (6m SE of Bradford, off M62 junct 26/27, follow brown heritage signs, turn off A652 onto Nutter Lane) *Map Ref: SE22*
☎ 01924 326240 📄 01924 326249
e-mail: oakwell.hall@kirklees.gov.uk

Oakwell Hall is a moated Elizabethan manor house, furnished as it might have looked in the 1690s. It is set in a 110-acre country park with a visitor information centre, period gardens, nature trails, an arboretum and a children's adventure playground. Charlotte Brontë visited Oakwell Hall in the 1830s and it became the model for Fieldhead in her novel *'Shirley'*.

Times: Open all year, daily Mon-Fri 11-5; Sat & Sun 12-5. Closed Good Fri & 24 Dec-1 Jan. **Fee:** ✱ Hall £1.40 (ch & wheelchair users 50p). Family ticket £3. Charges Mar-Oct. Free admission Nov-Feb. Vistor centre and park free all year. **Facilities:** 🅿 💷 ♿ (herb garden for the blind, large print & Braille guide) toilets for disabled shop ✖ (park only ex guide dogs) 🖃

WAKEFIELD   WAKEFIELD ART GALLERY

Wentworth Ter WF1 3QW
Dir: (N of city centre by Wakefield College and Clayton Hospital)
Map Ref: SE32
☎ **01924 305796** 📄 **01924 305770**
e-mail: museumsandarts@wakefield.gov.uk

Wakefield was home to two of Britain's greatest modern sculptors - Barbara Hepworth and Henry Moore. The art gallery, which has an important collection of 20th-century paintings and sculptures, has a special room devoted to these two local artists. There are frequent temporary exhibitions of both modern and earlier works.

Times: Open all year, Tue-Sat 10.30-4.30, Sun 2-4.30. **Facilities:** 🅿 (on street) (on street parking restricted to 2hrs) & shop ✈ (ex guide dogs)

WEST BRETTON   YORKSHIRE SCULPTURE PARK

WF4 4LG
Dir: (M1 junct 38, follow brown signs to A637. Left at rdbt, park signed) *Map Ref:* SE21
☎ **01924 832631** 📄 **01924 832600**
e-mail: info@ysp.co.uk

Set in the beautiful grounds and gardens of a 500-acre, 18th-century country estate, this park is one of the world's leading open-air galleries and presents a changing programme of international sculpture exhibitions. The landscape provides a variety of magnificent scenic vistas of the valley, lakes and 18th-century estate buildings and bridges. A number of temporary exhibitions are organised.

Times: Open all year 10-6 (summer) 10-4 (winter). Please phone for details of Xmas closures **Fee:** ✱ Free. (Donations welcome). Car parking £3, coaches £8 **Facilities:** 🅿 (charged) 💭 ✗ licensed & (free scooters, parking, trail accessible for wheelchairs) toilets for disabled shop ✈ (ex assist dogs)

Forest at Brantingham Dale

South & East England

The southeast region is dominated by the capital but also stretches up to the wild corners of the Fenlands and down across the water to the Channel Islands. Large cities, other than London, are the seaports of Portsmouth and Southampton, otherwise the county towns tend to be small and historic, but no less influential, with centres of academic excellence at Cambridge and Oxford, and major league cathedrals like Canterbury and Winchester. Other key ports are Felixstowe, Harwich and Dover, and the coast is dotted with popular seaside resorts: Yarmouth, Lowestoft, Southend, Margate, Brighton and Bournemouth. Diverse natural features include The Fens, Constable Country, the New Forest, The Needles and the South Downs.

The majority of the country's top tourist attractions are located in the region, including Madame Tussaud's; the Tower of London; the Natural History Museum; Legoland, Windsor; Chessington World of Adventure; the Science Museum; Canterbury Cathedral; Windsor Castle; Westminster Abbey; St Paul's Cathedral; London Zoo; the Victoria & Albert Museum; Thorpe Park; the British Museum, and the Tate Galleries.

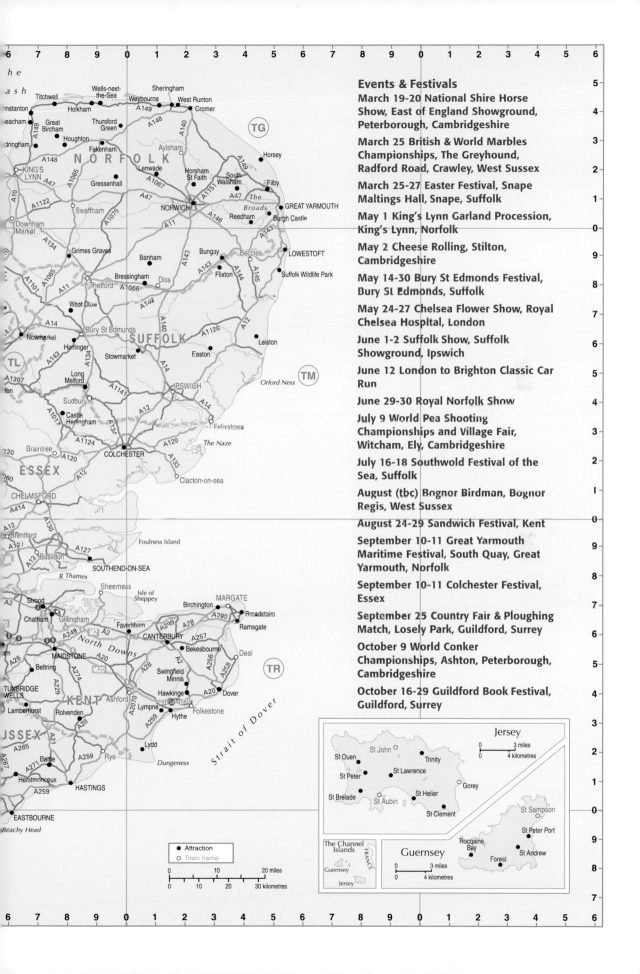

Events & Festivals

March 19-20 National Shire Horse Show, East of England Showground, Peterborough, Cambridgeshire

March 25 British & World Marbles Championships, The Greyhound, Radford Road, Crawley, West Sussex

March 25-27 Easter Festival, Snape Maltings Hall, Snape, Suffolk

May 1 King's Lynn Garland Procession, King's Lynn, Norfolk

May 2 Cheese Rolling, Stilton, Cambridgeshire

May 14-30 Bury St Edmonds Festival, Bury St Edmonds, Suffolk

May 24-27 Chelsea Flower Show, Royal Chelsea Hospital, London

June 1-2 Suffolk Show, Suffolk Showground, Ipswich

June 12 London to Brighton Classic Car Run

June 29-30 Royal Norfolk Show

July 9 World Pea Shooting Championships and Village Fair, Witcham, Ely, Cambridgeshire

July 16-18 Southwold Festival of the Sea, Suffolk

August (tbc) Bognor Birdman, Bognor Regis, West Sussex

August 24-29 Sandwich Festival, Kent

September 10-11 Great Yarmouth Maritime Festival, South Quay, Great Yarmouth, Norfolk

September 10-11 Colchester Festival, Essex

September 25 Country Fair & Ploughing Match, Losely Park, Guildford, Surrey

October 9 World Conker Championships, Ashton, Peterborough, Cambridgeshire

October 16-29 Guildford Book Festival, Guildford, Surrey

BEDFORD BEDFORD MUSEUM

Castle Ln MK40 3XD
Dir: (close to town bridge and Embankment) **Map Ref:** *TL04*
☎ 01234 353323 📄 01234 273401
e-mail: bmuseum@bedford.gov.uk

Embark on a fascinating journey through the human and natural history of north Bedfordshire, pausing briefly to glimpse at wonders from more distant lands. Go back in time and visit the delightful rural room sets and the Old School Museum, where Blackbeard's Sword, 'Old Billy' the record breaking longest-living horse and numerous other treasures and curiosities can be found. Housed in the former Higgins and Sons Brewery, Bedford Museum is situated within the gardens of what was once Bedford Castle, beside the Great Ouse embankment. The courtyard and galleries provide an excellent setting for the varied collections.

Times: Open all year, Tue-Sat 11-5, Sun 2-5. (Closed Mon ex BH Mon afternoon, Good Fri & Xmas). **Fee:** ✱ £2.30 (ch, pen & concessions free). Fri free for everyone. Annual ticket £9.20. **Facilities:** P (50mtrs) 💻 ♿ (lift available on request, subject to staff availability) toilets for disabled shop 🐕 (ex guide dogs) 📷

LEIGHTON BUZZARD LEIGHTON BUZZARD RAILWAY

Pages Park Station, Billington Rd LU7 4TN
Dir: (0.75m SE on A4146 signposted in and around Leighton Buzzard, near rdbt junct with A505) **Map Ref:** *SP92*
☎ 01525 373888 📄 01525 377814
e-mail: info@buzzrail.co.uk

The Leighton Buzzard Railway offers a 70-minute journey into the vanished world of the English light railway, with its sharp curves, steep gradients, level crossings and unique roadside running. Built in 1919 to serve the local sand industry, the railway has carried a steam passenger service, operated by volunteers, since 1968.

Times: Open Mar-Oct, Sun & BH wknds; Jul, Wed; Aug, Tue-Thu, Sat & BH wknds. **Fee:** ✱ Return ticket £5.50 (ch 2-15 £2.50, pen £4.50 & ch under 2 free). Party 10+. **Facilities:** P 💻 ♿ (platform & train access for wheelchairs) toilets for disabled shop 📷

LUTON STOCKWOOD CRAFT MUSEUM & GARDENS

Stockwood Country Park, Farley Hill LU1 4BH
Dir: (signposted from M1 junct 10 and from Hitchin, Dunstable, Bedford and from Luton town centre) **Map Ref:** *TL02*
☎ 01582 738714 & 546739 📄 01582 546763   FREE
e-mail: museum.gallery@luton.gov.uk

This museum of rural crafts and trades is set in parkland, two miles south of Luton town centre, where Stockwood House once stood. The Period Gardens reflect nine centuries of gardening history, including an Elizabethan knot garden and Victorian cottage gardens, while the classical-style Improvement Garden features sculptures by Scottish artist Ian Hamilton Finlay. The Mossman collection of over 50 horse-drawn vehicles traces the history of transport from Roman times to the 1940s. Craft demonstrations, events and activities are held throughout the year, please telephone for details.

Times: Open all year; Mar-Oct, Tue-Sun 10-5; Nov-Mar, wknds 10-4. (closed Xmas & 1 Jan) **Facilities:** P 💻 ♿ (stair lift, parking, induction loop, automatic door) toilets for disabled shop 🐕 (ex guide & hearing dogs)

OLD WARDEN — *THE SHUTTLEWORTH COLLECTION*
Old Warden Park SG18 9EA
Dir: (2m W from rdbt on A1, Biggleswade by-pass)
Map Ref: TL02
☎ **01767 627288** 📄 **01767 626229**

Housed in eight hangars on a classic grass aerodrome, 40 working historic aeroplanes span the progress of aviation with exhibits ranging from a 1909 Bleriot to a 1941 Spitfire. A garage of roadworthy motor vehicles explores the eras of the 1898 Panhard Levassor to the Railton sports car of 1937. The 19th-century coach house displays horse-drawn vehicles from 1880 to 1914.

Times: ✱ Open Apr-Oct 10-5 (last admission 4), Nov-Mar 10-4 (last admission 3). Closed Xmas-New Year. **Facilities:** 🅿 🍴 ✗ licensed ♿ toilets for disabled shop ✗ (ex guide dogs) 🎫

SANDY — RSPB NATURE RESERVE
The Lodge Shop SG19 2DL
Dir: (1m E, on B1042 Potton road) **Map Ref:** TL14
☎ **01767 680541** 📄 **01767 683508**
e-mail: claire.wallace@rspb.org.uk

This is the headquarters of the Royal Society for the Protection of Birds. The house and buildings are not open to the public, but there are waymarked paths and formal gardens, and two species of woodpecker, nuthatches and woodland birds may be seen, as may muntjac deer. Another feature is the specialist wildlife garden created in conjunction with the Henry Doubleday Association.

Times: Open all year, Mon-Fri 9-5, Sat, Sun & BHs 10-5. Closed 25-26 Dec. **Fee:** ✱ £3 (ch under 16 £1, concessions £1.50). Family ticket (2ad+2ch) £6. **Facilities:** 🅿 ♿ (partial access) toilets for disabled shop ✗ (ex in restricted areas) 🎫

WHIPSNADE — WHIPSNADE WILD ANIMAL PARK
LU6 2LF
Dir: (signposted from M1 junct 9 & 12) **Map Ref:** TL01
☎ **01582 872171** 📄 **01582 872649**

Set in 600 acres of countryside, Whipsnade is home to 3,000 creatures, and is one of the largest wildlife conservation centres in Europe. Visitors can see tigers, elephants, penguins, giraffes, bears, chimps, hippos and more. The newest addition is the Chimpnasium, added in 2004. There are regular special events and keeper talks, so phone for details, and remember that by coming to Whipsnade you are helping to protect endangered species and conserve natural habitats.

Times: Open all year, daily. (Closed 25 Dec). Telephone 01582 872171 or check website **Fee:** ✱ £13.50 (ch 3-15 & concessions £9.35). Car entry £10 Family ticket (2 ad & 2 ch) £42.50 **Facilities:** 🅿 (charged) 🍴 ♿ (free entry for disabled cars) toilets for disabled shop ✗ 🎫

Berkshire

WOBURN *WOBURN ABBEY*

MK17 9WA
Map Ref: SP93
☎ 01525 290666 📠 01525 290271
e-mail: enquiries@woburnabbey.co.uk

Standing in 3,000 acres of parkland, this palatial 18th-century mansion was originally a Cistercian Abbey, and the Dukes of Bedford have lived here since 1547. The art collection includes works by Canaletto, Rembrandt, Van Dyke and Gainsborough. Fourteen state apartments are on view, and the private apartments are shown when not in use. Special events are held during the year, including the De-Havilland Tiger Moth Fly-In and a garden show.

Times: ✱ Open Jan-23 Mar; Abbey Sat & Sun only 11-4, Deer park 10.30-3.45; 24 Mar-29 Sep; Abbey weekdays 11-4, Sun & BH 11-5; 5-27 Oct Sat & Sun only; Deer Park weekdays 10-4.30, Sun & BH 10-4.45. **Facilities:** 🅿 (charged) ☕ ✗ licensed ♿ (wheelchairs accommodated by prior arrangement) toilets for disabled shop 🐕 📷

WOBURN SAFARI PARK

Woburn Park MK17 9QN
Dir: (Signposted from M1 junct 13) *Map Ref:* SP93
☎ 01525 290407 📠 01525 290489
e-mail: info@woburnsafari.co.uk

Set in 3,000 acres of parkland belonging to Woburn Abbey, the Safari Park has an extensive collection of many species. The safari road passes through an African plains area stocked with eland, zebra, hippo and rhino, through tiger and lion enclosures and on past bears and monkeys. Animal encounters, underwater sea lion viewing and parrot shows are part of the fun, and other attractions include a boating lake, adventure playgrounds, railway train, walk-through aviary, squirrel monkey exhibit and 'the Australian Walkabout', with friendly wallabies.

Times: ✱ Open daily, 10 Mar-27 Oct, 10-5. **Facilities:** 🅿 ☕ ✗ licensed ♿ toilets for disabled shop 🐕 📷

BRACKNELL THE LOOK OUT DISCOVERY CENTRE

Nine Mile Ride RG12 7QW
Dir: (3m S of town centre. From M3 junct 3, take A322 to Bracknell and from M4 junct 10, take A329(M) to Bracknell. Follow brown tourist signs) *Map Ref:* SU86
☎ 01344 354400 📠 01344 354422
e-mail: thelookout@bracknell-forest.gov.uk

A hands-on, interactive science and nature exhibition where budding scientists can spend many hours exploring and discovering over 70 fun filled exhibits within five themed zones, linked to the National Curriculum. The new Woodland & Water Zone features Vortex, an amazing water tornado, a molehole and wormery and an ant colony at work. Climb the 88 steps to the Look Out tower (closed when wet) or enjoy a nature walk in the surrounding 2,600 acres of Crown Estate woodland.

Times: Open all year (Closed 24-26 Dec). **Fee:** £4.80 (ch & concessions £3.20). Family (2 adults + 2 ch or 1 adult + 3 ch) £12.80. **Facilities:** 🅿 ☕ ♿ lift to first floor toilets for disabled shop 🐕 (ex in grounds) 📷

HAMPSTEAD NORREYS *THE LIVING RAINFOREST*

RG18 OTN
Dir: (follow brown tourist signs from M4/A34) *Map Ref:* SU57
☎ **01635 202444** 📄 **01635 202440**
e-mail: enquiries@livingrainforest.org

By providing education and supporting research into the relationship between humanity and the rainforests, this wonderful attraction hopes to promote a more sustainable future. Visitors to the Living Rainforest will see plants and wildlife that are under threat in their natural habitat, and be encouraged to take part in a large variety of activities, workshops and exhibitions.

Times: ✱ Open daily 10-5.15. (Closed from 1pm 24 Dec & 25-26 Dec) **Facilities:** 🅿 💻 🚻 toilets for disabled shop ✖ (ex guide dogs) ◀

LOWER BASILDON *BEALE PARK*

Lower Basildon RG8 9NH
Dir: (M4 junct 12, follow brown tourist signs to Pangbourne, A329 towards Oxford) *Map Ref:* SU67
☎ **0118 984 5172** 📄 **0118 984 5171**
e-mail: bealepark@bun.com

Beale Park is home to an extraordinary bird collection including peacocks, swans, owls and parrots. It also offers a steam railway, rare breed farm animals, a great pets' corner, meerkats, wallabies, a deer park, two splash pools, a huge adventure playground, acres of gardens, sculptures, trails and environmental education in a traditional family park beside the Thames. There are summer riverboat trips and excellent lake and river fishing.

Times: ✱ Open Mar-Dec. **Facilities:** 🅿 💻 🚻 (wheelchair available, parking) toilets for disabled shop ✖ (ex guide dogs)

READING *MUSEUM OF ENGLISH RURAL LIFE*

University of Reading, Whiteknights RG6 6AG
Dir: (2m SE on A327) *Map Ref:* SU77
☎ **0118 378 8660** 📄 **0118 975 1264**
e-mail: merl@reading.ac.uk

This museum houses a national collection of agricultural, domestic and crafts exhibits, including wagons, tools and a wide range of other equipment used in the English countryside over the last 150 years. Special facilities such as videos and teaching packs are available for school parties. The museum also contains extensive documentary and photographic archives, which can be studied by appointment.

Times: ✱ Open all year, Tue-Sat, 10-1 & 2-4.30. (Closed BH's & Xmas-New Year). **Facilities:** 🅿 🚻 shop ✖

RISELEY WELLINGTON COUNTRY PARK

RG7 1SP
Dir: (signposted off A33, between Reading & Basingstoke)
Map Ref: *SU76*
☎ 0118 932 6444 📄 0118 932 6445
e-mail: info@wellington-country-park.co.uk

Wellington Country Park comprises 350 acres of woodland and meadows, set around a lake in peaceful countryside. Attractions at the park include a collection of farm animals, a miniature railway, crazy golf, an adventure playground and a sandpit. You can also fish and take a boat out on the 35-acre lake.

Times: Open Mar-Oct, daily 10-5.30. **Fee:** ✱ £4.80 (ch 5-15 £2.50, under 5 free) **Facilities:** 🅿 ☕ ♿ (fishing platform & nature trail for disabled) toilets for disabled shop ◀

WINDSOR LEGOLAND WINDSOR

Winkfield Rd SL4 4AY
Dir: (on B3022 Windsor to Ascot road well signposted from M3 junct 3 & M4 junct 6) ***Map Ref:*** *SU97*
☎ 08705 040404 01753 626111 📄 01753 626113
e-mail: customer.services@legoland.co.uk

LEGOLAND Windsor is an award-winning family theme park set in 150 acres of beautiful parkland. There are over 50 interactive rides in themed areas such as Wild Woods, Knight's Kingdom and Adventure Land; live shows; building workshops with Lego and Duplo bricks; driving schools with pedal cars and a hot air balloon gondola, and Sky Rider.

Times: Open daily 20 Mar-Oct (Xmas shopping 4/5, 11/22 Dec) **Fee:** ✱ Adult £21-£23 (ch under 3 free, ch 3-15 & pen £19-£20). Tickets can be booked in advance by telephoning 08705 040404. **Facilities:** 🅿 ☕ ✗ licensed ♿ (signing staff, wheelchair hire, parking) toilets for disabled shop ✖ (ex guide dogs) ◀

WINDSOR CASTLE

SL4 1NJ
Dir: (M4 junct 6 & M3 junct 3) ***Map Ref:*** *SU97*
☎ 020 7766 7304 📄 020 7930 9625
e-mail: windsorcastle@royalcollection.org.uk

Covering 13 acres, this is the official residence of HM The Queen and the largest inhabited castle in the world. Begun as a wooden fort by William the Conqueror, it has been added to by almost every monarch since. The Upper Ward includes the State Apartments, magnificently restored following the fire of 1992, and the Lower Ward where St George's Chapel is situated. The Doll's House designed for Queen Mary in the 1920s by Lutyens is also on display.

Times: Open all year, daily except Good Fri & 25-26 Dec. Nov-Feb, 9.45-4.15 (last admission 3), Mar-Oct 9.45-5.15 (last admission 4). As Windsor Castle is a royal residence the opening arrangements may be subject to change at short notice - 24hr info line - 01753 831118 **Fee:** ✱ £12 (ch 5-16 £6, under 5's free, pen & students £10) Family ticket £30 (2ad+3ch) **Facilities:** 🅿 (400yds) ♿ (ramps) toilets for disabled shop ✖ (ex guide dogs) ◀

BEACONSFIELD BEKONSCOT MODEL VILLAGE

Warwick Rd HP9 2PL
Dir: (M40 junct 2, 4m M25 junct 16) *Map Ref:* SU99
☎ 01494 672919 📄 01494 675284
e-mail: info@bekonscot.co.uk

Bekonscot Model Village depicts life in rural England in the 1930s on a miniature scale over a 1.5 acre site. It was created by Roland Callingham in 1929, since when it has raised £4 million for charity. A Gauge 1 model railway meanders through six little villages, each with their own tiny population. Rides on the sit-on miniature railway take place at weekends and during school holidays.

Times: Open mid Feb-Oct, 10-5. **Fee:** £5.30 (ch £3.20, concessions £4). **Facilities:** 🅿 ☕ ⴵ (wheelchair loan) toilets for disabled shop ✖ (ex guide dogs) 🚩

BLETCHLEY BLETCHLEY PARK

The Mansion, Bletchley Park MK3 6EB
Dir: (Approach Bletchley from V7 Saxon St. At rdbt, southern end of Saxon St. go under railway bridge towards Buckingham & follow signs to Bletchley Park) *Map Ref:* SP93
☎ 01908 640404 📄 01908 274381
e-mail: info@bletchleypark.org.uk

Known as 'Station X' during World War II, this was the home of the secret scientific team that worked to decipher German military messages sent using the Enigma code machine. Visitors can find out more about the Enigma machine; the 'bombes', computers used to crack the code; Alan Turing, one of the leading mathematicians of his day, who worked on the project; as well as see a number of other displays including the use of pigeons during the war, wartime vehicles, and a Churchill collection.

Times: Open daily 9.30-5.30 (Tours at 11 & 2). Weekends open 10.30-5. Closed 25 & 26 Dec. **Fee:** £10 (ch & concessions £8) Family £25 under 8's free. **Facilities:** 🅿 (charged) ☕ ✖ licensed ⴵ shop 🚩

CHALFONT ST GILES CHILTERN OPEN AIR MUSEUM

Newland Park, Gorelands Ln HP8 4AB
Dir: (M25 junct 17, M40 junct 2. Follow brown signs)
Map Ref: SU99
☎ 01494 871117 📄 01494 872774
e-mail: coamuseum@netscape.net

Saved from demolition and moved brick by brick to Newland Park, this collection of old buildings includes barns, granaries and even a tin chapel. Step back in time and get a feel of the 1940s in a fully furnished Prefab, or experience AD 50 at the Iron Age House. Demonstrations including brick making, rug making, blacksmithing and storytelling. Regular living history re-enactments are held.

Times: ✱ Open 31 Mar-Oct, daily 10-5. **Facilities:** 🅿 ☕ ⴵ (Braille guide books & taped guides available, wheelchairs) toilets for disabled shop ✖ (ex on lead) 🚩

QUAINTON   BUCKINGHAMSHIRE RAILWAY CENTRE

Quainton Rd Station HP22 4BY
Dir: (Signed off A41 Aylesbury-Bicester road at Waddesdon, 7m
NW of Aylesbury) *Map Ref:* SP72
☎ 01296 655720   📄 01296 655720
e-mail: bucksrailcentre@btopenworld.com

Housed in a Grade II listed building, the Centre features an interesting and varied collection of about 20 locomotives with 40 carriages and wagons from places as far afield as South Africa, Egypt and America. Items date from the 1800s up to the 1960s. Visitors can take a ride on full-size and miniature steam trains, and stroll around the 20-acre site to see locomotives and rolling stock. The Centre runs locomotive driving courses for visitors. Regular 'Days out with Thomas' events take place throughout the year.

Times: Open with engines in steam Apr-Oct, Sun & BH Mon; Jun-Aug, Wed; 10.30-5.30. Dec Sat & Sun Santa's Magical Steamings-advanced booking recommended. Also open for static viewing Wed-Sun. **Fee:** ✱ Steaming Days; £6 (ch & pen £4). Family ticket £18. BH wknds £7 (ch & pen £5). Family ticket £20. Static viewing £3 (ch & pen £2). **Facilities:** 🅿 🖥 ♿ (ramped bridge with wheelchair lift) toilets for disabled shop 🛒

WADDESDON   WADDESDON MANOR

HP18 0JH
Dir: (entrance off A41, 6m NW of Aylesbury) *Map Ref:* SP71
☎ 01296 653211, 653226 & 653203   📄 01296 653212
e-mail: suzy.barron@nationaltrust.org.uk

Waddesdon was built in the style of a French château of the 16th century and houses one of the finest collections of French 18th-century decorative arts in the world, including French furniture, Savronnerie carpets and Sèvres porcelain. There is also a collection of important portraits by Gainsborough and Reynolds, along with Dutch and Flemish masters of the 17th century. The garden is renowned for its seasonal displays, colourful shrubs, mature trees and parterre. There is a rococo-style aviary housing many exotic birds, a rose and children's garden.

Times: Open, Grounds & Aviary only, 3 Mar-Oct, Wed-Sun & BH Mon 10-5. House 31 Mar-Oct, Wed-Sun & BH Mon 11-4. Entrance by timed ticket. **Fee:** ✱ Grounds £4 (ch £2). Family £10. Group £3.20 each. House £7 (ch £6). Group £5.60 each. Tickets bookable in advance at booking charge (tel 01296 653226). **Facilities:** 🅿 ✕ licensed ♿ (wheelchairs, Braille guide, parking, scented plants) toilets for disabled shop 🐕 (ex guide dogs) 🦮 🛒

WEST WYCOMBE   THE HELL-FIRE CAVES

HP14 3AJ
Dir: (on A40 in West Wycombe) *Map Ref:* SU89
☎ 01494 524411 (office) & 533739 (caves)
📄 01494 471617
e-mail: mary@west-wycombe-estate.co.uk

The entrance to West Wycombe caves is halfway up the hill that dominates the village. On the summit stands the parish church and the mausoleum of the Dashwood family. The caves were dug on the orders of Sir Francis Dashwood between 1748 and 1752. He was Chancellor of the Exchequer and founder of the Hell Fire Club, whose members were reputed to have held outrageous parties in the caves, which extend approximately half a mile underground. At the entrance is a brick tunnel where tableaux and curiosities are exhibited.

Times: Open all year, Mar-Oct, daily 11-6; Nov-Feb, Sat & Sun 1-5. **Fee:** £4 (ch, pen & students £3). Family ticket £12 (max 3 ch) **Facilities:** 🅿 🖥 ♿ toilets for disabled shop 🐕 (ex guide dogs) 🛒

CAMBRIDGE *CAMBRIDGE & COUNTY FOLK MUSEUM*

2/3 Castle St CB3 0AQ
Dir: (off A14 onto A3019, museum NW of town) *Map Ref:* TL45
☎ 01223 355159
e-mail: info@folkmuseum.org.uk

This timber-framed building, formerly the White Horse Inn, houses items covering the everyday life of the people of Cambridgeshire from 1700 to the present day. It re-opens early in 2005 after a period of refurbishment. Please telephone for details of special exhibitions and children's activity days, which take place throughout the year.

Times: ✱ Open all year, Apr-Sep, Mon-Sat 10.30-5, Sun 2-5. Oct-Mar, Tue-Sat 10.30-5, Sun 2-5. (Last admissions 30 mins before closing). Closed 1 Jan, Good Fri, 24-31 Dec
Facilities: P (300yds) (pay and display on street parking) & (Braille touch tables, tape guides & large print guides) shop ✖ (ex guide dogs)

CAMBRIDGE UNIVERSITY BOTANIC GARDEN

Cory Lodge, Bateman St CB2 1JF
Dir: (1m S of city centre) *Map Ref:* TL45
☎ 01223 336265 ▤ 01223 336278
e-mail: enquiries@botanic.cam.ac.uk

The Cambridge University Botanic Garden is a 40-acre haven of beautifully landscaped gardens and glasshouses close to the heart of the historic city. Opened on its present site in 1846, the garden showcases a collection of some 8,000 plant species. This Grade II heritage landscape features the Rock Garden, with its alpine plants, the Winter and Autumn Gardens, tropical rainforest and seasonal displays in the Glasshouses, the historic Systematic Beds, the Scented Garden, herbaceous beds and the finest collection of trees in the east of England.

Times: Open all year daily 10-6 (summer), 10-5 (autumn & spring), (10-4) winter. Glasshouses 10-3.45. Closed 25 Dec-1 Jan. Entry by Bateman St & Station Rd gates on wkdays & by Bateman St gate only at wknds & BH. **Fee:** £3 (pen £2.50). **Facilities:** P (0.25km) (on street parking - pay & display) ☕ & (guiding service, manual & motorised wheelchairs-prebooked) toilets for disabled shop (open Mar-Oct) ✖ (ex guide dogs)

SCOTT POLAR RESEARCH INSTITUTE MUSEUM

Lensfield Rd CB2 1ER
Dir: (1km S of City Centre) *Map Ref:* TL45
☎ 01223 336540 ▤ 01223 336549   **FREE**
e-mail: rkh10@cam.ac.uk

An international centre for polar studies, including a museum featuring displays of Arctic and Antarctic expeditions, with special emphasis on those of Captain Scott. Other exhibits include Eskimo work and various arts of the polar regions, as well as displays on current scientific exploration. Public lectures run from October to December and February to April. Special exhibitions are a regular feature.

Times: Open all year, Tue-Sat 2.30-4. Closed some public & university hols.
Facilities: P (400mtrs) & shop ✖ (ex guide dogs)

DUXFORD IMPERIAL WAR MUSEUM DUXFORD

CB2 4QR
Dir: (off M11 junct 10, on A505) *Map Ref:* TL44
☎ 01223 835000 📄 01223 837267
e-mail: duxford@iwm.org.uk

Duxford is one of the world's most spectacular aviation heritage complexes with a collection of nearly 200 aircraft, the American Air Museum and a fine collection of military vehicles plus special exhibitions including The Battle of Britain, Normandy Experience and Monty. The Museum holds four Air Shows throughout the summer plus other special events such as the Military Vehicle Show.

Times: Open all year, mid Mar-mid Oct daily 10-6; mid Oct-mid Mar daily 10-4. (Closed 24-26 Dec) **Fee:** ✱ £8.50 (pen £6.50 & concessions £4.50). Ch under 16yrs free. Different rates apply for air shows. **Facilities:** 🅿 💺 ✗ licensed ♿ (wheelchair available-phone in advance) toilets for disabled shop ✖ (ex guide dogs) ▰

ELY ELY CATHEDRAL

CB7 4DL
Dir: (A10 or A142, 15m from Cambridge) *Map Ref:* TL58
☎ 01353 667735 📄 01353 665658
e-mail: receptionist@cathedral.ely.anglican.org

The Octagon Tower of Ely Cathedral can be seen for miles as it rises above the surrounding flat fenland. A monastery was founded on the site by St Etheldreda in 673, but the present cathedral church dates from 1083 and is a magnificent example of Romanesque architecture. Ely is a small place but the diocese of Ely covers some 1,500 square miles. Special events are held throughout the year, please telephone for details.

Times: Open daily, Summer 7-7, Winter 7.30-6 (5pm Sun). **Fee:** £4.80 (concessions £4.20). Ch free in family group. Group reductions (15+) **Facilities:** 🅿 (walking distance) 💺 ✗ licensed ♿ (touch tour for blind/partially sighted) toilets for disabled shop ✖ (ex guide dogs)

HAMERTON HAMERTON ZOO PARK

PE28 5RE
Dir: (off A1 junct 15, signed Sawtry) *Map Ref:* TL17
☎ 01832 293362 📄 01832 293677
e-mail: office@hamertonzoopark.com

Hamerton Zoo Park is a wildlife breeding centre, dedicated to the practical conservation of endangered species including gibbons, marmosets, lemurs, wildcats, meerkats, sloths and many more. There is also a large and varied bird collection, with several species unique to Hamerton, and over 120 species in all. Other attractions include a children's play area, and new 'creature contact' sessions.

Times: Open Summer daily 10.30-6; Winter daily 10.30-4. Closed 25 Dec **Facilities:** 🅿 💺 ♿ toilets for disabled shop ✖ ▰

LINTON LINTON ZOOLOGICAL GARDENS

Hadstock Rd CB1 6NT
Dir: (M11 junct 9/10, on B1052 off A1307 between Cambridge &
Haverhill, signposted) **Map Ref:** *TL54*
☎ **01223 891308** 📄 **01223 891308**

Linton Zoo places emphasis on conservation and education
where visitors can enjoy a combination of beautiful gardens and a
wealth of wildlife from all over the world. There are many rare
and exotic creatures to see including tapirs, snow leopards, tigers,
lions, Grevy's zebra, tamarin monkeys, lemurs, owls, parrots, giant
tortoises, snakes, tarantula spiders and many others. The zoo is
set in 16 acres of gardens with plenty of picnic areas, children's
play area and bouncy castle.

Times: Open daily 29 May-19 Sep 10-6; 20 Sep-30 Oct 10-5; 31
Oct-18 Mar 10.30-4, last admission 1 hr before closing. Closed 25-26
Dec. **Fee:** £6.50 (ch 2-13 £4.50) **Facilities:** 🅿 ☕ ♿ toilets for
disabled shop ✈ 🎦

PETERBOROUGH *FLAG FEN BRONZE AGE CENTRE*

The Droveway, Northey Rd PE6 7QJ
Map Ref: *TL19*
☎ **01733 313414** 📄 **01733 349957**
e-mail: office@flagfen.freeserve.co.uk

Although visitors enter this site through a 21st-century
roundhouse, the rest of their day will be spent in the Bronze Age,
some 3,000 years ago. Flag Fen is one of Europe's most
important Bronze Age sites, and contains reconstructions of Iron
Age as well as Bronze Age roundhouses. There is also a museum
of artefacts found on the site over the last 20 years, as well as a
Preservation Hall that contains a 60-foot mural depicting the fens
in ancient times.

Times: ✱ Open daily 10-4 (last admission). Site
closes 5pm. (Closed 24 Dec-2 Jan)
Facilities: 🅿 ☕ ♿ toilets for disabled shop
✈ (ex assistance dogs) 🎦

RAILWORLD

Oundle Rd PE2 9NR
Dir: (from A1(M) Peterborough, turn onto A1139 then off at junct
5 to city centre. At 1st rdbt, follow tourist signs for "Little Putter".
Entrance for Railworld is off Oundle Rd at city end through car
park) **Map Ref:** *TL19*
☎ **01733 344240**

Railworld is themed around modern international rail travel, with
a focus on environmental issues and the need for an integrated
system of transport. There are also sections for the town's railway
history, the era of steam, hand-on exhibits and a large model
railway. Outside exhibits include the unique RTV31, a Danish
Pacific 144-ton steam compound locomotive, and a pioneer USA
Alco Diesel Switcher, set amid pleasant gardens with a picnic
area.

Times: Mar-Oct daily 11-4, Nov-Feb Mon-Fri 11-4
Fee: £4 (ch £2, concessions £3) Family £10
Facilities: 🅿 ☕ ♿ (reasonable access) toilets
for disabled shop (ex guide dogs)

Cambridgeshire continued

WANSFORD   *NENE VALLEY RAILWAY*

Wansford Station, Stibbington PE8 6LR
Dir: (A1 at Stibbington, W of Peterborough, 1m S of A47 junct)
Map Ref: *TL09*
☎ **01780 784444** 📄 **01780 784440**
e-mail: nvrorg@aol.com

Visit Britain's International Steam Railway and see steam and
diesel engines, carriages and wagons from Europe including the
UK. All the sights and sounds of the golden age of steam come
alive here. Travelling between Yarwell Junction, Wansford and
Peterborough the 7.5 miles of track pass through the heart of the
500-acre Ferry Meadows Country Park. Nene Valley Railway is also
the home of Thomas - children's favourite engine.

Times: ✳ Train services operate on Sun from Jan; wknds from
Apr-Oct; Wed from May, plus other mid-week services in summer.
Facilities: 🅿 💺 ♿ (disabled access to trains) toilets for disabled
shop 🍴

WATERBEACH   *THE FARMLAND MUSEUM AND DENNY ABBEY*

Ely Rd CB5 9PQ
Dir: (on A10 between Cambridge and Ely) **Map Ref:** *TL46*
☎ **01223 860988** 📄 **01223 860988**
e-mail: f.m.denny@tesco.net

Explore two areas of rural life at this fascinating museum. The
Abbey tells the story of those who have lived there, including
Benedictine monks, Franciscan nuns, and the mysterious Knights
Templar. The farm museum features the craft workshops of a
wheelwright, a basketmaker and a blacksmith. Also on site are a
1940's farmworker's cottage and a village shop.

Times: Open daily Apr-Oct, noon-5pm
Fee: ✳ £3.80 (concessions £2.90, ch £1.60)
Facilities: 🅿 💺 ♿ toilets for disabled shop

CASTLE HEDINGHAM   *COLNE VALLEY RAILWAY & MUSEUM*

Castle Hedingham Station CO9 3DZ
Dir: (4m NW of Halstead on A1017) **Map Ref:** *TL73*
☎ **01787 461174**

Many former Colne Valley and Halstead railway buildings have
been rebuilt here. Stock includes seven steam locomotives plus
80 other engines, carriages and wagons, in steam from Easter to
October. Visitors can dine in style in restored Pullman carriages
while travelling along the line. Please telephone for a free
timetable and details of the many special events.

Times: Open all year, daily 10-dusk. Steam days,
rides from 12-4. Closed 23 Dec-1 Feb. Steam
days every Sun and BH from Mothering Sunday to
end Oct, Wed of school summer hols & special
events. Railway Farm Park open May-Sep. Phone
01787 461174 for timetable information or visit
website. **Fee:** Steam days: £6 (ch £3, pen £5)
Family ticket £18. Diesel days £5 (ch £2.50);
Family ticket £15. **Facilities:** 🅿 💺 ✗ licensed
♿ (ramps for wheelchairs to get onto carriages)
shop 🐕 (ex guide dogs) 🍴

COLCHESTER   COLCHESTER CASTLE MUSEUM

Castle Park, High St CO1 1TJ
Dir: (at E end of High St)   **Map Ref:** *TL92*
☎ **01206 282939** 🖷 **01206 282925**

The largest Norman castle keep in Europe - built over the remains of the magnificent Roman Temple of Claudius which was destroyed by Boudicca in AD60. Colchester was the first capital of Roman Britain, and the archaeological collections are among the finest in the country. Please telephone for details of a range of events held throughout the year.

Times: Open all year, Mon-Sat 10-5, Sun 11-5. Closed Xmas/New Year **Fee:** ✱ £4.50 (ch & concessions £2.90, under 5's free) **Facilities:** 🅿 (town centre) ♿ (all parts accessible except vaults/roof tour) toilets for disabled shop ✖ (ex guide dogs) 🍽

COLCHESTER ZOO

Stanway, Maldon Rd CO3 0SL
Dir: (turn off A12 onto A1124 and follow elephant signs)
Map Ref: *TL92*
☎ **01206 331292** 🖷 **01206 331392**
e-mail: enquiries@colchester-zoo.co.uk

One of England's finest zoos, Colchester Zoo has over 200 types of animals. Visitors can meet the elephants, handle a snake, and see parrots, seals, penguins and birds of prey all appearing in informative daily displays. New enclosures include Spirit of Africa, Elephant Kingdom, Penguin Shores, the Wilds of Asia for orang-utans, and Chimp World. There is also an undercover soft play complex, road train, four adventure play areas, eating places and gift shops, all set in 40 acres of gardens. The new PlayaPatagonia Sealion experience features a 2-metre underwater tunnel

Times: Open all year, daily from 9.30. Last admission 5.30 (1hr before dusk out of season). Closed 25 Dec. **Fee:** ✱ £11.99 (ch 3-14 £6.99, disabled £4.99, pen £ 8.99). **Facilities:** 🅿 🍽 ✖ licensed ♿ (easy route developed, but zoo has hills) toilets for disabled shop garden centre ✖ 🍽

NEWPORT   MOLE HALL WILDLIFE PARK

Widdington CB11 3SS
Dir: (M11 junct 8. Situated between Stansted & Saffron Walden, off B1383) **Map Ref:** *TL53*
☎ **01799 540400 & 541359** 🖷 **01799 542408**
e-mail: enquiries@molehall.co.uk

The 20-acre park has been lovingly developed by the Johnstone family over 40 years, and a wide variety of animals includes South American guanaco, red squirrels, serval cats and the Formosan sika deer, which is extinct in the wild. Mole Hall is also home to two species of otter, being the first regular breeders in the UK of the North American Otter. Other residents include chimpanzees, capuchins and lemurs. There is also a tropical butterfly pavilion, with tarantulas, snakes, leaf-eating ants, pools of aquatic life, small monkeys, tortoises and lovebirds.

Times: ✱ Open all year, daily 10.30-6 (or dusk). Closed 25 Dec. Butterfly House open mid Mar-Oct. **Facilities:** 🅿 🍽 ♿ (Difficult in wet weather for wheelchairs) toilets for disabled shop garden centre ✖ (ex guide dogs) 🍽

SOUTHEND-ON-SEA Southend Museum, Planetarium & Discovery Centre

Victoria Av SS2 6ES
Dir: (take A127 or A13 towards town centre. Museum is adjacent to Southend Victoria Railway Station) ***Map Ref:*** *TQ88*
☎ 01702 434449 🖹 01702 349806
e-mail: southendmuseum@hotmail.com

Southend's Central Museum is housed in the town's first free public library, a fine Edwardian building. It exhibits collections of archaeology, natural history and local history, and tells the human history of the south-east Essex area. It also has the only planetarium in the South East outside London. Ring for details of special events.

Times: Open Central Museum: Tue-Sat 10-5 (Closed Sun-Mon & BH); Planetarium: Wed-Sat, shows at 11, 2 & 4. **Fee:** Central Museum free. Planetarium £2.40 (ch & pen £1.70). Family tickets £7.50 Party rates on request. **Facilities:** P (50mtrs) (disabled only behind museum) ♿ (planetarium not accessible, disabled access to centre) shop (ex guide dogs)

STANSTED House on the Hill Museum Adventure

CM24 8SP
Dir: (off B1383 in the centre of Stansted Mountfitchet)
Map Ref: *TL52*
☎ 01279 813567 🖹 01279 816391
e-mail: mountfitchetcastle1066@btinternet.com

A large, privately-owned toy museum, housed on two floors covering 7,000 square feet. It shows a huge variety of toys, books and games from the late Victorian period up to the 1970s. There is a space display, Teddy Bears' picnic, Action Man, Sindy, Barbie, military displays and much more. Additional displays of film, theatre and television memorabilia are on show, plus end of the pier slot machines.

Times: Open daily, 10-5; (closed for a few days over the Xmas period & Mon in Jan & Feb) **Fee:** * £3.80 (ch under 14 £3, pen £3.50). Party 15+. **Facilities:** P (charged) shop (ex guide dogs)

Mountfitchet Castle & Norman Village

CM24 8SP
Dir: (off B1383, in centre of village. 5 min from M11 junct 8)
Map Ref: *TL52*
☎ 01279 813237 🖹 01279 816391
e-mail: mountfitchetcastle1066@btinternet.com

Mountfitchet is a Norman motte and bailey castle and village reconstructed as it was in the England of 1066, on its original historic site. A vivid illustration of village life in Domesday England, complete with houses, church, seige tower, seige weapons, and many types of animals roaming freely. Animated wax figures in all the buildings give historical information to visitors.

Times: Open daily, 13 Mar-13 Nov, 10-5. **Fee:** * £6 (ch under 2 free, ch 2-14 £5, pen £5.50). **Facilities:** P (charged) ♿ (laser commentaries) toilets for disabled shop (ex guide dogs)

WALTHAM ABBEY LEE VALLEY PARK FARMS

Stubbins Hall Ln, Crooked Mile EN9 2EG
Dir: (M25 junct 26, follow to Waltham Abbey. 2m from Waltham Abbey on B914) *Map Ref:* TL30
☎ **01992 892781 & 892291** 📄 **01992 892291**
e-mail: hayeshill@leevalleypark.com

Set in the heart of Lee Valley Country Park, Hayes Hill Farm offers young and old the chance to view many types of farm animals. Meet a variety of rare breeds in the traditional-style farmyard, and in the pet centre, see many other creatures from meerkats to chipmunks. During summer, there are tractor and trailer rides to Holyfield Hall, a 700-acre working dairy and arable farm.

Times: Open all year, Mon-Fri 10-4.30, wknds & BHs 10-5.30. **Fee:** £4 (ch 3+ £3, concessions £3.50). Family (2ad+3ch) £16 **Facilities:** P 🍽 🚾 (graded concrete paths, signed routes) toilets for disabled shop 🛍

ROYAL GUNPOWDER MILLS

Beaulieu Dr EN9 1JY
Dir: (M25 junct 26. Follow signs for A121 to Waltham Abbey at rdbt, entrance in Beaulieu Drive) *Map Ref:* TL30
☎ **01992 707370** 📄 **01992 707372**
e-mail: info@royalgunpowdermills.com

Set in 175 acres of parkland, this amazing scientific complex has 21 buildings of historical importance. Before it closed in 1991 this was the site of major scientific research and development, including work on Congreve's Rocket in the early 19th century, up to more recent work on ejector seats and fuel for rocket motors. Explosives were made in many of the buildings on the site which are connected by five miles of navigational canals.

Times: Open 30 Apr-25 Sep, 11-5, last entry at 3.30. (Wknds and BHs only) **Fee:** £5.50 (ch £3, concessions £4.70, under 5's free) Family £17 **Facilities:** P 🍽 🚾 (ramps, lift, tactile with audio tour) toilets for disabled shop ✈ (ex guide dogs) 🛍

FOREST GERMAN OCCUPATION MUSEUM

GY8 0BG
Dir: (Behind Forest Church near the airport)
☎ **01481 238205**

The museum has the Channel Islands' largest collection of items relating to the five-year occupation by the Germans during World War II. Displays, audio-visual presentations and tableaux of a period kitchen, bunker rooms and a street show what life was like for the islanders during the occupation. Liberation Day, 9 May, is celebrated with special events and exhibitions.

Times: Open Apr-Oct 10-5, Nov-Mar 10-1 (Closed Mon). **Facilities:** P 🍽 🚾 (ramps & handrails)

ROCQUAINE BAY FORT GREY AND SHIPWRECK MUSEUM

GY7 9BY
Dir: (on coast road at Rocquaine Bay)
☎ **01481 265036** 📄 **01481 263279**
e-mail: admin@museums.gov.gg

The fort is a Martello tower, built in 1804, as part of the Channel Islands' extensive defences. It is nicknamed the 'cup and saucer' because of its appearance, and houses a museum devoted to ships wrecked on the treacherous Hanois reefs nearby, including a display of salvaged artefacts and related illustrations.

Times: Open Apr-Sep, 10-5 **Fee:** ✳ Fort Grey, £2.50 (pen £1.25), 3 Venue Ticket £9 (pen £5) **Facilities:** P (opposite fort) shop ✈ (ex guide dogs) ◀

ST ANDREW GERMAN MILITARY UNDERGROUND HOSPITAL & AMMUNITION STORE

La Vassalerie GY6 8XR
Dir: (St Andrews Parish, centre of island)
☎ **01481 239100**

The largest structure created during the German occupation of the Channel Islands, a concrete maze of about 75,000 square feet, which took slave workers three-and-a-half years to complete, at the cost of many lives. Most of the equipment has been removed, but the central heating plant, hospital beds and cooking facilities can still be seen.

Times: Open Jul-Aug, daily 10-noon & 2-4.30; May-Jun & Sep, daily 10-noon & 2-4; Apr & Oct, daily 2-4; Mar & Nov, Sun & Thu 2-3. **Fee:** ✳ £3 (ch £1). **Facilities:** P ♿ shop

ST PETER PORT CASTLE CORNET

GY1 UG
Dir: (0.5m from town centre)
☎ **01481 721657** 📄 **01481 715177**
e-mail: admin@museums.gov.gg

The history of this magnificent castle spans eight centuries and its buildings now house several museums, the Refectory Café and a shop. Soldiers fire the noonday gun in a daily ceremony. Look for the Maritime Museum that charts Guernsey's nautical history, the 'Story of Castle Cornet' with its mystery skeleton and special exhibitions in the Royal Guernsey Militia Museum and the 201 squadron RAF Museum.

Times: Open Apr-Sep, daily 10-5. **Fee:** ✳ £6 (pen £4). 3 venue ticket £9 (pen £5) **Facilities:** P (100 yds) ☕ shop ✈ (ex guide dogs) ◀

ALDERSHOT   AIRBORNE FORCES MUSEUM

Browning Barracks, Queens Av GU11 2BU
Dir: (M3 take A325 to Aldershot then next left)   **Map Ref:** SU85
☎ **01252 349619** 📠 **01252 349203**
e-mail: airborneforcesmuseum@army.mod.uk.net

The Airborne Forces Museum traces the history of the Parachute Regiment and British Airborne Forces since 1940. Using weapons, equipment, dioramas and briefing models, it depicts the story of airborne actions such as the early raids, D-Day, Arnhem, the Rhine Crossing, and post-war campaigns such as Suez, the Falklands and Kosovo.

Times: Open all year, Mon-Fri 10-4.30 (last admission 3.45), Sat-Sun & BH 10-4. Closed Xmas. **Fee:** ✱ £3 (ch, pen & former members of the Regiment £1, under 5's free)
Facilities: 🅿 & (wheelchair ramps) shop ✖ (ex guide dogs)

AMPFIELD   THE SIR HAROLD HILLIER GARDENS & ARBORETUM

Jermyns Ln SO51 OQA
Dir: (3m NE of Romsey, signed off A3090 & B3057)
Map Ref: SU42
☎ **01794 368787** 📠 **01794 368027**

Established in 1953, this 180-acre public garden comprises the greatest collection of hardy trees and shrubs in the world. It is a garden for all seasons with a stunning range of seasonal colour and interest, featuring eleven national plant collections. You can also see champion trees, the Gurkha Memorial Garden and the largest winter garden in Europe.

Times: ✱ Open all year, Apr-Oct wkdays 10.30-6, wknds & Bl ls 9.30-6. Nov-Mar daily 10.30-5 or dusk if earlier. Closed Xmas.
Facilities: 🅿 ✖ licensed & (all ability path) toilets for disabled garden centre ✖ (ex guide dogs)

ANDOVER   FINKLEY DOWN FARM PARK

SP11 6NF
Dir: (signed from A303 & A343, 1.5m N of A303 & 2m E of Andover)   **Map Ref:** SU34
☎ **01264 352195** 📠 **01264 363172**
e-mail: admin@finkleydownfarm.co.uk

This fun family farm park is jam packed with things to do. You can join in with feeding time, groom a pony, cuddle a rabbit, or collect duck eggs. Lots of activities are scheduled throughout the day, or kids can just let off steam in the playground or on the trampolines. From chipmunks to chinchillas, pygmy goats to peacocks, and lambs to llamas, Finkley Down Farm has something for everyone!

Times: Open mid Mar-Oct, daily 10-6. Last admission 5.
Fee: ✱ £4.75 (ch £3.75, pen £4.25). Family ticket £16 (2ad+2ch).
Facilities: 🅿 🍽 & toilets for disabled shop ✖ (ex guide dogs) 🖥

ASHURST LONGDOWN DAIRY FARM

Longdown SO40 7EH
Dir: (off A35 between Lyndhurst & Southampton)
Map Ref: SU31
☎ 023 8029 3326 📄 023 8029 3376
e-mail: enquiries@longdownfarm.co.uk

Fun for all the family with a variety of hands-on activities every day, including small animal handling and pony grooming. There are indoor and outdoor play areas, with trampolines and ball pools, and while adults can have a go at Land Rover driving, children can take out the pedal tractors. Facilities also include a tearoom, picnic area and excellent gift shop.

Times: Open Feb-Dec, daily 10-5. **Fee:** ✱ £5 (ch 3-14 & pen £4.25). Saver ticket £17.50 (2ad+2ch). **Facilities:** P ☕ & (concrete path for wheelchairs) toilets for disabled shop ✖ (kennels provided) ◀

BASINGSTOKE MILESTONES - HAMPSHIRE'S LIVING HISTORY MUSEUM

Basingstoke Leisure Park, Churchill Way West RG21 6YR
Dir: (M3 junct 6, take ringway road (West) follow brown signs for Leisure Park) *Map Ref:* SU65
☎ 01256 477766 📄 01256 477784
e-mail: jane.holmes@hants.gov.uk

Milestones brings Hampshire's recent past to life through stunning period street scenes and exciting interactive areas, all under one enormous roof. Nationally important collections of transport, technology and everyday life are engagingly presented. Staff in period costumes, mannequins and a free audio guide narrated by Rory Bremner enrich the experience.

Times: Open Tue-Fri & BHs 10-5, Sat-Sun 11-5. Closed 25-26 Dec & 1 Jan. **Fee:** £6.50 (ch £3.50, concessions £5.75). Family ticket (2ad+2ch) £16.50. Group discounts 15+ (may be subject to change) **Facilities:** P ☕ & (induction loops, subtitles screens, scooters, wheelchairs) toilets for disabled shop ✖ (ex guide dogs) ◀

BEAULIEU BEAULIEU : NATIONAL MOTOR MUSEUM

SO42 7ZN
Dir: (M27 junct 2, A326, B3054, then follow tourist signs)
Map Ref: SU30
☎ 01590 612345 📄 01590 612624
e-mail: info@beaulieu.co.uk

In the heart of William the Conqueror's New Forest, on the banks of the Beaulieu River, stands this 16th-century house. It is now best known as the home of the National Motor Museum. Also on site are the picturesque abbey ruins, where an exhibition on life in the middle ages is shown along with Montagu family treasures and memorabilia. The Abbey recently celebrated the 800th anniversary of its founding with a special audio visual presentation.

Times: Open all year - Palace House & Gardens, National Motor Museum, Beaulieu Abbey & Exhibition of Monastic Life, May-Sep 10-6; Oct-Apr 10-5. Closed 25 Dec. **Fee:** ✱ £15 (ch 5-12 £7.50, 12-17 £8.50, pen £13.50). Family ticket £42. **Facilities:** P ☕ & (ramp access, lift to upper level, induction loop) toilets for disabled shop ◀

BREAMORE BREAMORE HOUSE & COUNTRYSIDE

SP6 2DF
Dir: (turn off A338, between Salisbury & Fordingbridge and follow signs for 1m) **Map Ref:** *SU11*
☎ **01725 512468** 📠 **01725 512858**
e-mail: breamore@ukonline.co.uk

The handsome manor house was completed in around 1583 and has a fine collection of paintings, china and tapestries. The museum has good examples of steam engines, and uses reconstructed workshops and other displays to show how people lived and worked a century or so ago. There is also a children's playground.

Times: Open Apr, Tue, Sun & Etr, May-Jul & Sep, Tue-Thu & Sat, Sun & all BH, Aug, daily 2-5.30 (Countryside Museum 1pm). **Fee:** £6 (ch £4). Party £5 each. **Facilities:** 🅿 ☕ ♿ (ramps, parking, recorded message & book about 2nd floor) toilets for disabled shop ✖ (ex guide dogs)

BUCKLER'S HARD BUCKLER'S HARD VILLAGE & MARITIME MUSEUM

SO42 7XB
Dir: (M27 junct 2, A326, B3054 then follow tourist signs to Beaulieu & Buckler's Hard) **Map Ref:** *SU40*
☎ **01590 616203** 📠 **01590 612624**
e-mail: info@bucklershard.co.uk

An enticing port of call, the picturesque shipbuilding village of Buckler's Hard is where ships from Nelson's fleet were built. After setting a course for the Buckler's Hard Story and authentically reconstructed 18th-century cottages, savour the sight and sounds of the countryside on a ramble along the Riverside Walk or enjoy a cruise in 'Swiftsure' on the Beaulieu River during the summer months.

Times: Open all year, Etr-Sep 10.30-5, winter 11-4. Closed 25 Dec. **Fee:** ✱ £5.25 (ch £3.75, pen £4.75). Family £16 **Facilities:** 🅿 ☕ ✖ licensed ♿ toilets for disabled shop ◧

EXBURY EXBURY GARDENS & RAILWAY

Exbury Estate Office SO45 1AZ
Dir: (from M27 W junct 2, 3m from Beaulieu, off B3054)
Map Ref: *SU40*
☎ **023 8089 1203** 📠 **023 8089 9940**

A 200-acre landscaped woodland garden on the east bank of the Beaulieu River, with one of the finest collections of rhododendrons, azaleas, camellias and magnolias in the world, as well as many rare and beautiful shrubs and trees. A labyrinth of tracks and paths enables you to explore the beautiful gardens and walks. Year round interest is ensured in various parts of the gardens and the steam railway has several features.

Times: Open 28 Feb-Oct, daily 10-5.30; Santa Steam Specials 11,12,18-21 Dec **Fee:** ✱ £4-£6 (ch under 5 free, ch 5-15 £1-£1.50, pen £3.50-£5.50, £5 Tue-Thu). Railway £2-£2.50. **Facilities:** 🅿 ✖ licensed ♿ (free wheelchair loans & access maps, buggy tours £3) toilets for disabled shop garden centre ◧

FAREHAM ROYAL ARMOURIES FORT NELSON

Downend Rd PO17 6AN
Dir: (from M27 junct 11, follow brown tourist signs for Royal
Armouries) *Map Ref:* SU50
☎ 01329 233734 ▤ 01329 822092
e-mail: fnenquiries@armouries.org.uk

FREE

Superbly restored 19-acre Victorian fort overlooking Portsmouth
Harbour providing visitors with spectacular views. It was built in
the 1860s to deter a threatened French invasion, and there are
secret tunnels, underground chambers and grass ramparts to
explore. Fort Nelson is home to the Royal Armouries' collection of
artillery, part of the National Museum of Arms and Armour, with
over 350 pieces from the Roman era to the infamous Iraqi
supergun.

Times: Open all year, daily. Closed 25-26 Dec.
Facilities: 🅿 ☕ ♿ (access & audio guide,
ramps, induction loop, wheelchair) toilets for
disabled shop ✖ (ex guide & hearing dogs) ◧

GOSPORT EXPLOSION! MUSEUM OF NAVAL FIREPOWER

Priddy's Hard PO12 4LE
Dir: (A32 and follow signs) *Map Ref:* SZ69
☎ 023 9250 5600 ▤ 023 9250 5605
e-mail: info@explosion.org.uk

Explosion! is set in the green Heritage Area of Priddy's Hard in
Gosport, on the shores of Portsmouth Harbour. It tells the story of
naval firepower from the days of gunpowder to modern missiles.
Come face to face with the atom bomb, the Exocet missile and
the Gatling Gun and find out about the men and women who
supplied the Royal Navy. Walk around the buildings that were a
state secret for 200 years and discover the Grand Magazine, an
amazing vault once packed full with gunpowder, now a stunning
multimedia film show.

Times: Open all year, Apr-Oct & all school hols,
daily 10-5.30; Nov-Mar, Thu, Sat & Sun 10-4.30.
Closed 24-26 Dec. **Fee:** ✱ £5 (ch £3.50, pen
£4.50). Family ticket £15 **Facilities:** 🅿 ☕
♿ toilets for disabled shop ✖ (ex guide dogs) ◧

ROYAL NAVY SUBMARINE MUSEUM & HMS ALLIANCE

Haslar Jetty Rd PO12 2AS
Dir: (M27 junct 11, follow signs for Submarine Museum)
Map Ref: SZ69
☎ 023 9252 9217 & 9251 0354 ▤ 023 9251 1349
e-mail: rnsubs@rnsubmus.co.uk

The great attraction of this museum is the chance to see inside a
submarine, and there are guided tours of 'HMS Alliance' as well
as displays exploring the development of submarines. Two
periscopes from 'HMS Conqueror' can be seen in the
reconstruction of a nuclear submarine control room, giving
panoramic views of Portsmouth Harbour. A new gallery shows the
development of submarine weapons from the tiny topedo to the
huge polaris nuclear missile. The navy's first submarine is back on
display in a new gallery and exhibition space.

Times: ✱ Open all year, Apr-Oct 10-5.30;
Nov-Mar 10-4.30. Closed 24 Dec-1 Jan. (Allow 3
hrs for visit. Last tour 1 hour before closing).
Facilities: 🅿 ☕ ♿ (information in Braille, lift to
upper gallery) toilets for disabled shop
✖ (ex guide dogs) ◧

HAVANT   STAUNTON COUNTRY PARK

Middle Park Way PO9 5HB
Dir: (off B2149, between Havant & Horndean) *Map Ref:* SU70
☎ 023 9245 3405   📄 023 9249 8156
e-mail: amanda.fallbrown@hants.gov.uk

This colourful Victorian Park offers a wonderful range of attractions for all age groups. Meet and feed the friendly animals at the Ornamental Farm where there is a broad range of animals from llama and shire horses to pigs and pigmy goats. Explore the Victorian tropical glasshouses with exotic flowers from around the world, including the giant Amazonian waterlily (summer months only). Also in the 1,000 acres of parkland are hidden follies to explore and an ornamental lake available for angling.

Times: Open 10-5 (4 winter). **Fee:** £4.50 (ch £3.30, pen £4). **Facilities:** 🅿 🍴 ✗ ♿ (wheelchair for visitors, most areas accessible) toilets for disabled shop ✗ (dogs in parkland only) 🔳

HIGHCLERE   *HIGHCLERE CASTLE & GARDENS*

RG20 9RN
Dir: (4.5m S of Newbury, off A34) *Map Ref:* SU45
☎ 01635 253210   📄 01635 255315
e-mail: theoffice@highclerecastle.co.uk

This splendid early Victorian mansion stands amid beautiful parkland. It has sumptuous interiors and numerous Old Master paintings. It has been in the same family since the late 17th century and the present Lord and Lady Carnarvon are very much involved in all the events that take place in their home. Also shown are early finds by the 5th Earl of Carnarvon, one of the discoverers of Tutankhamun's tomb.

Times: ✱ Open Jul-Aug (may occasionally be subject to closure during this period), Tue-Fri & Sun 11-5 (last admission 4); Sat 11-3.30 (last admission 2.30). Also open BH 25-26 May & 25 Aug. Closed 5 Jul. **Facilities:** 🅿 🍴 ✗ licensed ♿ (wheelchair available) toilets for disabled shop ✗ (ex guide dogs) 🔳

HURST CASTLE   HURST CASTLE

SO4 0FF
Dir: (on Pebble Spit S of Keyhaven) *Map Ref:* SZ38
☎ 01590 642344

Built by Henry VIII in 1544, Hurst Castle crouches menacingly on a shingle spit that extends 1.5 miles from the coast, the ideal spot for defending the western approach to the Solent. Indeed the castle was the pride of Tudor England's coastal defences. It has a fascinating history: Charles I was imprisoned in the castle in 1648 before his execution in London, and it was involved in the smuggling trade during the 17th and 18th centuries.

Times: Open Apr-Oct, daily 10.30-5. **Fee:** ✱ £3 (ch £1.80, concessions £2.70). Prices & opening times relate to 2004, for further details phone or log onto www.english-heritage.org.uk/visits
Facilities: 🍴 ✗ (ex on lead in certain areas) ⊞

LIPHOOK *BOHUNT MANOR*

GU30 7DL
Dir: (on old A3 opposite junct) *Map Ref:* SU83
☎ 01428 727936 📄 01428 727936
e-mail: eddie@bohuntmanor.freeserve.co.uk

Bohunt includes woodland gardens with a lakeside walk, a water garden, roses, tulips and herbaceous borders. There is also a collection of ornamental ducks, white swans and geese. Several unusual trees and shrubs include a handkerchief tree and a Judas tree. The property has been given to the Worldwide Fund for Nature.

Times: ✱ Open all year, daily 10-5.
Facilities: 🅿 ♿ garden centre ✖ (ex guide dogs)

HOLLYCOMBE STEAM COLLECTION

Iron Hill, Midhurst Rd GU30 7LP
Dir: (1m SE Liphook on Midhurst road, follow brown tourist signs) *Map Ref:* SU83
☎ 01428 724900 📄 01428 723682
e-mail: info@hollycombe.co.uk

The comprehensive collection of working steam-power at Hollycombe includes a large Edwardian fairground, three railways - one with spectacular views of the South Downs - traction engine hauled rides, steam agricultural machinery, a sawmill and even a paddle steamer engine. The pets' corner is an additional attraction.

Times: Open Etr-9 Oct, Sun & BHs; 1-29 Aug, daily 12-5
Fee: ✱ £8.50 (ch 3-15 & pen £7). **Facilities:** 🅿 💳 ♿ toilets for disabled shop 🛍

LYNDHURST *NEW FOREST MUSEUM & VISITOR CENTRE*

Main Car Park, High St SO43 7NY
Dir: (leave M27 at Cadnam & follow A337 to Lyndhurst. Museum signed) *Map Ref:* SU30
☎ 023 8028 3444 📄 023 8028 4236
e-mail: office@newforestmuseum.org.uk

The story of the New Forest - history, traditions, character and wildlife - is told through an audio-visual show, computer interactives and exhibition displays at this museum and visitor centre, which is owned and ruin by an independent charity. Exhibits include life-size models of forest characters, and the famous 25-foot-long New Forest embroidery. The Christopher Tower New Forest Reference Library is also accommodated here. This is the most comprehensive collection of New Forest material anywhere.

Times: Open daily, from 10. Closed 25 & 26 Dec.
Facilities: 🅿 ♿ toilets for disabled shop 🛍

MARWELL MARWELL ZOOLOGICAL PARK

Colden Common SO21 1JH
Dir: (M3 junct 11 or M27 junct 5. Zoo on B2177, follow brown tourist signs) **Map Ref:** SU52
☎ **01962 777407** 🖨 **01962 777511**
e-mail: marwell@marwell.org.uk

Marwell has over 200 species of rare and wonderful animals including tigers, snow leopards, rhino, meerkats, hippo and zebra. Highlights include The World of Lemurs, Encounter Village with unusual domesticated animals, Tropical World with its rainforest environment, Into Africa for giraffes and monkeys, Penguin World and Desert Carnivores. New additions include an exciting leopard enclosure. Marwell is dedicated to saving endangered species and every visit helps this conservation work. With road and rail trains, holiday activities, restaurant, gift shops and adventure playgrounds Marwell provides fun and interest for all ages.

Times: Open all year, daily, 10-6 (in summer), 10-4 (in winter). (Last admission 90 min before closing). Closed 25 Dec. **Fee:** ✱ £11.50 (ch £8, pen £9.50). Family ticket (2ad+2ch) £37.50.
Facilities: 🅿 💺 ✕ ♿ (wheelchairs & tours for visually impaired/disabled groups) toilets for disabled shop ✈ 🛍

MIDDLE WALLOP MUSEUM OF ARMY FLYING & EXPLORERS WORLD

SO20 8DY
Dir: (on A343, between Andover & Salisbury) **Map Ref:** SU23
☎ **01980 674421** 🖨 **01264 781694**
e-mail: enquiries@flying-museum.org.uk

One of the country's finest historical collections of military kites, gliders, aeroplanes and helicopters. Imaginative dioramas and displays trace the development of Army flying from before the First World War to more recent conflicts in Ireland, the Falklands and the Gulf. Sit at the controls of a real Scout helicopter and test your skills on the helicopter flight simulator, plus children's science and education centre.

Times: Open all year, daily 10-4.30. Closed week prior to Xmas. Evening visits by special arrangement. **Fee:** ✱ £5 (ch £3.50, pen & student £4) Family £15. Party 10+.
Facilities: 🅿 💺 ✕ licensed ♿ (lifts to upper levels) toilets for disabled shop 🛍

MOTTISFONT MOTTISFONT ABBEY GARDEN

SO51 0LP
Dir: (4.5m NW Romsey, 1m W of A3057) **Map Ref:** SU32
☎ **01794 340757** 🖨 **01794 341492**
e-mail: mottisfontabbey@nationaltrust.org.uk

In a picturesque setting by the River Test, Mottisfont Abbey is an 18th-century house adapted from a 12th-century priory. The garden has the national collection of old-fashioned roses. The estate includes Mottisfont village.

Times: Open Garden 5 Feb-20 Mar 11-4. Garden & House: 21 Mar-1 Jun, Sat-Wed 11-6; 5-27 Jun daily from 11-6 (garden to 8.30); 28 Jun-31 Aug, Sat-Thu 11-6; Sep-Oct, Sat-Wed 11-6. (Last admission to grounds 1hr before closing). **Fee:** £7 (ch £3.50) Family ticket £17.50
Facilities: 🅿 💺 ✕ licensed ♿ (Braille guide, wheelchair available, driven buggy) toilets for disabled shop closed 5 Feb-20 Mar garden centre ✈ (ex guide dogs) 🐾 🛍

NEW ALRESFORD WATERCRESS LINE

The Railway Station SO24 9JG
Dir: (stations at Alton & Alresford signed off A31, follow brown tourist signs) **Map Ref:** *SU53*
☎ **01962 733810** 🖷 **01962 735448**
e-mail: info@watercressline.co.uk

The Watercress Line is a heritage steam railway, operated by volunteers, running through ten miles of rolling countryside between Alton and Alresford. All four stations on the line are 'dressed' in period style, and there's a locomotive yard and picnic area at Ropley. Real ale, dining train and seasonal events are held throughout the year.

Times: Open May-Sep Tue-Thu & wknds; Jan-Apr & Oct wknds only.
Fee: ✱ Unlimited travel for the day, £10 (ch £5, pen £9). Family ticket £25. **Facilities:** 🅿 (charged) 💷 ✗ licensed ♿ (ramp access to trains) toilets for disabled shop (at Alresford, Alton & Ropley stations) charge for dogs ◀

NEW MILTON SAMMY MILLER MOTORCYCLE MUSEUM

Bashley Cross Rd BH25 5SZ
Dir: (signed off A35, 15m W of Southampton, 10m E of Bournemouth, N of New Milton town centre) **Map Ref:** *SZ29*
☎ **01425 620777** 🖷 **01425 619696**
e-mail: info@sammymiller.co.uk

Sammy Miller is a legend in motorcycling, a road racer who established himself as a leading trials rider in the 1950s and 1960s. His amazing collection has motorcycles dating back to 1900, some of them the only surviving example of their type. The Racing Collection features world record breaking bikes and their history, including the first bike to lap a grand prix course at over 100 miles per hour. Special events include marquee days.

Times: Open daily 10-4.30. (Closed 2 Jan-1 Feb for refurbishment) **Fee:** £4.50 (ch £2).
Facilities: 🅿 💷 ✗ licensed ♿ (special rates for disabled people) toilets for disabled shop ✗ (ex guide dogs) ◀

OWER PAULTONS PARK

SO51 6AL
Dir: (exit M27 junct 2, near junct A31 & A36) **Map Ref:** *SU31*
☎ **023 8081 4442** 🖷 **023 8081 3025**
e-mail: info@paultons.co.uk

Paultons Park offers a great day out with over 50 attractions, including two new drop rides, a roller coaster, bumper boats, six-lane astroglide, teacups, log flume, pirate ship swingboat, dragon roundabout, and wave-runner coaster. For younger children there's Kid's Kingdom, Tiny Tots Town, the Magic Forest, the World of Wind in the Willows and gentle rides. It is located in a beautiful parkland setting with 'Capability' Brown gardens, exotic birds, a lake and hedge maze. There is also the Romany Museum with a unique collection of gypsy wagons and the Village Life Museum.

Times: Open mid Mar-Oct, daily 10-6; Nov & Dec, wknds only until Xmas. **Fee:** ✱ £13.50 (ch under 14). Children under 1m tall enter for free. Range of Family Supersavers. **Facilities:** 🅿 💷 ✗ licensed ♿ (pre-booked wheelchair hire, some rides unsuitable) toilets for disabled shop ✗ (ex guide dogs) ◀

PORTCHESTER PORTCHESTER CASTLE

Castle St PO16 9QW
Dir: (off A27) **Map Ref:** *SU60*
☎ **01705 378291**

Discover 2,000 years of history at Porchester Castle, from its Roman beginnings to the years of medieval splendour. It is surrounded by the most complete Roman walls in Northern Europe, and there are fantastic views over Portsmouth, the harbour and the Solent from the massive keep. An interactive exhibition tells the story of the castle, and visitors can stand right where Henry V rallied his troops before setting out to the battle of Agincourt in 1415.

Times: Open all year, Apr Sep, daily 10-6; Oct-Mar, daily 10-4. Closed 24-26 Dec & 1 Jan.
Fee: ✱ £3.50 (ch £1.80, concessions £2.60). Prices & opening times relate to 2004, for further details phone or log onto www.english-heritage.org.uk/visits
Facilities: 🅿 ♿ shop ✖ (ex on lead in certain areas) ♯

PORTSMOUTH BLUE REEF AQUARIUM

Clarence Esplanade PO5 3PB
Dir: (on approach to city follow brown tourist signs to seafront or Aquarium. Located on Southsea seafront between D-Day Museum and The Hoverport) **Map Ref:** *SU60*
☎ **023 9287 5222** 📠 **023 9229 4443**
e-mail: portsmouth@bluereefaquarium.co.uk

The spectacular underwater walkthrough tunnels at Blue Reef offer some amazing sights of exotic coral reefs - home to sharks and shimmering shoals of brightly-coloured fish. Mediterranean and tropical waters are recreated in giant ocean tanks, where a stunning array of undersea life includes seahorses, puffer fish, coral, piranhas, and incredible crustaceans. Special events are also a feature.

Times: Open daily from 10. Closing times vary with season, please telephone for details.
Fee: ✱ £5.95 (pen £4.95, ch 3-16 £3.95)
Facilities: 🅿 (under 50m) 🍴 ♿ (all on 1 level) toilets for disabled shop ✖ (ex assist dogs) 🛒

CITY MUSEUM & RECORDS OFFICE

Museum Rd PO1 2LJ
Dir: (M27/M275 into Portsmouth, follow museum symbol signs)
Map Ref: *SU60*
☎ **023 9282 7261** 📠 **023 9287 5276**   **FREE**
e-mail: Christopher.Spendlove@ portsmouthcc.gov.uk

Dedicated to local history, fine and decorative art, 'The Story of Portsmouth' displays room settings showing life here from the 17th century to the 1950s. The 'Portsmouth at Play' exhibition features leisure pursuits from the Victorian period to the 1970s. The museum has a fine and decorative art gallery, plus a temporary exhibition gallery with regularly changing exhibitions. The Record Office contains the official records of the City of Portsmouth from the 14th century.

Times: Open all year, Apr-Oct daily 10-5.30; Nov-Mar daily 10-5. Closed 24-26 Dec and Record Office closed on public holidays.
Facilities: 🅿 🍴 ♿ (induction loops, lift & wheelchairs available, parking) toilets for disabled shop ✖ (ex guide & helper dogs)

D-Day Museum & Overlord Embroidery

Clarence Esplanade PO5 3NT
Dir: (M27/M275 into Portsmouth, follow D-Day Museum &
seafront signs) *Map Ref:* *SU60*
☎ 023 9282 7261 📄 023 9287 5276
e-mail: **Christopher.Spendlove@portsmouthcc.gov.uk**

Portsmouth's D-Day Museum tells the dramatic story of the Allied
landings in Normandy in 1944. The centrepiece is the magnificent
Overlord Embroidery, comprising 34 individual panels and
measuring 83 metres in length. Experience the world's largest
ever seaborne invasion, and step back in time to scenes of
wartime Britain. Military equipment, vehicles, landing craft and
personal memories complete this special story.

Times: Open all year, Apr-Oct daily 10-5.30. Nov-Mar, 10-5.
Fee: ✱ £5 (ch £3, pen £3.75). Family ticket £13.
Facilities: 🅿 (charged) ☕ ♿ (induction loops, sound aids, w/chairs
available) toilets for disabled shop ✖ (ex guide & helper dogs) 🔲

Natural History Museum & Butterfly House

Cumberland House, Eastern Pde PO4 9RF
Dir: (accessible from A3(M), A27 or A2030, follow signs to
seafront) *Map Ref:* *SU60*
☎ 023 9282 7261 📄 023 9282 5276
e-mail: **Christopher.Spendlove@portsmouthcc.gov.uk**

This museum focuses on the natural history and geology of
Portsmouth; its diverse habitats including riverbank, marshes,
woods and urban areas. The wildlife dioramas exhibited include a
riverbank scene with a fresh water aquarium. During the summer,
British and European butterflies fly free in the Butterfly House.
Fact sheets enable visitors to find out more about specific
creatures, such as bats, blue-tits and bee-eaters.

Times: Open all year daily, Apr-Oct 10-5.30;
Nov-Mar 10-5. **Fee:** ✱ Nov-Mar, £2 (ch £1.20,
accompanied child under 13 free, pen £1.50).
Apr-Oct, £2.50 (ch £1.50, accompanied ch under
13 free & pen £1.80). Family ticket £6.50.
Facilities: 🅿 (200mtrs) shop ✖ (ex guide &
helper dogs) 🔲

Portsmouth Historic Dockyard

HM Naval Base PO1 3LJ
Dir: (M27/M275 & follow brown historic ships sign)
Map Ref: *SU60*
☎ 023 9287 0999 📄 023 9229 5252
e-mail: **enquiries@historicdockyard.co.uk**

Portsmouth Historic Dockyard is home to the Royal Naval
Museum and the world's greatest historic ships: '*Mary Rose*', built
1510-1511, lost in 1545 and raised in 1982; '*HMS Victory*', Lord
Nelson's flagship in the Battle of Trafalgar, 1805; and '*HMS
Warrior*' built in 1860. Also on site is Action Stations, an attraction
demonstrating life on board a modern naval frigate. Many special
events are held throughout the year, please telephone for details.

Times: Open all year, Apr-Oct, daily 10-5.30;
Nov-Mar, daily 10-5. Closed 25 Dec. **Fee:** All
inclusive ticket: £15.50 (ch & pen £12.50, under
5's free). Family £45 **Facilities:** 🅿 (charged) ☕
✖ ♿ (wheelchairs, facilities for visually & hearing
impaired) toilets for disabled shop ✖ (ex guide
dogs) 🔲

SOUTHSEA CASTLE

Clarence Esplanade PO5 3PA
Dir: (accessible from M27, A27, A3M, A2030, follow castle signs)
Map Ref: SU60
☎ **023 9282 7261** 🖺 **023 9287 5276**
e-mail: Christopher.Spendlove@portsmouthcc.gov.uk

Part of Henry VIII's national coastal defences, this fort was built in 1544, and affords panoramic views of the Solent and the Isle of Wight. In the 'Time Tunnel' experience, the ghost of the castle's first master gunner guides you through the dramatic scenes from the castle's eventful history. There are underground passages, Tudor military history displays, artillery and an audio-visual presentation.

Times: Open all year, Apr-Sep, daily 10-5.30; Oct-Mar, daily 10-5. **Fee:** ✱ £2.50 (ch & students £1.50, ch accompanied under 13 free, pen £1.80). Family ticket £6.50.
Facilities: 🅿 ♿ (wheelchair available) shop ✖ (ex guide & helper dogs) 🍴

SPITBANK FORT

P O Box 129 PO12 2XY
Dir: (Ferries depart from HM Naval Base Portsmouth, Portsmouth Hard, Gosport Ferry Pontoon, by the side of Portsmouth Harbour Railway Stn and Gunwarf Quays shopping centre)
Map Ref: SU60
☎ **02392 504207** 🖺 **02392 504207**
e-mail: enquiries@spitbankfort.co.uk

Built in the 1860s as part of the coastal defences against the French, this massive granite and iron fortress stands a mile out to sea - a man-made island - with magnificent views across the Solent. The interior is a maze of passages connecting over 50 rooms on two levels, and is used for pub nights, parties, weddings and other functions. There is also a bolt passage within the armour of the fort that you can explore. Access at specific times of the year is by boat.

Times: Open Etr-Sep, Wed-Sun. (Weather permitting). **Fee:** ✱ £6.50 (ch £5) includes ferry charge. Boat ride takes approx 20 mins, visitors should allow 2hr to view. Pub nights: (Wed/Thu) £16 (ch £10). Parties: (Fri/Sat) £25 (adult only). Sun Lunch: £16 (ch £10) **Facilities:** 🅿 ☕ ✖ licensed (many steps) ✖ (ex guide dogs) 🍴

RINGWOOD MOORS VALLEY COUNTRY PARK

Horton Rd, Ashley Heath BH24 2ET
Dir: (1.5m from Ashley Heath rdbt on A31 near Three Legged Cross) **Map Ref:** SU10
☎ **01425 470721** 🖺 **01425 471656**
e-mail: moorsvalley@eastdorsetdc.gov.uk

Fifteen hundred acres of forest, woodland, heathland, lakes, river and meadows provide a home for a wide variety of plants and animals, and there's a Visitor Centre, Adventure Playground, picnic area, Moors Valley Railway, Tree Top Trail and 'Go Ape' - a high ropes course (book on 0870 444 5562). Cycle hire is also available.

Times: Open all year, 8-dusk. Visitor centre open 9.30-4.30 (later in summer). Closed 25 Dec. **Fee:** ✱ No admission charge but parking up to £5 per day. **Facilities:** 🅿 (charged) ☕ ✖ licensed ♿ (visitor centre & park mostly accessible, wheelchairs) toilets for disabled shop 🍴

ROCKBOURNE *ROCKBOURNE ROMAN VILLA*

SP6 3PG
Dir: (from Salisbury exit A338 at Fordingbridge, take B3078 westwards through Sandleheath & follow signs. Or turn off A354 Salisbury to Blandford road, W of Coombe Bissett)
Map Ref: SU11
☎ 01725 518541

Discovered in 1942, the site features the remains of a 40-room Roman villa and is the largest in the area. Displays include mosaics and a very rare hypocaust system. The museum displays the many artefacts found on the site during excavations. Roman re-enactments are performed from time to time - please ring for details.

Times: Open Apr-Sep, daily 10.30-6. (Last admission 5.30) **Facilities:** P 💻 & (ramps in & out of museum) toilets for disabled shop ✖ (ex guide/hearing dogs)

SELBORNE GILBERT WHITE'S HOUSE & THE OATES MUSEUM

High St GU34 3JH
Dir: (on village High St) *Map Ref:* SU73
☎ 01420 511275 📄 01420 511040

This charming 18th-century house was home to the famous naturalist, the Rev Gilbert White, author of '*The Natural History and Antiquities of Selborne*'. Also in the house are exhibitions on two famous members of the Oates family - Captain Oates who accompanied Scott to the South Pole, and Frank Oates, a Victorian explorer. Special events include a Gilbert White Day in July.

Times: Open daily Jan-24 Dec, 11-5. **Fee:** ✱ £5 (ch £3, concessions £4.50). **Facilities:** P 💻 ✖ & toilets for disabled shop ✖ (ex guide dogs) 🍴

SHERBORNE ST JOHN THE VYNE

RG24 9HL
Dir: (4m N of Basingstoke, off A340, signed from A33, A339 & A340) *Map Ref:* SU65
☎ 01256 883858 📄 01256 881720
e-mail: thevyne@nationaltrust.org.uk

Built in the early 16th century for Lord Sandys, Henry VIII's Lord Chamberlain, the house acquired a classic portico in the mid 17th-century, the first of its kind in England. It has a fascinating Tudor chapel, a Palladian staircase and fine furniture. There are attractive grounds.

Times: Open House & Gardens 20 Mar-Oct daily (ex Thu & Fri) 1-5, wknds 11-5. Gardens also open wknds in Feb & Mar, 11-5. (Gardens 11-5 Mon-Wed). **Fee:** ✱ House & Grounds £7 (ch £3.50). Family £17.50, Group £6. Grounds & Gardens only £4 (ch £2). NT members free. **Facilities:** P 💻 ✖ licensed & (Braille guides & touch tours) toilets for disabled shop ✖ (ex guide & hearing dogs) 🐾 🍴

SOUTHAMPTON MUSEUM OF ARCHAEOLOGY
God's House Tower, Winkle St SO14 2NY
Dir: (near the waterfront close to Queen's Park and the Town Quay) **Map Ref:** *SU41*
☎ 023 8063 5904 & 8083 2768 ≊ 023 8033 9601 FREE
e-mail: historic.sites@southampton.gov.uk

The museum is housed in an early fortified building, which dates from the 1400s and takes its name, God's House Tower, from the nearby medieval hospital, founded in 1196. Exhibits on the Roman, Saxon and medieval towns of Southampton are displayed in the three main galleries. The collection is designated in recognition of its national and international importance. There are resources for children and families, plus special events.

Times: Open Nov-Mar: Tue-Fri 10-4; Sat 10-12 & 1-4; Sun 1-4. Apr-Oct: Tue-Fri 10-12 & 1-5; Sat 10-12 & 1-4; Sun 2-5. Also open BH Mon.
Facilities: P (400 yds) (designated areas only, parking charges) & shop ✖ (ex guide dogs)

SOUTHAMPTON CITY ART GALLERY
Civic Centre, Commercial Rd SO14 7LP
Dir: (situated on the Watts Park side of the Civic Centre, a short walk from the station) **Map Ref:** *SU41*
☎ 023 8083 2277 ≊ 023 8083 2153
e-mail: art.gallery@southampton.gov.uk

The largest gallery in the south of England, with the finest collection of contemporary art in the country outside London. A diverse range of media is represented, including sculpture, photography, installation and video work among its 3,500 pieces. A notable collection of studio pottery is also shown. Varied displays of landscapes, portrait paintings or recent British art are always available, as well as a special display, selected by members of the public.

Times: Open all year, Tue-Sat 10-5, Sun 1-4. Closed 25-27 & 31 Dec. **Facilities:** P (50yds) (nearby street parking is 1hr only) ☕ ✖ licensed & (free BSL signed tours by arrangement, 'touch tour') toilets for disabled shop ✖ (ex guide dogs)

SOUTHAMPTON MARITIME MUSEUM
The Wool House, Town Quay SO14 2AR
Dir: (on the waterfront, near to the Town Quay) **Map Ref:** *SU41*
☎ 023 8022 3941 & 8063 5904 ≊ 023 8033 9601 FREE
e-mail: historic.sites@southampton.gov.uk

The Wool House was built in the 14th century as a warehouse for storing wool that was due to be exported to Flanders and Italy. In the early 19th century it was used as a prison, and the names of French prisoners can still be seen carved into the wooden beams. It now houses the Southampton Maritime Museum, with models and displays telling the history of the Victorian and modern port of Southampton. Features include exhibitions themed around the 'Titanic' and the 'Queen Mary', and there is an interactive area for children.

Times: Open Nov-Mar: Tue-Fri 10-4; Sat 10-1 & 2-4; Sun 1-4. Apr-Oct: Tue-Fri 10-1 & 2-5; Sat 10-1 & 2-4; Sun 2-5. Also open BH Mon.
Facilities: P (400yds) (metered parking adjacent) & (hearing loop on Titanic presentation) shop ✖ (ex guide dogs)

WEYHILL   THE HAWK CONSERVANCY AND COUNTRY PARK

SP11 8DY
Dir: (3m W of Andover, signed from A303) *Map Ref:* SU34
☎ 01264 772252 🖹 01264 773772
e-mail: info@hawk-conservancy.org

This is the largest centre in the south for birds of prey from all over the world, including eagles, hawks, falcons, owls, vultures and kites. Exciting birds of prey demonstrations are held daily at noon, 2pm and 3.30pm, including the 'Valley of the Eagles' at 2pm. Different birds are flown at these times and visitors may have the opportunity to hold a bird and adults can fly a Harris Hawk.

Times: Open Feb half term-Oct half term, daily from 10.30-5.30 (last admission 4).
Fee: ✱ £7.25 (ch £4.65, pen & student £6.70). Family ticket £23. **Facilities:** 🅿 ☕ ♿ (wheelchair area in flying grounds, viewing areas in hides) toilets for disabled shop 🐕 📷

WHITCHURCH   WHITCHURCH SILK MILL

28 Winchester St RG28 7AL
Dir: (halfway between Winchester & Newbury signposted clearly on the A34. Located in centre of the town) *Map Ref:* SU44
☎ 01256 892065 🖹 01256 893882
e-mail: silkmill@btinternet.com

The mill is idyllically located on the River Test. Whitchurch Silk Mill is the oldest surviving textile mill in Southern England. Fine silks and ribbons are still woven for interiors and fashion. See the 19th-century waterwheel pounding and learn about winding, warping and weaving. There is a programme of exhibitions, workshops and children's activities.

Times: Open Tue-Sun & BH Mon 10.30-5 (last admission 4.15). Closed 24 Dec-1 Jan.
Facilities: 🅿 ☕ ♿ (disabled parking adjacent site) toilets for disabled shop 🐕 (ex guide dogs) 📷

WINCHESTER   HOSPITAL OF ST CROSS

St Cross SO23 9SD
Dir: (on B3335, 0.5m from M3 junct 11) *Map Ref:* SU42
☎ 01962 851375 🖹 01962 878221
e-mail: visitors@stcrosshospital.co.uk

The Hospital of St Cross was founded in 1132 for the benefit of 13 poor men, and still functions as an almshouse. Throughout the Middle Ages the hospital handed out the Dole - bread and beer - to travellers, and this is still done. The Church of St Cross, Brethrens Hall, the medieval kitchen and the walled Master's Garden are all worthy of note.

Times: Apr-Oct, 9.30-5; Nov-Mar 10.30-3.30.
Fee: ✱ £2.50 (ch 50p, pen £2).
Facilities: 🅿 ☕ ♿ toilets for disabled shop 🐕 (ex guide dogs) 📷

INTECH - Hampshire Technology Centre & Technology Centre

Telegraph Way, Morn Hill SO21 1HX
Dir: (M3 junct 10 onto A31 then B3404, Alresford road)
Map Ref: *SU42*
☎ **01962 863791** 📄 **01962 868524**
e-mail: htct@intech-uk.com

This purpose-built 3,500 square metre building houses 100 interactive exhibits, which demonstrate the science and technology of the world around us in an engaging and exciting way. The philosophy is most definitely 'hands-on', and the motto of the centre is 'Doing is Believing'. Exhibits deal with things like viscosity, tornados, and Newton's Cradle among others.

Times: Open daily 10-4. Closed Xmas & 1 Jan.
Fee: ✱ £5.95 (pen £3.75, ch £4.30)
Facilities: 🅿 ➡ ♿ toilets for disabled shop 🐾 (ex guide dogs)

The Great Hall

Castle Av SO23 8PJ
Dir: (situated at top of High St. Park & Ride recommended)
Map Ref: *SU42*
☎ **01962 846476** 📄 **01962 841326**

The only surviving part of Winchester Castle, once home to the Domesday Book, this 13th-century hall was at the centre of court and government life. Built between 1222 and 1235, during the reign of Henry III, it is one of the largest and finest five bay halls in England to have survived to the present day. The Round Table based on the Arthurian Legend and built between 1230 and 1280 hangs in the hall. Queen Eleanor's Garden, a re-creation of a late 13th-century ornamental garden, was opened in 1986 by the Queen Mother.

Times: ✱ Open all year, Mar-Oct daily 10-5; Nov-Feb, daily 10-5, wknds 10-4. Closed 25-26 Dec. **Facilities:** 🅿 (200yds) ♿ toilets for disabled shop 🐾 (ex guide/hearing dogs) ◀

Winchester Cathedral

SO23 9LS
Dir: (in city centre - follow city heritage signs) **Map Ref:** *SU42*
☎ **01962 857200 & 866854** 📄 **01962 857201** 🅵🆁🅴🅴
e-mail: cathedral.office@
winchester-cathedral.org.uk

The longest medieval church in Europe, founded in 1079 on a site where Christian worship had already been offered for over 400 years. Among its treasures are the 12th-century illuminated Winchester Bible, the font, medieval wall paintings and Triforium Gallery Museum. Items of interest include Jane Austen's tomb and the statue of the Winchester diver, William Walker, who in 1905 saved the cathedral by underpinning its foundations, working up to six hours a day over a period of six years, often in 20 feet of water.

Times: Open all year, daily 8.30-5.30. Subject to services and special events.
Facilities: 🅿 (500mtrs) ➡ 🍴 licensed ♿ (chair lift to east end of Cathedral, touch & hearing model) toilets for disabled shop 🐾 (ex guide dogs) ◀

HATFIELD HATFIELD HOUSE, PARK AND GARDENS

AL9 5NQ
Dir: (2m from junct 4 A1(M) on A1000, 7m from M25 junct 23.
House is opposite railway station) *Map Ref:* TL20
☎ 01707 287010 📠 01707 287033
e-mail: visitors@hatfield-house.co.uk

The house, built by Robert Cecil in 1611, is the home of the
Marquess of Salisbury and is full of exquisite tapestries, furniture
and famous paintings. The 42 acres of gardens include formal,
knot, scented and wilderness areas, which reflects their Jacobean
history. Additional attractions are the national collection of model
soldiers and a children's play area.

Times: Open Etr Sat-Sep. House: Sat-Wed 12-4, guided tours only on
Mons, ex BH. Park & Gardens: Sat-Wed 11-5.30. **Fee:** House Park &
Gardens: £8 (ch £4). Park only £2 (ch £1). Park & Gardens: £4.50
(ch £3.50). Mon (Garden Connoisseurs' Day); Park & Gardens: £6.50.
House Tour, £5. **Facilities:** 🅿 ✕ licensed ♿ (lift to 1st floor,
wheelchairs) toilets for disabled shop ➷

KNEBWORTH KNEBWORTH HOUSE, GARDENS & COUNTRY PARK

SG3 6PY
Dir: (direct access from A1(M) junct 7) *Map Ref:* TL22
☎ 01438 812661 📠 01438 811908
e-mail: info@knebworthhouse.com

Home of the Lytton family since 1490, the original Tudor Manor
was transformed in 1843 by the spectacular high Gothic
decoration of Victorian novelist Sir Edward Bulwer Lytton. The
formal gardens, laid out by Edwin Lutyens, include a Gertrude
Jekyll herb garden, a maze, a walled garden and a dinosaur trail.
In the 250-acre park you'll find a miniature railway, adventure
playground and a deer park.

Times: Open daily 26 Mar-10 Apr, 28 May-5 Jun & Jul- Aug. Wknds &
BH's 19-20 Mar, 16 Apr-22 May, 11-26 Jun & 3-25 Sep. Park,
Playground & Gardens 11-5.30; House & Exhibition noon-5 (last
admission 4.15). **Fee:** Contact for details, visit website.
Facilities: 🅿 ☕ ♿ (transport to door, wheelchair, Carers free entry.)
toilets for disabled shop garden centre ✕ (ex guide dogs & in park) ➷

LONDON COLNEY DE HAVILLAND AIRCRAFT HERITAGE CENTRE

Salisbury Hall AL2 1EX
Dir: (M25 junct 22. Follow signs for 'Mosquito Aircraft Museum'
onto B556) *Map Ref:* TL10
☎ 01727 822051 & 826400 📠 01727 826400

The oldest aircraft museum in Britain opened in 1959 to preserve
and display the de Havilland Mosquito prototype on the site of its
conception. It is a working museum with displays of 20 de
Havilland aircraft and sections together with a comprehensive
collection of de Havilland engines and memorabilia. Selected
cockpits are open to enter. A maze-style education storyboard is a
new addition.

Times: Open first Sun Mar-last Sun Oct, Sun & BHs 10.30-5.30, Tue,
Thu & Sat 2-5.30. **Fee:** £5 (ch under 5 free, ch & pen £3) Family
ticket £13 (2ad+2ch) **Facilities:** 🅿 ☕ ♿ (wheelchairs available)
toilets for disabled shop (not accessible for wheelchairs) ➷

ST ALBANS   MUSEUM OF ST ALBANS

Hatfield Rd AL1 3RR
Dir: (city centre on A1057 Hatfield road)   *Map Ref:* *TL10*
☎ **01727 819340** 📄 **01727 837472**   FREE
e-mail: museum@stalbans.gov.uk

Exhibits at the Museum of St Albans include the Salaman collection of craft tools, and reconstructed workshops. The history of St Albans is traced from the departure of the Romans up to the present day. There is a special exhibition gallery with a wide variety of exhibitions and a wildlife garden with a picnic area.

Times: Open all year, daily 10-5, Sun 2-5. Closed 25-26 Dec. **Facilities:** 🅿 & toilets for disabled shop ✖ (ex guide dogs) 🍴

VERULAMIUM MUSEUM

St Michaels AL3 4SW
Dir: (follow signs for St Albans, museum signed)   *Map Ref:* *TL10*
☎ **01727 751810** 📄 **01727 859919**
e-mail: a.coles@stalbans.gov.uk

Verulamium was one of the largest and most important Roman towns in Britain. By the 1st century AD it was declared a 'municipium', giving its inhabitants the rights of Roman citizenship, the only British city granted this honour. A mosaic and under floor heating system can be seen, and the museum has wall paintings, jewellery, pottery and other domestic items. On the second weekend of every month legionaries occupy the galleries and describe the tactics and equipment of the Roman Imperial Army and the life of a legionary.

Times: Open all year wkdys 10-5.30, Sun 2-5.30. Closed 25-26 Dec. **Fee:** £3.30 (ch, pen & students £2). Family ticket £8. Subject to change. **Facilities:** 🅿 (charged) & (ramp access to main entrance) toilets for disabled shop ✖ (ex guide dogs) 🍴

TRING   THE WALTER ROTHSCHILD ZOOLOGICAL MUSEUM

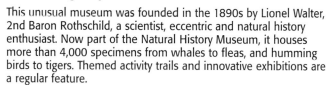

Akeman St HP23 6AP
Dir: (signed from A41)   *Map Ref:* *SP91*
☎ **020 7942 6171** 📄 **020 7942 6150**   FREE
e-mail: tring-enquiries@nhm.ac.uk

This unusual museum was founded in the 1890s by Lionel Walter, 2nd Baron Rothschild, a scientist, eccentric and natural history enthusiast. Now part of the Natural History Museum, it houses more than 4,000 specimens from whales to fleas, and humming birds to tigers. Themed activity trails and innovative exhibitions are a regular feature.

Times: Open all year, Mon-Sat 10-5, Sun 2-5. Closed 24-26 Dec.
Facilities: 🅿 🍴 & (ramps to shop & cafe, disabled parking space) toilets for disabled shop ✖ (ex guide dogs)

Hertfordshire continued

WARE SCOTT'S GROTTO

Scott's Rd SG12 9JQ
Dir: (off A119) ***Map Ref:*** *TL31*
☎ **01920 464131** 📄 **0870 120 6902**
e-mail: jg@ware-herts.org.uk

FREE

Scott's Grotto, built in the 1760s by the Quaker poet John Scott, has been described by English Heritage as 'one of the finest in England', and has been restored by the Ware Society. The grotto consists of underground passages and chambers decorated with flints, shells, minerals and stones, and extends 67 feet into the side of the hill. Visitors are advised to wear flat shoes and to bring a torch.

Times: Open Apr-Sep, Sat & BH Mon 2-4.30. Other times by appointment only.
Facilities: P (on street) ✈ 🚌

ST BRELADE JERSEY LAVENDER FARM

Rue du Pont Marquet JE3 8DS
Dir: (on B25 from St Aubin's Bay to Redhouses)
☎ **01534 742933** 📄 **01534 745613**
e-mail: admin@jerseylavender.co.uk

Jersey Lavender grows nine acres of lavender, distils the essential oil and creates a range of toiletry products. Visitors are able to see the whole process from start to finish. There is a national collection of lavenders, extensive gardens, herb beds and walks among the lavender fields. Other herbs are also grown and distilled, namely eucalyptus, rosemary and tea tree.

Times: Open 10 May-18 Sep, Mon-Sat 10-5.
Fee: £3.30 (ch under 14 free). **Facilities:** P 🍴 ♿ (free wheelchair loan) toilets for disabled shop garden centre 🍴

ST CLEMENT SAMARÈS MANOR

JE2 6QW
Dir: (2m E of St Helier on St Clements Inner Rd)
☎ **01534 870551** 📄 **01534 768949**
e-mail: barbara@samaresmanor.com

The manor, which dates back to Norman times, stands in 14 acres of beautiful gardens. There is a renowned herb garden and a Japanese garden occupying an artificial hill with a series of waterfalls cascading over Cumberland limestone. Other attractions are a craft centre, falconry, farm animals and a children's play area. Tours of the manor house, a family scavenger hunt and medieval music also feature.

Times: Open 3 Apr-16 Oct. **Fee:** £4.95 (ch under 16 £1.95, pen £4.50). Sat prices: £3.95 (ch under 16 £1.75, pen £3.50)
Facilities: P 🍴 ✕ licensed ♿ toilets for disabled shop garden centre ✈ (ex guide dogs) 🍴

ST HELIER MARITIME MUSEUM & OCCUPATION TAPESTRY GALLERY

New North Quay JE2 3ND
Dir: (alongside Marina, opposite Liberation Square)
☎ 01534 811043 ▤ 01534 874099
e-mail: marketing@jerseyheritagetrust

This converted 19th-century warehouse houses the tapestry consisting of 12 two-metre panels that tells the story of the occupation of Jersey during World War II. Each of the 12 parishes took responsibility for stitching a panel, making it the largest community arts project ever undertaken on the island. The Maritime Museum celebrates the relationship of islanders and the sea, including an award-winning hand-on experience, especially enjoyed by children.

Times: Open all year, daily 10-5. Winter closing at 4. **Fee:** ✱ £5.95 (ch under 6 free, pen & students £5.10). Discount and family tickets **Facilities:** P (paycards in public car parks) ㄥ (Braille books, audio guide etc) toilets for disabled shop ✖ (ex guide dogs) ◀

ST LAWRENCE GERMAN UNDERGROUND HOSPITAL

Les Charrieres Malorey JE3 1FU
Dir: (bus route 8A from St Helier)
☎ 01534 860808 ▤ 01534 860886
e-mail: info@jerseywartunnels.com

On 1 July 1940, the Channel Islands were occupied by German forces, and this vast complex dug deep into a hillside is the most evocative reminder of that occupation. A video presentation, along with a large collection of memorabilia, illustrates of the lives of the islanders at war and a further exhibition records their impressions during 1945, the year the island was liberated.

Times: Open 14 Feb-19 Dec, daily 9.30-5.30 (last admission 4). **Fee:** ✱ £8 (ch £4, students & serving armed forces £6 & pen £7). **Facilities:** P ▣ ✖ licensed ㄥ (ramp to restaurant & lift in Visitor Centre to restaurant) toilets for disabled shop ✖ (ex guide dogs) ◀

ST OUEN THE CHANNEL ISLANDS MILITARY MUSEUM

Five Mile Rd
Dir: (N end of Five Mile Rd, at rear of Jersey Woollen Mill & across road from Jersey Pearl)
☎ 01534 723136
e-mail: damienhorn@jerseymail.co.uk

The museum is housed in a German coastal defence bunker, which formed part of Hitler's Atlantic Wall. It has been restored, as far as possible, to give the visitor an idea of how it looked. The visitor can also see German uniforms, motorcycles, weapons, documents, photographs and other items from the 1940-45 occupation.

Times: Open week before Etr-Oct **Fee:** ✱ £4 (ch £2) Groups by arrangement. **Facilities:** P ▣ ㄥ (all parts accessible ex 1 small room) toilets for disabled shop ✖ (ex guide dogs)

Jersey continued

ST PETER THE LIVING LEGEND

Rue de Petit Aleval JE3 7ET
Dir: (from St Helier, along main esplanade & right to Bel Royal.
Left and follow road to attraction, signed from German
Underground Hospital)
☎ **01534 485496** ▤ **01534 485855**
e-mail: info@jerseyslivinglegend.co.je

Pass through the granite archways into the landscaped gardens
and the world of the Jersey Experience, where Jersey's exciting
past is recreated in a three dimensional spectacle. Learn of the
heroes and villains, the folklore and the story of the island's links
with the UK and its struggles with Europe. Other attractions
include an adventure playground, street entertainment, the Jersey
Craft and Shopping Village, a range of shops and the Jersey
Kitchen Restaurant. There are also two 18-hole adventure golf
courses suitable for all ages.

Times: Open daily, Mar-Nov 9.30-5, Sat-Sun 10-5
Fee: ✳ £7.10 (ch 7-13 £4.85, pen £6.80, student
£5.50, disabled £5.60). **Facilities:** 🅿 ☕
✗ licensed ♿ (wheelchair available) toilets for
disabled shop 🐕 (ex guide dogs) ◀

TRINITY DURRELL WILDLIFE CONSERVATION TRUST

Les Augres Manor, La Profunde Rue JE3 5BP
☎ **01534 860000** ▤ **01534 860001**
e-mail: info@durrell.org

This is Gerald Durrell's unique sanctuary and breeding centre for
many of the world's rarest animals. Visitors can see these
remarkable creatures, some so rare that they can only be found
here, in modern, spacious enclosures in the gardens of the 16th-
century manor house. Major attractions are the magical aye-ayes
from Madagascar and the world-famous family of lowland gorillas.
There is a comprehensive programme of keeper talks, animal
displays and activities.

Times: Open all year, daily 9.30-6 (summer); 9.30-5 (winter). Closed
25 Dec. **Fee:** ✳ £9.95 (ch 4-16 £7.25, pen £8.35).
Facilities: 🅿 ☕ ✗ ♿ toilets for disabled shop 🐕 ◀

BEKESBOURNE HOWLETTS WILD ANIMAL PARK

CT4 5EL
Dir: (off A2, 3m S of Canterbury, follow brown tourist signs)
Map Ref: TR15
☎ **01303 264647** ▤ **01303 264944**
e-mail: info@howletts.net

Set in 90 acres of parkland, Howletts is home to some of the
world's most rare and endangered animals. It boasts the UK's
largest group of African elephants, Indian and Siberian tigers,
many small cats and rare monkeys and the world's largest group
of Western Lowland gorillas. The glass fronted tiger enclosures,
children's adventure playground and the new Jurassic Mine with
an ice and gem cave are not to be missed.

Times: ✳ Open all year, daily 10-6 during summer (last admission
4.30), 10-dusk during winter (last admission 3). Closed 25 Dec.
Facilities: 🅿 ☕ ✗ ♿ toilets for disabled shop 🐕 (ex guide dogs) ◀

BELTRING HOP FARM & COUNTRY PARK

TN12 6PY
Dir: (on A228 at Paddock Wood) **Map Ref:** *TQ64*
☎ **01622 872068** 📄 **01622 872630**
e-mail: enquiry@thehopfarm.co.uk

The Hop Farm is a popular South East family visitor attraction and event location. Set among a large collection of Victorian Oast houses, attractions include museums and exhibitions, indoor and outdoor play areas, an animal farm and shire horses, a restaurant and a gift shop. Special events throughout the year include craft shows, motor shows, food and drink festivals and themed holiday weeks.

Times: Open from 10. Closed 24-26 Dec, 23 May & 20 June **Fee:** ✱ £7.50 (ch 4-15 £6.50). Family ticket (2ad+2ch) £27. **Facilities:** P 🍵 ✗ licensed 🚻 toilets for disabled shop 🛍

BIRCHINGTON POWELL-COTTON MUSEUM, QUEX HOUSE & GARDENS

Quex Park CT7 0BH
Dir: (W of Margate on A28. In Birchington right into Park Lane before rdbt in centre of town. Entrance 600yds on left)
Map Ref: *TR36*
☎ **01843 842168** 📄 **01843 846661**
e-mail: powell-cotton.museum@virgin.net

Major Powell-Cotton spent much of his life on the study of African animals and many different cultures. This museum, founded in 1895, is his legacy, consisting of animal dioramas, photographs, extensive notes, and artefacts from around the world. Also on display in Quex House, the family home, are collections of Eastern and Asian furniture, Kashmir walnut wall carvings, Chinese silk embroidery, and English period furniture.

Times: Open Apr-Oct, Tue-Thu, Sun & BH 11-5, Quex House 2-4.30. Nov & Mar Sun 11-4, Quex House closed. Closed Dec-Feb. **Fee:** ✱ Summer £5 (ch & pen £4, under 5's free), Family ticket (2ad+3ch) £14. Winter £4 (ch & pen £3), Family ticket (2ad+3ch) £10. Garden only £1.50 (ch & pen £1). **Facilities:** P 🍵 ✗ licensed 🚻 (two wheelchairs available) toilets for disabled shop ✈ (ex assistance dogs) 🛍

BROADSTAIRS BLEAK HOUSE DICKENS MARITIME & SMUGGLING

Fort Rd CT10 1EY
Dir: (off Eastern Esplanade, near Viking Bay) **Map Ref:** *TR36*
☎ **01843 862224**

The house was a favourite seaside residence of Charles Dickens, and he wrote all of 'David Copperfield' and other works here, and drafted the idea for 'Bleak House'. There are also exhibitions of relics salvaged from the Goodwin Sands, including a bronze canon and a ship's kettle, and Kent's only smuggling museum.

Times: ✱ Open mid Feb-mid Dec, daily; Jan-mid Feb wknds only, 10-6 **Facilities:** P (100 yds) 🚻 (provisions made for blind) shop

CANTERBURY CANTERBURY ROMAN MUSEUM

Butchery Ln, Longmarket CT1 2RA
Dir: (in centre close to cathedral and city centre car parks)
Map Ref: TR15
☎ **01227 785575** 🖹 **01227 455047**
e-mail: museums@canterbury.gov.uk

Step below today's Canterbury to discover an exciting part of the Roman town including the real remains of a house with fine mosaics. Experience everyday life in the reconstructed market place and see exquisite silver and glass. Try your skills on the touch screen computer, and in the hands-on area with actual finds. Use the computer animation of Roman Canterbury to join the search for the lost temple.

Times: Open all year, Mon-Sat 10-5 & Sun (Jun-Oct) 1.30-5. (Last admission 4). Closed Good Fri & Xmas period. **Fee:** ✱ £2.80 (ch 5-18, disabled, pen & students £1.75). Family ticket £7.20 **Facilities:** P (walking distance) ⅋ (lift) toilets for disabled shop ✖ (ex guide dogs)

THE CANTERBURY TALES

St. Margaret's St CT1 2TG
Dir: (in heart of city centre, follow finger signs) **Map Ref:** TR15
☎ **01227 479227** 🖹 **01227 765584**
e-mail: info@canterburytales.org.uk

Step back in time to experience the sights, sounds and smells of the Middle Ages in this reconstruction of 14th-century England. Travel from the Tabard Inn in London to St Thomas Becket's Shrine in Canterbury in the company off Chaucer's colourful pilgrims. Their tales of chivalry, romance and intrigue are vividly brought to life for you along your journey.

Times: Open all year, Mar-Jun 10-5, Jul-Aug 9.30-5, Sep-Oct 10-4 & Nov-Feb 10-4.30. Closed 25 Dec **Fee:** ✱ £6.95 (ch £5.25, pen £5.75, student £5.95) Family ticket (2 ad & 2 ch) £22.50 **Facilities:** P (200mtrs) 🍴 ⅋ (notice required for wheelchairs) toilets for disabled shop ✖ (ex guide dogs) ▰

CANTERBURY WEST GATE MUSEUM

St. Peter's St CT1 2RA
Dir: (at end of main street beside river. Entrance under main arch) **Map Ref:** TR15
☎ **01227 789576** 🖹 **01227 455047**
e-mail: museums@canterbury.gov.uk

The last of the city's fortified gatehouses sits astride the London road with the river as a moat. Rebuilt in around 1380 by Archbishop Sudbury, it was used as a prison for many years. The battlements give a splendid panoramic view of the city and are a good vantage point for photographs. Arms and armour can be seen in the guardroom, and there are cells in the towers. Brass rubbings can be made and children can try on replica armour.

Times: Open all year (ex Good Fri & Xmas period), Mon-Sat; 11-12.30 & 1.30-3.30. Last admission 15 mins before closure. **Fee:** ✱ £1.10 (ch, disabled, pen, students & UB40 70p). Family ticket £2.60. **Facilities:** P (100yds) shop ✖ (ex guide dogs)

DRUIDSTONE PARK & ART PARK

Honey Hill, Blean CT2 9JR
Dir: (3m NW on A290 from Canterbury) **Map Ref:** TR15
☎ 01227 765168 📄 01227 768860

Druidstone Park provides an idyllic garden setting for a range of sculptures, and enchanted woodland walks where the sleeping dragon lives. Here you can see the mystical oak circle and the old man of the oaks. Other attractions popular with the younger members of the family are the children's farmyard and play areas, plus the gift shop and cafeteria.

Times: Open Etr-Nov, daily, 10-5.30. **Fee:** £4.80 (ch £3.50 & pen £4). Family ticket £14.50 **Facilities:** 🅿 💺 ♿ toilets for disabled shop ✖ (ex guide dogs) 🍴

MUSEUM OF CANTERBURY

Stour St CT1 2RA
Dir: (in the Medieval Poor Priests' Hospital, just off St Margaret's St or High St) **Map Ref:** TR15
☎ 01227 475202 📄 01227 455047
e-mail: museums@canterbury.gov.uk

Discover the story of Canterbury in new interactive displays for all the family. See the city's treasures, including the famous Canterbury Cross. Try the fun activities in the Medieval Discovery Gallery, find out about the mysteries surrounding Christopher Marlowe's life and death, and spot friend or foe planes in the World War II Blitz gallery. Meet favourite children's TV character Bagpuss and friends, and enjoy the Rupert Bear Museum - full of adventure and surprises.

Times: Open all year, Mon-Sat 10.30-5 & Sun (Jun-Sep) 1.30-5 (last admission 4pm). (Closed Good Fri & Xmas period). **Fee:** ✱ £3.10 (concessions £2.10). Family ticket £8.20 (2 Adults + 3 ch) **Facilities:** 🅿 walking ♿ toilets for disabled shop ✖ (ex guide dogs)

CHATHAM *FORT AMHERST*

Dock Rd ME4 4UB
Dir: (adjacent to A231 dock road, 0.5m from Chatham Dockyard)
Map Ref: TQ76
☎ 01634 847747 📄 01634 830612
e-mail: amherstman2@hotmail.com

Amherst is a fine Georgian fortress set in over 15 acres of attractive parkland. A fascinating collection of caves, tunnels, gun-batteries and barracks gives visitors an insight into the life of the soldier anticipating a Napoleonic invasion. Two hundred years later the fort was made ready for a feared German invasion, and the civil defence museum reflects this period. Special events are a regular feature, including historic re-enactments. Please phone for details.

Times: ✱ Open daily Nov-Mar Sat & Sun 10-3.30. Apr-Oct daily 10-4 **Facilities:** 🅿 💺 ♿ (wheelchair provided, road access up to fort) toilets for disabled shop ✖ (ex guide dogs) 🍴

THE HISTORIC DOCKYARD CHATHAM

ME4 4TZ
Dir: (M20 & M2 junct 3, follow signs for Chatham on A229. Then A230 and A231, following brown tourist signs. Brown anchor signs lead to visitors' entrance) **Map Ref:** *TQ76*
☎ **01634 823800** ▤ **01634 823801**
e-mail: info@chdt.org.uk

The Historic Dockyard celebrates over 400 years of naval history in one 80-acre site. Exhibits include 'Battle Ships' with World War II destroyer '*HMS Cavalie*r' and the spy sub '*Ocelot*'; 'Lifeboat' with a display of 15 full size boats, archive film and artefacts; and 'Wooden Walls', which looks at the life of a carpenter's apprentice in the 18th century. The naval architecture is spectacular.

Times: Open mid Feb-early Nov, daily 10-6. Last entry 4. **Fee:** ✱ £10 (ch 5-15 £6.50, concessions £7.50). Family ticket (2ad+2ch) £26.50, additional child £3.25 **Facilities:** ▣ ▣ ✗ licensed & (wheelchair available, Braille guides, virtual tours) toilets for disabled shop ▰

DOVER *CRABBLE CORN MILL*

Lower Rd, River CT17 0UY
Dir: (A2 to Whitfield rdbt then 2nd turning down Whitfield Hill, left. At traffic lights right into River Crabble, under railway bridge and 1st right. Mill 500mtrs on left) **Map Ref:** *TR34*
☎ **01304 823292** ▤ **01304 823292**
e-mail: miller@ccmt.org.co.uk

Visit this beautifully restored working Kentish water mill dating from 1812, where there are regular demonstrations of the waterwheel working and making stoneground wholemeal flour from Kentish organic wheat. Flour is available to buy, and home-baked produce in the café. There is also an exhibition space displaying the work of local artists and craftspeople.

Times: Open all year, Mar-Sep, daily 11-5; Winter, Sun only (except by appointment). Open all year for groups by arrangement. Closed Xmas & Jan. **Facilities:** ▣ ▣ & shop ✗ (ex guide dogs)

DOVER CASTLE & SECRET WARTIME TUNNELS

CT16 1HU
Map Ref: *TR34*
☎ **01304 211067** ▤ **01304 214739**

Various exhibitions demonstrate how Dover Castle has served as a vital strategic centre from the Iron Age onwards. In May 1940 the tunnels under the castle, built during the Napoleonic Wars, became the nerve centre for 'Operation Dynamo' - the evacuation of Dunkirk. These wartime secrets are now revealed for all to see. The castle was first built as an earthwork in 1066 by William of Normandy, and it was rebuilt with the huge keep and concentric rings of defences, in the 1180s by Henry II.

Times: Open all year, Apr-Jun & Sep, daily 10-6; Jul-Aug, daily 9.30-6.30; Oct, daily 10-5; Nov-Jan, Thu-Mon 10-4; Feb-Mar, daily 10-4. Closed 24-26 Dec & 1 Jan. **Fee:** ✱ £8.50 (ch £4.30, concessions £6.40). Family £21.30 (2ad+2ch). Prices & opening times relate to 2004, for further details phone or log onto www.english-heritage.org.uk/visits **Facilities:** ▣ ✗ & shop ✗ (ex on lead in certain areas) ▥

EYNSFORD LULLINGSTONE ROMAN VILLA

Lullingstone Ln DA4 0JA
Dir: (0.5m SW off A225) **Map Ref:** *TQ56*
☎ **01322 863467**

This Roman villa was discovered in 1939 and the site was excavated after the war. It is an exciting find with wonderful mosaic floors, wall paintings and skeletal remains, now preserved by the erection of a building to cover it. Audio tours offer a fascinating insight into the life of a well-to-do Roman family.

Times: Open all year, Apr-Sep, daily 10-6; Oct-Nov, daily 10-4; Dec-Jan, Wed-Sun 10-4; Feb-Mar, daily 10-4. Closed 24-26 Dec & 1 Jan.
Fee: ✱ £3.50 (ch £1.80, concessions £2.60). Prices & opening times relate to 2004, for further details phone or log onto www.english-heritage.org.uk/visits
Facilities: 🅿 ✖ ♯

FAVERSHAM FLEUR DE LIS HERITAGE CENTRE

10-13 Preston St ME13 8NS
Dir: (3 minutes' drive from M2 junct 6) **Map Ref:** *TR06*
☎ **01795 534542**
e-mail: faversham@btinternet.com

Now expanded and updated, and housed in 16th-century premises, the heritage centre features colourful displays and room settings that vividly evoke the 2,000 year history of Faversham. Special features include the 'Gunpowder Experience' and a working old-style village telephone exchange, one of only two remaining in Britain. In July, during the Faversham Open House Scheme, over 20 historic properties in the town are opened to the public.

Times: Open all year, Mon-Sat, 10-4; Sun 10-1.
Fee: £2 (ch & pen £1) **Facilities:** 🅿 (200yds) ♿ toilets for disabled shop ◀

GROOMBRIDGE PLACE GROOMBRIDGE PLACE GARDENS & ENCHANTED FOREST

TN3 9QG
Dir: (M25 junct 5, A21 S, exit at A26 (signed Tunbridge Wells), then A264 - follow Groombridge village and Groombridge Place Gardens signs) **Map Ref:** *TQ53*
☎ **01892 863999** 📠 **01892 863996**
e-mail: office@groombridge.co.uk

These award-winning gardens, set in 200 acres, feature magnificent walled gardens and herbaceous borders, rose gardens, secret gardens, drunken topiary and much more, against the romantic backdrop of a 17th-century moated manor. In the ancient woodland of the 'Enchanted Forest' there's mystery, innovation and excitement for all ages.

Times: Open 21 Mar-5 Nov, daily 9.30-6 (dusk if earlier) **Fee:** £8.50 (ch 3-12 £7, pen £7.20). Family ticket (2ad+2ch) £29.50. Groups 20+ available on request. **Facilities:** 🅿 ✖ ♿ toilets for disabled shop ✖ (ex guide/hearing dogs) ◀

HAWKINGE *KENT BATTLE OF BRITAIN MUSEUM*

Aerodrome Rd CT18 7AG
Dir: (off A260, 1m along Aerodrome road) *Map Ref:* TR23
☎ 01303 893140
e-mail: kentbattleofbritainmuseum@btinternet.com

This former Battle of Britain Station now houses the largest collection of relics and related memorabilia of British and German aircraft involved in the fighting. Also shown are full-size replicas of the Hurricane, Spitfire and Me109 used in Battle of Britain films. The year 2000 was the 60th anniversary of the Battle of Britain and a new memorial has been dedicated. Artefacts on show, recovered from over 600 battle of Britain aircraft, all form a lasting memorial to all those involved in the conflict.

Times: ✱ Open Etr-Sep, daily 10-5; Oct, daily 11-4. (Last admission 1 hour before closing).
Facilities: 🅿 💻 ♿ shop ✖ (ex guide dogs)

HEVER *HEVER CASTLE & GARDENS*

TN8 7NG
Dir: (M25 junct 5 or 6, 3m SE of Edenbridge, off B2026)
Map Ref: TQ44
☎ 01732 865224 📠 01732 866796
e-mail: mail@hevercastle.co.uk

This enchanting, double-moated, 13th-century castle was the childhood home of Anne Boleyn. Restored by the American millionaire William Waldorf Astor at the beginning of the 20th century, it shows superb Edwardian craftsmanship. Astor also transformed the grounds, creating topiary, a yew maze, a 35-acre lake and Italian gardens.

Times: Open Mar-Nov, daily. Castle 12-6, Gardens 11-6. (Last admission 5). (Closes 4pm Mar & Nov). **Fee:** ✱ Castle & Gardens £8.80 (ch 5-14 £4.80, pen £7.40). Family ticket £22.40. Gardens only £7 (ch 5-14 £4.60, pen £6). Family ticket £18.60. Party 15+.
Facilities: 🅿 💻 ✖ licensed ♿ (wheelchairs available, book in advance) toilets for disabled shop garden centre 🛄

HYTHE *ROMNEY, HYTHE & DYMCHURCH RAILWAY*

TN28 8PL
Dir: (M20 junct 11, off A259 signed New Romney)
Map Ref: TR13
☎ 01797 362353 & 363256 📠 01797 363591
e-mail: rhdr@romneyrail.fsnet.co.uk

The world's smallest public railway, which opened in 1927, has its headquarters here. The concept of two enthusiasts coincided with Southern Railway's plans for expansion, and so the 13-and-a-half mile stretch of 15-inch gauge railway came into being, running from Hythe through New Romney and Dymchurch to Dungeness Lighthouse. Steam engine driving experience days can be booked.

Times: Open daily Etr-Sep, also wknds in Mar & Oct. For times apply to: The Manager, RH & DR, New Romney, Kent.
Facilities: 🅿 (charged) 💻 ♿ (stairlift to Toy & Model Museum) toilets for disabled shop (Dymchurch & Dungeness high season only) 🛄

IGHTHAM IGHTHAM MOTE

TN15 0NT
Dir: (2.5m S off A227, 6m E of Sevenoaks) **Map Ref:** *TQ55*
☎ **01732 810378 & 811145 (info line)** 📄 **01732 811029**
e-mail: igthammote@nationaltrust.org.uk

This moated manor house, nestling in a sunken valley, dates from 1330. The main features of the house span many centuries and include the great hall; old chapel and crypt; Tudor chapel with painted ceiling; drawing room with Jacobean fireplace, frieze and 18th-century hand painted Chinese wallpaper, and the billiards room. There is an extensive garden and interesting walks in the surrounding woodland.

Times: Open Apr-Nov, daily ex Tue & Sat, 10-5.30. Open Good Fri. (Last admission 5). **Fee:** ✱ £6.50 (ch £3). Family ticket £16.50. **Facilities:** 🅿 ☕ ✗ licensed ♿ (wheelchairs,special parking ask at office, virtual tour) toilets for disabled shop ✗ (ex hearing & guide dogs) 🐾

LAMBERHURST SCOTNEY CASTLE GARDEN

TN3 8JN
Dir: (1m S, of Lamberhurst on A21) **Map Ref:** *TQ63*
☎ **01892 891081** 📄 **01892 890110**
e-mail: scotneycastle@nationaltrust.org.uk

The beautiful gardens at Scotney were planned in the 19th century around the remains of the old, moated Scotney Castle. There is something to see at every time of year, with spring flowers followed by rhododendrons, azaleas and a mass of roses, and then superb autumn colours. Estate walks can be enjoyed all year through in the 770 acres of woodlands and meadows. A walker's guide is available.

Times: Garden: Apr-end Oct. Old Castle: May-mid Sep, Wed-Sun, 11-6 or sunset if earlier. BH Mon 11-6. Closed Good Fri. (Last admission 1hr before closing). **Fee:** Telephone for details. **Facilities:** 🅿 ♿ (wheelchair hire, Braille/large print guidebook, audio tape) toilets for disabled shop garden centre ✗ (ex guide & hearing dogs) 🐾 ☕

LYDD RSPB NATURE RESERVE

Boulderwall Farm, Dungeness Rd TN29 9PN
Dir: (off Lydd to Dungeness road, 1m SE of Lydd, follow tourist signs) **Map Ref:** *TR02*
☎ **01797 320588** 📄 **01797 321962**
e-mail: dungeness@rspb.org.uk

This coastal reserve comprises 2,106 acres of shingle beach and flooded pits. An excellent place to watch breeding terns, gulls and other water birds. Wheatears, great crested and little grebes also nest here, and outside the breeding season there are large flocks of teals, shovelers, and goldeneyes, goosanders, smews and both Slavonian and red-necked grebes.

Times: Open: Visitor Centre all year, daily 10-5 (10-4 Nov-Feb). Reserve open all year, daily 9am-9pm (or sunset if earlier). Closed 25-26 Dec. **Fee:** £3 (ch £1, concessions £2). **Facilities:** 🅿 ♿ (access by car to some hides) toilets for disabled shop ✗ (ex guide dogs) ☕

LYMPNE *PORT LYMPNE WILD ANIMAL PARK,MANSION & GARDEN*

CT21 4PD
Dir: (M20 junct 11, follow brown tourist signs) *Map Ref: TR13*
☎ 01303 264647 📠 01303 264944
e-mail: info@howletts.net

A 400-acre wild animal park that houses hundreds of rare animals: Indian elephants, rhinos, wolves, bison, snow leopards, Siberian and Indian tigers, gorillas and monkeys. The mansion designed by Sir Herbert Baker is surrounded by 15 acres of spectacular gardens. Inside, the most notable features include the restored Rex Whistler Tent Room, Moroccan patio and hexagonal library where the Treaty of Paris was signed after World War I. Visit the Spencer Roberts mural room and the Martin Jordan animal mural room.

Times: ✱ Open all year, daily 10-6 (closes at dusk in summer). (Last admission 4.30 summer, 3 winter. Closed 25 Dec. **Facilities:** 🅿 ☕ ✗ licensed ♿ (very limited access for disabled, special route available) toilets for disabled shop garden centre (in season) 🐾 ◀

MAIDSTONE LEEDS CASTLE

ME17 1PL
Dir: (7m E of Maidstone at junct 8 of M20/A20, clearly signed)
Map Ref: TQ75
☎ 01622 765400 📠 01622 735616
e-mail: enquiries@leeds-castle.co.uk

Set on two islands in the centre of a lake, Leeds Castle has been called the 'loveliest castle in the world', and was home to six medieval Queens of England, as well as being Henry VIII's royal palace. Daily falconry displays are given from April to September.

Times: Open daily, Mar-Oct 10-5 (Castle 11-5.30). Nov-Mar 10-3 (Castle 10-3). Closed 26 Jun; 3 Jul; 5 Nov; 25 Dec **Fee:** ✱ Mar-Oct: Castle, Park & Gardens, £12.50 (ch 4-15 £9, students & pen £11); Family ticket (2ad+3ch) £39. Nov-Feb: Castle, Park & Gardens £10.50 (ch £7, students & pen £9). Family ticket £33 **Facilities:** 🅿 ☕ ✗ licensed ♿ (Braille information, induction loops & wheelchair, lift) toilets for disabled shop garden centre 🐾 (ex guide dogs) ◀

MAIDSTONE MUSEUM & BENTLIF ART GALLERY

Saint Faith's St ME14 1LH
Dir: (close to County Hall & Maidstone E train stn)
Map Ref: TQ75
☎ 01622 602838 📠 01622 685022   〔FREE〕
e-mail: alexgurr@maidstone.gov.uk

Set in an Elizabethan manor house, which has been much extended over the years, this museum houses an outstanding collection of fine and applied arts, including watercolours, furniture, ceramics, and a collection of Japanese art and artefacts. The museum of the Queen's Own Royal West Kent Regiment is also accommodated here. Please apply for details of temporary exhibitions, workshops and events.

Times: Open all year, Mon-Sat 10-5.15, Sun & BH Mon 11-4. Closed 25-26 Dec. **Facilities:** 🅿 (150 mtrs) ☕ ♿ shop 🐾 (ex guide dogs) ◀

MUSEUM OF KENT LIFE

Lock Ln, Sandling ME14 3AU
Dir: (from M20 junct 6 onto A229 Maidstone road, follow signs
for Aylesford) *Map Ref:* TQ75
☎ **01622 763936** 📄 **01622 662024**
e-mail: enquiries@museum-kentlife.co.uk

Kent's award-winning open air museum is home to an
outstanding collection of historic buildings which house
exhibitions on life in Kent over the last 100 years. An early 20th-
century village hall and reconstruction of cottages from the 17th
and 20th-centuries are among the more recent buildings to be
viewed. A programme of events is run throughout the year.

Times: ✳ Open Feb-1 Nov, daily 10-5.30, in
winter open every wknd 10-3. **Facilities:** 🅿 💷
✗ licensed ♿ (wheelchairs available, ramps,
transport available) toilets for disabled shop 🛍

PENSHURST PENSHURST PLACE & GARDENS

TN11 8DG
Dir: (M25 junct 5 take A21 Hastings road then exit at
Hildenborough & follow signs) *Map Ref:* TQ54
☎ **01892 870307** 📄 **01892 870866**
e-mail: enquiries@penshurstplace.com

Built between 1340 and 1345, the original house is perfectly
preserved. It was enlarged by successive owners during the 15th,
16th and 17th centuries. There is a toy museum, venture
playground, woodland trail and 10 acres of walled formal gardens.

Times: Open: wknds from 5 Mar, daily from 19 Mar-30 Oct. Grounds
open 10.30-6. House open noon-5.30 (4 on Sat) **Fee:** ✳ House &
Grounds £7 (ch 5-16 £5, pen & students £6.50). Family £20.
Grounds only £5.50 (ch 5-16 £4.50, pen & students £5) Family £17.
Party 20+. Garden season ticket £35. **Facilities:** 🅿 ✗ licensed
♿ (ramp into Barons Hall, Braille & large print guides) toilets for
disabled shop 🐕 (ex guide dogs) 🛍

RAMSGATE MARITIME MUSEUM

Clock House, Pier Yard, Royal Harbour CT11 8LS
Dir: (follow Harbour signs) *Map Ref:* TR36
☎ **01843 587765 & 570622** 📄 **01843 582359**
e-mail: museum@ekmt.fsnet.co.uk

The Maritime Museum is housed in the early 19th-century Clock
House, right on the quayside at Ramsgate Harbour. Four galleries
depict various aspects of the maritime heritage of Ramsgate
andthe East Kent area: the harbour, navigation, fishing, lifeboats
and shipwrecks. The adjacent restored dry dock and floating
exhibits from the museum's historic ship collection include the
steam tug '*Cervia*' and the Dunkirk little ship motor yacht
'*Sundowner*'.

Times: Open Etr-Sep, Tue-Sun 10-5. Oct-Etr
Thu-Sun 10-4.30. **Fee:** ✳ Combined ticket for
museum £1.50. (ch & pen 75p). Family £4.
Facilities: 🅿 (charged) ♿ (restricted) shop 🐕

ROLVENDEN   C M BOOTH COLLECTION OF HISTORIC VEHICLES

Falstaff Antiques, 63 High St TN17 4LP
Dir: (on A28, 3m from Tenterden) **Map Ref:** *TQ83*
☎ **01580 241234**
e-mail: info@morganmuseum.co.uk

Not just vehicles, but various other items of interest connected with transport are included in this display. There is a unique collection of three-wheeled Morgan cars, dating from 1913, and the only known Humber tri-car of 1904, as well as a 1929 Morris van, a 1936 Bampton caravan, and various motorcycles and bicycles. A toy and model car display will be of particular interest to children.

Times: Open all year, Mon-Sat 10-5.30. Closed 25-26 Dec. **Fee:** £2 (ch £1)
Facilities: P (roadside) shop 🔲

STROOD   DIGGERLAND

Medway Valley Leisure Park ME2 2NU
Dir: (M2 junct 2, follow A228 towards Rochester. At rdbt turn right. Diggerland on right) **Map Ref:** *TQ76*
☎ **08700 344437** 📄 **09012 010300**
e-mail: mail@diggerland.com

An adventure park with a difference, where kids of all ages can experience the thrills of driving real earth moving equipment. Choose from various types of diggers and dumpers ranging from a ton to 8.5 tons. Supervised by an instructor, you can complete the Dumper Truck Challenge or dig for buried treasure. New rides include JCB Robots, the Supertrack, Landrover Safari and Spin Dizzy. Even under fives can join in, with mum or dad's help.

Times: Open all year, 10-5, wknds, BHs & school hols **Fee:** £2.50 for all over 2yrs (pen £1.25) Additional charges to ride/drive real machinery
Facilities: P 🍴 & toilets for disabled shop ✈ (ex guide dogs) 🔲

SWINGFIELD MINNIS   *THE BUTTERFLY CENTRE*

McFarlanes Garden Centre CT15 7HX
Dir: (on A260 by junction with Elham-Lydden road)
Map Ref: *TR24*
☎ **01303 844244**

The Butterfly Centre is set in a tropical greenhouse garden where scores of colourful butterflies from all over the world fly free among exotic plants such as bougainvillea, oleander and banana. The temperate section houses our native British butterflies, with many familiar and favourite species but also some rarer varieties.

Times: ✱ Open Apr-1 Oct, daily 10-5. Closed Etr Sun. **Facilities:** P 🍴 & shop garden centre ✈ (ex guide dogs) 🔲

TUNBRIDGE WELLS (ROYAL) TUNBRIDGE WELLS MUSEUM AND ART GALLERY

Civic Centre, Mount Pleasant TN1 1JN
Dir: (adjacent to Town Hall, off A264) *Map Ref:* *TQ53*
☎ **01892 554171 & 526121** 📠 **01892 534227** `FREE`

A local history museum showing Tunbridge ware, archaeology, toys and dolls, and domestic and agricultural bygones. There is also a natural history room with displays of British birds, local butterflies, live insects, geology, minerals and fossils. The art gallery has regularly changing art and craft exhibitions and touring displays from British and European museums. Educational workshops and special events are featured.

Times: Open all year, daily 9.30-5. Sun 10-4. Closed BHs & Etr Sat. **Facilities:** P (200 yds) ♿ (parking adjacent to building) shop ✖ (ex guide dogs)

EC2 BANK OF ENGLAND MUSEUM

Threadneedle St EC2R 8AH
Dir: (museum housed in Bank of London, entrance in Bartholomew Lane)
☎ **020 7601 5545** 📠 **020 7601 5808** `FREE`
e-mail: museum@bankofengland.co.uk

The museum tells the story of the Bank of England from its foundation in 1694 to its role in today's economy. Interactive programmes with graphics and video presentations help explain its many and varied roles. Collections, amassed over 300 years, include a unique array of coins and banknotes, books, furniture, pictures, photographs and cartoons. A popular exhibit is a genuine gold bar, which may be handled.

Times: Open all year, Mon-Fri 10-5. Closed wknds & BHs. Open on day of Lord Major's Show. **Facilities:** P (10 mins walk) ♿ (special need presentation, advance notice helpful) toilets for disabled shop

SE1 BRITISH AIRWAYS LONDON EYE

Riverside Building, County Hall, Westminster Bridge Rd SE1 7PB
Dir: (Underground - Waterloo/Westminster)
☎ **0870 500 0600** 📠 **0870 990 8882**
e-mail: customer.services@ba-londoneye.com

British Airways' London Eye is one of the most inspiring and visually dramatic additions to the London skyline. At 443 feet, it is the world's tallest observation wheel, allowing you to see the capital from a completely new perspective. It takes you on a gradual, 30-minute, 360-degree rotation, revealing parts of the city that are simply not visible from the ground. For Londoners and visitors alike, it is also a great way to see many of the celebrated landmarks. The Eye also caters for private parties with in-flight hospitality packages.

Times: Open May, Mon-Thu 9.30-8, Fri-Sun 9.30-9, (24-31 May last flight 10pm); June, Mon-Thu 9.30-9, Fri-Sun 9.30am-10pm; July-Aug daily 9.30am-10pm; Sep, Mon-Thu 9.30-8, Fri-Sun 9.30-9, (1-7 Sep last flight 10pm); Oct-Dec, daily 9.30-8. Closed 25 Dec. **Fee:** ✱ £11.50 (ch under 5 free, ch £5.75, disabled visitors £9, pen £9). Fast track entry £25. **Facilities:** P (500yds) 🍴 ♿ (Braille guidebooks, wheelchair hire, carer ticket) toilets for disabled shop ✖ (ex guide & hearing dogs) 💳

W12 BBC TELEVISION CENTRE TOURS

BBC Television Centre, Wood Ln W12 7RJ
Dir: (Underground - Central Line/White City)
☎ 0870 603 0304 🖹 020 8576 7466
e-mail: bbctours@bbc.co.uk

Take a look behind the scenes at the world's most famous TV centre. As the BBC TV Centre is a working building, no guarantees can be made as to what visitors will see, although dressing rooms, the News Centre, the Weather Centre, and various studios are all possible. The uncertain nature of the visit means that no two are the same, and that only pre-booked guided tours are available.

Times: Open Mon-Sat. Tours at 10, 10.20, 1.15, 1.30, 3.30 & 3.45. Closed 24 Dec-2 Jan. All tours must be pre-booked. **Fee:** ✱ £7.95 (concessions £6.95, student £5.95). Family ticket £21.95 **Facilities:** 🅿 & (wheelchair & sign language available) toilets for disabled shop ✖ (ex guide/hearing dogs) 🍴

WC1 BRITISH MUSEUM

Great Russell St WC1B 3DG
Dir: (Underground - Russell Sq, Tottenham Court Rd, Holborn)
☎ 020 7323 8000 🖹 020 7323 8616   FREE
e-mail: information@thebritishmuseum.ac.uk

Behind its imposing Neo-Classical façade the British Museum displays the rich and varied treasures which make it one of the great museums of the world. Founded in 1753, displays cover the works of humanity from prehistoric to modern times. The galleries are the responsibility of eight departments, including Egyptian, Greek and Roman, Japanese, Prehistory and Europe, Prints and Drawings, and Ethnography. Among the treasures to be seen are Egyptian mummies, sculptures from the Parthenon, Anglo-Saxon treasure from the Sutton Hoo ship burial and the Vindolanda Tablets from Hadrian's Wall. Young visitors can enjoy special children's trails.

Times: Open all year, Gallery: Mon-Sat 10-5.30 & Thu-Fri 10-8.30. Great Court: Sun-Wed 9-6, Thu-Sat 9am-11pm. Closed Good Fri, 24-26 Dec & 1 Jan. **Facilities:** 🅿 (5 mins walk) 🍵 ✖ licensed & (parking by arrangement) toilets for disabled shop ✖ (ex guide/companion dogs)

SW1 BUCKINGHAM PALACE

Buckingham Palace Rd SW1 1AA
Dir: (Underground - Victoria, Green Park, St James' Park)
☎ 020 7766 7300 🖹 020 7930 9625
e-mail: buckinghampalace@royalcollection.org.uk

Buckingham Palace has been the official London residence of Britain's sovereigns since 1837. Today it serves as both the home and office of Her Majesty the Queen. Its 19 state rooms, which open for eight weeks a year, form the heart of the working palace and more than 50,000 people visit each year as guests at state, ceremonial and official occasions and garden parties. After visiting the state rooms, visitors can enjoy a walk along the south side of the garden, which offers superb views of the west front of the palace and the 19th-century lake.

Times: Open Aug-Sep 9.30-6.30 (last admission 4.15). Entry by timed-ticket. **Fee:** ✱ £12.95 (ch under 17 £6.50, pen & student £11) Family ticket (2ad+3ch) £32.50. Tickets bought in advance £1 booking fee **Facilities:** 🅿 (200yds) (very limited, driving not recommended) & (ex gardens, pre-booking essential) toilets for disabled shop ✖ (ex guide dogs) 🍴

SW1   CABINET WAR ROOMS

Clive Steps, King Charles St SW1A 2AQ
Dir: (Underground - Westminster (exit 6) or St James Park)
☎ 020 7930 6961   📄 020 7839 5897
e-mail: cwr@iwm.org.uk

The underground emergency accommodation used to protect the
Prime Minister, Winston Churchill, his War Cabinet and the Chiefs
of Staff during World War II provides a fascinating insight into that
tense period. Among the 30 rooms are the Cabinet Room, the
Map Room (where information about operations on all fronts was
collected) and the Prime Minister's room, all carefully preserved
since the end of the war. A further nine rooms, including the
Churchill's kitchen, dining room and Mrs Churchill's bedroom,
were recently revealed to the public for the first time, and the
most recent addition is the new Churchill Museum.

Times: Open all year, daily 9.30-6. (Oct-Mar
10-6) (last admission 5.15). Closed 24-26 Dec.
Fee: ✱ £7.50 (ch under 16 free, students & pen
£6). Party 10+ £6 (students & pen £5.50)
Facilities: P (2 mins walk) (meter parking) 🍵
♿ (education service, object handling session,
induction loop) toilets for disabled shop
✖ (ex guide dogs) 🎧

SE10   CUTTY SARK CLIPPER SHIP

King William Walk, Greenwich SE10 9HT
Dir: (situated in dry dock beside Greenwich Pier)
☎ 020 8858 2698   📄 020 8858 6976
e-mail: info@cuttysark.org.uk

The fastest tea clipper ever, built in 1869, the *'Cutty Sark'* once
sailed 363 miles in a single day. The famous vessel has been
preserved in dry dock since 1957, her graceful lines dominating
the riverside at Greenwich. Visitors can climb aboard to explore,
and restoration work can be seen. Exhibitions and a video
presentation tell the story of the ship, built just as sailing ships
were becoming redundant.

Times: Open all year, daily 10-4.30 (Closed 24-27 Dec).
Fee: ✱ £4.25(concessions £3.25, ch £2.95). Family ticket £10.50.
Facilities: P (50mtrs) ♿ shop ✖ (ex guide dogs) 🎧

SE1   DESIGN MUSEUM

Shad Thames SE1 2YD
Dir: (Turn off Tooley St onto Shad Thames. Underground -
London Bridge or Tower Hill)
☎ 0870 909 9009   📄 0870 909 1909
e-mail: info@designmuseum.org

This is the first museum in the world to be dedicated to 20th and
21st century design. Since opening in 1989, it has become one of
London's most inspiring attractions and has won international
acclaim for its ground-breaking exhibition and education
programmes. As one of the leading museums of design, fashion
and architecture, the Design Museum has a changing programme
of exhibitions, combining compelling insights into design history
with innovative contemporary design.

Times: Open all year, daily 10-5.45 (last entry
5.15). Late opening on Fri, during summer
months only 9pm (last entry 8.30pm). Closed 25
Dec only. **Fee:** £6 (concessions £4) Family ticket
£16. **Facilities:** P (3 mins) (Gainsford St car
park is chargeable) 🍵 ✖ licensed ♿ (ramped
entrance, wheelchair & lift) toilets for disabled
shop ✖ (ex guide dogs) 🎧

SE1 THE FASHION & TEXTILE MUSEUM

83 Bermondsey St SE1 3XF
☎ **020 7403 0222** 🖹 **020 7407 8664**
e-mail: info@ftmlondon.org

The first exhibition space in London to dedicate itself to the global fashion industry, the Fashion & Textile Museum was founded by Zandra Rhodes and opened in 2003 on the South Bank. The museum aims to hold two or three major exhibitions a year, manage an education and outreach programme, and host an extensive digital fashion and textile archive.

Times: ✱ Open Tue-Sun 11-5.45 (last admission 5.15) **Facilities:** P & toilets for disabled shop ✖ ◀

SE18 FIREPOWER

Royal Arsenal, Woolwich SE18 6ST
Dir: (A205, right at Woolwich ferry onto A206, attraction signed)
☎ **020 8855 7755** 🖹 **020 8855 7100**
e-mail: info@firepower.org.uk

Firepower, the Royal Artillery Museum in the historic Royal Arsenal, houses Europe's widest collection of historic and modern artillery. Spanning 2,000 years it shows the development of artillery from the Roman catapult to the guided missile and self-propelled gun. Here you can put science into action with touchscreen displays and be awed by big guns from over the last 600 years. Special events, fairs and exhibitions are featured regularly, and you can even hold your child's party here.

Times: ✱ Open Wed-Sun & BHs 11-5.30. Phone for winter opening times. **Facilities:** P (charged) & (wheelchairs available) toilets for disabled shop ✖ (ex guide dogs) ◀

SE1 FLORENCE NIGHTINGALE MUSEUM

Gassiot House, 2 Lambeth Palace Rd SE1 7EW
Dir: (Underground - Westminster, Waterloo. On the site of St Thomas' Hospital)
☎ **020 7620 0374** 🖹 **020 7928 1760**
e-mail: info@florence-nightingale.co.uk

Florence Nightingale needs no introduction, but this museum shows clearly that she was more than 'The Lady with the Lamp'. Beautifully designed, the museum creates a personal setting in which a large collection of Florence's personal items are displayed, including childhood souvenirs, her dress, furniture from her houses and honours awarded to her in old age. There is a small military history collection of souvenirs from the Crimean War, including military medals and a military nursing uniform.

Times: Open all year, Mon-Fri 10-5; wknds & BHs 11.30-4.30. (Last admission 1hr before closing). Closed Good Fri, Etr Sun & 24 Dec-2 Jan. **Facilities:** P (20mtrs) (hospital parking limited and charged) & toilets for disabled shop ✖ (ex guide dogs) ◀

N7   FREIGHTLINERS CITY FARM
Sheringham Rd, Islington N7 8PF
Dir: (off Liverpool Rd)
☎ **020 7609 0467** 🖨 **020 7609 9934**   FREE
e-mail: robert@freightlinersfarm.org.uk

This working farm brings rural life into an urban setting in the heart of Islington. It was originally located on wasteland behind Kings Cross Station - hence the unusual name. A variety of animals can be seen at the farm, including cows, pigs, goats, sheep and poultry, and interesting buildings include a straw-bale construction, solar dome, an outside bread oven and a continental beehive. Farm grown fruit and vegetables is offered for sale.

Times: Winter: 10-4. Summer: 10-4.45.
Facilities: P (charged) 🖫 & toilets for disabled shop garden centre ✖ (ex guide dogs)

SE1   GOLDEN HINDE EDUCATIONAL MUSEUM
St Mary Overie Dock, Cathedral St SE1 9DE
Dir: (On the Thames path between Southwark Cathedral and the new Globe Theatre)
☎ **020 7403 0123** 🖨 **020 7407 5908**
e-mail: info@goldenhinde.co.uk

This is a full size replica of Sir Francis Drake's famous 16th-century galleon. Just like the original, this 'Golden Hinde' has circumnavigated the globe. You can explore the five decks, where replica furniture adds to the atmosphere. Special events include living history enactments, and there are holiday workshops for children. The ship is also available for private hire and children's pirate parties.

Times: ✱ Open all year, 9.30-5.30. Visitors are advised to check opening times as they may vary due to closures for functions. **Facilities:** P (on street parking) 🖫 shop ✖ (ex guide dogs) 🎞

SE1   HMS BELFAST
Morgans Ln, Tooley St SE1 2JH
Dir: (Underground - London Bridge/Tower Hill/Monument. Rail: London Bridge)
☎ **020 7940 6300** 🖨 **020 7403 0719**
e-mail: hmsbelfast@iwm.org.uk

Europe's last surviving big gun armoured warship from World War II, 'HMS Belfast' was launched in 1938 and served in the North Atlantic and Artic with the Home Fleet. She led the Allied naval bombardment of German positions on D-Day, and was saved for the nation in 1971. A tour of the ship will take you from the captain's bridge through nine decks to the massive boiler and engine rooms. You can visit the cramped mess decks, officers' cabins, galley, sick bay, dentist's and laundry.

Times: Open all year, daily. Mar-Oct 10-6 (last admission 5.15); Nov-Feb 10-5 (last admission 4.15). Closed 24-26 Dec. **Fee:** ✱ £7 (ch under 16 free, concessions £4.50). Party £5.50 per person. **Facilities:** 🖫 & (wheelchair lift for access on board) toilets for disabled shop ✖ (ex guide dogs) 🎞

SE1 IMPERIAL WAR MUSEUM

Lambeth Rd SE1 6HZ
Dir: (Underground - Lambeth North, Elephant & Castle or Waterloo)
☎ **020 7416 5000** 🖷 **020 7416 5374**
e-mail: mail@iwm.org.uk

Founded in 1917, this museum illustrates and records all aspects of the two World Wars and other military operations involving Britain and the Commonwealth since 1914. There are always special exhibitions and the programme of events includes film shows and lectures. The museum has a wealth of military reference material, although some reference departments are open to the public by appointment only.

Times: ✱ Open all year, daily 10-6. Closed 24-26 Dec. **Facilities:** P (on street, 100mtrs) (metered Mon-Fri) ☕ ✗ licensed ♿ (parking & wheelchair hire book in advance, study room) toilets for disabled shop ✖ (ex guide dogs) 🎧

N3 THE JEWISH MUSEUM

The Sternberg Centre, 80 East End Rd, Finchley N3 2SY
Dir: (Underground - Finchley Central, 10 mins' walk via Station Rd & Manor View)
☎ **020 8349 1143** 🖷 **020 8343 2162**
e-mail: enquiries@jewishmuseum.org.uk

The Jewish Museum traces the story of Jewish immigration and settlement in London, including a reconstruction of an East End tailoring workshop. It also has a Holocaust Education Gallery with an exhibition on Leon Greenman - British Citizen and Auschwitz survivor. There is a regular programme of changing exhibitions and events.

Times: Open all year, Sun 10.30-4.30, Mon-Thu 10.30-5. Closed Jewish festivals, public holidays & 24 Dec-4 Jan. Also closed Sun in Aug & BH wknds. **Fee:** ✱ £2 (ch free, concessions £1) **Facilities:** P (50mtrs) (on street parking) ☕ ♿ toilets for disabled shop ✖

NW1 THE JEWISH MUSEUM

Raymond Burton House, 129-131 Albert St, Camden Town NW1 7NB
Dir: (Underground - Camden Town, 3 mins walk from station)
☎ **020 7284 1997** 🖷 **020 7267 9008**
e-mail: marketing@jmus.org.uk

The Jewish Museum comprises attractive galleries illustrating Jewish history and religious life in Britain and beyond. It has one of the world's finest collections of Jewish ceremonial art, and a photographic archive of mainly black and white prints of Jewish life in London from the late 19th century onwards. There are constantly changing temporary exhibitions, events and workshops.

Times: Open Mon-Thu, 10-4, Sun 10-5. Closed Jewish Festivals & public holidays. **Fee:** ✱ £3.50 (ch, students, disabled & UB40 £1.50, pen £2.50) Family ticket £8. **Facilities:** P (outside museum) (pay & display parking) ♿ (induction loop in lecture room linked to audio-visual unit) toilets for disabled shop ✖ (ex guide dogs) 🎧

NW3 KENWOOD HOUSE

Hampstead Ln NW3 7JR
Dir: (Underground - Hampstead)
☎ **020 8348 1286** 📄 **020 7973 3891**   FREE

In splendid grounds beside Hampstead Heath, this outstanding neo-classical house contains one of the most important collections of paintings ever given to the nation. Works by Rembrandt, Vermeer, Turner, Gainsborough and Reynolds are all set against a backdrop of sumptuous rooms. Scenes from '*Notting Hill*' and '*Mansfield Park*' were both fimed here. Stroll through the lakeside gardens and woodland and see sculptures by Henry Moore and Barbara Hepworth.

Times: Open all year, Apr-Oct, daily 10-5; Nov-Mar, daily 10-4 (park stays open later, see notices). On Wed & Fri house opens at 10.30. Closed 24-26 Dec & 1 Jan. **Facilities:** 🅿 🚏 ✘ licensed ♿ toilets for disabled shop ♯

SE1 LONDON AQUARIUM

County Hall, Riverside Building, Westminster Bridge Rd SE1 7PB
Dir: (Underground-Waterloo & Westminster. On south bank next to Westminster Bridge, nr Big Ben & London Eye)
☎ **020 7967 8000** 📄 **020 7967 8029**
e-mail: info@londonaquarium.co.uk

The London Aquarium is one of Europe's largest displays of global aquatic life with over 350 species in over 50 displays, ranging from the mystical seahorse to the deadly stonefish. The huge Pacific display is home to a variety of jacks, stingrays and eight sharks. Come and witness the spectacular Atlantic feed where a team of divers hand feeds rays and native British sharks. The rainforest feed incorporates a frenzied piranha attack with the amazing marksmanship of the archerfish. There is also a range of education tours and literature to enhance your visit.

Times: ✱ Open all year, daily 10-6. (Last admission 1hr before closing). Closed 25 Dec. Late opening over summer months see website for details. **Facilities:** 🅿 (300mtrs) 🚏 ♿ (wheelchairs available) toilets for disabled shop 🐕 (ex guide & hearing dogs) ◀

SE1 LONDON DUNGEON

28-34 Tooley St SE1 2SZ
Dir: (Next to London Bridge Station)
☎ **020 7403 7221** 📄 **020 7378 1529**
e-mail: londondungeon@merlin-entertainments.com

The London Dungeon offers blood and guts, torture and terror, in re-enactments of some of the most gruesome events in British history. Brave the Great Fire of London, sail down the Thames towards Traitor's Gate, or visit Executioners Corner. You can also meet some especially Wicked Women. Step back to 1665 to dodge the rats inhabiting London's newest feature, 'The Great Plague'.

Times: ✱ Open all year, daily, Apr-Sep 10-5.30; Oct-Mar 10.30-5. Late night opening in the Summer. Telephone for exact times. **Facilities:** 🅿 (NCP 200yds) 🚏 ♿ toilets for disabled shop 🐕 (ex guide dogs) ◀

WC2 *LONDON'S TRANSPORT MUSEUM*

The Piazza, Covent Garden WC2E 7BB
Dir: (Underground - Covent Garden, Leicester Sq or Holburn)
☎ **020 7379 6344 & 020 7565 7299** 📄 **020 7565 7250**
e-mail: resourced@ltmuseum.co.uk

Covent Garden's original Victorian flower market is home to this excellent museum, which explores the colourful story of London and its famous transport system from 1800 to the present day. There are buses, trams, tube trains and posters, as well as touch-screen displays, videos, working models and tube simulators to bring the story to life.

Times: ✱ Open all year, daily 10-6, Fri 11-6. (Last admission 5.15). Closed 24-26 Dec.
Facilities: P (5 mins walk) (parking meters) 🍵 & (lift & ramps, touch & sign tours) toilets for disabled shop ✖ (ex guide dogs) 🖼

SW13 *LONDON WETLAND CENTRE*

Queen Elizabeth Walk SW13 9WT
Dir: (underground - Hammersmith)
☎ **020 8409 4400** 📄 **020 8409 4401**
e-mail: info@wetlandcentre.org.uk

This inspiring wetland landscape stretches over 105 acres, almost into the heart of London at Barnes. The award-winning centre has been designated as a Site of Special Scientific Interest (SSSI). Thirty wild wetland habitats have been created from a reservoir lagoon to ponds, lakes and reed beds and all of these are home to a wealth of wildlife, including nationally important numbers of gadwell and shoveler ducks. A diverse programme of events ranges from bird races to barbecues.

Times: Winter 9.30-4, Summer 9.30-5.
Fee: £6.75 (ch £4 & pen £5.50). Family ticket £17.50. Groups 10+. Car park £2 charge on Sun & BH's per vehicle. **Facilities:** P (charged) 🍵 ✖ licensed & (ramps, lifts) toilets for disabled shop ✖ (ex guide dogs)

NW1 *LONDON ZOO*

Regents Park NW1 4RY
Dir: (Underground - Camden Town or Regents Park)
☎ **020 7449 6235** 📄 **020 7586 5743**
e-mail: marketing@zsl.org

London Zoo is home to over 12,000 animals, insects, reptiles and fish. First opened in 1828, the Zoo can claim the world's first aquarium, insect and reptile house. Visit the cheeky, the deadly and the wild, and meet the world's largest lizards in the new Komodo dragon exhibit. Get closer to your favourite animals, learn about them at the keeper talks and watch them show off their skills at special events. By visiting London Zoo, visitors help protect endangered species, conserve natural habitats and bring learning to life for all ages.

Times: Open all year, daily from 10. Closed 25 Dec. **Fee:** ✱ £13 (ch 3-15 £9.75, concessions £11). Family £41. **Facilities:** P (charged) 🍵 ✖ licensed & (wheelchairs & booster scooter available) toilets for disabled shop ✖ 🖼

NW8 LORD'S TOUR & M.C.C. MUSEUM

Lord's Ground NW8 8QN
Dir: (Underground - St John's Wood)
☎ **020 7616 8595 & 7616 8596** 📄 **020 7266 3825**
e-mail: tours@mcc.org.uk

Established in 1787, Lord's is the home of the MCC (Marylebone Cricket Club) and the game of cricket itself. Guided tours take you behind the scenes, and highlights include the Long Room and the MCC Museum (the oldest sporting museum in the world), where the Ashes and a large collection of paintings and memorabilia are displayed. The museum is open on match days for spectators.

Times: Open all year, Oct-Mar tours at 12 & 2. Apr-Sep 10, 12 & 2 (restrictions on some match days). Telephone for details & bookings.
Fee: Guided tour £7 (ch £4.50, students & pen £5.50). Family ticket (2ad+2ch) £20. Party 25+. Museum only £2.50 (concessions £1) plus ground admission (match days only).
Facilities: 🅿 ✗ licensed ♿ (by arrangement) toilets for disabled shop ✈ (ex guide dogs) 🔲

NW1 MADAME TUSSAUD'S & THE LONDON PLANETARIUM

Marylebone Rd NW1 5LR
Dir: (Underground - Baker Street)
☎ **020 7935 6861** 📄 **020 7465 0862**
e-mail: csc@madame-tussauds.com

Madame Tussaud's world-famous waxwork collection was founded in Paris in 1770. It moved to England in 1802 and found a permanent home in London's Marylebone Road in 1884. The 21st century has brought new innovations and new levels of interactivity. Listen to Kylie Minogue whisper in your ear, become an A-list celeb in the 'Blush' nightclub, and take your chances in a high security prison populated by dangerous serial killers. Madame Tussaud's has been combined with the equally memorable London Planetarium, where visitors can now interact with characters from Disney's 'Treasure Planet'.

Times: ✱ Open all year 10-5.30 (9.30 wknds, 9 summer) **Facilities:** 🅿 (200mtrs) ✗ licensed ♿ (all parts accessible except Spirit of London ride) toilets for disabled shop ✈ (ex guide dogs) 🔲

E2 MUSEUM OF CHILDHOOD AT BETHNAL GREEN

Cambridge Heath Rd E2 9PA
Dir: (Underground - Bethnal Green)
☎ **020 8980 2415** 📄 **020 8983 5225**   FREE
e-mail: bgmc@vam.ac.uk

The Museum of Childhood houses a multitude of childhood delights. Toys, dolls and dolls' houses, model soldiers, puppets, games, model theatres, children's costume and nursery antiques are all included in its well planned displays. Art activities and soft play are available every weekend throughout the school holidays. There is a permanent under fives' play area and games zone with board games and giant snakes and ladders.

Times: Open all year, Mon-Thu & Sat-Sun 10-5.50. Closed Fri, 24-26 Dec & 1 Jan.
Facilities: 🅿 (metered parking) 🔲 ♿ (disabled parking by arrangement) toilets for disabled shop ✈

EC2 MUSEUM OF LONDON

150 London Wall EC2Y 5HN
Dir: (Underground - St Paul's, Barbican)
☎ **020 7600 3699** 📠 **020 7600 1058**
e-mail: info@museumoflondon.org.uk

Dedicated to the story of London and its people, the Museum of London exists to inspire a passion for London in all who visit it. As well as the permanent collection, the museum has a varied exhibition programme with three major temporary exhibitions and six topical displays each year. There are also smaller exhibitions in the newly-developed foyer gallery. A wide programme of lectures and activities is provided.

Times: ✱ Open all year, Mon-Sat 10-5.50, Sun 12-5.50. Closed 24-26 Dec & 1 Jan.
Facilities: 🅿 ☕ ♿ (wheelchairs available, lifts & induction loops, parking) toilets for disabled shop ✖ (ex guide dogs) ◼

WC2 MUSEUMS OF THE ROYAL COLLEGE OF SURGEONS

35-43 Lincoln's Inn Fields WC2A 3PE
Dir: (Underground - Holborn)
☎ **020 7869 6560** 📠 **020 7869 6564**
e-mail: museums@rcseng.ac.uk

FREE

The newly-refurbished Hunterian Museum houses the anatomical and pathological specimens collected by John Hunter FRS (1728-1793), a renowned surgeon and teacher of anatomy. The museum also contains the Science of Surgery Gallery which provides an insight into the development of surgical practice from the 18th century to the present day. The Collection Study Centre holds the museum's reserve collection and provides a dedicated space for learning, exploration and study.

Times: Due to reopen in Feb 2005, Mon-Fri 10-5
Facilities: 🅿 (15mtrs) (pay & display 8.30-6.30pm) ♿ (prior notice required, external lift) shop ✖ (ex guide dogs)

WC2 NATIONAL GALLERY

Trafalgar Square WC2N 5DN
Dir: (Underground - Charing Cross, Leicester Square, Embankment & Piccadilly Circus. Rail: Charing Cross. Located on N side of Trafalgar Sq)
☎ **020 7747 2885** 📠 **020 7747 2423**
e-mail: information@ng-london.org.uk

FREE

All the great periods of Western European painting from 1260-1900 are represented here. The Gallery's particular treasures include Velázquez's 'Toilet of Venus', Leonardo da Vinci's cartoon 'The Virgin and Child with Saints Anne and John the Baptist', Rembrandt's 'Belshazzar's Feast', Van Gogh's 'Sunflowers', and Titian's 'Bacchus and Ariadne'. The British paintings include Gainsborough's 'Mr and Mrs Andrews' and Constable's 'Haywain'.

Times: Open all year, daily 10-6, (Wed until 9). Special major charging exhibitions open normal gallery times. Closed 24-26 Dec & 1 Jan.
Facilities: 🅿 (100yds) ☕ ✖ licensed ♿ (wheelchair, induction loop, lift, deaf/blind visitor tours) toilets for disabled shop ✖ (ex guide & hearing dogs) ◼

SE10 NATIONAL MARITIME MUSEUM

Romney Rd SE10 9NF
Dir: (central Greenwich)
☎ 020 8312 6565 📄 020 8312 6632  FREE

Britain's seafaring history is represented in a series of exhibits in this impressive modern museum. Themes include exploration and discovery, Nelson, trade and empire, passenger shipping and luxury liners, maritime London, costume, art and the sea, and the future of the sea. There are interactive displays for children and a diverse programme of special exhibitions.

Times: Open all year, daily 10-5. Closed Xmas/New Year.
Facilities: P (50 yds) (parking in Greenwich limited) 🍽 ✕ licensed ♿ (wheelchairs, advisory service for hearing/sight impaired) toilets for disabled shop 🐕 (guide dogs) 📹

WC2 NATIONAL PORTRAIT GALLERY

St Martin's Place WC2H 0HE
Dir: (Underground - Charing Cross, Leicester Square. Buses to Trafalgar Square)
☎ 020 7306 0055 📄 020 7306 0056 FREE

The National Portrait Gallery is home to the largest collection of portraiture in the world featuring famous British men and woman who have created history from the Middle Ages until the present day. Over 1,000 portraits are on display across three floors form Henry VIII and Florence Nightingale to The Beatles and The Queen. And, if you want to rest those weary feet, visit the fabulous Portrait Restaurant on the top floor with roof-top views across London.

Times: Open all year, Mon-Wed & Sat-Sun 10-6, Thu-Fri 10-9. Closed Good Fri, 24-26 Dec & 1 Jan. (Gallery closure commences 10mins prior to stated time). **Facilities:** P (200yds) 🍽 ✕ licensed ♿ (stair climber,touch tours,audio guide,large print captions) toilets for disabled shop 🐕 (ex guide dogs) 📹

SW7 THE NATURAL HISTORY MUSEUM

Cromwell Rd SW7 5BD
Dir: (Underground - South Kensington)
☎ 020 7942 5000 📄 020 7942 5075 FREE
e-mail: marketing@nhm.ac.uk

The Natural History Museum - the UK's national museum of natural history - is a vast and elaborate Romanesque-style building covering an area of four acres, its terracotta facing decorated with relief mouldings of animals, birds and fishes. A collection of over 70 million specimens from all over the globe ranges from dinosaurs to diamonds and earthquakes to ants, and the exhibits take you on a journey into Earth's past, present and future. Permanent exhibitions include the Earth Galleries, the Darwin Centre, and the Wildlife Garden, the museum's first living exhibition. There is also a varied programme of special exhibitions and children's activities.

Times: Mon-Sat 10-5.50, Sun 11-5.50 (last admission 5.30). Closed 24-26 Dec.
Facilities: P (180yds) (limited parking, use public transport) 🍽 ✕ licensed ♿ (top floor/one gallery not accessible, wheelchair hire) toilets for disabled shop 🐕 (ex guide dogs) 📹

WC1 *PETRIE MUSEUM OF EGYPTIAN ARCHAEOLOGY*

Malet Place, Univerity College London WC1E 6BT
Dir: (on 1st floor of the D M S Watson building, in Malet Place, off
Torrington Place)
☎ **020 7679 2884** 📄 **020 7679 2886**
e-mail: petrie.museum@ucl.ac.uk

One of the largest and most inspiring collections of Egyptian
archaeology anywhere in the world. The displays illustrate life in
the Nile Valley from prehistory, through the era of the Pharaohs to
Roman and Islamic times. Especially noted for its collection of the
personal items that illustrate life and death in Ancient Egypt,
including the world's earliest surviving dress (c 2800 BC).

Times: ✱ Open all year, Tue-Fri 1-5, Sat 10-1.
Closed for 1 wk at Xmas/Etr. **Facilities:** 🍽 ✕
♿ toilets for disabled shop ✖ (ex guide dogs)

W1 *POLLOCK'S TOY MUSEUM*

1 Scala St W1T 2HL
Dir: (Underground - Goodge St)
☎ **020 7636 3452**
e-mail: info@pollocksmuseum.co.uk

Teddy bears, wax and china dolls, dolls' houses, board games, toy
theatres, tin toys, mechanical and optical toys, folk toys and
nursery furniture, are among the attractions to be seen in this
appealing museum. Items from all over the world and from all
periods are displayed in two small, interconnecting houses with
winding staircases and charming little rooms. Toy theatre
performances are available for groups.

Times: ✱ Open all year, Mon-Sat 10-5. Closed
BH, Sun & Xmas. **Facilities:** 🅿 (100yds) (Central
London restrictions) ♿ shop 🛍

NW9 ROYAL AIR FORCE MUSEUM

Grahame Park Way, Hendon NW9 5LL
Dir: (within easy reach of the A5, A41, M1 and North Circular
A406 roads. Tube on Northern Line to Colindale. Rail to Mill Hill
Broadway station. Bus route 303 passes the door)
☎ **020 8205 2266** 📄 **020 8358 4981**   ⟨FREE⟩
e-mail: groups@rafmuseum.org

Take off to the Royal Air Force Museum and soar through the
history of aviation from the earliest balloon flights to the latest
Eurofighter. A recent addition is the dramatic 'Milestones of Flight'
hall, with an exciting display of suspended aircraft and touch
screen technology. Visitors can experience the bi-plane era in the
beautifully restored Grahame-White factory, or have some hands-
on fun in the expanded Aeronauts Interactive centre. All this plus
a huge collection of aircraft, simulator rides, uniforms, light and
sound show, and much more.

Times: Open daily 10-6. (Last admission 5.30).
Closed 24-26 Dec & 1 Jan **Facilities:** 🅿 🍽
✕ licensed ♿ (lifts, ramps & wheelchairs
available) toilets for disabled shop ✖ (ex guide
dogs) 🛍

SE10 ROYAL OBSERVATORY GREENWICH

Greenwich Park, Greenwich SE10 9NF
Dir: (off A2, Greenwich Park)
☎ 020 8312 6565 📠 020 8312 6632   FREE

Charles II founded the Royal Observatory in 1675 with the purpose of 'perfecting navigation and astronomy'. It stands at zero meridian longitude and is the original home of Greenwich Mean Time. It houses an extensive collection of historic timekeeping, astronomical and navigational instruments. There are Planetarium shows throughout the year, and special events are planned for the school holidays.

Times: Open all year, daily 10-5. Closed 24-26 Dec & 1 Jan. **Facilities:** 🅿 (charged) ♿ toilets for disabled shop ✻ ◀

EC4 ST PAUL'S CATHEDRAL

St Pauls Courtyard EC4M 8AD
☎ 020 7246 8348 📠 020 7248 3104
e-mail: chapterhouse@stpaulscathedral.org.uk

Completed in 1710, Sir Christopher Wren's architectural masterpiece is the cathedral church of the Bishop of London, and arose, like so much of this area of London, from the ashes of the Great Fire of London in 1666. Among the worthies buried here are Nelson and the Duke of Wellington, while Holman Hunt's masterpiece, 'Light of the World' hangs in the nave. Impressive views of London can be seen from the Golden Gallery.

Times: Open Cathedral, Crypt, Ambulatory, Mon-Sat 8.30. Galleries 9.30. (Last admission 4). Cathedral may close for special services. **Fee:** ✱ £7 (ch £3, concessions £6) Family £17 (2ad+2ch). Groups 10+ £6.50 (ch £2.50, concessions £5.50) **Facilities:** 🅿 (400mtrs) (meter parking in area) 💻 ✗ licensed ♿ toilets for disabled shop ✻ (ex guide dogs) ◀

SW7 SCIENCE MUSEUM

Exhibition Rd, South Kensington SW7 2DD
Dir: (Underground - South Kensington, signed from tube stn)
☎ 020 7942 4000 📠 020 7942 4421
e-mail: sciencemuseum@nmsi.ac.uk

Ideal for children and adults too, the displays feature many working models with knobs to press, handles to turn and buttons to push to various different effects: exhibits are set in motion, light up, rotate and make noises. The collections cover science, technology, engineering and industry through the ages; there are galleries dealing with printing, chemistry, nuclear physics, navigation, photography, electricity, communications and medicine. The Wellcome Wing includes an IMAX cinema, six new galleries and a restaurant.

Times: ✱ Open all year, daily 10-6. Closed 24-26 Dec. **Facilities:** 💻 ✗ licensed ♿ (personal 2hr tour of museum) toilets for disabled shop ✻ (ex guide dogs) ◀

SE1 SHAKESPEARE'S GLOBE EXHIBITION AND THEATRE TOUR

21 New Globe Walk, Bankside SE1 9DT
Dir: (Underground - London Bridge, walk along Bankside.
Mansion House, walk across Southwark Bridge. St Pauls, walk
across Millennium Bridge)
☎ **020 7902 1500** ▤ **020 7902 1515**
e-mail: info@shakespearesglobe.com

Guides help to bring England's theatrical heritage to life at the
'unparalleled and astonishing' recreation of Shakespeare's famous
Globe Theatre. The exhibition is located in the theatre's
'Underglobe' and includes demonstrations of sword fighting and
how actors dress in Elizabethan costumes. Here you can discover
what an Elizabethan audience would have been like and find out
about the rivalry between the Bankside theatres. You can also
learn about bear baiting, the stews, the penny stinkards and what
a bodger is. Tours last about an hour and a half.

Times: Open all year, May-Sep, daily 9-12 (12-5
Rose Theatre tour); Oct-Apr 10-5. **Fee:** ✱ Oct-Apr
£8 (ch £5.50, pen & students £6.50). May-Sep
£8.50 (ch £6, pen & students £7) Group rates
available. **Facilities:** P (0.5m) (very limited
on-street parking) ➿ ✗ licensed ♿ (parking
spaces, 'touch tours' available by appointment)
toilets for disabled shop ✖ (ex guide & hearing
dogs) ◄

SW1 TATE BRITAIN

Millbank SW1P 4RG
Dir: (Underground - Pimlico)
☎ **020 7887 8000 & rec info 020 7887 8008**
e-mail: information@tate.org.uk

Tate Britain is the national gallery of British art from 1500 to the
present day, from Tudors to the Turner Prize. Tate holds the
greatest collection of British art in the world, including works by
Blake, Constable, Epstein, Gainsborough, Gilbert and George,
Hatoum, Hirst, Hockney, Hodgkin, Hogarth, Moore, Rossetti,
Sickert, Spencer, Stubbs and Turner. The gallery is the world
centre for the understanding and enjoyment of British art. The
opening of the Tate Centenary provides Tate Britain with ten new
and five refurbished galleries used for special exhibitions and the
permanent collection.

Times: Open daily 10-5.50. Closed 24-26 Dec.
Fee: Free. Donations welcomed. Prices vary for
special exhibitions. **Facilities:** P (100mtrs) (1hr
stay) ➿ ✗ licensed ♿ (wheelchairs on request,
parking by prior arrangement) toilets for disabled
shop ✖ (ex guide & hearing dogs) ◄

SE1 *TATE MODERN*

Bankside SE1 9TG
Dir: (Underground - Southwark, Blackfriars)
☎ **020 7887 8008 (info) & 020 7887 8888**
▤ **020 7401 5052**
e-mail: information@tate.org.uk

The Tate Modern, on the bank of the River Thames, is the world's
most popular art museum. It is housed in the former Bankside
Power Station with a stunning entrance hall in the vast turbine
hall. The three levels of galleries are topped with a two-storey
glass roof, which affords spectacular views over London. The Tate
Modern presents a permanent collection of modern and
contemporary art from 1900 to the present day. Admission to the
main gallery is free, but there is generally a fee for the special
exhibitions.

Times: Open all year, Sun-Thu 10-6, Fri & Sat
10am-10pm. Closed 24-26 Dec.
Facilities: P (very limited) ➿ ✗ licensed
♿ (parking & wheelchairs available call 020 7887
8888) toilets for disabled shop ✖ (ex guide
dogs) ◄

WC2 THEATRE MUSEUM

Russell St, Covent Gardent WC2E 7PR
Dir: (Underground - Covent Garden, Leicester Sq)
☎ **020 7943 4700** 🖷 **020 7943 4777** FREE
e-mail: tmenquiries@vam.ac.uk

Major developments, events and personalities from the performing arts, including stage models, costumes, prints, drawings, posters, puppets, props and a variety of other theatre memorabilia feature at the Theatre Museum. There are guided tours, demonstrations on the art of stage make-up, and you can dress up in costumes from National Theatre companies. Groups are advised to book in advance. Theatre and walking tours 2pm Saturdays.

Times: Open all year, Tue-Sun 10-6. Closed 24-26 Dec & 1 Jan. **Facilities:** P (meters, NCP 250yds) ♿ (Braille guides, audio tours) toilets for disabled shop ✖ (ex guide dogs) ▦

SE1 THE TOWER BRIDGE EXHIBITION

Tower Bridge Rd SE1 2UP
Dir: (Underground - Tower Hill or London Bridge)
☎ **020 7940 3985** 🖷 **020 7357 7935**
e-mail: enquiries@towerbridge.org.uk

Tower Bridge, dating from 1894, is one of the capital's most famous landmarks. The Tower Bridge Exhibition uses state-of-the-art effects to present the story of the bridge in a dramatic and exciting fashion. Much of the original machinery for working the bridge can be seen in the engine rooms, and the glass-covered walkways stand 142-feet above the Thames, affording panoramic views of the river.

Times: ✱ Open all year, 9.30-6 (last ticket sold 5). Closed 1 Jan & 24-25 Dec.
Facilities: P (100yds) ♿ toilets for disabled shop ✖ ▦

EC3 TOWER OF LONDON

Tower Hill EC3N 4AB
Dir: (Underground - Tower Hill)
☎ **0870 756 6060**

Perhaps the most famous castle in the world, the Tower of London has played a central part in British history. The White Tower, built by William the Conqueror, is an outstanding example of Norman military architecture. It was the notorious state prison for hundreds of years and two of Henry VIII's wives were executed here. The tower is protected by Yeoman Warders, or Beefeaters, and is home to the Crown Jewels, and the Royal Armouries, first viewed in 1489. Look out for the ravens, whose continued residence is said to ensure that the kingdom does not fall.

Times: ✱ Open all year, Mar-Oct, Mon-Sat 9-6, Sun 10-6 (last admission 5); Nov-Feb, Tue-Sat 9-5, Sun 10-5 (last admission 4). Closed 24-26 Dec & 1 Jan. **Facilities:** P (100yds) (NCP Lower Thames St) ▇ ✖ licensed ♿ (access guide can be obtained in advance call 020 7488 5694) toilets for disabled shop ✖ (ex guide dogs) ▦

SW7 VICTORIA AND ALBERT MUSEUM

Cromwell Rd, South Kensington SW7 2RL
Dir: (Underground - South Kensington, Museum situated on A4, Buses C1,14,74,414 stop outside the Cromwell Road entrance)
☎ **020 7942 2000**
e-mail: vanda@vam.ac.uk FREE

The world's finest museum of art and design has collections spanning 3,000 years, comprising sculpture, furniture, fashion and textiles, paintings, silver, glass, ceramics, jewellery, books, prints, and photographs from Britain and all over the world. Highlights include the national collection of paintings by John Constable, the Dress Court showing fashion from 1500 to the present day, a superb Asian collection, the Jewellery Gallery including the Russian Crown Jewels, and the 20th Century Gallery, devoted to contemporary art and design. The stunning British Galleries 1500-1900 tell the story of British design from the Tudor age to the Victorian era.

Times: Open all year, Mon-Sun 10-5.45. Closed 24-26 Dec. Wed & last Fri of month open late, 10am-10pm. **Facilities:** P (500yds) (limited, charged parking) ⬛ ✕ licensed ♿ (Facilities available. Call for details 020 7942 2211) toilets for disabled shop ✕ (ex guide dogs) ◀

SW1 WESTMINSTER ABBEY

Broad Sanctuary SW1P 3PA
Dir: (Underground - Westminster, St James's Park. Next to Parliament Square and opposite the Houses of Parliament)
☎ **020 7222 5152 7654 4900** 📠 **020 7233 2072**
e-mail: info@westminster-abbey.org

Westminster Abbey was originally a Benedictine monastery. In the 11th century it was re-founded by St Edward the Confessor. The great Romanesque abbey Edward built next to his royal palace became his burial place shortly after it was completed. Over the centuries many more kings and queens have been buried, and many great figures commemorated here. It has also been the setting for nearly every coronation since that of William the Conqueror in 1066, and for numerous other royal occasions. The present building, begun by Henry III in 1245, is one of the most visited churches in the world.

Times: Abbey: Mon-Fri 9.30-3.45, Sat 9-1.45. Wed late night opening 6-7. (Last admission 60 mins before closing). Cloister: daily 8-6. No tourist visiting on Sun, however visitors are welcome at services. The Abbey may at short notice be closed for special services & other events. **Fee:** ✱ £7.50 (ch 11-15 £5, under 11's free, pen & students £4). Family ticket (2ad+2ch) £15. **Facilities:** ⬛ ♿ (areas accessible induction loop) shop ✕ (ex guide dogs) ◀

SW1 WESTMINSTER CATHEDRAL

Victoria St SW1P 1QW
Dir: (300yds from Victoria Station)
☎ **020 7798 9055** 📠 **020 7798 9090** FREE
e-mail: barrypalmer@rcdow.org.uk

Westminster Cathedral is a fascinating example of Victorian architecture. Designed in the Early Christian Byzantine style by John Francis Bentley, its strongly oriental appearance makes it very distinctive. The foundation stone was laid in 1895 but the interior decorations are not fully completed. The Campanile Bell Tower is 273 feet high and has a four-sided viewing gallery with magnificent views over London. The lift is open daily 9am-5pm Mar-Nov but shut Mon-Wed from Dec-Feb.

Times: Open all year, daily 7am-7pm. **Facilities:** P (0.25m) (2hr metered parking) ⬛ ♿ (all parts accessible except side chapels) shop ✕ (ex guide dogs)

SE1 WINSTON CHURCHILL'S BRITAIN AT WAR EXPERIENCE

64/66 Tooley St SE1 2TF
Dir: (mid way down Tooley St, between London Bridge & Tower Bridge. 2 min walk from London Bridge Stn)
☎ **020 7403 3171** 🖷 **020 7403 5104**
e-mail: britainatwar@dial.pipex.com

Experience life on the home front during World War II, as the Britain at War Experience recreates the sensation of the London Blitz through special effects, including the sounds, sights and smells - the very dust and smoke - of an air raid. Take the lift to the underground, where many spent sleepless nights. Find out about evacuation, rationing, air-raids and the blackout, and tune into the latest war time news on the radio.

Times: Open all year, Apr-Sep 10-5.30; Oct-Mar 10-4.30. Closed 24-26 Dec. **Fee:** ✱ £8.50 (ch 5-16 £4.50, student & pen £5.50). Family ticket (2ad+2ch) £18. **Facilities:** Ⓟ (100mtrs) ♿ (wheelchair for loan) toilets for disabled shop (small) ✖ (ex guide dogs) ◀

BRENTFORD KEW BRIDGE STEAM MUSEUM

Green Dragon Ln TW8 0EN
Dir: (Underground - Kew Gardens, District line then 391 bus. Museum 100yds from N side of Kew Bridge. From M4 junct 2 follow A4 to Chiswick rdbt, take A315 to Kew Bridge, Green Dragon Ln 1st right after lights) **Map Ref:** TQ17
☎ **020 8560 4757** 🖷 **020 8569 9978**
e-mail: info@kbsm.org

This Victorian pumping station has steam engines and six beam engines, of which five are working and one is the largest in the world. A diesel house and waterwheel can also be seen along with London's only steam narrow-gauge railway, which operates every Sunday March to November. The Water for Life Gallery tells the story of London's water supply from Pre-Roman times. The newest exhibit is a water pump, once powered by horses.

Times: Open all year, daily 11-5. Engines in steam, wknds & BHs. Closed Good Fri, Xmas wk & New Year. **Fee:** ✱ Wkdays £4, wknds £5.20 (reductions for pen, students & ch). **Facilities:** Ⓟ ▣ ♿ (partially sighted tours, wheelchairs, large print guide) toilets for disabled shop ◀

CHESSINGTON CHESSINGTON WORLD OF ADVENTURES

Leatherhead Rd KT9 2NE
Dir: (M25 junct 9/10, on A243) **Map Ref:** TQ16
☎ **0870 444 7777** 🖷 **01372 725050**

Family theme park with rides, attractions and amusements divided into various areas. Animal Land features big cats, gorillas and other resident animals, which can also be seen from the Safari Skyway. Favourite rides include Dragon Falls in the Mystic East, the Runaway Train in Mexicana, Black Buccaneer in Pirates' Cove, Vampire in Transylvania and Rameses Revenge in the Forbidden Kingdom. A recent addition is Land of the Dragons, for two to eight-year olds, with the new ride Dragon's Fury. Younger children will also enjoy Beanoland, Toytown, and the 4-D magic of Hocus Pocus Hall.

Times: ✱ Open 10 Apr-2 Nov (excluding some off peak days) either 10-5, 10-6 or 10-7 (telephone for details). Open until 7.30 during Halloween Hocus Pocus. **Facilities:** Ⓟ ▣ ✖ licensed ♿ (some rides not accessible, disabled guide available) toilets for disabled shop ✖ (ex guide dogs & hearing dogs) ◀

CHISLEHURST CHISLEHURST CAVES

Old Hill BR7 5NB
Dir: (off A222 near Chislehurst railway stn. Turn into station approach, then right & right again into Caveside Close)
Map Ref: TQ47
☎ 020 8467 3264 📠 020 8295 0407
e-mail: enquiries@chislehurstcaves.co.uk

Grab a lantern and get ready for an amazing adventure. Visit the caves and your whole family can travel back in time as you explore the maze of passageways dug through the chalk deep beneath Chislehurst. Accompanied by an experienced guide on a 45-minute tour you'll see the tunnels made famous as a shelter during World War II, visit the cave's church, druid altar and the haunted pool.

Times: Open all year, Wed-Sun, 10-4. Daily during local school hols (incl half terms). Closed Xmas.
Fee: £4 (ch & pen £2). **Facilities:** 🅿 🍵 ✗ licensed shop ✖ (ex guide dogs) ◾

HAM HAM HOUSE

TW10 7RS
Dir: (W of A307, between Kingston & Richmond) *Map Ref:* TQ17
☎ 020 8940 1950 📠 020 8332 6903
e-mail: hamhouse@nationaltrust.org.uk

Built in 1610 and extended in the 1670s, Ham House is one of the most outstanding Stuart houses remaining. It was home to the renowned political schemer, the Duchess of Lauderdale, and was at the heart of Civil War politics and Restoration court intrigues. Beautiful grounds include the Cherry Garden, eight grass plats, a 17th-century orangery, a listed avenue of over 250 trees, and a flock of green parakeets.

Times: Open Gardens: all year, Sat-Wed 11-6 or dusk if earlier. Closed 25-26 Dec & 1 Jan. House: 3 Apr-Oct, Sat-Wed 1-5. (Last admission 4.30).
Fee: ✱ House £7.50 (ch £3.75). Family ticket £18.75. Garden only £3.50 (ch £1.75). Family ticket £8.75. **Facilities:** 🅿 (400yds) 🍵 ♿ (Braille guide, wheelchairs, stairclimber, lift, parking) toilets for disabled shop ✖ (ex guide/hearing dogs) ♥ ◾

HAMPTON COURT HAMPTON COURT PALACE

KT8 9AU
Dir: (on A308, close to A3, M3 & M25 exits. Train from Waterloo - Hampton Court, 2mins walk from station) *Map Ref:* TQ16
☎ 0870 752 7777 & 8781 9501 📠 020 8781 9669

With over 500 years of royal history, Hampton Court Palace has something to offer everyone, from the magnificent state apartments to the domestic reality of the Tudor kitchens. Costumed guides and audio tours bring the palace to life and provide an insight into how life in the palace would have been in the time of Henry VIII and William III.

Times: Open mid Mar-mid Oct, daily, 9.30-6 (10.15-6 on Mon); mid Oct-mid Mar, daily, 9.30-4.30 (10.15-4.30 on Mon).
Facilities: 🅿 (charged) 🍵 ✗ licensed ♿ (lifts, buggies for gardens, wheelchairs, wardens to assist) toilets for disabled shop (4 shops on site) ✖ (ex guide/hearing dogs) ◾

KEW KEW GARDENS (ROYAL BOTANIC GARDENS)

TW9 3AB
Dir: (Underground - Kew Gdns) *Map Ref:* TQ17
☎ **020 8332 5655** 📄 **020 8332 5197**
e-mail: info@kew.org

Kew Gardens is a paradise throughout the seasons. Lose yourself in the magnificent conservatories and discover plants from the world's deserts, mountains and oceans. Wide-open spaces, stunning vistas, listed buildings and wildlife contribute to the garden's unique atmosphere. As well as being famous for its beautiful gardens, Kew is world renowned for its contribution to botanical and horticultural science.

Times: Open all year, Gardens daily 9.30-between 4 & 7.30pm (seasonal, visit website or phone to verify). Closed 25 Dec & 1 Jan.
Fee: ✱ £8.50 (concessions £6.50, ch under 17 free).
Facilities: 🅿 (charged) 🍮 ✗ licensed ♿ (16 seat bus tour: enquiries ring 020 8332 5643) toilets for disabled shop ✈ (ex guide dogs) ◀

TWICKENHAM MARBLE HILL HOUSE

Richmond Rd TW1 2NL
Map Ref: TQ17
☎ **020 8892 5115** 📄 **020 8607 9976**

Marble Hill House is a magnificent Thames-side Palladian villa built for Henrietta Howard, mistress of King George II, set in 66 acres of riverside parklands. High points are the gilded decorations, early Georgian paintings and furniture, and the Lazenby Bequest Chinoiserie display. Free guided tours are held on a regular basis, when visitors can hear stories about the house's historical inhabitants, and the grounds are the venue for a programme of popular outdoor concerts.

Times: Open Apr-Oct, Sat 10-2, Sun & BHs 10-5. Closed Nov-Mar but pre-booked groups by arrangement. **Fee:** ✱ £3.50 (ch £2, concessions £3). Prices & opening times relate to 2004, for further details phone or log onto www.english-heritage.org.uk/visits
Facilities: 🅿 🍮 ✗ licensed ♿ toilets for disabled shop ✈ (ex on lead in certain areas) ⌗

MUSEUM OF RUGBY & TWICKENHAM STADIUM TOURS

Rugby Football Union, Rugby Rd TW1 1DZ
Dir: (A316, follow signs to museum) *Map Ref:* TQ17
☎ **020 8892 8877** 📄 **020 8892 2817**
e-mail: museum@rfu.com

Located beneath the east stand of the Twickenham Stadium, home of the England team and headquarters of the Rugby Football Union, the museum uses interactive displays, period set pieces and video footage to bring the history of the game to life. The tour includes a visit to the England dressing room, and magnificent views of the stadium from the top of the north stand. After that why not spend time in the Scrummery or Rugby Store.

Times: Open, Tue-Sat 10-5 (last admission 4.30), Sun 11-5 (last admission 4.30). Closed post Twickenham match days, Etr Sun, 24-26 Dec & 1 Jan. **Fee:** ✱ Museum Tour: £8 (concessions £5).
Facilities: 🅿 🍮 ✗ licensed ♿ toilets for disabled shop ✈ (ex guide dogs) ◀

London Outer continued

ORLEANS HOUSE GALLERY

Riverside TW1 3DJ
Dir: (Richmond road (A305), Orleans Rd is on right just past Orleans Park School) **Map Ref:** TQ17
☎ **020 8892 0221** 🖷 **020 8744 0501**
e-mail: m.denovellis@richmond.gov.uk

Stroll beside the Thames and through the woodland gardens of Orleans House, where you will find stunning 18th-century interior design and an excellent public art gallery. Visitors of all ages can try out their own artistic talents in pre-booked workshops, and wide-ranging temporary exhibitions are held throughout the year - please telephone for details.

Times: ✳ Open Oct-Mar, Tue-Sat 1-4.30, Sun & BH 2-4.30; Apr-Sep Tue-Sat 1-5.30, Sun & BH 2-5.30. **Facilities:** 🅿 ♿ (handling objects & large print labels for some exhibitions) toilets for disabled shop ✖ (ex guide dogs)

BANHAM   BANHAM ZOO

The Grove NR16 2HE
Dir: (on B1113, signed off A11 and A140. Follow brown tourist signs) **Map Ref:** TM08
☎ **01953 887771 & 887773** 🖷 **01953 887445**
e-mail: info@banhamzoo.co.uk

Banham Zoo is set in 35 acres of magnificent parkland, where you can see hundreds of animals ranging from big cats to siamangs (small acrobatic primates). Tiger Territory is a purpose-built enclosure for Siberian tigers, including a rock pool and woodland setting. See also Lemur Island and Tamarin and Marmoset Islands. The Heritage Farm Stables & Falconry displays Norfolk's rural heritage with majestic shire horses and birds of prey. Other attractions include the Children's Farmyard Barn and Adventure Play Area.

Times: Open all year, daily from 10. (Last admission 1 hour before closing). Closed 25 & 26 Dec. **Fee:** Please phone Zoo for details **Facilities:** 🅿 ▣ ✖ licensed ♿ (3 wheelchairs for hire, special parking) toilets for disabled shop ✖ ▰

BRESSINGHAM   BRESSINGHAM STEAM MUSEUM & GARDENS

IP22 2AB
Dir: (on A1066 2.5m W of Diss, between Thetford & Diss)
Map Ref: TM08
☎ **01379 686900 & 687386** 🖷 **01379 686907**
e-mail: info@bressingham.co.uk

Alan Bloom is an internationally recognised nurseryman and a steam enthusiast, and has combined his interests to great effect at Bressingham. There are three miniature steam-hauled trains, including a 15-inch gauge running through two and a half miles of the wooded Waveney Valley. The Dell Garden has 5,000 species of perennials and alpines; Foggy Bottom has wide vistas, pathways, trees, shrubs, conifers and winter colour (restricted opening). A steam roundabout is another attraction, and the Norfolk fire museum is housed here. Phone for details of special events.

Times: Open: Steam Museum, Dad's Army collection, Foggy Bottom & Dell Garden Apr-Sep, daily 10.30-5.30 (Mar & Oct 10.30-4.30). (Last admission 1 hour before closing time).
Fee: ✳ £7-£10 (ch 3-16 £5-£8, pen £6-£8). Family £21-£30. Season tickets available.
Facilities: 🅿 ▣ ✖ licensed ♿ (wheelchairs can be taken onto Nursery & Waveney lines) toilets for disabled shop garden centre ✖ (ex guide dogs) ▰

BURGH CASTLE   BERNEY ARMS WINDMILL

NR30 1SB
Map Ref: TG40
☎ **01493 700605**

One of the largest and best-preserved Victorian windmills in
Norfolk, the Berney Arms stands 20 metres tall and has seven
floors to explore. It was built to grind a constituent of cement and
its superb machinery is still in working order. The mill was
operational until 1951, though latterly it pumped water from the
surrounding marshland. The nearby pub is the most remote in
Britain, accessible only by boat and train (the station is nearby).

Times: Open Apr-Sep, pre-booked groups only. **Fee:** ✱ £2 (ch £1,
concessions £1.50). Prices & opening times relate to 2004, for further
details phone or log onto www.english-heritage.org.uk/visits
Facilities: shop ▥

FAKENHAM (See also Thursford Green)   PENSTHORPE WATERFOWL PARK & NATURE RESERVE

Pensthorpe NR21 0LN
Dir: (just outside Fakenham on the A1067 to Norwich)
Map Ref: TF93
☎ **01328 851465** 🖹 **01328 855905**
e-mail: info@pensthorpe.com

Covering 500 acres of beautiful Wensum Valley countryside, and
including five lakes, Pensthorpe Nature Reserve & Gardens are
home to one of the largest collections of waterfowl and waders in
Europe. Spacious walk-through enclosures and a network of hard
surfaced pathways ensure that visitors have close contact with
birds at the water's edge.

Times: Open Jan-Mar: daily 10-4. Apr-Dec: 10-5
Fee: £6 (ch £3, pen £5) **Facilities:** 🅿 ☕
♿ (network of hard surfaced pathways ensures
access) toilets for disabled shop ✕ (ex guide
dogs) ◼

FILBY   THRIGBY HALL WILDLIFE GARDENS

NR29 3DR
Dir: (on unclass road off A1064, between Acle & Caister-on-Sea)
Map Ref: TG41
☎ **01493 369477** 🖹 **01493 368256**
e-mail: mail@thrigbyhall.co.uk

The 250-year-old park of Thrigby Hall is now the home of a
collection of animals and birds from Asia, with ornamental
wildfowl populating the lake. There are tropical bird houses, a
unique blue willow pattern garden and tree walk and a summer
house as old as the park. The enormous jungle swamp hall has
special features such as underwater viewing of large crocodiles.

Times: Open all year, daily from 10.
Fee: ✱ £6.90 (ch 4-14 £4.90, pen £5.90).
Facilities: 🅿 ☕ ♿ (wheelchairs available, ramps,
parking) toilets for disabled shop ✕ (ex guide
dogs) ◼

GREAT BIRCHAM BIRCHAM WINDMILL

PE31 6SJ
Dir: (0.5m W off unclassified Snettisham road) **Map Ref:** TF73
☎ **01485 578393**
e-mail: birchamwindmill@btinternet.com

This windmill is one of the last remaining in Norfolk, where some 300 mills once ground the corn for flour, bread and animal feed. Bircham looks very much as it did over a century ago, and visitors can climb up its five floors. Sails turn on windy days, and the adjacent tea room serves home-made cakes, light lunches and cream teas. There is also a bakery shop and cycle hire.

Times: Open Etr-Sep, 10-5. **Fee:** *Prices not confirmed for 2005* **Facilities:** 🅿 ☕ ♿ toilets for disabled shop

GREAT YARMOUTH ELIZABETHAN HOUSE MUSEUM

4 South Quay NR30 2QH
Dir: (from A12 & A47 follow town centre signs, then Historic South Quay signs, leading onto South Quay) **Map Ref:** TG50
☎ **01493 855746** 📄 **01493 745459**
e-mail: yarmouth.museums@norfolk.gov.uk

Experience the lives of families who lived in this splendid quayside house from Tudor to Victorian times. Decide for yourself if the death of Charles I was plotted in the Conspiracy Room. Dress the family in Tudor costumes. Discover Victorian life, upstairs and downstairs, and what it was like to work in the kitchen and scullery. Children can play in the toy room, while parents relax in the small but delightful walled garden.

Times: Open 5 Apr-Oct, Mon-Fri 10-5; Sat & Sun 1.15-5. **Fee:** ✱ £2.70 (ch £1.50, concessions £2.30). Adult in a family group £2.20 **Facilities:** 🅿 (250yds) ♿ shop ✖ (ex guide dogs)

MERRIVALE MODEL VILLAGE

Wellington Pier Gardens, Marine Pde NR30 3JG
Dir: (Marine parade seafront, next to Wellington Pier)
Map Ref: TG50
☎ **01493 842097**

Set in more than an acre of attractive landscaped gardens, this comprehensive miniature village is built on a scale of 1:12, and features streams, a lake and waterfalls. Among the models are a working fairground, a stone quarry, houses, shops, and a garden railway. There are even illuminations at dusk! The new Penny Arcade gives you the chance to play old amusements.

Times: Open 3 Apr-28 May, 10-5. 29 May-12 Sep, 10-9. 13 Sep-Oct, 10-5 **Fee:** ✱ £3 (ch 3-16, pen £2.50). **Facilities:** 🅿 (opposite) ☕ ♿ toilets for disabled shop

GRESSENHALL ROOTS OF NORFOLK

Beech House NR20 4DR
Dir: (on B1146 3m NW of Dereham, follow brown signs from A47 or Dereham town centre) **Map Ref:** *TF91*
☎ **01362 860563** 🖷 **01362 860385**
e-mail: gressenhall.museum@norfolk.gov.uk

Set among 50 acres of beautiful Norfolk countryside, this museum looks at the folkways, history and traditions of the area. Visit a workhouse and hear stories of the people who lived there. Explore traditional cottages and village shops. Take a free cart ride round the farm and get up close with rare breed animals. Relax in the tranquil gardens, or let off steam in the adventure playground. Extra family activities during school holidays.

Times: Open 19 & 20 Feb, 11-4. 27 Feb-13 Mar: Sun 11-4. 20 Mar-30 Oct: daily 10-5. 6-27 Nov: Sun 11-4. **Fee:** ✳ £5.70 (ch £4.40, under 4's free, concessions £5) **Facilities:** 🅿 💷 ♿ (sound guide, wheelchair loan, induction loops) toilets for disabled shop ✖ 🍴

GRIMES GRAVES GRIMES GRAVES

IP26 5DE
Dir: (7m NW of Thetford off A134) **Map Ref:** *TL88*
☎ **01842 810656**

These unique and remarkable Neolithic flint mines are the earliest major industrial site in Europe - not graves at all. Here, miners working between 2200 and 2500 BC sunk shafts to find seams of flint which they used to make axes. Some extend to 30 feet below ground; an extraordinary piece of work considering the tools at the miners' disposal - antlers - according to archaeological finds from the site. One pit is open to the public: a 30-foot shaft with seven galleries.

Times: Open Mar; Thu-Mon, 10-5; Apr-Sep, daily 10-6; Oct, Thu-Mon 10-5. Closed Nov-Feb.
Fee: ✳ £2.60 (ch £1.30, concessions £2, family £6.50). Prices & opening times relate to 2004, for further details phone or log onto www.english-heritage.org.uk/visits
Facilities: 🅿 ♿ (exhibition area, grounds only, access track rough) shop ⌗

HEACHAM NORFOLK LAVENDER

Caley Mill PE31 7JE
Dir: (follow signs on A149 & A148. Car park entrance on B1454, 100yds E of junct with A149) **Map Ref:** *TF63*
☎ **01485 570384** 🖷 **01485 571176**
e-mail: admin@norfolk-lavender.co.uk

Norfolk Lavender is the largest lavender-growing and distilling operation in Britain, home to the National Collection of some 150 lavenders. The different coloured plants are grown in strips and harvested in July and August, and visitors can take guided tours of the distillery and gardens from May to September. The visitor centre is housed in Caley Mill, formerly a watered-powered grain mill dating from 1830s, and Norfolk Lavender has been here since 1936. Also on site are a fragrant meadow garden, herb gardens and a fragrant plant centre.

Times: Open all year, daily, Apr-Oct 10-5; Nov-Mar 10-4. (Closed 25-26 Dec & 1 Jan).
Fee: ✳ Admission to grounds free. Guided tours £2.25 (May-Sep). Trip to Lavender Field £4.50, mid Jun-mid Aug. **Facilities:** 🅿 💷 ✖ licensed ♿ (wheelchairs for loan) toilets for disabled shop garden centre 🍴

HOLKHAM HOLKHAM HALL & BYGONES MUSEUM

NR23 1AB
Dir: (off A149, 2m W of Wells-next-the-Sea) **Map Ref:** *TF84*
☎ **01328 710227** 🖻 **01328 711707**
e-mail: l.herrieven@holkham.co.uk

This classic Palladian mansion was built between 1734 and 1764 by Thomas Coke, 1st Earl of Leicester, and is home to his descendants. It has a magnificent alabaster entrance hall and the sumptuous state rooms house Roman statuary, fine furniture and paintings by Rubens, Van Dyck, Gainsborough and others. The Bygones Museum, housed in the stable block, has over 5,000 items of domestic and agricultural display - from gramophones to fire engines.

Times: Open May-Sep, Thu-Mon 1-5; Etr, May & Summer BHs also open Sat-Mon 11.30-5.
Fee: *Prices not confirmed for 2005*
Facilities: 🅿 🍵 ♿ (wheelchair ramps at all entrances) toilets for disabled shop garden centre (ex guide dogs) 🗕

HORSEY HORSEY WINDPUMP

NR29 4EF
Dir: (15m N of Great Yarmouth, on the B1159 4m NE of Martham) **Map Ref:** *TG42*
☎ **01493 393904**

Set in a remote part of the Norfolk Broads, the windpump mill was built 200 years ago to drain the area, and then rebuilt in 1912 by Dan England, a noted Norfolk millwright. It has since been restored again, having been struck by lightning in 1943. The windpump overlooks Horsey Mere and marshes, which are noted for their wild birds and insects and have been designated as a site of International Importance for Nature Conservation.

Times: ✱ Open 10.30-4.30, (last admission 4); Mar, Sat-Sun only; Apr-Jun, Wed-Sun; Jul-Aug, daily; Sep-Oct, Wed-Sun; Open BHs.
Facilities: 🅿 (charged) 🍵 ♿ (parking, ramps to ground floor) toilets for disabled shop ✈ (ex guide dogs) 🗕

HORSHAM ST FAITH CITY OF NORWICH AVIATION MUSEUM

Old Norwich Rd NR10 3JF
Dir: (follow brown tourist signs from A140 Norwich to Cromer Road) **Map Ref:** *TG21*
☎ **01603 893080** 🖻 **01603 893080**
e-mail: norwichairmuseum@hotmail.com

A massive Avro Vulcan bomber, veteran of the Falklands War, dominates the collection of military and civilian aircraft at the Norwich Aviation Museum. There are several displays relating to the aeronautical history of Norfolk, including some on the role played by Norfolk-based RAF and USAAF planes during World War II, and a section dedicated to the operations of RAF Bomber Command's 100 group.

Times: Open all year, Apr-Oct Tue-Sat, 10-5. Sun & BH Mons 12-5 (Mons during school hols). Nov-Mar, Wed & Sat 10-4. Sun 12-4.
Fee: ✱ £2.80 (ch & concessions £1.50, pen £2.30) Family ticket £8. **Facilities:** 🅿 🍵 ♿ (assistance available) shop ✈ (ex guide dogs) 🗕

HOUGHTON Houghton Hall

PE31 6UE
Dir: (1.25m off A148. 13m E of King's Lynn & 10m W of Fakenham on A148) **Map Ref:** *TF72*
☎ 01485 528569 📠 01485 528167
e-mail: administrator@houghtonhall.com

Houghton Hall was built in the 1720s by Sir Robert Walpole, Britain's first Prime Minister, and is one of the grandest surviving Palladian Houses in England. It is now owned by the 7th Marquess of Cholmondeley. The spectacular five-acre walled garden, restored by Lord Cholmondeley, has been divided into areas for fruit and vegetables, spacious herbaceous borders, and formal rose gardens with over 150 varieties. A collection of model soldiers contains over 20,000 models laid out in various battle formations.

Times: Open Etr-Sep, Wed, Thu, Sun & BHs. House open 2-5.30, grounds, museum, tea shop 1-5.30. **Fee:** * £6.50 (ch 5-16 £3, ch under 5 free). Excluding house £4 (ch 5-16 £2). **Facilities:** P ☕ ✕ licensed ♿ (lift, motorised buggies) toilets for disabled shop 🐕 (ex guide dogs)

HUNSTANTON Sea Life Aquarium & Marine Sanctuary

Southern Promenade PE36 5BH
Map Ref: *TF64*
☎ 01485 533576 📠 01485 533531

With over 30 fascinating displays of marine life, this aquarium and sanctuary offers close encounters with starfish, sharks, octopus, eels and many other underwater wonders. Visitors can see feeding demonstrations, and find out more about more about sea creatures and their environment through talks and special presentations. Otters are the latest addition to the creatures on site.

Times: * Open all year, daily from 10. (Closed 25 Dec) **Facilities:** P (charged) ☕ ✕ ♿ toilets for disabled shop 🐕 (ex guide dogs) 💳

LENWADE Dinosaur Adventure Park

Weston Park NR9 5JW
Dir: (9m from Norwich. Follow Weston Park signs from A47 or A1067) **Map Ref:** *TG01*
☎ 01603 876310 📠 01603 876315
e-mail: info@dinosaurpark.co.uk

Dinosaur Adventure Park is set in 100 acres of wooded parkland, nine miles from Norwich. Here children will have great fun coming face to face with lots of friendly farm animals (real), and giant dinosaurs (thankfully not real). Alongside the animals there are adventure play areas, a fossil dig, raptor racers, Jurassic putt, a Victorian walled garden, and the Neanderthal walk.

Times: * Open Etr-8 Sep & Oct half term, daily; 9 Sep-20 Oct, Fri, Sat & Sun. **Facilities:** P ☕ ♿ toilets for disabled shop 🐕 (ex guide dogs) 💳

NORWICH BRIDEWELL MUSEUM

Bridewell Alley NR2 1AQ
Dir: (in city centre) *Map Ref:* TG20
☎ 01603 629127 📄 01603 765651
e-mail: museums@norfolk.gov.uk

Built in the late 14th century, this flint-faced merchant's house was used as a prison from 1583 to 1828. It now houses displays illustrating the trades and industries of Norwich during the past 200 years, including a large collection of locally made boots and shoes. You can also see a reconstructed 1930's pharmacy, a pawnbroker's shop and a blacksmith's smithy.

Times: Open Apr-29 Oct, Tue-Fri 10-4.30; Sat 10-5. School hols, Mon-Sat 10-5. **Fee:** £2.20 (ch £1.30, concessions £1.80) Family ticket £5. **Facilities:** P (5 min walk) shop ✈ (ex guide dogs)

NORWICH CASTLE MUSEUM

Castle Meadow NR1 3JU
Dir: (in city centre) *Map Ref:* TG20
☎ 01603 493625 📄 01603 493623
e-mail: museums@norfolk.gov.uk

Norwich Castle keep was built in the 12th century, and the museum houses displays of art, archaeology, natural history, Lowestoft porcelain, Norwich silver, a large collection of paintings (with special emphasis on the Norwich School of Painters) and British ceramic teapots. There are also guided tours of the dungeons and battlements. A programme of exhibitions, children's events, gallery and evening talks takes place throughout the year. Please ring for details.

Times: Open all year, Mon-Fri 10-4.30, Sat 10-5, Sun 1-5; School hols, Mon-Sat 10-6, Sun 1-5. Closed 24-27 Dec & 1 Jan. **Fee:** All zones £5.25 (ch 4-16 £3.70, conc £4.50). Castle & History Zone £3.50 (ch £2.50, concessions £2.95). Art & Exhibitions Zone £3 (ch £2.10, concessions £2.55) **Facilities:** P (200mtrs) ☕ ♿ (lift to first floor, special parking by prior arrangement) toilets for disabled shop ✈ (ex guide dogs)

REEDHAM PETTITTS ANIMAL ADVENTURE PARK

NR13 3UA
Dir: (off A47 at Acle) *Map Ref:* TG40
☎ 01493 700094 & 701403 📄 01493 700933

Pettitts Animal Adenture Park is really three parks in one, aimed at the younger child. There are rides including a railway and roller coaster; an adventure play area with a golf course, ball pond and tearoom; and entertainment is provided by clowns, puppets and live musicians. Among the animals that can be seen are small horses, wallabies, birds of prey, goats, chickens and ducks.

Times: Open daily 27 Mar-Oct, 10-5/5.30. **Fee:** ✱ £7.75 (ch 3-15 £7.25, under 3's free, pen/disabled £5.85) **Facilities:** P ☕ ♿ (ramps to all areas) toilets for disabled shop ✈ 🍴

SANDRINGHAM SANDRINGHAM HOUSE, GROUNDS, MUSEUM & COUNTRY

PE35 6EN
Dir: (off A148) *Map Ref:* TF62
☎ **01553 772675 & 612908** 🖨 **01485 541571**
e-mail: visits@sandringhamestate.co.uk

A neo-Jacobean house built in 1870 for King Edward VII, Sandringham is the private country retreat of Her Majesty the Queen. The main rooms used by the Royal Family when in residence are all open to the public. Sixty acres of glorious grounds surround the house and offer beauty and colour throughout the season. Sandringham Museum exhibits fascinating displays of royal memorabilia.

Times: Open Etr Sat-mid Jul & early Aug-Oct. House open 11-4.45, Museum 11-5 & Grounds 10.30-5. **Fee:** ✱ House, Museum & Grounds: £6.50 (ch £4, pen £5). Family ticket £17. **Facilities:** 🅿 ☕ ✗ licensed ♿ (wheelchair loan, free transport in grounds, Braille guide) toilets for disabled shop garden centre ✖ (ex guide dogs) ◀

SHERINGHAM NORTH NORFOLK RAILWAY

Sheringham Station NR26 8RA
Dir: (from A148 take A1082. Next to large car park by rdbt in town centre) *Map Ref:* TG14
☎ **01263 820800** 🖨 **01263 820801**
e-mail: enquiries@nnrailway.com

North Norfolk Steam Railway, the Poppy Line, runs a 10.5 mile round trip through countryside designated as an Area of Outstanding Natural Beauty. At Sheringham Station there's a visitor centre, railway museum, shop and buffet. At Weybourne Station there is a restoration centre, buffet and picnic area. There is a 300 sq ft model railway open at weekends.

Times: Open mid Feb-Oct; daily steam trains; Dec & Jan, Santa specials. Telephone for details **Fee:** ✱ £8 (ch under 4 free, ch 4-15 £4.50, pen £7). Family ticket £23 (free brochure while stocks last). **Facilities:** 🅿 ☕ ♿ (ramps to trains, carriage converted for wheelchair access) toilets for disabled shop ◀

SOUTH WALSHAM FAIRHAVEN WOODLAND & WATER GARDEN

School Rd NR13 6DZ
Dir: (follow brown heritage signs from A47 onto B1140 to South Walsham. Left into School Rd) *Map Ref:* TG31
☎ **01603 270449** 🖨 **01603 270449**
e-mail: fairhavengardens@norfolkbroads.com

These delightful woodland and water gardens offer a combination of cultivated and wild flowers. In spring there are masses of primroses and bluebells, with azaleas and rhododendrons in several areas and in summer the wild flowers provide a habitat for butterflies, bees and dragonflies.

Times: Open daily 10-5, extended opening until 9 Wed & Thu, May-Aug. Closed 25 Dec. **Fee:** £4 (ch £1.50, under 5 free, pen & concessions £3.50). Single membership tickets £15. Family membership ticket £35. Dog membership £2.50. Wildlife Sanctuary £1.50. **Facilities:** 🅿 ☕ ♿ (ramp, grab rail) toilets for disabled shop garden centre ◀

THURSFORD GREEN   THURSFORD COLLECTION

NR21 0AS
Dir: (1m off A148. Halfway between Fakenham and Holt)
Map Ref: TF93
☎ **01328 878477**   📠 **01328 878415**
e-mail: admin@thursfordcollection.co.uk

This exciting collection of steam driven and mechanical items specialises in organs, with a Wurlitzer cinema organ, fairground organs, barrel organs and street organs among its treasures. There are live musical shows every day. The collection also includes showmen's engines, ploughing engines and farm machinery. There is a children's play area and a breathtaking 'Venetian gondola' switchback ride.

Times: Open Good Fri-last Sun in Sep, daily, 12-5. Closed Sat. **Fee:** £5.50 (ch under 4 free, ch 4-14 £3, students £4.75 pen £5.20). Party 15+ £4.75 each. **Facilities:** 🅿 🍵 ✗ licensed ♿ toilets for disabled shop (five different giftshops) ✈ (ex guide dogs) 🛍

TITCHWELL   RSPB NATURE RESERVE

PE31 8BB
Dir: (6m E of Hunstanton on A149, signed entrance)
Map Ref: TF74
☎ **01485 210779**   📠 **01485 210779**
e-mail: titchwell@rspb.org.uk   **FREE**

At this bird reserve a firm path takes you to three hides and on to the beach where a platform overlooking the sea is suitable for wheelchairs. A colony of avocets nests on the enclosed marsh along with gadwalls, tufted ducks, shovelers and black-headed gulls. During the season many migrants visit the marsh including wigeon, black-tailed godwits, curlews, and sandpipers.

Times: Open at all times. Visitor Centre daily 9.30-5 (4 Nov-Mar). **Facilities:** 🅿 (charged) 🍵 ♿ (ramps to hides, wheelchair bays in hides) toilets for disabled shop 🛍

WELLS-NEXT-THE-SEA   WELLS & WALSINGHAM LIGHT RAILWAY

NR23 1QB
Dir: (A149, Cromer road)   *Map Ref:* TF94
☎ **01328 711630**

The railway covers the four miles between Wells and Walsingham, and is the longest ten and a quarter inch gauge track in the world. The line passes through some very attractive countryside, particularly noted for its wild flowers and butterflies. This is the home of the unique Garratt Steam Locomotive specially built for this line.

Times: Open daily Good Fri-end Oct. **Fee:** ✱ £6.50 return (ch £5 return). **Facilities:** 🅿 🍵 ♿ shop

WELNEY WWT WELNEY

Hundred Foot Bank PE14 9TN
Dir: (off A1101, N of Ely) **Map Ref:** TL59
☎ **01353 860711** 🖹 **01353 860711**
e-mail: **welney@wwt.org.uk**

This important wetland site on the beautiful Ouse Washes is famed for the breathtaking spectacle of the wild ducks, geese and swans that spend the winter here. Impressive observation facilities, including hides, towers and an observatory, offer outstanding views of the huge numbers of wildfowl, which include Bewick's and whooper swans, wigeon, teal and shoveler. Floodlit evening swan feeds take place between November and February. There are two hides for wheelchair users.

Times: Open all year, daily 10-5. Closed 25 Dec.
Fee: ✱ £3.90 (ch £2.30, pen £3.20). Family ticket £10.50. **Facilities:** 🅿 🖳 & toilets for disabled shop ✖ (ex guide/hearing dogs) ◀

WEST RUNTON NORFOLK SHIRE HORSE CENTRE

West Runton Stables NR27 9QH
Dir: (off A149 in village of West Ranton half-way between Cromer & Sheringham, follow brown signs) **Map Ref:** TG14
☎ **01263 837339** 🖹 **01263 837132**
e-mail: **bakewell@norfolkshirehorse.fsnet.co.uk**

The Shire Horse Centre has a collection of draught horses and some breeds of mountain and moorland ponies. There are also exhibits of horse-drawn machinery, waggons and carts. Harnessing and working demonstrations are given twice every day. Other attractions include a children's farm, a photographic display of draught horses past and present, talks and a video show. There is also a riding school on the premises.

Times: Open 4 Apr-29 Oct, Sun-Fri; also Sat BHs. (Last admission 3.45) **Fee:** ✱ £5.50 (ch £3.50, pen £4.50). **Facilities:** 🅿 🖳 & (concrete yards all ramped) toilets for disabled shop ◀

WEYBOURNE THE MUCKLEBURGH COLLECTION

Weybourne Military Camp NR25 7EG
Dir: (on A149, coast road, 3m W of Sheringham) **Map Ref:** TG14
☎ **01263 588210 & 588608** 🖹 **01263 588425**
e-mail: **info@muckleburgh.co.uk**

The largest privately-owned military collection of its kind in the country, which incorporates the Museum of the Suffolk and Norfolk Yeomanry. Exhibits include restored and working tanks, armoured cars, trucks and artillery of WWII, and equipment and weapons from the Falklands and the Gulf War. Live tank demonstrations are run daily (except Sat) during school holidays.

Times: check website or phone for details
Fee: £5.50 (ch £3 & pen £4.50). Family ticket £13.50. **Facilities:** 🅿 🖳 ✖ & (ramped access, wheelchairs available) toilets for disabled shop ✖ (ex guide, kennels provided) ◀

BANBURY BANBURY MUSEUM

Spiceball Park Rd OX16 2PQ
Dir: (M40 junct 11 straight across at first rdbt into Hennef Way, left at next rdbt into Concord Ave, right at next rdbt & left at next rdbt, Castle Quay Shopping Centre & Museum on right)
Map Ref: *SP44*
☎ **01295 259855** 📄 **01295 269469** `FREE`
e-mail: banburymuseum@cherwell-dc.gov.uk

Banbury's stunning new museum is situated in an attractive canal-side location in the centre of town. Exciting modern displays tell of Banbury's origins and historic past. The Civil War, the plush manufacturing industry, the Victorian market town, costume from the 17th century to the present day, Tooley's Boatyard and the Oxford Canal, are just some of the subjects illustrated in this fine development.

Times: Open all year, Mon-Sat, 10-5, Sun 10.30-4.30. **Facilities:** P (500yds) 🍵 ✗ licensed ♿ toilets for disabled shop ✗ (ex guide dogs) 🔊

BURFORD COTSWOLD WILDLIFE PARK

OX18 4JW
Dir: (on A361 2m S of A40 at Burford) **Map Ref:** *SP21*
☎ **01993 823006** 📄 **01993 823807**

This 160-acre landscaped zoological park surrounds a listed Gothic-style manor house. There is a varied collection of animals from all over the world, many of which are endangered species, such as Asiatic lions, leopards, white rhinos and red pandas. There's an adventure playground, a children's farmyard, and train rides during the summer. The park has also become one of the Cotswold's leading attractions for garden enthusiasts, with its exotic summer displays and varied plantings offering interest all year.

Times: Open all year, daily from 10, (last admission 4.30 Mar-Sep, 3 Oct-Feb). Closed 25 Dec. **Fee:** £8.50 (ch 3-16 & pen £6). **Facilities:** P 🍵 ✗ licensed ♿ (parking, free hire of wheelchairs) toilets for disabled shop 🔊

DIDCOT DIDCOT RAILWAY CENTRE

OX11 7NJ
Dir: (on A4130 at Didcot Parkway Station) **Map Ref:** *SU58*
☎ **01235 817200** 📄 **01235 510621**
e-mail: didrlyc@globalnet.co.uk

Based around the original Great Western Railway engine shed, the Didcot Railway Centre is home to the biggest collection anywhere of Great Western Railway steam locomotives, carriages and wagons. A typical GWR station has been re-created and a section of Brunel's original broad gauge track relaid. Steam days and special events are featured, please telephone for details.

Times: Open all year, Sat & Sun, 25 Mar-17 Apr; 30 Apr-25 Sep, Steamdays Sat & Sun 23 Apr-2 Oct, Wed 13 Jul-Aug. 10-4 Steamdays & wknds Mar-Oct, 10-5. **Fee:** ✱ £4-£8 depending on event (ch £3-£7.50, pen £3.50-£6.50). **Facilities:** P (100yds) 🍵 ♿ (advance notice recommended, some awkward steps) toilets for disabled shop 🔊

HENLEY-ON-THAMES RIVER & ROWING MUSEUM

Mill Meadows RG9 1BF
Dir: (off A4130, signed to Mill Meadows) **Map Ref:** SU78
☎ **01491 415600** 🖨 **01491 415601**
e-mail: museum@rrm.co.uk

The award-winning River and Rowing Museum is the only museum in the world with galleries dedicated to rowing and the 'Quest for Speed', from the Greek Trireme to modern Olympic rowing boats; and the River Thames from source to sea with its rich history and varied wildlife. See the boats that won gold in Sydney and the riverside town of Henley featuring the Royal Regatta. The most recent addition is a permanent Wind in the Willows exhibition.

Times: Open Summer: May-Aug 10-5.30. Winter: Sep-Apr 10-5. Closed 24-25 & 31 Dec & 1 Jan. **Fee:** ✱ £6 (concessions £4, pens £5). Family ticket from £18. Party 10+. **Facilities:** 🅿 💺 ✗ licensed ♿ (lift access to upstairs galleries, ramps at entrance) toilets for disabled shop ✈ (ex guide dogs) 🎧

THE WIND IN THE WILLOWS™ at the River & Rowing Museum

MAPLEDURHAM MAPLEDURHAM HOUSE

RG4 7TR
Dir: (off A4074, follow brown heritage signs from Reading)
Map Ref: SU67
☎ **0118 972 3350** 🖨 **0118 972 4016**
e-mail: mtrust1997@aol.com

The small community at Mapledurham includes the house, a watermill and a church. The fine Elizabethan mansion, surrounded by quiet parkland that runs down to the River Thames, was built by the Blount family in the 16th century. The estate has literary connections with the poet Alexander Pope, with Galsworthy's 'Forsyte Saga' and Kenneth Graham's 'Wind in the Willows', and was the location for the film 'The Eagle has Landed'.

Times: Open Etr-Sep, Sat, Sun & BHs 2-5.30 Picnic area 2 5.30. (Last admission 5). Group visits midweek by arrangement. **Fee:** ✱ Combined house, watermill & grounds £6 (ch £3). House & grounds £4 (ch £2). Watermill & grounds £3 (ch £1.50). **Facilities:** 🅿 💺 ♿ shop 🎧

MAPLEDURHAM WATERMILL

RG4 7TR
Dir: (off A4074, follow brown heritage signs from Reading)
Map Ref: SU67
☎ **0118 972 3350** 🖨 **0118 972 4016**
e-mail: mtrust1997@aol.com

Close to Mapledurham House stands the last working corn and grist mill on the River Thames, still using traditional wooden machinery and producing flour for local bakers and shops. The watermill's products can be purchased in the shop. When Mapledurham House is open the mill can be reached by river launch.

Times: Open Etr-Sep, Sat, Sun & BHs 2-5.30. Picnic area 2-5.30. (Last admission 5). Groups midweek by arrangement. **Fee:** ✱ Watermill & grounds £3 (ch £1.50) **Facilities:** 🅿 💺 ♿ shop 🎧

OXFORD ASHMOLEAN MUSEUM OF ART & ARCHAEOLOGY

Beaumont St OX1 2PH
Dir: (city centre, opposite The Randolph Hotel) *Map Ref:* SP50
☎ **01865 278000** 📄 **01865 278018**

The oldest public museum in the country, opened in 1683, the Ashmolean contains Oxford University's priceless collections of art and archaeological artefacts. These are divided into five curatorial areas: Antiquities, the Cast Gallery (casts of sculptures from around the world), Eastern Art, the Heberden Coin Gallery and Western Art. Many important historical art pieces and artefacts are on display, including work from Ancient Greece through to the 20th century.

Times: Open all year, Tue-Sat 10-5, Sun & BH Mons 2-5. Closed Etr & during St.Giles Fair in early Sep, Xmas & 1 Jan. **Fee:** ✱ Free. Guided tours by arrangement. **Facilities:** P (100-200mtrs) (pay & display) ▆ ✗ licensed & (entry ramp from Beaumont St. Tel. before visit) toilets for disabled shop ✗ ▆

HARCOURT ARBORETUM

Nuneham Courtenay OX44 9PX
Dir: (400yds S of Nuneham Courtenay on A4074)
Map Ref: SP50
☎ **01865 343501** 📄 **01865 341828**
e-mail: piers.newth@botanic-garden.ox.ac.uk

The arboretum, six miles south of Oxford, consists of 75 acres of mixed woodland, meadow, pond, rhododendron walks and fine specimen trees and is a part of the plant collection of the Botanic Garden in central Oxford. The arboretum runs a diverse programme of events throughout the year, from bird spotting to plant sales, craft weekends to theatrical productions.

Times: Apr-Nov, daily 10-5, Dec-Mar, Mon-Fri 10-4.30. Closed 22 Dec-4 Jan. **Fee:** ✱ £2 pay & display for car park or £5 for 1yr season ticket. **Facilities:** P (charged) & ✗ (ex guide dogs)

MUSEUM OF THE HISTORY OF SCIENCE

Old Ashmolean Building, Broad St OX1 3AZ
Dir: (next to Sheldonian Theatre in city centre, on Bond St)
Map Ref: SP50
☎ **01865 277280** 📄 **01865 277288**
e-mail: museum@mhs.ox.ac.uk

The Museum of the History of Science is located in the first purpose built museum in Britain, the original Ashmolean Museum built in 1683 to accommodate the Ashmolean collection. It is now home to the world's finest collection of early scientific instruments used in astronomy, navigation, surveying, physics and chemistry.

Times: ✱ Open Tue-Sat 12-4, Sun 2-5. Closed Xmas wk. **Facilities:** P (300mtrs) (limited street parking, meters) & (lift) toilets for disabled shop ✗ (ex guide dogs) ▆

THE OXFORD STORY

6 Broad St OX1 3AJ
Dir: (follow signs for city centre then finger post signs to attraction, or use park & ride service) *Map Ref:* SP50
☎ 01865 728822 🖷 01865 791716
e-mail: info@oxfordstory.co.uk

The Oxford Story offers the best introduction to the city's world famous university, located in a three-storey former book warehouse. Climb aboard the indoor 'dark' ride to travel through the university's 900 years of history. In the interactive exhibition, 'Innovate' you can quiz experts from Oxford University on the issues that engage us today, from heart disease to climate change.

Times: Open Jan-Jun & Sep-Dec, Mon-Sat 10-4.30 & Sun 11-4.30. Jul & Aug daily 9.30-5. Closed 25 Dec. **Fee:** ✱ £6.95 (ch £5.25, pen £5.75 & students £5.95), Family ticket (2ad+2ch) £22.50
Facilities: P (300mtrs) & (advisable to phone in advance) toilets for disabled shop ✖ (ex guide dogs) ◀

OXFORD UNIVERSITY MUSEUM OF NATURAL HISTORY

Parks Rd OX1 3PW
Dir: (opposite Keble College) *Map Ref:* SP50
☎ 01865 272950 🖷 01865 272970
e-mail: info@oum.ox.ac.uk

Built between 1855 and 1860, this museum of 'the natural sciences' was intended to satisfy a growing interest in biology, botany, archaeology, zoology, entomology and so on. The museum reflects Oxford University's position as a 19th-century centre of learning, with displays of early dinosaur discoveries, Darwinian evolution and Elias Ashmole's collection of preserved animals. Although visitors to the Pitt-Rivers Museum must pass through the University Museum, the two should not be confused.

Times: Open daily 12-5. Times vary at Xmas & Etr.
Facilities: P (200mtrs) (meter parking) & toilets for disabled shop ✖

PITT RIVERS MUSEUM

South Parks Rd OX1 3PP
Dir: (10 min walk from city centre) *Map Ref:* SP50
☎ 01865 270927 🖷 01865 270943
e-mail: prm@prm.ox.ac.uk

The Pitt Rivers Museum is one of the city's most popular attractions, it is part of the University of Oxford and was founded in 1884. The collections held at the museum are internationally acclaimed, and contain many objects from different cultures of the world and from various periods, all grouped by type or purpose. A new research centre for the museum is currently under construction. Special exhibitions and events are regular features.

Times: Open Mon-Sat 12-4.30 & Sun 2-4.30. Closed Xmas & Etr, open BHs.
Facilities: & (audio guide, wheelchair trail and map to ground floor) toilets for disabled shop ✖ (ex guide dogs)

University of Oxford Botanic Garden

Rose Ln OX1 4AZ
Dir: (E end of High St on banks of River Cherwell)
Map Ref: SP50
☎ 01865 286690 📄 01865 286693
e-mail: postmaster@botanic-garden.ox.ac.uk

Founded in 1621, this botanic garden is the oldest in the country. It has an incredibly diverse national reference collection of over 7,000 plants from all over the world. The three main areas are the glass houses for tender plants; the walled garden where plants are grouped according to their country of origin or botanic family, and an area outside the wall garden where there is a rock garden, water garden and themed borders.

Times: Open all year daily: 9-4.30 Jan, Feb, Nov & Dec (last admission 4.15). 9-5 Mar, Apr & Oct (last admission 4.15). 9-6 May-Sep (last admission 5.15). 9-8 Thu in Jun, Jul & Aug (last admission 7.15). Closed Good Fri & 25 Dec. **Fee:** £2.50 (ch free in full time education accompanied by an adult family member/guardian, UB40 & disabled/carers, pen & students £2) **Facilities:** P (0.5m) (park and ride system) ♿ toilets for disabled ✖ (ex guide dogs)

WITNEY   Cogges Manor Farm Museum

Church Ln, Cogges OX28 3LA
Dir: (0.5m SE off A4022) *Map Ref:* SP31
☎ 01993 772602 📄 01993 703056
e-mail: info@cogges.org

This museum is dedicated to rural Oxfordshire life in the Victorian period, and characters from Cogges' past describe life on the farm in an audio tour. The lovely Cotswold farm is home to traditional breeds of animals, and milking and butter-making demonstrations are a feature. Rooms in the manor house are presented in period style, and visitors can meet the Victorian house maids as they go about their tasks of cleaning, cooking and washing. Special events take place through the season.

Times: Open Apr-Oct, Tue-Fri & BH Mon 10.30-5.30, Sat & Sun 12-5.30. Early closing Oct. Closed Good Fri. **Fee:** ✱ £4.40 (ch £2.30, pen, students & UB40 £2.85). Family ticket £12.90 (2ad+2ch). **Facilities:** P ☕ ♿ (wheelchair available,commentary/history file for 1st floor) toilets for disabled shop 🛍

WOODSTOCK   Blenheim Palace

OX20 1PX
Dir: (M40 junct 9, follow signs to Blenheim, on A44, 8m N of Oxford) *Map Ref:* SP41
☎ 08700 602080 📄 01993 810570
e-mail: admin@blenheimpalace.com

Home of the 11th Duke of Marlborough and birthplace of Sir Winston Churchill, Blenheim Palace is an English Baroque masterpiece. Fine furniture, sculpture, paintings and tapestries are set in magnificent gilded staterooms that overlook sweeping lawns and formal gardens. 'Capability' Brown landscaped the 2,100-acre grounds, which are open to visitors for pleasant walks and beautiful views.

Times: Palace & Gardens 12 Feb-11 Dec (ex Mon & Tue in Nov & Dec) daily 10.30-5.30 (last admission 4.45). Park daily all year 9-4.45. Closed 25 Dec. **Fee:** ✱ Palace, Park & Gardens £11-12.50 (ch £5.50-£7, concessions £8.50-£10). Park & Gardens £6-£7.50 (ch £2-£3.50, concessions £4-£5.50) **Facilities:** P ☕ ✖ licensed ♿ (ramps, disabled parking, buggies, wheelchairs) toilets for disabled shop 🛍

OXFORDSHIRE MUSEUM

Fletcher's House OX20 1SN
Dir: (A44 Evesham-Oxford, follow signs for Blenheim Palace.
Museum opposite church) **Map Ref:** SP41
☎ **01993 811456** 🖹 **01993 813239**
e-mail: oxon.museum@oxfordshire.go.uk   FREE

Situated in the heart of historic Woodstock, the award-winning
redevelopment of Fletcher's House is home to the new county
museum. Surrounded by attractive gardens, the museum
celebrates Oxfordshire in all its diversity and features collections
of local history, art, archaeology, landscape and wildlife as well as
a gallery exploring the country's innovative industries from nuclear
power to nano-technology. Interactive exhibits offer learning
experiences for visitors of all ages, and the museum's Garden
Gallery houses a variety of touring exhibitions.

Times: Open all year, Tue-Sat 10-5. (Last
admission 4.30). Closed Good Fri, 25 26 Dec & 1
Jan. Galleries closed on Mon, but open BH Mons,
2-5. **Facilities:** P (outside entrance) (free
parking) 🍵 ✗ licensed ♿ (chair lifts to all
galleries) toilets for disabled ✖ (ex guide dogs)

BUNGAY   *OTTER TRUST*

Earsham NR35 2AF
Dir: (off A143, 1m W of Bungay) **Map Ref:** TM38
☎ **01986 893470** 🖹 **01986 892461**

The Otter Trust's main aim is to breed this endangered species in
captivity in sufficient numbers so that it can re-introduce young
otters into the wild wherever suitable habitat remains. This re-
introduction programme has been running since 1983. The Otter
Trust covers 23 acres on the banks of the River Waveney. As well
as otter pens, there are three lakes with a large collection of
European waterfowl.

Times: ✶ Open Apr (or Good Fri if earlier)-Oct, daily 10.30-6.
Facilities: P 🍵 ♿ toilets for disabled shop ✖ (ex guide dogs)

EASTON   *EASTON FARM PARK*

IP13 0EQ
Dir: (signed from A12 at Wickam Market, and from A1120)
Map Ref: TM25
☎ **01728 746475** 🖹 **01728 747861**
e-mail: easton@eastonfarmpark.co.uk

Easton is an award-winning farm park on the banks of the River
Deben. It has lots of breeds of farm animals, including Suffolk
Punch horses, ponies, pigs, lambs, calves, goats, rabbits, guinea
pigs and poultry. Daily events include chicks hatching and egg
collecting, and pat-a-pet and pony ride opportunities. There is
also a Green Trail through the water meadows by the river.

Times: ✶ Open Mar-end Sep, daily 10.30-6. Also
open Feb & Oct half term hols. **Facilities:** P 🍵
♿ (special parking) toilets for disabled shop 🍴

FLIXTON NORFOLK & SUFFOLK AVIATION MUSEUM

Buckeroo Way, The Street NR35 1NZ
Dir: (off A143, take B1062, 2m W of Bungay) **Map Ref:** *TM38*
☎ **01986 896644**
e-mail: nsam.flixton@virgin.net

FREE

This aviation museum in the Waveney Valley has a collection of over 40 historic aircraft. You can also see a Bloodhound surface-to-air missile, the 446th Bomb Group Museum, RAF Bomber Command Museum, the Royal Observer Corps Museum, RAF Air-Sea Rescue and Coastal Command and a souvenir shop. Among the displays are Decoy Sites and Wartime Deception, Fallen Eagles - Wartime Luftwaffe Crashes - and an ex-Ipswich airport hangar made by Norwich company Boulton and Paul Ltd.

Times: Open Apr-Oct, Sun-Thu 10-5 (last admission 4); Nov-Mar, Tue, Wed & Sun 10-4 (last admission 3). Closed late Dec-early Jan.
Facilities: 🅿 💺 ♿ (helper advised, ramps/paths to all buildings) toilets for disabled shop ✖ (ex guide dogs)

HORRINGER ICKWORTH HOUSE, PARK & GARDENS

The Rotunda IP29 5QE
Dir: (2.5m S of Bury St Edmunds in village of Horringer on A143)
Map Ref: *TL86*
☎ **01284 735270** 🖷 **01284 735175**
e-mail: ickworth@ntrust.org.uk

The eccentric Earl of Bristol created this equally eccentric house, begun in 1795, to display his collection of European art. The Georgian silver collection is considered the finest in private hands. There is plenty to see outside, too, with parkland designed by 'Capability' Brown, a children's adventure playground, a deer enclosure, and some way-marked walks.

Times: Open: House 19 Mar-Oct, Mon, Tue, Fri, wknds & BH Mons 1-5 (4.30 in Oct). (Last admission 4.30); Garden open daily 19 Mar-Oct 10-5. (Last admission 4.30). Nov-22 Dec wkdays, 10-4; Park daily 7-7. **Fee:** ✱ House, Garden & Park £6.40 (National Trust members & ch under 5 free, ch £2.90) Garden & park £2.95 (ch 85p). Discount for pre-booked parties.
Facilities: 🅿 ✖ licensed ♿ (Braille guide, batricars, stairlift to shop & restaurant) toilets for disabled shop garden centre ✖ (ex guide dogs & in park) 🐾

LEISTON LONG SHOP STEAM MUSEUM

Main St IP16 4ES
Dir: (Turn off A12, follow B1119 from Saxmundham to Leiston. Museum is in the middle of town) **Map Ref:** *TM46*
☎ **01728 832189** 🖷 **01728 832189**
e-mail: longshop@care4free.net

Discover the magic of steam through a visit to the world famous traction engine manufacturers. Trace the history of the factory and Richard Garrett engineering. See the traction engines and road rollers in the very place that they were built. Soak up the atmosphere of the Long Shop, built in 1852 as one of the first production line engineering halls in the world. An award-winning museum with five exhibition halls full of items from the glorious age of steam and covering 200 years of local, social and industrial history.

Times: Open Apr-Oct, Mon-Sat 10-5, Sun 11-5.
Facilities: 🅿 ♿ (wheelchair available) toilets for disabled shop ✖ (ex guide dogs)

LONG MELFORD *KENTWELL HALL*

CO10 9BA
Dir: (signposted off A134, between Bury St Edmunds & Sudbury)
Map Ref: *TL84*
☎ **01787 310207** 📠 **01787 379318**
e-mail: info@kentwell.co.uk

Kentwell Hall is a moated red brick Tudor manor with gardens, woodland walks and a rare breeds farm. It is an award-winning attraction, restored over a period of 30 years from a state of neglect and abandonment. Kentwell was a pioneer of living history events and recreations of Tudor and World War II life are a regular feature. A programme of theatrical, music and other events is also operated, please telephone for details.

Times: Open: Gardens & Farm Sun during Mar, Apr-Jun. House, Gardens & Farm 14 Jul-early Sep daily; Oct, Sun only. Also open BH wknds & school hols. Historical recreations on selected wknds throughout year. **Facilities:** 🅿 💻 ♿ (wheelchair ramp & 2 wheelchairs for loan) toilets for disabled shop ✈ (ex guide dogs) 🍴

LOWESTOFT EAST ANGLIA TRANSPORT MUSEUM

Chapel Rd, Carlton Colville NR33 8BL
Dir: (3m SW of Lowestoft, follow brown signs from A12, A146 & B1384) ***Map Ref:*** *TM59*
☎ **01502 518459** 📠 **01502 584658**
e-mail: enquiries@eatm.org.uk

A particular attraction of this transport museum is the reconstructed 1930s street scene, which is used as a setting for working vehicles. Here, visitors can ride by tram, trolley bus and narrow gauge railway. Other motor, steam and electrical vehicles are exhibited, and there is a woodland picnic area served by trams.

Times: Open Good Fri & Ett Sat 2-4, Ett Sun-Ett Mon 11-5. May-Sep, Sun & BH's 11-5; Wed & Sat 2-5 (last entry 1 hour before closing). **Fee:** £5 (ch 5-15 & pen £3.50). Price includes rides. Party rates available. **Facilities:** 🅿 💻 ♿ toilets for disabled shop 🍴

NEW PLEASUREWOOD HILLS

Leisure Way, Corton NR32 5DZ
Dir: (off A12 at Lowestoft) ***Map Ref:*** *TM59*
☎ **01502 586000 (admin) & 508200 (info)**
📠 **01502 567393**
e-mail: info@pleasurewoodhills.co.uk

There are over 40 rides, shows and attractions at New Pleasurewood Hills, set in 50 acres of beautiful parkland. Old favourites such as the Tidal Wave Watercoaster and the Fairytale Fantasy Ride combine with more recent attractions such as Formula K Raceway Go-Karts, the 100-ft Drop Tower, the Crazy Coaster and the Double Decker Carousel.

Times: ✱ Open Apr-Oct & Xmas. Telephone for details. **Facilities:** 🅿 💻 ✕ licensed ♿ (all shows accessible, most ride operators able to assist) toilets for disabled shop ✈ (ex guide dogs) 🍴

NEWMARKET NATIONAL HORSERACING MUSEUM AND TOURS

99 High St CB8 8JH
Dir: (located in centre of High St) *Map Ref:* TL66
☎ **01638 667333** 📄 **01638 665600**

This friendly, award-winning museum tells the story of the people and horses involved in racing in Britain, including modern heroes like Lester Piggott and Frankie Dettori. You can have a go on the horse simulator in the hands-on gallery and chat to retired jockeys and trainers about their experiences. Special minibus tours visit the gallops, a stable and yard, and the horses' swimming pool. Temporary exhibitions with a racing theme are an additional feature.

Times: Open Etr-end Oct, Tue-Sun (also BH Mons & Mons in Jul & Aug) 11-5. 10 opening on race days. **Fee:** £4.50 (ch £1.50, concessions £3.50). Family ticket £10 (2ad+2ch).
Facilities: P (300yds) (coach drop off in front of museum) 🍽 ✕ licensed ♿ (ramps & lift) toilets for disabled shop ✖ (ex guide dogs) 🍴

STOWMARKET MUSEUM OF EAST ANGLIAN LIFE

IP14 1DL
Dir: (located in centre of Stowmarket, signed from A14 & B1115)
Map Ref: TM05
☎ **01449 612229** 📄 **01449 672307**
e-mail: meal@meal.fsnet.co.uk

This 70-acre, all-weather museum is set in an attractive river-valley site. There are reconstructed buildings, including a water mill, a smithy and a wind pump; and the Boby Building houses craft workshops. There are displays on Victorian domestic life, gypsies, farming and industry. These include working steam traction engines, the only surviving pair of Burrell ploughing engines of 1879, and a working Suffolk Punch horse. A more recent attraction is the William Bone Building illustrating the history of Ransomes of Ipswich.

Times: ✱ Open Apr-Oct. **Facilities:** P (adjacent) 🍽 ♿ (wheelchairs available, special vehicle facilities) toilets for disabled shop 🍴

SUFFOLK WILDLIFE PARK SUFFOLK WILDLIFE PARK

Kessingland NR33 7TF
Dir: (25min S of Gt. Yarmouth, just S of Lowestoft off the A12)
Map Ref: TM58
☎ **01502 740291** 📄 **01502 741104**
e-mail: info@suffolkwildlifepark.co.uk

Enjoy the atmosphere and excitement of your very own African Adventure here. Spend the whole day exploring the 100 acres of dramatic coastal parkland, filled with animals from the African continent and around the world. Guide your expedition to see giraffe, lion, buffalo, hyena and many more exciting animals. Capture the true splendour and atmosphere of the park by going walkabout amongst the large open paddocks or join the children's favourite - the Safari Roadtrain with its live commentary of fascinating animal facts.

Times: Open all year, daily from 10. Closed 25-26 Dec. **Fee:** ✱ Please call park reception for full admission prices **Facilities:** P 🍽 ✕ ♿ (wheelchairs available for hire) toilets for disabled shop ✖ 🍴

WEST STOW WEST STOW ANGLO SAXON VILLAGE

West Stow Country Park, Icklingham Rd IP28 6HG
Dir: (off A1101, follow brown heritage signs, 7m NW of Bury St Edmunds) **Map Ref:** *TL87*
☎ **01284 728718** 🖹 **01284 728277**
e-mail: weststow@stedsbc.gov.uk

The village is a reconstruction of a pagan Anglo-Saxon settlement dated AD 420-650. Seven buildings have been reconstructed on the site of the excavated settlement. There is a visitors' centre and a children's play area. The Anglo-Saxon Centre houses the original objects found on the site. The village is located in the 125-acre West Stow Country Park, which has a river, lake, woodland and heath, with many trails and paths.

Times: Open all year, daily 10-5. Last entry 4 (3.30 in Winter) **Fee:** ✱ £5 (ch £4). Family ticket £15. (Prices subject to changes for special events) **Facilities:** 🅿 🍽 ♿ (ramps) toilets for disabled shop 🐾 (ex guide dogs) 🚩

CHERTSEY *THORPE PARK*

Staines Rd KT16 8PN
Dir: (M25 junct 11 or 13 and follow signs via A320 to Thorpe Park) **Map Ref:** *TQ06*
☎ **0870 444 4466** 🖹 **01932 566367**

Thorpe Park is home to one of the world's most intense, disorientating and exhilarating rollercoasters - Nemesis Inferno - the legendary feet-free, suspended coaster with volcanic theming and effects, plus the wrenching Quantum, and Colossus, the world's first 10-looping rollercoaster. Another trio of 'must ride' thrill sensations are the explosive Detonator, awesome Vortex and spinning Zodiac. There is also Tidal Wave, one of Europe's highest water drop rides, the white water thrills of Ribena Rumba Rapids, X:/No Way Out, Loggers Leap, Pirates-4D, Neptune's Beach, Thorpe Farm and lots more besides.

Times: ✱ Open from 5 Apr-2 Nov (ex some off-peak days) 9/10-5/6 (times vary), 7.30 from 25 Jul-7 Sep, until 8 on fireworks night & from noon-11 on Fri nights. **Facilities:** 🅿 🍽 ✕ licensed ♿ (some rides not accessible, wheelchair hire available) toilets for disabled shop 🐾 (ex guide dogs) 🚩

FARNHAM *BIRDWORLD & UNDERWATERWORLD*

Holt Pound GU10 4LD
Dir: (3m S of Farnham on A325) **Map Ref:** *SU84*
☎ **01420 22140** 🖹 **01420 23715**
e-mail: bookings@birdworld.co.uk

Birdworld is the largest bird collection in the country and includes toucans, pelicans, flamingos, ostriches and many others. Underwater World is a tropical aquarium with brilliant lighting that shows off collections of marine and freshwater fish, as well as the swampy depths of the alligator exhibit. Visitors can also visit some beautiful gardens, the Jenny Wren farm and the Heron Theatre.

Times: Open daily, 10-6 (summer), 10-4.30 (winter).
Facilities: 🅿 🍽 ♿ (wheelchairs available) toilets for disabled shop garden centre 🐾 (ex guide dogs) 🚩

GODSTONE GODSTONE FARM

RH9 8LX
Dir: (M25 junct 6, S of village, signed) **Map Ref:** *TQ35*
☎ **01883 742546** 📄 **01883 740380**
e-mail: havefun@godstonefarm.co.uk

An ideal day out for children, Godstone Farm has lots of friendly animals, big sand pits and play areas. Chicks, rabbits and pigs are born all year round; lambs in spring, goats in summer, and then miniature Shetland ponies. The farm now also has llamas. Children are encouraged to get close to and to handle the animals. The Indoor Play Barn is ideal for wet weather and cost an additional £1.

Times: Open Mar-Oct, 10-6 (last admission 5); Nov-Feb 10-5 (last admission 4). Closed 25 & 26 Dec. **Fee:** ✱ Contact for admission prices. **Facilities:** 🅿 ☕ ♿ toilets for disabled shop ✖ (ex guide dogs) 💳

GUILDFORD DAPDUNE WHARF

Wharf Rd GU1 4RR
Dir: (off Woodbridge Rd to rear of Surrey County Cricket Ground) **Map Ref:** *SU94*
☎ **01483 561389** 📄 **01483 531667**
e-mail: riverwey@nationaltrust.org.uk

The visitor centre at Dapdune Wharf is the centrepiece of one of the National Trust's most unusual properties, the River Way Navigations. A series of interactive exhibits and displays allow you to discover the fascinating story of Surrey's secret waterway, one of the first British rivers to be made navigable. See where huge Wey barges were built and climb aboard *'Reliance'*, one of the last surviving barges. Children's trails and special events run throughout the season.

Times: Open Apr-Oct, Thu-Mon 11-5. River trips Thu-Mon 11-5 (conditions permitting) **Fee:** ✱ £2.50 (ch £1.50). Family ticket £6.50. National Trust Members free. **Facilities:** 🅿 ☕ ♿ (Braille guide) toilets for disabled shop 🍂

HASCOMBE WINKWORTH ARBORETUM

Hascombe Rd GU8 4AD
Dir: (2m NW on B2130, follow brown tourist signs from Godalming) **Map Ref:** *SU94*
☎ **01483 208477** 📄 **01483 208252**
e-mail: winkwortharboretum@nationaltrust.org.uk

This lovely woodland covers a hillside of nearly 100 acres, with fine views over the North Downs. The best times to visit are April and May, for the azaleas, bluebells and other flowers, and October for the autumn colours. A delightful Victorian boathouse is open April to October with fine views over Rowes Flashe lake. There are many rare trees and shrubs in group plantings for spring and autumn colour effect.

Times: Open all year, daily during daylight hours. (Could close when weather is bad) **Fee:** ✱ £4 (ch £2). Family ticket £10, additional family member £1.75. **Facilities:** 🅿 ☕ ♿ (suggested route, free entry for helpers) toilets for disabled shop 🍂 💳

OUTWOOD OUTWOOD WINDMILL

Outwood Common RH1 5PW
Dir: (M25 junct 6, take A25 through Godstone towards Redhill, after 1m turn S off A25 at Bletchingly, between The Prince Albert & The White Hart. Mill 3m on left) *Map Ref:* TQ34
☎ 01342 843458 & 843644 📄 01342 843458
e-mail: info@outwoodwindmill.co.uk

This award-winning example of a post mill dates from 1665. It is the oldest working windmill in England and one of the best preserved in existence. Standing 400 feet above sea level, it is surrounded by common land and National Trust property, and ducks and geese wander freely in the grounds. There is a play area for small children and a video room showing a presentation about windmills.

Times: Open Etr Sun-3rd Sun in Oct, Sun & BH Mons only 2-6. Other times for parties only by arrangement. **Fee:** ✱ £2 (ch £1).
Facilities: P (10yds) & toilets for disabled shop

PAINSHILL PARK PAINSHILL PARK

KT11 1JE
Dir: (W of Cobham on A245) *Map Ref:* TQ06
☎ 01932 868113 📄 01932 868001
e-mail: info@painshill.co.uk

Painshill Park, created by the Hon Charles Hamilton between 1738 and 1773, was a pleasure ground for fashionable society. His vision influenced the future of England's countryside, culture and gardening. Staged around a huge serpentine lake, surprises come at every turn - a Gothic temple, Chinese bridge, ruined abbey, grotto, Turkish tent, Gothic tower, spectacular waterwheel, 18th-century planting and a working vineyard.

Times: Open Mar-Oct, Tue-Sun & BH, 10.30-6. (last entry 4.30). Nov-Feb, Wed-Sun, & BH 11-4 (gates close 3). Closed 25 Dec.
Fee: *Prices not confirmed for 2005* **Facilities:** P 💺 ✕ licensed & (wheelchairs & buggies available - pre-booked) toilets for disabled shop ✖ (ex guide dogs) 📼

REIGATE REIGATE PRIORY MUSEUM

Bell St RH2 7RL
Dir: (next to Bell Street car park) *Map Ref:* TQ24
☎ 01737 222550   FREE

The museum is housed in Reigate Priory, a Grade I listed building, originally founded before 1200 and converted into a mansion in Tudor times. Notable features include the magnificent Holbein fireplace, the 17th-century oak staircase and murals. The small museum has changing exhibitions on a wide range of subjects, designed to appeal to both adults and children. The collection includes domestic bygones, local history and costume.

Times: Open Etr-early Dec, Wed & Sat, 2-4.30 in term time. **Facilities:** P (50yds) & (hands on facilities) shop ✖

Surrey continued

TILFORD RURAL LIFE CENTRE

Reeds Rd GU10 2DL
Dir: (off A287, 3m S of Farnham, signed) *Map Ref:* SU84
☎ 01252 795571 📄 01252 795571
e-mail: rural.life@lineone.net

The museum covers village life from 1750 to 1960. It is set in over ten acres of garden and woodland and incorporates purpose-built and reconstructed buildings, including a chapel. Displays show village crafts and trades, such as wheelwrighting, thatching, ploughing and gardening. The historic village playground provides entertainment for children and there is an arboretum featuring over 100 trees from around the world.

Times: Open late Mar-early Oct, Wed-Sun & BH 10-5; Winter Wed & Sun only 11-4 **Fee:** £5 (ch £3 & pen £4). Family ticket £14 (2ad+2ch) **Facilities:** 🅿 🍽 ✕ licensed ♿ (3 wheelchairs for use) toilets for disabled shop 🔊

WEYBRIDGE *BROOKLANDS MUSEUM*

Brooklands Rd KT13 0QN
Dir: (M25 junct 10/11, museum off B374) *Map Ref:* TQ06
☎ 01932 857381 📄 01932 855465
e-mail: info@brooklandsmuseum.com

Brooklands racing circuit was the birthplace of British motorsport and aviation. From 1907 to 1987 it was a world-renowned centre of engineering excellence. The Museum features old banked track and the 1-in-4 Test Hill. Many of the original buildings have been restored including the clubhouse, the Shell and BP petrol pagodas, and the Malcolm Campbell sheds in the motoring village. Many motorcycles, cars and aircraft are on display. Ring for details of special events.

Times: ✱ Open Tue-Sun & BHs 10-5 (4 in winter). **Facilities:** 🅿 🍽 ♿ toilets for disabled shop 🐕 (ex guide dogs) 🔊

ALFRISTON DRUSILLAS PARK

BN26 5QS
Dir: (off A27 between Brighton & Eastbourne) *Map Ref:* TQ50
☎ 01323 874100 📄 01323 874101
e-mail: info@drusillas.co.uk

Situated amidst the stunning scenery of the Cuckmere Valley at Alfriston, Drusillas is widely recognised as the Best Small Zoo in England. There are over 100 animal species in naturalistic environments, including meerkats, bats, penguins, monkeys, reptiles and creepy crawlies. There are also beautiful gardens, play areas, panning for gold, Jungle Adventure Golf, Explorers Lagoon and Mokomo's Jungle Rock.

Times: Open all year, daily 10-6 (winter 10-5). Closed 24-26 Dec. **Fee:** ✱ Family super saver tickets: Family of 3 £27.45, family of 4 £36.45, family of 5 £44.95 **Facilities:** 🅿 🍽 ✕ licensed ♿ (rear train carriage & sensory trails) toilets for disabled shop 🐕 (ex guide dogs) 🔊

BATTLE BUCKLEYS YESTERDAY'S WORLD

89-90 High St TN33 0AQ
Dir: (A21 onto A2100 towards Battle, opposite Battle Abbey)
Map Ref: *TQ71*
☎ 01424 775378 774269 📄 01424 775174
e-mail: info@yesterdaysworld.co.uk

A fun day out for all the family, as the past is brought to life. Walk down the cobbled streets of yesteryear and meet the colourful characters in over 30 shop and room settings including a 1930's grocer's and a Victorian kitchen. The exhibition contains many rarities from the 1850s onwards, including some of Queen Victoria's personal effects and letters written by the present queen. The museum is housed in beautiful gardens with children's play village, miniature golf and summer tea rooms.

Times: Open all year, Winter, daily 10-5; Summer, daily 10-6. Closed 25-26 Dec. **Fee:** ✱ £4.99 (ch £3.75, pen & students £4.75). Family ticket £16.75. Discount for special needs visitors & groups of 15+. **Facilities:** P (100yds) (£2 per day) 🍴 ⚹ (limited access for wheelchairs) toilets for disabled shop 📷

1066 BATTLE OF HASTINGS ABBEY & BATTLEFIELD

TN33 0AD
Dir: (A21 onto A2100) *Map Ref:* *TQ71*
☎ 01424 773792 📄 01424 775059

Explore the site of the Battle of Hastings where on 14 October 1066 one of the most famous events in English history took place. It was here that William the Conqueror defeated Harold, King of England. After just a day's fighting, the English army disintegrated and William was crowned king. A free interactive wand talks you around a tour of the battlefield and the atmospheric abbey ruins.

Times: Open all year, Apr-Sep, daily 10-6 (Oct 10 5); Nov-Mar, daily 10-4. Closed 24-26 Dec & 1 Jan. **Fee:** ✱ £5 (ch £2.50, concessions £3.80). Family £12.50. Prices & opening times relate to 2004, for further details phone or log onto www.english-heritage.org.uk/visits **Facilities:** P (charged) ⚹ shop ⊞

BRIGHTON BRIGHTON MUSEUM & ART GALLERY

Royal Pavilion Gardens BN1 1EE
Dir: (A23/M23 from London, in city centre near seafront. New entrance in Royal Pavilion Gardens) *Map Ref:* *TQ30*
☎ 01273 290900 📄 01273 292841   FREE

A £10 million redevelopment has transformed Brighton museum into a state-of-the-art visitor attraction. Dynamic and innovative new galleries, including fashion, 20th-century design and world art, feature exciting interactive displays appealing to all ages. The museum also benefits from a spacious new entrance located in the Royal Pavilion gardens and full disabled access.

Times: Open all year, Tue 10-7, Wed-Sat 10-5 & Sun 2-5. (Closed Mon ex BHs). **Facilities:** P (5 mins walk) (Church St NCP & on street) 🍴 ⚹ (lift,tactile exhibits,induction loops,ramps,automatic door) toilets for disabled shop ✖ (ex guide dogs)

ROYAL PAVILION

BN1 1EE
Dir: (M23/A23 from London, situated in city centre near seafront.
15 min walk from train station) *Map Ref:* TQ30
☎ **01273 290900** 📄 **01273 292871**
e-mail: visitor.services@brighton-hove.gov.uk

Acclaimed as one of the most exotically beautiful buildings in the
British Isles, the Royal Pavilion was the magnificent seaside
residence of George IV, originally a simple farmhouse which was
developed over 35 years into a Regency palace. The breathtaking
building is decorated in Chinese style, with a romanticised Indian
exterior, and is surrounded by restored Regency gardens.

Times: Open all year, Apr-Sep, daily 9.30-5.45 (last admission 5);
Oct-Mar, daily 10-5.15 (last admission 4.30). **Fee:** ✱ £5.95 (ch £3.50,
concessions £4.20) Family ticket £9.20-£15. Groups 20+ £4.95 each.
Family ticket (2ad+4ch) £15.40, (1ad+4ch) £9.45. **Facilities:** P (5
mins walk) (NCP & on Church St) 🍵 ♿ (tours by arrangement,
wheelchairs) toilets for disabled shop ✖ (ex guide dogs) ◀

SEA LIFE CENTRE

Marine Pde BN2 1TB
Dir: (next to Brighton Pier between Marine Parade and Madeira
Drive) *Map Ref:* TQ30
☎ **01273 604234** 📄 **01273 681840**
e-mail: slcbrighton@merlinentertainments.biz

Experience spectacular marine displays set in the world's oldest
functioning aquarium at the Brighton Sea Life Centre. Take a look
at over 100 species in their natural habitat, including seahorses,
sharks and rays. Over 40 exhibits include Adventures at 20,000
Leagues complete with NASA-designed walk-through observation
tunnel. Features also include a Captain Pugwash quiz trail, a soft
play area, a café and a gift shop.

Times: ✱ Open all year, daily 10-6. (Last
admission 5). Open later on wknds in summer &
school hols. Closed 25 Dec.
Facilities: P (200yds) (pay & display) 🍵
♿ toilets for disabled shop ✖ (ex guide dogs) ◀

EASTBOURNE   "HOW WE LIVED THEN" MUSEUM OF SHOPS & SOCIAL HISTORY

20 Cornfield Ter BN21 4NS
Dir: (just off seafront, between town centre & theatres, signed)
Map Ref: TV69
☎ **01323 737143**
e-mail: howwelivedthen@btconnect.com

Over the last 40 years, Jan and Graham Upton have collected over
100,000 items which are now displayed on four floors of
authentic old shops and room-settings, transporting visitors back
to their grandparents' era. Other displays, such as seaside
souvenirs, wartime rationing and royal mementoes, help to
capture 100 years of social history.

Times: Open all year, daily, 10-5.30 (last entry 5).
Winter times subject to change, telephone
establishment. **Fee:** £4 (ch 5-15 £3, under 5's
free, pen £3.50). Party 10+.
Facilities: P (outside) ♿ (no charge for
disabled) shop

WISH TOWER PUPPET MUSEUM

Martello Tower No 73, King Edward Pde BN21 4BU
Dir: (on seafront, W of pier) *Map Ref:* *TV69*
☎ **01323 417776** 📄 **01323 644440**
e-mail: puppet.workshop@virgin.net

This museum hosts a unique display of puppets from all over the world. From early shadow puppets of Asia, through over 300 years of Punch and Judy in England to television and film puppets of today. Puppet shows sometimes take place during the summer. The tower itself is one of a chain of Martello towers built along the south coast of England when there was a threat of invasion from Napoleon.

Times: ✱ Open May-mid Jul & Sep, wknds 11-5; mid Jul-Aug, daily 11-5. **Facilities:** ℙ (100mtrs) shop ✈ ◼

HALLAND BENTLEY WILDFOWL & MOTOR MUSEUM

BN8 5AF
Dir: (7m NE of Lewes, signposted off A22, A26 & B2192)
Map Ref: *TQ51*
☎ **01825 840573** 📄 **01825 841322**
e-mail: barrysutherland@pavilion.co.uk

Hundreds of swans, geese and ducks from all over the world can be seen on lakes and ponds along with flamingos and peacocks. There is a fine array of veteran, Edwardian and vintage vehicles, and the house has splendid antiques and wildfowl paintings. The gardens specialise in old fashioned roses. Other attractions include woodland walks, a nature trail, education centre, adventure playground and a miniature train.

Times: ✱ Open 17 Mar-Oct, daily 10.30-4.30. House open from noon, Apr-Nov, Feb & part of Mar, wknds only. Estate closed Dec & Jan. House closed all winter. **Facilities:** ℙ ◉ ♿ (wheelchairs available) toilets for disabled shop ✈ (ex guide dogs) ◼

HASTINGS SMUGGLERS ADVENTURE

St Clements Caves, West Hill TN34 3HY
Dir: (follow brown signs along A259 coast road through Hastings. Use seafront car park and then take West cliff railway or follow signed footpath) *Map Ref:* *TQ80*
☎ **01424 422964** 📄 **01424 721483**
e-mail: smugglers@discoverhastings.co.uk

Smugglers Adventure is a themed experience housed in a labyrinth of caverns and passages deep below the West Hill. Visitors first tour a comprehensive exhibition and museum, followed by a video theatre, before embarking on the Adventure Walk - a trip through several acres of caves with life-size tableaux, push-button automated models and dramatic scenic effects depicting life in the days of 18th-century smuggling.

Times: Open all year daily, Etr-Sep 10-5.30; Oct-Etr 11-4.30. Closed 24-26 Dec. **Fee:** ✱ £5.95 (ch £3.95, concessions £4.95). Family ticket £16.50. **Facilities:** ℙ (500yds) (parking meters on some streets) shop ✈ (ex guide dogs) ◼

HERSTMONCEUX THE OBSERVATORY SCIENCE CENTRE

BN27 1RN
Dir: (2m E of village on Boreham St to Pevensey Rd)
Map Ref: TQ61
☎ 01323 832731 📄 01323 832741
e-mail: info@the-observatory.org

From the 1950s to the 1980s this was part of the Royal Greenwich Observatory, and was used by astronomers to observe and chart movements in the night sky. Visitors can learn about not only astronomy, but also other areas of science in a series of interactive and engaging displays. There are also exhibitions, a discovery park, and a collection of unusual giant exhibits.

Times: Open Apr-Sep daily 10-6; Mar & Oct 10-5; Nov-Feb 10-4; (wknds only in Jan & Dec starting 10 Jan & finishing 12 Dec) **Fee:** ✱ £5.80 (ch 4-15 £4.20). Family ticket (2ad+3ch or 1ad+4ch) £17.50 **Facilities:** 🅿 🖳 ♿ (ramps & disabled entrance) toilets for disabled shop ✖ (ex guide dogs) ◼

HOVE BRITISH ENGINEERIUM-MUSEUM OF STEAM & MECHANICAL ANTIQUITIES

off Nevill Rd BN3 7QA
Dir: (signed off A27 from Worthing & Eastbourne)
Map Ref: TQ20
☎ 01273 559583 📄 01273 566403
e-mail: info@britishengineerium.com

This restored Victorian water pumping station has an original working beam engine of 1876, and a French Corliss horizontal engine which won first prize at the Paris International Exhibition of 1889. There are also traction engines, fire engines, and many other full-size and model engines. Also an exhibition of craftsmen's tools and domestic appliances. Boilers are fired up and in steam on special days.

Times: ✱ Open all year, daily 10-4. In steam first Sun in month & Sun & Mon of BHs. Telephone for details of days closed prior to Xmas. **Facilities:** 🅿 ♿ shop ✖ (ex guide dogs)

LEWES LEWES CASTLE & BARBICAN HOUSE MUSEUM

169 High St BN7 1YE
Dir: (N of High St off A27/A26/A275) *Map Ref:* TQ41
☎ 01273 486290 📄 01273 486990
e-mail: castle@sussexpast.co.uk

High above the town's medieval streets stands Lewes Castle, begun soon after the Norman Conquest by William de Warenne as his stronghold in Sussex and added to over the next 300 years, culminating in the magnificent Barbican. Thomas Read Kemp and his family owned and updated the ruins during Georgian times. Barbican House is next to the castle and is home to a museum covering the area from pre-history to the late medieval period. A 'sound and light' show in the museum tells the story of Lewes through the ages.

Times: ✱ Open daily, Tue-Sat 10-5.30, Sun & Mon 11-5.30. (Last admission 30 mins before closing). Closed Xmas & Mon in Jan. **Facilities:** 🅿 (on street parking) shop ✖ (ex guide dogs) ◼

NEWHAVEN PARADISE PARK & GARDENS

Avis Rd BN9 0DH
Dir: (signed off A26 & A259) **Map Ref:** TQ40
☎ **01273 512123** 📄 **01273 616005**
e-mail: enquiries@paradisepark.co.uk

A perfect day out for plant lovers whatever the season. Discover the unusual garden designs with waterfalls, fountains and lakes, including the Caribbean garden and the tranquil Oriental garden. The Conservatory Gardens complex contains a large variety of the world's flora divided into several zones. There's also a Sussex history trail and Planet Earth with moving dinosaurs and interactive displays, plus rides and amusements for children.

Times: Open all year, daily 9-6. Closed 25-26 Dec. **Fee:** ✱ £5.99 (ch £4.99). Family ticket £19.99 (2ad+3ch). **Facilities:** 🅿 🍽 ✗ licensed & (all areas level or ramped) toilets for disabled shop garden centre ✗ (ex guide dogs) 🛍

SHEFFIELD PARK STATION BLUEBELL RAILWAY

Sheffield Park Station TN22 3QL
Dir: (4.5m E of Haywards Heath, off A275) **Map Ref:** TQ42
☎ **01825 720800 & 722370** 📄 **01825 720804**
e-mail: info@bluebell-railway.co.uk

A volunteer-run heritage steam railway with nine miles of track running through pretty Sussex countryside. It was the first standard gauge passenger railway to be preserved in the UK, re-opening part of the Lewes to East Grinstead line of the old London Brighton & South Coast Railway in 1960. Visitors should note that there is no parking at Kingscote Station. If you wish to board the train here, catch the bus (service 473) which connects Kingscote and East Grinstead.

Times: Open all year, Sat & Sun, daily May-Sep & during school holidays. Santa Specials run Dec. For timetable and information regarding trains contact above. **Fee:** ✱ 3rd class return fare £9 (ch £4.50). Family ticket £25. Admission to Sheffield Park Station only £1.60 (ch 80p). Other tickets available on request. **Facilities:** 🅿 🍽 ✗ licensed & (special carriage for wheelchairs & carers with lift) toilets for disabled shop 🛍

AMBERLEY AMBERLEY WORKING MUSEUM

BN18 9LT
Dir: (on B2139, between Arundel and Storrington, adjacent to Amberley railway station) **Map Ref:** TQ01
☎ **01798 831370** 📄 **01798 831831**
e-mail: office@amberleymuseum.co.uk

This 36-acre open-air museum is dedicated to the industrial heritage of the southeast of England. Here you can see traditional craftspeople (including a blacksmith and potter), a working narrow-gauge railway and vintage bus collection, the Connected Earth telecommunications display, Seeboard Electricity Hall, stationary engines, a print workshop, woodturners, wheelwrights, nature trails, a restaurant, shop and much more.

Times: ✱ Open 12 Mar-2 Nov, Wed-Sun & BH Mon 10-5.30 (last admission 4.30). Also open daily during school hols. **Facilities:** 🅿 🍽 & (wheelchairs available for loan & large print guides) toilets for disabled shop 🛍

ARUNDEL ARUNDEL CASTLE

BN18 9AB
Dir: (on A27 between Chichester & Worthing) *Map Ref:* TQ00
☎ 01903 883136 ▤ 01903 884581
e-mail: info@arundelcastle.org

Set high on a hill in West Sussex, this magnificent castle and
stately home, seat of the Dukes of Norfolk for nearly 1,000 years,
commands stunning views across the River Arun and out to sea.
Here you can climb to the keep and battlements, marvel at a fine
collection of 16th-century furniture, tapestries and portraits by Van
Dyke, Gainsborough and Caneletto, and see the personal
possessions of Mary, Queen of Scots. Outside in the grounds are
the renovated Victorian flower and vegetable gardens.

Times: Open 25 Mar-Oct, Sun-Fri 11-5, Castle open 12-5. (Last
admission 4). Closed Sat **Fee:** ✱ £9 (ch 5-16 £5.50, pen £7). Family
ticket £24.50. Party 20+. **Facilities:** 🅿 🖳 ♿ toilets for disabled shop
✈ (ex guide dogs) ◀

WWT ARUNDEL

Mill Rd BN18 9PB
Dir: (signed from A27 & A29) *Map Ref:* TQ00
☎ 01903 883355 ▤ 01903 884834
e-mail: arundel@wwt.org.uk

More than a thousand ducks, geese and swans from all over the
world can be found here, many of which are so friendly that they
will eat from your hand. The reserve attracts a variety of birds and
includes a reedbed habitat considered so vital to the wetland
wildlife it shelters that it has been designated a Site of Special
Scientific Interest. Visitors can walk right through the reedbed on
a specially designed boardwalk. There is a packed programme of
events and activities throughout the year.

Times: Open all year, daily; summer 9.30-5;
winter 9.30-4.30. (Last admission summer 5;
winter 4). Closed 25 Dec. **Fee:** ✱ £5.75
(ch £3.50, pen £4.50). Family ticket £14.50.
Facilities: 🅿 🖳 ✗ licensed ♿ (level paths, free
wheelchair loan) toilets for disabled shop
✈ (ex guide & hearing dogs) ◀

BIGNOR BIGNOR ROMAN VILLA & MUSEUM

RH20 1PH
Dir: (6m S of Pulborough and 6m N of Arundel on A29, signed.
8m S of Petworth on A285, signed) *Map Ref:* SU91
☎ 01798 869259 ▤ 01798 869259
e-mail: bignorromanvilla@care4free.net

Rediscovered in 1811, this Roman house was built on a grand
scale. It is one of the largest known, and has spectacular mosaics.
The heating system can also be seen, and various finds from
excavations are on show. The longest mosaic in Britain (82 feet)
is on display here in its original position.

Times: Open Mar-Apr, Tue-Sun & BH 10-5; May
daily 10-5; Jun-Sep daily 10-6, Oct daily 10-5
Fee: ✱ £4 (ch 5-15 £1.70, pen £2.85). Party
10+. Guided tours by arrangement.
Facilities: 🅿 🖳 ♿ (most areas accessible) shop
✈ (ex guide dogs) ◀

CHICHESTER MECHANICAL MUSIC & DOLL COLLECTION

Church Rd, Portfield PO19 4HN
Dir: (1m E of Chichester, signposted off A27) *Map Ref:* SU80
☎ 01243 372646 📄 01243 370299

A unique opportunity to see and hear barrel organs, polyphons, musical boxes, fair organs etc - all fully restored and playing. The Mechanical Music & Doll Collection provides a magical musical tour to fascinate and entertain all ages. The doll collection contains fine examples of Victorian china and wax dolls, and felt and velvet dolls of the 1920s.

Times: Open Jun-Sep, Wed 1-4; Group bookings anytime in the year by prior arrangement.
Fee: ✱ £2.50 (ch £1.25). **Facilities:** 🅿 ♿ shop ✖ (ex guide dogs)

FISHBOURNE FISHBOURNE ROMAN PALACE

Salthill Rd PO19 3QR
Dir: (off A27 onto A259 into Fishbourne. Turn right into Salthill Rd & right into Roman Way) *Map Ref:* SU80
☎ 01243 785859 📄 01243 539266
e-mail: adminfish@sussexpast.co.uk

This is the largest known Roman residence in Britain. It was occupied from the 1st to the 3rd centuries AD, and has mosaic floors and painted walls. Twenty five of these mosaic floors can still be seen in varying states of completeness, including others rescued from elsewhere in the area. Outside, part of the garden has been replanted to its original 1st-century plan. The museum displays a collection of finds from the excavations and tells the story of the site's discovery. An audio-visual presentation helps bring the site back to life.

Times: ✱ Open all year, daily Feb-15 Dec. Feb, Nov-Dec 10-4; Mar-Jul & Sep-Oct 10-5; Aug 10-6. Winter wknds 10-4. **Facilities:** 🅿 ☕ ♿ (self guiding tapes & tactile objects for the blind) toilets for disabled shop garden centre ✖ (ex guide dogs) 🍴

GOODWOOD GOODWOOD HOUSE

PO18 0PX
Dir: (3m NE of Chichester) *Map Ref:* SU81
☎ 01243 755000 📄 01243 755005
e-mail: curator@goodwood.co.uk

Goodwood House has been the ancestral home of the Dukes of Richmond for 300 years. Following refurbishment, the state apartments have taken on new life, notably the restored tapestry drawing room. Goodwood was the country home of the scandalous and glamorous Lennox sisters, immortalised in the BBC TV production of 'Aristocrats'. Unrivalled as an English ancestral collection, the paintings include works by Van Dyck, Reynolds, Stubbs and Canaletto.

Times: ✱ Open 30 Mar-6 Oct, Sun & Mon; 3-28 Aug, Sun-Thu 1-5. Closed 13 Apr, 22 Jun, 6-7 & 13-14 Jul & 7 Sep. **Facilities:** 🅿 ☕ ♿ (ramp at front of house, disabled parking area) toilets for disabled shop ✖ 🍴

LITTLEHAMPTON LOOK & SEA! VISITOR CENTRE

63-65 Surrey St BN17 5AW
Dir: (on harbour front 10 mins' walk from Littlehampton Station)
Map Ref: TQ00
☎ **01903 718984** 📄 **01903 718036**
e-mail: info@lookandsea.co.uk

An interactive museum exploring the history and geography of
Littlehampton and the surrounding area. Inside the modern
waterfront building you can meet the 500,000-year-old Boxgrove
Man, become a ship's captain in an interactive computer game,
and enjoy spectacular panoramic views of the Sussex coast from
the circular glass tower.

Times: Open all year, daily 9-5 **Fee:** ✱ £2.95 (ch £2.50, pen &
student £2.50). **Facilities:** P 💻 ✗ ♿ toilets for disabled shop
🐕 (ex guide dogs) 🍴

LOWER BEEDING LEONARDSLEE LAKES & GARDENS

RH13 6PP
Dir: (4m SW from Handcross, at junct of B2110 & A281)
Map Ref: TQ22
☎ **01403 891212** 📄 **01403 891305**
e-mail: gardens@leonardslee.com

This Grade I listed garden is set in a peaceful valley with walks
around seven beautiful lakes. It is a paradise in spring, with banks
of rhododendrons and azaleas along paths lined with bluebells.
Wallabies live in parts of the valley, deer in the parks and wildfowl
on the lakes. Enjoy the Rock Garden, the fascinating Bonsai, the
new 'Behind the Doll's House' exhibition and the collection of
Victorian Motorcars (1889-1900).

Times: Open Apr-Oct, daily 9.30-6 **Fee:** Apr &
Jun-Oct £6, May (Mon-Fri) £8, (wknds & BH) £9
(ch £4 anytime). **Facilities:** P 💻 ✗ licensed
shop garden centre 🐕 🍴

PETWORTH PETWORTH HOUSE & PARK

GU28 0AE
Dir: (in town centre, A272/283) *Map Ref:* SU92
☎ **01798 342207 & 343929** 📄 **01798 342963**
e-mail: petworth@ntrust.org.uk

Petworth House is an impressive 17th-century mansion set in a
700-acre deer park, landscaped by 'Capability' Brown and
immortalised in Turner's paintings. At Petworth you will find the
National Trust's finest art collection including work by Van Dyck,
Titian and Turner as well as sculpture, ceramics and fine furniture.
Fascinating servants' quarters show the domestic side of life on
this great estate.

Times: Open 27 Mar-Oct (closed Thu & Fri) 11-5.30, (last entry 5)
Fee: ✱ £7 (ch £4). Family ticket £18. Party 15+ £6 each. NT
members free. Pleasure Ground £1.50 (ch free). **Facilities:** P 💻
✗ licensed ♿ (wheelchairs available, Braille guide) toilets for disabled
shop 🐕 (ex guide/hearing dogs) 👶 🍴

PULBOROUGH *PARHAM HOUSE & GARDENS*

Parham Park RH20 4HS
Dir: (midway between A29 & A24, off A283 between Pulborough & Storrington) **Map Ref:** TQ01
☎ **01903 744888 & 742021** 📄 **01903 746557**
e-mail: enquiries@parhaminsussex.co.uk

Surrounded by a deer park, fine gardens and 18th-century pleasure grounds, in a beautiful downland setting, this Elizabethan family home contains an important collection of paintings, furniture, carpets and rare needlework. A brick and turf maze has been created in the grounds - designed with children in mind, it is called 'Veronica's Maze'.

Times: ✱ Open Etr Sun-Sep, Wed, Thu, Sun & BH Dir: (also open Tue & Fri in Aug). Gardens open 12-6; House 2-6 (last entry 5). Guided tours on Wed & Thu mornings & Tue & Fri afternoons by special arrangement. **Facilities:** 🅿 ☕ & (wheelchairs, ramps, recorded tour tape, parking) toilets for disabled shop garden centre ✖ (ex guide dogs & in grounds) ▬

RSPB PULBOROUGH BROOKS NATURE RESERVE

Uppertons Barn Visitor Centre, Wiggonholt RH20 2EL
Dir: (signed on A283, 2m SE of Pulborough & 2m NW of Storrington) **Map Ref:** TQ01
☎ **01798 875851**
e-mail: pulborough.brooks@rspb.org.uk

Set in the scenic Arun Valley and easily reached via the visitor centre at Wiggonholt, this is an excellent reserve for year-round family visits. A nature trail winds through hedgerow lined lanes to viewing hides overlooking water meadows. Breeding summer birds include nightingales and warblers, ducks and wading birds, and nightjars and hobbies on nearby heathland. Unusual wading birds and hedgerow birds regularly pass through on spring and autumn migration.

Times: Open daily, Reserve: 9-9, (or sunset if earlier). Visitor centre: 10-5. Reserve closed 25 Dec, Visitor Centre closed 25-26 Dec. **Fee:** £3.50 (ch £1, concessions £2.50). Family ticket £7. **Facilities:** 🅿 ☕ & (free hire electric buggy for use on nature trail) toilets for disabled shop ✖ (ex guide dogs) ▬

SINGLETON WEALD & DOWNLAND OPEN AIR MUSEUM

PO18 0EU
Dir: (6m N of Chichester on A286) **Map Ref:** SU81
☎ **01243 811348** 📄 **01243 811475**
e-mail: office@wealddown.co.uk

This open-air museum is a showcase of English architectural heritage, where historic buildings have been rescued from destruction and rebuilt in a parkland setting. Vividly demonstrating the evolution of building techniques and use of local materials, these fascinating buildings bring to life the homes, farms and rural industries of the southeast over the past 500 years.

Times: Open all year, Mar-Oct, daily 10.30-6 (last admission 5); Nov-Feb, Sat & Sun 10.30-4, also 26 Dec-1 Jan daily & Feb half term, 10.30-4. **Fee:** £7.50 (ch £4, pen £6.50). Family ticket (2ad+3ch) £20. Party. **Facilities:** 🅿 ☕ & (separate entrance and ramps available for some buildings) toilets for disabled shop ▬

Sussex, West continued

TANGMERE TANGMERE MILITARY AVIATION MUSEUM TRUST

PO20 2ES
Dir: (off A27, 3m E of Chichester towards Arundel)
Map Ref: SU90
☎ **01243 775223** 📄 **01243 789490**
e-mail: admin@tangmere-museum.org.uk

Based at an airfield that played an important role during the
World Wars, this museum spans 80 years of military aviation.
There are photographs, documents, aircraft and aircraft parts on
display along with a Hurricane replica, Spitfire replica and cockpit
simulator. A hangar houses a Supermarine Swift and the record-
breaking aircraft Meteor and Hunter. Aircraft outside include
Lockheed T33, English Electric Lightning, Gloster Meteor and
Westland Whirlwind helicopter.

Times: Open Mar-Oct, daily 10-5.30; Feb & Nov,
daily 10-4.30. **Fee:** £5 (ch £1.50 & pen £4)
Family £11 (2ad+2ch). **Facilities:** 🅿 ☕
♿ (wheelchairs available) toilets for disabled shop
🐕 (ex guide dogs)

ALUM BAY THE NEEDLES OLD BATTERY

West High Down PO30 0JH
Dir: (at Needles Headland, W of Freshwater Bay and Alum Bay,
B3322) *Map Ref:* SZ38
☎ **01983 754772** 📄 **01983 756978**
e-mail: jean.pitt@nationaltrust.org.uk

In 1862, the threat of a French invasion prompted the
construction of this fort in its spectacular setting by the Needles
rocks. The Old Battery still retains its original gun barrels, and the
laboratory and searchlight position-finding cells have all been
restored. A 65-metre tunnel leads to stunning views of the
Hampshire and Dorset coastline.

Times: Open 28 Mar-Jun & Sep-Oct daily (closed Fri ex Good Fri)
10.30-5; Jul-Aug daily 10.30-5; Property closes in very bad weather.
Telephone on day of visit to check. **Fee:** ✱ £3.80 (ch £1.90). Family
ticket £8.50. Group £3.20 each **Facilities:** 🅿 (0.5m) ☕ ♿ (ramp &
audio tours) toilets for disabled 🐾 📷

THE NEEDLES PARK

PO39 0JD
Dir: (signed on B3322) *Map Ref:* SZ38
☎ **0870 458 0022** 📄 **01983 755260**
e-mail: info@theneedles.co.uk

Overlooking the Needles on the western edge of the island, the
park has attractions for all the family: included in the wide range
of facilities is the spectacular chair lift to the beach to view the
famous coloured sand cliffs, Needles Rocks and lighthouse. Other
popular attractions are Alum Bay Glass and the Isle of Wight
Sweet Manufactory.

Times: Open 23 Mar-30 Oct, daily 10-5. Hours extended in high
season & on special event days **Fee:** ✱ No admission charged for
entrance to Park. All day car park charge £3. Pay as you go attractions
or Supersaver Attraction discount ticket £7.50 (ch £5.50).
Facilities: 🅿 (charged) ☕ ✗ licensed ♿ (designated parking) toilets
for disabled shop 📷

ARRETON *ROBIN HILL COUNTRY PARK*

Downend PO30 2NU
Dir: (0.5m from Arreton village next to Hare & Hounds pub)
Map Ref: SZ58
☎ 01983 527352 ▤ 01983 527347

Set in 88 acres of downland and woods, Robin Hill offers a tree top trail, mazes, snake slides, Troll Island, Neptune Ride and jets, Squirrel Tower, forest sculptures and a countryside centre. All this and the three largest rides on the island (for over eights) - the 400-metre Toboggan Run, 28-seater motion platform cinema Time Machine, and the 42-seater swinging Colossus.

Times: ✱ Open 25 Mar-3 Nov, daily 10-5 (last admission 4). **Facilities:** P ▣ ✗ & (most areas are accessible, ramps access) toilets for disabled shop ▄

BEMBRIDGE *BEMBRIDGE WINDMILL*

PO35 5SQ
Dir: (0.5m S of Bembridge on B3395) *Map Ref:* SZ68
☎ 01983 873945

The last remaining windmill on the island to survive, Bembridge Mill was built about 1700 and was in use until 1913. The stone-built tower with its wooden cap and machinery have been restored since it was given to the National Trust in 1961. Quizzes and trails are available for children.

Times: Open 29 Mar-29 Oct, Sun-Fri, 10-5 (Closed Sat ex Etr Sat); Jul-Aug, daily 10-5. **Fee:** ✱ £2 (ch £1) Family £6. Group £1.70
Facilities: P (200yds) shop ✖ (ex guide dogs) ▨ ▄

BLACKGANG *BLACKGANG CHINE FANTASY PARK*

PO38 2HN
Dir: (follow signs from Ventnor for Whitnell & Niton. From Niton follow signs for Blackgang) *Map Ref:* SZ47
☎ 01983 730330 ▤ 01983 731267
e-mail: info@blackgangchine.com

Opened as scenic gardens in 1843 covering some 40 acres, the park has imaginative play areas, water gardens, maze and coastal gardens. Set on the steep wooded slopes of the chine are the themed areas Smugglerland, Nurseryland, Dinosaurland, Fantasyland and Frontierland. St Catherine's Quay has a maritime exhibition showing the history of local and maritime affairs.

Times: Open 22 Mar-Oct daily, 10-5; 18 Jul-4 Sep open until 10. **Fee:** ✱ Combined ticket to chine, sawmill & quay £7.50. Saver ticket (4 people) £27.
Facilities: P (charged) ▣ & (some paths steep) toilets for disabled shop ▄

BRADING ISLE OF WIGHT WAX WORKS

46 High St PO36 0DQ
Dir: (on A3055, in Brading High St) **Map Ref:** *SZ68*
☎ **0870 4584477** 📠 **01983 402112**
e-mail: waxworks@bradingisleofwight.fsnet.co.uk

Set in 0.75 of an acre in the historic 'Kynge's Towne' of Brading, the waxworks comprises the rectory mansion filled with famous and infamous characters from the past, the chamber of horrors, the great British legends gallery, world of nature, Professor Copperthwaithe's extraordinary collection of oddities, and demonstrations on the art of candle-carving.

Times: Open all year, Summer 10-5, Winter 10.30-4.30 (last admission 1hr before closing) **Fee:** £5.50 (ch 5-14, £3.75, under 5 free, pen £4.50). Family £17 (2ad+2ch), Family £20 (2ad+3ch). Party 20+. **Facilities:** 🅿 ☕ & (disabled route planner) toilets for disabled shop 🛍

LILLIPUT ANTIQUE DOLL & TOY MUSEUM

High St PO36 0DJ
Dir: (A3055 Ryde/Sandown road, in Brading High Street)
Map Ref: *SZ68*
☎ **01983 407231** 📠 **01983 404663**
e-mail: lilliput.museum@btconnect.com

This private museum contains one of the finest collections of antique dolls and toys in Britain. There are over 2,000 exhibits, ranging in age from 2000 BC to 1945 with examples of almost every seriously collectable doll, many with royal connections. Also dolls' houses, teddy bears and rare and unusual toys.

Times: Open all year, daily, 10-5. **Fee:** £1.95 (ch & pen £1.15, ch under 5 free). Party on request. **Facilities:** 🅿 (200 yds) & (ramps provided on request) shop 🛍

CARISBROOKE CARISBROOKE CASTLE

PO30 1XY
Dir: (1.25m SW of Newport, off B3401) **Map Ref:** *SZ48*
☎ **01983 522107** 📠 **01983 528632**

A royal fortress and prison to King Charles I, Carisbrooke is set on a sweeping ridge at the heart of the Isle of Wight. Until 1944 it was the official residence of the island's governor. Don't miss the donkeys that can be seen working a 16th-century wheel to draw water from the well. A museum of Isle of Wight history is located in the castle's medieval great hall.

Times: Open all year, Apr-Sep, daily 10-6; Oct-Mar, daily 10-4. Closed 24-26 Dec & 1 Jan. **Fee:** ✱ £5 (ch £2.50, concessions £3.80). Family £12.50. Prices & opening times relate to 2004, for further details phone or log onto www.english-heritage.org.uk/visits **Facilities:** 🅿 ☕ & shop ⊞

OSBORNE HOUSE OSBORNE HOUSE

PO32 6JY
Dir: (1m SE of East Cowes) **Map Ref:** *SZ59*
☎ 01983 200022 ▤ 01983 281380

The beloved seaside retreat of Queen Victoria offers a glimpse into the private life of Britain's longest reigning monarch. The royal apartments are full of treasured mementos. Queen Victoria's role as Empress of India is celebrated in the decoration of the Dunbar Room. Visit the gardens and the charming Swiss Cottage, a wooden chalet in the grounds, where Victoria's children learnt to cook and which now houses a museum.

Times: Open House: Apr-Sep, daily 10-6; Oct-Mar, Sun-Thu guided tours only. Closed 24-26 Dec & 1 Jan. **Fee:** ✱ House & Gardens: £8.50 (ch £4.30, concessions £6.40). Garden only: £5 (ch £2.50, concessions £3.80). Family £21.30 (2ad+3ch). Prices & opening times relate to 2004, for further details phone or log onto www.english-heritage.org.uk/visits **Facilities:** ℙ 🍴 & shop ✖ ♯

PORCHFIELD COLEMANS ANIMAL FARM

Colemans Ln PO30 4LX
Dir: (A3054 Newport to Yarmouth road, follow brown tourist signs) **Map Ref:** *SZ49*
☎ 01983 522831 ▤ 01983 537534
e-mail: info@colemansfarm.net

Ideal for young children, this extensive petting farm has donkeys, goats, rabbits, guinea pigs, pigs, Highland cattle, Shetland ponies, chickens, ducks and geese. There is also a fun barn with slides and swings, an adventure playground, a tractor fun park, and the Old Barn Café for adults who need to relax. Visitors can cuddle, stroke and feed the animals at special times throughout the day, and there are other events that run daily.

Times: Open 20 Mar-7 Nov, Tue-Sun 10-5. (Closed Mon, ex during school and BHs) **Fee:** £4.95 (ch & concessions £3.95) **Facilities:** ℙ 🍴 & toilets for disabled shop ◀

SHANKLIN SHANKLIN CHINE

12 Pomona Rd PO37 6PF
Dir: (turn off A3055 at lights, left into Hope Rd & continue onto Esplanade for entrance) **Map Ref:** *SZ58*
☎ 01983 866432 ▤ 01983 866145
e-mail: jill@shanklinchine.co.uk

Part of Britain's national heritage, this scenic gorge at Shanklin is a magical world of unique beauty and a haven for rare plants and wildlife. A path winds through the ravine with overhanging trees, ferns and other flora covering the steep sides. 'The Island - Then and Now' is an exhibition detailing the history of the Isle of Wight, including its military importance in World War II.

Times: Open daily, Apr-Oct (late May-late Sep illuminated after dusk) **Fee:** £3.50 (ch under 16 £2, pen & students £2.50). Family ticket £9 (2ad+2ch), £11 (2ad +3ch). Group rates available. **Facilities:** ℙ (450yds) 🍴 (access via lower entry only) shop

VENTNOR SMUGGLING MUSEUM

Botanic Gardens PO38 1UL
Dir: (on A3055, 1m W of Ventnor) **Map Ref:** *SZ57*
☎ **01983 853677**

Looks are deceptive at this unique museum; the small reception is the only part of the building visible at ground level. The collection is housed underground in extensive vaults where a 700-year history of smuggling is illustrated in three large galleries through a collection of over 300 exhibits, coming right up to present day practices. The collecting of the artefacts has been the lifelong work of Ron Dowling RNVR, who worked in contraband control in Aden in World War II.

Times: Open Apr-Sep, daily 10-5. **Fee:** £3 (ch, pen & students £1.50). Parties by arrangement. **Facilities:** 🅿 (charged) shop

VENTNOR BOTANIC GARDEN

Undercliff Dr PO38 1UL
Dir: (on A3055 coastal road, 1.5m W of Ventnor) **Map Ref:** *SZ57*
☎ **01983 855397** 📄 **01983 856756**
e-mail: alison.ellsbury@iow.gov.uk

Due to the unique microclimate of the Undercliff, plants that can only survive in a Mediterranean climate thrive on the Isle of Wight. Built on the site of a Victorian hospital for TB sufferers, the garden was founded in 1970 by Sir Harold Hillier, and opened in 1972 by Earl Mountbatten. The garden has plants from Australasia, Africa, America, the Mediterranean, and the Far East, and is a great day out for anyone remotely interested in exotic flora.

Times: Gardens: open all year; Visitor Centre & Green House: Mar-Oct, daily 10-5 & Nov-Feb, wknds only 10-4 **Fee:** Free admission to Gardens & Visitor Centre; Green House £1 **Facilities:** 🅿 (charged) 🍽 ♿ (lifts in garden, wheelchairs) toilets for disabled shop garden centre ✖ (ex guide dogs) ◀

A stone lion clutching a royal crest at Hampton Court

The West Country

The only two large cities in the region are Bristol and Plymouth, both major ports with a strong tradition of international trade. The coastline predominates, attracting huge numbers of visitors to fabulous beaches and a congenially mild climate in the English Riviera. The Jurassic Coast of Dorset and East Devon with its rich geology and wealth of fossils is designated a UNESCO World Heritage Site, and the South West Coast Path is the longest of the National Trails, extending 630 miles from Minehead to Poole Harbour.

Other natural features of the region are Exmoor, extending from the Heritage Coast of North Devon and Somerset, and Dartmoor in Devon – both National Parks. Further inland are the Mendips, including Wookey Hole and Cheddar Gorge, and the gentle Cotswolds, studded with pretty stone-built villages. The cathedral towns of Salisbury, Exeter, Gloucester and Wells are well worth exploring, as are the delightful old towns of Bath, Cheltenham, Dorchester and Glastonbury.

Top tourist attractions in the West Country are the Eden Project in Cornwall, the Roman Baths & Pump Room in Bath, Avebury Stone Circle and Stonehenge in Wiltshire.

Events & Festivals

April 30 Downton Cuckoo Fair, Wiltshire

May 1 Giant Bolster Festival, St Agnes, Cornwall (lantern procession with giant puppets and bonfire)

May 14-15 Re-enactment of the Battle of Stamford Hill, Bude, Cornwall

May 2-3 Weymouth International Beach Kite Festival, Dorset

May (tbc) Blackawton International Festival of Worm Charming, Normandy Arms, Blackawton, Devon

May 20-June 5 Bath International Music Festival, Somerset

June 17-July 3 Exeter Summer Festival

July (tbc) Okehampton Balloon Fiesta, Simmons Park, Okehampton, Devon

July 23-31 Lyme Regis Lifeboat Week, The Cobb, Lyme Regis, Dorset

July 30-August 2 Glastonbury Children's Festival

August Regattas in Fowey, Dartmouth and Falmouth

September 8 Widecombe Fair, Old Field, Widecombe-in-the-Moor, Devon

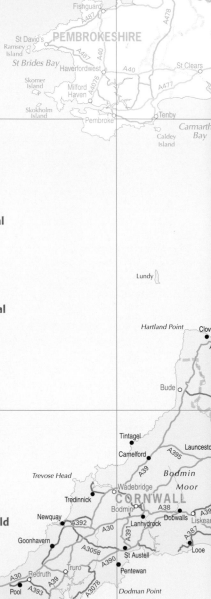

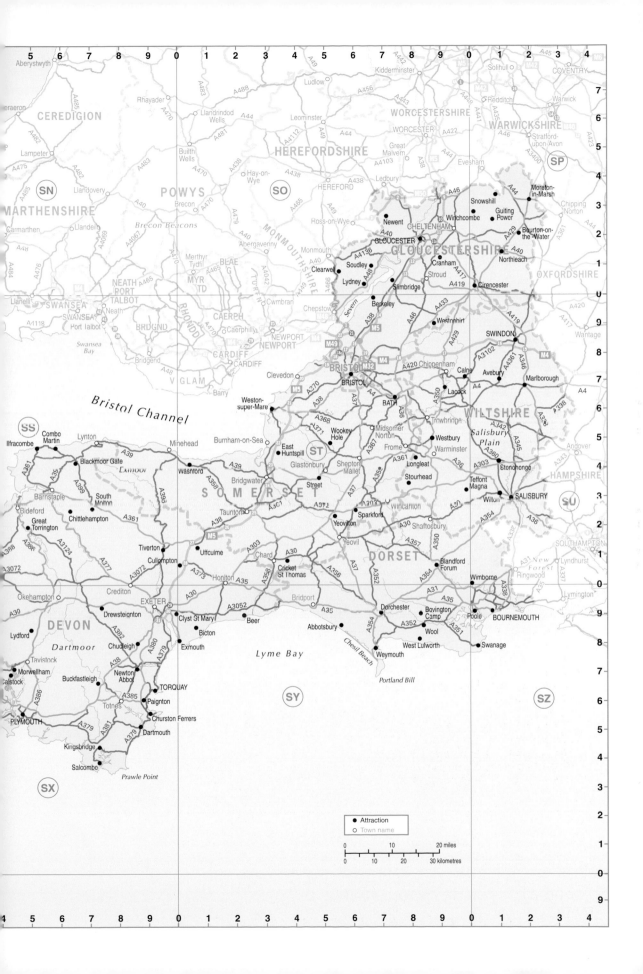

BRISTOL AT-BRISTOL

Anchor Rd, Harbourside BS1 5DB
Dir: (from city centre, A4 to Anchor Rd. Located on left opposite
Cathedral) *Map Ref:* *ST57*
☎ 0845 345 1235 📠 0117 915 7200
e-mail: information@at-bristol.org.uk

For the interactive adventure of a lifetime head for At-Bristol's
three attractions on the city's habourside. A clever fusion of sci-fi
architecture and historic buildings are home to 'Wildwalk', a
breathtaking journey through the plant and animal kingdoms;
Explore, the UK's most exciting hands-on science centre; and the
IMAX theatre, the largest cinema screen in the West of England.

Times: Open all year, term-time wkdays 10-5,
wknds & school hols 10-6. Closed 25 Dec.
Fee: Ticket for 3 attractions £16.50 (ch £11.45,
concessions £13.45). Family ticket £52.
Facilities: 🅿 (charged) 🍴 ✕ licensed
♿ (induction loop & mini com 0117 914 3475)
toilets for disabled shop ✖ (ex guide dogs) ▰

BLAISE CASTLE HOUSE MUSEUM

Henbury Rd, Henbury BS10 7QS
Dir: (4m NW of city, off B4057) *Map Ref:* *ST57*
☎ 0117 903 9818 📠 0117 959 3475   FREE
e-mail: general_museum@bristol-city.gov.uk

Blaise Castle is a folly built in 1766 by Thomas Farr and used as a
summer house by the Harford family, who later built Blaise Castle
House, which since 1949 has been a branch of the Bristol City
Museum and Art Gallery. The mansion is set in lovely parkland,
with wooded areas, rocks and pathways down to where the River
Trym flows through a gorge. Interesting buildings, a watermill and
cottages, are dotted about the grounds. Inside the museum you'll
find a Victorian school room, kitchens, laundry, toys, model trains,
costume displays and a Victorian Picture Room.

Times: Open all year, Sat-Wed, 10-5.
Facilities: 🅿 ♿ shop ✖ (ex guide dogs)

BRISTOL CITY MUSEUM & ART GALLERY

Queen's Rd, Clifton BS8 1RL
Dir: (follow signs to City Centre, then follow tourist board signs to
City Museum & Art Gallery) *Map Ref:* *ST57*
☎ 0117 922 3571 📠 0117 922 2047   FREE
e-mail: general_museum@bristol-city.gov.uk

Awarded Designated status by the Government, the City Museum
and Art Gallery is the largest in the region, with collections of
local, national and international importance. It is located in an
Edwardian Baroque building and offers a regularly changing
temporary exhibition programme in addition to its diverse
permanent collection. Art galleries upstairs include Old Masters,
French School, British Collection, Modern Art and Bristol School.
Museum galleries offer sections on archaeology, Egyptology, world
wildlife, the natural history of the Southwest (with a freshwater
aquarium), costume and pottery. Free events and activities feature
regularly.

Times: Open all year, daily 10-5. (Closed 25-26
Dec). **Facilities:** 🅿 (NCP 400yds) 🍴 ♿ (lift)
toilets for disabled shop ✖ (ex guide dogs)

BRISTOL INDUSTRIAL MUSEUM

Prince's Wharf, Prince St, City Docks BS1 4RN
Dir: (within walking distance of the city centre) *Map Ref:* ST57
☎ **0117 925 1470** 📄 **0117 729 7318** FREE
e-mail: general_museum@bristol-city.gov.uk

The museum is housed in a converted dockside transit shed.
Motor and horse-drawn vehicles from the Bristol area are shown,
with locally built aircraft and aero-engines. Railway exhibits
include the industrial locomotive *'Henbury'*. At weekends from
April to October there are trips around the harbour in the tug
'John King', the steam tug *'Mayflower'*, or the fire boat *'Pyronant'*.
Alternatively, there are trips around the dockside on the Bristol
Harbour Railway. On certain weekends visitors can watch the
steam crane and electric crane at work.

Times: Open all year Sat-Wed 10-5
Facilities: 🅿 (charged) ♿ toilets for disabled
shop ✖ (ex guide dogs)

BRISTOL ZOO GARDENS

Clifton BS8 3HA
Dir: (M5 junct 17, take A4018 then follow signs) *Map Ref:* ST57
☎ **0117 973 8951** 📄 **0117 973 6814**
e-mail: information@bristolzoo.org.uk

This award-winning zoo is dedicated to conservation and there
are 300 exotic and endangered species from the smallest tortoise
to the largest ape. See the diverse species found in the
threatened coastal rainforests of Brazil, and come face to face
with penguins and seals in their natural element through
transparent underwater walkways. Other favourites include Bug
World, Twilight World, and the Reptile House.

Times: Open all year, daily (ex 25 Dec) from 9. Closing times approx
5.30 (summer) 4.30 (winter) **Fee:** ✱ £9.50 (ch £6, concessions
£8.50). Family ticket (2ad+2 ch) £28. **Facilities:** 🅿 (charged) 🍽
✖ licensed ♿ (wheelchairs/electric scooters for use in zoo grounds)
toilets for disabled shop ✖ (kennels for service dogs) ◀

BRITISH EMPIRE & COMMONWEALTH MUSEUM

Station Approach, Temple Meads BS1 6QH
Dir: (in city centre, near Temple Meads station) *Map Ref:* ST57
☎ **0117 925 4980** 📄 **0117 925 4983**
e-mail: admin@empiremuseum.co.uk

Exploring the dramatic 500-year history of the rise and fall of the
British Empire and the emergence of the modern
Commonwealth, this internationally acclaimed museum uses
video stations, interactive exhibits, and computer games, as well
as more traditional techniques. Visitors have the opportunity to
dress in period costume, learn Morse code or sample exotic
spices. The museum is divided into three sections: Britain's first
empire 1500-1790, the British Empire at its height 1790-1914, and
Independence and Beyond, and is housed in a restored railway
terminus built by Brunel. Phone for details of special events and
activities.

Times: Open daily 10-5. Closed 25-26 Dec.
Fee: ✱ £6.50 (ch & pen £3.95, students £5.50)
Facilities: 🅿 (charged) 🍽 ♿ toilets for disabled
shop ✖ (ex guide dogs) ◀

HORSEWORLD

Staunton Manor Farm, Staunton Ln, Whitchurch BS14 0QJ
Dir: (A37 Bristol to Wells road, follow brown signs from Maes Knoll traffic lights) **Map Ref:** ST57
☎ **01275 540173** 🖹 **01275 540119**
e-mail: visitor.centre@horseworld.org.uk

One of the largest horse rescue centres in Britain, HorseWorld is located in Mendip-stone farm buildings on the edge of Bristol. Visitors get to meet the friendly horses, ponies and donkeys, and there is a miniature farm, 'touch and groom' areas, pony rides, daily presentations, nature trail, educational displays, video theatre and an adventure playground.

Times: Open 10-5 daily (Winter; closed Mon)
Fee: ✳ £4.50 (ch & pen £3) **Facilities:** 🅿 ☕ ✗ ♿ toilets for disabled shop 🛍

MARITIME HERITAGE CENTRE

Gas Ferry Rd BS1 6UN
Dir: (M5 junct 18, follow brown 'Anchor' signs) **Map Ref:** ST57
☎ **0117 926 0680** 🖹 **0117 925 5788**
e-mail: commerical@ss-great-britain.com

Bristol's Maritime Heritage Centre is located on the quayside at Great Western Dock, by 'SS Great Britain'. The museum explores 200 years of Bristol shipbuilding, with special reference to Charles Hill & Son, and their predecessor, James Hillhouse. An exhibition about 'SS Great Britain' looks at the vessel's history from its construction to its recent restoration.

Times: ✳ Open all year, daily 10-5.30, 4.30 in winter. (Closed 24 & 25 Dec).
Facilities: 🅿 (charged) ☕ ♿ toilets for disabled shop ✗ (ex guide dogs) 🛍

SS GREAT BRITAIN

Great Western Dock, Gas Ferry Rd BS1 6TY
Dir: (off Cumberland Rd) **Map Ref:** ST57
☎ **0117 926 0680** 🖹 **0117 925 5788**

Built and launched in Bristol in 1843, the 'SS Great Britain', designed by Isambard Kingdom Brunel, was the first ocean-going, propeller driven, iron ship. After a life as a passenger liner, troop transport and cargo carrier, she was abandoned in the Falkland Islands in 1886. But in 1970 she was towed back to Bristol and is now part of the Maritime Heritage Centre in Great Western Dock where she was built.

Times: ✳ Open all year daily 10-5.30, 4.30 in winter. (Closed 24 & 25 Dec).
Facilities: 🅿 (charged) ☕ ♿ shop ✗ 🛍

CALSTOCK COTEHELE

St Dominick PL12 6TA
Dir: (between Tavistock and Callington. Turn off A390 at St. Anne's Chapel, signposted 2.5m S of junct) **Map Ref:** *SX46*
☎ **01579 351346 & 352739 (info)** ▤ **01579 351222**
e-mail: cotehele@ntrust.org.uk

Cotehele is a medieval house of granite and slate built between 1485 and 1627 showing collections of tapestries, embroideries, furniture and armour. Outside, beautiful gardens on various levels lead down to the river. These include a formal Italian-style garden, a medieval stewpond, dovecote, and an 18th-century tower with lovely views. There is a restored water mill in the valley below, and at the Victorian riverside quay, an outstation of the National Maritime Museum.

Times: Open 19 Mar-30 Oct daily ex Fri (open Good Fri), 11-5 (11-4.30 Oct). Garden open all year, daily 10.30-dusk. **Fee:** ✱ House, Garden & Mill £7. Garden & Mill £4 (ch 1/2 price, under 5's & NT members free). Family ticket £16 for House, Garden and Mill, £9 for Garden and Mill only. Party £6 each. **Facilities:** ▣ ◪ ✗ licensed � (garden limited access, Braille guide, audio loop, wheelchairs) toilets for disabled shop garden centre ꕥ ◼

CAMELFORD BRITISH CYCLING MUSEUM

The Old Station PL32 9TZ
Dir: (1m N of Camelford on B3266 at junct with B3314)
Map Ref: *SX18*
☎ **01840 212811** ▤ **01840 212811**

This is the nation's foremost museum of cycling history from 1818 to the present day. Its collection comprises over 400 cycles, and more than 1,000 cycling medals, fobs and badges. There is also an extensive library; displays of gas, candle, battery and oil lighting; and many advertisements, posters and enamel signs.

Times: Open all year, Sun-Thu 10-5.
Fee: ✱ £2.90 (ch 5-17 £1.70).
Facilities: ▣ � shop ✖ (ex guide dogs)

DOBWALLS DOBWALLS FAMILY ADVENTURE PARK

PL14 6HB
Dir: (turn off A38 in centre of Dobwalls and follow the brown signs for approx 0.5m) **Map Ref:** *SX26*
☎ **01579 320325 & 321129** ▤ **01579 321345**
e-mail: dobwallsadventurepark@hotmail.com

There's plenty for everyone to do at this family adventure park, with stretches of miniature American railroads to ride - steam and diesel locos - including a Rio Grande ride through the forests and the Union Pacific route over the prairies. In Adventureland there are action-packed areas filled with both indoor and outdoor adventure play equipment.

Times: Open Etr to Oct, daily 10.30-5 (10-5.30 high season). Closed some days in Apr, May & Oct **Fee:** ✱ £8.95 (ch under 2 free, pen & disabled £5.50). Family tickets available from £17.50-£52.95. Groups 20+ £5.50 each. **Facilities:** ▣ ◪ � (manual wheelchairs subject to availability) toilets for disabled shop ◼

FALMOUTH NATIONAL MARITIME MUSEUM CORNWALL

Discovery Quay TR11 3QY
Dir: (follow signs from A39 for park/float ride and museum)
Map Ref: *SW83*
☎ **01326 313388** 📄 **01326 317878**
e-mail: enquiries@nmmc.co.uk

This award-winning museum has achieved wide national and international acclaim for its architecture, hands-on displays, world renowned boats and associated video footage, maritime heritage and interactive entertainment. It has one of only three natural underwater viewing locations in the world, plus breathtaking views from the 29-metre tower. You can also play with model boats on the 12-metre pool complete with wind tunnel.

Times: Open daily 10-5. Closed 25 & 26 Dec **Fee:** £6.50 (ch, pen & students £4.30). Family ticket (2ad&3ch) £17.
Facilities: 🅿 (charged) ☕ ✕ licensed ♿ (wheelchairs provided on arrival) toilets for disabled shop ✖ (ex guide dogs) ◀

GOONHAVERN *WORLD IN MINIATURE*

Bodmin Rd TR4 9QE
Dir: (turn off A30 at Boxheater junct onto B3285)
Map Ref: *SW75*
☎ **0870 458 4433** 📄 **01872 572829**
e-mail: info@worldinminiature.co.uk

There are six major attractions for the price of one at this theme park. Visitors can stroll amongst famous landmarks such as the Taj Mahal and the Statue of Liberty, all in miniature scale, set in spectacular gardens. Then there is Tombstone, a wild-west town complete with saloon, bank, shops, livery stable and jail. The Adventure Dome is the original super cinema 180 direct from the USA, which shows two exciting films. The 12-acre gardens are beautifully landscaped with over 70,000 plants and shrubs. See Jurassic Adventure World, Super X Simulator and children's fairground rides.

Times: ✱ Open Etr-Oct, daily from 10am.
Facilities: 🅿 ☕ ♿ toilets for disabled shop garden centre ◀

GWEEK NATIONAL SEAL SANCTUARY

TR12 6UG
Dir: (pass RNAS Culdrose & take A3293 & then B3291 to Gweek, the sanctuary is signed from village) ***Map Ref:*** *SW72*
☎ **01326 221361 & 221874** 📄 **01326 221210**
e-mail: slcgweek@merlin-entertainments.com

Britain's largest seal rescue facility, offering a unique opportunity to learn more about these beautiful creatures. Every year it rescues, rehabilitates and releases around 30 sick or abandoned seal pups. The sanctuary has a hospital and nursery, convalescence and resident pools. You can also see sea lions, ponies and goats that have also found sanctuary here.

Times: Open all year, daily from 10. Closed 25 Dec. **Fee:** *Prices not confirmed for 2005*
Facilities: 🅿 ☕ ♿ toilets for disabled shop ◀

HELSTON   THE FLAMBARDS EXPERIENCE

Culdrose Manor TR13 0QA
Dir: (0.5m SE of Helston on A3083, Lizard road) **Map Ref:** SW62
☎ **01326 573404** 📠 **01326 573344**
e-mail: info@flambards.co.uk

Three award-winning, all-weather attractions can be visited on one site here. Flambards Victorian Village is a recreation of streets, shops and houses from 1830-1910; Britain in the Blitz is a life-size wartime street and the Science Centre brings physics alive for the whole family. Along with the Thunderbolt and Extreme Force, there is also the Hornet Rollercoaster and the Family Log Flume plus much more.

Times: Open winter Nov-22 Mar, 11-4; closed Thu/Fri & 23 Dec-10 Jan. Open summer daily 23 Mar-Oct. **Fee:** ✱ £9.95 (ch 5-14 £8.45 over 55's £5.75). Family of 3 £27.31, of 4 £36, of 5 £44 of 6 £51.50 **Facilities:** 🅿 💺 ♿ (95% accessible, free loan of wheelchairs, route guides) toilets for disabled shop garden centre ✈ (ex guide dogs) 🍽

GOONHILLY SATELLITE EARTH STATION EXPERIENCE

Goonhilly Downs TR12 6LQ
Dir: (7m from Helston on B3293, Helston to St Keverne road)
Map Ref: SW62
☎ **0800 679593** 📠 **01326 221438**
e-mail: goonhilly.visitorscentre@bt.com

Making a dramatic impression on the Lizard Peninsula landscape, this is the largest earth station in the world, with over 60 dishes. Opened in 1962 with only one dish, Goonhilly now handles millions of e-mails, phone calls, and TV broadcasts. In the fully interactive visitors' centre, you can explore the world of communications, experience tomorrow's technology today, and see your own animated 3D virtual head.

Times: Open all year, daily 10-6 (last entry 5pm). After 1 Nov please call 0800 679593 for opening details. **Fee:** ✱ £5 (ch5-16 £3.50, under 4's free; pen £4) **Facilities:** 🅿 💺 ✗ licensed ♿ toilets for disabled shop ✈ (ex guide dogs) 🍽

LANHYDROCK   LANHYDROCK

PL30 5AD
Dir: (2.5m SE of Bodmin, signed from A30, A38 & B3268)
Map Ref: SX06
☎ **01208 265950** 📠 **01208 265959**
e-mail: lanhydrock@nationaltrust.org.uk

A part-Jacobean, part-Victorian building, Lanhydrock gives a vivid picture of life in Victorian times. The 'below stairs' sections have a huge kitchen, larders, dairy, bakehouse, cellars, and servants' quarters. The long gallery has a moulded ceiling showing Old Testament scenes, and overlooks the formal gardens with their clipped yews and bronze urns. The higher garden, famed for its magnolias and rhododendrons, climbs the hillside behind the house.

Times: Open Apr-Oct: House daily (ex Mon), 11-5.30 (11-5 in Oct), open BH Mon. Gardens daily from mid Feb, (last admission half hour before closing). Winter: Gardens, Nov-Feb during daylight hours. **Fee:** ✱ House & Grounds £7.50 (ch £3.75). Grounds £4.20 (ch £2.10). Family ticket £18.50 Party £6.50 each (ch £3.25 each) **Facilities:** 🅿 💺 ✗ licensed ♿ (lift, self drive buggy (pre-book), wheelchairs) toilets for disabled shop garden centre ✈ (ex on lead in park) 🐾 🍽

LAUNCESTON LAUNCESTON STEAM RAILWAY

St Thomas Rd PL15 8DA
Dir: (turn off A30 Launceston, well signed) **Map Ref:** SX38
☎ **01566 775665**

The Launceston Steam Railway links the historic town of Launceston with the hamlet of New Mills. Tickets are valid for unlimited travel on the day of issue and you can break your journey at various points along the track. Launceston Station houses railway workshops, a transport museum, gift shop and book shop.

Times: Open Good Fri for 8 days inclusive; Spring, BH Sun for 6 days; Jun, Sun-Wed; Jul-Sep, daily ex Sat; Oct half-term week. **Fee:** ✱ £6.50 (ch £4.25, pen £5). Family ticket £20 (2 ad & up to 4 ch). Dogs 50p. **Facilities:** 🅿 🖴 ⅋ shop

THE TAMAR OTTER SANCTUARY

North Petherwin PL15 8GW
Dir: (5m NW off B3254 Bude road) **Map Ref:** SX38
☎ **01566 785646** 🖹 **01986 892461**

The Tamar Otter Sanctuary has a breeding programme for the British otter and has to date bred and released over 100 otters into the wild. Visitors to the sanctuary can see otters in large natural enclosures, as well as fallow and muntjac deer, waterfowl and wallabies. Woodland running down to Bolesbridge Water is also home to the increasingly rare dormouse.

Times: Open Apr-Oct, daily 10.30-6 **Fee:** ✱ £6 (ch £3.50) **Facilities:** 🅿 🖴 ⅋ shop ✗ (ex guide dogs)

LOOE MONKEY SANCTUARY

St Martins PL13 1NZ
Dir: (signed on B3253 at No Man's Land between East Looe & Hessenford) **Map Ref:** SX25
☎ **01503 262532** 🖹 **01503 262532**
e-mail: info@monkeysanctuary.org

Visitors to the Looe Monkey Sanctuary can see a colony of Amazonian woolly monkeys in extensive indoor and outdoor territory. There are also conservation gardens, a children's play area, an activity room, display room and vegetarian café. In addition, there is a bat cave on site where visitors can watch a colony of rare 'horseshoe' bats.

Times: Open Sun-Thu 11-4.30 from the Sun before Etr-end Sep. Also open Autumn Half Term. **Fee:** ✱ £5 (under 5's free, ch £3 & concession £4). Family ticket (2 ad + 2 ch) £15. **Facilities:** 🅿 🖴 ⅋ toilets for disabled shop ✗ 🍴

MARAZION *St Michael's Mount*

TR17 0HT
Dir: (access is by Causeway on foot at low tide. 0.5m S of A394
at Marazion) *Map Ref:* SW53
☎ 01736 710507 & 710265 📄 01736 711544
e-mail: godolphin@manor-office.co.uk

Reached on foot by causeway at low tide, or by ferry at high tide
in the summer only, St Michael's Mount rises dramatically from
the sea, a medieval castle to which a magnificent east wing was
added in the 1870s. It is home to Lord St Leven, whose ancestor
John St Aubyn acquired it in the 17th century.

Times: ✱ Open 31 Mar-Oct, Mon-Fri 10.30-5.30. Last admission 4.45;
Nov-Mar, telephone for details. The Castle and grounds are open most
wknds during the summer season. Special charity open days, NI
members are also asked to pay. Group bookings 01736 710507.
Facilities: P (on mainland) ⬛ ✖ licensed (Braille guide) shop
✖ (ex guide dogs) 🐾 📇

MAWNAN SMITH *Glendurgan*

TR11 5JZ
Dir: (4m SW of Falmouth. 0.5m SW of Mawnan Smith on road to
Helford Passage) *Map Ref:* SW72
☎ 01872 862090 📄 01872 865808
e-mail: glendurgan@nationaltrust.org.uk

This delightful garden, set in a valley above the River Helford, was
started by Alfred Fox in 1820. The informal landscape contains
trees and shrubs from all over the world, including the Japanese
loquat and tree ferns from New Zealand. There is a laurel maze,
and a Giant's Stride, which is popular with children. The house is
not open to the public.

Times: Open mid Feb-Oct, Tue-Sat & BH Mon.
Last admission 4.30 (Closed Good Fri)
Fee: ✱ £4.20 (ch £2.10). Family ticket £10.50
Facilities: P ⬛ ♿ (Braille guide, limited access
to gardens/ground floor) toilets for disabled shop
garden centre ✖ (ex guide dogs) 🐾 📇

NEWQUAY *Blue Reef Aquarium*

Towan Promenade TR7 1DU
Dir: (from A30 follow signs to Newquay, follow Blue Reef
Aquarium signs to car park in town centre) *Map Ref:* SW86
☎ 01637 878134 📄 01637 872578
e-mail: info@bluereefaquarium.co.uk

Take the ultimate undersea safari at the Blue Reef Aquarium.
Discover Cornish marine life from native sharks and rays to the
incredibly intelligent and playful octopus. From here journey
through warmer waters to watch the magical seahorses, jet-
propelled cuttlefish and the vibrant, swaying tentacles of living
sponges and anemones. Continue through the underwater tunnel
in a tropical sea to encounter a coral reef alive with shoals of
brightly coloured fish and the graceful, black tip reef sharks which
glide silently overhead. Daily talks and regular feeding
demonstrations bring the experience to life.

Times: Open all year, daily 10-5. (Closed 25
Dec). Open until 6 during summer holidays.
Fee: £5.95 (ch £3.95, pen & student £4.95).
Family ticket £17.95 (2 ad & up to 3 ch)
Facilities: P (5mins walk) (prior contact for
disabled parking) ⬛ ♿ (lifts, wheelchair, ramps)
toilets for disabled shop ✖ (ex guide dogs &
service dogs) 📇

DAIRY LAND FARM WORLD

Summercourt TR8 5AA
Dir: (Signed from A30 at exit for Mitchell/Summercourt)
Map Ref: SW86
☎ 01872 510246 📠 01872 510349
e-mail: info@dairylandfarmworld.co.uk

Visitors can watch while the cows are milked to music on a spectacular merry-go-round milking machine. The life of a Victorian farmer and his neighbours is explored in the heritage centre, and a farm nature trail features informative displays along pleasant walks. Children will have fun getting to know the farm animals in the farm park. They will also enjoy the playground, assault course and indoor play areas.

Times: Open daily, late Mar-Oct 10.30-5. (Bull pen additional winter openings wknds & school hols, telephone for more information) **Fee:** £6.95 (ch £5.95, under 3s free, pen £4.95). Family Supersaver £22 (2 ad & up to 3 ch). Telephone for info about parties & groups. **Facilities:** 🅿 ☕ ♿ (wheelchairs for loan; disabled viewing gallery - milking) toilets for disabled shop ✈ 🍴

NEWQUAY ZOO

Trenance Gardens TR7 2LZ
Dir: (off A3075 and follow signs to Zoo) *Map Ref:* SW86
☎ 01637 873342 📠 01637 851318
e-mail: info@newquayzoo.org.uk

At Newquay Zoo you can explore the rainforest exhibit in the tropical house populated with a world of exotic animals. Water cascades down the ancient temple walls to pools filled with tropical fish. Spot the iguanas, sloths and flying foxbats, and explore the mini-beasts room. Among the sub-tropical lakeside gardens live hundreds of animals from around the world ranging from small monkeys to shy red pandas. Look out for meerkats, and endangered lemurs and fossa. The zoo gardens feature a Tarzan trail, children's play area and dragon maze.

Times: Open Apr-Oct, daily 9.30-6; Nov-Mar 10-dusk. (Closed 25 Dec) **Fee:** ✱ £6.95 (ch 3+ £4.45, pen £5.45, ch under 3 free). Family ticket £19.95. Check website for more details **Facilities:** 🅿 (charged) ☕ ✕ ♿ (85% free wheelchairs, guided tours & sensory sculptures) toilets for disabled shop ✈ (ex guide dogs) 🍴

PENDEEN   GEEVOR TIN MINES

TR19 7EW
Dir: (Geevor is beside the B3306 Lands End to St Ives coast road. From Penzance take A3071 towards St Just, then the B3318 towards Pendeen. From St Ives follow B3306 to Pendeen)
Map Ref: SW33
☎ 01736 788662 📠 01736 786059
e-mail: info@geevor.com

A preserved tin mine and museum provide an insight into the methods and equipment used in the industry that was once so important in the area. The Geevor Tin Mine only actually stopped operation in 1990. Guided tours let visitors see the tin treatment plant, and a video illustrates the techniques employed. The underground tour is well worth the trip.

Times: Open daily except Sat 9-5, closes at 4pm Nov-Mar. Closed 21-27 Dec & 1-2 Jan. **Fee:** ✱ £6.50 (ch & students £4, pen £6) Family £17.50 **Facilities:** 🅿 ☕ ✕ ♿ wheelchair, lift, ramps toilets for disabled shop (not underground) 🍴

PENTEWAN THE LOST GARDENS OF HELIGAN

PL26 6EN
Dir: (signposted from A390 & B3273) **Map Ref:** *SX04*
☎ **01726 845100** 📄 **01726 845101**
e-mail: info@heligan.com

Heligan, seat of the Tremayne family for more than 400 years, is one of the most mysterious estates in England. At the end of the 19th-century its thousand acres were at their zenith, but only a few years after the Great War, bramble and ivy were already drawing a green veil over this sleeping beauty. Today the garden offers 200 acres for exploration, which include productive gardens, pleasure grounds, sustainably-managed farmland, wetlands, and ancient woodlands.

Times: Open daily 10-6 (last admission 4.30pm): winter 10-dusk. Closed 24-25 Dec. **Fee:** ✱ £7.50. Please telephone to confirm concessions prices. **Facilities:** 🅿 🖭 ✗ licensed ♿ (free loan of wheelchairs and trained access advisors) toilets for disabled shop garden centre ✖ allowed Nov-Feb only ◼

POOL *CORNISH MINES & ENGINES*

TR14 7AW
Dir: (2m W of Redruth on A3047, signposted from A30, Pool exit)
Map Ref: *SW64*
☎ **01209 315027 & 210900** 📄 **01209 315027**
e-mail: info@trevithicktrust.com

Impressive relics of the tin mining industry, these great beam engines were used for pumping water from 2,000 feet down and for lifting men and ore from the workings below ground. The mine at East Pool has been converted into the Cornwall Industrial Heritage Centre which includes audio visual theatre giving background to all aspects of Cornwall's industrial heritage.

Times: ✱ Open 31 Mar-2 Nov, daily (ex Sat) 11-5; Aug open daily 11-5. Nov-Mar by arrangement. **Facilities:** 🅿 ♿ (lift to all levels, parking by arrangement, Braille guide) toilets for disabled shop ✖ (ex guide dogs) 🦮 ◼

ST MARY'S ISLES OF SCILLY MUSEUM

Church St, Hugh Town TR21 0LP
Dir: (Located in the centre of Hugh Town)
☎ **01720 422337**
e-mail: info@iosmuseum.org

A small, independent museum which seeks to safeguard and promote the islands' history and traditions, and reflect every aspect of life on the islands. In 2005 there will be an exhibition of material from the '*HMS Colossus*', a 72-gun frigate that sank close to the Scilly Isles in 1798.

Times: Etr-Sep, Mon-Sat 10-4.30. Oct-Etr, Mon-Sat 10-12 **Fee:** £2.50 (ch 50p sen & students £1.50) **Facilities:** 🖭 ♿

ST AUSTELL CHARLESTOWN SHIPWRECK & HERITAGE CENTRE

Quay Rd, Charlestown PL25 3NJ
Dir: (signed off A390 from St. Austell close to Eden Project)
Map Ref: SX05
☎ 01726 69897 🖷 01726 69897
e-mail: admin@shipwreckcharlestown.com

Charlestown is a small and unspoilt village with a unique sea-lock and china-clay port, which was purpose-built in the 18th century. The Shipwreck and Heritage Centre houses the largest display of shipwreck artefacts in the UK, along with local heritage and diving exhibits. There is also a 'Titanic' display.

Times: Open Mar-Oct, daily 10-5 (later in high season). (Last admission 1 hour before closing) **Fee:** £4.95 (ch under 10 free if accompanied by paying adult, ch under 16 £2.50, concessions £3.45). **Facilities:** 🅿 (charged) 🍵 ✗ licensed ♿ (ramps in place) toilets for disabled shop 🛒

EDEN PROJECT

Bodelva PL24 2SG
Dir: (overlooking St Austell Bay signposted from A390/A30/A391)
Map Ref: SX05
☎ 01726 811911 🖷 01726 811912
e-mail: information@edenproject.com

An unforgettable experience in a breathtaking location, the Eden Project is a gateway into the fascinating world of plants and human society. Space age technology meets the lost world in the biggest greenhouse ever built. Located in a 50-metre-deep crater the size of 30 football pitches are two gigantic geodesic conservatories: the Humid Tropics Biome and the Warm Temperate Biome. This is a startling and unique day out.

Times: ✶ Open daily Mar-Oct 10-6 (last admission 5pm), Nov-Feb 10-4.30 (last admission 3pm). Closed 24-25 Dec. **Facilities:** 🅿 🍵 ✗ licensed ♿ (wheelchairs, car shuttle to visitor centre/biomes) toilets for disabled shop garden centre 🐕 (ex guide dogs) 🛒

TINTAGEL TINTAGEL CASTLE

PL34 0HE
Dir: (on Tintagel Head, 0.5m along uneven track from Tintagel, no vehicles) *Map Ref:* SX08
☎ 01840 770328 🖷 01840 770328

Overlooking the wild Cornish coast, Tintagel is one of the most spectacular spots in the country and is associated with the legendary King Arthur and the magician Merlin. Recent excavations have revealed Dark Age connections between Spain and Cornwall, alongside the discovery of 'Arthnou' stone, suggesting that Tintagel was a royal place for the Dark Age rulers of Cornwall.

Times: Open all year, Apr-Sep, daily 10-6; Oct, daily 10-5; Nov-Mar, daily 10-4. (Closed 24-26 Dec & 1 Jan). **Fee:** ✶ £3.70 (ch £1.90, concessions £2.80). Prices & opening times relate to 2004, for further details phone or log onto www.english-heritage.org.uk/visits **Facilities:** 🅿 (in village) shop 🐕 (ex dogs on leads) ⛩

TREDINNICK   *CORNWALL'S CREALY GREAT ADVENTURE PARK*

Trelow Farm PL27 7RA
Dir: (signposted off A39) **Map Ref:** *SW97*
☎ **01841 541215**
e-mail: shirespark@tiscali.co.uk

This award-winning park offers fun for everyone with the ghoul-packed 'Haunted Castle', and 'Dragon Kingdom', the country's largest indoor adventure zone. Walk through the Enchanted Forest to Greengate Meadow and meet animated moles, Mr Badger and their woodland friends. Other attractions include Thunder Falls double log flume ride, Raging River Watercoaster and Viking Warrior Pirate Ship, plus acres of outdoor adventure play with the highest aerial bridges and the longest, steepest slides in Cornwall. There are also train rides around the lakes, shire horses and farmyard friends.

Times: Open Good Fri-end Oct, daily 10-5.
Facilities: 🅿 💺 ✗ licensed ♿ (most areas are ramped) toilets for disabled shop

WENDRON   *POLDARK MINE AND HERITAGE COMPLEX*

TR13 0ER
Dir: (3m from Helston on B3297 Redruth road, follow brown signs) **Map Ref:** *SW63*
☎ **01326 573173** 📄 **01326 563166**
e-mail: info@poldark-mine.com

The centre of this attraction is the 18th century tin mine where visitors can join a guided tour of workings which retain much of their original character. The site's museum explains the history of tin production in Cornwall from 1800 BC through to the 19th century and the fascinating story of the Cornish overseas. In addition to the museum, the audio-visual presentation gives more insight into Cornwall's mining heritage.

Times: Open Etr-1st wk Nov, 10-5.30 (last tour 4pm). **Facilities:** 🅿 💺 ♿ (newly refurbished museum allowing disabled access) shop ◀

ZENNOR   *WAYSIDE FOLK MUSEUM*

TR26 3DA
Dir: (4m W of St Ives, on B3306) **Map Ref:** *SW43*
☎ **01736 796945**

Founded in 1937, this museum covers every aspect of life in Zennor and the surrounding district from 3000 BC to the 1930s. Over 5,000 items are displayed in 12 workshops and rooms covering wheelwrights, blacksmiths, agriculture, fishing, wrecks, mining, domestic and archaeological artefacts. A photographic exhibition entitled 'People of the Past' tells the story of the village.

Times: Open Etr-end Oct, daily 10.30-5.30.
Fee: ✱ £2.75 (ch £1.50, over 60's £2.50). Party rates 10+. **Facilities:** 🅿 (50yds) ♿ (not suitable for wheelchair users) shop ✘ (ex guide dogs) ◀

BEER PECORAMA PLEASURE GARDENS

Underleys EX12 3NA
Dir: (from A3052 take B3174, Beer road, signed) **Map Ref:** *SY28*
☎ **01297 21542** 🖹 **01297 20229**

The pleasure gardens are located high on a hillside, overlooking Beer, and a miniature steam and diesel passenger line offers visitors a stunning view of Lyme Bay as it runs through. Attractions include an aviary, crazy golf, children's activity area and the Peco Millennium Garden. The main building houses an exhibition of railway modelling in various small gauges. There are souvenir and railway model shops, plus full catering facilities.

Times: Open Etr-Oct , Mon-Fri 10-5.30, Sat 10-1. Open Sun Etr & Whitsun-early Sep. **Fee:** ✱ £5.25 (ch 4-14 £3.50, pen £4.75, over 80 & under 4 free) **Facilities:** 🅿 ⛽ ✗ ♿ (access with helper, wheelchair. Garden steep in places) toilets for disabled shop ✗ (ex guide dogs) 🍴

BICTON BICTON PARK BOTANICAL GARDENS

East Budleigh EX9 7BJ
Dir: (2m N of Budleigh Salterton on B3178, leave M5 at junct 30 & follow brown tourist signs) **Map Ref:** *SY08*
☎ **01395 568465** 🖹 **01395 568374**
e-mail: info@bictongardens.co.uk

Bicton Park has unique Grade 1 listed gardens dating from the 18th century, with a palm house, orangery and plant collections. Additional attractions include an extensive countryside museum, indoor and outdoor activity play areas, a pinetum, arboretum, nature trail, woodland railway, garden centre and restaurant. All this set in 63 acres of beautiful parkland that has been cherished for 300 years.

Times: Open Winter 10-5, Summer 10-6. Closed 25 & 26 Dec.
Fee: ✱ £4.95 (ch & concessions £3.95). Family ticket £15.95.
Facilities: 🅿 ⛽ ✗ licensed ♿ (adapted carriage on woodland railway, wheelchairs) toilets for disabled shop garden centre 🍴

BLACKMOOR GATE EXMOOR ZOOLOGICAL PARK

South Stowford, Bratton Fleming EX31 4SG
Dir: (off A361 link road onto A399, follow brown tourist signs)
Map Ref: *SS64*
☎ **01598 763352**
e-mail: exmoorzoo@fsbdial.co.uk

Exmoor Zoo, open since 1982, is both personal and friendly. It is an ideal family venue, catering particularly for the younger generation. The zoo specialises in smaller animals, many endangered, such as the golden headed lion tamarind. Over 14 species of this type of primate are exhibited. Contact pens are provided throughout and children are encouraged to participate. There are twice daily guided tours at feeding times along with handling sessions.

Times: Open daily, Apr-Oct 10-6; Nov-Mar 10-4.
Fee: ✱ £6.95 (ch £4.95, concessions £5.95).
Facilities: 🅿 ⛽ ♿ toilets for disabled shop ✗ (ex guide dogs) 🍴

BUCKFASTLEIGH BUCKFAST BUTTERFLY FARM & DARTMOOR OTTER SANCTUARY

TQ11 0DZ
Dir: (off A38, at Dart Bridge junct, follow tourist signs)
Map Ref: *SX76*
☎ **01364 642916**
e-mail: info@ottersandbutterflies.co.uk

At this butterfly and otter centre, visitors can wander around a specially designed, undercover tropical garden, where free-flying butterflies and moths from around the world can be seen. The otter sanctuary has large enclosures with underwater viewing areas. Three types of otters can be seen - the native British otter along with Asian and North American otters.

Times: Open Good Fri-end Oct, daily 10-5.30 or dusk (if earlier). **Fee:** ✱ £5.95 (ch £4.50, pen £5.50). Family ticket £16.95. **Facilities:** 🅿 ☕ ♿ (wheelchair ramps) shop ✖ (ex guide dogs) ◀

CHITTLEHAMPTON COBBATON COMBAT COLLECTION

Cobbaton EX37 9RZ
Dir: (signed from A361 & A377) *Map Ref:* *SS62*
☎ **01769 540740** 📠 **01769 540141**
e-mail: info@cobbatoncombat.co.uk

World War II British and Canadian military vehicles, war documents and military equipment can be seen in this private collection. There are over 50 vehicles including tanks, one a Gulf War Centurian, and a there's a new added Warsaw Pact exhibit. There is also a display on 'Mum's War', and the Home Front which is now in new purpose-built accommodation.

Times: Open Apr-Oct, daily (ex Sat) 10-5; Jul-Aug daily. Winter most wkdays, phone for details. **Fee:** ✱ £4.75 (ch £3.25, pen £4.25). **Facilities:** 🅿 ☕ ♿ (most areas accessible) toilets for disabled shop ✖ (ex guide dogs, outside) ◀

CHUDLEIGH CANONTEIGN FALLS

EX6 7NT
Dir: (off A38 at Chudleigh/Teign Valley junct onto B3193 and follow tourist signs for 3m) *Map Ref:* *SX87*
☎ **01647 252434** 📠 **01647 52617**
e-mail: info@canonteignfalls.com

A magical combination of waterfalls, woodlands and lakes is found in the beautiful Teign Valley at Canonteign in Dartmoor. Here, the highest waterfall in England descends almost vertically for 220 feet. Other attraction on site include wonderful walks, quiz trails, a junior commando course, fern centre, a restaurant, picnic area and shop.

Times: Open all year, Mar-mid Nov, daily 10-5; Feb half term & Winter wknds. **Facilities:** 🅿 ☕ ✖ licensed (grounds partly accessible) shop garden centre ◀

CHURSTON FERRERS GREENWAY GARDEN

TQ5 0ES
Dir: (off A3022 into Galmpton. Follow Manor Vale Rd into village
then brown signs for Greenway Garden, establishment signed)
Map Ref: SX95
☎ 01803 842382 📠 01803 661900
e-mail: greenway@nationaltrust.org.uk

Greenway is a beautiful woodland garden set on the banks of the
River Dart. It is a garden held on the edge of wilderness,
renowned for rare half-hardy trees and shrubs, underplanted by
native wild flowers. There are many walks in the surrounding
estate with stunning views over the estuary. Greenway is not
easily accessible, as it has some steep and slippery paths, so care
should be taken. You can also travel by river to enjoy this peaceful
haven.

Times: Open 2 Mar-11 Oct, Wed-Sat.
Fee: ✱ £3.90 (ch £1.95). **Facilities:** 🅿 ☕
♿ (part access to garden, Braille guide) toilets for
disabled shop 🐾 (ex guide dogs & in Parkland) ♨

CLOVELLY THE MILKY WAY ADVENTURE PARK

EX39 5RY
Dir: (on A39, 2m from Clovelly) *Map Ref:* SS32
☎ 01237 431255 📠 01237 431735
e-mail: info@themilkyway.co.uk

One of the West Country's leading attractions for the biggest rides
and the best shows. These include Clone Zone, Europe's first
interactive adventure ride featuring a suspended roller coaster;
Time Warp indoor adventure play area; daily displays from the
North Devon Bird of Prey Centre; archery centre; golf driving nets;
railway; pets corner and more. A recent addition, 'Droid
Destroyers', invites pilots to save the Earth from the Vega Asteroid.

Times: ✱ Open Etr-Oct, daily 10.30-6. Telephone
for winter opening times. **Facilities:** 🅿 ☕
♿ (ramps) toilets for disabled shop 🍴

CLYST ST MARY CREALY ADVENTURE PARK

Sidmouth Rd EX5 1DR
Dir: (M5 junct 30 onto A3052 Exeter to Sidmouth road)
Map Ref: SX99
☎ 01395 233200 📠 01395 233211
e-mail: fun@crealy.co.uk

Among the exciting rides at Crealy Adventure Park are Tidal Wave
(Devon's first ever log flume), El Pastil Loco Coaster, Queen Bess
Pirate Ship, Techno Race Karts, Bumper Boats, a Victorian
Carousel, and huge indoor and outdoor playgrounds. Animal
Showtime is the showpiece of Crealy's Animal Realm, where you
can ride, feed, milk, groom or cuddle the friendly animals.
Unearth the Farming Realm's original Great Farm Adventures, and
discover the Summer Sunflower Maze.

Times: Open all year, Jan-mid July & 6 Sep-Dec,
daily 10-5. Closed winter term time Mon-Tue; mid
Jul-5 Sep, daily 10-6. **Fee:** ✱ £7.95-£8.95
(ch under 90cm free, pen £5.20-£6.20). Party 4+
£7.70-£8.70. **Facilities:** 🅿 ☕ ✕ licensed
♿ (carers admitted free, rollercoaster has disabled
facility) toilets for disabled shop 🍴

COMBE MARTIN   COMBE MARTIN WILDLIFE PARK & DINOSAUR PARK

EX34 0NG
Dir: (M5 junct 27 then A361 towards Barnstaple, turn right onto A399)   *Map Ref:* SS54
☎ **01271 882486**   📄 **01271 883869**
e-mail: info@dinosaur-park.com

The land that time forgot; a subtropical paradise with hundreds of birds and animals and animatronic dinosaurs, so real they're alive! Snow leopards, meerkats, timber wolves, apes and monkeys are just some of the animals you can see, plus sea lion shows, falconry displays and animal handling sessions. Additional attractions include a spectacular lightshow, destination Mars, and Earthquake Canyon, the most unusual train ride in the UK.

Times: Open 20 Mar-Oct, daily 10-4 (last admission 3). **Fee:** ✱ £10 (ch 3-15 £6, ch under 3 free, pen £7). Family (2ad+2ch) £29.
Facilities: 🅿 🍽 shop ✖ (ex guide dogs) 🍴

CULLOMPTON   DIGGERLAND

Verbeer Manor EX15 2PE
Dir: (M5 junct 27. E on A38 & at rdbt turn right onto A3181. Diggerland is 3m on left)   *Map Ref:* SS54
☎ **08700 344437**   📄 **0901 2010 300**
e-mail: mail@diggerland

An adventure park with a difference, where kids of all ages can experience the thrills of driving real earth moving equipment. Choose from various types of diggers and dumpers ranging from a ton to 8.5 tons. Supervised by an instructor, you can complete the Dumper Truck Challenge or dig for buried treasure. New rides include JCB Robots, the Supertrack, Landrover Safari and Spin Dizzy. Even under fives can join in, with mum or dad's help.

Times: Open 12 Feb-27 Nov, 12-5, wknds, BHs & school hols. **Fee:** £2.50 (pen £1.25, under 2's free). Additional charge to drive/ride machinery.
Facilities: 🅿 🍽 ♿ shop ✖ (ex guide dogs) 🍴

DARTMOUTH   WOODLANDS LEISURE PARK

Blackawton TQ9 7DQ
Dir: (W, off A3122)   *Map Ref:* SX85
☎ **01803 712598**   📄 **01803 712680**
e-mail: fun@woodlandspark.com

All weather fun with an outstanding range of indoor and outdoor attractions. Experience the biggest indoor venture centre in the UK, and enjoy 60 acres of outdoor attractions for all the family including three watercoasters, a 500-metre toboggan run, Arctic Gliders, Mystic Maze and 15 massive play zones. There is an indoor falconry centre, and a wide selection of animals and birds. New additions are The Master Blaster game and the rock'n'roll tugboat ride.

Times: Open 26 Mar-5 Nov daily, wknds & school hols.
Fee: ✱ £8.25. Family ticket £31.20 (2ad+2ch). **Facilities:** 🅿 🍽
♿ (ramps) toilets for disabled shop ✖ (ex guide dogs) 🍴

DREWSTEIGNTON   CASTLE DROGO

EX6 6PB
Dir: (5m S of A30 Exeter-Okehampton. Coaches turn off A382 at Sandy Park) *Map Ref: SX79*
☎ 01647 433306   📠 01647 433186
e-mail: castledrogo@nationaltrust.org.uk

India tea baron Julius Drewe's dream house, this granite castle, built between 1910 and 1930, is one of Sir Edward Lutyens' most remarkable works, combining the grandeur of a medieval castle with 20th-century comfort. It is a great country house with formal terraced gardens, a woodland spring garden, huge circular croquet lawn and colourful herbaceous borders. Standing at more than 900 feet, the house overlooks the wooded gorge of the River Teign and offers stunning views of Dartmoor.

Times: Castle open 20 Mar-7 Nov, daily (ex Tue) 11-5. Garden open all year, daily 10.30-5.30 (or dusk if earlier). **Fee:** ✱ Castle £6.20. Garden & grounds only £3.15 (ch half price, under 5's free). Family ticket £15. **Facilities:** 🅿 ☕ ♿ (Braille & large print guide, touch list) toilets for disabled shop garden centre ✈ (ex guide/hearing dogs) 🌿 🛍

EXMOUTH   *THE WORLD OF COUNTRY LIFE*

Sandy Bay EX8 5BU
Dir: (M5 junct 30, take A376 to Exmouth. Follow signs to Sandy Bay) *Map Ref: SY08*
☎ 01395 274533   📠 01392 273457

The World of Country Life is an all-weather family attraction including owl displays and a safari train that rides through a 40-acre deer park. Kids will enjoy the friendly farm animals, pets centre and animal nursery. There is also a Victorian street, working models and thousands of exhibits from a bygone age, including steam and vintage vehicles.

Times: ✱ Open Etr-Oct, daily 10-5.
Facilities: 🅿 ☕ ✗ ♿ (all parts accessible ex 'safari train') toilets for disabled shop ✈ (ex guide dogs) 🛍

GREAT TORRINGTON   DARTINGTON CRYSTAL

EX38 7AN
Dir: (Turn off A386 in centre of Great Torrington down School Lane (opposite church). Dartington Crystal is 200mtrs on left) *Map Ref: SS41*
☎ 01805 626242   📠 01805 626263
e-mail: sfrench@dartington.co.uk

Dartington Crystal has won many international design awards in recognition of its excellence. The factory tour allows visitors to watch the glassware being crafted, from the safety of elevated viewing galleries. All age groups are encouraged to have fun in the glass activity area and to discover the fascinating story of glass and the history of Dartington in the visitor centre.

Times: Open all year. Visitor centre, Factory tour, Pavilion Cafe and Shops Mon-Fri 9-5 (last tour 3.15), Sat 10-5, Sun 10-4 (tours closed wknds). For Xmas, New Year and BH opening please telephone for details. **Fee:** ✱ £4.50 (ch under 16 free, pen £3.50). Max 5 ch with every full paying adult. **Facilities:** 🅿 ☕ ✗ licensed ♿ toilets for disabled shop ✈ (ex guide dogs) 🛍

ILFRACOMBE   WATERMOUTH CASTLE & FAMILY THEME PARK

EX34 9SL
Dir: (3m NE off A399, midway between Ilfracombe & Combe
Martin) *Map Ref:* SS54
☎ **01271 863879** 📄 **01271 865864**
e-mail: enquiries@watermouthcastle.com

Watermouth Castle, overlooking Watermouth Cove, is the location
for this popular family attraction. The children's theme park,
aimed at 2-11 year olds, offers rides, indoor and outdoor play
areas, a driving school and amusements, such as a penny slot
arcade, fairytale carriages and a room of scientific mind-benders.
Favourite rides include the Fantasy Train, bumper boats, and
Cinderella's carousel.

Times: Open Apr-end Oct, closed Sat. (Also
closed some Mon & Fri off season). Ring for
further details. **Fee:** ✱ £9 (ch 3-13 £7.50 & pen
£6.50) **Facilities:** 🅿 💷 ♿ (special wheelchair
route) toilets for disabled shop 🐾 (ex guide
dogs) ◀

KINGSBRIDGE   COOKWORTHY MUSEUM OF RURAL LIFE

The Old Grammar School, 108 Fore St TQ7 1AW
Dir: (A38 onto A384, then A381 to Kingsbridge, museum at top
of town) *Map Ref:* SX74
☎ **01548 853235**
e-mail: wcookworthy@talk21.com

The museum founded to commemorate William Cookworthy,
father of the English china clay industry, is housed in a 17th-
century former grammar school. Reconstructed room-sets of a
Victorian kitchen and an Edwardian pharmacy, a costume room
and an extensive collection of local historical items illustrate
South Devon life. There is also a walled garden and farm gallery.
The Local Heritage Resource Centre is based here along with a
Devon record service point.

Times: Open all year, 21 Mar-Sep, Mon-Sat
10.30-5; Oct 10.30-4. Nov-Mar groups by
arrangement. Local Heritage Resource Centre
open all year, Mon-Thu 10-12 & Wed also 2-4,
other times by appointment. **Fee:** ✱ £2 (ch 90p,
pen £1.50). Family ticket £5 (2ad+4ch). Party
rates available. **Facilities:** 🅿 (100mtrs) (max
3hrs) ♿ (Braille labels on selected exhibits) toilets
for disabled shop 🐾 (ex guide dogs)

LYDFORD   LYDFORD GORGE

EX20 4BH
Dir: (off A386, between Okehampton & Tavistock)
Map Ref: SX58
☎ **01822 820320 & 820441** 📄 **01822 822000**
e-mail: lydfordgorge@nationaltrust.org.uk

The spectacular gorge has been formed by the River Lyd, which
has cut into the rock and caused swirling boulders to scoop out
potholes in the stream bed. This has created some dramatic
features, notably the Devil's Cauldron close to Lydford Bridge. At
the end of the gorge is the 90-foot-high White Lady Waterfall.

Times: Open Apr-Sep, daily 10-5.30; Oct, daily
10-4. (Nov-Mar, waterfall entrance only, daily
10.30-3). **Fee:** ✱ £4 (ch 5-16 £2, under 5 free)
Party £3.40 (ch £1.70). **Facilities:** 🅿 💷
♿ (easy access path above gorge, audio tapes)
toilets for disabled shop 🐾

MORWELLHAM MORWELLHAM QUAY

PL19 8JL
Dir: (4m W of Tavistock, off A390. Midway between Gunnislake & Tavisock. Signed) **Map Ref:** *SX47*
☎ **01822 832766 & 833808** 📄 **01822 833808**
e-mail: enquiries@morwellham-quay.co.uk

Morwellham was the greatest copper port in Queen Victoria's empire. Once the mines were exhausted the port area disintegrated into wasteland, until 1970 when a charitable trust was set up for its restoration. Visitors can ride by electric tramway underground into a copper mine, last worked in 1869. The staff wear Victorian costume and visitors can try on replica costumes in the Limeburner's Cottage.

Times: Open all year (ex Xmas wk) 10-6 (4.30 Nov-Etr). Last admission 3.30 (2.30 Nov-Etr). **Fee:** ✱ £8.90 (ch 5-16 £6, pen & students £7.80). **Facilities:** 🅿 🍽 ✕ licensed ♿ (smooth paths, but difficult areas in Victorian village) toilets for disabled shop ⬛

NEWTON ABBOT HEDGEHOG HOSPITAL AT PRICKLY BALL FARM

Denbury Rd, East Ogwell TQ12 6BZ
Dir: (1.5m from Newton Abbot on A381 towards Totnes, follow brown heritage signs) **Map Ref:** *SX87*
☎ **01626 362319 & 330685** 📄 **01626 330685**
e-mail: hedgehog@hedgehog.org.uk

See, touch and learn all about this delightful wild animal. In mid-season you can see baby hogs bottle feeding. Find out how to encourage hedgehogs into your garden and how they are put back into the wild. Talks on hedgehogs are held throughout the day, and short basic video information about hedgehogs is available.

Times: Open wk before Etr-end Oct, 10.30-5. (Last admission 1hr before closing) **Facilities:** 🅿 🍽 ♿ (large print menu, use of wheelchair, Braille menu) toilets for disabled shop garden centre ✖ (ex guide dogs) ⬛

PAIGNTON PAIGNTON & DARTMOUTH STEAM RAILWAY

Queens Park Station, Torbay Rd TQ4 6AF
Dir: (from Paignton follow brown tourist signs) **Map Ref:** *SX86*
☎ **01803 555872** 📄 **01803 664313**
e-mail: pdsr@talk21.com

Steam trains run for seven miles from Paignton to Kingswear on the former Great Western line. The views of the Torbay coast are superb and the trains stop at Goodrington Sands, Churston and Kingswear, connecting with the ferry crossing to Dartmouth. Combined river excursions are also available. Please ring for details of special events.

Times: Open Jun-Sep, daily 9-5.30 & selected days Oct & Apr-May. **Fee:** ✱ Paignton to Kingswear £7 (ch £5, pen £6.50). Family £22. Paignton to Dartmouth (including ferry) £8.50 (ch £5.80, pen £8). Family £26. **Facilities:** 🅿 (5mins walk) 🍽 ♿ (wheelchair ramp for boarding train) toilets for disabled shop ⬛

PAIGNTON ZOO ENVIRONMENTAL PARK

Totnes Rd TQ4 7EU
Dir: (1m from town centre on A3022) *Map Ref:* SX86
☎ 01803 697500 🖷 01803 523457
e-mail: info@paigntonzoo.org.uk

Paignton is one of Britain's biggest zoos, set in a secluded woodland valley, where new enclosures are spacious and naturalistic. A tour takes in some of the world's threatened habitats - Forest, Savannah, Wetland and Desert, with hundreds of species, many of them endangered and part of conservation breeding programmes. There are regular keeper talks and a children's play area.

Times: Open all year, daily 10-6 (5 in winter). Last admission 5 (4 in winter). Closed 25 Dec. **Fee:** ✱ £8.50 (ch 3-15 £6.20, students £7). Family ticket £26.70 **Facilities:** 🅿 🍽 ✗ licensed ♿ (some steep hills, wheelchair loan-booking essential) toilets for disabled shop ✖ (ex guide dogs) ◀

PLYMOUTH   PLYMOUTH DOME

The Hoe PL1 2NZ
Map Ref: SX86
☎ 01752 603300 & 600608 (recorded message)
🖷 01752 256361

This high-tech visitor centre lets you explore the sounds and smells of an Elizabethan street, walk the gun-deck of a galleon, dodge the press gang, stroll with film stars on an ocean liner, and witness the devastation of the Blitz. Examine satellite weather pictures as they arrive from space, keep up to date with shipping movements and monitor the busy harbour on radar. An excellent introduction to Plymouth and a colourful interpretation of the past. Ring for details of special events.

Times: Open Apr-Oct, daily 10-5; Nov-Mar, Tue-Sat 10-4 **Fee:** ✱ £4.75 (ch £3.25 ch under 5 free, pen & students £3.75). Family (2 ad+2 ch) £13. **Facilities:** 🅿 (200yds) 🍽 ♿ (audio descriptions, induction loop, wheelchairs available) toilets for disabled shop ✖ (ex guide dogs) ◀

SALCOMBE   OVERBECKS MUSEUM & GARDEN

Sharpitor TQ8 8LW
Dir: (1.5m SW of Salcombe, signed from Malborough & Salcombe, narrow approach road) *Map Ref:* SX73
☎ 01548 842893 🖷 01548 845020
e-mail: dovrcx@smtp.ntrust.org.uk

This garden is on the most southerly tip of Devon, and allows many exotic plants to flourish. The scientist Otto Overbeck lived here from 1928 to 1937, and the Edwardian house displays toys, dolls and a natural history collection. An exhibition of late 19th-century photographs relates to the local area, and there are nautical artefacts and ship-building tools. There is also a secret room for children, where they can search for 'Fred' the friendly ghost.

Times: Open Apr-Jul, Sun-Fri 11-5.30; Aug, daily 11-5.30; Sep, Sun-Fri 11-5.30; Oct, Sun-Thu 11-5. Gardens open all year, 10-6 (or sunset if earlier). **Fee:** ✱ Museum & gardens £4.60 (ch £2.30). Gardens only £3.40 (ch £1.70). Family ticket £11.50. **Facilities:** 🅿 🍽 ♿ (ramp from garden, Braille guide) shop ✖ (ex guide dogs) 🚐 🐾 ◀

SOUTH MOLTON   QUINCE HONEY FARM

EX36 3AZ
Dir: (3.5m W of A361, on N edge of South Molton)
Map Ref: SS72
☎ 01769 572401   🖹 01769 574704
e-mail: info@quincehoney.co.uk

Follow the story of honey and beeswax from flower to table. The exhibition allows you to see the world of bees close up in complete safety; hives open at the press of a button revealing the honeybees' secret life. After viewing the bees at work, sample the fruits of their labour in the café or shop.

Times: Open daily, Apr-Sep 9-6; Oct 9-5; Shop only Nov-Etr 9-5. Closed 25 Dec-4 Jan.
Fee: ✱ £3.50 (ch 5-16 £2, pen £2.80)
Facilities: 🅿 💻 ⅙ toilets for disabled shop ✖ (ex guide dogs) 🛍

TIVERTON   TIVERTON MUSEUM OF MID DEVON LIFE

Beck's Square EX16 6PJ
Dir: (in centre of town next to Beck's Square car park)
Map Ref: SS91
☎ 01884 256295
e-mail: curator@tivertonmusuem.org.uk

This large and comprehensive museum, now with 15 galleries, reopened after extensive rebuilding and refurbishment throughout. It is housed in a 19th-century school and the exhibits include a Heathcote Lace Gallery featuring items from the local lace-making industry. There is also an agricultural section with a collection of farm wagons and implements. Other large exhibits include two waterwheels and a railway locomotive with many GWR items.

Times: Open Feb-mid Dec, Mon-Fri 10.30-4.30, Sat 10-1. **Fee:** £3.50 (ch £1, pen £2.50)
Facilities: 🅿 (100yds) ⅙ (lift, induction loop) toilets for disabled shop ✖ (ex guide dogs)

TORQUAY   BABBACOMBE MODEL VILLAGE

Hampton Av, Babbacombe TQ1 3LA
Dir: (follow brown tourist signs from outskirts of town)
Map Ref: SX96
☎ 01803 328669 & 315315   🖹 01803 315173
e-mail: ss@babbacombemodelvillage.co.uk

Set in four acres of beautifully maintained, miniature landscaped garden, the village contains over 400 models and 1,200 feet of model railway. City Lights, an evening illuminations feature, depicts Piccadilly Circus in miniature. At the end of your visit, enjoy a new facility that offers breathtaking views over the model village. There are also free trips on an open-top bus, a computer presentation area, an undercover display area, a vintage model railway layout, and Aquaviva, an evening water, light and sound spectacular.

Times: Apr-May, 10-5.30; Jun-Aug, 10am-10.30pm; Sep, 10-9.30; Oct, 10-5; Nov-Feb 10-4.30. Closed 25 Dec. **Fee:** ✱ £6.40 (ch £3.95, pen £5.40). Family ticket £18.50.
Facilities: 🅿 (charged) 💻 ✖ ⅙ (push button audio information) toilets for disabled shop garden centre 🛍

'BYGONES'

Fore St, St Marychurch TQ1 4PR
Dir: (follow tourist signs into Torquay and St Marychurch)
Map Ref: SX96
☎ **01803 326108** 🖹 **01803 326108**

Step back in time at this life-size Victorian exhibition street of over 20 shops including a forge, pub and period display rooms, housed in a former cinema. Exhibits include a large model railway layout, illuminated fantasyland, railwayana and military exhibits, including a walk-through World War I trench. At Christmas the street is turned into a winter wonderland. A new set piece features Babbacombe's John Lee (the man they couldn't hang) in his cell.

Times: ✱ Open all year, Summer 10-9.30, (Fri-Sun 10-6); Spring & Autumn 10-6; Winter 10-4, wknds & school hols 10-5. (Last entry 1hr before closing). **Facilities:** P (50yds) ☕ (ramp) shop ✈ (ex guide dogs)

LIVING COASTS

Beacon Quay TQ1 2BG
Dir: (in Torquay follow A379 and brown tourist signs)
Map Ref: SX96
☎ **01803 202470** 🖹 **01803 202471**
e-mail: info@livingcoasts.org.uk

Living Coasts is an unusual and ambitious attraction that allows visitors to take a trip around the coastlines of the world without leaving Torquay. Specially designed environments are home to fur seals, puffins, penguins, ducks, rats, and waders among others. All the animals can be seen above and below the water, whilst the huge meshed aviary allows the birds to fly free over your head. Joint ticket for Paignton Zoo available.

Times: Open daily from 10. Closed 25 Dec. **Fee:** ✱ £5.70 (ch over 3 £4, pcn £4.40). Family ticket (2ad 1 2ch) £17.50 **Facilities:** P ☕ ✗ licensed & (wheelchair hire) toilets for disabled shop ✈ (ex assist dogs) 📷

UFFCULME   COLDHARBOUR MILL WORKING WOOL MUSEUM

Coldharbour Mill EX15 3EE
Dir: (2m from M5 junct 27, off B3181. Follow signs to Willand, then brown signs to museum) **Map Ref:** ST01
☎ **01884 840960** 🖹 **01884 840858**
e-mail: info@coldharbourmill.org.uk

The Picturesque Coldharbour Mill is set in idyllic Devon countryside. It has been producing textiles since 1799 and is now a working museum, still making knitting wools and fabrics on period machinery. The Fox Gallery exhibits a variety of temporary exhibitions including textiles, photography, mixed media and craft. With machine demonstrations, a water wheel and steam engines, Coldharbour Mill is a wonderful and very different family day out.

Times: Open Mar-Oct, daily 10.30-5. Shop & Restaurant open all year. **Fee:** ✱ £5.75 (ch 5-16 £2.75, pen £5.25). Family ticket £16. **Facilities:** P ☕ ✗ licensed & (helpful guides & lift, indoor restaurant not accessible) toilets for disabled shop ✈ (ex guide dogs or in grounds) 📷

ABBOTSBURY *ABBOTSBURY SWANNERY*

New Barn Rd DT3 4JG
Dir: (turn off A35 at Winterborne Steepleton near Dorchester.
Abbotsbury on B3157 coastal road, between Weymouth and
Bridport) ***Map Ref:*** *SY58*
☎ 01305 871858 ▤ 01305 871092
e-mail: info@abbotsbury-tourism.co.uk

Abbotsbury is the breeding ground of the only managed colony of
mute swans. The swans can be seen safely at close quarters, and
the site is also home or stopping point for many wild birds. The
highlight of the year is the cygnet season, end of May to the end
of June, when there may be over 100 nests on site. Visitors can
often take pictures of cygnets emerging from eggs at close
quarters. There is an audio-visual show, as well as mass feeding
at noon and 4pm daily, and an ugly duckling trail.

Times: ✱ Open 24 Mar-2 Nov, daily 10-6, last
admission 5. **Facilities:** ℙ ☕ ✕ licensed
& (free wheelchair loan, herb garden for blind)
toilets for disabled shop ✈ 📽

BLANDFORD FORUM ROYAL SIGNALS MUSEUM

Blandford Camp DT11 8RH
Dir: (signed off B3082 Blandford/Wimborne road & A354
Salisbury road. Follow brown signs for Museum) ***Map Ref:*** *ST80*
☎ 01258 482248 ▤ 01258 482084
e-mail: info@royalsignalsmuseum.com

The Royal Signals Museum depicts the history of military
communications, science and technology from the Crimea to the
Gulf. As well as displays on all the major conflicts involving British
forces, there are stories of the ATS, the Long Range Desert Group,
Air Support, Airborne, Para and SAS Signals. For children there are
trails and interactive exhibits.

Times: Open Mon-Fri 10-5, Mar-Oct Sat-Sun 10-4.
Closed 10 days over Xmas & New Year **Fee:** £5
(ch £3, pen £4). Family £13 **Facilities:** ℙ ☕
& (ramps & lifts) toilets for disabled shop
✈ (ex guide dogs) 📽

BOURNEMOUTH OCEANARIUM

Pier Approach, West Beach BH2 5AA
Dir: (from A338 Wessex Way, follow Oceanarium tourist signs)
Map Ref: *SZ09*
☎ 01202 311993 ▤ 01202 311990
e-mail: oceanarium@reallive.co.uk

Explore the secrets of the ocean in an adventure that will take
you to some of the world's most amazing waters. The
Oceanarium brings you face to face with a vast array of creatures
from piranhas and clownfish to tiny freshwater turtles. Take a
walk through our amazing underwater tunnel to get even closer
to sharks, sea turtles, stingrays and eels.

Times: Open all year, daily from 10. Closed 25
Dec. **Fee:** ✱ Telephone for admission charges.
Facilities: ℙ (100mtrs) ☕ & (wheelchair for
hire) toilets for disabled shop ✈ (ex guide
dogs) 📽

BOVINGTON CAMP THE TANK MUSEUM

BH20 6JG
Dir: (off A352 or A35, follow brown tank signs from Bere Regis & Wool) *Map Ref:* SY88
☎ **01929 405096** ▤ **01929 405360**
e-mail: info@tankmuseum.co.uk

The Tank Museum houses the world's finest international collection of armoured fighting vehicles. Tanks in Action displays are held every Thursday at noon from July to September and every Tuesday from the end of July to August Bank Holiday. Armoured vehicle rides are available throughout the summer, and various special events take place - please telephone for details.

Times: Open all year, daily 10-5. Closed 23-28 Dec. **Fee:** £8 (ch £6, pen £7.50). Family saver £23 (2ad+2ch); £22 (1ad+3ch). Group rates available. **Facilities:** 🅿 ☕ ✗ licensed ♿ (wheelchairs available, Braille & audio tours) toilets for disabled shop ✈ (ex guide dogs) 📷

DORCHESTER DINOSAUR MUSEUM

Icen Way DT1 1EW
Dir: (off A35 into Dorchester, museum in town centre just off High East St) *Map Ref:* SY69
☎ **01305 269880** ▤ **01305 268885**
e-mail: info@thedinosaurmuseum.com

This award-winning museum is the only one in Britain dedicated to dinosaurs, a topic of endless fascination to people of all ages. The exhibits are an appealing mixture of fossils, skeletons, life-size reconstructions and interactive displays such as the 'feelies'. There are audio-visual presentations and computer displays providing an all-round family attraction with new displays each year.

Times: Open all year, daily 9.30-5.30 (10-4.30 Nov-Mar). Closed 24-26 Dec. **Fee:** ✱ £6 (ch £4.50, pen & student £5.25, under 4's free). Family ticket £18.50 **Facilities:** 🅿 (50yds) ♿ (many low level displays) shop 📷

DORSET TEDDY BEAR MUSEUM

Antelope Walk, Cornhill DT1 1BE
Dir: (off A35, museum in town centre near Tourist Information Centre) *Map Ref:* SY69
☎ **01305 263200** ▤ **01305 268885**
e-mail: info@teddybearmuseum.co.uk

A visit to the museum begins with the home of Edward Bear and his extended family of human-sized teddy bears. Then, in a more traditional museum setting, view hundreds of teddy bears from throughout the last century in atmospheric and evocative displays. There is also a period-style shop selling teddy bears and teddy bear related goods.

Times: Open daily, Mon-Sat 9.30-5, Sun 10-4.30. Closed 25-26 Dec. **Fee:** ✱ £3.50(ch £2.50, under 4's free). Family £10.50 **Facilities:** 🅿 (500mtrs) shop ✈ (ex guide dogs) 📷

TUTANKHAMUN EXHIBITION

High West St DT1 1UW
Dir: (off A35 into Dorchester town centre) *Map Ref: SY69*
☎ 01305 269571 📄 01305 268885
e-mail: info@tutankhamun-exhibition.co.uk

The exhibition recreates the excitement of one of the world's greatest discoveries of ancient treasure. A reconstruction of the tomb and recreations of its treasures are displayed. The superbly preserved mummified body of the boy king can be seen, wonderfully recreated in every detail. Facsimiles of some of the most famous treasures, including the golden funerary mask and the harpooner can be seen in the final gallery.

Times: Open all year daily, Apr-Oct, 9.30-5.30; Nov-Mar wkdays 9.30-5, wknds 10-4.30. Closed 24-26 Dec. **Fee:** ✱ £6 (ch £4.50, pen & student £5.25, under 5's free). Family ticket £18.50
Facilities: P (200yds) ♿ shop ✖ (ex guide dogs) ▄

POOLE WATERFRONT MUSEUM

4 High St BH15 1BW
Dir: (off Poole Quay) *Map Ref: SZ09*
☎ 01202 262600 📄 01202 262622
e-mail: museums@poole.gov.uk

FREE

The museum tells the story of Poole's seafaring past. Learn of the Roman occupation and see material raised from the Studland Bay wreck. Scaplen's Court, just a few yards from the museum, is a beautifully restored domestic building dating from the medieval period. Although it is only open to the public in August, Scaplen's Court is not to be missed, with a Victorian school room, a kitchen and scullery.

Times: Museum: open Apr-Oct, Mon-Sat 10-5, Sun noon-5; Nov-Mar, Mon-Sat 10-3, Sun noon-3. Scaplen's Court: Aug, Mon-Sat 10-5, Sun noon-5.
Facilities: P (250mtrs) ♿ (Scaplen's Court not accessible) toilets for disabled ✖ (ex guide dogs) ▄

SWANAGE *SWANAGE RAILWAY*

Station House BH19 1HB
Dir: (signed from A351) *Map Ref: SZ09*
☎ 01929 425800 📄 01929 426680
e-mail: general@swanrail.freeserve.co.uk

The railway from Swanage to Wareham was closed in 1972, and in 1976 the Swanage Railway took possession and has gradually restored the line, which now runs for six miles from Swanage to Norden, passing the ruins of Corfe Castle. It is a premier standard gauge steam railway, largely run by volunteers, whose aim is to restore the line as far as Wareham. Ring for details of special events.

Times: ✱ Open every wknd throughout year, daily Apr-Oct.
Facilities: P ☕ ✖ licensed ♿ (special disabled persons coach) toilets for disabled shop (shop at Swanage Station) ▄

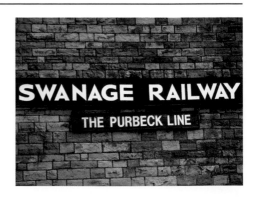

WEST LULWORTH   *LULWORTH CASTLE*

BH20 5QS
Dir: (from Wareham, W on A352 for 1m, left onto B3070 to E
Lulworth, follow tourist signs) **Map Ref:** *SY88*
☎ **01929 400352**   📄 **01929 400563**
e-mail: estate.office@lulworth.com

Glimpse life below stairs in the restored kitchen, and enjoy
beautiful views from the top of the tower of this historic castle set
in beautiful parkland. The 18th-century chapel is the first Catholic
chapel built in England after the Reformation. Children will enjoy
the animal farm, play area, indoor activity room and pitch and
putt.

Times: ✱ Open Castle: Summer 10.30-6; Winter
10.30-4. Lulworth Castle House open Wed 28
May-30 Jul, 2-5. **Facilities:** 🅿 ☕ ♿ (limited in
castle due to grade one listing) toilets for disabled
shop 🛍

WEYMOUTH   *DEEP SEA ADVENTURE & SHARKY'S PLAY & PARTY*

9 Custom House Quay, Old Harbour DT4 8BG
Dir: (A35 to Weymouth, then Old Harbour North, attraction is
located between pavillion and town bridge) **Map Ref:** *SY67*
☎ **0871 222 5760**   📄 **0871 222 5760**
e-mail: enquiries@deepsea-adventure.co.uk

A fascinating attraction telling the story of underwater exploration
and marine exploits. Discover the history of Weymouth's Old
Harbour, with compelling tales of shipwreck survival; explore the
Black Hole and search for Ollie the Oyster. There is also a unique
display relating the 'Titanic' disaster. Sharky's Play Area is four
floors of fun-packed adventure, with a separate area for the under
fives.

Times: Open all year, daily 9.30-7 (high season
9.30-8). Closed 25-26 Dec & 1 Jan).
Fee: ✱ Sharky's Play Zone: Adults free
(ch £3.30). Deep Sea Adventure: £3.75 (ch 5-15
£2.75, pen & student £3.25). Combined ticket for
both attractions, ch £4.75.
Facilities: 🅿 (100yds) ✕ licensed ♿ (lift & sign
language for deaf) toilets for disabled shop
✈ (ex guide dogs) 🛍

RSPB NATURE RESERVE RADIPOLE LAKE

The Swannery Car Park DT4 7TZ
Dir: (close to seafront & railway station) **Map Ref:** *SY67*
☎ **01305 778313**   📄 **01305 778313**

Covering an area of 222 acres, this RSPB Reserve offers firm
paths, a hide and a visitor centre with viewing windows
overlooking the lake. Visitors can expect to see several types of
warblers, mute swans, gadwalls, teals and great crested grebes.
Please phone for details of special events.

Times: Open daily 9-5 **Fee:** *Prices not confirmed
for 2005* **Facilities:** 🅿 (charged) ♿ toilets for
disabled shop 🛍

SEA LIFE PARK

Lodmoor Country Park DT4 7SX
Dir: (on A353) **Map Ref:** SY67
☎ **01305 788255** 📠 **01305 760165**
e-mail: simongrove@merlinentertainments.biz

The Sea Life Park at Weymouth is located in the beautiful Lodmoor Country Park. Here you can marvel at the mysteries of the deep and discover amazing sea creatures from around our own shores in spectacular marine displays. Sea Life has a captive breeding programme for seahorses, and a tropical shark lagoon set in the hull of a sunken wreck. Other interesting creatures you are likely to encounter are puffer fish, mantis shrimp and horseshoe crabs.

Times: ✱ Open all year, daily from 10am. (Closed 25 Dec). **Facilities:** 🅿 (charged) 🍽 ✗ ♿ toilets for disabled shop ✖ (ex guide dogs) 🎞

WIMBORNE   KINGSTON LACY HOUSE, GARDEN & PARK

BH21 4EA
Dir: (1.5m W of Wimborne, B3082) **Map Ref:** SZ09
☎ **01202 883402 (Mon-Fri) & 842913 (wknds)**
📠 **01202 882402**
e-mail: kingstonlacy@nationaltrust.org.uk

Kingston Lacy House was the home of the Bankes family for over 300 years. The original house is 17th century, but in the 1830s was given a stone façade. The Italian marble staircase, Venetian ceiling, treasures from Spain and an Egyptian obelisk were also added. There are outstanding pictures by Titian, Rubens, Velasquez, Reynolds and Van Dyck. No photography is allowed in the house.

Times: House 20 Mar-Oct, 11-5, Wed-Sun. Garden & Park 10.30-6, all week 5 Nov-19 Dec, 10.30-4, Fri-Sun 5 Feb-20 Mar, 10.30-4, Sat-Sun. **Fee:** ✱ House, Garden & Park £7.20 (ch £3.60) Family £19. Park & Gardens only £3.60 (ch £1.80) Family £9.50. **Facilities:** 🅿 🍽 ✗ licensed ♿ (4 manual wheelchairs, Braille guides, parking) toilets for disabled shop ✖ (ex on leads in park & wood) 🐾

PRIEST'S HOUSE MUSEUM AND GARDEN

23-27 High St BH21 1HR
Map Ref: SZ09
☎ **01202 882533** 📠 **01202 882533**
e-mail: priestshouse@eastdorset.gov.uk

This award-winning local history museum is set in a historic house with a Victorian kitchen. Regular cooking demonstrations are held here on the fourth Saturday in the month, 2-5pm. There are nine other rooms to see, along with regular special exhibitions, a new costume and textile gallery and a beautiful 300-ft long walled garden.

Times: ✱ Open Apr-Oct, Mon-Sat, 10-4.30. Also every Sun Jul-Aug & BH wknds 2-5. **Facilities:** 🅿 (200yds) 🍽 ♿ (hands on archaeology gallery, audio tapes) shop ✖ (ex guide dogs)

STAPEHILL ABBEY

Wimborne Rd West BH21 2EB
Dir: (2.5m E off A31 at Canford Bottom rdbt) **Map Ref:** *SZ09*
☎ 01202 861686 📄 01202 894589

This early 19th-century abbey, home for nearly 200 years to Cistercian nuns, is now a busy working crafts centre with many attractions under cover. There are many acres of award-winning landscaped gardens, parkland and picnic spots, and the Power to the Land exhibition. Within the abbey you can see the Victorian parlour and laundry room, the nun's chapel and cloisters. Telephone for details of special events.

Times: Open Etr-Sep, daily 10-5; Oct-Etr, Wed-Sun 10-4. Closed 22 Dec-Feb. **Fee:** ✱ £7.50 (ch 4-16 £4.50, students & pen £7). Family ticket (2ad+2ch) £19.50. **Facilities:** 🅿 ☕ ♿ toilets for disabled shop garden centre ✖ (ex guide dogs) 🔇

WOOL MONKEY WORLD

Longthorns BH20 6HH
Dir: (1m N of Wool on Bere Regis rd) **Map Ref:** *SY88*
☎ 01929 462537 & 0800 456600 📄 01929 405414
e-mail: apes@monkeyworld.org

Set up in order to rescue monkeys and apes from abuse and illegal smuggling, Monkey World houses over 100 primates in 60 acres of Dorset woodland. There are 45 chimps, the largest grouping outside Africa, as well as orang-utans, gibbons, woolly monkeys, lemurs, macaques and marmosets. Those wishing to help the centre continue in its quest to rescue primates from lives of misery may like to take part in the adoption scheme which includes free admission to the park for one year.

Times: Open daily 10-5 (Jul-Aug 10-6). (Last admission 1 hour before closing) **Facilities:** 🅿 ☕ ✖ ♿ toilets for disabled shop ✖ (ex guide dogs) 🔇

BERKELEY BERKELEY CASTLE

GL13 9BQ
Dir: (just off A38 midway between Bristol & Gloucester. From M5 take junct 14 or 15) **Map Ref:** *ST69*
☎ 01453 810332 📄 01453 512995
e-mail: info@berkeley.castle.com

Berkeley Castle is the amazing fortress home of the Berkeley family, who have lived in the building since the keep was completed in 1153. The castle is still intact, from dungeon to elegant drawing rooms, and reflects nearly a thousand years of English history: a king's murder, the American Colonies, and London's Berkeley Square.

Times: Open Apr-2 Oct, Tue-Sat & BH Mon 11-4, Sun 2-5; Oct, Sun only 2-5. **Fee:** ✱ Castle & Gardens & Butterfly House: £7 (ch 5-15 £4, pen £5.50). Family ticket (2ad+2ch) £18.50. **Facilities:** 🅿 ☕ ♿ Special tours can be arranged shop ✖ (ex guide dogs) 🔇

BOURTON-ON-THE-WATER   BIRDLAND

Rissington Rd GL54 2BN
Dir: (on A429)   *Map Ref:* SP12
☎ **01451 820480** 📄 **01451 822398**
e-mail: sb.birdland@virgin.net

Birdland is a natural setting of woodland, river and gardens, which is inhabited by over 500 birds; flamingos, pelicans, penguins, cranes, storks, cassowary and waterfowl can be seen on various aspects of the water habitat. There are over 50 aviaries of parrots, falcons, pheasants, hornbills, touracos, pigeons, ibis and many more. Tropical, Toucan and Desert Houses are home to the more delicate species.

Times: Open all year, Apr-Oct, daily 10-6; Nov-Mar, daily 10-4. (Last admission 1hr before closing). Closed 25 Dec. **Fee:** ✱ £4.85 (ch 4-14 £2.85, pen £3.85). Family ticket (2ad+2ch) £14. Party 10+. **Facilities:** P (adjacent) 🍴 ♿ toilets for disabled shop 🛍

MODEL VILLAGE

Old New Inn GL54 2AF
Map Ref: SP12
☎ **01451 820467** 📄 **01451 810236**
e-mail: reception@theoldnewinn.co.uk

The model at Bourton-on-the-Water is built of Cotswold stone to a scale of one-ninth, and is a perfect replica of the village. It includes a miniature River Windrush, a working model of a waterwheel, churches and shops, with tiny trees, shrubs and alpine plants. It was built by an inn owner and a team of craftsmen in the 1930s and was opened on the Coronation day of King George VI and Queen Elizabeth in 1937.

Times: Open all year 9-5.45 (summer), 10-dusk (winter). Closed 25 Dec. **Facilities:** P (500yds) 🍴 ✗ licensed shop 🐕 (ex guide dogs) 🛍

CIRENCESTER   CORINIUM MUSEUM

Park St GL7 2BX
Dir: (in town centre)   *Map Ref:* SP00
☎ **01285 655611**
e-mail: museums@cotswold.gov.uk

Discover the treasures of the Cotswolds at the new Corinium Museum. Two years and over £5 million in the making, it has been transformed into a must-see attraction. It features archaeological and historical material from Cirencester and the Cotswolds, from prehistoric times to the 19th century. The museum is known for its Roman mosaic sculpture and other material from one of Britain's largest Roman towns. New on display are Anglo-Saxon treasures from Lechlade bringing to life this little known period. The museum also houses medieval, Tudor, Civil War and 18th-19th century displays.

Times: Open Mon-Sat 10-5, Sun 2-5. Closed 25-26 Dec & 1 Jan. **Fee:** ✱ £3.50 (ch & students £2, pen £2.50). Family ticket £8. **Facilities:** P (2mins walk) 🍴 ✗ ♿ toilets for disabled shop 🐕 🛍

CLEARWELL   CLEARWELL CAVES ANCIENT IRON MINES

GL16 8JR
Dir: (1.5m S of Coleford town centre, off B4228 follow brown
tourist signs) *Map Ref:* SO50
☎ 01594 832535   📄 01594 833362
e-mail: jw@clearwellcaves.com

These impressive natural caves have been mined since the
earliest times for paint pigment and iron ore. Today, visitors can
explore nine large caverns with displays of local mining and
geology. Small scale ochre mining still continues in the traditional
way. There is a colour room where ochre pigments are produced
and blacksmith's shop.

Times: Open Mar-Oct daily 10-5. Jan-Feb Sat-Sun
10-5. Christmas Fantasy 1-24 Dec, daily 10-5.
Fee: ✱ £4 (ch £2.50, concessions £3.50) Family
ticket £11. **Facilities:** 🅿 🍽 ♿ (hands-on
exhibits, braille guide book, contact in advance)
toilets for disabled shop ✈ (ex guide & hearing
dogs) ◀

CRANHAM   PRINKNASH BIRD & DEER PARK

GL4 8EU
Dir: (M5 junct 11a, A417 Cirencester. Take 1st exit signed A46
Stroud. Follow brown tourist signs) *Map Ref:* SO81
☎ 01452 812727   📄 01452 812727

Nine acres of parkland and lakes make a beautiful home for black
swans, geese and other water birds. There are also exotic birds
such as white and Indian blue peacocks and crown cranes, as
well as tame fallow deer and pygmy goats. The Golden Wood is
stocked with ornamental pheasants, and leads to the reputedly
haunted monks' fishpond, which contains trout. An 80-year-old,
free-standing, 16-ft tall Wendy House in the style of a Tudor house
has now been erected near the picnic area.

Times: Open all year, daily 10-5 (4 in winter).
Closed 26 Dec & Good Fri. **Fee:** ✱ £4 (ch £2.50,
pen £3.50). Party 10+ £3.50 (ch £2, pen £3).
Facilities: 🅿 🍽 shop ✈

GLOUCESTER   GLOUCESTER CITY MUSEUM & ART GALLERY

Brunswick Rd GL1 1HP
Dir: (centre of Gloucester) *Map Ref:* SO81
☎ 01452 396131   📄 01452 410898
e-mail: city.museum@gloucester.gov.uk

There is something for everyone at this city museum and art
gallery: an impressive range of Roman artefacts including the
Rufus Sita tombstone; the Iron Age Birdlip Mirror; one of the
earliest backgammon sets in the world; dinosaur fossils; and
paintings by Turner and Gainsborough. You can also see full-sized
dinosaurs; Gloucestershire wildlife; and beautiful antique
furniture, glass, ceramics and silver. Hands-on displays, computer
quizzes and activity workstations add to the fun, and there's an
exciting programme of temporary exhibitions. Look out for
children's holiday activities and special events.

Times: Open all year, Tue-Sat 10-5. **Facilities:** 🅿 (500yds) ♿ toilets
for disabled shop ✈ (ex guide dogs) ◀

GLOUCESTER FOLK MUSEUM

99-103 Westgate St GL1 2PG
Dir: (A40 & A48 from W, A38 & M5 from N, A40 & B4073 from E & A4173 & A38 from S) *Map Ref:* SO81
☎ 01452 396467 🖹 01452 330495   FREE
e-mail: folk.museum@gloucester.gov.uk

Three floors of splendid Tudor and Jacobean timber-framed buildings dating from the 16th and 17th centuries, along with new buildings housing the dairy, ironmonger's, wheelwright and carpenters' workshops. Local history, domestic life, crafts, trades and industries from 1500 to the present are reflected in the exhibits. Special exhibitions, hands-on activities, events, demonstrations and role play sessions are held. Plus a cottage garden and courtyard for events.

Times: Tue-Sat, 10-5 (For ten weeks only during half terms and holidays) **Facilities:** P (500yds) & (hands-on displays, virtual tour of Protal gallery) shop ✖ (ex guide dogs) 🖿

THE NATIONAL WATERWAYS MUSEUM

Llanthony Warehouse, The Docks GL1 2EH
Dir: (follow signs for historic docks from M5 and A40 and also within the city) *Map Ref:* SO81
☎ 01452 318200 🖹 01452 318202
e-mail: bookingsnwm@thewaterwaystrust.org

Based in Gloucester Docks, this museum takes up three floors of a seven-storey Victorian warehouse, and documents the 200-year history of Britain's water-based transport. The emphasis is on hands-on experience, including working models and engines, interactive displays, actual craft, computer interactions and the national collection of inland waterways. Boat trips are also available between Easter and October.

Times: Open all year, daily 10-5. (Last admission 4). Closed 25 Dec. **Facilities:** P (charged) 🍷 & (wheelchair, lifts, limited access to floating exhibits) toilets for disabled shop ✖ (ex guide dogs) 🖿

NATURE IN ART

Wallsworth Hall, Tewkesbury Rd, Twigworth GL2 9PA
Dir: (0.5m off A38 2m N of Gloucester. Follow brown tourist signs from village) *Map Ref:* SO81
☎ 01452 731422 0845 4500233 🖹 01452 730937
e-mail: ninart@globalnet.co.uk

Nature is the theme at this museum and art gallery, and there are many outstanding exhibits including sculpture, tapestries and ceramics. There is a comprehensive 'artist in residence' programme for ten months of the year, and events include regular talks, films, temporary exhibitions and art courses. Work from over 60 countries spanning 1,500 years is included.

Times: Open all year, Tue-Sun & BHs 10-5. Closed 24-26 Dec.
Fee: £3.60 (ch, pen & students £3.00, ch under 8 free). Family ticket £11. Party 15+. **Facilities:** P 🍷 ✖ licensed & (lift & ramps at entrance) toilets for disabled shop ✖ (ex guide dogs)

GUITING POWER   COTSWOLD FARM PARK

GL54 5UG
Dir: (signed off B4077 from M5 junct 9) *Map Ref:* SP02
☎ 01451 850307 ▤ 01451 850423
e-mail: info@cotswoldfarmpark.co.uk

At the Cotswold Farm Park there are nearly 50 breeding herds and flocks of the rarest British breeds of sheep, cattle, pigs, goats, horses and poultry. Activities for children including cuddling rabbits and guinea pigs, bottle feeding lambs and calves, tractor and trailer rides, battery powered tractors and safe, rustic-themed play areas indoors and out. Lambing occurs in early May, followed by shearing and then milking demonstrations later in the season.

Times: Open 20 Mar-12 Sep, daily 10.30 5 (then open wknds only until end Oct & Autumn half term 10.30-4). **Fee:** ✱ £4.95 (ch £3.50, pen £4.65). Family ticket £15.50 **Facilities:** ▣ ⬛ ♿ (ramps, wheelchair to let) toilets for disabled shop ✖ (ex guide dogs) ◀

LYDNEY   DEAN FOREST RAILWAY

Norchard Railway Centre, New Mills, Forest Rd GL15 4ET
Dir: (At Lydney turn off A48, follow brown tourist signs to Norchard Railway Centre, on B4234) *Map Ref:* SO60
☎ 01594 843423 (info) & 845840 ▤ 01594 845840
e-mail: commercial@deanforestrailway.co.uk

Just north of Lydney lies the headquarters of the Dean Forest Railway, where a number of steam locomotives, plus lots of coaches, wagons and railway equipment are on show and guided tours are available by prior arrangement. A standard gauge passenger service on steam haulage runs from Norchard to Lydney Junction and back to Norchard, the diesel train runs from Lydney Junction to Tufts and back to Lydney Junction.

Times: Open Apr-Oct, Sun; June-Sep, Wed, Sat, Sun; Aug, Thu; Dec wknds (Santa Specials) **Fee:** ✱ £6.50 (under 5's free, ch £4.50, pen £5.50) **Facilities:** ▣ ⬛ ✖ licensed ♿ (specially adapted coach for wheelchairs, phone for details) toilets for disabled shop ◀

MORETON-IN-MARSH   BATSFORD ARBORETUM

Admissions Centre, Batsford Park GL56 9QB
Dir: (1.5m NW, off A44 from Moreton-in-Marsh) *Map Ref:* SP23
☎ 01386 701441 ▤ 01386 701829
e-mail: batsarb@batsfound.freeserve.co.uk

Batsford Arboretum has one of the largest private collections of trees in Great Britain and wonderful views across the Vale of Evenlode. Visitors can stroll amongst the spring flowers that cascade down the hillside, and see many rare and unusual trees. There is an impressive display of colour during autumn, and peace and tranquillity are ever present. View the Buddha and cave and try to negotiate the waterfall without getting too wet. Sheer Cotswold magic.

Times: Open Feb-mid Nov, daily 10-5; mid Nov-Jan, wknds only 10-4. **Fee:** £5 (ch 4-15 £1, concessions £4). Party 12+. **Facilities:** ▣ ⬛ ♿ (some steep, slippery paths, wheelchair available) toilets for disabled shop garden centre ◀

COTSWOLD FALCONRY CENTRE

Batsford Park GL56 9QB
Dir: (1m W of Moreton-in-Marsh on A44) **Map Ref:** SP23
☎ 01386 701043
e-mail: geoffdalton@yahoo.co.uk

Conveniently located by the Batsford Park Arboretum, the Cotswold Falconry gives daily demonstrations in the art of falconry. The emphasis here is on breeding and conservation, and eagles, hawks, owls and falcons can be seen. Flying displays are held daily at 11.30am, 1.30pm, 3pm and 4.30pm (when the light allows), and each display lasts for about an hour.

Times: Open mid Feb-mid Nov, 10.30-5.30. (Last admission 5pm). **Fee:** £5 (ch 4-15 £2.50, concession £4). Joint ticket with Batsford Arboretum £8.50 (ch 4-15 £3, concession £8). **Facilities:** 🅿 & (no steps, wide doorways) toilets for disabled shop garden centre ✈ (ex on leads in arboretum) ◀

NEWENT   THE NATIONAL BIRDS OF PREY CENTRE

GL18 1JJ
Dir: (follow A40, right onto B4219 towards Newent. Follow brown tourist signs from Newent town) **Map Ref:** SO72
☎ 0870 9901992 📄 01531 821389
e-mail: katherine@nbpc.co.uk

At this national centre, trained birds can be seen at close quarters in the Hawk Walk and the Owl Courtyard and there are also breeding aviaries. Birds are flown three times daily in summer and winter, in an exciting and informative display. There are over 80 aviaries on view with 40 species. Facilities also include a gift shop, bookshop, picnic areas, coffee shop and children's play area.

Times: Open Feb-Oct, daily 10.30-5.30. **Fee:** ✱ £6.75 (ch £4, pen £5.75). Family ticket £18.50 (2ad+2ch). **Facilities:** 🅿 ☕ & (special tours available, pre-booking required) toilets for disabled shop ✈ ◀

THE SHAMBLES

Church St GL18 1PP
Dir: (close to town centre near church) **Map Ref:** SO72
☎ 01531 822144

Cobbled streets, alleyways, cottages and houses have been re-created on this site which covers over an acre close to the contemporary streets of the country town of Newent. There are display shops and trades, even a tin chapel and cottage garden to produce the period look and atmosphere of a Victorian village.

Times: Open mid Mar-end Oct, Tue-Sun & BHs 10-5 (or dusk); Nov-Dec wknds only. **Fee:** ✱ £4.25 (ch £2.65, pen £3.65). **Facilities:** 🅿 (100yds) ☕ & toilets for disabled shop ◀

NORTHLEACH KEITH HARDING'S WORLD OF MECHANICAL MUSIC

The Oak House, High St GL54 3ET
Dir: (at crossroads of A40 & A429) *Map Ref: SP11*
☎ 01451 860181 📠 01451 861133
e-mail: keith@mechanicalmusic.co.uk

At Keith Harding's World of Mechanical Music, a fascinating collection of antique clocks, musical boxes, automata and mechanical musical instruments are displayed in a period setting and played during regular tours. The exhibits having been restored and maintained in the world famous workshops. There is also an exhibition of coin operated instruments which visitors can have a go on.

Times: Open all year, daily 10-6. Last tour 5. Closed 25-26 Dec.
Fee: ✳ £5 (ch £2.50, pen & students £4). Discounts for families & groups. **Facilities:** 🅿 ♿ (Safety rails, non-slip floor) toilets for disabled shop 🐕 (ex guide dogs) 🍴

SLIMBRIDGE WWT SLIMBRIDGE

GL2 7BT
Dir: (off A38, signed from M5 junct 13 & 14) *Map Ref: SO70*
☎ 01453 891900 📠 01453 890827
e-mail: slimbridge@wwt.org.uk

Slimbridge is home to the world's largest collection of exotic wildfowl and the only place in Europe where all six types of flamingo can be seen. Up to 8,000 wild birds winter on the 800-acre reserve of flat fields, marsh and mudflats on the River Severn. Facilities include a tropical house, discovery centre, shop and restaurant.

Times: Open all year, daily from 9.30-5 (winter 4). Closed 25 Dec. **Fee:** ✳ £6.75 (ch £4, pen £5.50). Family ticket £17.50. **Facilities:** 🅿 🍴 ✕ licensed ♿ (wheelchair loan, tapes for blind, hearing pads & loops) toilets for disabled shop 🐕 (ex guide & hearing dogs) 🍴

SNOWSHILL SNOWSHILL MANOR

WR12 7JU
Dir: (3m SW of Broadway, off A44) *Map Ref: SP03*
☎ 01386 852410 📠 01386 842822
e-mail: snowshillmanor@nationaltrust.org.uk

Arts and crafts garden designed by its owner Charles Paget Wade in collaboration with M H Baillie Scott, as a series of outdoor rooms to complement his traditional Cotswold manor house. The first National Trust garden to be managed following organic principles, it has a vibrant mix of cottage flowers and stunning views across Cotswold countryside. The house is filled with his unique collection of craftsman-made items including musical instruments, clocks, toys, bicycles and Japanese armour.

Times: House: 25 Mar-2 May, 12-5, Thu-Sun, 4 May-30 Oct, 12-5, Wed-Sun. Garden: 25 Mar-2 May, 11-5.30, Thu-Sun, 4 May-30 Oct, 11-5.30, Wed-Sun. Shop: As garden, also 5 Nov-11Dec, 12-4, Sat & Sun. Restaurant: As shop **Fee:** House & Garden: £7, (ch £3.50). Family £17.80 Garden, Restaurant & Shop: £4, (ch £2). Family £10 **Facilities:** 🅿 ✕ licensed ♿ (Braille guides, audio tapes, 2 manual wheelchairs) toilets for disabled shop 🐕 (ex guide dogs) 🍴

SOUDLEY DEAN HERITAGE CENTRE

Camp Mill GL14 2UB
Dir: (on B4227, in Forest of Dean) *Map Ref:* SO61
☎ **01594 822170** 📄 **01594 823711**
e-mail: deanmuse@btinternet.com

The centre tells the story of this unique area and its people, from pre-historic times to the present day. Displays include a reconstructed cottage, a working beam engine from Lightmore Colliery, a charcoal burners' camp and an art gallery. There are also nature trails with animals, and an adventure playground that includes a maze and swing bridge. Library and research facilities are available by appointment.

Times: Open all year, daily, British Winter 10-4, British Summer 10-5.30. Closed 24-26 Dec & 1 Jan. **Fee:** £4.50 (ch £2.50, under 5's free, pen & concessions £3.50). Family ticket £13.
Facilities: 🅿 ☕ ♿ (lift, ramps, help from establishment staff) toilets for disabled shop ✖ (ex guide dogs) 🛍

WESTONBIRT WESTONBIRT ARBORETUM

GL8 8QS
Dir: (3m S Tetbury on A433) *Map Ref:* ST88
☎ **01666 880220** 📄 **01666 880559**

Begun in 1829, this arboretum contains one of the finest and most important collections of trees and shrubs in the world. There are 18,000 specimens, planted from 1829 to the present day, covering 600 acres of landscaped Cotswold countryside. Enjoy magnificent displays of rhododendrons, azaleas, magnolias and wild flowers in season, and in the autumn a blaze of colour from the national collection of Japanese maples.

Times: Open all year, daily 10-8 or sunset. Visitor centre & shop all year. Closed Xmas & New Year. **Fee:** ✱ Jun-Nov £7.50 (pen £6.50) Family ticket £15. Nov-Mar £5 (pen £4) Family ticket £11. Apr-Jun £6 (pen £5) Family ticket £12
Facilities: 🅿 ☕ ✖ licensed ♿ (electric & manual wheelchair for loan, telephone to book) toilets for disabled shop garden centre 🛍

WINCHCOMBE SUDELEY CASTLE & GARDENS

GL54 5JD
Dir: (B4632 to Winchcombe, Castle is signed) *Map Ref:* SP02
☎ **01242 602308** 📄 **01242 602959**
e-mail: marketing@sudeley.org.uk

Sudeley Castle was home to Katherine Parr, who is buried in the chapel. Henry VIII, Anne Boleyn, Lady Jane Grey and Elizabeth I all stayed or visited here; and it was Prince Rupert's headquarters during the Civil War. There is a famous rose collection.

Times: Open daily Mar-Oct, Grounds, Gardens, Exhibition, Shop & Plant Centre 10.30-5.30. 29 Mar-2 Nov, Castle apartments, Church & restaurant 11-5. **Fee:** ✱ Castle & Gardens £6.85-£7.85 (ch 5-15 £3.85-£4.85 & concessions £5.85-£6.85). Gardens only £5.50-£6.50 (ch £2.75-£3.75 & concessions £4.50-£5.50). Family ticket (2ad+2ch) £18.50-£22. Party 20+ £5.85 (ch £3.85, concessions £4.85).
Facilities: 🅿 ✖ licensed ♿ (limited access to gardens only, parking) toilets for disabled shop garden centre ✖ (by request on arrival) 🛍

BATH AMERICAN MUSEUM

Claverton Manor BA2 7BD
Dir: (2.5m SE) **Map Ref:** *ST76*
☎ **01225 460503** ▤ **01225 469160**
e-mail: info@americanmuseum.org

Claverton Manor is just two miles southeast of Bath, in a beautiful setting above the River Avon. The house was built in 1820 by Sir Jeffrey Wyatville, and is now a museum of American decorative arts. The gardens are well worth seeing, and include an American arboretum and a replica of George Washington's garden at Mount Vernon. The Folk Art Gallery and the New Gallery are among the many exhibits in the grounds, along with seasonal exhibitions.

Times: Open 14 Mar-30 Oct, Tue-Sun 2-5. Gardens 12-6. Open Mon in Aug & BHs.
Fee: £6.50 (ch £3.50, pen £5.50).
Facilities: ☐ ☐ & toilets for disabled shop ☐

BATH POSTAL MUSEUM

8 Broad St BA1 5LJ
Dir: (M4 junct 18. A46 to Bath, on entering city fork left at mini rdbt. After all lights into Walcot St. Car park opp) **Map Ref:** *ST76*
☎ **01225 460333** ▤ **01225 460333**
e-mail: info@bathpostalmuseum.org

Discover how 18th-century Bath influenced and developed the postal system, including the story of the penny post. The first letter with a stamp was sent from this very building. Visitors can explore the history of written communication from Egyptian clay tablets, thousands of years ago, to the first airmail flight from Bath to London in 1912.

Times: ✱ Open all year, Mon-Sat 11-4.30. (Last admission Mar-Oct 4.30, Oct-Mar 4). Closed Sun, 25 26 Dec & 1 Jan.
Facilities: ☐ (150yds) (no on street parking) ☐ & (films and computer games for hearing impaired) toilets for disabled shop ✖ (ex guide dogs)

THE BUILDING OF BATH MUSEUM

Countess of Huntingdons Chapel, The Vineyards, The Paragon BA1 5NA
Dir: (M4 junct 18, follow A46 towards Bath city centre. Take A4, 2nd exit at mini rdbt. Along road on right) **Map Ref:** *ST76*
☎ **01225 333895** ▤ **01225 445473**
e-mail: cathryn@bathmuseum.co.uk

This new museum relates the fascinating story of how Georgian Bath was created. 17th-century Bath was a medieval market town but in the space of a hundred years it was transformed into one of the most beautiful and glamorous cities in Europe. The exhibition depicts elegant society life in Beau Nash's spa resort and explains how the houses were constructed. After a visit, the street scene outside seems like an extension of the exhibition. Ring for details of special events such as concerts and lectures.

Times: ✱ Open 15 Feb-1 Dec, Tue-Sun & BHs 10.30-5. **Facilities:** ☐ (500mtrs) & shop ✖ (ex guide dogs) ☐

MUSEUM OF COSTUME

Bennett St BA1 2QH
Dir: (M4 junct 18, follow A46 into Bath. Museum near city centre)
Map Ref: ST76
☎ **01225 477785** 📠 **01225 477743**
e-mail: costume_bookings@bathnes.gov.uk

The Museum of Costume is one of the finest collections of fashionable dress in the world, covering the period from the late 16th century to the present day. It is housed in Bath's famous 18th-century Assembly Rooms designed by John Wood the Younger in 1771. Entrance to the Assembly Rooms is free.

Times: Open all year, daily 10-4.30. Closed 25 & 26 Dec. **Fee:** ✱ £6 (ch £4). Family ticket £16.50. Combined ticket with Roman Baths, £12 (ch £7). **Facilities:** 🅿 (5 mins walk) (park & ride recommended) ☕ ♿ (audio guides available) toilets for disabled shop ✖ (ex guide dogs) ▰

ROMAN BATHS & PUMP ROOM

Abbey Church Yard BA1 1LZ
Dir: (M4 junct 18, A46 into city centre) *Map Ref:* ST76
☎ **01225 477785** 📠 **01225 477743**
e-mail: romanbaths_bookings@bathnes.gov.uk

The remains of the Roman baths and temple give a vivid impression of life nearly 2,000 years ago. Built next to Britain's only hot spring, the baths served the sick and the pilgrims visiting the adjacent Temple of Sulis Minerva. The Pump Room became a popular meeting place in the 18th century. No visit is complete without a taste of the famous spa water.

Times: Open all year, Mar-Jun & Sep-Oct, daily 9-5; Jul & Aug daily 9am-10pm; Jan-Feb & Nov-Dec, daily 9.30-4.30. Closed 25-26 Dec. (Last exit 1hr after closing). **Fee:** ✱ £9 (ch £5). Family ticket £24. Combined ticket with Museum of Costume £12 (ch £7). Disabled visitors free admission to ground floor areas. **Facilities:** 🅿 (5 mins walk) (park & ride recommended) ✖ licensed ♿ (sign language & audio tours) toilets for disabled shop ✖ (ex guide dogs) ▰

SALLY LUNN'S REFRESHMENT HOUSE & MUSEUM

4 North Pde Passage BA1 1NX
Dir: (centre of Bath, follow signs, next to Bath Abbey)
Map Ref: ST76
☎ **01225 461634** 📠 **01225 447090**
e-mail: david@sallylunns.co.uk

This Tudor building is Bath's oldest house and was a popular 17th-century meeting place. The traditional 'Sally Lunn' is similar to a brioche, and it is popularly believed to carry the name of its first maker who came to Bath in 1680. The bun is still served in the restaurant, and the original oven, Georgian cooking range and a collection of baking utensils are displayed in the museum.

Times: Open all year, Museum - Mon-Fri 10-6, Sat 10-5, Sun 11-5. Closed 25-26 Dec & 1 Jan.
Fee: ✱ 30p (concessions free).
Facilities: 🅿 (2-3 min walk) (cards required for street parking) ☕ ✖ licensed ♿ (Braille menu for the blind) shop ✖ (ex guide dogs) ▰

CRICKET ST THOMAS   *THE WILDLIFE PARK AT CRICKET ST THOMAS*

TA20 4DB
Dir: (3m E of Chard on A30, follow brown heritage signs. Clearly signed from M5 junct 25) *Map Ref:* ST30
☎ **01460 30111** 📄 **01460 30817**
e-mail: teresa.white2@bourne-leisure.co.uk

The Wildlife Park offers you the chance to see more than 60 species of animals at close quarters. Visitors can learn about what is being done to save endangered species, take a walk through the lemur wood, ride on the safari train or visit the children's farm. During peak season, park mascot Larry the Lemur stars in his own show.

Times: Open all year, daily 10-dusk, last admission 4 in summer. Closed 25 Dec.
Facilities: 🅿 🍴 ✕ licensed ♿ (some steep slopes) toilets for disabled shop ✖ (ex guide dogs) 🔊

SPARKFORD   HAYNES MOTOR MUSEUM

BA22 7LH
Dir: (from A303 follow A359 towards Castle Cary, museum clearly signed) *Map Ref:* ST62
☎ **01963 440804** 📄 **01963 441004**
e-mail: info@haynesmotormuseum.co.uk

Haynes Motor Museum has a spectacular collection of historic cars, motorcycles and motoring memorabilia. Vehicles range from a 1903 Oldsmobile to sports cars of the 50s and 60s and modern day classics. Also at the museum is a 70-seat video cinema, the Hall of Motorsports, a millennium hall and a picnic area and children's adventure playground.

Times: Open all year, Mar-Oct, daily 9.30-5.30; Nov-Feb, 10-4.30. Closed 24-26 Dec & 1 Jan.
Fee: ✱ £6.50 (ch £3.50, concessions £5). Family £8.50 (1ad+1ch), £19 (2ad+3ch).
Facilities: 🅿 ✕ licensed ♿ (ramps & loan wheelchairs available) toilets for disabled shop ✖ (ex guide dogs & in grounds) 🔊

STREET   THE SHOE MUSEUM

C & J Clark Ltd, High St BA16 0YA
Dir: (M5 junct 23, A39 to Street, follow signs for Clarks Village)
Map Ref: ST43
☎ **01458 842169** 📄 **01458 442226**   FREE

The museum is in the oldest part of the shoe factory set up by Cyrus and James Clark in 1825. Here the company made rugs, mops and chamois leather from sheepskins, before they began producing shoes in 1830. The museum's collections include shoes from Roman times to the present, along with buckles, engravings, fashion plates, machinery, hand tools and advertising material.

Times: Open all year, Mon-Fri 10-4.45, Sat 10-1.30 & 2-5, Sun 11-1.30 & 2-5. Closed 10 days over Xmas. **Facilities:** 🅿 ♿ (access wkdays only) shop ✖ (ex guide dogs)

WASHFORD *TROPIQUARIA ANIMAL AND ADVENTURE PARK*

TA23 0QB
Dir: (on A39, between Williton and Minehead) *Map Ref:* ST04
☎ 01984 640688 🖹 01984 641105
e-mail: office@tropiquaria.co.uk

Tropiquaria is housed in a 1930's BBC transmitting station. The main hall has been converted into an indoor jungle with a 15-foot waterfall, tropical plants and free-flying birds. (Snakes, lizards, iguanas, spiders, toads and terrapins are caged!) Downstairs is the submarine crypt with local and tropical marine life. Two new full size pirate adventure ships are moored on the front lawn accessible to pirates of all ages, and the park has an indoor play castle for adventure and fun whatever the weather. Other attractions are landscaped gardens, the Shadowstring Puppet Theatre, and the 'Wireless in the West' museum.

Times: ✻ Open Apr-Sep, daily 10-6 (last entry 4.30); Oct daily 11-5 (last entry 4); Nov-Mar wknds 11-4 (last entry 3). **Facilities:** 🅿 ☕ ♿ (ramp to pirate galleon & indoor castle) toilets for disabled shop ✖ (ex guide dogs) ◀

WESTON-SUPER-MARE THE HELICOPTER MUSEUM

The Heliport, Locking Moor Rd BS24 8PP
Dir: (outskirts of town on A371, nr M5 junct 21) *Map Ref:* ST36
☎ 01934 635227 🖹 01934 645230
e-mail: office@helimuseum.fsnet.co.uk

This is the world's largest rotary-wing collection and the only helicopter museum in Britain. More than 70 helicopters and autogyros are on display - including examples from France, Germany, Poland, Russia and the United States. These date from 1935 to the present day, with displays of models, engines and other components explaining the history and development of the rotorcraft. Special events include 'Open Cockpit Days', when visitors can learn more about how the helicopter works.

Times: Open all year, Nov-Mar, Wed-Sun 10-4.30; Apr-Oct 10-5.30. Open daily during Etr & Summer school hols 10-6.30. Closed 24-26 Dec & 1 Jan. **Fee:** ✻ £4.95 (ch under 5 free, ch 5-16 £2.95, pen £3.95). Family ticket (2ad+2ch) £13, (2ad+3ch) £15. Party 12+. **Facilities:** 🅿 ☕ ♿ (large print and Braille information sheet) toilets for disabled shop ◀

NORTH SOMERSET MUSEUM

Burlington St BS23 1PR
Map Ref: ST36
☎ 01934 621028 🖹 01934 612526
e-mail: museum.service@n-somerset.gov.uk

This museum, housed in the former workshops of the Edwardian Gaslight Company, has displays on the seaside holiday, an old chemist's shop, a dairy and Victorian pavement mosaics. Adjoining the museum is Clara's Cottage, a Westonian home of the 1900s with period kitchen, parlour, bedroom and back yard. One of the rooms has an additional display of Peggy Nisbet dolls. Other displays include wildlife gallery, Mendip minerals, mining and local archaeology, costume, ceramics and cameras.

Times: Open all year: Mon-Sat 10-4.30. Closed 25-26 Dec & 1 Jan. **Fee:** £3.50 (ch free when accompanied by an adult, pen £2.50) **Facilities:** 🅿 (800yds) (some disabled parking outside museum) ☕ ♿ toilets for disabled shop ✖ (ex guide dogs) ◀

WOOKEY HOLE WOOKEY HOLE CAVES & PAPERMILL

BA5 1BB
Dir: (M5 junct 22 follow signs via A38 & A371, from Bristol & Bath
A39 to Wells then 2m to Wookey Hole) *Map Ref:* ST54
☎ 01749 672243   📄 01749 677749
e-mail: witch@wookey.co.uk

Some of Europe's most spectacular caves, carved out by the River
Axe, are located at Wookey Hole, the legendary haunt of the
Witch of Wookey. Cave tours are enhanced by atmospheric
lighting and fascinating folklore. But there is much more to see
and do whatever the weather, including authentic Victorian Pier
attractions and Britain's last surviving handmade paper mill.
Special events are a regular feature throughout the year.

Times: Open all year, Nov-Mar, daily 10.30-5.30
(last admission 4); Apr-Oct, daily 10-7 (last
admission 5) **Fee:** ✱ £8.80 (ch 4-14,
concessions £5.50, under 4's free).
Facilities: 🅿 ✕ licensed ♿ (papermill only
accessible) toilets for disabled shop ✖ (ex guide
dogs) ▬

YEOVILTON *FLEET AIR ARM MUSEUM*

Royal Naval Air Station BA22 8HT
Dir: (on B3151, just off A303) *Map Ref:* ST52
☎ 01935 840565   📄 01935 842630
e-mail: info@fleetairarm.com

The Fleet Air Arm Museum is a national museum in a rural setting
with an area the size of a football pitch under cover. It is the only
British Museum sited next to an operational military airfield. The
museum shows over 40 aircraft within the many exhibitions
throughout the four large halls. 'Leading Edge' tells the story of
aircraft from early biplanes to Concorde and the Sea Harrier.
Innovative touch screen displays show how aircraft fly, and give
information on the aircraft and the men who flew them.

Times: Open all year, daily 10-5.30 (4.30 Nov-Mar). Closed 24-26
Dec. **Facilities:** 🅿 💺 ✕ licensed ♿ (wheelchairs available) toilets
for disabled shop ✖ (ex guide dogs) ▬

AVEBURY ALEXANDER KEILLER MUSEUM

High St SN8 1RF
Dir: (6m W of Marlborough. 1m N of A4 (Bath Rd) on A4361 and
B4003) *Map Ref:* SU06
☎ 01672 539250   📄 01672 539388
e-mail: avebury@nationaltrust.org.uk

The Avebury Stone Circle is one of the most important megalithic
monuments in Europe, and was built before Stonehenge, and is
believed to have served a religious and ceremonial service. The
museum, including an exhibition in the 17th-century threshing
barn, presents the full archaeological story of the stones using
finds from the site, along with inter-active and audio-visual
displays.

Times: Open Apr-Oct, daily 10-6 or dusk if earlier;
Nov-Mar 10-4 .Closed 24-26 Dec **Fee:** ✱ £4.20
(ch £2.10) Family £10 (2ad+3ch) Family £7
(1ad+3ch) **Facilities:** 🅿 (charged) 💺
✕ licensed ♿ (Braille guide, large print guide,
drop off point) toilets for disabled shop
✖ (ex guide dogs) ⊞ ♨ ▬

CALNE BOWOOD HOUSE & GARDENS

SN11 0LZ
Dir: (off A4 Chippenham to Calne road, in Derry Hill village)
Map Ref: SU97
☎ **01249 812102** 📠 **01249 821757**
e-mail: houseandgardens@bowood.org

Built in 1624, the house was finished by the first Earl of Shelburne, who employed celebrated architects, notably Robert Adam, to complete the work. Adam's library is particularly admired, and also of note is the laboratory where Dr Joseph Priestley discovered the existence of oxygen in 1774. The house overlooks terraced gardens towards the 40-acre lake and some beautiful parkland. The gardens were laid out by 'Capability' Brown in the 1760s and are carpeted with daffodils, narcissi and bluebells in spring. There is also an adventure playground and new soft play area.

Times: Open Apr-Oct, daily 11-6, including BH. Rhododendron Gardens (separate entrance off A342) open 6 weeks during mid Apr-early Jun, 11-6. **Fee:** ✱ House & Gardens £6.40 (ch 2-4 £3.25; 5-15 £4.10; pen £5.30). Rhododendrons only £3.60 or £2.60 if combined with a vist to Bowood House & Gardens on the same day. Children free. **Facilities:** 🅿 🍽 ✕ licensed ♿ (parking by arrangement) toilets for disabled shop ✖ (ex guide & hearing dogs) ◀

LACOCK LACKHAM COUNTRY PARK

Wiltshire College, Lackham SN15 2NY
Dir: (3m S of Chippenham, on A350. 6m S of M4 junct 17)
Map Ref: SU96
☎ **01249 466800** 📠 **01249 444474**
e-mail: daviaj@wiltscoll.ac.uk

Various visitor attractions are situated within the 210-hectare estate of Wiltshire College - Lackham. Thatched and refurbished farm buildings accommodate the farm museum and the grounds feature a walled garden, glasshouses, and a farm park. Also grown in this garden was the largest citron (large lemon) which earned a place in the Guinness Book of Records. There is also a self-guided picturesque woodland walk.

Times: Open Etr-Aug, Sun & BH Mon, Tue-Thu in Aug 10-5. (Last admission 4) **Fee:** ✱ £2 (concessions £1.50, up to 2 ch under 16 free). **Facilities:** 🅿 🍽 ♿ (wheelchair available, parking for disabled) toilets for disabled shop garden centre

LACOCK ABBEY, FOX TALBOT MUSEUM & VILLAGE

SN15 2LG
Dir: (3m S of Chippenham, E of A350, car park signed)
Map Ref: SU96
☎ **01249 730227 (abbey) 01249 730459**
📠 **01249 730501**
e-mail: courtsgarden@nationaltrust.org.uk

Lacock Abbey was founded in the 13th century, but at the Dissolution it was sold to William Sharington, who destroyed the church and turned the rest into a grand home, though there are remains of the fine cloister court. The abbey was the venue for a series of innovative photographic experiments by William Henry Fox Talbot, and in 1840 he discovered the negative/positive photographic process. The museum is dedicated to his life and work. The picturesque village, with its many attractive buildings, has changed little since the 13th century.

Times: Museum, Cloisters & Grounds, Mar-Oct, daily 11-5.30. Closed Good Fri. Abbey, 27 Mar-Oct daily, ex Tue, 1-5.30. Closed Good Fri. **Fee:** ✱ Museum, Abbey, Grounds & Cloisters £7 (ch £3.50) Family ticket £17.90 (2ad+2ch). Cloisters & Museum only £4.40 (ch £2.20) Family ticket £11.20. Abbey Cloisters & garden only £5.60 (ch £2.80) Family ticket £14.30. Museum (Winter) £3 (ch £1.50). Family £7.70. **Facilities:** 🅿 ♿ (manual wheelchairs, Braille/large print & audio guides) toilets for disabled shop ✖ ⛔

LONGLEAT LONGLEAT

The Estate Office BA12 7NW
Dir: (turn off A36 onto A362) **Map Ref:** *ST84*
☎ **01985 844400** 📄 **01985 844885**
e-mail: enquiries@longleat.co.uk

One of the most beautiful stately homes open to the public, Longleat House was built in 1580 by Sir John Thynne and has remained in the family ever since. It has many treasures, including paintings by Tintoretto and Wooton and exquisite Flemish tapestries. Longleat is also renowned for its safari park, where hundreds of animals can be seen in woodland and parkland settings, including the famous pride of lions, white tiger, wolves, rhesus monkeys and zebra. Other attractions are the hedge maze, adventure castle, Longleat Railway, pets' corner and safari boats.

Times: Open 12 Feb-6 Nov. Telephone for opening times
Fee: ✱ Longleat passport: £16 (ch 3-14 yrs & pen £13)
Facilities: 🅿 🍽 ✗ licensed ♿ (informative leaflet available or see website) toilets for disabled shop ✖ (kennels for safari) 🎫

MARLBOROUGH CROFTON BEAM ENGINES

Crofton Pumping Station, Crofton SN8 3DW
Dir: (signed from A4/A338/A346 & B3087 at Burbage)
Map Ref: *SU16*
☎ **01672 870300**
e-mail: enquiries@croftonbeamengines.org

The oldest working beam engine in the world still in its original building and still doing its original job, the Boulton and Watt 1812 can be found in this rural spot. Its companion is a Harvey's of Hayle of 1845. Both are steam driven, from a hand-stoked, coal-fired boiler, and pump water into the summit level of the Kennet and Avon Canal with a lift of 40 feet.

Times: Open daily 9 Apr 26 Sep, 10.30-5 (last entry 4.30). 'In Steam' Etr, BH wknds & last wknd of Jun, Jul & Sep **Fee:** ✱ In Steam wknd: £4.50 (ch £1, under 5 free & pen £3.50). Family ticket £10. Non-In Steam days £3 (ch £1, pen £2.50) Family £7 **Facilities:** 🅿 (charged) 🍽 ♿ (phone warden in advance, sighted guides provided) shop

SALISBURY THE MEDIEVAL HALL (SECRETS OF SALISBURY)

Cathedral Close SP1 2EY
Dir: (look for signs within Salisbury Cathedral Close)
Map Ref: *SU12*
☎ **01722 412472 & 324731** 📄 **01722 339983**
e-mail: medieval.hall@ntworld.com

Visit the historic 13th-century Medieval Hall and watch the fascinating 40-minute sound and picture guide to the city and region. A witty and informative soundtrack (sometimes available in other languages), specially composed music and some startling effects accompany hundreds of images to provide an insight into Salisbury's extraordinary past, the colourful city of today, and many of the attractions in the area. Enjoy refreshments while you watch. Contact the hall for full details of special events.

Times: Open Apr-Sep, from 11-5. Also open throughout year for pre-booked groups. Occasionally closed for special events.
Fee: ✱ £2.25 (ch under 18 £1.75, ch under 6 free). Family tickets available
Facilities: 🅿 (charged) 🍽 ♿ (ramp access) shop

SALISBURY CATHEDRAL

33 The Close SP1 2EJ
Dir: (S of city centre & Market Sq) *Map Ref:* SU12
☎ 01722 555120 ▤ 01722 555116
e-mail: visitors@salcath.co.uk

Built in one phase between 1220 and 1258, the cathedral is probably Britain's finest piece of medieval architecture. The spire is 123 metres tall, making it the tallest in England. The Chapter House displays a frieze depicting scenes from Genesis and Exodus, also the finest surviving Magna Carta. The choir continues a tradition that began around 800 years ago, with performances at daily services. The surrounding Cathedral Close contains two museums, two small stately homes and acres of lawn.

Times: Open all year, daily 7.15am-6.15pm; Jun-Aug, Mon-Sat 7.15am-7.15pm. **Fee:** ✱ Suggested voluntary donations: £3.80 (ch 5-17 £2, pen & students £3.30). Family £8.50. **Facilities:** P (100yds) ▆ ✗ licensed & (loop system, interpretative model for blind, wheelchairs) toilets for disabled shop (closed 25 Dec) ◀

STONEHENGE   STONEHENGE

SP4 7DE
Dir: (2m W of Amesbury on junct A303 and A344/A360)
Map Ref: SU14
☎ 01980 624715

Britain's greatest and best loved prehistoric monument is located on Salisbury Plain and has been designated a World Heritage Site. What visitors see today are the substantial remains of the last in a series of monuments erected between c3000 and 1600 BC. The dramatic stone circle is surrounded by more than 300 burial sites and other pre-historic remains. The Stonehenge project is planning to improve the site and add a visitor centre.

Times: Open all year, 16 Mar-May, daily 9.30-6; Jun-Aug, daily 9-7; Sep-15 Oct, daily 9.30-6. 16 Oct-15 Mar, daily 9.30-4. Closed 24-26 Dec & 1 Jan. **Fee:** ✱ £5.20 (ch £2.60, concessions £3.90). Prices & opening times relate to 2004, for further details phone or log onto www.english-heritage.org.uk/visits.
Facilities: P ▆ & shop ✗ (ex guide & hearing dogs) ⊞

STOURHEAD   STOURHEAD GARDEN & HOUSE

Stourhead Estate Office BA12 6QD
Dir: (At Stourton off B3092, 3m NW Mere A303, follow brown tourist signs) *Map Ref:* ST73
☎ 01747 841152 ▤ 01747 842005
e-mail: stourhead@nationaltrust.org.uk

An outstanding example of the English landscape style, this splendid garden was designed by Henry Moore II and laid out between 1741 and 1780. Classical temples, including the Parthenon and Temple of Apollo, are set around the central lake at the end of a series of vistas, which change as the visitor moves around the paths and through the mature woodland with its extensive collection of exotic trees.

Times: Garden open all year 9-7 (or dusk if earlier). House open 19 Mar-Oct ,11-5 (closed Wed & Thu); King Alfred tower open 19 Mar-Oct, daily 12-5. **Fee:** ✱ Garden & House £9.40, ch £4.50, Garden or House £5.40, ch £3, Garden only (Nov- end Feb) £4.10, ch £2, King Alfred Tower £2, ch £1. **Facilities:** P ▆ ✗ licensed & (wheelchairs, electric buggy, telephone in advance) toilets for disabled shop garden centre ✗ (ex in gardens Nov-Feb only) ✿ ◀

SWINDON STEAM - MUSEUM OF THE GREAT WESTERN RAILWAY

Kemble Dr SN2 2TA
Dir: (from M4 junct 16 & A420 follow brown signs to 'Outlet
Centre' and Museum) **Map Ref:** *SU18*
☎ **01793 466646** 📠 **01793 466615**
e-mail: steampostbox@swindon.gov.uk

Nominated for European Museum of the Year, this fascinating
attraction tells the story of the men and women who built,
operated and travelled on the Great Western Railway. Hands-on
displays, world-famous locomotives, archive film footage and the
testimonies of ex-railway workers bring the story to life. A
reconstructed station platform, posters and holiday memorabilia
recreate the glamour and excitement of the golden age of steam.
Located next door to the McArthurGlen Designer Outlet, Steam
offers a great day out for all. Good value group packages, special
events and exhibitions, shop and café.

Times: Open daily 10-5. Closed 25-26 Dec & 1
Jan **Fee:** ✱ £5.95 (ch £3.80, pen £3.90) Family
ticket £14.70 (2ad+2ch) **Facilities:** 🅿 (charged)
☕ ♿ (wheelchair or scooter can be pre-booked)
toilets for disabled shop ✈ (ex guide dogs) 💳

TEFFONT MAGNA FARMER GILES FARMSTEAD

SP3 5QY
Dir: (11m W of Stonehenge, off A303 to Teffont. Follow brown
tourist signs) **Map Ref:** *ST93*
☎ **01722 716338** 📠 **01722 716993**
e-mail: tdeane6995@aol.com

At this 40-acre working farm you can learn about farming and
enjoy visiting the animals. There are indoor and outdoor play areas
with a straw stack and bouncy castle, tractor tours, exhibitions, a
pets' corner and the opportunity to feed the lambs, groom a
donkey or milk a cow. The landscaped grounds include a lake and
waterfall, plus nature walks such as the beech belt. Facilities
extend to a barn restaurant, bar, picnic area and gift shop.

Times: Open 18 Mar-5 Nov, daily 10-6, wknds in winters, 10-dusk.
Party bookings all year. **Fee:** ✱ £3.95 (ch £2.85, under 2's free & pen
£3.50) Family ticket £13. **Facilities:** 🅿 ✗ licensed ♿ (complete access
for disabled/wheelchairs available for use) toilets for disabled shop 💳

TISBURY OLD WARDOUR CASTLE

SP3 6RR
Dir: (2m SW) **Map Ref:** *ST92*

This 14th-century castle was built by John, 5th Lord Lovel and
stands in a romantic lakeside setting. During the Civil War
(1642-48) gunpowder mines were laid in a drainage tunnel
beneath the castle and when they exploded a large part of the
castle collapsed. The damage caused was considered beyond
repair. Today landscaped grounds and an elaborate rockwork
grotto surround the unusual hexogonal ruins. Scenes from *Robin
Hood, Prince of Thieves*, starring Kevin Costner were filmed here.

Times: Open all year, Apr-Jun & Sep, daily 10-5;
Jul-Aug 10-6; Oct 10-4; Nov-Mar, Sat-Sun 10-4
(Closed 24-26 Dec & 1 Jan). **Fee:** ✱ £2.80
(ch £1.40, concessions £2.10). Prices and opening
times relate to 2004, for further details phone or
log onto www.englishheritage.org.uk/visits
Facilities: 🅿 ♿ ♿

WESTBURY BROKERSWOOD COUNTRY PARK

Brokerswood BA13 4EH
Dir: (off A36 at Bell Inn, Standerwick. Follow brown signs)
Map Ref: ST85
☎ 01373 822238 & 823880 🖹 01373 858474
e-mail: woodland.park@virgin.net

Brokerswood Country Park's nature walk leads through 80 acres of woodlands, with a lake and resident wildfowl. Facilities include a woodland visitor centre (covering wildlife and forestry), two children's adventure playgrounds (Easter to October school holidays and weekends only), guided walks and the woodland railway, which is over a third of a mile long.

Times: Open all year; Park open daily 10-5. Closed 25-26 Dec & 1 Jan. Ring for museum opening hours. **Fee:** ✳ £3 (ch 3-16yrs £2, pen £2.50) **Facilities:** 🅿 ☕ ♿ (ramp access to cafe) toilets for disabled shop 💳

WILTON (NEAR SALISBURY) WILTON HOUSE

SP2 0BJ
Dir: (3m W of Salisbury, on A30, 10m from Stonehenge & A303)
Map Ref: SU03
☎ 01722 746720 & 746729(24 hr line) 🖹 01722 744447
e-mail: tourism@wiltonhouse.com

This fabulous Palladian mansion amazes visitors with its treasures, including magnificent art, fine furniture and interiors by Inigo Jones. The traditional and modern gardens, some designed by the 17th Earl, are fabulous throughout the season and continue to delight visitors, while the adventure playground is a firm favourite with children.

Times: Open 2 Apr-Oct, daily, 10.30-5.30. (Last admission 4.30). House closed Mon, ex BHs. **Fee:** ✳ £9.75 (ch 5-15 £5.50, students & pen £8). Family ticket £24. **Facilities:** 🅿 ☕ ♿ (induction loop) toilets for disabled shop garden centre ✖ (ex service dogs) 💳

The world-famous stones of Stonehenge

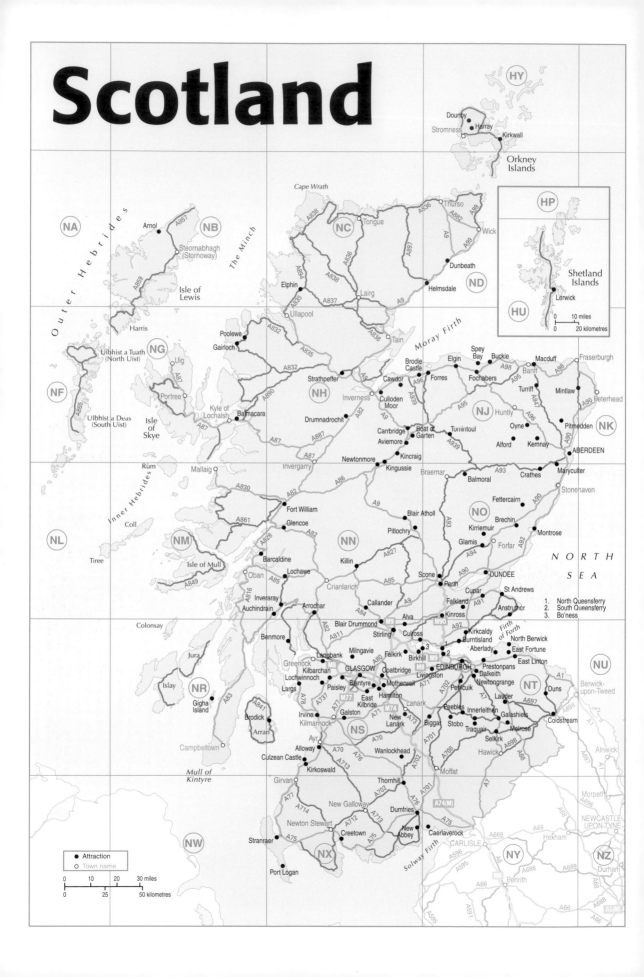

Go west and north for grandeur: the broad beaches where Atlantic waves crash after a 3,000-mile journey; classic mountains (the highest in Britain); islands of romance and unparalleled beauty; and remote, haunting landscapes.

Spread across the centre of the country and up the east coast are the commercial and cultural dynamos of Scotland – Dundee, Edinburgh, Glasgow and Aberdeen – thrust by the Enlightenment and the Industrial Revolution onto the forefront of the world stage. Nowadays, Scottish cities jostle for attention, with multitudes of attractions, with Edinburgh Castle still top of the list. Everywhere, high-tech businesses such as oil and electronics are comfortable bedfellows with the legacy of a dramatic past.

Further south lie the relatively unvisited Southern Uplands, great rolling ranges where turbulent times of border tension between powerful neighbours cannot be forgotten.

Local Events & Festivals 2005

March 25-28 Edinburgh Easter Festival, free events in Princes Street Garden and Easter Sunday Parade

April 2-12 Edinburgh International Science Festival, various venues

April 30 Beltane Fire Festival, Carlton Hill, Edinburgh

May 19-30 Perth Festival of the Arts

May 24-30 Bank of Scotland Children's International Theatre Festival, Edinburgh

June 3-12 Highland Festival, in and around Inverness: dance, music, arts, culture

June 10-26 West End Festival, Glasgow: theatre, music, exhibitions, film, markets and Midsummer Carnival

June 17-22 St Magnus Festival, Orkney: music, drama, dance and visual arts

June 23-26 Royal Highland Show, Ingliston, Edinburgh

August 4-14 Aberdeen International Youth Festival, various venues

August 5-27 Edinburgh Military Tattoo

late August-early September Largs Viking Festival, Largs, Ayrshire

September 3 Braemar Gathering, The Princess Royal and Duke of Fife Memorial Park, Braemar

September 3-4 Edinburgh Mela

September 10 RAF Leuchars Airshow, Leuchars, Fife

October 21-30 Scottish International Storytelling Festival, Edinburgh

December 29-Jan 1 Edinburgh's Hogmanay Festival

Above: The cliffs of St Abb's Head

ABERDEEN   CRUICKSHANK BOTANIC GARDEN

University of Aberdeen, St Machar Dr AB24 3UU
Dir: (enter by gate in Chanonry, in Old Aberdeen)
Map Ref: NJ90
☎ 01224 272704   📄 01224 272703
e-mail: pss@abdn.ac.uk

FREE

Developed at the end of the 19th century, the 11 acres include
rock and water gardens, a rose garden, a fine herbaceous border,
an arboretum and a patio garden. There are collections of spring
bulbs, gentians and alpine plants, and a fine array of trees and
shrubs. The garden is part of the University of Aberdeen and is
used for teaching and research purposes.

Times: Open all year, Mon-Fri 9-4.30; also Sat &
Sun, May-Sep 2-5. **Facilities:** P (200mtrs) & ✈

SATROSPHERE ("HANDS-ON" SCIENCE & TECHNOLOGY CENTRE)

179 Constitution St AB24 5TU
Dir: (located very close to Beach Esplanade. Follow signs to fun
beach, then attraction) *Map Ref:* NJ90
☎ 01224 640340   📄 01224 622211
e-mail: info@satrosphere.net

Satrosphere, the Discovery Place, is different from many museums
or exhibition centres. It is an interactive centre where everything is
'hands-on'. Displays aren't locked in glass cases and there are
certainly no 'do not touch' signs. The emphasis is on doing and
finding out, not just looking and standing back. There are over
100 exhibits, interactive shows, workshops and special weekend
events.

Times: Open all year, Mon-Sat 10-5, Sun 11.30-5.
Closed 25-26 Dec & 1-2 Jan. **Fee:** ✱ £5.25
(under 3's free, ch & concessions £3.75).
Facilities: P 🍽 & toilets for disabled shop
✈ (ex guide dogs) 🛍

ALFORD   ALFORD VALLEY RAILWAY

AB33 8AD
Dir: (A944 Alford Village) *Map Ref:* NJ51
☎ 019755 62326 & 62811   📄 019755 63182

This narrow-gauge passenger railway runs for approximately a
mile between Alford and Haughton Park Station, a scenic route
with views of Bennachie. At the park there is a large play and
picnic area with walkways down to the River Don. The railway line
offers diesel traction and steam on peak weekends. Exhibitions
are also featured.

Times: Open Apr, May & Sep wknds 1-5, Jun-Aug
daily from 1pm (30 min service). Party bookings
also available at other times. **Fee:** *Prices not
confirmed for 2005* **Facilities:** P & (ramps at
station platforms) toilets for disabled shop

BALMORAL *BALMORAL CASTLE GROUNDS & EXHIBITION*

AB35 5TB
Dir: (on A93 between Ballater & Braemar) *Map Ref:* NO29
☎ 013397 42534 🖹 013397 42034
e-mail: info@balmoralcastle.com

Queen Victoria and Prince Albert first rented Balmoral Castle in 1848, and Prince Albert bought the property four years later. He commissioned William Smith to build a new castle, which was completed by 1856 and is still the Royal Family's Highland residence. Country walks and pony trekking can be enjoyed, and an exhibition of paintings and other works of art can be seen in the castle ballroom, together with a travel and carriage exhibition and a wildlife exhibition.

Times: Open Apr-Jul, daily 10-5. **Facilities:** P (100yds) ☕ ♿ (wheelchairs & battricars available, reserved parking) toilets for disabled shop 🐕 (ex guide dogs/in grounds) ▰

CRATHES *CRATHES CASTLE & GARDEN*

AB31 5QJ
Dir: (On A93, 3m E of Banchory) *Map Ref:* NO79
☎ 01330 844525 🖹 01330 844797
e-mail: crathes@nts.org.uk

This impressive 16th-century castle with magnificent interiors has royal associations dating from 1323. Of particular interest are the Jacobean painted ceilings uncovered in 1877. There is a large walled garden and a notable collection of unusual plants, including yew hedges dating from 1702. The grounds contain six nature trails, one suitable for disabled visitors, and an adventure playground.

Times: Open. Castle & Visitor Centre: Apr-Sep, daily 10-5.30, Oct daily 10-4.30. To help enjoy your visit & for safety reasons, admission to the castle is by timed ticket (limited numbers: entry may be delayed). Garden & grounds all year, daily 9-sunset. Times may change for 2005 please telephone or check on www.nts.org.uk **Fee:** ✱ £9 (concessions £6.50) Admission free to NTS members. For other details please phone 0131 243 9387 or check website.
Facilities: P ✕ licensed ♿ (tape for visually impaired) toilets for disabled shop 🐕 (ex guide dogs) ♨

FETTERCAIRN *FASQUE*

AB30 1DN
Dir: (0.5m N on B974) *Map Ref:* NO67
☎ 01561 340569 & 340202 🖹 01561 340325 & 340569

Fasque has been the home of the Gladstone family since 1829, and W E Gladstone, four times Prime Minister, lived here from 1830 to 1851. There are impressive state rooms and a handsome, sweeping staircase, as well as extensive servants' quarters to be seen. Red deer and Soay sheep are resident in the spacious park.

Times: ✱ Open Jul-Aug, daily 11-5. (Closed 5.30). Groups by arrangement. **Facilities:** P ☕ ♿ (wheelchairs available) shop 🐕

KEMNAY   CASTLE FRASER

AB51 7LD
Dir: (off A944, 4m N of Dunecht) *Map Ref:* NJ71
☎ 01330 833463
e-mail: castlefraser@nts.org.uk

The massive Z-plan castle was built between 1575 and 1636 and is one of the grandest of the Castles of Mar. The interior was remodelled in 1838 and decoration and furnishings of that period survive in some of the rooms. A formal garden inside the old walled garden, estate trails, a children's play area and a programme of concerts are among the attractions.

Times: Open Apr-Jun & Sep, Fri-Tue 12-5.30, Jul-Aug, daily 11-5.30. Times may change for 2005 please telephone or check on www.nts.org.uk **Fee:** ✱ £7 (concessions £5.25) Groups adult £5.60, child £1, please book groups in advance. Admission free to NTS members. For other details please phone 0131 243 9387 **Facilities:** 🅿 ☕ & shop garden centre ✖ (ex guide dogs, certain areas) ♨

MACDUFF   MACDUFF MARINE AQUARIUM

11 High Shore AB44 1SL
Dir: (off A947 to Macduff, attraction signed) *Map Ref:* NJ76
☎ 01261 833369   📄 01261 831052
e-mail: macduff.aquarium@aberdeenshire.gov.uk

Exciting displays at this aquarium feature local sealife. The central exhibit, unique in Britain, holds a living kelp reef. Divers feed the fish in this tank. Other displays include an estuary exhibit, splash tank, rock pools, deep reef tank and ray pool. Young visitors especially enjoy the touch pools. There are talks, video presentations and feeding shows throughout the week.

Times: Open 10-5 daily (last admission 4.15). Closed 25-26 Dec & 31 Dec-2 Jan **Fee:** ✱ £4.50 (ch £2, concessions £2.50). Family ticket (2ad+2ch) £11.50. Groups 10+ **Facilities:** 🅿 & (audio tour for visually impaired) toilets for disabled shop ✖ (ex guide dogs) 🍴

MARYCULTER   STORYBOOK GLEN

AB12 5FT
Dir: (5m W of Aberdeen on B9077) *Map Ref:* NO89
☎ 01224 732941   📄 01224 732941

This is a child's fantasy land, where favourite nursery rhyme and fairytale characters are brought to life in life-size model form. Grown-ups can enjoy the nostalgia and also the 20 acres of Deeside country, full of flowers, plants, trees and waterfalls. Also on site is Dingle Dell, the new garden centre, and a large restaurant.

Times: Open Mar-Oct, daily 10-6; Nov-Feb, daily 10-4. **Fee:** ✱ £4.15 (ch £3.10, pen £3.25). **Facilities:** 🅿 ☕ ✖ licensed & toilets for disabled shop garden centre ✖ (ex guide dogs) 🍴

MINTLAW ABERDEENSHIRE FARMING MUSEUM

Aden Country Park AB42 5FQ
Dir: (1m W of Mintlaw on A950) *Map Ref:* NJ94
☎ **01771 622906** 📄 **01771 622884**
e-mail: **heritage@aberdeenshire.gov.uk**   FREE

The farm museum is housed in 19th-century farm buildings, once part of the estate which now makes up the Aden Country Park. Two centuries of farming history and innovation are illustrated, and the story of the estate is also told. The reconstructed farm of Hareshowe shows how a family in the northeast farmed during the 1950s. Access is by guided tour only.

Times: Open May-Sep, daily 11-4.30; Apr & Oct, wknds only noon-4.30. (Last admission 30 mins before closing). Park open all year, Apr-Sep 7-10, winter 7-7. **Facilities:** 🅿 (charged) 🍵 ♿ (sensory garden) toilets for disabled shop 🐕 (ex guide dogs)

OYNE ARCHAEOLINK

Berryhill AB52 6QP
Dir: (1m off A96 on B9002) *Map Ref:* NJ62
☎ **01464 851500** 📄 **01464 851544**
e-mail: **info@archaeolink.co.uk**

A stunning audio-visual show, the Myths and Legends Gallery and a whole range of interpretation techniques help visitors to explore what it was like to live 6,000 years ago. In addition there are landscaped walkways and outdoor activity areas, including an Iron Age farm, Roman marching camp and Stone Age settlement in the 40-acre park. Enjoy daily hands-on activities for all ages, guided tours with costume guides or relax in the coffee shop. Special events are held regularly at weekends.

Times: Open all year, daily 11-5. **Fee:** ✱ £4.75 (ch 3-16 £3.25, concessions £4.25) Family from £11.25 **Facilities:** 🅿 🍵 ✕ licensed ♿ (induction loop in theatre, wheelchair) toilets for disabled shop 🐕 (ex guide dogs) 💳

PITMEDDEN PITMEDDEN GARDEN

AB41 7PD
Dir: (1m W of Pitmedden on A920) *Map Ref:* NJ82
☎ **01651 842352** 📄 **01651 843188**
e-mail: **aclipson@nts.scot.demon.co.uk**

This fine walled garden was originally laid out by Sir Alexander Seton, 1st Baronet of Pimedden in 1675, and has been authentically restored, with sundials, pavilions and fountains dotted among the parterres. The estate extends to 100 acres and includes the Museum of Farming Life, a visitor centre, herb garden, ponds and a woodland walk.

Times: Open May-Sep, daily 10-5.30. Grounds: all year, daily. Times may change for 2005 please telephone or check on www.nts.org.uk **Fee:** ✱ £5 (concessions £3.75) Family ticket £13.50. Groups adult £4 (ch/school £1). Please book groups in advance. Admission free to NTS members. For other details please phone 0131 243 9387 or check website. **Facilities:** 🅿 🍵 ♿ (2 wheelchairs available) toilets for disabled shop 🐶

TURRIFF FYVIE CASTLE

Fyvie AB53 8JS
Dir: (8m SE of Turriff on A947) *Map Ref:* NJ75
☎ 01651 891266 🖹 01651 891107
e-mail: aclipson@nts.scot.demon.co.uk

This superb castle, founded in the 13th century, has five towers, each built in a different century, and is one of the grandest examples of Scottish Baronial architecture. It contains the finest wheel stair in Scotland and a 17th-century morning room, lavishly furnished in Edwardian style. The collection of portraits is exceptional, and there are also displays of arms and armour and tapestries.

Times: Open Apr-Jun & Sep, Fri-Tue 12-5; Jul-Aug, daily 11-5. Grounds all year, daily, 9.30-sunset. Times may change for 2005 please telephone or check on www.nts.org.uk **Fee:** ✱ £7 (concessions £5.25) Family ticket £19. Groups adult £5.60 (ch/school £1). Please book groups in advance. Admission free to NTS members. For other details please phone 0131 243 9387 **Facilities:** 🅿 ☕ ♿ (small lift, Braille sheets) toilets for disabled shop ✖ (ex guide dogs) 🐾

BRECHIN PICTAVIA VISITOR CENTRE

DD9 6RL
Dir: (off A90) *Map Ref:* NO66
☎ 01356 626813 🖹 01356 626814
e-mail: renniedg@angus.gov.uk

At Pictavia you can find out about the ancient pagan nation of the Picts, who lived in Scotland nearly 2,000 years ago. Visitors can learn about Pictish culture, art and religion through film, interactive displays and music. Pictavia is set in the Brechin Castle Park, where there are nature and farm trails, a pets' corner, an adventure playground, coffee shop and garden centre.

Times: Open daily, Apr-Sep, Mon-Sat 9.30-5.30, Sun 10.30-5.30; Oct-Mar, Mon-Sat 9.30-5, Sun 10-5. Closed 25-26 Dec & 1 Jan **Fee:** £3.25 (ch & concessions £2.25) **Facilities:** 🅿 ☕ ✖ licensed ♿ toilets for disabled shop garden centre 🛒

GLAMIS ANGUS FOLK MUSEUM

Kirkwynd Cottages DD8 1RT
Dir: (off A94, in Glamis) *Map Ref:* NO34
☎ 01307 840288 🖹 01307 840233

A row of stone-roofed, late 18th-century estate cottages now houses the splendid Angus Folk Collection.The domestic equipment and cottage furniture on show reflect Scottish rural life over a period of 200 years. Exhibits include reconstructions of a traditional cottage, a farm bothy and a minister's parlour. Across the wynd, an Angus stone steading houses 'The Life on the Land' exhibition.

Times: Open Apr-Jun & Sep, Fri-Tue 12-5; Jul & Aug 12-5. Times may change for 2005 please telephone or check on www.nts.org.uk **Fee:** ✱ £5 (concessions £3.75) Groups adult £4 (ch/school group £1), groups please book in advance. Family ticket £13.50. Admission free to NTS members. For other details please phone 0131 243 9387 or check web **Facilities:** 🅿 ♿ toilets for disabled ✖ (ex guide dogs) 🐾

Angus

GLAMIS CASTLE

DD8 1RJ
Dir: (5m W of Forfar on A94) **Map Ref:** *NO34*
☎ **01307 840393** 📄 **01307 840733**
e-mail: enquires@glamis-castle.co.uk

Glamis Castle is the family home of the Earls of Strathmore and Kinghorne and has been a royal residence since 1372. It is the childhood home of the late Queen Mother, the birthplace of the late Princess Margaret and the setting for Shakespeare's play *Macbeth*. The castle is set in lovely grounds with an Italian garden, a mass of rhododendrons and azaleas in summer, a pinetum, and daffodils lining the mile-long avenue leading up to the castle in spring. There is also a nature trail by the banks of the Glamis Burn.

Times: Open Mar-Oct, 10-6. (Last admission 4.30). **Fee:** ✱ Castle & grounds £6.80 (ch £3.70, pen & students £5.50). Family ticket £19, Grounds only £3.50 (ch, pen & students £2.50). Group 20+ **Facilities:** 🅿 ✗ licensed & (castle tour not suitable due to stairs) toilets for disabled shop ✖ (ex in grounds, guide dogs) ◀

KIRRIEMUIR   J M BARRIE'S BIRTHPLACE

9 Brechin Rd DD8 4BX
Dir: (on A90/A926, 6m NW of Forfar) **Map Ref:** *NO35*
☎ **01575 572646**
e-mail: acllpson@nts.scot.demon.co.uk

The creator of Peter Pan, Sir James Barrie, was born in Kirriemuir in 1860. The upper floors of No 9 Brechin Road are furnished as they may have been when Barrie lived there, and the adjacent house, No 11, houses an exhibition about him. The wash-house outside was his first 'theatre' and gave him the idea for Wendy's house in *Peter Pan*.

Times: Open Apr-Jun & Sep, Fri-Tue 12-5; Jul-Aug, daily 12-5. Times may change for 2005 please telephone or check on www.nts.org.uk **Fee:** ✱ £5 (concessions £3.75) Groups adult £4 (ch/school £1), please book groups in advance. Family ticket £13.50. Admission free to NTS members. For other details please phone 0131 243 9387 or check web site **Facilities:** 🅿 (100yds) 📖 & (stairlift, audio programmes) shop ✖ (ex guide dogs) ♟

MONTROSE   HOUSE OF DUN

DD10 9LQ
Dir: (on A935, 3m W of Montrose) **Map Ref:** *NO75*
☎ **01674 810264** 📄 **01674 810722**
e-mail: houseofdun@nts.org.uk

This Georgian house, overlooking the Montrose Basin, was built for Lord Dun in 1730 and is noted for the exuberant plasterwork of the interior. Family portraits, fine furniture and porcelain are on display, and royal mementos connected with a daughter of King William IV and the actress Mrs Jordan, who lived here in the 19th century. Outside there is a walled garden and woodland walks.

Times: Open House: Apr-Jun, & Sep, Fri-Tue 12-5, Jul-Aug, daily 12-5. Garden & grounds all year daily 9.30-sunset. Times may change for 2005 please telephone or check on www.nts.org.uk **Fee:** ✱ £7 (concessions £5.25) Family ticket £19. Groups adult £5.60 (ch/school £1). Please book groups in advance. Admission free to NTS members. For other details please phone 0131 243 9387 or check web site **Facilities:** 🅿 ✗ & (Braille sheets, house wheelchair & stair lift) toilets for disabled shop ✖ (ex guide dogs) ♟

269

ARROCHAR ARGYLL FOREST PARK

Forest Enterprise, Ardgartan Visitor Centre G83 7AR
Dir: (on A83 at foot of "The Rest and Be Thankful")
Map Ref: NN20
☎ **01301 702597** 📄 **01301 702597** FREE
e-mail: robin.kennedy@forestry.gsl.gov.uk

The Argyll Forest Park extends over a large area of mountains, glens, lochs and forest, and is noted for its rugged beauty. It was the first Forest Park to be established for public enjoyment, as far back as 1935. Numerous forest walks and picnic sites allow for plenty of exploration; the arboretum walks and the route between the Younger Botanic Gardens and Puck's Glen are particularly lovely.

Times: Open all year. **Facilities:** 🅿 shop 🖼

AUCHINDRAIN AUCHINDRAIN TOWNSHIP-OPEN AIR MUSEUM

PA32 8XN
Dir: (6m SW of Inverarary on A83) *Map Ref:* NN00
☎ **01499 500235**

Auchindrain is an ancient West Highland township, the only communal tenancy township to have survived on its centuries-old site. The town's buildings have been furnished and equipped to present a fascinating glimpse of Highland life during various historical periods. Facilities on the site include a visitor centre, picnic area and gift shop.

Times: Open Apr-Sep, daily 10-5. **Fee:** £4.50 (ch £2.20, pen £3.50). Family ticket £12. **Facilities:** 🅿 shop

BARCALDINE SCOTTISH SEA LIFE SANCTUARY

PA37 1SE
Dir: (10m N of Oban on A828 towards Fort William)
Map Ref: NM94
☎ **01631 720386** 📄 **01631 720529**
e-mail: obansealife@merlinentertainments.biz

Set in one of Scotland's most picturesque locations on the shores of Loch Creran, the Scottish Sea Life Sanctuary provides dramatic views of native undersea life, including stingrays, seals, octopus and catfish. There are daily talks and feeding demonstrations, and during the summer young seals can be viewed prior to their release back into the wild. Recent additions are the otters in their large naturally landscaped enclosure with a deep diving pool and underwater viewing. Facilities include a children's play park, nature trail, restaurant and gift shop.

Times: Open all year, mid Feb-Nov, daily 10-5. Dec & Jan; Sat-Sun & school hols only **Fee:** £7.95 (ch £5.50, pen £6.50). Group 15+. **Facilities:** 🅿 🍽 ✕ ♿ (assistance available for wheelchairs) toilets for disabled shop ✈ (ex guide dogs) 🖼

BENMORE BENMORE BOTANIC GARDEN

PA23 8QU
Dir: (7m N of Dunoon on A815) *Map Ref:* NS18
☎ 01369 706261 📄 01369 706369
e-mail: benmore@rbge.org.uk

From the formal gardens through the hillside woodlands, follow the paths to a stunning viewpoint with a spectacular outlook across the garden and the Holy Loch to the Firth of Clyde and beyond. Amongst many highlights at Benmore are the stately conifers, the magnificent avenue of giant redwoods, and an extensive magnolia and rhododendron collection.

Times: Open Mar & Oct daily 10-5, Apr-Sep daily 10-6 **Fee:** ✱ £3.50 (ch £1, concessions £3). Family £8. Party rates. **Facilities:** 🅿 ☕ ✕ licensed ♿ toilets for disabled shop garden centre ✖ (ex guide dogs) ◀

GIGHA ISLAND *ACHAMORE GARDENS*

PA41 7AD
Map Ref: NR64
☎ 01583 505267 & 505254 📄 01583 505244
e-mail: william@isle-of-gigha.co.uk

These wonderful woodland gardens of rhododendrons and azaleas were created by Sir James Horlick, who bought the little island of Gigha in 1944. Many of the plants were brought in laundry baskets from his former home in Berkshire. Sub-tropical plants flourish in the rich soil and virtually frost-free climate, and there is a walled garden for some of the finer specimens.

Times: ✱ Open all year, daily. **Facilities:** 🅿 ♿

INVERARAY INVERARAY CASTLE

PA32 8XE
Dir: (on A83 Glasgow to Campbeltown road) *Map Ref:* NN00
☎ 01499 302203 📄 01499 302421
e-mail: enquiries@inveraray-castle.com

The third Duke of Argyll engaged the London architect Roger Morris to build the castle that you see today in 1743; in the process the old Burgh of Inveraray was demolished and a new town built nearby. The 5th Duke commissioned the magnificent interiors, which were completed between 1770 and 1789. The great armoury hall and staterooms are of particular note.

Times: Open 1st Sat in Apr-last Sun in Oct. Apr-May, Oct, Mon-Thu & Sat 10-1 & 2-5.45. Sun 1-5.45; Jun-Sep, Mon-Sat 10-5.45, Sun 1-5.45. (Last admission 12.30 & 5). **Fee:** ✱ £5.90 (ch under 16 £3.90, concessions £4.90) Family ticket £16. School parties. Groups 20+. **Facilities:** 🅿 ☕ ♿ toilets for disabled shop ✖ (ex guide dogs) ◀

Argyll & Bute continued

INVERARAY JAIL

Church Square PA32 8TX
Dir: (on A82/A83 Campbeltown road) *Map Ref:* NN00
☎ 01499 302381 📄 01499 302195
e-mail: inverarayjail@btclick.com

Enter Inveraray Jail and step back in time. See furnished cells and experience prison sounds and smells. Ask the 'prisoner' how to pick oakum; turn the heavy handle of an original crank machine, and take 40 winks in a hammock or listen to Matron's tales of day-to-day prison life. Visit the magnificent 1820 courtroom and hear trials in progress. Imaginative exhibitions including 'Torture, Death and Damnation' and 'In Prison Today'. A recent addition is a fully preserved 'Black Maria' built in 1891.

Times: Open all year, Nov-Mar, daily 10-5 (last admisssion 4); Apr-Oct, daily 9.30-6 (last admission 5). Closed 25 Dec & 1 Jan.
Fee: £5.75 (ch £2.80, pen £3.75). Family ticket £15.70. **Facilities:** P (100 yds) & (wheelchair ramp at rear, induction loop in courtroom) toilets for disabled shop 🎧

LOCHAWE CRUACHAN POWER STATION

Visitor Centre, Dalmally PA33 1AN
Dir: (A85 18m E of Oban) *Map Ref:* NN12
☎ 01866 822618 📄 01866 822509
e-mail: visit.cruachan@scottishpower.com

This is an extraordinary technical achievement - a vast cavern hidden one kilometre inside Ben Cruachan, which contains a 400,000-kilowatt hydro-electric power station, driven by water drawn from a high-level reservoir up the mountain. A 30-minute guided tour takes you inside the mountain and reveals the generators in their underground hideaway.

Times: Open Etr-Nov, daily 9.30-5 (last tour 4.15). Aug 9.30-6 (last tour 5.15) **Fee:** £4 (ch 6-16 £1.50, concessions £3)
Facilities: P 🅿 & toilets for disabled shop ✕ (ex guide dogs) 🎧

EDINBURGH CAMERA OBSCURA & WORLD OF ILLUSIONS

Castlehill, Royal Mile EH1 2ND
Dir: (next to Edinburgh Castle) *Map Ref:* NT27
☎ 0131 226 3709 📄 0131 225 4239
e-mail: info@camera-obscura.co.uk

A unique view of Edinburgh - as the lights go down, a brilliant moving image of the surrounding city appears. The scene changes as a guide operates the camera's system of revolving lenses and mirrors. The Magic Gallery is a wonder of light and illusion, and there are hologram displays in the Light Fantastic. Edinburgh Vision images range from Victorian 3D cityscapes to live viewcams, which you can control.

Times: ✻ Open all year, daily, Apr-Oct 9.30-6; Nov-Mar 10-5. Closed 25 Dec. Open later Jul-Aug, phone for details. **Facilities:** P (300mtrs) shop ✕ (ex guide dogs) 🎧

DYNAMIC EARTH

Holyrood Rd EH8 8AS
Dir: (on edge of Holyrood Park, opposite Palace of Holyrood House) *Map Ref:* NT27
☎ **0131 550 7800** ◈ **0131 550 7801**
e-mail: enquiries@dynamicearth.co.uk

Experience the phenomenal force of nature at this exciting attraction with interactive and hands-on exhibits throughout. Dynamic Earth explores the extremes of planet Earth. Here you can travel back in time to witness the Big Bang and feel the earth shaken by an erupting volcano; fly over glaciers and feel the chill of polar ice, and get caught in a tropical rainstorm.

Times: Open Apr-Oct daily & Nov-Mar Wed-Sat 10-5, (last entry 3.50); Jul-Aug daily, 10-6, (last entry 4.50). Closed 24-26 Dec. **Fee:** £8.95 (ch £5.45). Family ticket (2ad+2ch) £24.50. **Facilities:** 🅿 (charged) 🍽 ✗ licensed ♿ (audio guides, large print gallery guides) toilets for disabled shop ✖ (ex guide dogs) ◀

EDINBURGH CASTLE

EH1 2NG
Map Ref: NT27
☎ **0131 225 9846**

This historic stronghold stands on the precipitous crag of Castle Rock. One of the oldest parts is the 11th-century chapel of the saintly Queen Margaret, but most of the present castle evolved later, during its stormy history of sieges and wars, and was altered again in Victorian times. The Scottish crown and other royal regalia are displayed in the Crown Room. Also notable is the Scottish National War Memorial.

Times: Open all year, Apr-Sep daily 9.30-6.30; Oct-Mar 9.30-4.30. Closed 25-26 Dec & 1-2 Jan. **Fee:** ✱ £9.50 (ch £2, concessions £7). Prices valid until 2 Jan 2005. Please phone for further details. **Facilities:** 🅿 (charged) 🍽 ✗ licensed ♿ (free transport to top of Castle Hill lift) toilets for disabled shop ✖ ◀

THE EDINBURGH DUNGEON

31 Market St EH1 1QB
Dir: (close to Waverly Train Station) *Map Ref:* NT27
☎ **0131 240 1000 & 240 1002** ◈ **0131 240 1002**
e-mail: edinburghdungeon@merlinentertainments.biz

From the team that brought you The London Dungeon, there comes a Scottish 'feast of fun with history's horrible bits'. A mixture of live actors, rides, shows and special effects takes the brave visitor back into a dark past that includes such delights as the 18th-century Judgement of Sinners, the 17th-century Plague, and the new attraction, Clan Wars, which attempts to recreate the horror of the Glencoe Massacre of 1692.

Times: Open all year. Nov-Feb 11-4, wknds 10.30-4.30, Mar 10.30-4.30, Apr-Jun 10-5, Jul-Aug 10-7, Sep-Oct 10-5. Closed 25 Dec. **Fee:** ✱ £9.95 (ch 4-9 £4.95, ch 10-14 £6.95) **Facilities:** 🅿 (100mtrs) (metered bays limited to 1-2hrs) ♿ toilets for disabled shop ✖ (ex guide dogs) ◀

EDINBURGH ZOO

Murrayfield EH12 6TS
Dir: (3m W of city centre on A8 towards Glasgow)
Map Ref: NT27
☎ 0131 334 9171 ▤ 0131 314 0382
e-mail: marketing@rzss.org.uk

Scotland's largest wildlife attraction, Edinburgh Zoo is set in 80 acres of leafy hillside parkland, just ten minutes from the city centre. With over 1,000 animals ranging from the tiny poison arrow frog to massive white rhinos, including many threatened species. See the world's largest penguin pool with underwater viewing, and the Darwin Maze, based on the theme of evolution.

Times: Open all year, Apr-Sep, daily 9-6; Oct & Mar, daily 9-5; Nov-Feb, daily 9-4.30. **Fee:** £8.50 (ch 3-14 & disabled £5.50, student £6.50, pen £6). **Facilities:** ▣ (charged) ▩ ✗ licensed ♿ (wheelchair loan free, 1 helper free - phone in advance) toilets for disabled shop ✖ (ex guide dogs) ◀

GEORGIAN HOUSE

7 Charlotte Square EH2 4DR
Dir: (2 mins walk W end of Princes St) *Map Ref:* NT27
☎ 0131 226 3318 ▤ 0131 226 3318
e-mail: thegeorgianhouse@nts.org.uk

The house is part of Robert Adam's splendid north side of Charlotte Square, the epitome of Edinburgh New Town architecture. The lower floors of No 7 have been restored in the style of the early 1800s, when the house was new. There are also videos of life in the New Town, and this house in particular.

Times: Open Apr-Oct, daily 10-5; Mar & Nov-24 Dec daily 11-3. Times may change for 2005 please telephone or check on www.nts.org.uk **Fee:** ✱ £5 (concessions £3.75) Family ticket £13.50. Groups adult £4 (ch/school £1). Please book groups in advance. Admission free for NTS members. For other details please phone 0131 243 9387 or check web site. **Facilities:** ▣ (100 yds) (meters, disabled directly outside) ♿ (induction loop, Braille guide) shop ✖ (ex guide dogs) ❦

MUSEUM OF CHILDHOOD

42 High Street, Royal Mile, EH1 1TG
Dir: (On the Royal Mile) *Map Ref:* NT27
☎ 0131 529 4142 ▤ 0131 558 3103

The Museum of Childhood was one of the first museums of its kind, and was massively expanded in the mid 1980s. Children and adults alike will be delighted by this wonderful collection of toys, games and other belongings of children through the ages. A programme of temporary exhibitions and special events means that there is always something new to enjoy. Please ring for details.

Times: Open all year, Mon-Sat, Jun-Sep 10-6; Oct-May 10-5; (also Sun 12-5 in Jul-Aug). **Facilities:** ▣ ♿ (3 floors only) toilets for disabled shop ✖ (ex guide dogs)

MUSEUM OF SCOTLAND

Chambers St EH1 1JF
Map Ref: NT27
☎ 0131 247 4219 ▤ 0131 220 4819
e-mail: info@nms.ac.uk

The museum is a striking new landmark in Edinburgh's historic Old Town. It houses more than 10,000 of the nation's most precious artefacts, as well as everyday objects that throw light on life in Scotland through the ages. Admission to the Royal Museum, which is adjacent to the Museum of Scotland, is also free. Please telephone for details of special events.

Times: Open all year, Mon, Wed-Sat 10-5, Tue 10-8 & Sun 12-5.
Facilities: P ☕ ✗ licensed & toilets for disabled shop ✖ (ex assist dogs) ◀

NATIONAL GALLERY OF SCOTLAND

The Mound EH2 2EL
Dir: (off Princes St) *Map Ref:* NT27
☎ 0131 624 6200 ▤ 0131 343 3250
e-mail: enquiries@nationalgalleries.org

Occupying a handsome neo-classical building designed by William Playfair, the gallery is home to Scotland's greatest collection of European paintings and sculpture from the Renaissance to Post-Impressionism. It contains notable collections of works by Old Masters, Impressionists and Scottish artists. Special exhibitions at the National Gallery of Scotland focus on European and British art from the 14th to the 19th century.

Times: ✱ Open all year, Mon-Sat 10-5, Sun 12-5. Extended opening hours during the Edinburgh Festival period. Closed 25-26 Dec.
Facilities: P (150yds) & (ramps & lift, room A1 not accessible) toilets for disabled shop ✖ (ex guide dogs) ◀

NATIONAL WAR MUSEUM OF SCOTLAND

Edinburgh Castle EH1 2NG
Map Ref: NT27
☎ 0131 225 7534 ▤ 0131 225 3848
e-mail: info@nms.ac.uk

Explore the Scottish experience of war and military service over the last 400 years at the National War Museum of Scotland. Exhibits include uniforms, insignia, equipment, medals, decorations, weapons, paintings, silverware, documents, diaries and photographs, plus the stories of people's personal experiences and how they have affected them. Access to the museum is included in the admission price to Edinburgh Castle.

Times: Open all year, daily, Apr-Oct, 9.45-5.45; Nov-Mar, daily, 9.45-4.45 **Facilities:** P & toilets for disabled shop ✖ (ex assist dogs)

PALACE OF HOLYROODHOUSE

EH8 8DX
Dir: (at east end of Royal Mile) *Map Ref:* NT27
☎ **0131 556 5100** 📄 **020 7930 9625**
e-mail: holyrood@royalcollection.org.uk

The palace grew from the guest house of the Abbey of the Holyrood, said to have been founded by David I after a miraculous apparition. Mary, Queen of Scots had her court here from 1561 to 1567, and Bonnie Prince Charlie held levees at the palace during his occupation of Edinburgh. The palace is still used by the Royal Family, but can be visited when they are not in residence. The picture gallery is notable for its series of Scottish monarchs.

Times: Open daily, Apr-Oct 9.30-6 (last admission 5.15); Nov-Mar 9.30-4.30 (last admission 3.45). Closed 25-26 Dec and when The Queen is in residence. **Fee:** ✱ £8 (ch under 17 £4, pen & students £6.50). Family ticket (2ad+3ch) £20. Under 5's free **Facilities:** 🅿 (charged) 🍵 ♿ (first floor by lift, wheelchair available) toilets for disabled shop ✖ (ex guide dogs) ◼

THE PEOPLE'S STORY

Canongate Tolbooth, 163 Canongate, Royal Mile EH8 8BN
Dir: (on the Royal Mile) *Map Ref:* NT27
☎ **0131 529 4057** 📄 **0131 556 3439**

The museum, housed in the 16th-century Canongate Tolbooth, tells the story of the ordinary people of Edinburgh from the late 18th century to the present day, their home life, working life and leisure time. Reconstructions include a prison cell, a 1930's pub, a 1940's kitchen and a wash house, supported by photographs, displays, sounds and smells.

Times: Open, Mon-Sat 10-5. Also open Sun during Edinburgh Festival 2-5.
Facilities: 🅿 (100yds) (parking meters) ♿ (lift, induction loop in video room, touch facilities) toilets for disabled shop ✖ (ex guide dogs)

THE REAL MARY KING'S CLOSE

2 Warriston's Close, High St EH1 1PG
Dir: (off High St, opposite St. Giles Cathedral) *Map Ref:* NT27
☎ **08702 430160** 📄 **0131 225 0671**
e-mail: info@realmarykingsclose.co.uk

Step back in time to walk through a warren of hidden streets deep beneath The Royal Mile, where between the 17th and 18th centuries people lived out their lives - a site believed to be the most haunted in Scotland. Meet some of the real characters who used to inhabit these closes and hear tales of extraordinary apparitions as you are guided through dramatic episodes from Edinburgh's hidden past.

Times: Open all year daily, tours run every 20mins from 10. (Last tour Apr-Oct 9pm, Nov-Mar 4pm Sun-Fri & 9pm Sat). Closed 25 Dec
Fee: ✱ £7 (ch £5, pen & student £6). Family ticket (2ad+2ch) £21
Facilities: 🅿 ♿ toilets for disabled shop ✖ (ex guide dogs) ◼

ROYAL BOTANIC GARDEN EDINBURGH

20A Inverleith Row EH3 5LR
Dir: (1m N of city centre, off A902) **Map Ref:** NT27
☎ **0131 552 7171** 📠 **0131 248 2901**   FREE
e-mail: info@rbge.org.uk

Established in 1670, on an area the size of a tennis court, the Royal Botanic Garden in Edinburgh now extends over 70 acres of beautifully landscaped grounds. Spectacular features include the Rock Garden and the Chinese Hillside. The amazing glasshouses feature Britain's tallest palm house and there are magnificent woodland gardens and an arboretum.

Times: Open all year, daily; Apr-Sep, 10-7; Mar & Oct, 10-6; Nov-Feb, 10-4. Closed 25 Dec & 1 Jan. (Facilities close 30 mins before Garden) **Facilities:** P (restricted at certain times) ☕ ✗ licensed ♿ (wheelchairs available at east/west gates) toilets for disabled shop garden centre ✈ (ex guide dogs) ◀

ROYAL MUSEUM

Chambers St EH1 1JF
Dir: (5min from Edinburgh Castle and Royal Mile)
Map Ref: NT27
☎ **0131 247 4219 (info)** 📠 **0131 220 4819**
e-mail: info@nms.ac.uk

This magnificent museum houses extensive international collections in 36 galleries, covering the decorative arts, natural history, science, technology and working life, and geology. The lofty Main Hall has a 'bird cage' design, with fountains and fish ponds, and is a wonder in its own right. Temporary exhibitions, films, lectures and concerts take place throughout the year.

Times: Open all year, Mon-Sat 10-5, Sun 12-5 (Tue late opening till 8). Closed 25 Dec. Phone for times on 26 Dec/1 Jan. **Facilities:** P ☕ ✗ licensed ♿ (induction loops) toilets for disabled shop ✈ (ex assist dogs) ◀

THE ROYAL YACHT BRITANNIA

Ocean Terminal, Leith EH6 6JJ
Dir: (follow signs to North Edinburgh & Leith. Situated within Ocean Terminal) **Map Ref:** NT27
☎ **0131 555 5566** 📠 **0131 555 8835**
e-mail: enquiries@tryb.co.uk

Visit the Royal Yacht Britannia, now in Edinburgh's historic port of Leith. Discover Britannia's fascinating story in the visitor centre. Then step aboard for a self-led audio tour around five decks giving a unique insight into what life was like for the Royal Family and crew. Highlights include the state apartments, admiral's cabin, engine room, laundry, sick bay and Royal Marine barracks.

Times: Open Jan-Mar & Oct-Dec: 10-3.30 (close 5). Apr-Sep 9.30-4.30 (close 6). Closed 25 Dec & 1 Jan **Fee:** ✱ £8 (ch under 5 free, 5-17 £4, pen £6). Family ticket (2ad+3ch) £20. **Facilities:** P ♿ (lift to ship, all areas ramped, written scripts) toilets for disabled shop ✈ (ex guide dogs) ◀

City of Edinburgh continued

SCOTTISH NATIONAL GALLERY OF MODERN ART

Belford Rd EH4 3DR
Dir: (in West End, 20min walk from Haymarket station)
Map Ref: *NT27*
☎ **0131 624 6200** 📄 **0131 343 3250**
e-mail: enquiries@nationalgalleries.org

An outstanding collection of 20th-century painting, sculpture and graphic art is shown at the Scottish National Gallery of Modern Art. It includes major works by Matisse, Picasso, Bacon, Moore and Lichtenstein and an exceptional group of Scottish paintings. The gallery is set in leafy grounds with a sculpture garden. Facilities include a good bookshop and café.

Times: ✱ Open all year, Mon-Sat 10-5 & Sun 12-5. Extended opening hours during the Edinburgh Festival. Closed 25-26 Dec.
Facilities: 🅿 ☕ & (ramps & lift) toilets for disabled shop ✖ (ex guide dogs) ▆

SOUTH QUEENSFERRY HOPETOUN HOUSE

EH30 9SL
Dir: (2m W of Forth Road Bridge, off A904) **Map Ref:** *NT17*
☎ **0131 331 2451** 📄 **0131 319 1885**
e-mail: marketing@hopetounhouse.com

Hopetoun House, just a short drive from Edinburgh, was built some 300 years ago and is one of the most splendid examples of the work of Scottish architects Sir William Bruce and William Adam. It shows some of the finest examples in Scotland of carving, wainscoting and ceiling painting. The house is set in 100 acres of parkland including a deep park, and the gardens are full of colour and interest through the seasons. After a gentle walk you can indulge yourself with a traditional tea and a browse through the shop.

Times: Open daily Etr-Sep **Fee:** ✱ £6.50 (ch £3.50). Grounds £3.50 (ch £2). **Facilities:** 🅿 ☕ & (ramps) toilets for disabled shop ▆

GLASGOW BURRELL COLLECTION

2060 Pollokshaws Rd G43 1AT
Dir: (3.5m S of city centre) **Map Ref:** *NS56*
☎ **0141 287 2550** 📄 **0141 287 2597**
e-mail: museums@cls.glasgow.gov.uk

[FREE]

Set in Pollok Country Park, this award-winning building makes the priceless works of art on display seem almost part of the woodland setting. Shipping magnate Sir William Burrell's main interests were medieval Europe, Oriental art and European paintings. Colourful pictures and stained glass depict details of medieval life; rugs, ceramics and metalwork represent the art of Islam, and there is an impressive collection of Chinese and other Oriental ceramics. Furniture, sculpture, armour and weapons complete the picture. Notable paintings on display include works by Bellini, Rembrandt and the French Impressionists.

Times: Open all year, Mon-Thu & Sat 10-5, Fri & Sun 11-5. Closed 24-25 & 31 [pm] Dec & 1-2 Jan
Facilities: 🅿 (charged) ☕ ✗ licensed & (wheelchairs available, tape guides, lifts) toilets for disabled shop ✖

CLYDEBUILT

Braehead Shopping Centre, King Inch Rd G51 4BN
Dir: (M8 junct 25A, 26, follow signs for Braehead Shopping Centre, then Green car park) *Map Ref:* NS56
☎ 0141 886 1013 📄 0141 886 1015
e-mail: clydebuilt@tinyworld.co.uk

On the banks of the River Clyde, home of the Scottish shipbuilding industry, visitors can discover how Glasgow's famous ships were built, from the design stages through to the launch. There are also displays on the textile and cotton industries, iron and steel, and tobacco. Hands-on activities allow you to operate a real ship's engine, become a ship's riveter, and steer a virtual ship up the Clyde.

Times: Open Mon-Thu & Sat 10-5.30; Sun 11-5. Closed Fri, open on local hols **Fee:** £3.50 (ch & concessions £1.75). Family ticket £8
Facilities: P & (lift/ramps/wheelchairs from shopping centre) toilets for disabled shop ✖ (ex guide dogs)

GALLERY OF MODERN ART

Royal Exchange Square G1 3AH
Dir: (just off Buchanan St & close to Central Station & Queen St Stn) *Map Ref:* NS56
☎ 0141 229 1996 📄 0141 204 5316   FREE
e-mail: museums@cls.glasgow.gov.uk

Glasgow's Gallery of Modern Art is located in the heart of the city in the historic Royal Exchange building. It shows work by local and international artists, as well as addressing contemporary social issues through its major biannual projects. A thought-provoking programme of temporary exhibitions and workshops helps to maintain the vitality of this impressive post-war collection.

Times: Open all year, Mon-Tue & Sat 10-5, Thu 10-8, Fri & Sun 11-5. **Facilities:** P (200yds) 🍵 & toilets for disabled shop ✖ (ex guide dogs)

GLASGOW SCIENCE CENTRE

50 Pacific Quay G51 1EA
Dir: (M8 junct 24 or M77 junct 21, follow brown signs, across Clyde from SECC) *Map Ref:* NS56
☎ 0141 420 5000 📄 0141 420 5011
e-mail: admin@glasgowsciencecentre.org

Glasgow Science Centre presents the world of science and technology in new and exciting ways. The centre is home to many entertaining and exciting attractions and contains hundreds of interactive exhibits. Highlights include the Scottish Power Space Theatre, Scotland's only IMAX cinema and the 12-metre Glasgow Tower, a remarkable free-standing structure that gives breathtaking views of the city (check availability before visiting).

Times: Open daily 10-6. **Fee:** ✱ Science Mall* or Imax: £6.95 (ch & concessions £4.95).Science Mall & Imax: £9.95 (ch & concessions £7.95). 10% off for groups 4+. * Scottish Power Space Theatre extra £2. **Facilities:** P 🍵 & (induction loops) toilets for disabled shop ✖ (ex guide/hearing dogs) 🍴

MUSEUM OF TRANSPORT

1 Bunhouse Rd G3 8DP
Dir: (1.5m W of city centre) **Map Ref:** NS56
☎ **0141 287 2720** 📄 **0141 287 2692** FREE
e-mail: museums@cls.glasgow.gov.uk

Visit the Museum of Transport and the first impression is of
gleaming metalwork and bright paint. All around you there are
cars, caravans, carriages and carts, fire engines, buses, steam
locomotives, prams and trams. The museum uses its collections
of vehicles and models to tell the story of transport by land and
sea, with a unique Glasgow flavour. Visitors can even go window
shopping along the recreated Kelvin Street of 1938. Upstairs, 250
ship models tell the story of the great days of Clyde shipbuilding.

Times: Open all year, Mon-Thu & Sat 10-5, Fri &
Sun 11-5. **Facilities:** 🅿 (charged)
& (assistance available) toilets for disabled shop
✖ (ex guide dogs)

PEOPLE'S PALACE AND WINTER GARDENS

Glasgow Green G40 1AT
Dir: (1m SE of city centre) **Map Ref:** NS56
☎ **0141 271 2951** 📄 **0141 271 2960** FREE
e-mail: museums@cls.glasgow.gov.uk

Glasgow grew from a medieval town by the cathedral to the
second city of the British Empire. Trade with the Americas, and
later industry, made the city rich. But not everyone shared in
Glasgow's wealth. The People's Palace on historic Glasgow Green
shows how ordinary Glaswegians worked, lived and played.
Visitors can discover how a family lived in a typical one-room
Glasgow 'single end' tenement flat, see Billy Connolly's amazing
banana boots, learn to speak Glesga, take a trip 'doon the watter'
and visit the Winter Gardens.

Times: Open all year, Mon-Thu & Sat 10-5, Fri &
Sun 11-5. Closed 24-25 & 31 Dec [pm] & 1-2 Jan
Facilities: 🅿 (50yds) & (lifts) toilets for
disabled shop garden centre ✖

ST MUNGO MUSEUM OF RELIGIOUS LIFE & ART

2 Castle St G4 0RH
Dir: (1m NE of city centre) **Map Ref:** NS56
☎ **0141 553 2557** 📄 **0141 552 4744** FREE
e-mail: museums@cls.glasgow.gov.uk

The award-winning St Mungo Museum explores the importance
of religion in people's everyday lives and art. It aims to promote
understanding and respect between people of different faiths and
of none. Highlights of the collection include the Salvador Dali
painting *Christ of St John of the Cross*. The museum also features
stained glass, objects, statues and video footage. Within the
grounds is Britain's first Japanese zen garden.

Times: Open all year, Mon-Thu & Sat 10-5, Fri &
Sun 11-5. **Facilities:** 🅿 (50yds) 💭 & (taped
information & lift) toilets for disabled shop
✖ (ex guide dogs)

THE SCOTTISH FOOTBALL MUSEUM

The National Stadium, Hampden Park G42 9BA
Dir: (3m S of city centre, follow brown tourist signs)
Map Ref: NS56
☎ **0141 616 6139** 🖹 **0141 616 6101**
e-mail: info@scottishfootballmuseum.org.uk

Using 2,500 pieces of footballing memorabilia, the Scottish Football Museum covers such themes as football's origins, women's football, fan culture, other games influenced by football, and even some social history. The exhibits include the world's oldest football, trophy and ticket, a reconstructed 1903 changing room and press box, and items of specific importance, such as Kenny Dalglish's silver cap, Jimmy McGrory's boots, and the ball from Scotland's 5-1 win over England in 1928.

Times: Open Mon-Sat 10-5, Sun 11-5. Closed match days, special events and Xmas/New Year, please telephone in advance for confirmation
Fee: Museum or stadium tour £5 (concessions & ch under 16 £2.50). Combined ticket £7.50 (concessions & ch under 16 £3.75)
Facilities: 🅿 💻 ♿ (ramps throughout) toilets for disabled shop ✈ (ex guide dogs) ◀

THE TALL SHIP AT GLASGOW HARBOUR

100 Stobcross Rd G3 8QQ
Dir: (from M8 junct 19 onto A814, follow signs for attraction)
Map Ref: NS56
☎ **0141 222 2513** 🖹 **0141 222 2536**
e-mail: info@thetallship.com

Visit The Tall Ship at Glasgow Harbour and step back into the days of sail. Experience Glasgow's maritime history at first hand and explore the UK's only remaining Clydebuilt sailing ship, the *Glenlee*. Exhibitions on board and in the quayside visitor centre tell the story of the ship and the Glasgow Harbour area, and children can join in the hunt for Jock, the ship's cat. The Tall Ship offers guided tours, changing exhibitions, children's activities, a nautical gift shop and café.

Times: Open daily Mar-Oct 10-5, Nov-Feb 10-4.
Fee: £4.50 (concessions £3.25, 1 ch free with paying adult/concession, additional ch £2.50).
Facilities: 🅿 💻 ✕ licensed ♿ toilets for disabled shop ◀

TENEMENT HOUSE

145 Buccleuch St, Garnethill G3 6QN
Dir: (N of Charing Cross) *Map Ref:* NS56
☎ **0141 333 0183**
e-mail: tenementhouse@nts.org.uk

This shows an unsung but once-typical side of Glasgow life: it is a first-floor flat, built in 1892, with a parlour, bedroom, kitchen and bathroom, furnished with the original recess beds, kitchen range, sink, and coal bunker, among other articles. The home of Agnes Toward from 1911 to 1965, the flat was bought by an actress who preserved it as a 'time capsule'. The contents vividly portray the life of one section of Glasgow society.

Times: Open Mar-Oct, daily 2-5. Wkday morning visits available for pre-booked educational & other groups. Times may change for 2005 please telephone or check on www.nts.org.uk
Fee: ✱ £3.50 (concessions £2.60) Family ticket £9.50. Groups adult £2.80 (ch/school £1). Admission free to NTS members. For other details please phone 0131 243 9387
Facilities: 🅿 (100yds) (restricted, recommend parking in town) (Braille guide) ✈ (ex guide dogs) ♨

ALVA MILL TRAIL VISITOR CENTRE

Glentana Mill, West Stirling St FK12 5EN
Dir: (on A91 approx 8m E of Stirling) *Map Ref: NS89*
☎ 01259 769696 📄 01259 763100   FREE

In the heart of Scotland's woollen mill country, the centre
recounts the history of Scotland's woollen and tweed traditions,
and features machines ranging from spinning wheels to large
motorised looms of the type in use today. Hear 12-year-old Mary
describe her working day as a mill girl 150 years ago, and then
contrast her story with our modern working woollen mill. Factory
bargains and local crafts are for sale and there is a tourist
information centre and café.

Times: Open all year, Jan-Jun 10-5; Jul-Aug 9-5;
Sep-Dec 10-5. **Facilities:** 🅿 🖥 ♿ toilets for
disabled shop ✖ (ex guide dogs) 🎞

CAERLAVEROCK WWT CAERLAVEROCK

Eastpark Farm DG1 4RS
Dir: (9m SE of Dumfries, signed from A75) *Map Ref: NY06*
☎ 01387 770200 📄 01387 770539
e-mail: caerlaverock@wwt.org.uk

This internationally important wetland is the winter habitat of the
entire Svalbard population of Barnacle Geese, which spends the
winter on the Solway Firth. Observation facilities include 20 hides,
three towers and a heated observatory. A wide variety of other
wildlife can be seen, notably the rare natterjack toad and a family
of barn owls, which can be observed via a CCTV system.

Times: Open daily 10-5. Closed 25 Dec.
Fee: ✱ £4 (ch £2.50 & concessions £3.25).
Family ticket £10.50 **Facilities:** 🅿 🖥 ♿ toilets
for disabled shop ✖ (ex guide dogs)

CREETOWN CREETOWN GEM ROCK MUSEUM

Chain Rd DG8 7HJ
Dir: (follow signs from A75 at Creetown bypass) *Map Ref: NX45*
☎ 01671 820357 & 820554 📄 01671 820554
e-mail: gem.rock@btinternet.com

The Gem Rock is the leading independent museum of its kind in
the UK, and is renowned worldwide. Crystals, gemstones,
minerals, jewellery and fossils - the Gem Rock displays some of
the most breathtaking examples of nature's wonders. See the
audio-visual presentation 'Fire in the Stones', explore the Crystal
Cave, and relax in the Prospector's Study.

Times: Open Etr-Sep, daily 9.30-5.30; Oct-Nov &
Mar-Etr, daily 10-4; Dec-Feb, wknds 10-4 or by
appointment wkdays. Closed 23 Dec-Jan.
Fee: ✱ £3.50 (ch £2 under 5 free, concessions
£3). Family ticket £9 (2ad+3ch).
Facilities: 🅿 🖥 ♿ (ideal attraction for
wheelchair users) toilets for disabled shop
✖ (ex guide dogs) 🎞

DUMFRIES DUMFRIES MUSEUM & CAMERA OBSCURA

The Observatory, Rotchell Rd DG2 7SW
Dir: (A75 from S Carlisle or SW from Castle Douglas, museum in Maxwellton area of Dumfries) ***Map Ref:*** *NX97*
☎ **01387 253374** 🖹 **01387 265081**
e-mail: dumfriesmuseum@dumgal.gov.uk

The museum is situated in and around an 18th-century windmill tower. Its collections were started over 150 years ago and exhibitions trace the history of the people and landscape of Dumfries and Galloway. The historic camera obscura is to be found on the top floor of the windmill tower, offering panoramic views over the town and for miles beyond on a clear day.

Times: Open all year, Apr-Sep Mon-Sat 10-5, Sun, 2-5; Oct-Mar, Tue-Sat 10-1 & 2-5. **Fee:** Free except Camera Obscura £1.55 (concessions 80p) **Facilities:** 🅿 ♿ (camera obscura, parking available) toilets for disabled shop

---

NEW ABBEY SHAMBELLIE HOUSE MUSEUM OF COSTUME

DG2 8HQ
Dir: (7m S of Dumfries, on A710) ***Map Ref:*** *NX96*
☎ **01387 850375** 🖹 **01387 850461**
e-mail: info@nms.ac.uk

Shambellie House is a beautiful Victorian country house set in attractive wooded grounds. You are invited to step back in time and experience Victorian and Edwardian grace and refinement. See period costume from the 1850s to the 1950s displayed in appropriate room settings with accessories, furniture and decorative art. Telephone for details of special events.

Times: Open Apr (or Good Fri if earlier)-Oct, 11-5. **Facilities:** 🅿 💻 ♿ (house inaccessible for wheelchair users) shop 🐕 (ex guide/hearing dogs) 🍴

PORT LOGAN LOGAN BOTANIC GARDEN

DG9 9ND
Dir: (on B7065, 14m S of Stranraer) ***Map Ref:*** *NX04*
☎ **01776 860231** 🖹 **01776 860333**
e-mail: logan@rbge.org.uk

This is probably the most exotic garden in the country, as Logan's exceptionally mild climate (courtesy of the Gulf Stream) allows a colourful array of tender plants to thrive out of doors. Among the many highlights are tree ferns, cabbage palms, unusual shrubs, climbers and tender perennials, found within the setting of the walled, water, terrace and woodland gardens. Self guided audio tours are available and monthly guided tours. Also on site are the Discovery Centre, Salad Bar and Botanics Shop.

Times: Open Mar-Oct, Mar & Oct daily 10-5. Apr-Sep 10-6 **Fee:** ✱ £3.50 (ch £1, concessions £3). Family £8 **Facilities:** 🅿 ✗ licensed ♿ (access limited, wheelchairs available for loan) toilets for disabled shop garden centre 🐕 (ex guide dogs) 🍴

STRANRAER   CASTLE KENNEDY GARDENS

Stair Estates, Rephad DG9 8BX
Dir: (5m E of Stranraer on A75, signed at Castle Kennedy Village)
Map Ref: NX06
☎ **01776 702024** 📄 **01776 706248**
e-mail: info@castlekennedygardens.co.uk

Situated on a peninsula between two lochs, the gardens around the old castle were first laid out in the early 18th century. They are noted for their rhododendrons and azaleas (at their best in May and early June) and the walled kitchen garden with fine herbaceous borders (best seen in August and September). The gardens have many avenues and walks amid beautiful scenery.

Times: Open Etr-Sep, daily 10-5 **Fee:** ✱ £4 (ch £1, pen £3). Party 20+ 10% discount.
Facilities: 🅿 ☕ ♿ (tearoom to enable access) toilets for disabled shop garden centre 🗃

THORNHILL   DRUMLANRIG CASTLE

DG3 4AQ
Dir: (4m N of Thornhill off A76)   **Map Ref:** NX89
☎ **01848 331555** 📄 **01848 331682**
e-mail: bre@drumlanrigcastle.org.uk

This unusual pink sandstone castle was built in the late 17th century in Renaissance style. It contains an outstanding collection of fine art, French furniture, silver and relics of Bonnie Prince Charlie. The old stable block has a craft centre with resident craft workers, and the grounds offer a garden plants centre, a working forge, mountain bike hire and woodland walks. Please phone for details of special events.

Times: Open early May-late Aug, Castle open seven days a week. Guided tours and restricted route may operate at various times, please verify before visiting. **Fee:** ✱ £6 (ch £2 & pen £4. Grounds only £3. Party 20+ £4 each. **Facilities:** 🅿 ✗ licensed ♿ (lift for wheelchair users) toilets for disabled shop 🐾 (ex in park on lead) 🗃

WANLOCKHEAD   MUSEUM OF LEAD MINING

ML12 6UT
Dir: (signed from M74 and A76)   **Map Ref:** NS81
☎ **01659 74387** 📄 **01659 74481**
e-mail: ggodfrey@goldpan.co.uk

Wanlockhead is Scotland's highest village, set in the beautiful Lowther Hills. Visitors can see miners' cottages and the miners' library as well as the 18th-century lead mine, where you can go underground for a guided tour. The area is also gold rich, so you can also try your hand at panning for gold.

Times: ✱ Open Apr-2 Nov, daily 10.30-4.30; Jul & Aug 10-5.
Facilities: 🅿 ☕ ✗ licensed ♿ (induction loops) toilets for disabled shop 🐾 (ex guide dogs) 🗃

DUNDEE CAMPERDOWN COUNTRY PARK

Coupar Angus Rd DD2 4TF
Dir: (A90 to Dundee then onto A923 (Coupar-Angus road), left at 1st rdbt to attraction) **Map Ref:** *NO43*
☎ 01382 431818 📄 01382 431810
e-mail: camperdown@dundeecity.gov.uk

The 19th-century mansion of Camperdown House was built for the son of Admiral Lord Duncan, who defeated the Dutch at the Battle of Camperdown in 1797. The house is set in nearly 400 acres of fine parkland, which includes a wildlife centre, an adventure play area and an extensive network of footpaths and forest trails to follow.

Times: Open Park: all year. Wildlife Centre: Apr-Sep, daily 10-3.45, Oct-Mar 10-2.45.
Fee: ✱ Park - free admission. Wildlife Centre charged. **Facilities:** 🅿 ♿ (ramps) toilets for disabled shop ✖ (ex guide dogs)

DISCOVERY POINT & RRS DISCOVERY

Discovery Quay DD1 4XA
Dir: (follow brown heritage signs for Historic Ships)
Map Ref: *NO43*
☎ 01382 201245 📄 01382 225891
e-mail: info@dundeeheritage.sol.co.uk

Discovery Point is the home of *RRS Discovery*, Captain Scott's famous Antarctic ship. Spectacular lighting, graphics and special effects re-create key moments in the Discovery story. The restored bridge gives a captain's view over the ship and the River Tay. Learn what happened to the ship after the expedition, during World War I and the Russian Revolution, and find out about her involvement in the first survey of whales' migratory patterns.

Times: ✱ Open Apr-Oct, Mon-Sat 10-6, Sun 11-6; Nov-Mar, Mon Sat 10-5, Sun 11-5. **Facilities:** 🅿 (charged) ☕ ♿ (in-house wheelchairs & lifts, parking, ramps onto ship) toilets for disabled shop ✖ (ex guide & hearing dogs) 🎞

HM FRIGATE UNICORN

Victory Dock DD1 3JA
Dir: (from W follow A85 from A90 at Invergowrie. From E follow A92. Near N end of Tay Road Bridge) **Map Ref:** *NO43*
☎ 01382 200900 & 200893 📄 01382 200923
e-mail: frigateunicorn@hotmail.com

The *Unicorn* is the oldest British-built warship afloat, and Scotland's only example of a wooden warship. She was built at Chatham Dockyard for the Royal Navy and launched in 1824, and is a unique survivor of the transitional period between the wooden sailing ship and the iron steamship. Today she houses a museum about life in the Royal Navy during the days of sail, with guns, models and displays.

Times: Open all year Apr-Oct, daily 10-5; Nov-Mar, Wed-Fri 12-4, Sat & Sun 10-4.Closed Mon-Tue & 2 weeks at Xmas & New Year.
Fee: £3.50 (concessions £2.50). Family ticket £7.50-£9.50. Groups 10+ £2 each.
Facilities: 🅿 ☕ ♿ (audio visual presentations, introductory video) shop ✖ 🎞

Dundee City continued

Mills Observatory

Balgay Park, Glamis Rd DD2 2UB
Dir: (1m W of city centre, in Balgay Park, on Balgay Hill. Vehicle entrance at Glamis Rd gate to Balgay Park) **Map Ref:** *NO43*
☎ **01382 435967** ▤ **01382 435962**
e-mail: mills.observatory@dundeecity.gov.uk

The observatory was built in 1935, and has a Victorian 10-inch Cooke refracting telescope among its instruments. The gallery has displays on astronomy and space exploration, and visitors can view a safe projection of the sun on bright days. There is a small planetarium for booked groups only. Open nights are held during the winter months and children's activities during the summer holidays.

Times: Open all year, Apr-Sep, Tue-Fri 11-5, Sat & Sun 12.30-4; Oct-Mar, Mon-Fri 4-10, Sat & Sun 12.30-4. Closed 25-26 Dec & 1-3 Jan. **Fee:** Free except for planetarium shows extra, £1 (ch 50p) Groups £10. **Facilities:** 🅿 ♿ (portable telescopes available, images on screen) toilets for disabled shop ✖ (ex guide dogs)

Verdant Works

West Henderson's Wynd DD2 5BT
Dir: (follow brown tourist signs) **Map Ref:** *NO43*
☎ **01382 225282** ▤ **01382 221612**
e-mail: info@dundeeheritage.sol.co.uk

Dating from 1830, this old jute mill covers 50,000 square feet and has been restored as a living museum of Dundee and Tayside's textile history, and is an award-winning European Industrial Museum. Phase I explains what jute is, where it comes from and why Dundee became the centre of its production. Working machinery illustrates the production process from raw jute to woven cloth. Phase II deals with the uses of jute and its effects on Dundee's social history.

Times: Open Apr-Oct; Mon-Sat 10-5, Sun 11-5. Nov-Mar; Mon-Sat 10-4, Sun 11-4. Venue closes 1hr after last entry. Please check for winter opening times. Closed 25-26 Dec & 1-2 Jan)
Facilities: 🅿 (charged) ♿ (wheelchairs, induction loops) toilets for disabled shop ✖ (ex guide & hearing dogs) ▤

GALSTON　LOUDOUN CASTLE THEME PARK

KA4 8PE
Dir: (signed from A74(M), from A77 and from A71)
Map Ref: *NS53*
☎ **01563 822296** ▤ **01563 822408**
e-mail: loudouncastle@btinternet.com

Loudoun Castle is an imposing ruin of a building dating from the 1800s, which encompassed a 15th-century keep and a 17th-century extension, destroyed by fire in 1941. It provides a romantic backdrop to this popular family theme park, which offers rides, live entertainment and McDougal's Farm, where there are live animals, tractors and pony rides. Favourite rides are the Twist n' Shout rollercoaster; The Slitherin (for *Harry Potter* fans); The Black Pearl (inspired by *Pirates of the Caribbean*); and The Captain's Wheel, guaranteed to give you a wild ride.

Times: Open Apr-Aug & following days in Sep 3, 9-10, 16-17, 22-25, 29-30. Also 1-2, 7-8, 14-22 Oct. **Fee:** ✱ Height: over 1.25m £10, over 0.90m £9, under 0.90m free (pen £5). Family ticket £25 (2ad+2ch). **Facilities:** 🅿 🍽 ✖ licensed ♿ toilets for disabled shop ✖ (ex guide dogs) ▤

MILNGAVIE MUGDOCK COUNTRY PARK

Craigallian Rd G62 8EL
Dir: (N of Glasgow on A81, signed) *Map Ref:* NS57
☎ 0141 956 6100 956 6586 🖹 0141 956 5624 FREE
e-mail: lain@mcp.ndo.co.uk

This country park incorporates the remains of Mugdock and Craigend castles, and is set in beautiful landscapes. Facilities at the park include an exhibition centre and craft shops, an orienteering course and many walks. There are over 30 organised activities throughout the year, plus barbecue site hire, pond dipping and mini beast studies.

Times: Open all year, daily. **Facilities:** 🅿 🍴 ♿ toilets for disabled shop garden centre ◀

ABERLADY MYRETON MOTOR MUSEUM

EH32 0PZ
Dir: (1.5m from A198, 2m from A1) *Map Ref:* NT47
☎ 01875 870288 & 07947 066666 🖹 01368 860199

The museum has on show a collection of over 50 cars, bicycles, motorcycles and commercial vehicles dating from as early as 1896, and military vehicles from World War II. Models include a 1896 Arnold Benz, a 1898 Leon Bollee, a 1902 Wolseley, a 1907 De Deon Bouton, and a 1927 Rolls Royce. There is also a large display of period advertising, posters and enamel signs.

Times: Open, Apr-Oct daily 11-4, Nov-Mar weekends only 11-3 **Fee:** £5 (ch £2). **Facilities:** 🅿 ♿ ✖ (ex guide dogs)

EAST FORTUNE *MUSEUM OF FLIGHT*

East Fortune Airfield EH39 5LF
Dir: (signed from A1 near Haddington. Onto B1347, past Athelstaneford) *Map Ref:* NT57
☎ 01620 880308 🖹 01620 880355
e-mail: info@nms.ac.uk

Situated on 63 acres of one of Britain's best preserved wartime airfields, the museum has three hangars, with more than 50 aeroplanes, plus engines, rockets and memorabilia. Items on display include two Spitfires, a Vulcan bomber and Britain's oldest surviving aeroplane, built in 1896. Recent exhibits include a Phantom jet fighter and Harrier jump-jet.

Times: Open daily, 10.30-5, Apr-Oct; 11-4, wknds only Nov-Mar **Facilities:** 🅿 🍴 ♿ toilets for disabled shop ✖ (ex assist dogs) ◀

EAST LINTON PRESTON MILL & PHANTASSIE DOOCOT

EH40 3DS
Dir: (signed from A1) *Map Ref:* NT57
☎ **01620 860426**

This attractive mill, with a conical roofed kiln and red pantiled roof, is the oldest working water-driven meal mill to survive in Scotland, and was last used commercially in 1957. It is in an attractive setting by a millpond with ducks and geese. Nearby is the charming Phantassie Doocot (dovecote), built for 500 birds.

Times: Open Apr-Sep, Thu-Mon 12-5, Sun 1-5. Times may change for 2005 please telephone or check on www.nts.org.uk **Fee:** ✱ £3.50 (concession £2.60) Family ticket £9.50. Groups adult £2.80 (ch/school £1). Admission free to NTS members. For other details please phone 0131 243 9387 **Facilities:** ▣ ♿ toilets for disabled shop ✖ (ex guide dogs) ♟

NORTH BERWICK SCOTTISH SEABIRD CENTRE

The Harbour EH39 4SS
Dir: (A1 from Edinburgh, then A198 to North Berwick. Brown heritage signs clearly marked from A1) *Map Ref:* NT58
☎ **01620 890202** ▤ **01620 890222**
e-mail: info@seabird.org

Get close to nature with a visit to this award-winning centre. The area is a haven for wildlife with panoramic views over the islands of the Firth of Forth and sand-fringed bays of North Berwick. Use state-of-the-art 'Big Brother' cameras to see a wide variety of wildlife action live - including a gannet colony, hundreds of puffins, seals and sometimes bottlenose dolphins. There is a wildlife boat safari with landings on the islands and a passenger ferry to Fife in the summer.

Times: Open all year, Apr-Oct 10-6 (every day), Nov-Jan 10-6 (Mon-Fri) 10-5.30 (Sat & Sun), Feb-Mar 10-5 (Mon-Fri) 10-5.30 (Sat & Sun). Closed Xmas **Fee:** £5.95 (ch & concessions £3.95). Family ticket (4 persons) £16.50. **Facilities:** ▣ 🅿 ♿ (1 w/chair, parking on site, walking frame available) toilets for disabled shop ✖ (ex guide dogs)

PRESTONPANS PRESTONGRANGE MUSEUM

Prestongrange
Dir: (on B1348) *Map Ref:* NT37
☎ **0131 653 2904** ▤ **01620 828201**
e-mail: elms@eastlothian.gov.uk

The oldest documented coal mining site in Scotland is at Prestongrange, with 800 years of history, and this museum shows a Cornish Beam Engine and on-site evidence of associated industries such as brick-making and pottery. It is located next to a 16th-century customs port. Special events for all the family are held at weekends during July and August.

Times: ✱ Open end Mar-mid Oct, daily 11-4. Last tour 3. **Fee:** *Prices not confirmed for 2005* **Facilities:** ▣ 🅿 ♿ (grounds partly accessible) toilets for disabled shop ✖ (ex guide dogs or outside)

BIRKHILL *THE BIRKHILL FIRECLAY MINE*

EH51 9AQ
Dir: (A706 from Linlithgow, A904 from Grangemouth, follow
brown signs to Steam Railway & Fireclay Mine) ***Map Ref:*** *NS97*
☎ **01506 825855** 📄 **01506 828766**
e-mail: mine@srps.org.uk

Tour guides will meet you at Birkhill Station and lead you down
into the ancient woodland of the beautiful Avon Gorge, and then
into the caverns of the Birkhill Fireclay mine. Here you can see
how the clay was worked and what it was used for. You can also
search for 300-million-year-old fossils in the roof of the mine.

Times: Open 3 Apr-Oct wknds only; Jul-Aug
Tue-Sun. **Facilities:** 🅿 ◼

BO'NESS *BO'NESS & KINNEIL RAILWAY*

Bo'ness Station, Union St EH51 9AQ
Dir: (A904 from all directions, signed) ***Map Ref:*** *NT08*
☎ **01506 822298** 📄 **01506 828233**
e-mail: railway@srps.org.uk

Historic railway buildings, including the station and train shed,
have been relocated from sites all over Scotland to the Bo'ness &
Kinneil Railway, and the Scottish Railway Exhibition tells the story
of the development of railways and their impact on the people of
Scotland. Take a seven mile return trip by steam train to the
tranquil country station at Birkhill. Special events take place
throughout the year.

Times: Open Apr-Jun & Sep-Oct, Sat-Sun; Jul-Aug,
Tue-Sun. Steam trains daily, depart 11, 12.15,
1.45 & 3, diesel departs at 4.15. Ring for details
of special events. **Facilities:** 🅿 ◼ ✕ ♿ (ramps
to station & adapted carriage) toilets for disabled
shop ◼

ANSTRUTHER *SCOTTISH FISHERIES MUSEUM*

St Ayles, Harbour Head KY10 3AB
Dir: (A917 through St Monans & Pittenweem to Anstruther)
Map Ref: *NO50*
☎ **01333 310628** 📄 **01333 310628**
e-mail: info@scottish-fisheries-museum.org

This award-winning National museum tells the story of Scottish
fishing and its people from the earliest times to the present. There
are ten galleries, two large boatyards, and a restored fisherman's
cottage to see, which contain many fine paintings and photographs,
boat models and actual boats, clothing and items from daily life.

Times: Open all year, Apr-Sep, Mon-Sat 10-5.30, Sun 11-5; Oct-Mar,
Mon-Sat 10-4.30, Sun 12-4.30. Closed 25-26 Dec & 1-2 Jan. (Last
admission 1 hr before closing). **Fee:** £4.50 (concessions £3.50).
Party 12+ £3 (primary ch £1, accompanied ch free, concessions £2)
Facilities: 🅿 (20yds) (charge in summer) ◼ ♿ (ramps throughout
to provide full access) toilets for disabled shop ✕ (ex guide dogs) ◼

BURNTISLAND BURNTISLAND EDWARDIAN FAIR MUSEUM

102 High St KY3 9AS
Dir: (in the centre of Burntisland) *Map Ref:* NT28
☎ **01592 412860** 📄 **01592 412870**   FREE

Burntisland Museum, located within the public library, has recreated a walk through the sights and sounds of the town's fair in 1910, based on a painting of the scene by local artist Andrew Young. You can see reconstructed rides, stalls and side shows of the time. There is also a local history gallery.

Times: Open all year, Mon, Wed, Fri & Sat 10-1 & 2-5; Tue & Thu 10-1 & 2-7. Closed PHs)
Facilities: P (20m) (on street parking) ✖ (except guide dogs)

CULROSS CULROSS PALACE, TOWN HOUSE & THE STUDY

West Green House KY12 8JH
Dir: (off A985, 3m E of Kincardine Bridge) *Map Ref:* NS98
☎ **01383 880359** 📄 **01383 882675**

A royal burgh, Culross dates from the 16th and 17th centuries and has remained virtually unchanged since. It prospered from the coal and salt trades, and when these declined in the 1700s, Culross stayed as it was. It owes its present appearance to the National Trust for Scotland, which has been gradually restoring it. In the Town House is a visitor centre and exhibition; in the building called The Study can be seen a drawing room with a Norwegian painted ceiling, and The Palace itself has painted rooms and terraced gardens.

Times: Open Palace, Study & Town House: Good Fri-Sep, daily 12-5. Garden all year 10-6 or sunset if earlier. Times may change for 2005 please telephone or check on www.nts.org.uk **Fee:** ✱ £5 (concessions £3.75). Family ticket £13.50. Groups adult £4 (ch/school £1). Please book groups in advance. Admission free to NTS members. For other details phone 0131 243 9387
Facilities: P 💻 ♿ toilets for disabled shop ✖ (ex guide dogs) ♉

CUPAR THE SCOTTISH DEER CENTRE

Bow-of-Fife KY15 4NQ
Dir: (3m W of Cupar on A91) *Map Ref:* NO31
☎ **01337 810391** 📄 **01337 810477**

Guided tours of the Scottish Deer Centre take about 30 minutes and allow you to meet and stroke the deer, of which there are some 140 from nine different species. Falconry displays are a regular feature, and there is a viewing platform, treetop walkway and scenic pathways for some pleasant walks. Indoor and outdoor adventure play areas are provided for children.

Times: Open daily, Etr-Oct 10-6, Nov-Etr 10-5.
Fee: ✱ £4.95 (ch 3-15 £3.45) **Facilities:** P 💻 ♿ (special parking bay, loan of wheelchairs) toilets for disabled shop ✖ (ex guide dogs) ◀

FALKLAND   FALKLAND PALACE & GARDEN

KY15 7BU
Dir: (off A912, 11m N of Kirkaldy) **Map Ref:** NO20
☎ 01337 857397   🖹 01337 857980

The hunting palace of the Stuart monarchs, this fine building, with a French-Renaissance style south wing, stands in the shelter of the Lomond Hills. The beautiful Chapel Royal and King's Bedchamber are the palace's most notable features, and recorded sacred music is played hourly in the chapel. The gardens comprise a wide lawn with beautiful herbaceous borders, including a spectacular delphinium display, and are also home to the oldest royal tennis court in Britain, dating from 1539.

Times: Open Mar-Oct, Mon-Sat 10-6, Sun 1-5. Times may change for 2005 please telephone or check on www.nts.org.uk **Fee:** ✱ £7 (concessions £5.25). Family ticket £19. Groups adult £5.60 (ch/school £1). Garden only £3.50 (concessions £2.60). Family ticket £9.50. Groups adult £2.80 (ch/school £1). Admission free to NTS members. For other details please phone 0131 243 9387 **Facilities:** 🅿 & shop ✖ (ex guide dogs) 🍽

KIRKCALDY   KIRKCALDY MUSEUM & ART GALLERY

War Memorial Gardens KY1 1YG
Dir: (next to train station) **Map Ref:** NT29
☎ 01592 412860   🖹 01592 412870   FREE
e-mail: kirkcaldy.museum@fife.gov.uk

Set in the town's lovely memorial gardens, the museum houses a collection of fine and decorative art, including 18th to 21st-century Scottish paintings; among them the works of William McTaggart and S J Peploe. An award-winning display, 'Changing Places', tells the story of the social, industrial and natural heritage of the area.

Times: Open all year, Mon-Sat 10 30-5, Sun 2-5. Closed local hols **Facilities:** 🅿 🖳 & (ramp to main entrance & lift to 1st floor galleries) toilets for disabled shop ✖ (ex guide dogs)

NORTH QUEENSFERRY   DEEP SEA WORLD

KY11 1JR
Dir: (from N, M90 take exit for Inverkeithing. From S follow signs to Forth Rd Bridge, 1st exit left) **Map Ref:** NT17
☎ 01383 411880   🖹 01383 410514
e-mail: info@deepseaworld.co.uk

The world's longest underwater tunnel gives you a diver's eye view of an underwater world. Come face to face with sand tiger sharks, and watch divers hand feed a wide array of sea life. Visit the Amazon experience with ferocious piranhas and electric eels and the amazing amphibian display featuring the world's most poisonous frog. The really brave will enjoy the dangerous animals tank.

Times: Open all year daily, Nov-Mar 10-5, Apr-Oct 10-6 wknds & school hols 10-6 **Fee:** ✱ £7.50 (ch 3-5 £5.50, concessions £6). Family ticket & group discounts available. **Facilities:** 🅿 🖳 & (ramps & disabled parking) toilets for disabled shop ✖ (ex guide dogs) 🍴

ST ANDREWS   BRITISH GOLF MUSEUM

Bruce Embankment KY16 9AB
Dir: (opposite Royal & Ancient Golf Club) *Map Ref:* NO51
☎ 01334 460046 460053 📄 01334 460064
e-mail: alisonwood@randa.org

Where better to find out about golf than in St Andrews, the home
of the game. Using a range of displays and exciting interactive
exhibits, the British Golf Museum explores the history of British
golf from its origins to the personalities of today. The 18th Hole is
fun for all the family, with dressing up, a mini-putting green and
loads to do!

Times: Open all year, Etr-mid Oct daily 9.30-5.30;
mid Oct-Etr Thu-Mon 11-3. Closed Tue & Wed.
Fee: ✱ £4 (ch 15 £2, pen & students £3). Family
ticket £10. Group 10+ **Facilities:** 🅿 (charged)
& toilets for disabled shop ✖ (ex guide dogs) 🍴

CASTLE & VISITOR CENTRE

KY16 9AR
Map Ref: NO51
☎ 01334 477196

This 13th-century castle is the former Bishop's Palace, the
residence of the Archbishops of St Andrews. Over the centuries
the castle has been besieged many times and witnessed some
grisly deeds, including the martyrdom of George Wishart and the
murder of Cardinal Beaton. It was destroyed in the Reformation
and only ruins remain, but there is an exhibition about the castle
in the visitor centre and you can still visit the infamous bottle
dungeon.

Times: Open all year, Apr-Sep, daily 9.30-6.30; Oct-Mar, daily
9.30-4.30. Closed 25-26 Dec & 1-2 Jan. **Fee:** ✱ £3 (ch £1,
concessions £2.30). Joint ticket with St Andrews Cathedral available
£4 (ch £1.25, concessions £3). Groups 11+ 10% discount. Rates
valid until 2 Jan 2005. Please phone for further details.
Facilities: 🅿 & toilets for disabled shop ✖ ▮

ST ANDREWS AQUARIUM

The Scores KY16 9AS
Dir: (signed in town centre) *Map Ref:* NO51
☎ 01334 474786 📄 01334 475985

There are over 30 exhibition tanks at this continually expanding
aquarium, where you can see shrimps, sharks, seahorses, eels,
octopus, seals and rays, plus deadly piranhas in the Amazonian
section. Some of the sea creatures can even be handled. A recent
addition is the Tropical Treats area with miniature fresh water
turtles called cooters, giant air-breathing gourami, tiger cat fish
and poison dart frogs. The Sea Mammal Research Unit at the
aquarium is committed to the care of sea mammals and their
environment.

Times: ✱ Open daily from 10. Please phone for
winter opening **Facilities:** 🅿 (charged) 🍷
✖ licensed & toilets for disabled shop
✖ (ex guide dogs) 🍴

AVIEMORE STRATHSPEY STEAM RAILWAY

Aviemore Station, Dalfaber Rd PH22 1PY
Dir: (from A9 take B970 for Coylumbridge, on B9152, left after railway bridge, car park 0.25m on left. Other stations: Boat of Garten in village; Broomhill, off A95, 3.5m S of Grantown-on-Spey) **Map Ref:** NH81
☎ **01479 810725**
e-mail: information@strathspeyrailway.co.uk

This steam railway covers the ten miles from Aviemore via Boat of Garten to Broomhill. The journey takes about 40 minutes, but allow around two hours for the round trip. Shorter trips are possible and timetables are available from the station and the tourist information centre. Special events include visits from Thomas the Tank Engine. Please telephone for details of dates.

Times: Open daily Etr, 23-29 Mar, 29 May-30 Sep; Apr, Wed & Sun; May & Oct, Wed-Thu, Sat-Sun & BH Mon, 9.30-4.30 **Fee:** £9 basic roundtrip (ch £4.50); £21 Family roundtrip. Day Rover £12 (ch £6) Family £30 **Facilities:** 🅿 ☕ ✗ & (ramps) toilets for disabled shop ◀

BALMACARA BALMACARA ESTATE & LOCHALSH WOODLAND GARDEN

IV40 8DN
Dir: (3m E of Kyle of Lochalsh, off A87) **Map Ref:** NG82
☎ **01599 566325** 🖨 **01599 566359**
e-mail: balmacara@nts.org.uk

The Balmacara estate comprises some 5,600 acres and seven crofting villages, including Plockton, which is an Outstanding Conservation Area. There are also excellent views to be had of Skye, Kintail and Applecross. The visitor centre at Balmacara Square offers an interactive CD-ROM, walk guides and other visitor information. The main attraction, however, is the Lochalsh Woodland Garden, which offers sheltered loch-side walks with Scots pines, oak and beech trees, rhododendrons, hydrangeas, fuchsias, bamboos and ferns.

Times: Open Estate: all year. Woodland garden daily 9-sunset. Balmacara Square Visitor Centre, Apr-Sep, daily, 9-5 (Fri 9-4). Times may change for 2005 please telephone or check on www.nts.org.uk **Fee:** ✳ Garden £2 (concessions £1). Visitor Centre £1 (honesty box). Admission free to NTS members. For other details please phone 0131 243 9387 **Facilities:** 🅿 ☕

BOAT OF GARTEN LOCH GARTEN OSPREY CENTRE

RSPB Reserve Abernethy Forest, Forest Lodge, Nethybridge PH25 3EF
Dir: (signed from B970 & A9 at Aviemore, follow 'RSPB Ospreys' signs) **Map Ref:** NH91
☎ **01479 831476** 🖨 **01479 821069**

Home of the Loch Garten Osprey Centre, this reserve holds one of most important remnants of Scots Pine forest in the Highlands. Within its 30,760 acres are forest bogs, moorland, mountain top, lochs and crofting land. In addition to the regular pair of nesting ospreys, there are breeding Scottish crossbills, capercaillies, black grouse and many others. The ospreys can be viewed through telescopes and there is a live TV link to the nest.

Times: Osprey Centre open daily, Apr-Aug 10-6. **Fee:** ✳ £2.50 (ch 50p, concessions £1.50). **Facilities:** 🅿 & (low level viewing slots & optics) toilets for disabled shop ✗ (ex guide dogs in centre) ◀

CARRBRIDGE LANDMARK FOREST THEME PARK

PH23 3AJ
Dir: (off A9 between Aviemore & Inverness) **Map Ref:** *NH92*
☎ **01479 841613 & 0800 731 3446** 📄 **01479 841384**
e-mail: landmarkcentre@btconnect.com

This innovative centre is designed to provide a fun and educational visit for all ages. Microworld takes a close up look at the incredible microscopic world around us; and there is a 70-foot forest viewing tower and a treetop trail. Attractions include a three-track watercoaster, a maze and a large covered adventure play area, mini electric cars, and a remote controlled truck arena. Also look out for demonstrations of timber sawing on a steam-powered sawmill, and log hauling by a Clydesdale horse throughout the day.

Times: Open all year, daily, Apr-mid Jul 10-6; mid Jul-mid Aug 10-7; Sep-Oct 10-5.30; Nov-Mar 10-5.
Fee: ✱ Apr-Oct: £7.90 (ch £5.90); Nov-Mar £2.80 (ch £2.15). Family tickets available.
Facilities: 🅿 💺 ✗ licensed ♿ (ramps) toilets for disabled shop ◀

CAWDOR CAWDOR CASTLE

IV12 5RD
Dir: (on B9090, off A96) **Map Ref:** *NH85*
☎ **01667 404401** 📄 **01667 404674**
e-mail: info@cawdorcastle.com

Home of the Thanes of Cawdor (reference Shakespeare's Scottish play) since the 14th century, this lovely castle has a drawbridge, an ancient tower built round a tree, and a freshwater well inside the house. The Gardens Weekend event takes place in June, with guided tours of the gardens and Bluebell Walk in Cawdor Big Wood.

Times: Open May-9 Oct, daily 10-5.30. Last admission 5.
Fee: ✱ £6.50 (ch 5-15 £3.70, pen £5.50). Family ticket £19. Party 20+ £5.70 each. Gardens, grounds & nature trails only £3.50.
Facilities: 🅿 💺 ✗ licensed ♿ (ramps to restaurants, shops and gardens) toilets for disabled shop ✖ (ex guide dogs) ◀

CULLODEN MOOR CULLODEN BATTLEFIELD

IV2 5EU
Dir: (B9006, 5m E of Inverness) **Map Ref:** *NH74*
☎ **01463 790607** 📄 **01463 794294**
e-mail: culloden@nts.org.uk

A cairn recalls the Battle of Culloden, the last battle fought on mainland Britain, on 16 April 1746, when the Duke of Cumberland's forces routed Bonnie Prince Charles Edward Stuart's army. The battlefield has been restored to its state on the day of the battle, and in summer there are living history enactments. This is a most atmospheric evocation of tragic events. Telephone for details of guided tours.

Times: Open Site: all year, daily. Visitor Centre: Feb-Mar & Nov-Dec, daily 11-4; Apr-Jun & Sep-Oct, daily 9-6; Jul-Aug, daily 9-7. Times may change for 2005 please telephone or check on www.nts.org.uk **Fee:** ✱ £5 (concessions £3.75) Family ticket £13.50. Group adult £4 (ch/school £1). Please book groups in advance. Admission free to NTS members. For other details please phone 0131 243 9387 **Facilities:** 🅿 ✗ ♿ (wheelchair, induction loop, raised map) toilets for disabled shop ✖ (ex guide dogs) ♨

DRUMNADROCHIT OFFICIAL LOCH NESS MONSTER EXHIBITION CENTRE

IV3 6TU
Dir: (on A82, 12m S Inverness) **Map Ref:** NH52
☎ **01456 450573 & 450218** 📄 **01456 450770**
e-mail: brem@loch-ness-scotland.com

The Official Loch Ness Monster Exhibition is a fascinating and popular multi-media presentation lasting 30 minutes. Seven themed areas cover the story from the pre-history of Scotland, through the cultural roots of the legend in Highland folklore, and into the 50-year controversy which surrounds it. Using latest technology in computer animation, lasers and multi-media projection systems.

Times: ✱ Open all year; Etr-May 9.30-5.30; Jun-Sep 9.30-6 (9-8.30 Jul & Aug); Winter 10-4. (Last admission 30mins before closing).
Facilities: 🅿 🍺 ✕ licensed & (parking) toilets for disabled shop ✖ (ex in grounds/guide dogs) 🍴

DUNBEATH LAIDHAY CROFT MUSEUM

KW6 6EH
Dir: (1m N of Dunbeath on A9) **Map Ref:** ND12
☎ **01593 731244**

The museum gives visitors a glimpse of a long-vanished way of life. The main building is a thatched Caithness longhouse, with the dwelling quarters, byre and stable all under one roof. It dates back some 200 years, and is furnished as it might have been 100 years ago. A collection of early farm tools and machinery is also shown. Near the house is a thatched winnowing barn with its roof supported on three 'Highland couples', or crucks.

Times: Open Etr-Oct, daily 10-6. **Fee:** £2 (ch 50p) **Facilities:** 🅿 🍺 & toilets for disabled

ELPHIN HIGHLAND & RARE BREEDS FARM

IV27 4HH
Dir: (on A835 in Elphin) **Map Ref:** NC21
☎ **01854 666204** 📄 **01854 666204**

At the Highland & Rare Breeds Farm you can see highland cattle, traditional four-horned sheep with coloured fleeces, Scottish ewes and lambs, and rare breeds of pigs and goats. There are many types of poultry, duck ponds, and a farm walk among the animals. Also on display are farm tools, crofting history exhibits, wool crafts and hand-spinning.

Times: Open Jul & Aug only **Fee:** ✱ £3.95 (ch £2.95, students & pen £3.50)
Facilities: 🅿 & (assistance available) toilets for disabled shop ✖ 🍴

FORT WILLIAM WEST HIGHLAND MUSEUM

Cameron Square PH33 6AJ
Dir: (museum next door to tourist office) *Map Ref:* NN17
☎ 01397 702169 🖹 01397 701927
e-mail: info@westhighlandmuseum.org.uk

Displays at the West Highland Museum illustrate traditional Highland life and history, through pictures, photographs, artefacts, archaeology, geology and archives. There are numerous Jacobite relics, including the 'secret portrait' of Bonnie Prince Charlie, which looks like meaningless daubs of paint but reveals a portrait when reflected in a metal cylinder. Popular activities are provided for children during the summer.

Times: Open all year Jun-Sep, Mon-Sat 10-5 (also July-Aug, Sun 2-5); Oct-May, Mon-Sat 10-4.
Fee: £3 (ch 50p, concessions £2)
Facilities: P (100yds) (charge May-Oct, max. 2hrs stay) & toilets for disabled shop ✈ (ex guide dogs)

GAIRLOCH GAIRLOCH HERITAGE MUSEUM

Achtercairn IV21 2BP
Dir: (on junct of A382 & B8021 near police station & public car park) *Map Ref:* NG87
☎ 01445 712287
e-mail: info@gairlochheritagemuseum.org.uk

A converted farmstead now houses the award-winning museum, which shows the way of life in this typical West Highland parish from early times to the 20th century. There are hands-on activities for children and reconstructions of a croft house room, a school room, a shop, and a smugglers' cave. You can also view Gairloch through one of the largest lenses assembled by the Northern Lighthouse Board.

Times: Open Apr-Sep, Mon-Sat 10-5; Oct, Mon-Fri 10-1.30 (last admission 4.30). Winter months by arrangement. **Facilities:** P & shop ✈ (ex guide dogs)

GLENCOE GLENCOE & NORTH LORN FOLK MUSEUM

PH49 4HS
Dir: (turn off A82 at Glencoe x-roads then immediately right into Glencoe village) *Map Ref:* NN15
☎ 01855 811664

Two heather-thatched cottages in the main street of Glencoe house the collections of the Glencoe and North Lorn Folk Museum. These feature items connected with the Macdonalds, the massacre at Glencoe and the Jacobite risings. A variety of local domestic and farming exhibits, dairying and slate-working equipment, costumes and embroidery are also shown.

Times: Open 20 May-Sep, Mon-Sat 10-5.30.
Fee: ✱ £2 (ch free, concessions £1.50).
Facilities: P & shop

GLENCOE VISITOR CENTRE

PA39 4HX
Dir: (on A82, 17m S of Fort William) *Map Ref:* NN15
☎ **01855 811307 & 811729** 📄 **01855 811772**

Glencoe has stunning scenery and some of the most challenging climbs and walks in the Highlands. Red deer, wildcats, eagles and ptarmigan are among the wildlife. It is also known as a place of treachery and infamy. The Macdonalds of Glencoe were hosts to a party of troops who, under government orders, fell upon them, men, women and children, in a bloody massacre in 1692. The visitor centre tells the story.

Times: Open: Site all year, daily. Visitor Centre Apr-Aug, 9.30-5.30; Mar-Apr & Sep-Oct, daily 10-5; Nov-Feb, Fri-Mon 10-4 (last admission 30 mins before closing). Times may change for 2005 please telephone or check on www.nts.org.uk
Fee: ✶ 50p (ch & pen 30p). Includes parking. For more details phone 0131 243 9387
Facilities: 🅿 💻 ♿ (induction loop in video programme room) toilets for disabled shop ✖ (ex guide dogs) ♉

HELMSDALE TIMESPAN

Dunrobin St KW8 6JX
Dir: (off A9 in centre of village, by Telford Bridge)
Map Ref: ND01
☎ **01431 821327** 📄 **01431 821058**
e-mail: admin@timespan.org.uk

Located in a historic fishing village, this museum relates to the social and natural history of the area, and the art gallery shows changing exhibitions of contemporary art and works by local artists. The garden has over 100 varieties of herbs and plants. There is a gift shop, and a café with beautiful views of the Telford Bridge.

Times: Open Apr- Oct, Mon-Sat 10-5, Sun 12-5.
Fee: £4 (ch £2 pen & student £3). Family ticket £10. **Facilities:** 🅿 (150 mtrs) 💻 ♿ (lift) toilets for disabled shop garden centre ✖ (ex guide dogs) 🖼

KINCRAIG HIGHLAND WILDLIFE PARK

PH21 1NL
Dir: (on B9152, 7m S of Aviemore) *Map Ref:* NH80
☎ **01540 651270** 📄 **01540 651236**
e-mail: info@highlandwildlifepark.org

As you drive through the main reserve at this wildlife park, you can see awe-inspiring European bison grazing alongside wild horses, red deer and highland cattle plus a wide variety of other species. Then in the walk-round forest, woodland and moorland habitats prepare for close encounters with animals such as wolves, capercaillie, arctic foxes, wildcats, pine martens, otters and owls. Special events are held every weekend April to October.

Times: Open throughout the year, weather permitting. Apr-Oct, 10-6; Jun-Aug 10-7; Nov-Mar 10-4. (Last entry 2 hours before closing). **Fee:** £8 (child £5.50, pen £7). **Facilities:** 🅿 💻 ♿ toilets for disabled shop ✖ 🖼

KINGUSSIE HIGHLAND FOLK MUSEUM

Duke St PH21 1JG
Dir: (12m SW of Aviemore off A9 at Kingussie) *Map Ref:* NH70
☎ 01540 661307 📄 01540 661631
e-mail: highland.folk@highland.gov.uk

First established in 1935, this was Britain's first open air museum. For a glimpse of life in a Blackhouse or a look at farming implements and domestic objects and furniture, the Kingussie museum offers an internationally renowned collection of items. The Museum Store, not accessible to visitors in previous years, now displays in excess of 1,500 objects.

Times: Open Apr-Aug, Mon-Sat 9.30-5.30; Sep & Oct Mon-Fri, 9.30-4.30 **Fee:** ✱ £2.50 (ch & pen £1.50) **Facilities:** 🅿 ♿ (ramp, door, rails) toilets for disabled shop ✖ (ex guide dogs) 🎩

NEWTONMORE HIGHLAND FOLK MUSEUM

Aultlarie Croft PH20 1AY
Dir: (on A86, follow signs off A9) *Map Ref:* NN79
☎ 01540 661307 📄 01540 661631
e-mail: highland.folk@highland.gov.uk

An early 18th-century farming township with turf houses has been reconstructed at this award-winning museum. A 1930's school houses old world maps, little wooden desks and a Coates library. Other attractions include a working croft with rare breed animals and a tailor's workshop. Vintage buses run throughout the site.

Times: Open Apr-Aug, Mon-Sun 10.30-5.30; Sep Mon-Sun, 11-4.30; Oct Mon-Fri, 11-4.30 **Fee:** ✱ £5 (ch & pen £3) **Facilities:** 🅿 ☕ ♿ (vintage bus with full disabled access) toilets for disabled shop ✖ (ex guide dogs) 🎩

POOLEWE INVEREWE GARDEN

IV22 2LG
Dir: (6m NE of Gairloch, on A832) *Map Ref:* NG88
☎ 01445 781200 📄 01445 781497
e-mail: inverewe@nts.org.uk

The influence of the North Atlantic Drift enables this remarkable 50-acre garden to grow rare and sub-tropical plants. It was created by Osgood Hanbury Mackenzie, who began the work in 1863, and carried on by his daughter Mairi T Sawyer, who gave the Inverewe Estate to the National Trust for Scotland in 1953. At its best in early June, but full of beauty from March to October, Inverewe has a backdrop of magnificent mountains and is set on a peninsular on the shore of Loch Ewe. There is visitor centre and marked footpaths.

Times: Open: Garden all year, Apr-Oct, daily 9.30-9 (or sunset if earlier). Nov-Mar, 9.30-4. Visitor Centre Apr-Sep, daily 9.30-5; Oct, daily 9.30-4. Times may change for 2005 please telephone or check on www.nts.org.uk **Fee:** ✱ £7 (concessions £5.25) Family ticket £19. Groups adult £5.60 (ch/school £1). Admission free to NTS members. For other details please phone 0131 243 9387 **Facilities:** 🅿 ✖ licensed ♿ (some paths difficult) toilets for disabled shop ✖ (ex guide dogs) 🌿

STRATHPEFFER   HIGHLAND MUSEUM OF CHILDHOOD

The Old Station IV14 9DH
Dir: (5m W of Dingwall on A834) **Map Ref:** NH45
☎ **01997 421031** 📄 **01997 421031**
e-mail: info@highlandmuseumofchildhood.org.uk

Located in a renovated Victorian railway station of 1885, the museum tells the story of childhood in the Highlands amongst the crofters and townsfolk; a way of life recorded in oral testimony, displays, and evocative photographs. An award-winning video, *A Century of Highland Childhood*, is shown. There are also doll and toy collections.

Times: Open Apr-Oct, daily 10-5, (Sun 2-5) also Jul & Aug evenings open to 7. Other times by arrangement. **Fee:** £2 (ch, pen & students £1.50). Family ticket £5 (2ad+3ch).
Facilities: 🅿 🖭 ♿ (tape tour with induction loop for partially sighted) shop ✖ (ex guide dogs) ◀

DALKEITH   EDINBURGH BUTTERFLY & INSECT WORLD

Dobbies Garden World, Lasswade EH18 1AZ
Dir: (0.5m S of Edinburgh city bypass at Gilmerton junct or Sherrithall rdbt) **Map Ref:** NT36
☎ **0131 663 4932** 📄 **0131 654 2774**
e-mail: info@edinburgh-butterfly-world.co.uk

Richly coloured butterflies from all over the world can be seen flying among exotic rainforest plants, trees and flowers. The tropical pools are filled with giant water lilies and colourful fish, and are surrounded by lush vegetation. Scorpions, leaf cutting ants, beetles, tarantulas and other remarkable creatures are also shown, and there is a unique honeybee display and daily insect handling sessions.

Times: Open Summer daily 9.30-5.30; Winter daily 10-5. Closed 25-26 Dec & 1 Jan.
Fee: ✱ £4.70 (ch, concessions & students £3.60). Family ticket £15 (2ad+2ch). Party 10+.
Facilities: 🅿 🖭 ♿ toilets for disabled shop garden centre ✖ (ex guide dogs) ◀

NEWTONGRANGE   SCOTTISH MINING MUSEUM

Lady Victoria Colliery EH22 4QN
Dir: (10m S of Edinburgh on A7, signed from bypass)
Map Ref: NT36
☎ **0131 663 7519** 📄 **0131 654 0952**
e-mail: visitorservices@scottishminingmuseum.com

Based at the Lady Victoria Colliery at Newtowngrange, Scotland's national mining museum offers an outstanding visit to Britain's finest Victorian colliery. Guided tours with miners, magic helmets, exhibitions, theatres, interactive displays and a visit to the coal face make this a fascinating day out. The museum is also home to Scotland's largest steam engine.

Times: Open all year, daily Mar-Nov, 10-5. (Last entry 3.30). Dec-Feb daily 10-4. (Last entry 2.30) **Fee:** ✱ £4.95 (ch & concessions £3.30). Family ticket £15. Party 20+. **Facilities:** 🅿 🖭 ✖ ♿ (Tactile Opportunites, interactive, audio tours) toilets for disabled shop ✖ (ex guide dogs) ◀

Midlothian continued

PENICUIK EDINBURGH CRYSTAL VISITOR CENTRE
Eastfield EH26 8HB
Dir: (on A701Edinburgh to Peebles road) *Map Ref:* NT26
☎ 01968 675128 🗎 01968 674847
e-mail: visitorcentre@edinburgh-crystal.co.uk

Watch skilled craftsmen as they take molten crystal and turn it into intricately decorated glassware. Not only can you talk to the craftsmen themselves but there is also video footage, story boards, artefacts and audio listening posts to help you understand the 300-year-old history of glassmaking. The shop includes the largest selection of Edinburgh crystal plus seconds at bargain prices.

Times: Open Mon-Sat 10-5, Sun 11-5.
Fee: ✱ Tours £3.50 (concessions £2.50). Family ticket £9. Party 12+. **Facilities:** 🅿 🍽 ✕ licensed 🅰 (ramp to first floor) toilets for disabled shop ✖ (ex guide dogs) ◀

BRODIE CASTLE BRODIE CASTLE
IV36 2TE
Dir: (4.5m W of Forres, off A96) *Map Ref:* NH95
☎ 01309 641371 🗎 01309 641600
e-mail: brodiecastle@nts.org.uk

The Brodie family lived here for hundreds of years before passing the castle to the National Trust for Scotland in 1980. It contains many treasures, including furniture, porcelain and paintings. The extensive grounds include a woodland walk and an adventure playground. Wheelchairs for disabled visitors are available. Please telephone for details of recitals, concerts, open air theatre and other events.

Times: Open Apr & Jul-Aug, daily 12-4; May-Jun & Sep, Sun-Thu 12-4. Grounds all year, daily, 9.30-sunset. Times may change for 2005 please telephone or check on www.nts.org.uk **Fee:** ✱ £5 (concessions £3.75) Groups adults £4 (ch/school £1), please book groups in advance. Family ticket £13.50. Garden, grounds & car parking £1. Admission free to NTS members. For other details please phone 0131 243 9387 **Facilities:** 🅿 🍽 🅰 (audio tape & information sheet in Braille) toilets for disabled shop ✖ (ex guide dogs) ❦

BUCKIE BUCKIE DRIFTER MARITIME HERITAGE CENTRE
Freuchny Rd AB56 1TT
Dir: (off A98 at March Rd Industrial Estate. Continue N to rdbt, straight ahead then left. Car park on right at bottom of hill)
Map Ref: NJ46
☎ 01542 834646 🗎 01542 835995
e-mail: buckie.drifter@moray.gov.uk

An exciting maritime heritage centre, where you can discover what life was like in the fishing communities of Moray District during the herring boom years of the 1890s and 1930s. Sign on as a crew member of a steam drifter and find out how to catch herring. Try your hand at packing fish in a barrel.

Times: ✱ Open end Mar-end Oct **Facilities:** 🅿 🍽 🅰 (car parking, touch display on lower floor) toilets for disabled shop ✖ (ex assistance dogs) ◀

ELGIN *ELGIN MUSEUM*

1 High St IV30 1EQ
Dir: (E end of High St, follow brown heritage signs)
Map Ref: NJ26
☎ **01343 543675** 🖨 **01343 543675**
e-mail: curator@elginmuseum.org.uk

This award-winning museum, independently run by the Moray
Society, is internationally famous for its fossil fish, fossil reptiles
and its Pictish stones. Collections of some 36,000 items include a
locally discovered Roman hoard. Other displays relate to the
natural and human history of Moray, and a recent acquisition is a
set of miniatures of the Parthenon Frieze - the Elgin Marbles - by
John Henning.

Times: Open Apr-Oct, Mon-Fri 10-5, Sat 11-4, Sun
2-5. **Facilities:** P (50mtrs) & (handrails, case
displays at sitting level with large fonts) toilets for
disabled shop ✖ (ex guide dogs)

FOCHABERS *BAXTERS HIGHLAND VILLAGE*

IV32 7LD
Dir: (1m W of Fochabers on A96) *Map Ref:* NJ35
☎ **01343 820666** 🖨 **01343 821790**   **FREE**
e-mail: highland.village@Baxters.co.uk

The Baxters food firm started here over 130 years ago and now
sells its products in over 60 countries. Visitors can see the shop
where the story began, watch an audio-visual display, and visit
five shops. See the great hall, audio-visual theatre and cooking
theatre. A food tasting area is a new addition.

Times: Open all year, Jan-Mar 10-5; Apr-Dec
9-5.30. **Facilities:** P ✖ licensed & (parking
facilities) toilets for disabled shop ✖ (ex guide
dogs) 🍴

FORRES *FALCONER MUSEUM*

Tolbooth St IV36 1PH
Dir: (11m W of Elgin, 26m E of Iverness) *Map Ref:* NJ05
☎ **01309 673701** 🖨 **01309 673701**
e-mail: museums@moray.gov.uk

This museum was founded by bequests made by two brothers,
Alexander and Hugh Falconer. Hugh was a distinguished scientist,
friend of Darwin, recipient of many honours and Vice-President of
the Royal Society. On display are fossil mammals collected by
him, and items relating to his involvement in the study of
anthropology. Other displays are on local wildlife, geology,
archaeology and history. You can also see the Forres
Quincentennial Time Capsule.

Times: Open all year Apr-Oct, Mon-Sat 10-5;
Nov-Mar, Mon-Thu 11-12.30 & 1-3.30. Closed
Good Fri & May Day **Fee:** ✱ Donations welcome
Facilities: P & (induction loop system) shop
✖ (ex guide dogs)

Moray continued

SPEY BAY THE MORAY FIRTH WILDLIFE CENTRE

IV32 7PJ
Dir: (off A96 onto B9014 at Fochabers, follow road approx 5m to village of Spey Bay. Turn left at Spey Bay Hotel and follow road for 500mtrs) **Map Ref:** NJ36
☎ 01343 820339 ▤ 01343 829109   FREE
e-mail: enquiries@mfwc.co.uk

This wildlife centre, owned and operated by the Whale and Dolphin Conservation Society, lies at the mouth of the River Spey and is housed in a former salmon fishing station, built in 1768. There is a free exhibition about the Moray Firth dolphins and the wildlife of Spey Bay. Visitors can browse through a well-stocked gift shop and enjoy refreshments in the cosy tea room.

Times: Open Apr-Oct 10.30-5. Check for winter opening times **Facilities:** ℙ ☕ ♿ toilets for disabled shop ✖ (ex guide dogs & outside) ◀

TOMINTOUL TOMINTOUL MUSEUM

The Square AB37 9ET
Dir: (on A939, 13m E of Grantown) **Map Ref:** NJ11
☎ 01309 673701 ▤ 01309 673701
e-mail: museums@moray.gov.uk

Tomintoul is one of the highest villages in Britain and the museum is located in the village square. The exhibits feature reconstructions of a crofter's kitchen and smiddy, with other displays on the area's wildlife, the story of Tomintoul, the local skiing industry and Glenlivet. Incorporated into the museum are a Tourist Information Centre and a shop.

Times: Open 25 Mar-May, Mon-Fri 9.30-12 & 2-4; Jun-Aug, Mon-Sat, 9.30-12 & 2-4.30; Sep, Mon-Sat, 9.30-12 & 2-4; 30 Sep-25 Oct, Mon-Fri, 9.30-12 & 2-4. Closed May Day & Good Fri.
Fee: ✱ Donations welcome.
Facilities: ℙ ♿ (induction loop and sound commentaries) shop ✖ (ex guide dogs)

IRVINE SCOTTISH MARITIME MUSEUM

Harbourside KA12 8QE
Dir: (Follow AA signs from Irvine) **Map Ref:** NS34
☎ 01294 278283 ▤ 01294 313211
e-mail: smm@tildesley.fsbusiness.co.uk

The museum has displays that reflect all aspects of Scottish maritime history. Vessels can be seen afloat in the harbour and under cover, and you can experience life in a 1910 shipyard worker's tenement flat. The Linthouse Engine Shop, originally built in 1872, is being developed and holds a substantial part of the museum's collection in open store.

Times: Open Apr-Oct 10-5 **Fee:** ✱ £2.50 (ch & pen £1.75). Family ticket £5. **Facilities:** ℙ ☕ ♿ (audio tapes for blind) toilets for disabled shop ✖ (ex guide dogs)

VENNEL GALLERY

10 Glasgow Vennel KA12 0BD
Map Ref: NS34
☎ **01294 275059** 🖨 **01294 275059** FREE
e-mail: vennel@north-ayrshire.gov.uk

The Vennel Gallery has a reputation for exciting and varied exhibitions, ranging from international to local artists. Behind the museum is the heckling shop where Robert Burns, Scotland's most famous poet, spent part of his youth learning the trade of flax dressing. In addition to the audio-visual programme on Burns, there is a reconstruction of his lodgings at No 4 Glasgow Vennel, Irvine.

Times: Open all year Thu-Sun 10-1 & 2-5
Facilities: P (residential area) & shop
✖ (ex guide dogs)

LARGS   KELBURN CASTLE AND COUNTRY CENTRE

Fairlie KA29 0BE
Dir: (2m S of Largs, on A78) *Map Ref:* NS25
☎ **01475 568685** 🖨 **01475 568121**
e-mail: admin@kelburncountrycentre.com

Historic home of the Earls of Glasgow, Kelburn is famous for its romantic glen, family gardens, unique trees and spectacular views over the Firth of Clyde. The centre offers glen walks, a riding and trekking centre, an adventure course, activity workshop, Kelburn Story Cartoon Exhibition and a family museum. The 'Secret Forest', Scotland's most unusual attraction, is a chance to explore the Giant's Castle, Maze of the Green Man and Secret Grotto. A recent addition is the Falconry Centre.

Times: Open all year, Etr-end Oct, daily 10-6; Nov-Mar, 11-dusk, Grounds only. **Fee:** ✱ £5 (concessions £3.50). Family tickets £15.
Facilities: P ✖ licensed & (Ranger service to assist disabled) toilets for disabled shop ◀

VIKINGAR!

Greenock Rd KA30 8QL
Dir: (on A78, 0.5m into Largs, opposite RNLI lifeboat station)
Map Ref: NS25
☎ **01475 689777** 🖨 **01475 689444**
e-mail: anyone@vikingar.co.uk

This award-winning attraction is located next to Largs promenade with fantastic views over the Firth of Clyde and the Isles of Cumbrae. It is an exciting multi-media experience that takes you from the first Viking raids in Scotland to their defeat at the Battle of Largs. The experience comes complete with Viking sounds and smells.

Times: ✱ Open daily, Apr-Sep, Mon-Fri & Sun 10.30-5.30, Sat 12.30-3.30; Oct-Mar, daily 10.30-3.30; Nov & Feb, wknds only, Sat 12.30-3.30, Sun 10.30-3.30. Closed Dec & Jan.
Facilities: P & toilets for disabled shop ✖ (ex guide dogs) ◀

COATBRIDGE SUMMERLEE HERITAGE TRUST

Heritage Way, West Canal St ML5 1QD
Dir: (follow main routes towards town centre, adjacent to Coatbridge central station) **Map Ref:** NS76
☎ 01236 431261 📄 01236 440429 FREE
e-mail: museums@northlan.gov.uk

A 20-acre museum of social and industrial history centring on the remains of the Summerlee Ironworks, which were put into blast in the 1830s. The exhibition hall features displays of social and industrial history including working machinery and recreated workshop interiors. Outside, Summerlee operates the only working tram in Scotland, a coal mine and reconstructed miners' rows with interiors dating from 1840.

Times: Open daily 10-5. Nov-Mar 10-4. Closed 25-26 Dec & 1-2 Jan. **Facilities:** 🅿 ☕ & (wheelchair available & staff assistance) toilets for disabled shop ✸ (ex guide dogs)

MOTHERWELL MOTHERWELL HERITAGE CENTRE

High Rd ML1 3HU
Dir: (A723 for town centre. Left at top of hill, after pedestrian crossing and just before railway bridge) **Map Ref:** NS75
☎ 01698 251000 📄 01698 268867 FREE
e-mail: museums@northlan.gov.uk

This award winning audio-visual experience, 'Technopolis', traces the history of the area from Roman times to the rise of 19th-century industry and the post-industrial era. There is also a fine viewing tower, an exhibition gallery and family history research facilities. A mixed programme of community events and touring exhibitions occur throughout the year.

Times: Open Wed-Sat 10-5 (Thu 10-7), Sun 12-5. Closed Mon & Tue, ex BHs
Facilities: 🅿 & (lifts, audio info & Braille buttons) toilets for disabled shop ✸ (ex guide dogs)

BLAIR ATHOLL BLAIR CASTLE

PH18 5TL
Dir: (off A9 at Blair Atholl & follow signs) **Map Ref:** NN86
☎ 01796 481207 📄 01796 481487
e-mail: office@blair-castle.co.uk

Blair Castle is the ancient seat of the Dukes of Atholl and the Atholl Highlanders, the Duke's unique private army. The castle dates back to the 13th century but was altered in the 18th, and later given a castellated exterior. The oldest part is Cumming's Tower, built in about 1270. There are paintings, furniture, porcelain, historic artefacts, Jacobite relics, and Masonic regalia. The extensive grounds include a deer park, and a restored 18th-century walled garden. Events are held throughout the year.

Times: Open 2 Nov-15 Mar, Tue-Sat 9.30-12.30 (last admission); 19 Mar-28 Oct, daily 9.30-4.30 (last admission). **Fee:** Prices not confirmed for 2005 **Facilities:** 🅿 ☕ ✕ licensed & (scooter, parking) shop ✸ (ex guide dogs) ◀

KINROSS   LOCH LEVEN CASTLE

Castle Island KY13 7AR
Dir: (on an island in Loch Leven accessible by boat from Kinross)
Map Ref: NO10
☎ **01786 450000**

Mary Queen of Scots was imprisoned here in this five-storey castle in 1567 - she escaped 11 months later and gave the 14th-century castle its special place in history. The castle stands on an island in the middle of Loch Leven, which is accessible by boat from the main pier opposite Kirkgate Park.

Times: Open Apr-Sep, daily 9.30-6.30.
Fee: ✶ £3.50 (ch £1.20, concessions £2.50). Charge includes ferry trip. Groups 11+ 10% discount. Rates valid until 2 Jan 2005. Please phone for further details. **Facilities:** 🅿 shop ✖ ▯

RSPB NATURE RESERVE VANE FARM

By Loch Leven KY13 9LX
Dir: (2m E of M90 junct 5, on S shore of Loch Leven, entered off B9097 to Glenrothes) *Map Ref:* NO10
☎ **01577 862355** 🖶 **01577 862013**
e-mail: vane.farm@rspb.org.uk

This RSPB reserve is well placed beside Loch Leven, with a nature trail and hides overlooking the Loch and a woodland trail with stunning panoramic views. It is noted for its pink-footed geese, and the area also attracts whooper swans, greylag geese and great spotted woodpeckers, amongst others. Details of special events are available from the visitors centre.

Times: Open daily, 10-5. Closed 25-26 Dec & 1-2 Jan. **Fee:** £3 (ch 50p, concessions £2). Family £6. **Facilities:** 🅿 ▆ ♿ (wheelchair extensions, ramps, telescopes) toilets for disabled shop ✖ (ex guide dogs) ◂

PITLOCHRY   SCOTTISH & SOUTHERN ENERGY VISITOR CENTRE, DAM & FISH PASS

PH16 5ND
Dir: (off A9, 24m N of Perth) *Map Ref:* NN95
☎ **01796 473152** 🖶 **01882 634 709**

The visitor centre at Scottish & Southern Energy features an exhibition showing how electricity is brought from the power station to the customer, and there is access to the turbine viewing gallery. The salmon ladder viewing chamber allows you to see the fish as they travel upstream to their spawning ground.

Times: Open Apr-Sep, Mon-Fri 10-5.30. Wknd opening Jul, Aug & BHs **Fee:** *Prices not confirmed for 2005* **Facilities:** 🅿 ♿ (monitor viewing of salmon fish pass) toilets for disabled shop ✖ (ex guide dogs) ◂

QUEEN'S VIEW   QUEEN'S VIEW VISITOR CENTRE

PH16 5NR
Dir: (7m W of Pitlochry on B8019) *Map Ref:* NN85
☎ 01350 727284   📄 01350 728635
e-mail: peter.fullarton@forestry.gsi.gov.uk

Queen Victoria admired the view on a visit here in 1866; it is possibly one of the most famous views in Scotland. The area, in the heart of the Tay Forest Park, has a variety of woodlands that visitors can walk or cycle in. A new exhibition and audio-visual display 'The Cradle of Scottish Forestry' tells the history of the people and the forests of highland Perthshire.

Times: Open Apr-Oct, daily 10-6. **Fee:** *Prices not confirmed for 2005* **Facilities:** 🅿 (charged) ☕ & toilets for disabled shop 🛍

SCONE   SCONE PALACE

PH2 6BD
Dir: (2m NE of Perth on A93) *Map Ref:* NO12
☎ 01738 552300   📄 01738 552588
e-mail: visits@scone-palace.co.uk

Scottish kings were crowned at Scone until 1651 and it was the site of the famous coronation Stone of Destiny from the 9th century until the English seized the Stone in 1296. The castellated edifice of the present palace dates from 1803 but incorporates the 16th-century and earlier buildings. The interior houses objets d'art, including French and Scottish furniture, an extensive porcelain collection and paintings. The grounds include a pinetum, the original Douglas Fir, the unique Murray Star Maze, woodland walks and herbaceous plantings. There is also the David Douglas Trail.

Times: Open Apr-Oct. **Fee:** *Prices not confirmed for 2005* **Facilities:** 🅿 ☕ ✕ licensed & (stairlift which gives access to all state rooms) toilets for disabled shop 🛍

WEEM   CASTLE MENZIES

PH15 2JD
Dir: (follow signs from main roads) *Map Ref:* NN84
☎ 01887 820982   📄 01887 820982
e-mail: menziesclan@tesco.net

Restored seat of the Chiefs of Clan Menzies, and a fine example of a 16th-century Z-plan fortified tower house. Prince Charles Edward Stuart stayed here briefly on his way to Culloden in 1746. The whole of the 16th-century building can be explored, and there is a small clan museum.

Times: Open Apr-13 Sep, Mon-Sat 10.30-5, Sun 2-5. **Fee:** £3.50 (ch £2, concessions £3). **Facilities:** 🅿 & toilets for disabled shop ✕ (ex guide dogs)

KILBARCHAN WEAVER'S COTTAGE

The Cross PA10 2JG
Dir: (off A737, 12m SW of Glasgow) **Map Ref:** NS46
☎ **01505 705588**
e-mail: aclipson@nts.scot.demon.co.uk

The last of the 800 looms working in this village in the 1830s is housed at this delightful 18th-century cottage museum. It is a typical handloom weaver's cottage, built in 1723, and on display is a collection of weaving equipment and other domestic utensils. The weaving craft is regularly demonstrated, and there is a DVD presentation on the village's links with the production of Paisley shawls.

Times: Open Apr-Sep, Fri-Tue, 1-5; morning visits available for pre-booked groups. Times may change for 2005 please telephone or check on www.nts.org.uk **Fee:** ✱ £3.50 (concessions £2.60) Family ticket £9.50. Groups adult £2.80 (ch/school £1). Please book groups in advance. Admission free to NTS members. For other details please phone 0131 243 9387
Facilities: P ✖ (ex guide dogs) ✿

LANGBANK FINLAYSTONE COUNTRY ESTATE

PA14 6TJ
Dir: (on A8 W of Langbank, 10m W of Glasgow Airport, follow Thistle signs) **Map Ref:** NS37
☎ **01475 540505** 🖷 **01475 540285**
e-mail: info@finlaystone.co.uk

Finlaystone is a beautiful country estate with views over the Firth of Clyde, woodland walks, waterfalls and imaginative play areas for children. It also has historic formal gardens which are renowned for their natural beauty. The 'Dolly Mixture', an international collection of dolls, can be seen in the visitor centre. The estate is managed by the family of the Chief of the Clan MacMillan.

Times: Open all year Woodland & Gardens daily, 10-5.
Fee: ✱ Garden & Woods £3 (ch & pen £2). 'The Dolly Mixture' Doll Museum free. **Facilities:** P 🍴 ♿ (lift to second floor pathways for wheelchairs) toilets for disabled shop 🛍

LOCHWINNOCH RSPB LOCHWINNOCH NATURE RESERVE

Largs Rd PA12 4JF
Dir: (on A760, Largs road, opposite Lochwinnoch station, 16m SW of Glasgow) **Map Ref:** NS35
☎ **01505 842663** 🖷 **01505 843026**
e-mail: Lochwinnoch@rspb.org.uk

The reserve, one of the few remaining wetland sites in the west of Scotland, is part of Clyde-Muirshiel Regional Park and a Site of Special Scientific Interest. It comprises two shallow lochs fringed by marsh, which in turn is fringed by scrub and woodland. There are two trails leading to three hides and a visitor centre with a viewing tower and telescopes.

Times: Open all year, daily 10-5. Closed 1-2 Jan & 25-26 Dec. **Fee:** *Prices not confirmed for 2005*
Facilities: P ♿ (hides are all wheelchair accessible) toilets for disabled shop ✖ 🛍

Renfrewshire continued

PAISLEY COATS OBSERVATORY

49 Oakshaw St West PA1 2DE
Dir: (M8 junct 27, follow signs to town centre to Gordon St
(A761). Left onto Causeyside St, left onto New St then left onto
High St) **Map Ref:** NS46
☎ **0141 889 2013** 🖹 **0141 889 9240**   **FREE**
e-mail: museums.els@renfrewshire.gov.uk

The Observatory, funded by Thomas Coats and designed by John
Honeyman, was opened in 1883. It houses a five-inch telescope
under the dome at the top. Weather recording activities have
been carried out here continuously since 1884. There is also
earthquake-measuring equipment and the Renfrewshire
Astronomical Society holds regular meetings here.

Times: Open all year, Tue-Sat 10-5, Sun 2-5. Last
entry 15 minutes before closing.
Facilities: P (150yds) (meters/limited street
parking) shop ✖ (ex guide dogs)

COLDSTREAM HIRSEL

Douglas & Angus Estates, Estate Office, The Hirsel TD12 4LP
Dir: (0.5m W on A697, on N outskirts of Coldstream)
Map Ref: NT84
☎ **01890 882834 & 882965** 🖹 **01890 882834**
e-mail: rogerdodd@btconnect.com

The Hirsel is the seat of the Home family, the grounds of which
are open all year. The focal point is the Homestead Museum, craft
centre and workshops. From there, nature trails lead around the
lake, along the Leet Valley and into woodland, which is noted for
its rhododendrons and azaleas.

Times: Garden & Grounds open all year, daylight
hours. Museum 10-5. Craft Centre Mon-Fri, 10-5,
wknds noon-5. **Fee:** ✱ £2 per car
Facilities: P (charged) 💻 ✖ ♿ toilets for
disabled shop

DUNS MANDERSTON

TD11 3PP
Dir: (2m E of Duns on A6105) **Map Ref:** NT75
☎ **01361 883450 882636** 🖹 **01361 882010**
e-mail: palmer@manderston.co.uk

This grandest of grand houses gives a fascinating picture of
Edwardian life above and below stairs. Completely remodelled for
the millionaire racehorse owner Sir James Miller, the architect was
told to spare no expense, and so the house boasts the world's
only silver staircase. The state rooms are magnificent, and there
are fine formal gardens, with a woodland garden and lakeside
walks. Manderston has been the setting for a number of films,
most recently *The Edwardian Country House.*

Times: Open mid May-end Sep, Thu & Sun 2-5
(also late May & Aug English BH Mons). Gardens
open until dusk. **Fee:** ✱ House & Gardens £6.50
(ch £3); Gardens only £3.50 (ch £1.50).
Facilities: P 💻 ♿ shop ✖ (ex guide dogs & in
gardens)

GALASHIELS LOCHCARRON OF SCOTLAND VISITOR CENTRE
Waverley Mill, Huddersfield St TD1 3BA
Dir: (32m S of Edinburgh on A7, follow signs to mill)
Map Ref: NT43
☎ 01896 752091 & 751100 📄 01896 758833
e-mail: quality@lochcarron.com

The museum is located in the Lochcarron of Scotland's mill, where pure new wool tartans and cashmere is woven. Guided tours of the mill take about 40 minutes and show you the process from spun yarn to finished fabric. The museum brings the town's past to life, and the focal point is a display on the woollen industry. The mill shop sells a range of knitwear, tartan and tweeds.

Times: Open all year, Mon-Sat 9-5, Sun (Jun-Sep) 12-5. Mill tours Mon-Thu at 10.30, 11.30, 1.30 & 2.30, Fri am only. **Fee:** Museum free. Mill tour £2.50 (ch 14 free). **Facilities:** 🅿 ♿ toilets for disabled shop 🍴

INNERLEITHEN ROBERT SMAIL'S PRINTING WORKS
7/9 High St EH44 6HA
Map Ref: NT33
☎ 01896 830206
e-mail: smails@nts.org.uk

The buildings at Robert Smail's Printing Works comprise a Victorian office, a paper store with a reconstructed waterwheel, a composing room and a press room. The machinery is in full working order and visitors may view the printer at work and have a go at typesetting in the composing room. The works were in the Smail family for over a hundred years, but were acquired by the National Trust for Scotland when Cowan Smail retired in 1986.

Times: Open Good Fri-Etr Mon & Jun-Sep, Thu-Mon 12-5, Sun 1-5. Times may change for 2005 please telephone or check on www.nts.org.uk **Fee:** ✱ £3.50 (concessions £2.60) Family ticket £9.50. Groups adult £2.80 (ch/school £1). Admission free for NTS members. For other details please phone 0131 243 9387 **Facilities:** 🅿 (300yds) ♿ shop ✖ (ex guide dogs) 🍴

LAUDER *THIRLESTANE CASTLE*
TD2 6RU
Dir: (off A68, S of Lauder) *Map Ref:* NT54
☎ 01578 722430 📄 01578 722761
e-mail: admin@thirlestanecastle.co.uk

One of the seven 'Great Houses of Scotland' this fairytale castle has been the home of the Maitland family, the Earls of Lauderdale, since the 12th century. Some of the most splendid plasterwork ceilings in Britain may be seen in the 17th-century state rooms. The family nurseries house a sizeable collection of antique toys and dolls. The informal riverside grounds, with their views of the grouse moors, include a woodland walk, picnic tables and adventure playground. There is also a vaulted dungeon display.

Times: ✱ Open Apr-Oct **Facilities:** 🅿 ☕ shop ✖ (ex guide dogs) 🍴

MELROSE ABBOTSFORD

TD6 9BQ
Dir: (2m W off A6091, on B6360) **Map Ref:** NT53
☎ **01896 752043** 📄 **01896 752916**
e-mail: abbotsford@melrose.bordernet.co.uk

Set on the River Tweed, Sir Walter Scott's romantic mansion remains much the same as it was in his day. Inside there are many mementoes and relics of his remarkable life and also his historical collections, armouries and library, with some 9,000 volumes. Scott built the mansion between 1811 and 1822, and lived here until his death ten years after its completion.

Times: Open daily from 3rd Mon in Mar-Oct, Mon-Sat 9.30-5. Sun in Mar-May & Oct 2-5. Sun Jun-Sep 9.30-5. **Fee:** ✱ £4.50 (ch £2.25). Party £3.70 (ch £1.85) **Facilities:** 🅿 💻 & (parking at private entrance, ramps at entrance) toilets for disabled shop ✖ (ex guide & hearing dogs) 🕮

PEEBLES KAILZIE GARDENS

EH45 9HT
Dir: (2.5m SE on B7062) **Map Ref:** NT24
☎ **01721 720007** 📄 **01721 720007**
e-mail: angela@buchan-hepburn.freeserve.co.uk

These extensive grounds, with their fine old trees, provide a burn-side walk flanked by bulbs, rhododendrons and azaleas. A walled garden contains herbaceous and shrub rose borders, greenhouses and a formal rose garden. There is a large stocked trout pond and rod hire available, and an 18-hole putting green. Some recent additions at Kailzie are the open bait pond, ornamental duck pond and osprey viewing centre.

Times: Open 25 Mar-Oct, daily 11-5.30. Grounds close 5.30. Garden open all year. **Fee:** mid Mar-Jun £2.50, Jun-Oct £3, end Oct-mid Mar £2 honesty box (ch 5-12 80p) **Facilities:** 🅿 💻 ✖ licensed & (ramps in garden) toilets for disabled shop

SELKIRK BOWHILL HOUSE AND COUNTRY PARK

TD7 5ET
Dir: (3m W of Selkirk off A708) **Map Ref:** NT42
☎ **01750 22204** 📄 **01750 22204**
e-mail: bht@buccleuch.com

An outstanding collection of pictures, including works by Van Dyck, Canaletto, Reynolds, Gainsborough and Claude Lorraine, are displayed at Bowhill. Memorabilia of people such as Queen Victoria and Sir Walter Scott, and a restored Victorian kitchen add further interest inside the house. Outside, the wooded grounds are perfect for walking. A small theatre provides a full programme of music and drama.

Times: Open, Park: Apr-Aug daily 12-5 (ex Fri). House & park: Jul, daily 1-4.30. Please phone for details as may vary. **Fee:** House & grounds £6 (ch under 5 & wheelchair users free, pen & groups £4). Grounds only £2. **Facilities:** 🅿 💻 ✖ licensed & (guided tours for the blind by appointment) toilets for disabled shop ✖ (ex in park on leads) 🕮

HALLIWELLS HOUSE MUSEUM

Halliwells Close, Market Place TD7 4BC
Dir: (off A7 in town centre) **Map Ref:** *NT42*
☎ **01750 20096** ▤ **01750 23282**
e-mail: museums@scotborders.gov.uk

A row of late 18th-century town cottages has been converted to create Halliwells House museum. Displays recreate the building's former use as an ironmonger's shop and home, and tell the story of the Royal Burgh of Selkirk. The Robson Gallery hosts a programme of contemporary art and craft exhibitions.

Times: ✱ Open Apr-Sep, Mon-Sat 10-5, Sun 10-12; Jul-Aug, Mon-Sat 10-5.30, Sun 10-12; Oct, Mon-Sat 10-4. **Facilities:** ⓟ (charged) ♿ (lift to first floor, large print, interpretation) toilets for disabled shop ✖ (ex guide dogs) ◼

STOBO   DAWYCK BOTANIC GARDEN

EH45 9JU
Dir: (8m SW of Peebles on B712) **Map Ref:** *NT13*
☎ **01721 760254** ▤ **01721 760214**
e-mail: dawyck@rbge.org.uk

From the landscaped walks of this historic arboretum an impressive collection of mature specimen trees can be seen - some over 40 metres tall. Particularly notable is the unique Dawyck beech-stand. Other features include the Swiss Bridge, a fine estate chapel and stonework and terracing produced by Italian craftsmen in the 1820s.

Times: Open daily 14 Feb-14 Nov. Feb & Nov 10-4. Mar-Oct 10-5. Apr-Sep 10-6 **Fee:** ✱ £3.50 (ch £1, concessions £3). Family ticket £8 **Facilities:** ⓟ 🍽 ♿ toilets for disabled shop garden centre ✖ (ex guide dogs) ◼

TRAQUAIR   TRAQUAIR HOUSE

EH44 6PW
Dir: (at Innerleithen take B709, house in 1m) **Map Ref:** *NT33*
☎ **01896 830323 & 830785** ▤ **01896 830639**
e-mail: enquiries@traquair.co.uk

Said to be Scotland's oldest inhabited house, Traquair House dates back to the 12th century, and 27 Scottish monarchs have stayed here. William the Lion Heart held court here, and the house has associations with Mary, Queen of Scots and the Jacobite risings. The Bear Gates were closed in 1745, not to be reopened until the Stuarts should once again ascend the throne. There is croquet, a maze and woodland walks by the River Tweed, craft workshops and a children's mini adventure playground. Also a brewery museum and shop, and an antiques shop.

Times: Open Etr-Oct **Fee:** Please telephone for admission costs. **Facilities:** ⓟ 🍽 ✖ licensed ♿ toilets for disabled shop ◼

ALLOWAY BURNS NATIONAL HERITAGE PARK

Murdoch's Lone KA7 4PQ
Dir: (2m S of Ayr) **Map Ref:** NS31
☎ 01292 443700 🖹 01292 441750
e-mail: info@burnsheritagepark.com

Alloway is the birthplace of Robert Burns, Scotland's national poet. The Burns National Heritage Park consists of a museum, Burn's Cottage, a visitor centre, tranquil landscaped gardens and historical monuments. It provides an introduction to the life of Burns, with an audio-visual presentation and a multi-screen 3D experience describing the Tale of Tam O'Shanter. A full programme of events includes the annual Burns an' a' That festival.

Times: Open all year, Apr-Sep 9.30-5.30, Tam O'Shanter experience 10-5.30, Oct-Mar 10-5. Closed 25-26 Dec & 1-2 Jan **Fee:** Adult passport £5 (pen & ch passport £2.50). **Facilities:** 🅿 ☕ ✗ licensed ♿ (wheelchair available) toilets for disabled shop ✗ (ex guide & hearing dogs) ◀

CULZEAN CASTLE CULZEAN CASTLE & COUNTRY PARK

KA19 8LE
Dir: (4m W of Maybole, off A77) **Map Ref:** NS21
☎ 01655 884455 🖹 01655 884503
e-mail: culzean@nts.org.uk

This 18th-century castle stands on a cliff in spacious grounds and was designed by Robert Adam for the Earl of Cassillis. It is noted for its oval staircase, circular drawing room and plasterwork. The Eisenhower Room explores the American general's links with Culzean. The 563-acre country park has a wide range of attractions - the shoreline, woodland walks, parkland, an adventure playground and gardens.

Times: Open Castle: Apr-Oct, daily 10.30-5 (last entry 4). Visitor centre: Apr-Oct, daily 9-5.30; Nov-Mar, wknds 11-4. Country Park: open all year 9.30-sunset. Times may change for 2005 please telephone or check on www.nts.org.uk **Fee:** ✱ £9 (concessions £6.50). Groups adult £9 (concessions £6.50) Family ticket £23. Country Park only Apr-Oct £5 (concessions £3.75). Family ticket £13.50. Group adult £4 (ch/school £1) Admission free to NTS members. For other details please phone 0131 243 9387 **Facilities:** 🅿 ☕ ✗ licensed ♿ (wheelchairs, lift in castle, Braille guides) toilets for disabled shop garden centre ✗ (ex castle, ex guide dogs) ♨

KIRKOSWALD SOUTER JOHNNIE'S COTTAGE

Main Rd KA19 8HY
Dir: (on A77, 4m SW of Maybole) **Map Ref:** NS20
☎ 01655 760603
e-mail: aclipson@nts.scot.demon.co.uk

'Souter' means cobbler and the village cobbler who lived in this 18th-century cottage was the inspiration for Burns' character Souter Johnnie, in his ballad *Tam O'Shanter*. The cottage is now a Burns museum and life-size stone figures of the poet's characters can be seen in the restored ale-house in the cottage garden.

Times: Open Apr-Sep, Fri-Tue 11.30-5. Times may change for 2005 please telephone or check on www.nts.org.uk **Fee:** ✱ £2.50 (concessions £1.90) Family ticket £7. Groups adult £2 (ch/school £1). Please book in advance for groups. Admission free to NTS members. For other details please phone 0131 243 9387 **Facilities:** 🅿 (75yds) ♿ (only one small step into cottage) ✗ (ex guide dogs) ♨

BIGGAR   GLADSTONE COURT MUSEUM

ML12 6DT
Dir: (On A702 40m from Glasgow, 30m from Edinburgh, entrance by 113 High St) *Map Ref:* NT03
☎ 01899 221050   ▤ 01899 221050
e-mail: margaret@bmtrust.freeserve.co.uk

An old-fashioned village street is portrayed in this museum, which is set out in a century-old coach-house. On display are reconstructed shops, complete with old signs and advertisements. These include a bank, a telephone exchange and photographer's booth. And there are plenty more interesting glimpses into the recent past. Activity sheets are available.

Times: Open Etr-Oct, Mon-Sat 11-4.30, Sun 2-4.30. **Fee:** ✱ £2 (ch £1, pen £1.50). Family ticket £4. Party £1.25 each. **Facilities:** ▣ & shop ✖ (ex guide dogs)

MOAT PARK HERITAGE CENTRE

ML12 6DT
Dir: (On A702, 30m from Edinburgh, 40m from Glasgow)
Map Ref: NT03
☎ 01899 221050   ▤ 01899 221050
e-mail: margaret@bmtrust.co.uk

The centre illustrates the history, archaeology and geology of the Upper Clyde and Tweed valleys with interesting models of early dwellings, mottes, castles and bastle houses. There are displays on rural, church, school and agricultural life, and a natural history section with a colony of live bees and a fun 'touch table'.

Times: Open all year, Apr-Oct, daily 11.30-4.30, Sun 2-4.30; Nov-Feb, wkdays during office hours. Other times by prior arrangement. **Fee:** ✱ £2 (ch £1, pen £1.50). Party £1.25 each. **Facilities:** ▣ & (upper floor with assistance on request) toilets for disabled shop ✖ (ex guide dogs)

BLANTYRE   DAVID LIVINGSTONE CENTRE

165 Station Rd G72 9BT
Dir: (M74 junct 5 onto A725, then A724, follow signs for Blantyre, right at lights. Centre is at foot of hill) *Map Ref:* NS65
☎ 01698 823140   ▤ 01698 821424

Share the adventurous life of Scotland's greatest explorer, David Livingstone, from his childhood in the Blantyre Mills to his explorations in the heart of Africa, dramatically illustrated in the historic tenement where he was born. Attractions include an art gallery, social history exhibit, children's animated display, a jungle garden, African playground, riverside walks, a gift shop and tearoom. Various events are planned throughout the season.

Times: Open Apr-24 Dec, Mon-Sat 10-5, Sun 12.30-5. Times may change for 2005 please telephone or check on www.nts.org.uk
Fee: ✱ £3.50 (concessions £2.60) Family ticket £9.50. Groups adult £2.80 (ch/school £1). Please book groups in advance. Admission free to NTS members. For other details please phone 0131 243 9387 **Facilities:** ▣ ▆ & toilets for disabled shop ✖ (ex guide dogs/lead grounds) ♨ ◀

EAST KILBRIDE *MUSEUM OF SCOTTISH COUNTRY LIFE*

Wester Kittochside G76 9HR
Dir: (From Glasgow take A749 to East Kilbride. From Edinburgh follow M8 to Glasgow, turn off junct 6 onto A725 to East Kilbride. Kittochside is signed before East Kilbride) *Map Ref:* NS65
☎ 01355 224 181 🖷 01355 571290
e-mail: info@nms.ac.uk

The Museum of Scottish Country Life offers an insight into the working lives of people in rural Scotland. It is a fascinating museum built on a 170-acre farm, complete with dairy cows and sheep. A programme of events runs throughout the year, demonstrating machinery from the working collection and contrasting modern and traditional farming methods. You can take a ride in the tractor trailer up to the Georgian farmhouse.

Times: Open daily 10-5. Closed 25-26 Dec & 1-2 Jan
Facilities: 🅿 ☕ ♿ (disabled parking, exhibition building is fully accessible) toilets for disabled shop ✖ (ex assist dogs) ◀

HAMILTON CHATELHERAULT COUNTRY PARK

Ferniegair ML3 7UE
Dir: (2.5km SE of Hamilton on A72 Hamilton-Larkhall/Lanark Clyde Valley tourist route) *Map Ref:* NS75
☎ 01698 426213 🖷 01698 421532   **FREE**

Designed as a hunting lodge by William Adam in 1732, Chatelherault is built of unusual pink sandstone and has been described as a gem of Scottish architecture. It is situated close to the motorway, and there is a visitor centre, shop and adventure playground. Look out for the herd of white Cadzow cattle.

Times: Open all year, Mon-Sat 10-5, Sun 12-5. House closed all day Fri & Sat. **Facilities:** 🅿 ☕ ♿ (ramps, parking, large print guide) toilets for disabled shop garden centre ✖ (ex in grounds & guide dogs) ◀

NEW LANARK NEW LANARK VISITOR CENTRE

New Lanark Visitor Centre, Mill 3, New Lanark Mills ML11 9DB
Dir: (4m S of Lanark) *Map Ref:* NS84
☎ 01555 661345 🖷 01555 66538
e-mail: trust@newlanark.org

Founded in 1785, New Lanark became well known in the early 19th century as a model community managed by enlightened industrialist and educational reformer Robert Owen. Surrounded by woodland and situated close to the Falls of Clyde, this unusual heritage site explores the philosophies of Robert Owen, using theatre, interactive displays, and the 'New Millennium Experience', a magical chair ride through history. Accommodation is also available at the New Lanark Mill Hotel.

Times: Open daily 11-5. Closed 25 Dec & 1 Jan
Fee: ✱ £5.95 (ch, concessions £3.95) family ticket (2ad+2ch) £16.95 family ticket (2ad+4ch) £19.95 **Facilities:** 🅿 ☕ ✖ licensed ♿ (ramps, disabled parking) toilets for disabled shop ✖ (ex guide dogs) ◀

BLAIR DRUMMOND *BLAIR DRUMMOND SAFARI & LEISURE PARK*

FK9 4UR
Dir: (M9 junct 10, 4m on A84 towards Callander)
Map Ref: NS79
☎ 01786 841456 & 841396 ▤ 01786 841491
e-mail: enquiries@safari-park.co.uk

Drive through the wild animal reserves where zebras, North American bison, antelope, lions, tigers, white rhino and camels can be seen at close range. Other attractions at Blair Drummond include the sea lion show, a ride on the boat safari through the waterfowl sanctuary and around Chimpanzee Island, an adventure playground, giant astraglide, and pedal boats. There are also African elephants, giraffes and ostriches.

Times: ✱ Open Apr-1 Oct, daily 10-5.30. (Last admission 4.30) **Facilities:** 🅿 ▣ ✕ licensed 🦽 (special menus & waitress service if booked in advance) toilets for disabled shop ✈ (ex guide dogs)

CALLANDER ROB ROY AND TROSSACHS VISITOR CENTRE

Ancaster Square FK17 8ED
Dir: (on A84) *Map Ref:* NN60
☎ 01877 330342 ▤ 01877 330784
e-mail: robroy&t@aillst.ossian.net

From Highland hero to Hollywood legend, follow the story of Scotland's most famous Highlander, Rob Roy. At this visitor centre attraction you can hear his innermost thoughts and witness his exploits. Step back in time and explore a reconstructed 18th-century farmhouse, just as it would have been in Rob Roy's time.

Times: Open Apr-May, daily 10-5; Jun-Sep, 10-6; Oct 10-5; Nov-Feb 11-4; Mar 10-5. (Winter openings may vary, please contact) **Fee:** *Prices not confirmed for 2005* **Facilities:** 🅿 🦽 toilets for disabled shop ✈ ◀

KILLIN BREADALBANE FOLKLORE CENTRE

Falls of Dochart FK21 8XE
Dir: (on A85) *Map Ref:* NN53
☎ 01567 820254 ▤ 01567 820764
e-mail: killin@aillst.ossian.net

Overlooking the beautiful Falls of Dochart, the Folklore Centre gives a fascinating insight into the legends of Breadalbane - Scotland's 'high country'. Learn of the magical deeds of St Fillan and hear tales of mystical giants, ancient prophesies, traditional folklore and clan history. The centre is housed in historic St Fillans Mill, which features a restored waterwheel. There is a Tourist Information Centre and gift shop on site.

Times: Open Mar-May & Oct, daily 10-5; Jun & Sep, daily 10-6; Jul-Aug, daily 9.30-6.30. Closed Nov-Feb. **Fee:** *Prices not confirmed for 2005* **Facilities:** 🅿 (30mtrs) 🦽 shop ✈ ◀

STIRLING NATIONAL WALLACE MONUMENT

Abbey Craig, Causewayhead FK8 2AD
Dir: (from A907 [Stirling to Alloa road] follow brown tourist signs)
Map Ref: NS79
☎ 01786 472140 📠 01786 461322
e-mail: nationalwallacemonument@aillst.ossian.net

Meet Scotland's national hero, William Wallace, and join his epic struggle for a free Scotland. Step into Westminster Hall and witness his trial. Climb the Wallace Monument's 220-foot tower, built in 1869 on the site of an ancient Pictish hillfort, and experience one of the finest views in Scotland. You can also see Wallace's fearsome two-handed broad sword on show at the monument.

Times: Open all year Jan-Feb & Nov-Dec, daily 10.30-4; Mar-May & Oct, daily 10-5; Jun, daily 10-6; Jul-Aug, daily 9.30-6.30; Sep, daily 9.30-5. **Fee:** ✱ £6 (ch & pen £4, student £4.50). Family ticket £16.
Facilities: 🅿 💻 ♿ (limited access) shop ✈ 🍴

OLD TOWN JAIL

Saint John St FK8 1EA
Dir: (follow signs for castle up hill, jail on left at top of Saint John's St) *Map Ref:* NS79
☎ 01786 450050 📠 01786 471301
e-mail: otjva@aillst.ossian.net

Experience life in a Victorian prison at the Old Town Jail, where living history performances bring the past to life. Here you can expect to come face to face with Stirling's notorious hangman and you may even witness an attempted jailbreak. A multi-lingual audio tour is available, and there is a stunning rooftop panorama.

Times: Open Apr-Sep, daily 9.30-5.30; Oct & Mar, daily 9.30-4.30; Nov-Feb, daily 9.30-3.30 (last admission) **Fee:** ✱ £5.50 (ch & pen £3.65, student £4.25). Family ticket £14.65.
Facilities: 🅿 ♿ toilets for disabled shop ✈ 🍴

STIRLING CASTLE

Upper Castle Hill FK8 1EJ
Map Ref: NS79
☎ 01786 450000

Sitting on top of a 250 foot rock, Stirling Castle has a strategic position on the Firth of Forth. As a result it has been the scene of many events in Scotland's history. James II was born at the castle in 1430. Mary Queen of Scots spent some years here, and it was James IV's childhood home. Among its finest features are the splendid Renaissance palace built by James V, and the Chapel Royal, rebuilt by James VI.

Times: Open all year, Apr-Sep, daily 9.30-6; Oct-Mar, daily 9.30-4.30. Closed 25-26 Dec & 1-2 Jan. **Fee:** ✱ £8 (ch £2, concessions £6). Groups 11+ 10% discount. Prices valid until 2 Jan 2005. Please phone for further details.
Facilities: 🅿 (charged) ✗ licensed ♿ toilets for disabled shop ✈ 🚩

LIVINGSTON ALMOND VALLEY HERITAGE CENTRE

Millfield EH54 7AR
Dir: (2m from M8 junct 3) *Map Ref:* NT06
☎ 01506 414957 🖹 01506 497771
e-mail: info@almondvalley.co.uk

The Heritage Centre offers a combination of fun and educational potential which is ideal for children. Almond Valley has a petting zoo of farm animals, an interactive museum on the shale oil industry, a narrow gauge railway, and tractor rides. Special events are held throughout the year, please telephone for details.

Times: Open all year, daily 10-5. **Fee:** £3 (ch £2). Family (2ad+4ch) £10.
Facilities: 🅿 🍴 ♿ toilets for disabled shop 🛍

ARRAN, ISLE OF BRODICK BRODICK CASTLE, GARDEN & COUNTRY PARK

KA27 8HY
Dir: (Ferry from Ardrossan-Brodick or Lochranza-Kintyre - frequent in summer, limited in winter) *Map Ref:* NS03
☎ 01770 302202 & 302462 🖹 01770 302312
e-mail: brodick@nts.org.uk

The site has been fortified since Viking times, but the present castle dating from the 13th century was a stronghold of the Dukes of Hamilton. Splendid silver, fine porcelain and paintings acquired by generations of owners can be seen, including many sporting pictures and trophies. There is a magnificent woodland garden, started by the Duchess of Montrose in 1923, world famous for its rhododendrons and azaleas.

Times: Open Apr-Oct, daily 11-4.30 (closes 3.30 in Oct). Country Park: open all year, daily 9.30-sunset. Times may change for 2005 please telephone or check on www.nts.org.uk **Fee:** ✱ £8 (concessions £6) Groups adult £6 (ch/school £2), please book groups in advance. Family ticket £20. Country Park only Apr-Oct £4 (concessions £3) Groups adult £3 (ch/school £2). Family ticket £12. £2. Admission free to NTS members.
Facilities: 🅿 ✗ ♿ (Braille, wheelchairs motorised buggy & stairlift) toilets for disabled shop 🐕 (ex guide dogs) ♨

LEWIS, ISLE OF ARNOL BLACK HOUSE MUSEUM

PA86 9DB
Dir: (11m NW of Stornoway on A858) *Map Ref:* NB34
☎ 01851 710395

The museum is located in a traditional Hebridean dwelling, the black house, which was built without mortar, using peat or earth to fill in the gaps. The roof is thatched over a timber framework, and while there is a central peat fire in the kitchen, no chimney is provided. The byre for the animals would be under the same roof, at the other end of the building.

Times: Open all year, Apr-Sep, Mon-Sat 9.30-6.30; Oct-Mar, Mon-Sat 9.30-4.30. Closed 25-26 Dec & 1-2 Jan. **Fee:** ✱ £3 (ch £1, concessions £2.30). Groups 11+ 10% discount. Prices valid until 2 Jan 2005. Please telephone for further details. **Facilities:** 🅿 ♿ toilets for disabled shop 🐕 ♨

MULL   CRAIGNURE   MULL & WEST HIGHLAND NARROW GAUGE RAILWAY

Craignure (old pier) Station PA55 6AY
Dir: (0.25m from Ferry Terminal, just off road to Iona)
Map Ref: NM73
☎ **01680 812494 (in season) or 01680 300389**
▤ **01680 300595**
e-mail: mullrail@dee-emm.co.uk

The first passenger railway on a Scottish island, opened in 1984. Both steam and diesel trains operate on the ten-and-a-quarter inch gauge line, which runs from Craignure to Torosay Castle. The 1.25 mile line offers dramatic woodland and mountain views taking in Ben Nevis, Glencoe and the Isle of Lismore.

Times: Open Etr-mid Oct **Facilities:** ▣ ♿ (provision to carry person seated in wheelchair on trains) shop ▬

ORKNEY   DOUNBY   SKARA BRAE

KW16 3LR
Dir: (19m W of Kirkwall on B9056) *Map Ref:* HY22
☎ **01856 841815**

This remarkable group of well-preserved Stone Age dwellings was revealed in 1850 when heavy storms washed away the sand that had kept Skara Brae hidden over centuries. It is the most outstanding pre-historic village in Britain, probably dating from around 3200 BC. There are eight houses linked by alleyways and stone furniture and a fireplace can be seen.

Times: Open all year, Apr-Sep, daily 9.30-6.30; Oct-Mar, daily 9.30-4.30. Closed Sun am in winter, 25-26 Dec & 1-2 Jan. **Fee:** ✳ £5 (ch £1.30, concessions £3.75). Groups 11+ 10% discount. Prices valid until 2 Jan 2005. Please phone for details. **Facilities:** ▣ ✕ ♿ toilets for disabled shop ✖ ▮

HARRAY   CORRIGALL FARM & KIRBUSTER MUSEUM

KW17 2JR
Map Ref: HY31
☎ **01856 771411 & 771268** ▤ **01856 874615**

The museum consists of two Orkney farmhouses with outbuildings. Kirbuster (Birsay) represents an improved farmhouse and steading, better than most, where the animals are housed separately from the family. Corrigall (Harray), a working museum, is the last surviving example of a 'Firehoose' with its central hearth and stone 'neuk' bed. Traditional crafts are demonstrated at both sites.

Times: ✳ Open Mar-Oct, Mon-Sat 10.30-1 & 2-5, Sun 2-7. **Facilities:** ▣ ♿ shop ✖ (ex guide dogs) ▬

KIRKWALL SCAPA FLOW VISITOR CENTRE & MUSEUM

Hoy KW15 1DH
Dir: (on A964 to Houton, ferry crossing takes 45 mins, visitors centre 2 mins from ferry terminal) **Map Ref:** HY41
☎ **01856 791300** ▤ **01856 871560**
e-mail: museum@orkney.gov.uk

Also known as the Lyness Interpretation Centre, this fascinating museum is home to a large collection of military equipment used in the defence of the Orkneys during the First and Second World Wars. There are also guns salvaged from the German ships scuppered in World War II. Visitors arrive at the island after a short boat trip from the Orkney mainland.

Times: ✱ Open all year: Mon-Fri 9-4.30 (mid May-Oct also Sat, Sun 10.30-3.30)
Facilities: 🅿 ▣ ⅃ toilets for disabled shop ✖ (ex guide dogs) ◀

THE ORKNEY MUSEUM

Broad St KW15 1DH
Dir: (town centre) **Map Ref:** HY41
☎ **01856 873191** ▤ **01856 874616**
e-mail: museum@orkney.gov.uk

One of the finest vernacular town houses in Scotland, located opposite the 12th-century St Magnus Cathedral, this 16th-century building, known as Tankerness House, accommodates The Orkney Museum. Displays cover the past 5,000 years of Orkney history, including the islands' fascinating archaeology, refurbished Neolithic/Bronze Age galleries and exhibits on 'Life and Death in Viking Orkney', and 'Medieval Orkney'. Smuggling activities are also reflected, and the rise of the merchant lairds in the 16th and 17th centuries. There is also a programme of temporary exhibitions.

Times: ✱ Open, Oct-Mar Mon-Sat, 10.30-12.30 & 1.30-5, Apr-Sep, 10.30-5 Mon-Sat.
Facilities: 🅿 (50yds) ⅃ shop ✖ (ex guide dogs) ◀

SHETLAND LERWICK SHETLAND MUSEUM

Lower Hillhead ZE1 0EL
Map Ref: HU44
☎ **01595 695057** ▤ **01595 696729**   FREE
e-mail: shetland.museum@sic.shetland.gov.uk

The massive brass propeller blade outside the building is from the 17,000-ton liner *Oceanic*, wrecked off Foula in 1914. The archaeology gallery covers Neolithic burials, axe-making, Bronze-Age houses, Iron-Age farming and domestic life. There are also agricultural and social history displays, including peat-working, corn harvest, local businesses, medals, boot-making and Shetland weddings. Changing exhibitions of contemporary art are also shown.

Times: Open until 31 Mar, Wed-Sat 10-5. (Closed 31 Mar 2005 & new Museum opens early 2006)
Facilities: 🅿 ⅃ (lift, wheelchair available) toilets for disabled shop ✖ (ex guide dogs) ◀

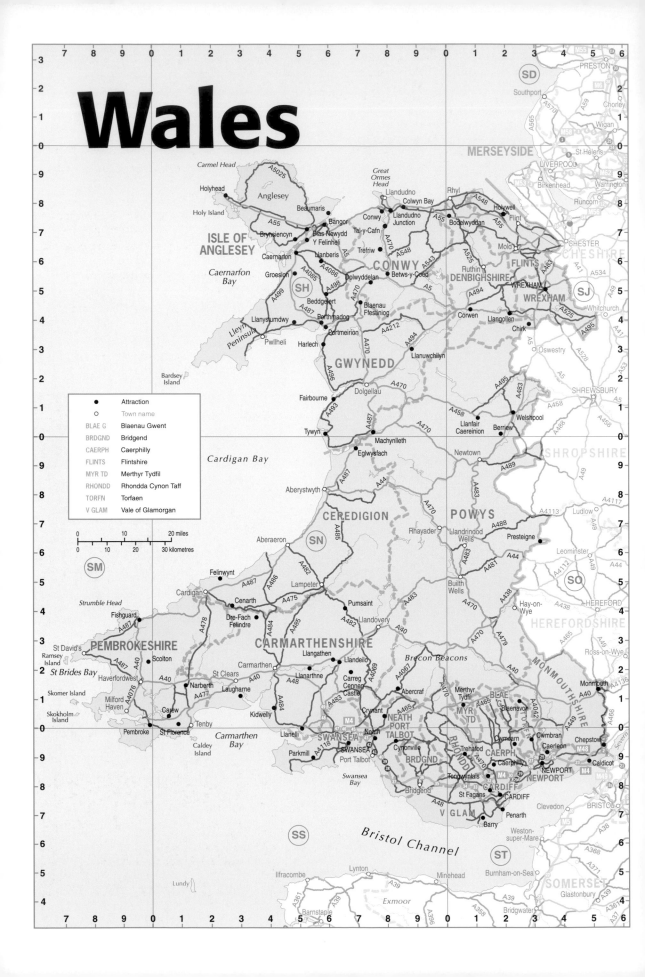

A country fiercely proud of its culture and identity, Wales is known both for its wild natural beauty and its cosmopolitan city life. The glorious coastline of Wales offers the largest concentration of award-winning beaches in the UK, and its mountainous landscapes, cut with lakes and rivers, are breathtakingly scenic.

The seaside and mountain resorts that sprung up when the railways brought Victorian holidaymakers from the factories of England retain a special charm, particularly along the north coast and into Snowdonia. Train lovers today can relish the sights, sounds and smells of more steam railways here than anywhere else in the UK.

Minerals made the country: slate from the monumental quarries and caverns of the north; iron and coal from the mines in the south, where the valleys run steeply down to the major ports of Swansea and Cardiff.

Tourist attractions centre on the castles and gardens of Wales, the industrial heritage sites and Portmeirion, the romantic Italianate village built by Clough Williams-Ellis between 1925 and 1975 on the coast of Snowdonia.

Events & Festivals

February (tbc) Y Grael, the Cauldron of Inspiration, Caernarfon Castle

April 1-17 International Festival of Musical Theatre, Cardiff

May 18-22 Llantilio Crossenny, Festival of Music & Drama

May 27-June 5 Hay Festival of Literature, Hay-on-Wye

May 28-June 5 St David's Cathedral Festival, St David's, Pembrokeshire

June (tbc) Llandudno Festival, Llandudno

July 5-10 Llangollen International Musical Eisteddfod, International Pavilion, Abbey Road, Llangollen

July 18-21 Royal Welsh Show, Royal Welsh Showground, Builth Wells

July 30-August 6 Royal National Eisteddfod of Wales, Tredegar Park, Newport

August 1-9 Talgarth Festival of the Black Mountains

August 29 World Bog Snorkelling Championship, Llanwrtyd Wells

August (tbc) Anglesey County Show, Anglesey Showground, Gwalchmai, Holyhead

Above: Looking north from Foel Cynwch, the Precipice Walk starts in Dolgellau

CAERPHILLY CAERPHILLY CASTLE

CF8 1JL
Dir: (on A469) *Map Ref:* ST18
☎ 029 2088 3143

The concentrically planned castle was begun in 1268 by Gilbert de Clare and completed in 1326. It is the largest in Wales, and has extensive land and water defences. A unique feature is the ruined tower - the victim of subsidence - which manages to out-lean even Pisa! The south dam platform, once a tournament-field, now displays replica medieval siege-engines.

Times: Open Apr-May & Oct, daily 9.30-5; Jun-Sep, daily 9.30-6; Nov-Mar, Mon-Sat 9.30-4, Sun 11-4. Telephone for Xmas opening times. **Fee:** £3 (ch 5-15, pen & students £2.50, disabled visitors and assisting companion free). Family ticket (2ad+3ch) £8.50. Group rates available. Prices quoted apply until 31 Mar 2005.
Facilities: P & shop ✈ ☺ 🍴

LLANCAIACH FAWR MANOR

Gelligaer Rd, Nelson CF46 6ER
Dir: (M4 junct 32, A470 to Merthyr Tydfil. Towards Ystrad Mynach A472, follow brown heritage signs) *Map Ref:* ST18
☎ 01443 412248 🖷 01443 412688
e-mail: allens@caerphilly.gov.uk

Step back in time to the Civil War period at this fascinating living history museum. The year is 1645 and visitors are invited into the manor to meet the servants of Colonel Edward Prichard. You can hear all the gossip about the Civil War raging between king and parliament, and see where their allegiances lie.

Times: Open Mon-Fri 10-3.30 (last admission), Sat & Sun 10-4.30. Closed Mon, Nov-Feb & 24 Dec-2 Jan. **Fee:** £4.95 (ch & concessions £3.25). Family ticket £13. **Facilities:** P 🍴 ✕ licensed & (personal stereo, photo album & Braille map) toilets for disabled shop ✈ (ex guide dogs) 🍴

CWMCARN CWMCARN FOREST DRIVE

Nantcarn Rd NP11 7FA
Dir: (8m N of Newport on A467, follow brown tourist signs) *Map Ref:* ST29
☎ 01495 272001 🖷 01495 271403
e-mail: cwmcarn-vc@caerphilly.gov.uk

Cwmcarn is a mature conifer forest including the beautiful Nantcarn Valley. The seven-mile scenic forest drive offers spectacular views over the Bristol Channel and surrounding countryside. Visitor centre facilities include barbecues, picnic and play areas, and forest and mountain walks. Special events are held throughout the year; please ring for details.

Times: ✱ Open Forest Drive: Mar & Oct 11-5; Apr-Aug 11-7 (11-9 wknds during Jul & Aug); Sep, 11-6; Nov 11-4 (wknds only). Visitor Centre: all year except between Xmas & New Year.
Facilities: P 🍴 & toilets for disabled shop 🍴

CARDIFF CARDIFF CASTLE

Castle St CF10 3RB
Dir: (from M4, A48 & A470 follow signs to city centre)
Map Ref: ST17
☎ **029 2087 8100** 🖷 **029 2023 1417**
e-mail: cardiffcastle@cardiff.gov.uk

Cardiff Castle is situated in the heart of the city. Contained within its mighty walls is a history spanning nearly 2,000 years, dating from the coming of the Romans to the Norman Conquest. Discover spectacular interiors on your guided tour, and enjoy magnificent views of the city from the top of the 12th century Norman keep.

Times: Open all year, daily (ex 25-26 Dec & 1 Jan) including guided tours, Mar-Oct, 9.30-6 (last tour 5); Nov-Feb, 9.30-5.30 (last tour 4). Royal Regiment of Wales Museum closed Tue. Queen's Dragoon Guards Museum closed Fri. **Fee:** Full conducted tour, military museums, green, Roman Wall & Norman Keep £6 (ch & pen £3.70). Family £17.60. Roman Wall, Norman Keep, & military museum £2.90 (ch & pen £1.80).
Facilities: P (200 yds) 💺 & (access to Castle Green & Museum) toilets for disabled shop ✖ (ex in grounds & guide dogs) 🖻

MILLENNIUM STADIUM TOURS

Millennium Stadium, Westgate St, Gate 3 CF10 1JA
Dir: (A470 to city centre. Westgate St opposite Castle far end)
Map Ref: ST17
☎ **029 2082 2228** 🖷 **029 2082 2040**

In the late 1990s this massive stadium was completed as part of an effort to revitalise Welsh fortunes. It replaced Cardiff Arms Park, and now hosts major music events, exhibitions, and international rugby and soccer matches. Its capacity of around 75,000 and its retractable roof make it unique in Europe. It is currently the home of five controlling bodies: Welsh Rugby, Welsh Football, English Football ASS, Football league (English) and British Speedway.

Times: Open Mon-Sat, 10-5; Sun 10-4
Fee: ✱ £5 (ch up to 16 £2.50, ch under 5 free, concessions £3). Party 20+
Facilities: P (opposite gate 3) 💺 & (lifts, escalators, disabled parking) toilets for disabled shop ✖ (ex guide dogs) 🖻

NATIONAL MUSEUM & GALLERY CARDIFF

Cathays Park CF10 3NP
Dir: (in Civic Centre, 5 mins walk from city centre & 20 mins walk from bus and train station) **Map Ref:** ST17
☎ **029 2039 7951** 🖷 **029 2037 3219** 〔FREE〕
e-mail: post@nmgw.ac.uk

This establishment is unique among British museums and galleries in its range of art and science displays. 'The Evolution of Wales' exhibition takes visitors on a spectacular 4,600-million year journey, tracing the world from the beginning of time and the development of Wales. There are displays of Bronze-Age gold, early Christian monuments, Celtic treasures, silver, coins and medals, ceramics, fossils and minerals. A significant collection of French Impressionist paintings sits alongside the work of Welsh artists, past and present, in the elegant art galleries.

Times: Open all year, Tue-Sun 10-5. Closed Mon (ex BHs) & 24-26 Dec. **Facilities:** P (charged) 💺 ✖ licensed & (wheelchair available, Tel 029 2057 3509 for access guide) toilets for disabled shop ✖ (ex guide dogs) 🖻

TECHNIQUEST

Stuart St CF10 5BW
Dir: (A4232 to Cardiff Bay) *Map Ref:* ST17
☎ **029 2047 5475** 🖨 **029 2048 2517**
e-mail: info@techniquest.org

There is always something new to explore at this exciting science discovery centre, located in the heart of Cardiff Bay. The attraction is aimed at engaging people of all ages in science through interactive exhibits and live demonstrations. You can journey into space in the planetarium, enjoy a Science Theatre show or experience one of the 160 hands-on exhibits. Visitors also get the chance to experiment in the Laboratory and Discovery Room.

Times: Open all year, Mon-Fri 9.30-4.30; Sat-Sun & BHs 10.30-5, school hols 9.30-5. Closed Xmas. **Fee:** ✱ £6.75 (ch 5-16 & concessions £4.65). Family ticket £18.50 (2ad+3ch). Friend season ticket £48. Groups 10+ **Facilities:** 🅿 (50mtrs) (limited parking for disabled visitors) 🍴 ♿ (lift, hearing loop) toilets for disabled shop ✖ (ex guide dogs) ◀

ST FAGANS MUSEUM OF WELSH LIFE

CF5 6XB
Dir: (4m W of Cardiff on A4232) *Map Ref:* ST17
☎ **029 2057 3500** 🖨 **029 2057 3490**   `FREE`
e-mail: post@nmgw.ac.uk

A stroll around the indoor galleries and 100 acres of beautiful grounds at this museum will give you a fascinating insight into how people in Wales have lived, worked and spent their leisure hours since Celtic times. You can see people practising the traditional means of earning a living, the animals they kept and at certain times of year, the ways in which they celebrated the seasons.

Times: Open all year daily, 10-5. Closed 24-26 Dec. **Facilities:** 🅿 (charged) 🍴 ✖ licensed ♿ (wheelchairs available on a 'first come-first served' basis) toilets for disabled shop ✖ (ex in grounds if on lead) ◀

TONGWYNLAIS CASTELL COCH

CF4 7YS
Dir: (A470 to Tongwynlais junct, then B4262 to castle on top of hill) *Map Ref:* ST18
☎ **029 2081 0101**

Castell Coch is Welsh for red castle, an appropriate name for this fairy-tale building with its red sandstone walls and conical towers. The castle was originally built in the 13th century but fell into ruin, and the present castle is a late 19th-century creation. Inside, the castle is decorated in fantasy style.

Times: Open Apr-May & Oct, daily 9.30-5; Jun-Sep, daily 9.30-6; Nov-Mar, Mon-Sat 9.30-4, Sun 11-4. Telephone for Xmas opening times. **Fee:** £3 (ch 5-15, pen & students £2.50, disabled visitors and assisting companion free). Family ticket (2ad+3ch) £8.50. Group rates available. Prices quoted apply until 31 Mar 2005. **Facilities:** 🅿 shop ✖ ☺ ◀

CARREG CENNEN CASTLE CARREG CENNEN CASTLE

SA19 6UA
Dir: (unclass road from A483 to Trapp village) **Map Ref:** SN61
☎ **01558 822291**

A steep path leads up to the castle, which is spectacularly sited on a limestone crag. It was first built as a stronghold of the native Welsh and then rebuilt in the late 13th century. Most remarkable among the impressive remains is a mysterious passage, cut into the side of the cliff and lit by loopholes. The farm at the site has a rare breeds centre.

Times: Open all year, Apr-Oct, daily 9.30-6.30; Nov-Mar, daily, 9.30-dusk. Telephone for Xmas opening times. **Fee:** £3 (ch 5-15, pen & students £2.50, disabled visitors & assisting companion free). Family ticket (2ad+3ch) £8.50. Group rates available. Prices quoted apply until 31 Mar 2005. **Facilities:** 🅿 💻 shop ✈ ☺ 🍴

DRE-FACH FELINDRE NATIONAL WOOLLEN MUSEUM

SA44 5UP
Dir: (16m W of Carmarthen off A484, 4m E of Newcastle Emlyn)
Map Ref: SN33
☎ **01559 370929** FREE

The National Woollen Museum has recently re-opened following a £2.6 million redevelopment programme. It is housed in the former Cambrian Mills and has a comprehensive display tracing the evolution of the woollen industry from its beginnings to the present day. Demonstrations of the fleece to fabric process are given on 19th-century textile machinery.

Times: Open Apr-Sep, daily 10-5; Oct-Mar, Tue-Sat 10-5. **Facilities:** 🅿 💻 ♿ (wheelchair access to ground floor & ample seating) toilets for disabled shop ✈ (ex guide dogs) 🍴

KIDWELLY KIDWELLY INDUSTRIAL MUSEUM

Broadford SA17 4LW
Dir: (signed from Kidwelly by-pass & town, stack visible from by-pass) **Map Ref:** SN40
☎ **01554 891078** FREE

Two of the great industries of Wales are represented in this museum: tinplate and coal mining. The original buildings and machinery of the Kidwelly tinplate works, where tinplate was hand made, are now on display to the public. There is also an exhibition of coal mining with pit-head gear and a winding engine, while the more general history of the area is shown in a separate exhibition.

Times: Open Etr, Jun-Sep, BH wknds, Mon-Fri 10-5, Sat-Sun 12-5. Last admission 4. Other times by arrangement for parties only. **Facilities:** 🅿 💻 ♿ (ramps on entrances) toilets for disabled shop

LAUGHARNE LAUGHARNE CASTLE

King St SA33 4SA
Dir: (on A4066) **Map Ref:** SN31
☎ **01994 427906**

Newly opened to the public, picturesque Laugharne Castle stands on a low ridge overlooking the wide Taff Estuary. A medieval fortress converted into an Elizabethan mansion, it suffered a Civil War siege and later became the backdrop for elaborate Victorian gardens, now recreated. Laugharne Castle has also inspired two modern writers - Richard Hughes and Dylan Thomas.

Times: Open Apr-Sep, daily 10-5. **Fee:** £2.75 (ch 5-15, pen & students £2.25, disabled visitors & assisting companions free). Family ticket (2ad+3ch) £7.75. Group rates available. Prices quoted apply until 31 Mar 2005.
Facilities: P (150mtrs) & toilets for disabled shop ✸ ☺ ◼

LLANARTHNE MIDDLETON, THE NATIONAL BOTANIC GARDEN OF WALES

Middleton Hall SA32 8HG
Dir: (8m E of Carmarthen on A48, dedicated intersection - signed) **Map Ref:** SN52
☎ **01558 668768** ▤ **01558 668933**
e-mail: info@gardenofwales.org.uk

Set in 568 acres of parkland in the beautiful Towy Valley, the garden's centrepiece is the Great Glasshouse, a tilted glass dome with a six-metre ravine. Here you can experience the aftermath of an Australian bush fire, pause in an olive grove or wander through fuchsia collections from Chile. A 22-metre herbaceous broad walk forms the spine of the garden and leads to the children's play area, the 360° surround screen cinema and the Old Stables Courtyard, where there is an art gallery, shop and restaurant. Land train tours take visitors to lakes surrounding the garden.

Times: ✱ Open 30 Mar-25 Oct 10-6, 26 Oct-27 Mar 10-4.30 **Facilities:** P ▣ ✗ licensed & (Braille interpretation wheelchairs/scooters shuttle svc) toilets for disabled shop garden centre ✸ (ex guide dogs) ◼

LLANDEILO DINEFWR PARK

SA19 6RT
Dir: (off A40 Carmarthenshire, on W outskirts of Llandeilo)
Map Ref: SN62
☎ **01558 823902** ▤ **01558 822036**
e-mail: dinefwr@nationaltrust.org.uk

At the heart of Welsh history for a thousand years, the park as we know it today took shape in the years after 1775 when the medieval castle, house, gardens, woods and deer park were integrated into one vast and breathtaking landscape. Access to Church Woods and Dinefwr Castle is through the landscaped park.

Times: Open Mar-Oct, daily (ex Tue & Wed) 11-4.30. (Last admission 30 mins before closing)
Fee: *Prices not confirmed for 2005*
Facilities: P (charged) ▣ & toilets for disabled ✸ (ex outer park on lead) ♨ ◼

LLANELLI NATIONAL WETLAND CENTRE WALES

Penclacwydd, Llwynhendy SA14 9SH
Dir: (3m E of Llanelli, off A484) **Map Ref:** *SN50*
☎ **01554 741087** 🖹 **01554 741087**
e-mail: wwtllanelli@aol.com

A wide variety of wild birds, including oystercatchers, redshanks, curlews, little egrets and occasionally ospreys, can be seen here during the right season. The grounds are beautifully landscaped, and include CCTV transmitting pictures of wild birds on the reserve, a wetland craft area and a flock of colourful Caribbean flamingos. There is also a discovery centre and outdoor activities for visitors to take part in. Facilities for the disabled include easy access on level paths, special viewing areas and wheelchair loan.

Times: Open summer 9.30-5; winter 9.30-4.30. Closed 24-25 Dec. **Fee:** ✱ £5.50 (ch £3.50, pen £4.50). Family £14.50. **Facilities:** 🅿 🖥 ✗ ♿ toilets for disabled shop ✖ (ex guide/hearing dogs) ◀

LLANGATHEN ABERGLASNEY GARDENS

SA32 8QH
Dir: (4m W of Llandeilo, follow signs from A40) **Map Ref:** *SN52*
☎ **01558 668998** 🖹 **01558 668998**
e-mail: info@aberglasney.org.uk

With a history stretching back to the 15th century, Aberglasney was reworked by the 17th-century Bishop of St David's, the 18th-century poet John Dyer and the 19th-century surgeon John Walters Phillips. Falling into disrepair through the 20th century, the house and its gardens were eventually rescued in 1995, and are now largely restored to their original Jacobean splendour. A mysterious and beautiful day out.

Times: Open all year, Apr-Oct, daily 10-6 (last entry 5); Nov-Mar, daily 10.30-4. Closed 25 Dec **Fee:** £6 (ch £3, pen £5). Party 10+ £5.50 (ch £3, pen £4.50). **Facilities:** 🅿 ✗ licensed ♿ (most areas accessible, wheelchairs available) toilets for disabled shop garden centre ✖ (ex guide dogs) ◀

PUMSAINT DOLAUCOTHI GOLD MINES

SA19 8RR
Dir: (on A482, signed both directions) **Map Ref:** *SN64*
☎ **01558 650177** 🖹 **01588 650707**
e-mail: dolaucothi@nationaltrust.org.uk

Here is an opportunity to spend a day exploring the gold mines and to wear a miner's helmet and lamp while touring the underground workings. The information centre and a walk along the Miners' Way disclose the secrets of 2,000 years of gold mining. This is the only place in Britain where the Romans mined gold.

Times: Open end Mar-end Oct, daily 10-5. **Fee:** *Prices not confirmed for 2005* **Facilities:** 🅿 🖥 ♿ toilets for disabled shop ⚘ ◀

CENARTH *THE NATIONAL CORACLE CENTRE*

Cenarth Falls SA38 9JL
Dir: (on A484 between Carmarthen and Cardigan, centre of Cenarth village, beside bridge and river) **Map Ref:** *SN24*
☎ **01239 710980**
e-mail: martinfowler.coraclecentre@virgin.net

Situated by the beautiful Cenarth Falls, this fascinating museum has a unique collection from all over the world, including Tibet, India, Iraq, Vietnam, and North America. Cenarth has long been a centre for coracle fishing, and coracle rides are often available in the village during the summer holidays. Look out for the salmon leap by the flour mill.

Times: ✱ Open Etr-Oct, Sun-Fri 10.30-5.30. All other times by appointment. **Facilities:** 🅿 ☕ ♿ shop 🛍

EGLWYSFACH RSPB NATURE RESERVE

Cae'r Berllan SY20 8TA
Dir: (6m S of Machynlleth on A487 in Eglwys-Fach. Signed from main road) **Map Ref:** *SN69*
☎ **01654 700222** 🖨 **01654 700333**
e-mail: ynyshir@rspb.org.uk

With the mixture of different habitats, this reserve is home to an abundance of birds and wildlife. The salt marshes in winter support the only regular wintering flock of greenland white-fronted geese in England and Wales in addition to peregrines, hen harriers and merlins. The sessile oak woodland is home to pied flycatchers, wood warblers and redstarts in the summer but woodpeckers, nut hatches, red kites, sparrow hawks and buzzards are here all year round. Otters, polecats, 30 butterfly and 15 dragonfly species are also present.

Times: Open daily, 9am-9pm (or sunset if earlier). Visitor Centre: Apr-Oct 9-5 daily; Nov-Mar 10-4 (Wed-Sun) **Fee:** ✱ £3.50 (ch £1, concessions £2.50) Family £7 RSPB members free. **Facilities:** 🅿 ♿ (Can take car to viewpoint) 🐕 (ex guide dogs) 🛍

FELINWYNT *FELINWYNT RAINFOREST & BUTTERFLY CENTRE*

Rhosmaen SA43 1RT
Dir: (from A487 Blaenannerch Airfield turning, onto B4333. Signed 6m N of Cardigan) **Map Ref:** *SN25*
☎ **01239 810882 & 810250** 🖨 **01239 810465**
e-mail: dandjdevereux@btinternet.com

A chance to wander among free-flying exotic butterflies accompanied by the recorded wildlife sounds of the Peruvian Amazon is offered at the Rainforest & Butterfly Centre. A waterfall, ponds and streams contribute to a humid tropical atmosphere and provide a habitat for fish and native amphibians. See the exhibition of rainforests of Peru and around the world. Free paper and crayons to borrow for children.

Times: Open daily from Etr-Oct. **Fee:** ✱ £3.90 (ch 4-14 £1.50, pen £3.50) **Facilities:** 🅿 ☕ ♿ toilets for disabled shop 🐕 (ex guide dogs) 🛍

Conwy

BETWS-Y-COED CONWY VALLEY RAILWAY MUSEUM

Old Goods Yard LL24 0AL
Dir: (signed from A5 into Old Church Rd, adjacent to train station) **Map Ref:** *SH75*
☎ **01690 710568** 📠 **01690 710132**

The two large museum buildings have displays on both the narrow and standard gauge railways of North Wales, including railway stock and other memorabilia. There are working model railway layouts, a steam-hauled miniature railway in the four-acre grounds, and a 15-inch gauge tramway to the woods. The latest addition is the quarter-size steam *Britannia* loco now on display. For children there are mini-dodgems, Postman Pat, a school bus and Toby Tram.

Times: Open daily, 10-5.30. Closed Xmas
Fee: ✱ £1 (ch & pen 50p). Family ticket £2.50. Steam train ride £1. Tram ride 80p.
Facilities: 🅿 🍽 ♿ (ramps & clearances for wheelchairs) toilets for disabled shop ▪

COLWYN BAY WELSH MOUNTAIN ZOO

Old Highway LL28 5UY
Dir: (A55 junct 20 signed Rhos-on-Sea) **Map Ref:** *SH87*
☎ **01492 532938** 📠 **01492 530498**
e-mail: welshmountainzoo@enterprise.net

The zoo is set in a 37-acre estate overlooking Colwyn Bay, with magnificent views of the coast and mountains. The animals are housed in natural settings, interspersed with gardens and woodland. The traditional range of zoo animals can be seen, from lions and elephants to penguins and parrots, and the zoo also attracts a variety of local wildlife. There are falconry displays during the summer months, sea lion feeding sessions, and chimp encounters. Additional attractions for children are the Jungle Adventureland and Tarzan Trail activity area, and the Children's Farm.

Times: Open all year, Mar-Oct, daily 9.30-6; Nov-Feb, daily 9.30-5. Closed 25 Dec
Facilities: 🅿 ✗ ♿ toilets for disabled shop ✈ ▪

CONWY SMALLEST HOUSE

The Quay LL32 8BB
Dir: (leave A55 at Conwy sign, through town, at bottom of High St for the quay, turn left) **Map Ref:** *SH77*
☎ **01492 593484** 📠 **01492 593484**

For a tiny place, this is a major tourist attraction. The *Guinness Book of Records* lists it as the smallest house in Britain, at just six feet wide by ten feet high. It is located on the quayside and is furnished in the style of a mid-Victorian Welsh Cottage. There isn't even room for a lavatory - that's outside in the old-fashioned way.

Times: Open Apr-May & Oct 10-5; Jun & Sep, 10-6, first half Jul 10-6 rest of Jul & Aug 10-9
Fee: ✱ 75p (ch under 16 50p, under 5 free).
Facilities: 🅿 (100yds) ♿ shop

DOLWYDDELAN DOLWYDDELAN CASTLE

LL25 0EJ
Dir: (on A470 Blaenau Ffestiniog to Betws-y-Coed)
Map Ref: SH75
☎ **01690 750366**

The castle is reputed to be the birthplace of Llywelyn the Great. It was captured in 1283 by Edward I, who immediately began strengthening it for his own purposes. A restored keep from around 1200, and a 13th-century curtain wall can be seen. An exhibition on the castles of the Welsh Princes is located in the keep.

Times: Open all year, Apr-Sep, Mon-Sat 9.30-6.30 & Sun 11-4; Oct-Mar, Mon-Sat 9.30-4, Sun 11-4. Telephone for Xmas opening times. **Fee:** £2 (ch 5-15, pen & students £1.50, disabled visitors & assisting companion free). Family ticket (2ad+3ch) £5.50. Group rates available. Prices quoted apply until 31 Mar 2005. **Facilities:** 🅿 ✖ ⊕ 🖃

LLANDUDNO JUNCTION RSPB NATURE RESERVE

LL31 9XZ
Dir: (off A55, signed) *Map Ref:* SH77
☎ **01492 584091**
e-mail: alan.davies@rspb.org.uk

The visitor centre at the Conwy RSPB Reserve has a viewing area which overlooks the estuary and Conwy Castle, and there's a nature trail and four hides for viewing lapwings and shelduck among many other species of bird. The shallow pools by the estuary are ideal for ducks and wading birds. Landscaping of the reserve is ongoing and thousands of trees are being planted.

Times: Open all year, daily, 10-5. Closed 25 Dec **Fee:** £2.50 (ch £1, concessions £1.50) **Facilities:** 🅿 ♿ (use of wheelchair & audio trail) toilets for disabled shop ✖ (ex guide dogs) 🖃

TAL-Y-CAFN BODNANT GARDEN

LL28 5RE
Dir: (8m S of Llandudno & Colwyn Bay off A470) *Map Ref:* SH77
☎ **01492 650460** 🖷 **01492 650448**
e-mail: office@bodnantgarden.co.uk

Set above the River Conwy with beautiful views over Snowdonia, these gardens are a delight. There are five Italian-style terraces constructed below the house, and on the lowest terrace is a canal pool with an open-air yew hedge stage and a reconstructed Pin Mill. The garden is renowned for its collections of magnolias, camellias, rhododendrons and azaleas and the famous Laburnum Arch. Telephone for details of open air theatre events.

Times: Open mid Mar-12 Nov, daily 10-5 (last admission half hour before closing) **Fee:** ✱ £5.50 (ch £2.75) Party of 20+ £5 **Facilities:** 🅿 💻 ♿ (ramps to gardens, wheelchairs & Braille guides) toilets for disabled shop garden centre ✖ (ex guide dogs) ❄ 🖃

TREFRIW TREFRIW WOOLLEN MILLS

LL27 0NQ
Dir: (on B5106 in centre of Trefriw, 5m N of Betws-y-Coed)
Map Ref: SH76
☎ 01492 640462 🖨 01492 641821 **FREE**
e-mail: info@t-w-m.co.uk

Established in 1859, the mill is situated beside the fast-flowing Afon Crafnant, which drives two hydro-electric turbines to power the looms. All the machinery of woollen manufacture can be seen here: blending, carding, spinning, dyeing, warping and weaving. In the Weaver's Garden, there are plants traditionally used in the textile industry, mainly for dyeing. Hand-spinning demonstrations are a feature.

Times: Mill open Etr-Oct, Mon-Fri 10-1 & 2-5. Weaving demonstrations & turbine house: open all year, Mon-Fri 10-1 & 2-5. Handspinning & weaver's garden Jun-Sep Tue-Thu Jul-Aug Mon-Fri 10-5 **Facilities:** P (35yds) 🍽 ♿ (access to shop, cafe, weaving & turbine house) shop 🐾 (ex in grounds on lead) 🎫

BODELWYDDAN BODELWYDDAN CASTLE

LL18 5YA
Dir: (just off A55, near St Asaph, follow brown signs)
Map Ref: SJ07
☎ 01745 584060 🖨 01745 584563
e-mail: enquiries@bodelwyddan-castle.co.uk

Bodelwyddan Castle houses over 100 portraits from the National Portrait Gallery's 19th century collection. The portraits hang in beautifully refurbished rooms and are complemented by sculpture and period furnishings. Interactive displays show how portraits were produced and used in the Victorian era. The Castle Gallery hosts a programme of temporary exhibitions and events. The castle is set within 200 acres of woodland.

Times: ✱ Open Apr-Sep, daily 10.30-5. Oct-Apr, 10.30-4. Closed Mon & Fri **Facilities:** P 🍽 ♿ (lift to first floor, Braille & audio guides) toilets for disabled shop 🐾 (ex guide dogs) 🎫

CORWEN EWE-PHORIA SHEEPDOG CENTRE

Glanrafon, Llangwm LL21 0PE
Dir: (off A5 to Llangwm, follow signs) *Map Ref:* SJ04
☎ 01490 460369
e-mail: info@ewe-phoria.co.uk

Ewe-Phoria is an Agri-Theatre and Sheepdog Centre that details the life and work of the shepherd and his sheepdog on a traditional Welsh farm. The Agri-Theatre has unusual living displays of sheep with accompanying lectures on their history and breed, while outside sheepdog handlers put their dogs through their paces. Visitors can meet the lambs and puppies and see sheep-shearing demonstrations.

Times: ✱ Open Etr-end Oct, Tue-Fri & Sun. Closed Sat & Mon ex BHs **Facilities:** P 🍽 ✗ licensed ♿ toilets for disabled shop 🐾 (ex guide dogs) 🎫

Pen-Y-Bryn Farm Park

LL21 9PP
Dir: (off A5 onto B5105. 5m from Cerrigydrudion)
Map Ref: SJ04
☎ **01490 420244 &** 🖷 **01490 420244**

Proudly catering to all ages, Pen-y-Bryn Park promises a fun day out on the farm surrounded by beautiful North Wales scenery. The farm has a petting zoo, falconry, and Solo the llama - probably the star of the show - with lots of his animal friends. There is free parking, a café and picnic area.

Times: ✱ Open Etr-Oct, Tue-Sun & BHs, 10-5
Facilities: P ☕ ﻋ toilets for disabled shop garden centre

LLANGOLLEN Horse Drawn Boats Centre

The Wharf, Wharf Hill LL20 8TA
Dir: (A5 onto Llangollen High St, across river bridge to T-junct. Wharf opposite) *Map Ref:* SJ24
☎ **01978 860702 & 01691 690322** 🖷 **01978 860799**
e-mail: sue@horsedrawnboats.co.uk

Take a horsedrawn boat trip along the beautiful Vale of Llangollen. Visit the canal museum, inside the motor museum, approx one metre along the towpath from the wharf, which illustrates the heyday of canals in Britain. The displays include working and static models, photographs, murals and slides. Another option is a narrowboat trip that crosses Pontcysyllte Aqueduct, the largest navigable aqueduct in the world. There is a full bar on board and a commentary throughout.

Times: Open Etr-end Oct, daily 10-5. May be closed wkdays in Oct except school hols
Fee: *Prices not confirmed for 2005*
Facilities: P (400yds) ☕ ﻋ (alighting/pick-up point available) toilets for disabled shop ◀

Llangollen Railway

Abbey Rd LL20 8SN
Dir: (Llangollen Station - off A5 at Llangollen traffic lights onto A539, cross river bridge. Station on left at T-junct. Carrog Station - from A5 at Llidiart-y-Parc take B5437, station on right downhill after crossing railway bridge) *Map Ref:* SJ24
☎ **01978 860979 & 860951(timetable)** 🖷 **01978 869247**
e-mail: office@llangollen-railway.co.uk

This heritage railway line features steam and classic diesel services along the picturesque Dee Valley. The journey consists of a 15-mile round trip between Llangollen and Carrog. A special coach for the disabled is available on some services. Special events, such as steam galas, diesel galas, days out with Thomas and Santa Specials are run throughout the year. Please telephone for more information.

Times: Open Station wknds, reduced services off peak, daily services Apr-Oct. Principally steam hauled, diesel trains please refer to timetable for off peak services. **Fee:** ✱ 2nd class return fare for full journey £8 (ch 3-16 £4, pen £6) Family ticket £18 (2ad+2ch) **Facilities:** P (400yds) (free parking at Carrog Station) ☕ ﻋ (special coach for disabled on some trains, notice required) toilets for disabled shop (at Llangollen only) ◀

HOLYWELL *GREENFIELD VALLEY HERITAGE PARK*

Greenfield Rd CH8 7GH
Map Ref: *SJ17*
☎ **01352 714172** 📠 **01352 714791**
e-mail: info@greenfieldvalley.com

This fascinating park covers one and a half miles of woodlands, reservoirs, ancient monuments and industrial history. Among the multitude of sights are a footpath that was once a railway line, the remnants of a number of mills relating to the copper industry, an environment centre, the shrine of St Winefride's Well, and Basingwerk Abbey.

Times: ✱ Park open all year. Museum & farm Apr-Oct, 10-4.30. **Facilities:** 🅿 ☕ ♿ (ramps to enter buildings) toilets for disabled shop

BANGOR *PENRHYN CASTLE*

LL57 4HN
Dir: (1m E of Bangor, off A5122 at Llandegai) **Map Ref:** *SH57*
☎ **01248 353084** 📠 **01248 371281**
e-mail: penrhyncastle@nationaltrust.org.uk

A massive 19th-century castle built on the profits of Jamaican sugar and Welsh slate, Penrhyn is crammed with fascinating artefacts such as a one-ton slate bed made for Queen Victoria and a grand staircase that took ten years to build. The castle also houses a doll museum, two railway museums and one of the finest collections of Old Master paintings in Wales. Regular events are held throughout the season.

Times: Open 23 Mar-Oct, daily (ex Tue) Castle 12-5. Grounds and stableblock exhibitions 11-5 (Jul & Aug 10-5.30). (Last admission 4.30). Last audio tour 4. **Fee:** All inclusive ticket: £7 (ch £3.50). Family ticket £17.50. Party 15+ £5.50 each. Grounds & stableblock only £5 (ch £2.50). **Facilities:** 🅿 ✗ licensed ♿ (wheelchairs & golf buggies pre bookable) toilets for disabled shop 🐾

BEDDGELERT *SYGUN COPPER MINE*

LL55 4NE
Dir: (1m E of Beddgelert on A498) **Map Ref:** *SH57*
☎ **01766 510100 & 01766 510101** 📠 **01766 890595**
e-mail: sygunmine@aol.com

A spectacular all-weather audio-visual underground experience, where visitors can explore the workings of this 19th-century copper mine and see the magnificent stalactite and stalagmite formations. Other activities include archery, panning for gold, metal detecting and coin making. Marvel at the fantastic coin collection from Julius Caesar to Queen Elizabeth II, and visit the Time-Line Museum with Bronze-Age and Roman artefacts.

Times: Open all year, 10-5 **Fee:** £7.95 (ch £5.95, pen £6.95). **Facilities:** 🅿 ☕ ♿ (wide access) toilets for disabled shop 📷

BLAENAU FFESTINIOG LLECHWEDD SLATE CAVERNS

LL41 3NB
Dir: (beside A470, 1m outside Blaenau Ffestiniog)
Map Ref: SH74
☎ **01766 830306** 🖨 **01766 831260**
e-mail: quarrytours@aol.com

The miners' underground tramway carries visitors into areas where early conditions have been recreated, while the deep mine is reached by an incline railway and has an unusual audio-visual presentation. Free surface attractions include several exhibitions and museums, a slate mill and the Victorian village which has period shops, a bank, the Miners Arms pub, lock-up and working smithy.

Times: Open all year, daily from 10. Last tour 5.15 (Oct-Feb 4.15). Closed 25-26 Dec & 1 Jan **Fee:** ✱ Single Tour £8.25 (ch £6.25, pen £7). Reductions for both tours **Facilities:** 🅿 ☕ ✗ licensed & toilets for disabled shop (also Victorian shops in the Village) ✗ (ex on surface) ◀

CAERNARFON CAERNARFON CASTLE

LL55 2AY
Map Ref: SH46
☎ **01286 677617**

Edward I began building the castle and extensive town walls in 1283 after defeating the last independent ruler of Wales. Completed in 1328, it has unusual polygonal towers, notably the 10-sided Eagle Tower. There is a theory that these features were copied from the walls of Constantinople, to reflect a tradition that Constantine was born nearby. Edward I's son and heir was born and presented to the Welsh people here, setting a precedent that was followed in 1969, when Prince Charles was invested as Prince of Wales.

Times: Open Apr-May & Oct, daily 9.30-5; Jun-Sep, daily 9.30-6; Nov-Mar, Mon-Sat 9.30-4, Sun 11-4. Telephone for Xmas opening times. **Fee:** £4.50 (ch 5-15, pen & students £3.50, disabled visitors & assisting compainion free). Family ticket (2 ad & 3 ch) £12.50. Group rates available. Prices quoted apply until 31 Mar 2005. **Facilities:** 🅿 shop ✗ ✿ ◀

SEGONTIUM ROMAN MUSEUM

Beddgelert Rd LL55 2LN
Dir: (on A4085 to Beddgelert approx 1m from Caernarfon)
Map Ref: SH46
☎ **01286 675625** 🖨 **01286 678416**   FREE
e-mail: info@segontium.org.uk

Segontium Roman Museum tells the story of the conquest and occupation of Wales by the Romans and displays the finds from the auxiliary fort of Segontium, one of the most famous in Britain. You can combine a visit to the museum with exploration of the site of the Roman Fort, which is in the care of Cadw: Welsh Historic Monuments. The exciting discoveries displayed at the museum vividly portray the daily life of the soldiers stationed in this remote outpost of the Roman Empire.

Times: Open Tue-Sun 12.30-4. Closed Mon except BH **Facilities:** 🅿 ✗ (ex guide dogs) ◀

WELSH HIGHLAND RAILWAY

St. Helen's Rd LL55 2YD
Dir: (SW of Caernarfon Castle beside harbour. Follow brown signs) *Map Ref:* SH46
☎ **01286 677018 & 01766 516000** 📄 **01286 677018**
e-mail: info@festrail.co.uk

The Welsh Highland Railway is a Millennium funded project to restore the old railway line from Caernarfon to Porthmadog, which closed in the 1930s. Half the total length is now open, and you can experience the stunning scenery of Snowdonia National Park as the narrow gauge, steam and diesel trains travel between Caernarfon and Rhyd Ddu at the foot of Snowdon.

Times: Open daily May-Oct, Etr & limited service in Winter, Feb half-term, 26 Dec-1 Jan.
Fee. ✱ £14 adult return **Facilities:** 🅿 (charged) ♿ (prior booking advisable) toilets for disabled 🖱

FAIRBOURNE *FAIRBOURNE RAILWAY*

Beach Rd LL38 2PZ
Dir: (on A493 follow signs for Fairbourne, main terminus is just past level crossing on left) *Map Ref:* SH61
☎ **01341 250362** 📄 **01341 250240**
e-mail: enquiries@fairbourne-railway.co.uk

One of the most unusual of Wales's 'little trains', built in 1890 as a horse-drawn railway to carry building materials and later converted to steam. It now covers two-and-a-half miles, running between Fairbourne Station and Penrhyn Point. Its route passes one of the loveliest beaches in Wales, with views of the beautiful Mawddach Estuary. There is a station museum at Fairbourne, showing photographs, documents and railway memorabila.

Times: ✱ Open early/mid Apr-mid/late Sep, times vary according to season and events. Trains will run during Oct half term holiday and Santa Specials at Xmas. **Facilities:** 🅿 🖱 shop 🖱

GROESLON INIGO JONES SLATEWORKS

LL54 7UE
Dir: (on A487, 6m S of Caernarfon towards Porthmadog)
Map Ref: SH45
☎ **01286 830242** 📄 **01286 831247**
e-mail: slate@inigojones.co.uk

Inigo Jones Slateworks was established in 1861 primarily to make school writing slates. Today the company uses the same material to make architectural, monumental and craft products. A self-guided audio/video tour takes visitors round the slate workshops, and displays the various processes used in the extraction and working of Welsh slate.

Times: Open all year, daily 9-5. Closed 25-26 Dec & 1 Jan. **Fee:** £4 (ch & pen £3.50).
Facilities: 🅿 🖱 ♿ toilets for disabled shop 🐕 (ex guide dogs) 🖱

HARLECH HARLECH CASTLE

LL46 2YH
Dir: (from A496) *Map Ref: SH53*
☎ 01766 780552

Harlech Castle was built in 1283-81 by Edward I, with a sheer drop to the sea on one side. Owain Glyndwr starved the castle into submission in 1404 and made it his court and campaigning base. Later, the defence of the castle in the Wars of the Roses inspired the song 'Men of Harlech'. Today the sea has slipped away, and the castle's great walls and round towers stand above the dunes.

Times: Open Apr-May & Oct, daily 9.30-5; Jun-Sep, daily 9.30-6; Nov-Mar, Mon-Sat 9.30-4, Sun 11-4. Telephone for Xmas opening times.
Fee: £3 (ch 5-15, pen & students £2.50, disabled visitors & assisting companion free). Family ticket (2ad+3ch) £8.50. Group rates available. Prices quoted apply until 31 Mar 2005.
Facilities: ▣ (disabled spaces in car park) shop ✖ ♿ ◖

LLANBERIS LLANBERIS LAKE RAILWAY

Padarn Country Park LL55 4TY
Dir: (off A4086 at Llanberis) *Map Ref: SH56*
☎ 01286 870549 🖹 01286 870549
e-mail: info@lake-railway.co.uk

Llanberis Lake Railway steam locomotives dating from 1889 to 1948 carry passengers on a five-mile return journey along the shore of Padarn Lake. The terminal station is adjacent to the Welsh Slate Museum, in the Padarn Country Park. The railway was formerly used to carry slate. A new extension to Llanberis village opened in 2003.

Times: Open Etr-late Oct. Trains run frequently Sun-Fri (Sat in Jul & Aug), 11-4.30 in peak season. Send for free timetable. **Fee:** ✱ £6 (ch £4). Family ticket available. Reduced rates for groups.
Facilities: ▣ (charged) ◖ ♿ (disabled carriage available) toilets for disabled shop (on trains, not in Cafe) ◖

SNOWDON MOUNTAIN RAILWAY

LL55 4TY
Dir: (on A4086, Caernarfon to Capel Curig road. 7.5m from Caernarfon) *Map Ref: SH56*
☎ 0870 4580033 🖹 01286 872518
e-mail: info@snowdonrailway.co.uk

The journey of just over four-and-a-half miles takes passengers more than 3,000 feet up to the summit of Snowdon; breathtaking views include, on a clear day, the Isle of Man and the Wicklow Mountains in Ireland. The round trip to the summit and back takes two and a half hours including a half hour at the summit. The rack and pinion railway was built 1894-1896 - an incredible feat of engineering - and has been running ever since, using both steam and diesel engines and electric diesel rail cars.

Times: Open 15 Mar-5 Nov, daily from 9 (weather permitting). **Fee:** Return £20 (ch £14). Early bird discount on 9am train, (not for Jul & Aug) **Facilities:** ▣ (charged) ◖ ♿ (some carriages suitable for wheelchairs - must notify) toilets for disabled shop ✖ (ex guide dogs) ◖

WELSH SLATE MUSEUM

Gilfach Ddu, Padarn Country Park LL55 4TY
Dir: (0.25m off A4086. Museum within Padarn Country Park)
Map Ref: SH56
☎ **01286 870630** 🖨 **01286 871906**   **FREE**
e-mail: slate@nmgw.ac.uk

Set among the towering quarries at Llanberis, the Welsh Slate Museum is a living, working site located in the original workshops of Dinorwig Quarry, which once employed 15,000 men and boys. You can see the foundry, smithy, workshops and mess room which make up the old quarry, and view original machinery, much of which is still in working order.

Times: Open Etr-Oct, daily 10-5; Nov-Etr, Sun-Fri 10-4. **Facilities:** 🅿 (charged) 🏪 & (all parts accessible except patten loft) toilets for disabled shop ✗ (ex guide dogs) 🎧

LLANUWCHLLYN   BALA LAKE RAILWAY

The Station LL23 7DD
Dir: (off A494 Bala to Dolgellau road) **Map Ref:** SH83
☎ **01678 540666** 🖨 **01678 540535**

Steam locomotives which once worked in the slate quarries of North Wales now haul passenger coaches for four and-a-half miles from Llanuwchllyn Station along the lake to Bala. The railway has one of the few remaining double-twist lever locking framed GWR signal boxes, installed in 1896. Some of the coaches are open and some closed, so passengers can enjoy the beautiful views of the lake and mountains in all weathers.

Times: Open Etr-last wknd in Sep, daily. (Closed certain Mon & Fri, telephone for details). **Fee:** ✱ £6.70 return (pen £6.20). Family ticket £16 (2ad+2ch). **Facilities:** 🅿 🏪 & (wheelchairs can be taken on train) shop

LLANYSTUMDWY   LLOYD GEORGE MUSEUM & HIGHGATE VICTORIAN COTTAGE

LL52 0SH
Dir: (on A497 between Pwllheli & Criccieth) **Map Ref:** SH43
☎ **01766 522071** 🖨 **01766 522071**
e-mail: amgueddfeydd-museums@gwynedd.gov.uk

This museum is dedicated to David Lloyd George (1863-1945), one of the greatest statesmen of the 20th century, who led the country in World War I, gave women the vote and introduced the old age pension. His boyhood home is recreated as it would have been when he lived here between 1864 and 1880, along with his Uncle Lloyd's shoemaking workshop.

Times: Open Etr, daily 10-5; May-Jun, Mon-Fri 10.30-5 (open Sat in Jun); Jul-Sep daily 10.30-5; Oct, Mon-Fri, 11-4. Other times by appointment, telephone 01286 679098 for details. **Facilities:** 🅿 & (induction loop in audio visual theatre, shop & cottage) toilets for disabled shop ✗ (ex guide dogs) 🎧

PORTHMADOG   FFESTINIOG RAILWAY

Harbour Station LL49 9NF
Dir: (SE end of town, on A487) *Map Ref:* SH53
☎ 01766 516000 📠 01766 516006
e-mail: info@festrail.co.uk

A narrow gauge steam railway running for 13.5 miles through Snowdonia National Park, with breathtaking views and superb scenery. A buffet service is provided on all trains including a licensed bar (in corridor carriages). The company also runs the Welsh Highland Railway, which will eventually link up with the Ffestiniog Railway. Please telephone for details of special events.

Times: Open daily late Mar to end Oct. Limited Winter service mid week trains Nov & early Dec. Santa specials in Dec. Open Feb half term. Fee: ✱ Full distance return £13.80 (1 ch free with each ad, pen £11.10). Other fares available. Facilities: 🅿 (charged) 🍵 ✗ licensed ♿ (Wheelchair ramps, trains mostly accessible) toilets for disabled shop (closed 24-25 Dec) 📧

PORTMEIRION   PORTMEIRION

LL48 6ET
Dir: (off A487 at Minffordd) *Map Ref:* SH53
☎ 01766 770000 📠 01766 771331
e-mail: info@portmeirion-village.com

Welsh architect Sir Clough Williams Ellis built his fairy-tale, Italianate village on a rocky, tree-clad peninsula on the shores of Cardigan Bay. A bell-tower, castle and lighthouse mingle with a watch-tower, grottos and cobbled squares among pastel-shaded picturesque cottages let as holiday accommodation. The 60-acre Gwyllt Gardens include miles of dense woodland paths and are famous for their fine displays of rhododendrons, azaleas, hydrangeas and sub-tropical flora. There is a mile of sandy beach and a playground for children. The village is probably best known as the major location for 1960s cult TV show, *The Prisoner*.

Times: Open all year, daily 9.30-5.30. Fee: £6 (ch £3, pen £5). Party 15+. Facilities: 🅿 🍵 ✗ licensed ♿ toilets for disabled shop garden centre ✖ (ex guide dogs) 📧

TYWYN   TALYLLYN RAILWAY

Wharf Station LL36 9EY
Dir: (A493 Machynlleth to Dolgellau for Tywyn station, B4405 for Abergynolwyn) *Map Ref:* SH50
☎ 01654 710472 📠 01654 711755
e-mail: enquiries@talyllyn.co.uk

Talyllyn is the oldest 27-inch gauge railway in the world, built in 1865 to run from Tywyn on Cardigan Bay to Abergynolwyn slate mine, some seven miles inland. The railway climbs the steep sides of the Fathew Valley, with stops on the way at Dolgoch Falls and the Nant Gwernol Forest. The return trip takes 2.5 hours. All scheduled passenger trains are steam hauled.

Times: Open Sun mid Feb-Mar, daily; Apr-early Nov & 26 Dec-2 Jan. Ring for timetable. Fee: ✱ £10 Day Rover (ch accompanied £2). Intermediate fares available. Facilities: 🅿 (charged) 🍵 ♿ (prior notice useful) toilets for disabled shop 📧

Y FELINHELI GREENWOOD FOREST PARK

LL56 4QN
Dir: (A55 junct 11, follow Llanberis signs onto A4244, signed from next rdbt) *Map Ref: SH56*
☎ 01248 670076 📠 01248 670069
e-mail: info@greenwood-centre.co.uk

This forest park provides a wide range of exciting activities for the whole family. Try the Great Green Run - the longest slide in Wales, shoot a real longbow, build dens in the woods and saw a log. Ride the Green Dragon, the world's first people powered family rollercoaster. Try the Jungle Boat Adventure and explore the rainforest. There are large interactive exhibitions in the oak framed great hall and the Forest Theatre stages shows during school holiday. The Toddlers village is ideal for young children.

Times: Open daily mid Mar-end Oct 10-5.30 (Sep & Oct 10-5). Fee: ✱ Varies with time of year. £4.95-£6.95 (ch £3.95-£5.95, pen £4.50-£6.30, disabled 20% discount). Family ticket (2ad+2ch) £15.65-£22.70; (2ad+3ch) £19.10-£27.95; (2ad+4ch) £22.60-£33.15. Facilities: 🅿 🍽 ♿ (grounds partly accessible, parking) toilets for disabled shop 🎁

BEAUMARIS BEAUMARIS CASTLE

LL58 8AP
Map Ref: SH67
☎ 01248 810361

Beaumaris was built by Edward I and took from 1295 to 1312 to complete. In later centuries it was plundered for its lead, timber and stone. Despite this it remains one of the most impressive and complete castles built by Edward I. It has a perfectly symmetrical, concentric plan, with a square inner bailey and curtain walls, round corner towers and D-shaped towers in between. There are also two great gatehouses, but these were never finished.

Times: Open Apr-May & Oct, daily 9.30-5; Jun-Sep, daily, 9.30-6; Nov-Mar, Mon-Sat 9.30-4, Sun 11-4. Telephone for Xmas opening times. Fee: £3 (ch 5-15, pen & students £2.50, disabled visitors and assisting companion free). Family ticket (2ad+3ch) £8.50. Group rates available. Prices quoted apply until 31 Mar 2005. Facilities: 🅿 ♿ shop 🐾 🚻 🎁

BEAUMARIS GAOL & COURTHOUSE

Steeple Ln LL58 8EW
Map Ref: SH67
☎ 01248 810921 & 724444 📠 01248 750282

With its treadmill and grim cells, the gaol is a vivid reminder of the tough penalties exacted by 19th-century law. Visitors can handle chains and fetters worn by prisoners. The courthouse, built in 1614 and renovated early in the 19th century, is a unique example of an early Welsh court. This is an all-weather attraction with a gift shop.

Times: ✱ Open Etr-Sep, daily 10.30-5. Other times by arrangement only. Facilities: 🅿 (500yds) ♿ (narrow gates may restrict some wheelchairs) shop 🐾 (ex guide dogs)

MUSEUM OF CHILDHOOD

1 Castle St LL58 8AP
Dir: (on A545 opposite Beaumaris Castle) **Map Ref:** SH67
☎ **01248 712498** 🖷 **01248 716869**

The museum illustrates the life and interests of children and families over the last 150 years. There are around 2,000 items in the museum's collection, shown in a series of nine rooms in two adjoining buildings. These include money boxes, dolls, educational toys and games, early clockwork trains, cars and aeroplanes, push toys and cycles.

Times: Open daily 10.30-5.30, Sun 12-5. (Last admission 4.30, Sun 4). Closed Nov-2nd wk Mar **Fee:** ✱ £3.50 (ch £2, pen & students £3). Family ticket £9.50. Free entry for wheelchairs.
Facilities: Ⓟ (50yds) ♿ shop ✖ (ex guide dogs)

BRYNSIENCYN ANGLESEY SEA ZOO

LL61 6TQ
Dir: (1st turning off Britannia Bridge onto Anglesey then follow Lobster signs along A4080 to zoo) **Map Ref:** SH46
☎ **01248 430411** 🖷 **01248 430213**
e-mail: info@angleseyseazoo.co.uk

Anglesey Sea Zoo, by the Menai Straits, is Wales's largest marine aquarium, and an all-weather undercover attraction with over 50 species of marine life. Exhibits include a shipwreck bristling with conger eels, a lobster hatchery, a seahorse nursery, exotic clownfish and piranhas, crashing waves and the enchanting fish forest. Children can even have a go at crab fishing. Outside there is an adventure playground, radio controlled boats and Aquablaster.

Times: Open 12 Feb-30 Oct. 10-6. (Last admission 1hr before site closes). **Fee:** ✱ £5.95 (ch & student £4.95, pen & UB40 £5.50). Family ticket £14.95-£21.95. Party 10+. Please telephone to confirm 2005 prices. **Facilities:** Ⓟ ▣
✖ licensed ♿ (2 wheelchairs available, Braile tour notes) toilets for disabled shop ✖ (ex guide dogs) ◀

FOEL FARM PARK

Foel Farm LL61 6TQ
Dir: (left off Britannia Bridge A55 onto A5/A4080 to Llanfairpwllgwyngyll, left on A4080 to Brynsiencyn & follow signs)
Map Ref: SH46
☎ **01248 430646** 🖷 **01248 430066**
e-mail: foelfarm@btinternet.com

Children will love this friendly farm experience on a genuine working farm, where they can meet animals big and small, feed them and even do some milking. They will also enjoy the adventure playground and tractor and trailer rides. A luxury handmade chocolate business is located in the park, as well as a tea room and gift shop, bistro and bar.

Times: Open daily Mar-Oct 10.30-5.30; Also wknds Nov-Feb 10.30-4.30. Also open half term Feb. **Facilities:** Ⓟ ▣ ✖ licensed ♿ toilets for disabled shop ✖ (ex guide dogs) ◀

HOLYHEAD RSBP NATURE RESERVE SOUTH STACK CLIFFS

Plas Nico, South Stack LL65 1YH
Dir: (A5 or A55 to Holyhead then follow brown heritage signs)
Map Ref: SH28
☎ 01407 764973 📄 01407 764973   **FREE**

High cliffs with caves and offshore stacks, backed by the maritime
heathland of Holyhead Mountain, make this an ideal reserve for
watching seabirds. Live video pictures of breeding seabirds are
shown in the cliff-top information centre during the summer.
Choughs, guillemots, razorbills, fulmars and puffins are among the
species that may be seen.

Times: Open: Information Centre daily, Etr-Sep,
11-5. Reserve open daily at all times.
Facilities: 🅿

PLAS NEWYDD PLAS NEWYDD

LL61 6DQ
Dir: (2m S of Llanfairpwll, on A4080) **Map Ref:** SH56
☎ 01248 714795 📄 01248 713673
e-mail: plasnewydd@nationaltrust.org.uk

Set amidst breathtakingly beautiful scenery, this elegant 18th-
century house was built by James Wyatt. The interior, restyled in
the 1930s, is famous for its association with Rex Whistler. His
largest painting is here, and an exhibition about his work. A
military museum contains campaign relics of the 1st Marquess of
Anglesea, who commanded the cavalry at the battle of Waterloo.
There is a fine spring garden and Australasian arboretum; a
summer terrace and, later, massed hydrangeas and autumn
colour. A woodland walk gives access to a marine walk on the
Menai Straits.

Times: Open Apr-Oct, Sat-Wed. House 12-5;
Garden 11-5.30. (Last admission 4.30)
Fee: ✱ £5 (ch £2.50). Family £12 (2ad+3ch).
Parties 15+ £4.50 **Facilities:** 🅿 ✗ licensed
& (close parking, wheelchairs, garden shuttle,
Braille guide) toilets for disabled shop
✗ (ex assistance dogs) 🐾

MERTHYR TYDFIL BRECON MOUNTAIN RAILWAY

Pant Station, Dowlais CF48 2UP
Dir: (follow Mountain Railway signs from A470 or A465 N of
Merthyr Tydfil) **Map Ref:** SO00
☎ 01685 722988 📄 01685 384854

Opened in 1980, this narrow-gauge railway follows part of an old
British Rail route which closed in 1964 when the iron industry in
South Wales fell into decline. The present route starts at Pant
Station and continues for 3.5 miles through the beautiful scenery
of the Brecon Beacons National Park, as far as Taf Fechan
reservoir. The train is pulled by a vintage steam locomotive and is
one of the most popular railways in Wales.

Times: Opening times on application to The
Brecon Mountain Railway, Pant Station, Merthyr
Tydfil. **Fee:** ✱ Fares are under review, please ring
for details. **Facilities:** 🅿 ◀ ✗ licensed
& (adapted carriage) toilets for disabled shop ◀

Monmouthshire

Merthyr Tydfil continued

Cyfarthfa Castle Museum & Art Gallery

Cyfarthfa Park CF47 8RE
Dir: (off A470, N towards Brecon, follow brown heritage signs)
Map Ref: SO00
☎ 01685 723112 📄 01685 723112
e-mail: museum@cyfarthfapark.freeserve.co.uk

FREE

Set in wooded parkland beside a beautiful lake, this imposing Gothic mansion now houses a superb museum and art gallery. The museum, located in the basement, provides a fascinating glimpse into 3,000 years of the town's history. Upstairs in the restored Regency rooms are the galleries of fine art and interesting objects from around the world.

Times: Open Apr-Sep: Mon-Sun 10-5.30; Oct-Mar, Tue-Fri 10-4, Sat-Sun 12-4. Closed between Xmas & New Year **Facilities:** 🅿 ☕ & (stair lift & wheelchair available) toilets for disabled shop ✈ (ex guide dogs)

CALDICOT Caldicot Castle, Museum & Countryside Park

Church Rd NP26 4HU
Dir: (M4 junct 23A onto B4245. From M48 junct 2 follow A48 & B4245. Signed from B4245) *Map Ref:* ST48
☎ 01291 420241 📄 01291 435094
e-mail: caldicotcastle@monmouthshire.gov.uk

Caldicot Castle's well-preserved fortifications were founded by the Normans and fully developed by the late 14th century. Restored as a family home by a wealthy Victorian, the castle offers the chance to explore medieval walls and towers in a setting of tranquil gardens and wooded country parkland, plus the opportunity to play giant chess or draughts.

Times: ✳ Open Mar-Oct, daily 11-5. **Facilities:** 🅿 ☕ & (taped tour, level trails, induction loop, access guide) toilets for disabled shop 🛍

CHEPSTOW Chepstow Castle

NP6 5EZ
Map Ref: ST59
☎ 01291 624065

Built by William FitzOsbern, in a strategic spot above the Wye, Chepstow is the first recorded Norman stone castle. It was strengthened in the following centuries, but was not besieged (as far as is known) until the Civil War, when it was twice lost to the Parliamentarians. The remains of the domestic rooms and the massive gatehouse, with its portcullis grooves and ancient gates, are still impressive, as are the walls and towers.

Times: Open Apr-May & Oct, daily 9.30-5; Jun-Sep, daily 9.30-6; Nov-Mar, Mon-Sat 9.30-4, Sun 11-4. Telephone for Xmas opening times. **Fee:** £3 (ch 5-15, pen & students £2.50, disabled visitors and assisting companion free). Family ticket (2ad+3ch) £8.50. Group rates available. Prices quoted apply until 31 Mar 2005. **Facilities:** 🅿 & shop ✈ ☺ 🛍

MONMOUTH NELSON MUSEUM & LOCAL HISTORY CENTRE

New Market Hall, Priory St NP25 3XA
Dir: (in town centre) **Map Ref:** SO51
☎ **01600 710630**
FREE
e-mail: nelsonmuseum@monmouthshire.gov.uk

Commemorative glass, china, silver, medals, books, models, prints and Admiral Nelson's fighting sword feature at this museum and local history centre. The local history displays deal with Monmouth's past as a fortress market town, and include a section on the co-founder of the Rolls Royce company, Charles Stewart Rolls, who was also a pioneer balloonist, aviator and, of course, motorist.

Times: Open all year, Mon-Sat 10-1 & 2-5; Sun 2-5. Closed Xmas & New Year. **Facilities:** P (200yds) (small daily charge) & toilets for disabled shop ✖ (ex guide dogs) ◀

CRYNANT CEFN COED COLLIERY MUSEUM

SA10 8SN
Dir: (1m S of Crynant, on A4109) **Map Ref:** SN70
☎ **01639 750556** 🖷 **01639 750556**

The museum is on the site of a former working colliery, and tells the story of mining in the Dulais Valley. A steam-winding engine has been kept and is now operated by electricity, and there is also a simulated underground mining gallery, boilerhouse, compressor house, and exhibition area. Outdoor exhibits include a stationary colliery locomotive. Exhibitions relating to the coal mining industry are held on a regular basis.

Times: ✱ Open daily, Apr-Oct 10.30-5; Nov-Mar, groups welcome by prior arrangement. **Facilities:** P & toilets for disabled shop

CYNONVILLE SOUTH WALES MINERS MUSEUM

Afan Argoed Country Park SA13 3HG
Dir: (M4 junct 40 onto A4107, 6m NE of Port Talbot)
Map Ref: SS89
☎ **01639 850564** 🖷 **01639 850446**
e-mail: boastam@sagainternet.co.uk

South Wales Mining Museum, with the most picturesque of settings in the Afan Argoed Countryside Centre, gives a vivid picture of the life of a miner in the South Wales valleys. Visitors get to see coal faces, pit gear and miners' equipment, and guided tours of the museum are available on request. The country park has a visitor centre, forest walks and picnic areas, and outdoor exhibits include a blacksmith's shop.

Times: Open all year daily, Apr-Sep 10.30-5 (Sat & Sun 10.30-6); Oct-Feb 10.30-4 (Sat & Sun 10.30-5). Closed Xmas week. **Fee:** ✱ £1.20 (ch & pen 60p). Concessionary rate for advance bookings. **Facilities:** P (charged) ◳ ✖ & (mechanical & manual wheelchairs on request) toilets for disabled shop ✖ (ex guide dogs) ◀

Neath Port Talbot continued

NEATH GNOLL ESTATE COUNTRY PARK

SA11 3BS
Dir: (follow brown heritage signs from town centre)
Map Ref: SS79
☎ 01639 635808 📄 01639 635694   FREE

The extensively landscaped country park is based in 18th-century
landscaped gardens, easily accessible from the centre of Neath,
with lakes, cascades and a grotto. It offers tranquil woodland
walks, picnic areas, stunning views, children's play areas, an
adventure playground, a nine-hole golf course, and coarse fishing.
A varied programme of events is scheduled along with school
holiday activities.

Times: Open all year - Vistor centre, daily from
10. Closed 24 Dec-2 Jan **Facilities:** P 🅿
& (wheelchair & scooter for hire, designated
parking) toilets for disabled shop ✈ (ex guide
dogs)

CAERLEON ROMAN LEGIONARY MUSEUM

High St NP18 1AE
Dir: (close to Newport, 20 min from M4, follow signs from Cardiff
& Bristol) *Map Ref:* ST39
☎ 01633 423134 📄 01633 422869   FREE
e-mail: roman@nmgw.ac.uk

The museum illustrates the history of Roman Caerleon and the
daily life of its garrison. On display are arms, armour and
equipment, with a collection of engraved gemstones, a labyrinth
mosaic and finds from the legionary base at Usk. Please
telephone for details of children's holiday activities - 01633
423134.

Times: Open all year: Mon-Sat 10-5, Sun 2-5.
Facilities: P (100yds) & toilets for disabled
shop ✈ (ex guide dogs) ◀

NEWPORT TREDEGAR HOUSE & PARK

NP10 8YW
Dir: (2m W of Newport, signed from A48 and M4 junct 28)
Map Ref: ST38
☎ 01633 815880 📄 01633 815895
e-mail: tredegar.house@newport.gov.uk

Home to one of the greatest of Welsh families, the Morgans, later
Lords Tredegar, for over five centuries, Tredegar House gives a
fascinating insight into life above and below stairs. The house and
gardens are set in a 90-acre landscaped park, where carriage
rides, formal gardens, self-guided trails, craft workshops, boating,
and an adventure playground provide plenty to do and see.

Times: Open Etr-Sep **Facilities:** P 🅿
& (wheelchairs for loan) toilets for disabled
shop ◀

CAREW CAREW CASTLE & TIDAL MILL

SA70 8SL
Dir: (on A4075, just off A477 Pembroke to Kilgetty road)
Map Ref: SN00
☎ **01646 651782** 🖶 **01646 651782**
e-mail: enquiries@carewcastle.com

This magnificent Norman castle has royal links with Henry Tudor and was the setting for the Great Tournament of 1507. Nearby is the Carew Cross (Cadw), an impressive 13-foot Celtic cross dating from the 11th century. Carew Mill is one of only four restored tidal mills in Britain, with records dating back to 1558.

Times: Open 25 Mar-5 Nov **Fee:** *Prices not confirmed for 2005* **Facilities:** 🅿 ♿ toilets for disabled shop ◀

FISHGUARD OCEANLAB

The Parrog, Goodwick SA64 0DE
Dir: (A40 to Fishguard, turn at by-pass, follow signs for Stenaline ferry terminal, pass 2 garages, turn right at rdbt & follow signs to attraction) **Map Ref:** SM93
☎ **01348 874737** 🖶 **01348 872528**
e-mail: fishguardharbour-tic@pembrokeshire.gov.uk

Overlooking the Pembrokeshire coastline, OceanLab is a multifunctional centre which aims to provide a fun-filled experience for the family. The Ice Age exhibition stars a replica woolly mammoth called Oscar, and there is a hands-on Ocean Quest exhibition. Additional facilities include a soft play area and a cyber café where visitors can surf the Internet.

Times: Open Apr-Oct 10-6, Nov-Mar 10-4. **Fee:** Telephone for details **Facilities:** 🅿 🍽 ♿ (lift, flat even ground) toilets for disabled shop ✖ (ex guide dogs) ◀

NARBERTH OAKWOOD PARK

Canaston Bridge SA67 8DE
Dir: (M4 W junct 49, take A48 to Carmarthen, signed)
Map Ref: SN11
☎ **01834 861889** 🖶 **01834 891380**
e-mail: park@oakwood-leisure.com

Wales' premier theme park, featuring the world's no 1 wooden rollercoaster Megafobia, the 50-metre high sky coaster Vertigo, the shot n' drop tower coaster The Bounce, and Snake River Falls. For young children there is KidzWorld featuring The Wacky Factory, The Lost Kingdom, Techniquest and Playtown. In summer there are firework displays and light shows at night.

Times: Open daily 3 Apr-3 Oct, from 10 (closing times vary) **Fee:** ✱ £13.75 (under 2's free, ch 3-9 £12.95, pen & disabled £9.50). Family ticket £49, Party 20+ tickets available £11.75 **Facilities:** 🅿 🍽 ✖ ♿ (wheelchair hire, special access to some rides) toilets for disabled shop ✖ (ex guide dogs) ◀

PEMBROKE PEMBROKE CASTLE

SA71 4LA
Dir: (W end of main street) *Map Ref: SM90*
☎ 01646 681510 & 684585 🖹 01646 622260
e-mail: pembroke.castle@talk21.com

This magnificent castle commands stunning views over the Milford estuary. Discover its rich medieval history, and that of Henry VII, the first Tudor king, through a variety of exhibitions. There are lively guided tours and events each Sunday in July and August. Before leaving, pop into the Brass Rubbing Centre and make your own special souvenir. To complete the day, wander round the tranquil millpond and medieval town walls which surround various architectural gems from Tudor and Georgian times.

Times: Open all year, daily, Apr-Sep 9.30-6; Mar & Oct 10-5; Nov-Feb, 10-4. Closed 24-26 Dec & 1 Jan. **Fee:** £3 (ch under 16 & pen £2, ch under 5 & wheelchairs users free). Family ticket £8.
Facilities: P (100yds) 🍽 & (induction loop, handrails, portable ramp) toilets for disabled shop 📻

ST FLORENCE MANOR HOUSE WILDLIFE & LEISURE PARK

Ivy Tower SA70 8RJ
Dir: (on B4318 between Tenby & St Florence) *Map Ref: SN00*
☎ 01646 651201 🖹 01646 651201

The park is set in 35 acres of delightful wooded grounds and award-winning gardens. The wildlife includes exotic birds, reptiles and fish. Also here are a pets' corner, a children's playground with free rides on an astraglide slide, and roundabouts. Other attractions include a natural history museum, a go-kart track, model railway exhibition and daily falconry displays. Telephone for details of displays and animal feeding times.

Times: ✱ Open Etr-end Sep, daily 10-6. Please telephone for late opening Jul & Aug.
Facilities: P 🍽 & toilets for disabled shop 🐕 📻

SCOLTON SCOLTON VISITOR CENTRE

SA62 5QL
Dir: (5m N of Haverfordwest, on B4329) *Map Ref: SM92*
☎ 01437 731328 (Mus) & 731457 (Park) 🖹 01437 731743

Scolton Manor Museum is situated in Scolton Country Park. The early Victorian mansion, refurbished stables and exhibition hall illustrate the history and natural history of Pembrokeshire. There are new displays in the house and stables, plus a Pembrokeshire Railways exhibition. The 60-acre grounds, partly a nature reserve, have fine specimen trees and shrubs. There is an environmentally friendly visitor centre, alternative energy and woodland displays, guided walks and children's play areas.

Times: Open Museum Apr-Oct, Tue-Sun & BHs 10.30-1 & 1.30-5.30; Country Park all year, Etr-Sep 10-7, Oct-Etr 10-6. Closed 25-26 Dec. **Fee:** *Prices not confirmed for 2005* **Facilities:** P (charged) 🍽 & (disabled parking area near house) toilets for disabled shop 🐕 (ex guide dogs & in grounds)

ABERCRAF *Dan-Yr-Ogof The National Showcaves Centre for Wales*

SA9 1GJ
Dir: (M4 junct 45, midway between Swansea & Brecon on A4067, follow brown tourist signs) *Map Ref: SN81*
☎ **01639 730284 & 730801** 📠 **01639 730293**
e-mail: info@showcaves.co.uk

This award winning attraction includes three separate caves, a dinosaur park, Iron Age farm, museum, shire horse centre and covered children's play area. The show caves, among the most spectacular in Northern Europe, were discovered by the Morgan brothers in 1912. Dan-Yr-Ogof is a wonderland of lakes, stalagmites and stalagtites, and Bone Cave is so called because 42 human skeletons have been found here. Cathedral Cave, where dramatic music and lighting intensifies the experience, is entered by an easy access tunnel, and has an exhibit on the lives of those who once lived here.

Times: Open Apr-Oct, daily from 10 (last admission 3). **Facilities:** 🅿 🍽 shop ♿

BERRIEW *Glansevern Hall Gardens*

Glansevern SY21 8AH
Dir: (signed on A483 between Welshpool and Newtown)
Map Ref: SJ10
☎ **01686 640200** 📠 **01686 640829**

Glansevern Hall was built in the Greek Revival style for Arthur Davies Owen, who chose a romantically positioned site on the banks of the River Severn. The current owners have developed the gardens, respecting the plantings and features of the past, and added a vast collection of new and interesting species. There are many fine and unusual trees, a lakeside walk, walled garden, water gardens and a rock garden with lamp-lit grotto.

Times: Open May-Sep, BH Mon, Fri-Sat 12-6. Parties other dates by arrangement.
Fee: ✱ £3.50 (pen £3, ch under 15 free).
Facilities: 🅿 🍽 ♿ (most areas accessible) toilets for disabled shop

---

LLANFAIR CAEREINION *Welshpool & Llanfair Light Railway*

SY21 0SF
Dir: (beside A458, Shrewsbury-Dolgellau road) *Map Ref: SJ10*
☎ **01938 810441** 📠 **01938 810861**
e-mail: info@wllr.org.uk

The Welshpool & Llanfair Railway is one of the great Little Trains of Wales. It offers a 16-mile round trip through glorious scenery by narrow gauge steam train. The line is home to a collection of engines and coaches from all round the world. The station at Llanfair has a shop, café and picnic area. Please ring for details of special events.

Times: Open wknds Etr-end Oct, daily during holiday periods, phone for timetable enquiries.
Fee: ✱ £9.50 return (ch £1, pen £8.50).
Facilities: 🅿 🍽 ♿ (three coachs adapted for wheelchairs) toilets for disabled shop ♿

MACHYNLLETH *CELTICA*

Y Plas, Aberystwyth Rd SY20 8ER
Dir: (well signed to south of town) *Map Ref:* *SH70*
☎ **01654 702702** 📄 **01654 703604**
e-mail: celtica@celticawales.com

Located in a restored mansion house, Celtica is an exciting heritage centre introducing the history and culture of the Celtic people. The sights and sounds of Celtic life are brought alive as you go on a journey portraying the Celtic spirit of the past, present and future. There's an interpretive centre dedicated to Welsh and Celtic history, a children's indoor play area, and conference rooms. Education resources are available and groups are welcome. Storytelling, lectures, music and craft events take place.

Times: ✱ Open daily 10-6. Closed Xmas, New Year & some dates in Jan. **Facilities:** 🅿 💻 ✗ licensed ♿ (lift & ramps to public areas, induction loop) toilets for disabled shop ✖ (ex guide dogs) 🍴

CENTRE FOR ALTERNATIVE TECHNOLOGY

SY20 9AZ
Dir: (3m N of Machynlleth, on A487) *Map Ref:* *SH70*
☎ **01654 705950**
e-mail: info@cat.org.uk

The Centre for Alternative Technology promotes practical ideas and information on sustainable technologies. The exhibition includes displays of wind, water and solar power, organic gardens, low-energy dwellings, and a unique water-powered railway which ascends a 200-foot cliff from the car park. The wave tank and the underground 'mole-hole' are particularly popular with children.

Times: Open 7 Apr-Oct, daily 10-5; Nov-6 Apr, daily 10-4. **Facilities:** 🅿 💻 (wheelchair available) shop ✖ (ex guide dogs) 🍴

KING ARTHUR'S LABYRINTH

King Arthur's Labyrinth, Corris SY20 9RF
Dir: (on A487 between Machynlleth and Dolgellau)
Map Ref: *SH70*
☎ **01654 761584** 📄 **01654 761575**
e-mail: king.arthurs.labyrinth@corris-wales.co.uk

This exciting and unusual attraction takes you into a labyrinth of tunnels carved deep into the ancient rock of Wales. It begins with an underground journey by boat through the great waterfall. Then you are led through tunnels and caverns while tales of King Arthur and other legends are told through tableaux and audio presentations with special lighting effects.

Times: Open 19 Mar-6 Nov, daily 10-5. **Fee:** ✱ £5 (ch £3.50, pen £4.45). **Facilities:** 🅿 💻 ♿ toilets for disabled shop ✖ (ex guide dogs) 🍴

PRESTEIGNE THE JUDGE'S LODGING

Broad St LD8 2AD
Dir: (in town centre, off B4362, signed from A44 & A49)
Map Ref: SO36
☎ **01544 260650** ▤ **01544 260652**
e-mail: info@judgeslodging.org.uk

The Judge's Lodging is a restored Victorian town house with integral courtroom, cells and service areas. Here you can step back into the 1860s, accompanied by an eavesdropping audio tour of voices from the past. Explore the fascinating world of the Victorian judges, their servants and felonious guests at this award winning, 'hands on', historic house.

Times: Open daily, Mar-Oct 10-6; Nov-Dec Wed-Sun 10-4. Closed Jan-Feb. **Fee:** £4.50 (ch £3.50, concessions £3.95). Family ticket £13.50. Party rates available.
Facilities: P (200mtrs) & (lift, disabled pack for inaccessible items) shop ✗ (ex guide dogs)

WELSHPOOL POWIS CASTLE

SY21 8RF
Dir: (1m S of Welshpool, signed off A483) **Map Ref:** SJ20
☎ **01938 551920** ▤ **01938 554336**
e-mail: ppcmsn@smtp.ntrust.org.uk

Laid out in the Italian and French styles, these world famous castle gardens retain their original lead statues, and feature an orangery and an aviary on the terraces. The medieval castle contains one of the finest collections of paintings and furniture in Wales and a beautiful collection of treasures from India. The 19th-century state coach and livery is now on display in the recently opened coach house.

Times: ✱ Open Castle & museum: Apr-Jun and Sep-Oct, Wed-Sun 1-5; Jul-Aug Tue-Sun 1-5; Open all BHs in season. Garden open same days as castle and museum 11-6. (Last admission to all parts 30 mins before closing)
Facilities: P ✗ licensed (photos of interior available from tearoom) shop garden centre ✗ (ex guide dogs) 🐾 ▤

TREHAFOD RHONDDA HERITAGE PARK

Lewis Merthyr Colliery, Coed Cae Rd CF37 7NP
Dir: (between Pontypridd & Porth, off A470, follow brown heritage signs from M4 junct 32) **Map Ref:** ST09
☎ **01443 682036** ▤ **01443 687420**
e-mail: reception@rhonddaheritagepark.com

Based at the Lewis Merthyr Colliery, the Heritage Park is a fascinating living history attraction. You can take the cage ride to 'Pit Bottom' and explore the underground workings of a 1950's pit, guided by men who were miners themselves. There are children's activities, an art gallery and a museum illustrating living conditions in the Rhondda Valley. Special events are held throughout the year, please phone for details.

Times: Open all year, daily 10-6. Closed Mon from Oct-Etr. (Last admission 4.30). Closed 25 Dec-3 Jan. **Fee:** ✱ £5.60 (ch £4.30, pen £4.95). Family ticket £16.50. **Facilities:** P ▟ ✗ licensed & (wheelchair available, accessible parking, lifts) toilets for disabled shop ✗ (ex guide dogs) ▤

PARKMILL GOWER HERITAGE CENTRE

Y Felin Ddwr SA3 2EH
Dir: (follow signs for South Gower on A4118 W from Swansea.
W side of Parkmill village) *Map Ref:* SS58
☎ 01792 371206 📠 01792 371471
e-mail: info@gowerheritagecentre.co.uk

Based around a 12th-century water-powered corn mill, the
heritage centre also includes a museum of rural life, a miller's
cottage and a number of craft workshops, all set in attractive
countryside in an Area of Outstanding Natural Beauty. Children
will enjoy the two play areas, the small animals, chickens and
ducks.

Times: Open daily, Mar-Oct 10-5.30; Nov-Feb 10-4.30. Closed 25
Dec. **Fee:** ✽ £3.70 (ch under 5 free, concessions £2.60). Family
ticket £12 **Facilities:** 🅿 🖳 ✗ ♿ (ramp entrance access) toilets for
disabled shop 🛍

SWANSEA PLANTASIA

Parc Tawe SA1 2AL
Dir: (M4 junct 42, follow A483 into Swansea, follow car park
signs for attraction) *Map Ref:* SS69
☎ 01792 474555 📠 01792 652588
e-mail: swansea.plantasia@swansea.gov.uk

A unique, giant hot house garden located in the city centre,
Plantasia houses a huge variety of unusual and exotic plants of
great interest, including several species that are extinct in the
wild. You can also visit the Butterfly House and see a variety of
species fly freely and observe various stages of butterfly
development.

Times: Open Tue-Sun 10-5 (BH Mons & all Mons
Jun-Aug) **Fee:** ✽ £3 (concessions £2.10)
Facilities: 🅿 🖳 ♿ toilets for disabled shop
✖ (ex guide dogs) 🛍

SWANSEA MUSEUM

Victoria Rd, Maritime Quarter SA1 1SN
Dir: (M4 junct 42, on main road into city centre) *Map Ref:* SS69
☎ 01792 653763 📠 01792 652585   **FREE**
e-mail: swansea.museum@swansea.gov.uk

This is the oldest museum in Wales, showing the history of
Swansea from the earliest times until today. The museum has a
tram shed and, in the summer months, there are floating boats to
explore. A continuous programme of temporary exhibitions and
events is run all year round.

Times: Open all year, Tue-Sun 10-5 (last
admission 4.45). Closed Mon except BH Mon,
25-26 Dec & 1 Jan. **Facilities:** 🅿 (50yds)
(charged) ♿ toilets for disabled shop ✖ (ex guide
dogs) 🛍

BLAENAVON *BIG PIT NATIONAL MINING MUSEUM OF WALES*

NP4 9XP
Dir: (M4 junct 25/26, follow signs on A4042 & A4043 to
Pontypool & Blaenavon. Signed off A465) *Map Ref:* SO20
☎ 01495 790311 ▤ 01495 792618
e-mail: bigpit@nmgw.ac.uk

For the authentic underground experience, Big Pit is the UK's
leading mining museum. It is a real colliery and was the place of
work for hundreds of men, woman and children for over 200
years. Go 300 feet down for a guided tour of the mine with a real
miner and experience life on the coal face. Visit colliery buildings
and learn about modern mining from interactive exhibits.

Times: ✱ Open Mid Feb-End Nov, daily 9.30-5,
telephone to confirm **Facilities:** 🅿 💻
♿ (underground tours by prior arrangement)
toilets for disabled shop

BLAENAVON IRONWORKS

North St
Map Ref: SO20
☎ 01495 792615

The Blaenavon Ironworks were a milestone in the history of the
Industrial Revolution. Constructed in 1788-99, they were the first
purpose built, multi furnace ironworks in Wales. By 1796,
Blaenavon was the second largest ironworks in Wales, eventually
closing down in 1904. The importance of the town's industrial
heritage has been recognised by Blaenavon's designation as a
World Heritage Site.

Times: Open 5 Apr-Oct, Mon-Fri 9.30-4.30, Sat
10-5, Sun 10-4.30. For details of opening outside
this period, telephone Torfaen County Borough
Council on 01633 648081. **Fee:** £2 (ch 5-16,
pen & students £1.50, disabled visitors & assisting
companion free). Family ticket (2ad+3ch) £5.50.
Group discounts available. Prices quoted apply
until 31 Mar 2005. **Facilities:** 🅿 ✈ ☺ 🍴

CWMBRAN *GREENMEADOW COMMUNITY FARM*

Greenforge Way NP44 5AJ
Dir: (follow signs for Cwmbran then brown heritage signs)
Map Ref: ST29
☎ 01633 862202 ▤ 01633 489332
e-mail: greenmeadow_community_farm@
compuserve.com

This is one of Wales's leading tourist attractions - a community
farm that was built during the 1980s on land threatened by
developers. There are milking demonstrations, tractor and trailer
rides, a dragon adventure play area, a farm and nature trail and
more. Phone for details of lambing weekends, shearing, country
fair and agricultural shows, Halloween and Christmas events.

Times: Open Summer 10-6, Winter 10-4. Closed 25 Dec. **Fee:** ✱ £4
(ch £3) Family (2ad+3ch) £14 **Facilities:** 🅿 💻 ♿ (tractor & trailer
rides for wheelchair users) toilets for disabled shop 🍴

BARRY *WELSH HAWKING CENTRE*

Weycock Rd CF62 3AA
Dir: (on A4226) *Map Ref:* ST16
☎ 01446 734687 📄 01446 739620

There are over 200 birds of prey at this centre, including eagles, hawks, owls, buzzards and falcons. They can be seen and photographed in the mews and some of the breeding aviaries. There are flying demonstrations at regular intervals during the day. A variety of tame, friendly animals, such as pigs, lambs and rabbits will delight younger visitors.

Times: ✱ Open end Mar-end Sep, daily 10.30-5, 1hr before dusk in winter. **Facilities:** 🅿 💺 ♿ toilets for disabled shop ✖ 🎦

PENARTH *COSMESTON LAKES COUNTRY PARK & MEDIEVAL VILLAGE*

Lavernock Rd CF64 5UY
Dir: (on B4267 between Barry and Penarth) *Map Ref:* ST17
☎ 029 2070 1678 📄 029 2070 8686
e-mail: NColes@valeofglamorgan.gov.uk

Deserted during the plagues and famines of the 14th century, the original village was rediscovered through archaeological excavations. The buildings have been faithfully reconstructed on the excavated remains, creating a living museum of medieval village life. Special events throughout the year include re-enactments and living history. The country park, a former limestone quarry, provides over 90 hectares of lakes, woodland and meadows.

Times: Open all year, daily 11-5 in Summer, 11-4 in Winter. Closed 25 Dec. Country park open at all times. **Fee:** ✱ Entry to Village £3.50, (concessions £2) Family ticket £8. Entry to Country Park free. **Facilities:** 🅿 💺 ✖ ♿ (access ramps & wheelchair hire) toilets for disabled shop

CHIRK *CHIRK CASTLE*

LL14 5AF
Dir: (8m S of Wrexham, signed off A483) *Map Ref:* SJ23
☎ 01691 777701 📄 01691 774706
e-mail: pcwmsn@smtp.ntrust.org.uk

Chirk Castle is one of a chain of late 13th-century Marcher castles. Its high walls and drum towers have hardly changed, but the inside shows the varied tastes of 700 years of occupation. One of the least altered parts is Adam's Tower. Many of the medieval-looking decorations were by Pugin in the 19th century. Varied furnishings include fine tapestries.

Times: ✱ Open 29 Mar-Sep, Wed-Sun & BH Mon 12-5 (castle), 11-6 (gardens); Oct, Wed-Sun 12-4 (castle), 11-5 (gardens). (Last admission 30 mins before closing). **Facilities:** 🅿 ✖ licensed ♿ (stairclimber) toilets for disabled shop ✖ (ex guide dogs) 🐾